LADY MARY, POPE, AND KNELLER: THE PORTRAIT SCENE. *See p.* 112.

THE

QUEENS OF SOCIETY.

BY

GRACE AND PHILIP WHARTON.

Illustrated by

CHARLES ALTAMONT DOYLE AND THE BROTHERS DALZIEL.

NEW YORK:
HARPER & BROTHERS, PUBLISHERS,
FRANKLIN SQUARE.
1861.

PREFACE.

WHEN the guardian-demon of the unbless'd was asked how many monarchs he had among the souls in his keeping, he replied, "All that ever reigned." So says fable; we are very far from intending to indorse it. But there may be some people who think that the monarchs of society—those uncrowned heads, whose dominions are the minds and hearts of their fellow-beings—present as few exceptions as those sovereigns who build up history. There may be many who imagine that the "Queens of Society" have won their titles with no better qualifications than wit and beauty; that their position has rendered them vain, if not imperious; and that they have lived in the world and for the world only. No opinion could be more erroneous; it is a libel on society to suppose its judgment so distorted; and a glance at the names of the women who have held this proud position will show that this is the case. Of the eighteen ladies whom we have selected as best fitted to represent this class, no less than six have been as celebrated for their literary talents as for their social position. Of these, Lady Morgan and Lady Caroline Lamb wrote novels which were eagerly devoured in their day; the Countess of Pembroke and Mrs. Thrale were miscellaneous writers; L. E. L. was a charming poetess; and Madame de Staël may be justly held up as the greatest authoress of France. Letter-writing, again, has been the produce of six others, of whom Lady Hervey, Mrs. Montagu, and Madame de Maintenon are only of less celebrity than Madame de Sévigné and Madame du Deffand, always cited as *the* letter-writers of France, while Lady Mary Wortley Montagu holds the same place in this country. Seven, again, have been eminent political leaders; one of them, indeed, Madame de Maintenon, though uncrowned, having been virtually Queen of France; and though Madame Récamier and the Duchesses of Gordon and Devonshire may have had comparatively little influence on the fate of their respective countries, the same can not be said of Madame Roland; while the names of De Staël and "Queen Sarah" are historical.

Nor was it their talent only that recommended these women to the electress-ships of their respective circles. Though society may do without a good heart, it will not dispense with that appearance of it which we call amiability of manner. With some few exceptions the "Queens of Society" have been kindly, amiable, and even gentle people. While Sarah of Marlborough and Madame du Deffand were as notorious for their high tempers as for their wit, Madame Roland, L. E. L., Mrs. Montagu, and Mrs. Damer were all as amiable women and as thoroughly good-hearted as possible; Byron himself, never too liberal of his praise, has testified to the vast fund of good-nature in "De l'Allemagne," as he calls Madame de Staël; Madame de Sévigné is a model of maternal affection; and Mrs. Thrale won Johnson—in spite of her silliness—by the kindness she showed the poor invalid. I think those who remember Lady Morgan will readily add her name to the list.

The talents of society—wit, conversational powers, and a knowledge of the world—are, of course, necessary ingredients in the characters of these charming women; but that there was in most of them a depth of mind not always accorded to the other sex may be safely deduced from the fact that, with few exceptions, every one of them has been the intimate friend—often, indeed, the counselor—of some great man. To run through the list before us: "Queen Sarah" was the friend of Marlborough; Madame Roland of the leaders of the Gironde; Lady Mary both friend and foe to Pope; the Duchess of Devonshire the active partisan of Fox; Madame de Sévigné the intimate of the Arnaulds and La Rochefoucauld; Madame Récamier of Châteaubriand; Madame du Deffand of Voltaire and Walpole, of whom the latter was devoted also to Mrs. Damer; Necker received advice from Schlegel, and was the companion of Madame de Staël; Mrs. Thrale was the friend of Johnson; Lady C. Lamb of Byron; Mrs. Montagu of Beattie; Lady Pembroke of Sir Philip Sidney; and Madame de Maintenon the consoler of Scarron, the buffoon, and the adviser of Louis Quatorze.

These facts must necessarily add much to the interest of lives which, even apart from them, have no ordinary attraction. But perhaps the greatest interest to the general reader will be found in the varied phases of society in which these women moved. The history of society collectively remains to be written; but it is written disjointedly in the life of every man or woman who has taken a high social position. It is, indeed, only in these that we are introduced to scenes of past life, which history, fully concerned with monarchs, parliaments, and nations, can not condescend to depict. The writers have therefore selected certain periods to illustrate by the lives in question. The profligate courts of Louis XIV. and Louis XV., the earlier and later periods of the French Revolution, the Empire, and the Restoration, are here touched upon in the memoirs of French women of society, while, for our own country, there is a life to illustrate every period from the reign of Elizabeth down to our own times, from the Countess of Pembroke to Lady Morgan, although a chronological arrangement has, for certain reasons, not been followed.

It remains only to point out that while the selection has generally been made from women of irreproachable moral character, one or two have been chosen by way of contrast and by way of warning. The temptations of society are very great; yet how far more easy it is to attain the honor—if honor it be—of reigning in its circles by strictly virtuous than by lax conduct may be seen from the memoirs to which the reader is now introduced.

In many cases the lives of the ladies selected have been written at greater length by other biographers; in some, however, none but short notices, prefixed to their letters or works, have hitherto been published, and in one or two, we believe, no consecutive memoirs have ever been written.

That the reader may not be misled, it should perhaps be stated that the mode of writing Lady Morgan's name was that adopted by herself.

Lastly, the illustrations have been executed with especial attention to costume and known peculiarities of dress; and, whenever it was found possible, the artists have introduced portraits of the persons represented.

CONTENTS.

LIST OF ILLUSTRATIONS.

THE QUEENS OF SOCIETY.

THE QUEENS OF SOCIETY.

SARAH, DUCHESS OF MARLBOROUGH.

Stung by the aspersions cast on her by her political enemies, this celebrated woman, whom Pope has satirized under the name of Atossa, published her own Memoirs. "I have been," she wrote, "a kind of author." She penned with great spirit her own vindication; nor would she have condescended to do so, had not her best feelings been wounded by the impressions entertained against her by the widow of Bishop Burnet; so alive was this celebrated woman to the good opinion of others.

Yet, though even Henry Fielding, whose father, Edward, had served under the Duke of Marlborough, wrote a vindication of the "duchess's character in general," as well as an answer to the attacks upon her, it is strange that neither her birthplace, nor the spot where she died, have been positively known, even to the descendants of this beautiful, arrogant, all-powerful female courtier. The fact, perhaps, was, that those who succeeded to her loved her little; while "Jack Spencer," as he was usually styled, her reckless favorite grandson and heir, was not a man to search out for the annals of an aged grandmother, and still less to dwell upon the scenes of her death-bed.

She was born, however, as careful and recent researches have proved, in a small house at Holywell, near St. Alban's; so called because the nuns of Sopwell, a monastery in the vicinity, used to dip their crusts in that well when too hard otherwise to be eaten; and on the 29th of May, 1660, the future "viceroy," as this leader in fashion and politics was termed, first saw the light.

Her father, Richard Jennings, was a plain country gentleman, possessing lands to the value of four thousand pounds yearly, derived from his estate at Sandridge, near St. Alban's, and other manors in Kent and Somersetshire: and her mother, Frances Thornhurst, was the daughter and heiress of Sir Giffard Thornhurst, of Agnes Court, in Kent. Sandridge, where once the family chiefly lived, is a straggling, uninteresting village: there seems not to have been any good house on the estate, until, sold by the extravagant grandson of the duchess, her darling spendthrift, Jack Spencer, a handsome house was built on it by a prosperous gentleman retired from trade.

Destined by fortune to affluence, Sarah Jennings was fated to see three of her father's offspring, two sons and a daughter, taken from her home by early death; so that, except herself, only one daughter survived, the beautiful and famous Frances Jennings, afterward the belle of the court of Charles II., and the unhappy wife of the Duke of Tyrconnel.

These two celebrated women passed their girlhood during the tranquil period which preceded the death of that monarch chiefly at Holywell. The opinions of men were, indeed, even then, forming themselves into the three great political parties—Jacobite, Whig, and Tory; but those factions in which "Queen Sarah" afterward mingled so conspicuously were still dormant. Her father and her forefathers had been zealous adherents to the Stuart cause, but were also strict Protestants.

Frances was the elder of the two sisters; and she, as well as Sarah, early displayed those talents which, with beauty, were likely to gain an ascendency in the court of either of the last Stuart kings. England was then what France has since been termed—"*le Paradis des Femmes.*"

"Love ruled the court, the camp, the grove,
And earth below, and heaven above."

But of heaven the well-bred in those times thought but little: they were either tainted by French morals, or perverted by bigoted views of religion, which was mournfully mixed up with politics and party views.

It may, therefore, easily be imagined into what peril the two lovely sisters, Frances and Sarah Jennings, were consigned, when their parents, impelled by their devotion to the Stuarts, resolved to send them to court. Frances went first. She was one of those blonde beauties—with luxuriant flaxen hair, a bright, delicate complexion, pretty, and somewhat insignificant features, who seemed born to grace the gallery at Whitehall, and to be painted by Lely. She had no sooner shown herself in that dangerous circle, the avowed leader of which was Lady Castlemaine, than her youth and innocence were assailed by every idler of the iniquitous region. But she was shrewd, and, though a coquette, had a principle of virtue within her that kept her respectable, though it did not render her modest. La belle Jennings, as she was called, had great wit, great penetration, great fearlessness in all she said, and she had courage even to turn into ridicule the compliments and addresses of James II., then Duke of York, who persecuted her with his admiration.

The sisters were nominally under the protection of Anne Hyde, Duchess of York; and at twelve years of age, Sarah Jennings entered the service of that intelligent though not irreproachable woman. Anne had the weakness of wishing to surround her own plain person with youth and loveliness, in order to challenge comparison with Katharine of Braganza, the queen of Charles II., an excellent princess, who had brought from Portugal some of the plainest maids of honor that had ever set foot on English shores. It seems, however, that Anne Hyde had chiefly encouraged the very early admission of Sarah Jennings into her court, in order that she might be a playmate to the Princess Anne, afterward queen: and this companionship, which produced in after days such signal effects, was continued after the death of Anne Hyde in 1671, and the marriage of Mary of Modena, her successor, to James II.

Frances, precocious and vain, was fluttering in the giddy court. Sarah was withdrawn from such influences. Anne from her youth was staid, if not prudish; and her mother, the Duchess of York, was one of the most sensible and prudent of women, under whose guidance Sarah enjoyed singular advantages.

But during the year 1671 the scene in which Sarah figured was changed. Anne Hyde died, and with her the ascendency of Protestant principles: and the "Queen of Tears," as Mary Beatrix D'Esté, was called, was selected for the bride of the royal widower James.

This lovely princess, the adopted daughter of Louis XIV., became henceforth the mistress of Sarah; and during the twelve years that she continued to be Duchess of York, there was kindness on the one side, respect on the other. Mary Beatrix was, indeed, about the same age as the young maid of honor. Young and light-hearted, she soon obtained the affection of all classes: her brilliant complexion, her dark hair and eyes, the sweet expression of her countenance, her exquisite form and dignity, gained her the reputation of great beauty, which her portraits do not seem to verify.

Sarah lived occasionally only in the duchess's household; and, under the influence of her example, grew up into a prudent and well-conducted woman, endowed with singular intelligence and ready wit. To these qualities was added a beauty so rare, and yet so enduring, that at the age of sixty, Sarah was still lovely: "a grandmother without a gray hair." Her face was round and small, with soft, deep-blue eyes; a nose somewhat retroussée; a delicate, rosy mouth, on which no trace of *temper* had settled; a forehead white as marble; and a form of easy grace: her hair was especially beautiful; blonde, thick, long, and glossy. Even in a court famed for beauty, Sarah was considered surpassingly lovely.

It happened that, on the marriage of the Duke of York to Mary of Modena, Colonel John Churchill was appointed one of his gentlemen of the bedchamber. He was the son of Sir Winston Churchill of Ashe, in Dorsetshire, where he had been chiefly brought up in seclusion, until, after becoming page to James, Duke of York, he had obtained, at the age of sixteen, a commission in the army.

He was singularly handsome, and when Sarah first knew him was even then esteemed a gallant soldier. Above the middle height, with regular features, a noble brow, thoughtful eyes, and a mouth expressive of sweetness, Churchill might well attract the fancy of a young girl who must have seen him almost daily. His merits as an officer had even then been owned by Turenne, who had added to his praise of the young soldier the *sobriquet* of the Handsome Englishman; and then his manner, Lord Chesterfield has declared, "was irresistible either by man or woman." It was this, that competent authority decides, which made his fortune. Colonel Churchill, however, was, like many others, pushed on by interest. Although his family were Cavaliers of stern integrity themselves, they had not blushed to see Sir Winston's daughter Arabella the avowed mistress of James II. during his first marriage, and the mother of several children, among others of James Fitz-James, Duke of Berwick, whose family is still traceable in France. John Churchill is also generally believed to have been indebted to his cousin Barbara Villiers, Lady Castlemaine, for the means to appear at court, and for the royal patronage which led to an early promotion. She gave him, during the brief continuance of her mad passion for him, while he was only an ensign in the Guards, five thousand pounds (probably public money), with which he bought an annuity from the Earl of Halifax.

It was at the age of twenty-four that Colonel Churchill became enamored of Sarah Jennings. During three years their engagement continued; and even when their marriage took place, it was in privacy, the kind Mary Beatrix being the only confidante. They first met at court; and when Sarah, then in her sixteenth year, saw the hero figure in a dance, her fancy was captivated. It is said that at that age he could scarcely spell. He excelled, however, in the courtier-like accomplishment of dancing. "Every step he took carried death in it," and Sarah, who was then the star of the court, felt that her heart was gone forever. She immediately rejected the addresses of the Earl of Lindsay and others, and accepted the eager love-suit of Colonel Churchill.

For some time their attachment could only be expressed by letters. Those from the duke, poor as was his orthography, display the most ardent tenderness. The replies he received from Sarah were, like herself, variable, petulant, and haughty. Nevertheless, after the fashion of men, Churchill loved her all the more. His family objected to the marriage; for Sarah's portion was scanty, and Churchill's patrimonial estate encumbered, like those of most of the landholders who had clung to the fortunes of Charles I. The estate of Sandridge, to which Sarah was coheiress, was also burdened by provisions for collateral relatives; so that the matter seemed hopeless, until Mary Beatrix offered pecuniary aid, and Churchill purchased with his ill-gained five thousand pounds the annuity from Halifax. But while all this was being arranged, the lovers, as is too often the case in long engagements, fell out perpetually. Once, indeed, matters went so far that Sarah begged of her lover to "give up an attachment which might injure his prospects," and declared that she should set off with her sister Frances to Paris, and so "end the matter." This spirited conduct, coupled with terms of abuse, in which Sarah was pre-eminent, brought matters to a crisis, and the lovers were forthwith united.

Still he continued to address his wife, by letter, as Miss Jennings, probably in order that she might retain her post. "My soul's soul," the brave soldier wrote to her from Antwerp, "I do, with all my heart and soul, long to be with you, you being dearer to me than my own life." Two years afterward, when Churchill was made master of the robes by the Duke of York, the young couple continued in the service of their kind patrons, and with them and the Princess Anne visited the Hague and Brussels. They went subsequently to Edinburgh, the journey to which lasted a month. In 1681, a daughter, Henrietta, afterward Duchess of Marlborough in her own right, was born in London, and the domestic happiness of the young couple seemed to be complete. It is curious to find the great Marlborough, the terror of Europe, writing to his young wife about their child in these terms, thus affording a proof that the bravest hearts are often the tenderest:

"I hope," he says, "all the red spots of our child will be gone against I see her, and her nose straight, so that I may fancy it to be like the mother, for she has your colored hair. I would have her to be like you in all things else." While these domestic incidents were gladdening the father's heart, public affairs wore the darkest aspect. The Rye-House Plot, and its woful results; the death of the Earl of Essex, who, like Raleigh, sought to avert his fate by suicide; the execution of

Russell; all served to show the real character of James II., even before he ascended the throne, and induced Churchill to wish for retirement. He had now been created Baron Churchill of Eyemouth in Scotland, and his favor with his royal master daily increased. Lady Churchill, meantime, as Sarah was now styled, was winning the affections of the Princess Anne, then in maturer age. Anne had her own secrets to pour into the breast of her young confidante. She loved, as far as her placid nature could love, the Earl of Mulgrave, whose addresses to her had been refused by her father. George I. had looked at her with matrimonial intent, but left England without offering. Prince George of Denmark, a staid bachelor, ten years older than the princess, was the husband eventually selected. Without love on either side, there was sympathy. The prince was a Tory at heart; Anne inclined to those sentiments. He loved the pleasures of the table, and taught his wife to do so in time; and they formed as dull and respectable a couple as ever won the suffrages of society.

It may easily be supposed what a court these two illustrious personages must have around them, and how essential Lady Churchill's society was to the heavy-minded Anne. And yet the princess and her favorite were dissimilar. Anne was a martinet in trifles. Every one knows the anecdote of Lord Bolingbroke's presenting himself before her in a Ramillies tie, and her remark "that his lordship would soon come to court in his nightcap." She had her servants marshaled before her every day that she might see if their ruffles were clean, and their periwigs dressed. In her reign, her bust on the gold coin was draped by her command. She had a calm good sense, but few ideas beyond her nursery, Prince George, her evening's rubber of whist, and her favorite, in whom, indeed, all that Anne ever showed of heart seemed to be bound up. She was also a rigid, uncompromising Protestant; while Lady Churchill, who detested trifles, was a latitudinarian in religion, or, rather, she could not bear to have the Church made the watchword for intolerance.

Anne was taciturn from having nothing to say. Sarah was sarcastic, restless, and buoyant. She had been imperfectly educated, but had made the most of what knowledge she possessed. Playing at cards was the only diversion Anne could endure. The lively Sarah soon, therefore, grew weary of a court life. Still she was bound to the princess by many early associations; and, with regard to Anne, she did not insist upon subserviency. "A friend," she said, "was what she most wanted." For the sake of friendship she wished all forms laid aside. "Your highness" displeased her, so she proposed to the lady in waiting that when separated they should adopt less alarming titles. "My frank, open temper," says Lady Churchill, "led me to pitch upon Freeman," and so the princess took the name of Morley; and from this time Mrs. Morley and Mrs. Freeman began to address each other as equals, made so by affection and friendship. But, unhappily, the affection was all on one side. In after life the duchess, though she allowed that Queen Anne possessed a certain majesty of deportment, depicted her as wearing a constant and sullen frown, showing "a gloominess of soul and a cloudiness of disposition:" terms which one would not readily employ when referring to any one who had ever been the object of our genuine attachment. Yet there is something noble and spirited in the following sentiment, expressed by the duchess in her vindication: "Young as I was when I became this high favorite, I laid it down as a maxim that flattery was falsehood to my trust, and ingratitude to my dearest friend." Anne, on the other hand, begged of her not to call her "highness" at every word, but to speak her mind freely in all things.

Henceforth, Lady Churchill remained in the Household of Anne until faction turned their friendship into enmity. Lady Churchill, located at Whitehall, now became the star of that minor court, noted for dullness and respectability, which assembled in Anne's private apartments to play whist, or quadrille, or to drink caudle after the birth of a young prince or princess. From this stately retirement, Lady Churchill witnessed the course of events: the death of Charles II., heartbroken by Monmouth's ingratitude; the accession of James II. During this period the beautiful Mrs. Freeman appears to have held aloof from masquerading, which was the fashion of the day. Her sister Frances, attired as an orange-girl, had passed her basket round in the pit of the theatre under the very eyes of Mary Beatrix, her patroness, and, her disguise half suspected, had vaunted of the compliments paid her. But Sarah abstained from lowering herself; and though afterward reigning over fashion as over politics, was little seen except in the performance of her duties.

Hyde Park was then only a country drive, a field, in fact, belonging to a publican. Sometimes the Princess Anne might be seen there, driving with her beloved Freeman, in her coach, panneled only, without glass windows, which were introduced by Charles II. There they encountered Lady Castlemaine and Miss Stuart, whose quarrel which should first use the famous coach presented by Grammont to the king was the theme of Whitehall. Sometimes from the groves and alleys of Spring Gardens they emerged, perhaps, into the broad walks of St.

James's Park, between the alleys of which, cafés, such as those permitted in the gardens of the Tuileries, were resorted to by the gay and titled. Sometimes the Princess Anne, followed by the haughty Freeman in her hood and mantle, descended Whitehall Stairs, and took her pleasure in her barge on the then calm and fresh waters of the Thames, beyond which were green fields and shady trees. These were all inexpensive pleasures; and both Mrs. Morley and Mrs. Freeman were economical. The princess's allowance from the privy purse was small, and Lord Churchill's means were moderate.

More frequently, however, the two friends sat in the princess's boudoir, then termed her closet, and in that sanctum discussed passing events with bitterness—the dramatic close of the days of Charles II., who begged pardon of his surrounding courtiers for being "so long a-dying;" the accession and unpopularity of his brother James; and, afterward, the event that roused even Anne from her apathy and made her malicious—the birth of the prince whom we southrons call the Pretender.

Kind, gentle, and correct as she was, Mary Beatrix was secretly the object of Anne's dislike. A step-mother is born to be hated: dislike begets dislike; and Mary Beatrix was not wholly faultless in her conduct to the princess. Anne was then the mother of a son of two years of age, and William, Duke of Gloucester, as he had been created, was the heir presumptive to the crown. Doubts were raised: and Anne, touching on the subject of the queen's confinement, provoked her majesty to throw a glove at her face, upon which the princess retired from court, and went to Bath: she was, therefore, as well as Lady Churchill, absent when the birth of James Stuart, afterward styled the Chevalier, took place.

Hitherto Sarah, as well as her lord, had been wholly devoted to the Stuarts, and to that party, not then designated, until a later date, Tories, which holds to the reigning family, right or wrong. But Lord Churchill, attached to the Protestant faith, had ample reason, from the gross tyranny of James II., to withdraw from the court as much as possible, and to decline either new honors or offices of trust under that monarch.

One by one friends and courtiers deserted James II.: but Prince George of Denmark still remained near him during his flight into Salisbury. Whenever any fresh desertion took place, Prince George, with some diplomacy, merely exclaimed, "*Est-il possible?*" At last he went too. Upon hearing of his withdrawal, James, with a degree of humor which we would rather have expected from Charles II., exclaimed—"What! is *Est-il possible* gone too?" On his return, however, to his capital, James found that Anne had also fled: her apartments at the

Cockpit, in Westminster, were empty. "God help me!" cried the disconsolate king; "my own children have forsaken me."

Anne had indeed, from a fear of being involved in disturbances which might injure the succession of her son, taken flight upon the return of *Est-il possible* to Whitehall. In the dead of the night she left her apartments, creeping down by the back stairs, in a hackney-coach, Lady Churchill accompanying her mistress; and protected by the Bishop of London, Dr. Compton, who had been Anne's tutor, they passed through the streets, and, unobserved, arrived at the episcopal palace, then in the city. On the ensuing day the fugitives went to Copt Hall, the seat of the Earl of Dorset: thence to the Earl of Northampton's, and then to Nottingham, where the country, and in particular the adherents of William of Orange, collected to welcome and support Anne. It must have been a simple cortège, of which Mrs. Morley and Mrs. Freeman now formed the main features: for the good Bishop Compton, firing up on the occasion, and recalling his youthful days, in which he had been a cornet of dragoons, rode at the front, with a drawn sword in his hand and a pair of pistols at his saddlebow.

Amid those who assembled at Nottingham was the famous Colley Cibber the dramatist, whose "Provoked Husband" and "Careless Husband" are among the most choice productions of a period rich in dramatic literature. Colley was then a young man, destined for Oxford: and his father, whose famous figures denoting Melancholy Madness and Raving Madness, of the size of life, in the Bethlehem Hospital, have never been excelled, was then usually working at Chatsworth, and altering the old Gothic pile into a Grecian structure. When Colley arrived at Chatsworth, he found that his father had gone to Nottingham to serve in the volunteer corps that had mustered for the protection of Princess Anne; and thither he also went. Now old Caius Cibber was by no means a hero, though the sculptor of heroes; and, on beholding his son full of ardor, he begged him to take his military duties on his young shoulders, and persuaded the Earl of Devonshire, who was the colonel of the corps, to allow of his having this substitute: so Colley, as he described it, jumped into his father's saddle, and figured away in the old man's regimentals.

Soon after this occurred, the corps were ordered to meet the princess on the London road, and to form a guard round her person while she entered Nottingham. The excitement in the town was very great, for a report prevailed that there were two thousand of the King's Dragoons in pursuit of the princess: but the cavalcade reached the Earl of Devonshire's quarters in safety. That night there was a supper. Anne was now the darling of the Protestant party; and all the persons of distinction in the town were eager to accept "my Lord Devonshire's invitation" to supper with him. The guests were many, the attendants few; and Colley Cibber being well known to the Earl of Devonshire's *maître d'hôtel*, was pressed into the service. It must have been a singular and an animated scene. The Princess Anne, stately, but heavy, was attended by two ladies of her bedchamber, both remarkable for their beauty; but Lady Churchill far outshone Lady Fitzhardinge, the other lady, in loveliness. As young Cibber, afterward so noted for his delineation of a woman of haut ton in Lady Modish, stood behind Lady Churchill, his eyes were riveted by her graceful beauty. He could see nothing, hear nothing else.

"Being so near the table," he wrote fifty years afterward, "you may naturally ask me what I might have heard to have passed in conversation at it, which I certainly should tell you had I attended to above two words that were uttered there, and those were, '*Some wine and water;*'" and these came from the "fair guest" whom Colley took such pleasure to wait upon. "Except," he says, "at that single sound, all my senses were collected into my eyes, which, during the whole entertainment, wanted no better amusement than that of stealing now and then the delight of gazing on the fair object so near me." This was Lady Churchill, who sat unconscious of a gaze which the juvenile enthusiast described as "a regard that had something softer than the most profound respect in it;" nor did he see why he was not free to express this admiration, "since beauty, like the sun, must," he thought, "sometimes lose its power to choose, and shine into equal warmth the peasant and the courtier." It was half a century after that evening that Colley, young still in fancy, described in those glowing terms the impression made on him by that brief interview. Lady Churchill was wholly passive in this flight of Anne's, although the blame of it was thrown on her by political writers. The metropolis, however, was in commotion when all was discovered. Every one believed that step to have been premeditated, since six weeks previously Anne had ordered a private stair-case to be made. She had evidently seen the storm afar off. She returned, however, to Whitehall, to see her royal sister Mary occupying the apartments of Mary Beatrix in that palace, and William holding his court at St. James's, escorted by Dutch guards. This was a result which Lady Churchill does not seem to have anticipated, if we may trust her own account.

"I do solemnly protest," she afterward wrote, "that if there be truth in any mortal, I was so very simple a creature that I never once dreamt of his (William III.) being king." Nevertheless, the responsibility was believed by every one to rest in some measure with Lady Churchill, since it was through her advice, it was thought, that Anne gave her consent to the crown being settled on William for life; whereas after Mary she would have been the rightful successor.

At this critical juncture, Lady Churchill wisely sought the advice of persons older and more competent to judge than herself. The widowed Lady Rachel Russell was still living at Southampton House, Bloomsbury, in deep and mournful seclusion. She sought her; and they consulted together, and, with the aid of Archbishop Tillotson, decided on the course to be adopted. It was in Southampton House, therefore, that edifice the sight of which had drawn tears from Lord Russell as he went to execution in Lincoln's Inn Fields, that it was resolved that Anne should henceforth turn from her father's cause, and embrace that of the Revolution. Lady Rachel was then in her prime; and the blindness which added to the sorrows of her old age, a blindness caused by incessant weeping, had not then commenced.

These preliminaries being settled, Lady Churchill endeavored to like, as well as to acknowledge the new queen who had succeeded the heroic, patient, and good Mary of Modena. But the court was indeed altered. Mary of Orange, on taking possession of her apartments at Whitehall, showed too plainly that she wanted feeling still more than the phlegmatic Anne. It was Lady Churchill's duty to attend her Majesty that day to the very rooms which had lately been occupied by Mary Beatrix, with her ill-starred infant son. Mary little suspected that the first lady of her sister's bedchamber was watching her with no friendly gaze. "She ran about," Lady Churchill relates, "looking into every closet and conveniency, and turning up the quilts on the bed, as people do when they come into an inn, and with no other sort of concern in her appearance but such as they express:" and, although at that time Mary was gracious and even caressing to the favorite, Lady Churchill thought her behavior very strange and unbecoming. Decorum, she felt, should have suggested some sadness of countenance when Mary passed through the rooms, and paused to examine the very bed from which her father, King James, had been so lately driven. But these thoughts she kept to herself. Two days afterward the very hall of that palace whence James had fled, and at the gate of which Charles I. had been beheaded, witnessed the proclamation which made William king and

Mary queen. In the present day, the faintest attempt to place a foreign monarch of another dynasty on the throne would produce revolution: in those it was hailed as a refuge against despotism. Two days previously, Lord Churchill having been created Earl of Marlborough, the aspiring Sarah gained another step in the course of her aggrandizement, and became the Countess of Marlborough. But she hated the hand whence this new honor came, and the reign of Mary was imbittered to both the daughters of James II. by the incessant bickerings of the two sisters, and by endless disputes and affronts which Lady Marlborough did not attempt to soothe. She had abandoned, it is true, the friend and patron of her youth, the confidante of her marriage, Mary Beatrix; but she could not avoid feeling that Mary of Orange, with her cold virtues, would never replace that warm and fascinating patroness. The royal sisters also, it was soon perceived, did not assimilate. Mary was a model queen, a model wife; that unpleasant personage, a pattern of excellence. She possessed what Pope calls, "not a science, but worth all the seven, prudence." She began to reform the court, to send away doubtful characters, to set an example of industry in needlework, and of regularity in public devotion as well as in private. She found fault, it appears, with Lady Marlborough's laxity in this last respect; and to hint a blemish in Lady Marlborough was to offend Anne mortally. Then Mary was an *esprit fort*, a great historian and politician, and a great talker; and she found her younger sister, from whom she had been separated for years, as silent as she was stupid, just answering a question, nothing more. William III., too, was intensely jealous of Anne's popularity, a state of things that sometimes is the result of perfect insignificance of character in high station. There soon arose a pretense for disputes, and an outbreak followed of course.

The Princess Anne, as we have seen, lived in that part of Whitehall called from its entrance the Cockpit. St. James's Park, which, in the time of Henry VIII., belonged to the Abbot of Westminster, was bought by that monarch and converted into a park, a tennis-court, and a cock-pit, which was situated where Downing Street now is. The park was approached by two noble gates, and, until the year 1708, the Cockpit Gate, which opened into the court where Anne lived, was standing. It was surmounted with lofty towers and battlements, and had a portcullis, and many rich decorations. Westminster Gate, the other entrance, was designed by Hans Holbein, and some foreign architect doubtless erected the Cockpit Gate.

The scene of the cruel diversion of cock-fighting was, indeed, obliterated before Anne's time, and the palace, which was one long range of apartments and offices reaching to the river, extended over that space.

The locality was pleasant enough. From her windows Anne could see the pleasant village of Charyng: Westminster Abbey, without the towers, stood in an open space, and the Park peopled with singing birds; and though merry King Charles was no longer to be seen there feeding his ducks, and talking pleasantly to every one, there was a grand mall in fine weather, to which lords and ladies, shopwomen, Mohawks and roaring boys, maccaronies (or dandies) of both sexes repaired and sat, in gay dresses and periwigs, under the trees. Yet the Princess Anne was not contented: she had the bad taste to wish to remove to the very rooms once occupied by the Duchess of Portsmouth, mistress to her late uncle, Charles II., a personage who, with other disreputable ladies, had been routed by Queen Mary from the now saintly precincts of Whitehall. The difficulties and discussions induced by Anne's wish to remove, produced endless heartburnings, and ended in Anne's taking the duchess's rooms for her children's use, and remaining at the Cockpit.

Here, at this period, resorted the gay, the learned, the intriguing, attracted, not by Queen Anne and her dull consort, but by the grace, the wit, and busy political turn of Lady Marlborough. She stands at the head of those who have been "queens of society," for she governed the *beau monde* of her own time. It is true she was not in her climax until Anne was on the throne; but she was in the radiance of her youth when her friend Mrs. Morley dwelt in the Cockpit. Unlettered, she was the counselor of her famous husband, the leading star of his ambition. Her plain, shrewd sense, without one grain of sentiment, riveted him. They had but one heart, one soul between them: while her loveliness, her dignified ease, her vivacity, fascinated a man of powerful understanding and noble qualities—the celebrated minister, Sidney Godolphin.

The very name Godolphin, signifying a white eagle, recalled in those days one of the heroes of the Great Rebellion, the ill-fated Sidney Godolphin. Like most others of Charles's adherents, the minister of Queen Anne belonged to an impoverished race, and it was even contemplated by his friends to place him in some trade. The young Cornishman had, however, all the shrewdness of the west countrymen; and, being a page to Charles II., when once in the precincts of a court, he made the best of his opportunities. Nothing, however, in the public service so accorded with his inclinations as being made chamberlain to Mary Beatrix. He admired, he respected, he almost loved this young and amiable queen, and continued to befriend her until the close of his own career.

That career was a struggle between principle and affection. When James II. showed his true designs to his indignant people, Godolphin, like an honest man, clung to the standard of civil and religious liberty; but his heart was with his early patrons. Courageous, but tender-hearted, he set his party at defiance, accompanied James II. to the seashore, before his final departure for France, and continued to correspond with him, which he honestly confessed to William III., until the death of the exiled monarch. Godolphin was Lord Treasurer to James II., and he was retained in that office by William III. Although one of the plainest of men, he had attracted, early in her youth, Queen Anne's regard: he was now, according to slanderous report, the favored lover of Sarah, Countess of Marlborough. Deeply marked with the small-pox, his countenance was harsh; and no one could have imagined that Godolphin could weep like a woman when his feelings were touched, and that he was prone to sentiment. His smile, however, when it broke forth from his plain, hard features, was most winning, and his eyes were dark and penetrating. Such was the man, to whose honor be it spoken that he even cherished for Mary of Modena a romantic and generous devotion, and to injure whom it was alleged by contemporaries that the wife of his friend and coadjutor, Marlborough, was the object of a passion by no means platonic. There existed at that period a paid regiment of writers, whose works were at once calumnious and adulatory. As "Queen Sarah," as she was now styled, was often the subject of the latter, so she sometimes became the butt of the former style of writing. Patronized by Dean Swift, among the venal defamers of the day, appears the notorious Rivella, *alias* Mrs. de la Riviere Manley, whose "Atalantis," "History of Prince Mirabel," "Secret History of Queen Zarah and the Zarazians," were thought worthy of being preserved by Swift among the state tracts. Rivella was a woman of abandoned character, the pupil, in her youth, of the infamous Madame Mazarin, the confidante of the Duchess of Cleveland, and the tool, for party purposes, of the malignant Swift. It was her aim, of course, at once to lower the Marlborough ascendency with the public, and to cut short an intimacy beneficial to all concerned, by tainting it with her foul and absurd aspersions; but Queen Sarah could not be aspersed. Her moral character was invulnerable. She rose superior to the assault, and retained the all-important friendship of Godolphin to her latest day. A woman of prudence and virtue has, in fact, a far greater latitude of action in her conscious innocence than those who dare not defy calumny. Marlborough was, indeed, continually absent; the very first campaign in Ireland tore him from his home. His letters were full of tenderness to her whom he left. "Put your trust in God," he wrote to his wife, in the very midst of his triumphs, "and be assured that I think I can't be unhappy as long as you are kind." And after the battle of Ramilies—"Pray believe me when I assure you that I love you more than I can express." Yet Sarah had now passed the bloom of her youth, and her temper had lost its equanimity. Still the hero pined for repose with her. "As God has been pleased to bless me," he writes in another letter, "I do not doubt but He will reward me with some years to end my days with you; and if that be with quietness and kindness, I shall be much happier than I have ever been yet."

Lady Marlborough was, indeed, every way blessed: to please her, her husband now purchased the share in the family estate, from her coheiresses Frances and Barbara, and built a large mansion on the spot where she was born, called Holywell House, a stately structure, which she left only when Blenheim was given them by the nation, and in which some remember the old Lady Spencer, the mother of the beautiful Duchess of Devonshire, living in great comfort and suitable style.

Some clouds, nay, some storms there were at times in this serene atmosphere; but these were almost essential to keep Queen Sarah alive, in the dull court of the Princess Anne. Like most spoiled women, she had one pet aversion, and that was King William, whom she called "Caliban." Other names that she gave him were not even so decorous as that offensive sobriquet. The dry, cold manner of William affronted her: the king despised talkers, and one of Lady Marlborough's greatest gifts was conversation. Then she hated his character, which, she thought, was exhibited in its true colors by William's eating up a dish of early peas all himself, while Anne, near her confinement, was dying to partake of them. "Europe and the back stairs," Horace Walpole remarks, "shared in her mind in importance;" and while every-day incidents affected her mind to phrensy, it became hard to take a broad and generous view of affairs.

The court now assumed a formality that disgusted one who hated surface-piety. William, while Lady Orkney was his mistress, paraded virtue in the plainest of forms. His sententious remarks, his deep reserve, his chilling demeanor, formed a singular contrast with the easy politeness and mirth of Charles II., and the stately courtesy of King James. At Hampton Court, whither he retired with Mary, his "Roman eagle" nose, his sparkling eyes—conspicuous on a face deeply seamed with the small-pox—his thin, small figure, made him look like a caricature of mankind. Like Napoleon III., he had the grand secret of hiding all he thought, and much that he felt. The royal actor on that stage whereon the pageant of royalty had of late passed so suddenly away, had the talent so much commended, for silence. The automaton monarch, however, broke the peaceful stillness by his deep convulsive cough, and the weakness which was bearing him to the grave recalled the conviction that he was human.

Lady Marlborough now passed much of her time at Hampton Court, to which William was adding that mass of building which looks upon the gardens, and where he was planning, with a lingering fondness for his Dutch palace at Loo, the noble gardens upon the model of those of his regretted home. Amid the ornaments of the presence-chambers, none formed a more suitable embellishment than Queen Mary herself. She was every inch a queen, and far more agreeable in appearance than her sister Anne. Tall, majestic, with a fine open face—though weak-eyed—Mary moved with infinite grace. Fond of society, she endeavored to obviate the impression made by the king's rudeness and taciturnity by talking herself, and by bringing around her those who could adorn the now exclusive circle of Hampton Court and Kensington. But she could not succeed in making the dull receptions of her court cheerful, or even endurable; for all the fashion, wit, and talent centered round Lady Marlborough.

Little did Mary love her sister Anne; yet she ascribed all the bickerings that now arose to the favorite, henceforth called the "dictatress," and resolved, if she could, to accomplish her dismissal. In spite of Lord Marlborough's great services to the crown, he had been detected in carrying on a correspondence bordering on treason with James II.; and, a still more fatal error, he was also discovered to have told his wife of a design of William's to surprise the important port of Dunkirk. That project had transpired—and failed. It had been mentioned by Lady Marlborough to a Lady Oglethorpe; by Lady Oglethorpe to Frances Jennings, now Lady Tyrconnel; by *her* it was transmitted to the French court. Jean Bart, the pirate, a native of Dunkirk, had cut through the English ships which blockaded the harbor, and saved the town.

Marlborough was disgraced, and his wife was led to conclude that she would be forbidden the court; nevertheless, with her usual courage, emboldened also by the advice of Godolphin, she attended Anne, when the princess conceived it to be her duty to visit her royal sister at Kensington.

No details of the audience are extant; but it may be readily pictured to a mind conversant with that period. The interior of Kensington Palace was then dark and cheerless; the walls were oak paneled; the roof richly embossed. Beneath a canopy of state sat Mary, in her accustomed deep-blue gown, with flowing skirts, and a chemisette of point lace opening in the front of the bust. Her plump throat is encircled with a collar of pearls; her hair is flowing down her back: in front it is raised high on the head in a toupee form, intermingled on either side with pearls. She wears a "commode" to set out her train, and has raised heels. Her aim is to be delicate and regal, for Mary has never worn her petticoats short since those days of youthful folly when she skated on the Scheldt with the Duke of Monmouth, whom it was William's policy to allure to his Dutch court. In vain has she tried to model her dress strictly by the rules of modesty, though angry with Kneller for continuing to paint her in a costume which looks as if it were likely to drop off altogether.

By her side sits the king in a French peruke, which almost obliterated his face, except his eagle nose, and fell down to his small waist. He wears a field-marshal's uniform, with the star and garter, a costume rarely altered by him; and his cough might be heard, dry and asthmatic, even at the very entrance of the presence-chamber.

Courtiers of every grade, silver sticks and gold sticks, the grand chamberlain and pages, stand in their appointed places, some in waving flaxen perukes, called by wags, "the silver fleeces," others in frosted wigs, which had just begun to succeed the dark, curling perukes of Charles II. and his time. The higher the rank of each individual, the larger the wig. (Shame on Louis XIV., by whom this absurdity was introduced, and in whose reign even statues were bewigged!) The king's feet are mounted on high-heeled shoes, and buckles of diamonds, set in silver, shine on the step on which they rested. William's brow darkens as he beholds the princess enter, for he has heard that when the disgrace of Marlborough was announced to her, Anne had shed tears. She knew what was next to happen.

Near the king stood Bentinck, afterward Duke of Portland, and once page to his Dutch majesty. Bentinck was one of Lady Marlborough's most powerful foes, for he had secured William's whole power of affection by nursing him, at the peril of his own life, through the small-pox—as great an act of friendship in those days, when that scourge was wholly unmitigated, as can be conceived. Bentinck had taken the disease, and his placid face, seamed and disfigured, could never fail to recall to the king his act of devotion. To him we owe the taste of gardening, which England, until his time, but little appreciated. Anne, when queen, never forgave his dislike of her dear Mrs. Freeman, but deprived him of his post as keeper of Windsor Great Park. The princess with her consort, Prince George, in his full dress as lord high admiral, may be easily pictured. The rubicund face of *Est-il possible* is now somewhat weather-beaten. He has lately distinguished himself fighting against his father-in-law's troops at the Battle of the Boyne; nevertheless, the king and queen treat the brave nonentity with no more respect, as Queen Sarah declares, "than if he had been a page of the back stairs."

Anne scowling, though Kensington would never have been too light, is handed by her consort with an air of injured innocence. There is a resemblance observable between the royal sisters, but the difference is the absence of intelligence and grace. Anne is clumsy in her stateliness; Mary is perfect in every attitude. Anne has a somewhat good housewife air, and looks like the respectable mother of a family. Mary is a Stuart and a queen. As Anne, in a cinnamon-colored gown, with a crimson train, a falling jewel on her brow, and her hair in thick short curls high on her forehead, moves heavily forward, a whisper runs through the presence-chamber. "What! Lady Marlborough? and her husband dismissed from his command, and she the cause?" Yes, she is coming in all her matured beauty, with her light hair all in wavy curls on her head; one tendril intruding upon her brow whiter than snow. The hair systematically careless is thrown back so as to show the ears, and the delicate region of the cheek, the chin, the throat; and falls in tresses far away, undulating, glossy tresses over the left shoulder. While all around are blazing with jewels, she wears not one: her dress is white satin, and could stand alone; but she, too, has a "commode:" her white arm has a string of pearls round it, and that is all.

On the left side of the queen walks Lady Fitzhardinge, whom Sarah loved—a rare distinction—and who betrayed her friends to William, an event so rare in courts; and followed by the usual silver sticks, and the complement of pages, they make their way up to the Cloth of Estate amid the smiles and murmurs of all present.

The reception—to return from this ideal picture to fact—was perfectly freezing; and, early in the next day, Mary intimated to her sister that since she had allowed Lady Marlborough to go to Kensington with her, her "lady of the bedchamber must not stay" in the princess's service: Anne's taking her "was the very strangest thing ever done, and was very unkind in a sister, and would have been very uncivil in an equal." She could pass over most things, but could not pass over Lady Marlborough's going to court on that occasion.

To this message Anne returned a calm but resolute reply,

said to have been suggested by Godolphin. No answer was sent to it, except a messenger from the lord chamberlain to Lady Marlborough, commanding her to leave the Cockpit; that being in Whitehall was considered within the queen's rights. The princess thereupon, resolved not to separate from her friend, packed up, and went away also, accepting, for a time, the loan of Sion House from the Duke of Somerset.

So far Queen Sarah was triumphant; but even her spirits and health were affected by her husband's continued disgrace. "Do, for God's sake," Anne wrote to her, "have a little care of your dear self. Give way as little to melancholy as you can. Try asses' milk." And she was miserable at the necessity of Mrs. Freeman's being "let blood."

The feud between the two sisters went on for some time; but Anne was as obstinate as any Stuart. Lady Marlborough, meantime, lost her infant son, Lord Brackley; and the princess taking a chair, braved royal anger, and went to see her. In vain did Mrs. Freeman offer to give up her post to insure peace. Anne answered her offers in letters which her dear friend afterward described as very "indifferent both in sense and spelling," with great repetitions of a few passionate expressions.

Anne's court, meantime, was almost deserted; and when she went to Bath, her uncle, Lord Rochester, wrote to the mayor (a tallow-chandler), forbidding any respect to be shown to her; yet Anne was scarcely vexed. Her favorite's smiles or frowns affected her more than the tallow-chandler's not being allowed to light up Bath. "Dear Mrs. Freeman must give me leave to ask her," she humbly wrote one night, "if any thing has happened to make her uneasy. I thought she looked to-night as if she had the spleen; and I can't help being in pain whenever I see her so." Mary even ordered that the text of the sermon at St. James's, where Anne went to church, should not be put into her pew according to custom; but that "noble design," as Mrs. Freeman termed it, was dropped by the advice of ministers.

These woman-like disputes were going on when Mary was attacked with the small-pox, and died, owing to the mistaken treatment of Dr. Radcliffe. The two sisters never met more, and the audience at Kensington was their last interview.

After a time, when William's bitter anguish was somewhat assuaged, he was reconciled to the Princess Anne; and forthwith crowds were seen hastening to Berkeley House, and Queen Sarah was once more in her glory. How thoroughly she despised those who now caressed her as the "dictatress" once more! How intensely diverted she seems to have been with the half-witted Lord Carmarthen's saying to Anne, as he stood by her in the circle: "I hope your highness will remember that I came to wait upon you when none of this company did;" and a burst of laughter shook the courtly assembly.

In spite of the reconciliation, however, William continued to show all the malice of a little mind toward his successor and sister-in-law. When Anne waited on his majesty at Kensington, no more respect was paid to her than to any other lady until this neglect was talked about; and then Lord Jersey saw her to her coach, but no one higher than a page of the back stairs ever came to meet her. Often was the princess kept waiting for an hour and a half. These annals of a wardrobe, as Horace Walpole terms them, are characteristic; and, as such, it is to be regretted that Hook the historian, to whom the duchess intrusted the arrangement of her Memoirs, thought it prudent to cut out some of the most amusing and impertinent passages. Time, however, softened all these heart-burnings; and William, how bitter soever his dislike to the Lady Marlborough, did justice at last to her husband. When the Duke of Gloucester, Anne's only surviving child, became old enough to require a governor, William confided him to Marlborough: "Teach him, my lord, to be like yourself," were William's words to Marlborough; "and my nephew can not want accomplishments." Bishop Burnet was appointed the little duke's tutor by Marlborough; and between them they so overtrained the poor hot-house plant, that in two years it ceased to exist. Five daughters and one son seemed to fill up the measure of Lord and Lady Marlborough's felicity. But of all human sources of happiness, none excite so much hope, none often cause such bitter disappointment, as children. The son, Lord Blandford, died early; the daughters were beautiful and virtuous, but had tempers like their mother, and, as they grew up, there was little family union. Lady Henrietta Churchill, in her eighteenth year, was married to Lord Rialton, the eldest son of the minister Godolphin; she afterward became Duchess of Marlborough in her own right, but died before her mother. Of her it is told that, being devotedly attached to Congreve, the dramatist, she had, after his death, a wax figure made resembling him, which was placed in his usual seat at her table, a cover always being laid for "Mr. Congreve." Henrietta's temper was not unperceived by her father, who deeply regretted the quarrels between his wife and daughters as the latter grew up.

Lady Anne, the second of the great Marlborough's daughters, and the loveliest, was married to Lord Sunderland, son of the disgraced minister, Sunderland, and through her descendants the titles and estates of the Churchills have been enjoyed by the Spencers. She was all goodness; but her union was infelicitous. Beneath a frigid demeanor, Lord Sunderland concealed fiery passions; with a cold heart, a republican in public, a tyrant in private life, when, a young widower, he sought the hand of Lady Anne Churchill, what affections he had were buried in the tomb of his first wife, Lady Arabella Cavendish. On this account Lord and Lady Marlborough long hesitated before they would intrust their best-beloved daughter to him. They were married, however, and Lady Sunderland became a leader of fashion; to compass which she must needs be a politician. "The *little Whig*," as she was called, from the smallness of her stature, used to wear her patches on the left side, while the Tory ladies wore theirs on the right; so that all society was divided by this social freemasonry. Lady Sunderland died at an early age of consumption.

Next came Lady Elizabeth, married to the Earl of Bridgewater:

> "Hence Beauty, waking, all her forms supplies,
> An angel's sweetness in Bridgewater's eyes."*

She also died of consumption, and is buried in Gaddesden Church, Hertfordshire.

Then came "Angel Duchess Montagu," Lady Mary Churchill, married to the Duke of Montagu; but, although Pope gave her that name, she seems to have been a complete shrew. Her mother and she were long at variance.

"I wonder you and your mother can not agree," said Marlborough, worn out, in old age, by their squabbles; "you are so alike."

The daughter of the Duchess of Montagu, the good and gay Duchess of Manchester, was a great favorite of Queen Sarah's.

"Duchess of Manchester," said her grandmother to her one day, "you are a good creature, but you *have* a mother."

"And *she*, too, has a mother," was the ready, fearless retort.

For her daughters, the "dictatress" procured so many places, that Queen Anne's court was said to consist only of one family. Yet, though they added lustre to her life, they were not the solace of her age.

The death of William III., in 1702, formed an era in the life of Queen Sarah. She was forty-three years of age, and her husband fifty-three, when, Anne coming to the throne, their prosperity was raised to the acme. Queen Sarah was now captivating as a wit rather than as a beauty; yet her loveliness remained still; and her hair, preserved by the use of

* Pope.

honey-water, was abundant still, and untouched by time. Her haughtiness had now grown into insolence, and her temper was chiefly vented upon her royal patroness, whom for ten years she governed without a rival. The courtiers, who had been weeping at the bedside of William, now rushed from Kensington to the more congenial atmosphere of St. James's, which was crowded with loyal subjects, congratulating her whom they had deserted when she had held her court in the privacy of Berkeley House.

The coronation followed in a few months, when Lady Marlborough was seen in all her glory, attending on the queen, who was carried in a low chair from the hall at Westminster to the abbey. Even then the watchful courtiers observed that when holding the queen's gloves, or presenting them to her majesty, the "dictatress" used to turn away her head, "as if she had an ill smell under her nose." But Anne took this insolence passively, and heaped honors and pensions on her two favorites.

In the midst of all Lady Marlborough's triumphs, however, a blow came which might have chastened a less proud spirit. Her son, the Marquis of Blandford, caught the small-pox at Cambridge: the disease appeared in its most malignant form. His mother, now, by the creation of her husband, Duchess of Marlborough, hastened to him. The queen sent two of her physicians in one of the royal carriages to see him. For some time there was a slight, slight hope. In this suspense the great heart of Marlborough was poured out thus to his wife:

"If we must be so unhappy as to lose this poor child," such were his words, "I pray God to enable us both to behave ourselves with that resignation which we ought to do. If this uneasiness which I now lie under should last long, I think I could not live. For God's sake, if there be any hope of recovery, let me know it."

A few hours after writing this letter, the unhappy father, unable to bear the delay of a reply, set off for Cambridge, where he arrived only in time to see his son expire. The youth was buried in King's College Chapel, the place where his prayers had been regularly and fervently uttered ever since his residence at college. Marlborough mourned like a father and a Christian; but he was summoned to the seat of war, and, in the excitement of battle, strove to bear his loss and to believe it for the best. It did not wean his wife from the world in which her whole soul was fatally bound up. The bereaved couple were separated by the French war for many months.

The duchess was now for many years, if not queen indeed, the queen of society. Lord Somers and the Earl of Halifax, of whose poetry Horace Walpole observes time has indeed "withered the charms," Pope, who satirized her as Atossa, Gay, Steele, Addison, Congreve, all mingled in the circles which, in the Friary in St. James's, where Queen Sarah latterly resided, were assembled. She delighted also in the society of Lady Mary Wortley Montagu, then a young and brilliant member of society. In after days Lady Mary and Lady Bute used to visit the duchess, and even sit by her while she was at dinner, or when casting up her accounts, which she did in the very midst of all her busy life. In the course of conversation with these two charming women, the duchess used to relate how proud the duke had formerly been of her luxuriant hair. One day, however, he offended her, and Sarah in a fury punished him. She cut off all those fair tresses, and laid them in a room through which Marlborough was obliged to pass, that he might see them, and be vexed. To her surprise, the duke took no notice of the loss of her locks. Years afterward she found them, however, in a cabinet among the most precious of his possessions, treasured up. At this point of her story the duchess used to melt into tears. The kind heart that had loved and pardoned her was, when Lady Mary Wortley heard the anecdote, in the grave, and the cold, undutiful members of the family alone remained.

Among the votaries of the duchess, Colley Cibber, in a scarlet and gold livery—for he was now one of the royal comedians, and styled "a gentleman of the great chamber"—still admired the charms of the "grandmother without a gray hair." Mrs. Oldfield, the original Lady Betty Modish, was also admitted, frail as she was, into the aristocratic saloons then thrown open widely to talent. Here she learned to personate the woman of fashion. She was the mistress of William Maynwaring, who, at forty, had become attached to the first-rate actress with all the passion and with more than the constancy of a first love. In vain did Maynwaring's best friends, and among others the Duchess of Marlborough, try to turn him from a connection so discreditable. Maynwaring was *ami de la maison* to the duke and duchess, and died at Holywell, after walking in the gardens there, very suddenly. He divided his property between Mrs. Oldfield and his sister, for which he was blamed by Swift, who knew not one generous sentiment, and defended by Sir Robert Walpole.

During the reign of Queen Sarah at Court, Maynwaring had often warned her of the risk she ran in treating the queen with contemptuous familiarity. Dr. Hare, Bishop of Chichester, recommended self-control on still higher grounds, while the famous Dr. Garth was, in all emergencies, not only a physician but a friend. But nothing could pacify her implacable haughty spirit, and it brought its own reward.

Favored so eminently by fortune, the duke and duchess had still their trials. Among the bitterest enemies of the Whig party was Dean Swift. He had set out in life as a violent Whig. When James II. left Whitehall, the dean declared that nothing would purify that ancient palace after the Stuarts had lived there.

> "He's gone—the rank infection still remains,
> Which to repel requires eternal pains."

The "mad parson," as Swift was called at Button's Coffee House, before his name was known there, excited the curiosity of many persons. The appearance of the "Tale of a Tub," in 1704, betrayed the renegade to his former friends. The "Examiner," conducted by Swift, Atterbury, Bolingbroke, and Prior, all Tory writers, made both the Duke and Duchess of Marlborough the objects of its skill and satire. The Whig party now began to decline, and, in spite of the great victories of Ramilies and Blenheim, which ought to have re-enforced Marlborough and Godolphin, a change of ministry took place, and Harley, Earl of Oxford, the very head and front of the High Church and Tory party, became prime minister. It is true that he endeavored by every possible means to gain the favor of the power behind the throne—Queen Sarah; but whatever were her failings, she was fearlessly sincere—and she defied him: she would not bend to his flatteries, nor scarcely listen to him when he spoke.

The duchess had, since the battle of Blenheim, become a princess of the German empire. Her pride was now almost too great for her attendance at court to continue: she was becoming weary of her duties; but, although willing to go out, was by no means inclined "to be turned out," and possibly her reign would have endured until the last, had it not been for one fatal error in her tactics.

It is often poor relations, or humble friends, who prove the worst foes of the incautious.

One of the queen's dressers, by name Abigail Hill, had owed the post to the Duchess of Marlborough, to whom she was related. Abigail was the "Becky" of Queen Anne's back stairs. Her father had been a Turkey merchant, and had failed; and she had even been reduced so low as to become a servant to Lady Rivers; but her kinswoman had rescued her, and placed her in the queen's household.

Her motives for this charitable act originated in that old-fashioned claim of consanguinity which is too often disallowed in the present day. Sir John Jennings, the duchess's grandfather, had had two-and-twenty children; and though he had an estate of four thousand a year, Mrs. Hill, the mother of Abigail, came in for a share of five hundred pounds only; and her husband having speculated, the family were reduced to indigence.

One day a lady ventured at Whitehall to tell the lofty Sarah that she had relations who were destitute. The dictatress, though by no means fond of parting with money, pulled ten guineas out of her purse and sent it for present use. Mrs. Hill's eldest daughter, Abigail, after this became an inmate of the duchess's house at Holywell, and was brought up in a wholesome state of fear of her patroness. In due time Abigail was promoted to be one of the Princess Anne's bedchamber women or dressers; "for," the duchess states, "as I found rockers (from the royal nursery) in King James's reign were promoted to that office," she did not see why she might not ask for it for poor Abigail Hill, whose younger sister was made laundress to the little Duke of Gloucester. Another member of this indigent family was Jack Hill, who was at first put into the Customs, and afterward rose to be a general, and commanded in the expedition to Quebec: nevertheless this "ragged boy, the honest Jack Hill, a good-for-nothing lad," was afterward, says the duchess, "persuaded by his sisters to get up, wrap himself in warmer clothes than those I had given him, and go to the House to vote against the duke."

The end might be conjectured, even if the often-told story of ingratitude and meanness on the one hand, and insolence and generosity on the other, had not been circumstantially told by the duchess in her "Vindication."

The queen and her favorite differed, it seemed, on several important points. Anne hated the idea of the Hanoverian succession, and pined to bring her brother back to England. Sarah was all for George I. and that dynasty, and showed her temper whenever Anne dared to rebel against her opinion. No sooner had she left the palace than Anne sent for Mrs. Hill to confide to her how ill treated she was. Mrs. Hill was willing to go all lengths, and to be a Jacobite heart and soul. Her manner was flattering and humble; and she had the additional advantage of being connected with Harley, Earl of Oxford, whose sentiments were Tory. In the midst of all this back-stairs intriguing, Miss Abigail married, privately, Mr. Samuel Masham, the eighth son of Sir Francis Masham, baronet, a groom of Prince George's bedchamber. But though the Duchess of Marlborough was not informed of this secret union, Queen Anne was a confidante in the affair, and had even attended the ceremony secretly, as Queen Sarah found out from a boy who waited on the upper servants in Anne's household: "back stairs" again!

The deception had been carried on some time. Whenever the duchess went to see the queen, in stepped Mrs. Masham, with the boldest and gayest air possible. At the sight of her benefactress she stopped short, changed her manner, and dropping a solemn courtesy, with a—"*Did* your majesty ring?" retired with demure humility.

As the duchess was, as she expressed it, "apt to tumble out her mind," she did not scruple to express herself very openly when her suspicions were confirmed; and to her horror she found that the queen began to take her cousin's part. Offense followed offense: there was no reasoning with worthy Queen Anne, who had a habit of repeating the same thing over and over again, till Sarah was almost ready to rush from the room in a rage. Mrs. Masham had offended her Grace of Marlborough by never going near her; and when the duchess complained of this one day, the queen said that it was very natural Mrs. Masham should keep away, since the duchess was angry with her; and she was quite in the right. "My cousin," cried Sarah, "has no need to be afraid, uuless she is conscious of some crime." Then Queen Anne began again—(this tiresome way of repeating the one idea in her mind had been inherited from her father)—"It was very natural, and she was very much in the right:" upon which, exasperated beyond measure, "Mrs. Freeman," as she was now only occasionally styled, got up, went away, and shut the door of the closet, in which she and the queen sat, with such violence that the very walls shook, and the corridor echoed with the sound.

Mrs. Masham, terrified, did at last call on the incensed duchess. Reproaches and recriminations proved that the poor queen was in the right; her interview made matters worse. During the ensuing Christmas holidays the duchess made one more attempt to see the queen. They were still Mrs. Freeman and Mrs. Morley in words; but all confidence was gone. Queen Anne stood during the interview, as if to give a hint that it was to be short; and when they parted, merely gave her hand to the duchess, who stooped to kiss it. "She took me up," the duchess relates, "with a very cold embrace, and then, without one kind word, let me go." The duchess, nevertheless, made another effort. She wrote to the queen, promising never to name her cousin Abigail again, and begging her majesty before she received the holy communion to examine herself; quoting, also, passages from the "Whole Duty of Man," then the handbook of the religious world, and Jeremy Taylor; but, in spite of her lecture to Queen Anne and her promise, calling Mrs. Masham "a wretch."

Neither argument nor promise availed. The Duke and Duchess of Marlborough were obliged, by the influence of Abigail, to resign their offices; and from the moment of their retirement, Queen Anne ceased either to be great abroad or respected at home. Henceforth, whenever Anne addressed her former favorite, it was in the tone of command. Mrs. Morley and Mrs. Freeman had ceased to exist.

They met, however, once more. When Prince George of Denmark lay expiring, the duchess hastened to Kensington, and was present at his last moments. When all was over, the duchess, in the warmth of a generous heart, kneeling, entreated her majesty to let her accompany her to St. James's, and to leave the scene of sorrow. Queen Anne was touched, but quailed at the idea of offending her "poor Masham," who was not in the room. She assented, however; but placing her watch in Sarah's hand, bade her retire till the finger should reach a certain hour; meantime to send Mrs. Masham to her. A crowd was collected outside the antechamber. The duchess, who perceived that all chance of regaining the queen's favor was at an end, resolved that the failure of her favor should not be disclosed to the expectant courtiers. She ordered them to retire while her majesty should pass through; she gave directions that her own coach should be ready for the queen's use: then she returned to the royal closet. "Your majesty," said the lofty dictatress, "must excuse my not delivering your message to Mrs. Masham; your majesty can send for her to St. James's how and when you please." Then she gave her arm to the queen, who, looking to the right and to the left, afraid of wounding her dear Masham, on whom she bestowed a glance of kindness, moved along the gallery. But no reconciliation ensued, and Queen Anne, when at St. James's, chose to sit in the very closet latterly occupied by Prince George, because the "back stairs" belonging to it communicated with Mrs. Masham's apartment; and Abigail could thus bring to her any one with whom she chose to carry on political intrigues.

Well might Shakspeare's lines in his Richard II., in speaking of the farewell between Anne and her once dear Mrs. Freeman, be recalled:

> "And say, what store of parting tears were shed,
> Faith none by me, except the north-east wind
> (Which then blew bitterly against our faces)
> Awak'd the sleepy rheum, and so by chance,
> Did grace our bitter parting with a tear."

Henceforth the duchess must be considered as the head of the Opposition. Swift now attacked her more fiercely than ever in the "Examiner," and accused her of taking enormous bribes when in office, and of peculating as mistress of the wardrobe. When Queen Anne heard of these charges, she remarked: "Every body knows that *cheating* is not the Duchess of Marlborough's crime."

Still Swift was in close alliance with the Masham faction, and directed against the Duke and Duchess of Marlborough those lines beginning,

"A widow kept a favorite cat,
At first a gentle creature:
But when he was grown sleek and fat,
With many a mouse and many a rat,
He soon disclosed his nature."

The erection of a ducal residence at Blenheim henceforth occupied the duke and duchess's retirement. It was designed by Sir John Vanbrugh, an architect who was the object of Sarah's inveterate hatred. Vanbrugh built the Haymarket Theatre: there he assisted Betterton as manager, and brought out two plays, "The Relapse" and the "The Provoked Wife," at once witty and immoral.

Vanbrugh was completing Castle Howard when he was engaged to build Blenheim. To his fantastic taste we owe St. John's Church, Westminster; not to mention his own residence, now pulled down, at Whitehall, of which Swift writes,

"At length they in the rubbish spy
A thing resembling a goose pie."

He was comptroller of the royal works, on which account, and being a man, on his mother's side, of good family, and of an agreeable exterior, he had been cherished in the society of the great. Having once been confined in the Bastile, and having been humanely treated, he built a house for himself on that model at Greenwich. He now began Blenheim, a work of which Swift says,

"That if his Grace* were no more skilled in
The art of battering walls than building,
We might expect to see next year
A mousetrap-man chief engineer."

The duchess and Vanbrugh began very soon to quarrel: she thought "sevenpence halfpenny per bushel for lime a very high price, when it could be made in the park," and he did not hesitate to call her very "foolish and troublesome."

She, in a manuscript letter never yet published, taunted him with going down to Blenheim in a coach with six horses; while old Wren, she said, was carried up and down to the top of St. Paul's in a basket, and though with ten times his genius,

* The Duke of Marlborough.

never grumbled. Vanbrugh, to do him justice, wished to restore the old Manor House of Woodstock (idolized by Sir Walter Scott). It was a picturesque building, quadrangular, with a court, and standing on an elevation near the then small stream, the Glyme, on whose banks old Chaucer wandered. Within the precincts of this tenement was the famous labyrinth "Rosamond's Bower;" and there was a gate-house in front of the ancient palace, from the window of which Queen Elizabeth, when a captive there, is said to have envied a milkmaid whom she saw passing, and to have written with charcoal those lines which are still extant, describing her wish for freedom. The Roundheads, too, had sheltered themselves in the Manor House. Yet, in spite of all these associations, the duchess ordered the house to be pulled down, Godolphin, without one atom of taste, aiding her by declaring "that he would as soon hesitate about taking a wen from his face as delay removing so unsightly an object from the brow of the hill." Down, therefore, it went; and the hill being of an "intractable shape," as Vanbrugh said, was lowered. Among other relics found in the earth was a ring with the words—"Remember the Covenant." It was given by the masons to Lady Diana Spencer. Blenheim was begun in 1705: in 1714 the shell of the building was not complete. It had then cost two hundred and twenty thousand pounds of public money.

The duke and duchess had begun to fear the enormous expense of living in such a palace, and to calculate about tons of coals and wax candles. When the Duke of Marlborough died, he left the duchess, however, ten thousand pounds, as the duchess said, to spoil Blenheim her own way; and twelve thousand a year to keep herself clean with and go to law. She finished the house, which altogether cost three hundred thousand pounds. The triumphal arch and the column were erected by her at her own expense. But a stout war was carried on between her and Vanbrugh, whom she would never allow to enter the house, even years after its completion. He consoled himself by calling her that "wicked woman of Marlborough," because she had seen through that remorseless jobbery which has ruined almost every national building in England.

The dictatress was, in fact, a woman of wonderful shrewdness. When the South Sea scheme was broached she predicted its fatal result. She had a great art of getting and hoarding money, yet she knew not one rule of arithmetic: when she added up, she set down her figures at random, as if a child had been scribbling on the paper; yet her sums, done chiefly in her head, always came right.

In 1716, the Duke of Marlborough was attacked by palsy,

partly in consequence of the death of his favorite daughter, Anne, Countess of Sunderland, "the little Whig." His mind never recovered its tone, and his nerves were far more shattered by the duchess's temper than by his battles or the turmoil of politics. One day when Dr. Garth, who was attending him, was going away, the duchess followed him down stairs and *swore* at him for some offense. Vainly did the duke try the Bath waters. He recovered partially, and his memory was spared. It is therefore wrong to couple him, as he has been in the following lines, with Swift, who became a violent lunatic, and died in moody despondency:

> "From Marlborough's eyes the tears of dotage flow,
> And Swift expires, a driveler and a show."

Marlborough was active and calculating to the last. While at Bath he would walk home from the rooms to his lodgings to save sixpence; and left a million and a half to his descendants to squander. When gazing at a portrait of himself, the great general is said to have exclaimed, "That *was* a man." He lingered six years after his first attack, still, to the last, attending the debates in the Lords, and settling his money matters himself. He had one difficulty, *too much* money, and once wrote to a friend to help him. "I have now," he said, "one hundred thousand pounds dead, and shall have fifty more next week; if you can employ it in any way, it will be a very great favor to me."

As he was expiring, the duchess asked him whether he had heard the prayers which had been read to him.

"Yes, and I joined in them," were the last words which the great Marlborough uttered. He sank to rest with her whom, with all her faults, he had loved more than all by his side.

The virtues of Marlborough were great; and one can not but accord with Lord Bolingbroke, who, hearing his penuriousness spoken of, stopped the parasite who had hoped to please him by abusing a foe:

"He was so very great a man that I forget he had that vice."

Swift, however, took care that it should not be forgotten. "I dare hold a wager," he said, "that the Duke of Marlborough in all his campaigns was never known to lose his baggage."

It is said that the great general scolded his servant for lighting four candles in his tent when Prince Eugene came to hold a conference with him. His habits were simple, like those of Wellington; his dress plain, except on set occasions; his table plain, too plain also, many thought who would have comprehended ostentation better. He kept few servants: nothing he dreaded so much as a numerous retinue; yet he was known to give a thousand pounds to a young soldier who wanted to purchase a commission. He was buried in the mausoleum at Blenheim, built by Rysbrach at the expense of the duchess.

She was now the richest peeress in England, with an income of forty thousand pounds a year; and not many months had passed after Marlborough's death before a suitor appeared in the person of a Whig peer, Lord Coningsby, whose admiration appears to have commenced before the duke's death; when, during the decline of the illustrious invalid, it was plain that Sarah would soon become a fine mark for the designing. "Friendship," however, had covered with its convenient garment his secret wishes: as a friend he and the duchess had corresponded; as a friend, four months after Marlborough had expired, he thus addresses the opulent widow:

"When I had the honor to wait on your grace at Blenheim, it struck me to the heart to find you, the best, the worthiest, and the wisest of women, with regard to your health, and, consequently, your precious life, in the worst of ways. Servants," he added, "were very sorry trustees for any thing so valuable, and the indifference of her grace, when she lay ill, had lain dreadfully heavy on his thoughts ever since." Then he reminds her of the loss her death would be to her two grandchildren, Lady Sunderland's children, whom she had adopted; and draws a parallel in his own case, saying that when he had himself lain on a bed of sickness, the idea of leaving his "two dearest innocents" to trustees and guardians, who, "ten millions to one, that they would become merciless and mercenary, had almost killed him." Of Lord Coningsby's "dearest innocents" there were five, the eldest of whom had lately been created Baroness Coningsby, so that a little of the duchess's wealth would have been a great addition to this newly-acquired title.

The duchess, being now in her sixty-second year, was not, it is certain, taken in by this devotion. However, Lord Coningsby wrote again, and his letter has been disinterred by a worthy Dryasdust from amid a heap of accounts and catalogues. This time she was his "dearest, dearest Lady Marlborough;" his despair at her intention of not going to London that winter; his desire to see her, if only for one moment; his hopes that she was going to make him the happiest man in the world, while he was to make her (who was already the wisest and the best) the happiest of women; ends with a postscript, which was, perhaps, the only part interesting to the matter-of-fact duchess:

"There is no cattle or sheep, as your grace desires, to be had till July next."

Unhappily, Queen Sarah's reply to all this devotion has not been preserved. We can imagine her reading the letter, swearing a little, and throwing it in with her bills, among which it has been found a hundred and fifty years after it was penned.

Charles, Duke of Somerset, second duke of England, commonly called the "Proud Duke," offered to the still beautiful Duchess of Marlborough within a year after the duke's death. This nobleman was a peer of the stamp of which one hopes the "mould and fashion" are destroyed. Never did he condescend to speak to a servant; he conveyed his commands by signs. Never were his children allowed to sit in his august presence. It was his custom to doze a little in the afternoon, when he required that one of his daughters should stand by him while he slept. One day, Lady Charlotte Seymour venturing to sit down, since she was tired, he left her twenty thousand pounds less than her sister. When he traveled, the duke ordered the roads to be cleared of all obstruction and idle bystanders. The duke was a widower of sixty-five, and his first wife having been a Percy, he thought he did her memory honor in offering his hand to the widow of Marlborough. He was, however, promptly refused. "The widow of Marlborough shall never become the wife of any other man," was the reply. He bowed to the decision, and begged the duchess to advise him whom to marry, as marry he would. "Ask Lady Charlotte Finch," was her counsel. He asked, and was accepted; but he never forgot the distinction between a Percy and a Finch. A gulf severed the two unequal families. The last duchess once tapped him familiarly with her fan. He turned round angrily, "My first duchess was a Percy, and she never took such a liberty."

Twenty-two long years did Queen Sarah survive her husband. She was the head of the Whig party, who filled the saloons of Marlborough House, while the Duchess of Buckingham, the natural daughter of James II., was the "queen" of the Jacobite circles. This eccentric lady, when her husband died, made as splendid a funeral for him as Queen Sarah had made for the defunct Marlborough, and when her son died, sent to borrow the funeral car which had carried the hero to the tomb.

"It carried my lord of Marlborough," cried the duchess, fiercely, "and it shall never carry any other."

"'Tis of no consequence," retorted the Duchess of Buckingham. "I have consulted the undertaker, and he can make me as good a one for twenty pounds."

Each duchess despised the other. Pope's famous character

of "Queen Sarah" was shown to her by a friend (friends being the people who always show such brochures), as if it had referred to her Grace of Buckingham. But the shrewd old Sarah saw through it. "I see what you mean," she called out, as the friend went on reading; "and I can't be imposed upon." She gave Pope a thousand pounds to suppress the character.

Women of the duchess's character have always a pet aversion, and Sir Robert Walpole had the honor of holding that post in her grace's mind. Her latter years, after she had done with the "Duke of Buckingham's widow," as she called her, were passed in quarreling with Walpole about a hundred thousand pounds she had lent to government; and with the Duke of St. Alban's, about coming *ad libitum* into Windsor Park, of which she was ranger, under pretense of supervising what he called the fortifications, but what she termed "the ditch around the castle." The duke's powers only extended to the castle and the forest; nevertheless, he had, the duchess said, besieged her in both parks, and been willing to forage them at pleasure.

It was the lot of the duchess to survive three of her lovely daughters: Henrietta, Duchess of Marlborough, after her father's death, in her own right; Anne, Lady Sunderland; and Elizabeth, Countess of Bridgewater. Lady Harriet Churchill was married, after her father's death, to the minister, Pelham Holles, Duke of Newcastle. She died before her mother, and with the only daughter who survived her Queen Sarah was in a state of perpetual warfare. The obligations of a courtier's life did not, perhaps, permit the duchess time to cultivate the affections or to form the characters of her children. She seems to have indulged her grandchildren with all the fondness that was never shown to their parents. One of the few objects she took pride in was the Lady Diana Spencer, Lady Sunderland's daughter. Though she detested Queen Caroline, the consort of George II., the duchess was pleased when her majesty said, at a drawing-room, "Tell my Dy to come back that I may bid her to hold up her head;" "a thing," said the duchess, "I was always telling her to do." Yet her Dy, who married Lord John Russell, the Duke of Bedford of Junius, only survived that union four years. There was another darling of the old dowager's heart, John, commonly called Jack Spencer, whom she styled her "Torrismond." Torrismond was more fond of the tavern, more frequently in the watch-house, than became his rank, name, and character; yet she still loved him, and hoped she might live to see him well married. In common with his elder brother, Lord Charles, he had squandered away the great sums left them, figured in all sorts of wild pranks, borrowed money from Jews at twenty per cent., and mortgaged his grandmother's jointure as soon as she died. She acted with sense and forbearance; but, at last, an amicable lawsuit, as it was called, between the Jews and his grandmother, was brought, to settle some disputed portion of the property. To the surprise of all, the aged duchess appeared in court to plead her own cause. The diamond-hilted sword given by the Emperor Charles was claimed by her grandson.

"What!" cried the duchess, "shall I suffer *that* sword, which my lord would have carried to the gates of Paris, to be sent to a pawnbroker's, to have the diamonds picked out one by one?"

Jack Spencer died, after a profligate career, at six-and-thirty, because, as Horace Walpole says, "he would not be abridged of those invaluable blessings of a British subject, namely, brandy, small beer, and tobacco." His grandmother, nevertheless, left him a clear thirty thousand a year.

Lady Anne Egerton, the only child of Lady Bridgewater, was undutiful, according to the duchess's notions, and to be insulted and derided, of course. So Lady Anne's picture was blackened by her grandmother at once; and writing on the frame, "She is blacker far within," was placed in her grace's sitting-room, that all visitors might see it.

Wretched, however, from the frequent losses in her family, the duchess now began to say that, having gone through so many misfortunes without being ill, "Nothing but distempers and physicians could kill her."

Her latter years were spent in resisting Vanbrugh's lawsuits, and in compiling her Memoirs. These were put together from scraps she had written: such as the character of Queen Anne; the account of Dr. Sacheverell's deeds; her opinions of Halifax, Somers, Lord Cowper, Swift, Prior, and others. Lord Hailes wrote a manuscript preface to her "Opinions." At the age of eighty-two the duchess became, as she said, "a kind of author." She published her Memoirs. Nathaniel Hooke, who wrote "The History of Rome," prepared them for the press. Hooke had suffered from the South Sea bubble, and was then, as he said, just worth nothing. He received four thousand pounds for his trouble; though he and the duchess quarreled violently about religion while he was compiling the work.

At last the health of this remarkable woman began to fail. "Old Marlborough" was dying, was the court news of the day. Her doctors said she must be blistered, or she must die. "I won't be blistered," she cried out; "and I won't die." She began to say that she cared not how "soon the stroke of death came." She still dictated to Hooke from her bed six hours a day, and played on a hand-organ, the eight tunes of which

THE DUCHESS OF MARLBOROUGH PLEADING HER OWN CAUSE.

pleased her, she said, more than an opera. She had three dogs, whom she esteemed more than human beings. She was wrapped up in flannels, and carried about like a child, or wheeled in a chair; nevertheless, she continued to snarl and rail at the world, to hate Sir Robert Walpole and Queen Caroline, yet to remain a Whig, and to be as keen and as clear in all that concerned her immense property as ever.

She was alive to any depredation. Having sent a rich suit of clothes to be made by Mrs. Buda, a fashionable dressmaker, she missed some yards in her dress when it came home. She resolved to punish the fraud. Mrs. Buda had a costly diamond ring on her finger. The duchess pretended to admire this ring, and asked a loan of it for a pattern. In a few days she sent it to Mrs. Buda's forewoman, saying it was to be shown to her mistress as a pledge that a certain piece of cloth should be returned. The cloth came back, upon which the ring was placed on Mrs. Buda's finger, the duchess at the same time convicting her of her offense.

She was now fading slowly but surely away; bitter to the last. She seems to have rested much on the fact that she had never "deceived any one." She performed some generous actions. Child's bank being nearly ruined by a quarrel with the Bank of England, she drew a check upon the Bank of England in favor of Child's for a hundred thousand pounds.

Until the 6th of October, 1744, she was capable of transacting her own business; on the 18th of that month she sank to rest at Marlborough House, aged eighty-four. She had been the favorite of nature and of fortune; but, as a wife and a woman, her character was at once wanting in sweetness and in elevation. She left, independent of many bequests, sixty thousand pounds per annum to each of her heirs.

Her funeral was, in accordance with her wish, strictly private. She was buried in the mausoleum at Blenheim. No mourning was to be given to any but the servants who attended at her interment. She did not, however, forget her poor chairmen, who had each twenty-five pounds. Her jewels must of themselves have been a fortune. Notwithstanding her conduct to Queen Anne, she left inscribed on the statue of that princess at Blenheim an epitaph full of eulogium. Her last sentiments, as far as concerned her own feelings, were those of a misanthropy which ill became one on whom so many blessings had been showered.

"I think one can't leave the world at a better time than now, when there is no such thing as real friendship, truth, justice, honor, or, indeed, any thing that is agreeable in life."

MADAME ROLAND.

About the year 1763 there lived on the Quai des Orfévres, on the banks of the Seine, at Paris, a jeweler of the name of Gratien Phlippon. His shop, filled with objects of art, is large, and gives evidence of a certain amount of prosperity. Phlippon is not strictly a jeweler, but an engraver; but as a restless and speculative man he has sought to enlarge his business, buys diamonds and other precious stones, which he takes care to sell at a good profit, and deals, too, in sculpture and engravings. He is a stout, healthy-looking man, active and loud-voiced, and intent on making money. While he sits in one corner of his room, receiving artists, giving directions to his apprentices, and himself plying the engraving-tool, there is not far from him a far more interesting character employed in a very different manner.

A little alcove adjoining the workshop has been turned into a miniature bedroom. There is here a tiny cot-bed, a small table, a chair, and a few shelves. By the table there sits a girl of nine years old, slight in figure, dark in complexion, with rich black hair, small sharp features, and very deep-blue eyes. Sombrely, almost solemnly, she is conning in that little corner a translation of "Plutarch's Lives." She has noticed that one of her father's young men, named Courson, leaves his books in a corner of the workshop, and from her hiding-place she has sallied out when no one was by and taken a volume stealthily to her little room. This she has repeated again and again, replacing the volumes when she has devoured them. The young man has peceived their disappearance; her mother, too, has detected her, but neither of them has said a word to her. Rather they are pleased to encourage this worship of books, and she is left in peace to wonder at the greatness of ancient Greeks and Romans, and to ask herself where such men are to be found in her own day. Nor is Plutarch her only joy: she has read the "Adventures of Telemachus," and been fired by the spirit of Tasso through a translation of the "Gerusalemme Liberata;" but Plutarch is her especial favorite, and during Lent that year, when she was obliged to go to mass every day, she has carried it to church with her, and read it there instead of her mass-book. It is then that she receives those impressions which make her republican without knowing it. And such at nine years old is Marie-Jeanne Phlippon, destined in after years, as the wife of Jean-Marie Roland, to be the centre of that band of fiery ambitious spirits who pulled down monarchy in France to raise up the guillotine, to which she who had encouraged them was herself to fall a victim.

Born in 1754, Marie-Jeanne was the second child of Gratien Phlippon and his wife Marguerite Bimont. Five other children were born to this couple, but all, including the eldest, died young, except this one precocious girl. Being sent into the country to be nursed by a worthy peasant woman near Arpajon, the little Manon (a *sobriquet* for Marie, equivalent to our Molly), as her parents called her, grew up healthy and strong, for that short but desperate battle of life she was to fight in after years. She gave early proof of a character which could be led by affection, but never driven by force. Her mother, a woman of good sense and delicate feelings, and far superior to her husband, whom she had married as a matter of duty, had no need to punish the little Manon. The single word *Mademoiselle*, pronounced with frigid dignity, was sufficient to recall her at any moment to obedience; and the child, thus addressed, would run and nestle at her mother's side and beg to be taken back to favor. But her father, who seems to have had a sharp temper, failed to bring her to her duty even by the application of the rod.

Once, indeed, when about six years old, she silently, and without a tear, suffered three severe beatings rather than take some medicine which she disliked. The child was ill, and the correction was so severe that it brought on a bad attack of illness, and from that time her father changed his system.

Her mother was a pious woman after the manner of her age and religion, and she early instructed her daughter in the mysteries of her faith. At the age of seven the little Manon was sent every Sunday to the catechising class, at which the curé of the parish, M. Garat, prepared the children for their confirmation. In a corner, or side chapel of the parish church, the children were ranged on benches, the boys separated from the girls, while the priest sat on a chair in the midst of them. The collect, gospel, and epistle of the day were repeated one by one. Then came the portion of the catechism which had been the task for the week. Often the fond mothers would come and stand behind their children, and great was Madame Phlippon's pride when her little Manon answered the curé's questions in a manner which proved, even at that age, her mental superiority and especially the strength of her memory.

To this instruction was added that of masters in writing,

geography, music, and dancing. To each of these studies the child applied herself with energy and delight in her little room, and made rapid progress. In her love of reading she devoured every thing she could get in the way of books. She found in her father's small library a folio edition of the "Lives of the Saints," and an old French version of the Bible. The heroic stories of the former were just suited to her peculiar mind, and the latter, with its quaint old-fashioned language won her heart, and she returned often to it. When other books failed, she even studied a treatise on heraldry, and began, but could not quite digest, another on contracts! The Abbé Bimont, a brother of Madame Phlippon, and a gay, lazy, merry priest, undertook to teach her Latin, and the little girl eagerly consented. She used to go to him three times a week, but he was always either busy with parish affairs, or scolding the choristers, or breakfasting with a friend; and his niece, in spite of her zeal, never mastered the language.

At home her father taught her a little of his own art, though he had no desire that she should be educated as an artist. Still, she rapidly succeeded with the graving pencils, as with every thing else, and would present her relations with specimens of her skill in the shape of flowers or complimentary verses neatly engraved on a well-polished plate. In return, she received a new dress or some such offering. Her mother, simple enough in her own person, was proud of arraying her only child in expensive clothes, far too good for her station in life, but had sense enough not to allow this to engender vanity in the little girl, and on week days would take her to market in the commonest attire, send her round to a neighboring shop for parsley and lettuces, and expect her to do her share of the cooking.

The miscellaneous reading of this forward child did not, fortunately, raise up a self-confident spirit; on the contrary, it seems to have turned her thoughts from the material to the invisible world, and to have bred an anxiety and timidity of mind, well fitted to receive religious impressions. The "Lives of the Saints" inspired her, too, with a longing to devote herself to the cause of religion. In her quiet retirement she felt, even at the age of eleven, the high value of this life, this short, black line of time, so prominent in the bright endless stream of eternity, knew that now was the moment of free-will, now the day of choice, and resolved to make the most of it. She felt, and trembled before the presence of the all-pervading Spirit, and humbly hoped to appease Him.

The period of her first communion was approaching. The doctrine of transubstantiation gives to this sacrament a solemnity even greater than that which invests it in our faith. The strict Romanist held that there was no salvation for those who, being of age to receive it, neglected to do so. The Church which could absolve readily from the greatest sins could find no pardon for neglect of her own rites. The preparation for an act of faith on which eternity depended was indeed of awful moment; and, impressed with a sense of this, the young girl was dissatisfied with her present life, and longed for the solemn shelter of a convent. One night she threw herself on her knees, and implored her parents to allow her to enter one for the period of her preparation. They consented, and made inquiries as to the best establishment in which to place her, fixing, at last, on that of La Congregation, which had a house in the Rue Neuve St. Etienne, in the Faubourg St. Marcel. Here she entered as a pupil in May, 1765. The worthy sisters undertook gratuitously the education of thirty-four young ladies from the age of eighteen down to that of six. Here, among girls who had been sent hither by their parents after the custom of Roman Catholic countries, and who felt but little reverence or enthusiasm in the matter, the sombre child who now entered produced a favorable impression on the sisters. She was placed among the older girls, whom she soon equaled in their studies by unwonted diligence and quickness of apprehension. The calm seclusion of the cloister seemed to cheer and strengthen rather than depress her. The high-walled garden, jealously shut out from the busy, wrangling world beyond; the lofty, dimly-lighted chapel, filled with the swell of solemn music, when from time to time some high sweet woman's voice rose like an angel's above the deep murmur of the organ; the sober silence that reigned through the whole building, all brought out in full glow that peculiar feeling which in women seems to take the place of actual religion. It was easy to believe that one loved God where there could be no temptation to love the world, and where all that was beautiful and majestic seemed to bring Him near to the humbled spirit. But then it required a certain piety and humility to be truly impressed with these effects. To many of her associates probably they were but tedious and commonplace. The little Manon was happy, too, in her confessor, a kind old man, with more sense than the majority of his class. Perhaps the explanation which Mad. de Sévigné gives for the attachment which women feel for their confessors, namely, that they would rather talk ill of themselves than not at all, may account in part for the affection which the young girl felt for this old man. In after years she could explain very sensibly the impression which all this made upon her.

"It must be confessed," she writes, "that the Catholic religion, though little suited to a healthy and enlightened judgment which subjects the objects of its belief to the rules of reason, is well adapted to captivate the imagination, which it strikes by the grand and terrible; while it takes possession of the senses by means of mysterious ceremonies alternately cheerful and melancholy. Eternity forever present to the mind of the sectarian, calls him to contemplation, and renders him a severe examiner of good and evil; while, on the other hand, the daily religious exercises and imposing ceremonies rather relieve and support the attention, and offer easy means of advancing toward the end in view. Women have a wonderful facility for performing these religious exercises and investing ceremonies such as these with every thing that can lend them beauty or effect; and the sisters of the convent excelled in this art."

While she was at the convent a novice took the vows, and the scene so often described, and in which all possible accessories are brought into requisition to heighten the effect of youth, beauty, and gayety embracing voluntarily a spiritual death, had a deep effect on the young girl who witnessed it. With some few of the inmates of the convent she formed close friendships. Among these, Angélique Boufflers, who went by the convent-name of Ste. Agathe, had been a victim to the vile system of sacrificing a daughter, that her proper portion of the family fortune might go to the sons, a system then even more common in France than now, and one but little better in principle than the female infanticide of India, at which a French mother would probably shudder sincerely enough. But we may ask of sensible people which is the worse—to drown your little child at the age of one or two in the waters of the Ganges—waters, remember, whose sacred character gives, in the eyes of Hindoo mothers, a kind of sacrificial sanctity to the act, or to condemn them, after the enjoyment of a few years of sunny youth, to perpetual imprisonment, perpetual virginity, and a morbid hankering after active life—to condemn them to this against their wills, and to gild the gallows by the palpable lie that it is a religious life.

But Ste. Agathe had known her destiny from the first. It was the fate of poverty, and she must be resigned to it. After all it was not so very hard to a French girl, for there was but one alternative—forced celibacy on the one hand, or forced marriage, perhaps with a man she hated, on the other. No wonder, when French girls are subjected to such a life, they should console themselves after marriage with all that is frivolous and vain, if not absolutely sinful.

St. Agathe grew much attached to her little charge, to whom she gave a duplicate key of her cell, where the thoughtful child devoured such meagre works of devotion as were allowed to a convent miss. The good sisters, still fond of a joke, used to quiz Ste. Agathe on her affection for the little pupil—and why not? They had no one more important to quiz her about. Agathe was then twenty-four years old. Some thirty years later the Revolution released her from the imprisonment of a convent, but too late. It had become a second nature to her, and she was as miserable at leaving her ill-furnished cell as Pellisson was to quit his tamed spiders in the Bastile. Habit reconciles human beings to every thing. Affection grows by and depends on habit. Offer them a palace and rob them of their relics, and are they happy? No; even death, which gives Heaven in exchange for a wretched life, is looked to by even the most miserable of us with horror.

When, at the end of the year for which she had entered, the young Phlippon left the convent, she was grieved to the heart. She found, too, that her father was too much engaged in the affairs of the commune to which he belonged to attend entirely to his business, and her mother had to take his place, and could not, therefore, give much attention to her daughter. She transferred her, therefore, to her grandmother Phlippon, a good-humored round-about little widow of sixty-five, who had failed once in trade, and come at last into a moderate fortune. Her sister Angélique lived with her—a meek, enduring, willing creature, with pale face, prominent jaw, and spectacles, who, without murmuring, filled the place of general servant to her more fortunate sister.

With this quiet couple, dwelling in the Isle St. Louis—a dreary, old-fashioned collection of moss-grown streets in the middle of the Seine—the future leader of the Girondists passed a calm life, quite happy if she could get a new book or a fresh nosegay from time to time. It was now the *Philothée* of St. Francis de Sales, "the most lovable of all the saints" as she confesses, and, we may add, always a great favorite with the women; now the Manual of St. Augustine, which led her thoughts back from the world into a realm of contemplation. But even now her mind developing gradually, becoming weaker to imagine, but stronger to reason and apter to observe, began to ask, if not yet to doubt, and the controversial works of Bossuet encouraged the tendency. Is it possible to ask without doubting? Does complete faith need to question? Does it not accept without investigation? Or is this a blind, contemptible faith, the mere child of indolence? We, who shudder at the mere thought of skepticism, have we not all been skeptics at one time? Can we investigate without doubting, and is not doubt skepticism? And does not real, sincere, manly faith imply a previous investigation? Can any of us say that we are *reasonable* believers, and have yet never doubted for a moment? Yet too often the weak mind has not power to return from its doubts, too often mere inquiry overthrows all faith, and in women especially. In after years Madame Roland confessed that these studies were the first step to infidelity. She passed on to Jansenism, the mildest form of dissent from Romanism, and thence, as if naturally, to the philosophy of Descartes, just as Madame de Grignan, the daughter of Madame de Sévigné, the Jansenist, had, before her, become a Cartesian. From Cartesian Madame Roland became Stoic; from Stoic, Deist; and from that she never returned.

How completely her mind was bent on reasoning at this period we may guess from her incapacity for singing, while she eagerly grasped the science of music. Her master was repeatedly saying to her, "Put more soul into it. You sing a ballad as a man does the Magnificat." To this Madame Roland, with the egotism of an autobiographist, adds, "The poor man did not see that I had too much soul to put it into a song."

The first thing which inspired a doubt of the truth of Romanism was the universal damnation pronounced on all who did not adhere to it, whether they had had it preached to them or not. This, indeed, is a great stumbling-block in the way of the success of that Church among civilized people, just as it is, perhaps, one of the secrets of its progress among the ignorant and superstitious; and unhappily those who dissent from it on this ground are not content to examine the more liberal doctrines of Protestantism, but fly off at once to philosophy or deism. Even at the present day immense numbers of nominal Romanists in France and Germany are Deists or Atheists; and at a time when the influence of Voltaire's writings was so great and general, it is not surprising that thinking men should have adopted the same course. The love of classical heroism, the admiration of the virtues of Socrates and of the superiority of many heretical writers, made it difficult to believe that perdition would depend on so little as the rejection or ignorance of the doctrines of Rome; and the moment this point was disputed by the inquirer, the Church might count him as lost to her.

To the cruelty of universal perdition succeeded the absurdity of infallibility, as an obstacle to blind belief; and one by one the arrogant assumptions of the Church of Rome were subjected to the test of reason. The young girl felt herself failing, and had recourse to her confessor, who, to save himself the trouble of going into controversy, supplied her with a collection of the defenders of Catholicism, such as Abbadie, Holland, and the Abbé Bergier. She read them and made notes on them, which she left in the volumes as she returned them to the curé. Here, too, she was introduced to the opposite party, and from the defenders themselves learned the doctrines of the accusers of her faith.

It is true that neither her reading nor the spirit of the age under a government which proclaimed by law that there was no God, ever brought Madame Roland to that terrible, hopeless, dreary goal where man, the impotent, the creature, the plaything of circumstance, dares to shout from the midst of his wretchedness that he is an Atheist, that he neither believes in nor cares for a Creator of the universe and a Protector of himself and his fellows. Her life was too pure and simple for such a creed. It has been doubted whether any man, tracking out truth patiently and with the humility attendant on the true student, ever does in his heart believe that there is no God. He may declare it in his works, or preach it openly; but there come moments when, in spite of himself, he trembles before that unknown Power, or in his weakness and misery turns to Him for aid with too ready belief. Perhaps, indeed, the very word atheist should be interpreted as one who lives without God, who *forgets* His existence, rather than one who, making that existence the subject of study, confidently *denies* it at last. The Atheist denies God in his life, but scarcely in his mind; and if we examine the case of real or asserted atheism, we shall generally find that the lives of its maintainers were such as to make them too glad to believe that there was no Judge to condemn them.

But Madame Roland, in later life, confessed that though not an Atheist, there were many unsolved and unsolvable questions on which, in the calm of a chamber and the impossibility of argument, she would agree with a partisan of atheism. Still her heart could never second her mind. "In the midst of the country," she wrote, "and in the contemplation of nature, my heart, moved by it, rises toward the enlivening Principle which animates it, the Intelligence which orders it, the goodness which in it supplies me with so many delights. And when," she adds, in her prison-cell, "measureless walls separate me from what I love, and all the evils of society together strike me as if to punish me for having desired its highest good, I look beyond the limits of this life to the reward of our sacrifices and the happiness of meeting again." One sees that this is not Christianity, nor, in our ideas, even religion; but it is the nearest approach to religion that a Romanist turned Deist can make.

"I could live with the Atheist," she goes on, "better than with the devotee, for he reasons more; but he is wanting in feeling, and my soul could not coalesce with his. He is cold to the most enchanting spectacle, and seeks a syllogism, when I can only give thanks." We see in all this the influence of her reading. Voltaire had taught her to despise, as he himself sneered at, revelation. Rousseau, setting up a faith in the place of that which the other had knocked down, had bid her seek the true revelation in nature itself. It is strange that a woman of her sense should give to such writers the implicit faith which she refused to men like St. Paul and St. John; but this, too, was the fashion of the age. A novelty was demanded even in religion, and they got only a poor miserable revival of the deism of Greece, a faith—if it be a faith and not a feeling—which had turned out an utter failure.

Marie Phlippon seems to have wanted the courage to proclaim or maintain her opinions. Indeed, what Atheist does not feel some qualm in doing so? and she was not even an Atheist. She continued to observe the ceremonial of Christianity, on account, she weakly confesses, of her sex, her age, and her situation. Nay, perhaps, even her affection for her mother restrained her from an open avowal of her want of belief; and we gladly seize hold of such a symptom to show how little zeal there is in infidelity. Her life was morally faultless. She owns that, with the exception of a desire to please—the narrow ambition of a woman—she had no sins to confess to her spiritual father. She might, indeed, have added the worse fault of judging others.

She had already, urged probably by her reading, made many observations on the falsity of social distinctions. On one occasion, these followed on a visit which she made with her grandmother to a certain Madame Boismorel, who, being above them in station, treated them with insulting condescension; on another, it was in accompanying a Madlle. d'Hannaches, a dry, disagreeable old maid, who boasted of her family tree, to the houses of certain people in authority, and noticing the attention paid to the birth and name of her companion, while she herself, the daughter of a mere engraver, was slighted. Then, again, she made one short visit to Versailles, where the old *régime*, with all its faults, called forth her contempt and disgust. "I preferred the statues in the gardens," she says, "to the people I saw there." Lastly, even the relatives of her intimate friend, Sophie de Cannet, who in their small way were comparatively aristocratic, excited her indignation. One was proud, another so fond of money and so insensible to fame, that, seeing the success of a tragedy written by a relation of his, he exclaimed, "Why did not my father teach me to write tragedies? I could have knocked them off on the Sundays." Certainly the state of society at that time favored the revolutionary sentiments which it produced; and while the despised working classes were meditating on the "virtues" of ancient Greece, birth, rank, and wealth were running into greater extravagancies and more painful absurdities than ever.

But whatever her reflections on men and nature, Marie Phlippon had soon a most practical part to play in the world; and she who had hitherto been "wedded in the spirit" to Socrates and Alcibiades, was now sought after by the butchers, bakers, and jewelers of her own class with a view to more substantial matrimony. Like the young ladies of the present day who are "all soul," she seems never to have been positively in love. She confesses that at an early age she was captivated by the voice and face of a young artist, named Tuboral, who came to her father's shop on matters of business. Whenever, hidden in her little alcove, she heard his gentle voice, she would steal out, and pretend to be looking for a pencil or some other trifle which she was supposed to have left in the workshop. The young man, who was one-and-twenty, and had "*une figure tendre*," blushed at seeing her more than she did, but as no intimacy arose nothing ensued from these little meetings.

Her appearance at seventeen—the marrying age in France—was of that kind which attracts Frenchmen, less on account of its beauty than of its interest. Her features, though not ill-proportioned, were not in themselves beautiful. Her profile was better than her full face, which was round rather than oval. The point of the nose was thick, and in the dilating nostril you saw more ambition than taste. The mouth was large, but the smile soft and the expression gentle and kind. The brow was high, broad, and calm, as if inclosing a large brain. Above it the hair parted freely, and fell in long luxuriant curls over her shoulders. The eyes of a deep blue, which looked in some lights brown, were full of thought and animation. The eyebrow was peculiarly elevated, dark, and full, so that it gave to the face an expression of frankness and loftiness combined with vigor. The whole frame of the woman had more strength than loveliness about it, the bust being full and high, the shoulders broad and manly, the figure slight, tall, and supple. But in the thoughtful and daring expression of the face was a charm which, in after years, gave her a command over the wild spirits of the Revolution, and made even the men, who despised woman as a chattel, her willing servants.

Added to this face, she had a fortune of twenty thousand francs, being an only child; and it was natural that many suitors should seek her, some from admiration of herself and her talents, others from affection for her ducats.

At the age of eighteen, however, she was attacked by the small-pox; but though the illness was long and severe, her face, on recovery, bore no traces of the disease. The chief effect of the attack was to interfere with those matrimonial projects which had hitherto been made for her.

These were so numerous that we need only cite a few instances. Her first admirer was her music-master, a Spaniard of colossal figure, with hands as rough as those of Esau. He announced himself as a noble of Malaga, whose misfortunes had driven him to teach the guitar, and employed a friend to make the offer for him. The ambitious father was not likely to listen to the proposal of a penniless teacher, and, after the manner of the day, ordered him never to set foot in the house again. A multitude of offers followed this one; and the jeweler, who enjoyed with a certain pride the popularity of his daughter, used to bring her the letters of proposal to answer: that is to say, she replied to them in her father's name, and he copied out her answers with his own pen. The next admirer was the butcher the family dealt with. His second wife had lately died, and he had amassed a fortune of some two thousand pounds, which he wished to increase. Accordingly, for about a whole summer he regularly met Madlle. Phlippon and her mother in their walks, dressed in a fine black suit with very good lace, and made them a dignified bow, without venturing to accost them. At length the usual manœuvring was effected through the medium of a person called Madlle. Michon, who boldly offered the butcher's fortune and business to the consideration of the ambitious jeweler. M. Phlippon's ambition was limited to a love of money; the butcher had it to offer, and he favored his suit. But his daughter was not so easily won. Now that marriage was so much talked of, she made up her mind to wed a man of her ideal cast — a philosopher, or, at least, a thinker, some one above the common mould. This was all very well; but it is amusing to see the contempt which this girl, who fretted so angrily at the condescension of the well-born, felt for those of her own class. She confesses that she abhorred trade, and would never marry a trader. What she aspired to does not appear; what she finally accepted was indeed a poverty of choice. But to return:

the butcher had wasted his time and worn out his clothes to no purpose. *Il fut congedié*, and there was an end to it.

An end, at least, to the hopes of the man of joints; but only a beginning to a difference of feeling between father and daughter, which later developed into absolute ill-will. Phlippon knew nothing and cared nothing for romance, learning, philosophy, or even feeling. He loved his daughter after a fashion; but like many a father, English as well as French, he wished to make that love an excuse for murdering her. He wanted to say to the world, "See how anxious I am for my daughter's future comfort and ease; I will not let her marry any but a rich man." But he knew well enough that that daughter preferred, as any girl of right feeling must do, to marry a man she could respect to all the ducats that butchers or jewelers could produce in the good city of Paris. Phlippon cared not a wisp for his daughter. That pretense was all sham. He cared only to have a wealthy son-in-law, a grandson who should be an honor of wealth to his race, a connection, in short, of which he could be proud; and in his vulgarity he could not be proud of high talents, fine honor, real breeding, and noble worth, but only of that eternal relay of gold louis and silver écus, which to his narrow mind represented all the rest. But why rail against Phlippon? Honest—yet, as the event showed, not excellent—workman as he was, he did no more than half the fathers of England are doing this very day; and those too, some of them, as proud as Lucifer of birth and position. Just as the jeweler of the Quai des Orfèvres shut his door upon the needy music-master, who had nothing but his guitar to offer, and hugged to his bosom the greasy flesh-monger, so my friend the baronet thrusts from his house the aspiring young tutor, and greets with a smile the wealthy representative of the great brewing firm of Malt, Barm, Kilderkin, & Co.; and my friend the baronet sees no vulgarity in so doing.

Marie Phlippon had not much romance in the matter. She knew well enough that she must marry a man whom she had no chance of loving before the wedding, but she wished at least to wed with one whose acquirements should be on a par with her own, who could understand her, and be a companion to her; and as she could not hope to discover much of such qualities from the slight intercourse which French manners permitted between herself and an aspirant for her hand and fortune, she was constrained to judge by circumstances rather than personal recommendations. So when a young physician, named Gardanne, was mentioned to her as a suitor, she rather caught at the idea, thinking that one of that profession must at least have a certain amount of instruction, and a certain knowledge of books. Hitherto she had often noticed that at church a pair of male eyes were fixed steadily upon her, or that in her walks with her mother a bow of peculiar meaning would be given by some stranger; and when, after these tokens, she saw her parents in anxious colloquy, she guessed what was the purport of these attentions. She was now to undergo another kind of manœuvre.

Walking one day to the Luxembourg with Madame Phlippon, she was suddenly stopped by her mother exclaiming that it was sure to rain, though the sky appeared calm enough. They happened—of course by accident—to be opposite the house of a lady friend, Madlle. de la Barre (it is generally a single lady of a certain age who undertakes these delicate transactions). They at once took refuge from the imaginary shower in this house, were served with a collation, and had not been seated many minutes, when, by pure accident, the young physician and a gentleman friend happened to call on the maiden lady. The doctor chattered away, ill at ease, cracked a bon-bon, and remarked that he loved *sweets*. This was considered a favorable sign, and papa Phlippon was ready to join their hands and pronounce a blessing at once; but his daughter did not encourage the bashful young doctor, partly because the wig, then worn by the faculty, gave him a ridiculous appearance. However, she expressed no repugnance this time, and the affair was on the point of being settled. It proceeded so far that the young lady and her mamma took the usual fortnight's journey to the country, in order to be out of the way while papa made inquiries into the character and position of the aspirant. This the worthy jeweler, who was not quite pleased with the match, did only too scrupulously; wrote letters of inquiry to Provence, the country of the physician, and even set people to take observations of his conduct at home. These movements came to the doctor's knowledge, and he was naturally indignant. The various go-betweens interfered, and, as a simple consequence, quarreled; and so, one way or another, the young girl was relieved from the necessity of deciding for herself as to the wearer of the ugly wig.

New matches might soon have been put forward, and the same part have been played again and again, but for a terrible blow which now fell on the family. In the spring of 1775, when Marie was about twenty-one, her excellent mother was suddenly struck with paralysis. She had long been unwell, and had shown symptoms of unnatural languor and weakness. The attack was fearfully violent, and ended in death. The daughter, mad with grief, lay ill for many days after this event. In losing her mother she lost all her family. Her father had never merited much affection, and he soon became utterly estranged from her. He had already taken to bad habits, from which his child had sought in vain to wean him. He passed his evenings, no one knew where, away from home, and was cold to his wife. Her death seemed to recall him for a time, but he soon relapsed into his old ways; and, now that the restraint his wife had imposed was gone, became worse than ever.

Her mother's death left Marie to a solitude which she could only fill up by reading. Her father found little society at home. The daughter perceived that he needed it, and strove to make herself more a companion to him. But this was impossible. Phlippon, caring for little but money and amusement, could not enter at all into her ideas, nor she into his. He soon formed a connection with a person of bad character, wasted his money, and to make it good took to gambling. His daughter was left completely alone, but her mind seems to have taken a more religious tone after her mother's sudden death, and she read with avidity the works of Bossuet, Fléchier, Bourdaloue, and Massillon. She was vexed to find how much these celebrated preachers talked of the "mysteries" of their faith, rather than of the high morals of Christianity, and she determined to try if a practical sermon were not easy to write. She wrote one on the love of one's neighbor, showed it to her uncle, the abbé, and received considerable commendation from him. What has become of this curious essay we do not know, but feel convinced that it would, if extant, have a peculiar interest, coming from the pen of a woman who, even in prison, with the guillotine waiting for her, could write in so masterly a manner as that of her Memoirs.

In the following December, however, began a new phase of her life. Her dearest friend at the convent had been Sophie Cannet, who, living now with her family at Amiens, corresponded regularly with Marie Phlippon, and was on the most affectionate terms with her, whenever she came up to Paris. Sophie, lamenting the stupidity of the society at Amiens, had often talked to her bosom friend of one exception in the person of a well-informed and clever man of middle age, who, however, was not much at home, passing several months of the year in Paris, and often making longer journeys into Italy or Germany. To this person, on the other hand, she had praised the talents of her old schoolfellow, showed him her portrait, and raised in him a desire to make her acquaintance. At last, one day in the winter of 1775, he told her that he was going to Paris, and offered to take a letter for her to her friend

Marie. In this manner Marie Phlippon made the acquaintance of M. Roland de la Platière. The introduction from her bosom friend was a sufficient recommendation; but there was nothing in the appearance or manners of M. Roland to excite any feeling keener than respect. He was past forty, tall, thin, and yellow, with a bald head and rather stiff manner. When, however, he opened his mouth, he at once charmed the delicate ear of Marie Phlippon by the softness of his voice; and she confesses that attraction with her entered by the ears rather than the eyes. His conversation, though calm and simple, was that of a thinking man. He was fond of being listened to, and Marie had the rare and excellent gift of listening well. In short their minds had much in common; and the conversation of a man who had traveled and thought was an enjoyment which this young woman had rarely met with among the friends of her parents. For eight or nine months he repeated his visits, not, indeed, very frequently, but making long ones when he came. In the summer of 1776 he made a journey to Italy, and before leaving begged to be allowed to deposit his MSS. with Madlle. Phlippon, till he should return to claim them.

This peculiar mark of esteem was not lost upon her; and the MSS. left with her served to make her more fully acquainted with M. Roland's mind. They consisted of notes of travel, reflections, and outlines of works, and displayed strength of character, strict principles, austere probity, mingled with taste and learning. In addition to this he wrote her a series of learned letters from Italy, intended as notes for a work on that country, and utterly free from any touch of romance or mark of affection.

The previous life of Roland had been sensible rather than romantic. He was of a family which, though in trade, were rather proud of their claims to antiquity, a weakness from which the austere philosopher was not himself free, since in 1784 he attempted to revive his lost dignity by applying for letters of nobility. He was undoubtedly a vain man, as he proved in subsequent transactions; but of all vanity this pride of family was perhaps the most contemptible in a man affecting republican principles. He was the youngest of five brothers, and there were only two careers open to him—to embark in trade or take holy orders. He shrank from both, and to avoid being compelled to embrace a mode of life which he detested, he ran away from home at the age of nineteen. He arrived at Nantes, and engaged himself with a shipbuilder to go to India. Fortunately, perhaps, for his future fame, he burst a blood-vessel, and was obliged to abandon the project.

At Rouen he had a relation named Godinot, the superintendent of a large manufactory, and at his suggestion Roland entered this establishment. He distinguished himself by his zeal, activity, and valuable head-piece, and worked up till he was himself appointed superintendent of a factory at Amiens. The government soon detected his abilities in matters connected with manufactures, and employed him to inspect those of Germany and Italy; and in this manner he was enabled to travel abroad, a rare advantage in those days among his fellow-countrymen.

After an absence of a year and a half in Italy, Roland returned to Paris, and renewed his visits at the house of Phlippon. Marie found in him a friend worth having. In his severe respectability she saw the *beau-idéal* of a philosopher, and, as she had long since resolved to marry for mind rather than heart, she readily listened to the declaration of attachment which Roland at last uttered in her ears. She accepted for herself; but, with a self-denial which was perhaps the less trying because her liking for Roland was purely based on esteem and admiration, and had nothing to do with love, she told him honestly how poor a match this would be for him in a worldly point of view. Her father had dissipated his fortune and hers, he was daily losing more than he made by his business, and had heavy debts to encumber him. Roland, very honorably for him, only insisted the more on the marriage. Though he was perhaps incapable of any thing like a passion, and would have thought it unworthy of his dignity to indulge one, he was not insensible to the attractions of a handsome girl twenty years his junior, with a mind vastly superior to his own, and who freely returned his admiration. He returned to Amiens, wrote to the jeweler to demand his daughter's hand, and was bluntly and even insolently refused. Phlippon had never liked Roland, which perhaps was natural; he had seen in him a severe moralist, who would have no pity for his father-in-law's vices and follies: Roland was nearly of his own age, and he was jealous of his superior mind and character. Considering that the new applicant was in a far better position than the aspiring butcher, and was likely to rise higher still, and that his own daughter had nearly reached the (in France) hopeless age of spinsterhood—five-and-twenty—the refusal of Phlippon can be accounted for only by a very strong personal dislike of Roland.

The daughter, however, was old enough now to take the matter into her own hands. Though she could not marry against her father's wishes, she could take an independent step of another kind. From her mother's fortune she had saved about twenty pounds per annum, and, resolving to live on this meagre income apart from a father with whom she could no longer agree, she retired to the Convent of La Congrégation, hired a small garret there, and set to work to parcel out her twenty pounds in such a manner as to cover the cost of her wants for a year. It can well be imagined that her economy was very severe. Her dinner, which she cooked herself, consisted of potatoes, rice, and a few vegetables, and with this she was fain to be content. In her garret she shut herself up with her books, receiving only the society of Ste. Agathe, her old friend of former days. Roland still wrote to her affectionately, but for six months did not repeat his proposal. He then came to Paris, and had an interview with her across the jealous grating of the convent door, and was more determined than ever to make this fascinating woman of spirit his wife. The independent position which she held as the inmate of a convent released her from her father's control, and she accepted, and was married to the man whom she esteemed the most in the world. That there was little more than esteem on either side may well be conceived; and this match, founded on the basis of cold regard, would have been a failure but for the high moral principles of Madame Roland. She confesses that she "often felt that similarity was wanting" between them; that if they lived quietly she had often "very trying hours to pass," and if they went into society she was "liked by persons, some of whom, she feared, might affect her too closely." The hard work which her husband exacted, and she willingly undertook, was the only safeguard against cherishing such thoughts as these; but the fact that they should often have arisen, proves how completely the union was one of reason rather than love.

Thus ended the girlhood of Marie Phlippon, much in the manner that one might expect—cold, rational, intellectual, and uncomfortable to the last, yet, in its very abnegation of comfort, grand and consistent with her whole character. Without, perhaps, knowing it, she was deeply ambitious, and she chose by instinct the path which should lead her to a clear field for her ambition.

The first year of their marriage was passed in Paris, the next two at Amiens. One child, a girl, was the whole fruit of it; but the birth of this child, and the delicate health of Roland, were two new ties to her husband, which even developed her esteem into something of wifely affection. In 1784 they moved to Lyons, where Roland had obtained a similar appointment to the one he held at Amiens. In the neighborhood of this city was the Clos La Platière, the humble paternal mansion of the Roland family, who took their *surnom de noblesse* from it, just as if Smith, who has half an acre of kitchen garden in Hog-lane, or Jones, who has inherited a two-roomed cottage in Green Bottom, should appear in the London world as Smith de Hog-lane, or Green-Bottom Jones, Esq. This silly pretension is rare in England, though, we believe, common in Scotland, where every Thomson or Johnson gives himself an air of antiquity by tacking on to his name the "of" some few yards of land or tumble-down manse. The Revolution tried to root out out this vanity of the people in France, but in vain. The people who left "Monsieur le Comte de St. Cyr" without any surname by the declaration that there were no more monsieurs, no more counts, no more "de's," no more saints, and, lastly, no more *sires*, were still prone to such little weaknesses as that with which Roland called himself Roland *de la Platière*, and in the present day no butcher, baker, or candlestick-maker, however republican in sentiment, retires from trade and buys a petty freehold without instantly claiming a "de" something or other to beautify his humble "Vidal" or "Lefèvre."

In this quiet country nook, however, Madame Roland *de la Platière* came out in more amiable colors than she had ever appeared in. Always ready to sacrifice herself for the good of others, and discovering that she was the only person in the neighborhood who knew any thing of medicine, she was ready to obey the most extravagant claims on her time and trouble, and would go three or four leagues at any moment to relieve a sick peasant. In 1789 she passed twelve days without taking off her clothes once, attending by the bedside of her husband, who was dangerously ill, and this devotion raised a new bond of affection between the husband and wife. In this year, too, the first echoes of the Revolution reached them in their retirement, and both sprang up joyfully to greet what they regarded as the emancipation of suffering mankind. Roland was soon famous for his opinions in Lyons; and that city sent him as her first deputy to the Constituent Assembly. On the 20th of February, 1791, Madame Roland returned once more to Paris, where for two short years she was to lead, and be the soul of, a new movement, which repaid her zeal, as it did that of so many another disciple, with the knife of the guillotine. Thus at the age of thirty-seven her private life, which would have left her without a name in history, ended; and she began the brief brilliant career which has surrounded it with a halo of blood-red light.

The rise of the French Revolution is too well known to need a review here; but it is necessary to show how the Rolands were drawn into the circle of the Girondins, and came to take so leading a part in the movements of that party.

The soul and originator of it was Brissot, a man of some virtues, more vices, but faithful to the last to the cause of the Republic. He was the son of a pastry-cook at Chartres. Born a democrat (unless making tarts and brioches be claimed as the aristocratic part of the business of a baker), a democrat by principles, education, convictions, he had yet that same aristocratic vanity which induced Roland to add "de la Platière" to his plebeian name. Brissot, ashamed of his, assumed the cognomen of De Warville. He received a good education, and turned to literature as a means of living. He had great talents, and a powerful pen, but he used both unscrupulously for money, writing on every possible subject with little regard to political principle, and even, so he was accused, inditing libels for the press. He was sent to London by Turgot on a secret mission, and there became editor of the "Courrier de l'Europe," a paper at that time bearing a not very good reputation. He was there associated with a set of foreigners of the worst character; and if the accusations against him be true, he himself sank so low as to embezzle sums of money, and to have led a vicious life in the purlieus of London. At the first symptoms of the Revolution he returned to Paris, and became the editor of a revolutionary paper, "Le Patriote Français," and in this paper went so far, that even Robespierre, who at that time desired liberty and not anarchy, reproached him with kindling a dangerous flame. Brissot was attacked in the papers; his character and early iniquities exposed; and though he defended himself ably, and his courageous political stand made him friends, he was never quite exculpated. Madame Roland was among those who saw in him the bold leader of her own party, a zealous soldier of liberty, and refused to lend an ear to the stories of his former days. He had some redeeming points: a tender affection for a girl he had married in spite of the opposition of his family, and a courage which he maintained even on the scaffold. Like herself, he believed in God, and confessed this belief by the side of the guillotine, adding that he died for it. She says of him: "He is the best of mortals, a good husband, tender father, faithful friend, and upright citizen: his society is as agreeable as his character is easy: bold even to imprudence, gay, simple, ingenuous as a boy of fifteen, he was made to live with the wise and be the dupe of the bad."

Brissot had from time to time sent Roland copies of his works, and an acquaintance was thus formed between them even before they met in the Constituent Assembly. Madame Roland was rather shocked at his want of dignity, so different from the sedate, old-gentlemanly bearing of her husband, and at that levity of manner which the life of an adventurer invariably gives in time. But Brissot's courage and love of liberty were more than equivalents in the eyes of the Rolands for this levity of manner, and he became their intimate friend. He brought with him to their house a better man, and fellow-townsman, Pétion—afterward called King Pétion, when, as Mayor of Paris, he sat in state at the Palais Royal—who had already achieved a name by his speeches. Pétion and Brissot were the friends of La Fayette, and sincere lovers of liberty.

Another intimate, and more than intimate, of Madame Roland, was Buzot. Young, handsome, and even elegant, he had none of the coarseness, none of the ferocity, of the heroes of the Revolution. He was by nature a gentleman, gentle in manner, in heart, in hopes. Like Madame Roland, he had long groaned at the corruption of the court and aristocracy, and the degradation of the people. He longed ardently for the freedom of his country, but would not buy it at the cost of blood and anarchy. She has drawn his character in the most pleasing colors: "An impassioned observer of nature, feasting his imagination with all the charms she can offer, and his soul with the principles of the most touching philosophy, he seems made to obtain and enjoy domestic happiness. He would forget the universe in the pleasure of home virtues with a heart worthy of him. But once launched upon public life, he ignores all but the rules of severe justice, and defends them at the cost of all. Readily indignant at injustice, he persecutes it warmly, and will never make a compromise with crime. A friend of humanity, susceptible of the tenderest affections, and capable of the sublimest impulses and noblest resolutions, he comes forward as a republican; but as a severe judge of individuals, and slow in developing his regard for them, he gives it to few. This reserve, combined with the energy with which he expresses himself, has brought upon him the accusation of pride, and made him many enemies." "Buzot is the kindest man on earth to his friends, the most bitter opponent of charlatans." He detested and opposed the excesses of the revolutionists, and in their turn they accused him of a partiality for royalism. He and Pétion perished even more terribly than those of their companions who mounted the scaffold. After the condemnation of the moderate Girondins, they took refuge, in company with Guadet, Barbaroux, and Salles, at the house of Madame Bouquey, at St. Emilion, near Bordeaux. Thence they were hunted by the soldiers, and rushed into the fields and woods. Barbaroux shot himself, and was dragged back, still half alive, to Bordeaux, where the guillotine put an end to his misery. The gleaners some days after found remnants of garments, clotted masses of tangled hair, bones, and flesh, about the fields. Whose were these? The wolves had been down from the hills. Had they devoured Pétion and Buzot, who had escaped the wolves of the Reign of Terror? None knew, but a silent belief that it was so passed through the country. Buzot and Pétion were heard of no more. To be torn to pieces by wild animals was not much worse than to be massacred by their own kind. In one sense it was better. These men had loved their own fellow-men; they had never loved the wolves of the forest. It is better to die by a hated than by a loved hand. Perhaps it was better to be torn to death bit by bit by wolves than to be carried to the scaffold amid the derisive jeers of the people they had sought to lead to better things.

The house of Madame Roland was chosen as a rendezvous for these patriots chiefly on account of its vicinity to their homes. They met there four times a week in the evening. The quiet, modest wife sat apart at a little table, working, or writing letters, but listening with both ears. None of the party suspected that this gentle woman was to play so prominent a part in the drama of their power and their fall. She who had dreamed of liberty as a glorious reprieve, who had thought of a Platonic republic, of the establishment of a grand reign of free thought and noble laws, was shocked and almost disgusted at the levity and bravura of these new-fledged patriots, who spoke of the constitution as a game in their hands. Often she longed to be up and speaking boldly among them. The words of her own husband, so calm and unenthusiastic, irritated her to phrensy. She saw, or dreamed of, purer, bolder motives, and could not sit to listen to such worldly prudence. She was a woman, not a man. While they strove to be practical and real, she longed to be grand and ideal. Yet she had to curb her tongue, and to learn from them the worldliness of even a Republican. The example of antiquity, the theories of Plato, the dreams of her youth, must be quenched in the strong, vulgar necessity of the times. She listened and said nothing.

There came, however, a new man among this small circle, and inspired her with hope. Small, feeble, and angular in figure, with an ugly but not hideous face, heavy brows, sharp eyes sunk deep within the forehead, yet glaring forth with a terrible fire, a small, sharp, impetuous nose, puffing at the nostrils with a wild anxiety, a large, thin-lipped mouth, without passion, with no token of sympathy or affection, and with a sneer grafted there from youth upward, and a strong, selfish determination that seemed to ask all earth and hell for its own —for of heaven it had no ambition—Robespierre, the king of blood, the apostle of hate, came among these men with a dominant resolution.

In their meetings he was a silent listener. He gathered up the gist of all that was there proposed and advanced it as his own at the Assembly. Yet Madame Roland saw in him at the first a sincere friend of liberty. He was born at Arras, of an honest, respectable family. The bishop of the diocese defrayed the expenses of his education, little thinking he was preparing a man who should denounce all religion as childish. When he came to Paris there was nothing to recommend him. He was a poor speaker compared with the excited men of the day; talked bad French, and when he spoke at all had all the obstinacy and determination of a man whose mind was made up and whose object was long since fixed upon. Biting his nails, and grinning calmly at all that passed, he waited for the more enthusiastic spirits to clear the way. They talked of the Republic. Robespierre asked what a republic meant. Such a man, with some fine fancies of the beauties of liberty, but selfish and unsympathizing, was just fitted to play the part he afterward did play without respect for persons or care for friends. He was, in fact, incapable of friendship, as he was insensible to kindness. The man who sent Madame Roland to the scaffold had been offered safety by the same woman in the hour of need. After the massacre of the Champ de Mars he had been accused of conspiring with the originators of the petition of forfeiture, and was obliged to conceal himself. Madame Roland, who knew the young man's hiding-place, went to him to offer him an asylum in her own house. He was gone; but Madame Roland, believing him worthy of her sympathy, sought out her friend Buzot and begged him to do his best to save the suspected man. Buzot agreed to do so, and in after years he, like Madame Roland, was the victim of his ingratitude.

Such society, if society it can be called, did Madame Roland, the daughter of the jeweler, receive in her salon, and watch with a yearning in their earliest struggles after liberty and reason. Roland had a good reputation among these men. He was disinterested, and true to the highest principles of freedom. He represented the almost old-fashioned ideas which had oozed up timidly under the *ancien régime*, the aspirations for a perfect republic or a pure constitution. He was calm, silent, secure as a rock, a philosopher rather than politician. He was, in fact, a safe man, one whom in days when every man's hand was against his brother could be trusted to perform the part his principles dictated without the ambition to shine. At times he was brilliant, but no one knew that his wife had inspired him; at times he was bold, but few guessed that Madame Roland had pushed him on. It was this secure character which led the Girondins to choose him as Minister of the Interior.

At the dissolution of the Constituent Assembly, the Rolands had returned to their seclusion at La Platière; but having once tasted the excitement of political life, they could not long remain in a small country village, and soon returned to Paris. In the mean time, Vergniaud and Brissot, the leading spirits of the Revolution, had overthrown first M. de Narbonne, and then M. de Lessart. The poor king, weak in his despair, and willing to make any concession to popular feeling, determined to choose a ministry from among his foes. The victorious party sought out men who were likely to serve without displacing them—tools not masters. They fixed on Roland for the interior and Dumouriez for foreign affairs.

Roland was too vain to see the position in which his party held him; but Dumouriez, less blind, was glad to use this office as a stepping-stone to a conquest over that very party. Dumouriez was a dashing, handsome soldier, who had passed his life in various adventures, all more or less romantic. An unfortunate love affair had been his first incentive to ambition. He had fallen desperately in love with a beautiful cousin; his father had forbidden their union. The young girl retired to a convent, and her lover took poison, which, unfortunately for his future name in history, did not have the desired effect. Awake to his folly, but not cured of his love, he sought relief in action. In Corsica, Portugal, and Poland he accepted missions which were half diplomatic and half military, and played more honorably with his sword than with his portfolio. He was told that his beloved one had given him up, and was about to take the veil, and out of pique entered on a new connection. On his return to France he was sent to the Bastile for having too well carried out his instructions, but after the imprisonment of a year his sentence was commuted to an exile at Caen, in Normandy. Here in a convent he found again the cousin whom he had so long loved, learned that rumor had been false, that she had neither forgotten him nor taken the veil, and then married her. In time he was appointed commandant of Cherbourg; and it is interesting to learn that he first formed those plans of fortifying that harbor which the present emperor has lately completed. By the time the Revolution broke out he had reached the rank of general, and was fifty years of age, yet gay and adventurous as ever.

Such was the man who, on being introduced to Madame Roland, thought to win more than her esteem, even her affection. But her keen observation detected his careless ambition. "Beware of this man," she said to Roland; "he has a false eye, and must be mistrusted more than any one. He has expressed great satisfaction at your being called to the ministry, but I should not wonder if he got you turned out one day."

Roland, however, trusted him implicitly. This staid philosopher entered on his duties with secret delight, and was resolved to show the king what a Republican was. He appeared at his first audience in a black coat, round hat, and dirty shoes. The king was disgusted, but Dumouriez turned it into a joke. The chamberlain pointed indignantly to the dusty shoes which had no buckles. "Ah!" laughed Dumouriez; "all is lost! No more etiquette; no more monarchy."

Madame Roland now took her place as the centre of the ministry in its private councils. They met at her house every Friday, and the cat's-paws of the Girondist party elicited her contempt. There was De Grave in the War-office, a mild, sleepy man, walking delicately on the tips of his toes; Lacoste, commissioner for the navy, a bureaucrat of the old school, cold, respectable, but narrow-minded; Duranton at the head of justice, a doting old woman; Clavière, the finance minister, irascible and self-opinioned; and, lastly, Dumouriez, with more talent but less principle than any of them. With these men, the actual holders of office, came those who were the real masters of the ground, the chiefs of the Girondin Club, Brissot, Pétion, Guadet, Gensonné, and Vergniaud; but Robespierre was no longer a visitor at Madame Roland's. His own ambition clashed with that of the moderate Girondins, who wished for a constitution while waiting for a democracy. He detested Brissot too, who from his small room on a fourth story could quietly make or depose ministers. He saw that the government which the nation supposed to be carried on in the Assembly and the king's council-chamber, really existed in the unpretending salon of Madame Roland. He had withdrawn and joined the rival Jacobins, where he led on Danton, Marat, and Camille Desmoulins.

It was, however, Madame Roland who drove Dumouriez from her salons. She had the penetration to see that, clever and daring as he was, he was not sincere in his adhesion to the Girondins, and suggested to her husband suspicions of him, which were imparted to the rest of the club. The Girondins were all respectable in their lives. Dumouriez was openly profligate, and it was said that he wasted money, which had been granted for the secret service, on his own pleasures. The Girondins, fearful that this open immorality would bring opprobrium on the cause of liberty, in which they believed they were laboring, remonstrated with him at Madame Roland's. Dumouriez treated the matter laughingly, but did not again come to the house.

This first Ministry of the People, as it was called, was by no means successful. The ministers might be diligent, but, with the exception of Dumouriez, were unfit to cope with the royal party. The councils at the palace were turned into mere parties of conversation. The poor king, forced to give in on every point to his new ministers, contented himself with accepting the decrees, and then chatted and even laughed with his directors. Roland was delighted with his affability; but his wife, who longed for the establishment of a systematic democracy, saw that all this was merely a delay of the great crisis. She took a step which has been much blamed. She foresaw that the nation would one day call these trifling ministers to account. She wished to save her husband; and with this view persuaded him to take to the council, and read to the king, a letter which she herself dictated, and which, if produced in the hour of need, would prove to the country that Roland had protested against the king's delays. The occasion of it was especially the refusal of Louis to sanction the decree against the nonjuring priests. The country demanded it with threatening gestures. France was in a ferment greater than ever. The Revolution went on while the monarchy survived. The letter called upon the king earnestly to take the proper measures to pacify the people. As we read it, it was sensible and excusable; but it has been affirmed that Roland and his wife, in thus providing a future defense for themselves, laid up a protest which would criminate the monarch Roland was serving. His own party even viewed it in this light. The letter was read, but the king held out; his conscience forbade him to sanction a step which he held to be destructive of the church he belonged to. At last the moment Madame Roland had foreseen arrived. The king remained inflexible, and dismissed from the ministry Roland, Clavière, and Servan. Roland rose in the Assembly and read out his letter. It was applauded; the king was blamed more than ever. Roland left the chamber a hero, and affected to think he had fallen by his own boldness.

Thus ended Roland's first ministry and his wife's first movements in the Revolution. Her husband's fall increased rather than diminished her influence. In an apartment high up in a house in the Rue St. Jacques, the young spirits of the day, yearning some for fame, some for power, some for the establishment of that democracy of which they had long dreamed, collected round her, attracted by her talents, her enthusiasm, and her beauty. She received the ministers and the leaders of the Gironde at dinner twice a week; but, with the same modesty she had always shown, maintained a reserve proper to her sex, for she was the only woman present at these meetings. Her female friends were always few, the wife of Pétion being among the most intimate of them. There was, in fact, little female society at this time. The court circles were too depressed to enjoy it, and the *bourgeoisie* was too intent on the struggle which was going on to care for merely social meetings. The gatherings of clubs in which stormy debates arose took the place of balls, parties, and the amusements of more peaceful times.

But of the political society of the day Madame Roland was the one centre. She was, in fact, almost the only woman who appeared in it, and every new "patriot" made a point of being introduced to her. Though the Jacobins were rising rapidly into popularity and power, the Girondists still and for long after held the field. They represented order, the constitution, and the medium between the king and the country. Their position as a ministry made them the apex of all the society of Paris, and the person who rallied them was Madame Roland. It was a proud position for the jeweler's daughter, yet she can scarcely be accused of abusing it. Her counsels to Roland, the measures she concerted with his party, the impulse she gave to their movements, were all, if not good and right in the abstract, the best in her view. She contrived to act on the principles with which she set out—the desire for liberty, equality, and fraternity in her country, the hatred of old pride, the contempt for old prejudices, and the hope for new institutions which should inaugurate a perfect Republic.

Even if our space permitted us to follow Madame Roland from the first ministry through the storms that now burst over France, and deluged it with a rain of blood, to do so would be only to recapitulate history. Madame Roland is from this period an historical character. Without any intimate friends but statesmen, actual or future, with no near relations left but her husband and daughter, she quenched her private in her public life. Madame Roland was now one of the Gironde faction, and in reality its soul. Her position as a woman gave her more power to move, more independence of action than the others had.

The times were critical. The Gironde, no longer connected with the monarch, now plotted to establish a liberal democracy, and Madame Roland was their most enthusiastic counselor. The morality of this conspiracy need scarcely be discussed here. The right of nations to depose their sovereigns, and even to subvert the institutions of ages, may be admitted in a country which glories in its two revolutions. The right to do so by bloodshed, terrorism, and the lowest weapons of rebellion, will not be admitted by the wise. It must first, too, be shown what a nation is, and proved that the nation, in its entirety, wills and effects the change. It can not be admitted that a mob of the ferocious and unthinking, roused by the voices of demagogues, is a nation, or even a fitting representative of a nation. The Girondins had recourse to such a rabble, to the scum of Paris, to alter the whole constitution of France. They had recourse to the violent measures, which this rabble, roused and let loose, could not be restrained from taking. Such a revolution, thus effected, was in fact nothing more than the most shameful tyranny to the rest of France. If France had wanted to overthrow the monarchy, France would have done it in time. To impose the will of a furious mob on France was worse despotism than any French king had ever been guilty of. The Gironde knew what they were about; and their act was punished by the very hands they had employed. The hell-dogs they set upon the royal family turned on themselves when blood was wanting; and the Girondins were among the earliest victims of a reign of terror which they had first made possible.

The excuse, if any there be, for this conspiracy, was the danger of delay. Already the army under La Fayette and Dumouriez was being driven out of Belgium—always a disastrous field for French armies—and the Austrians, it was reckoned, would in six weeks be in Paris, the monarchy be reinstated with more absolute powers than ever, and all hope of a constitution—still more of a democracy—lost forever. The king's refusal to sanction the decrees was looked upon as a shilly-shallying means of gaining time. He was in correspondence with the enemies of the Revolution. Peaceful means had already been tried; the decisions of the Assembly had been nullified by the king's scruples or obstinacy. There was but one alternative—to wait till Austrian bayonets should foist upon them the despotism they feared, and maintain, as they have since done in more than one case, a dynasty of *fainéant* Bourbons, or to strike at the throne itself. When we of 1860 look at the countries where the line of this family has been supported by foreign aid, and compare them with what France now is, we may well say with reverence that the Revolution, bloody and frantic as it was, was an instrument in the hands of a foreseeing Father to save one of the foremost nations of the earth from a degradation far worse than any slavery: we may almost excuse the violent measures to which the Girondins now resorted.

Whatever blame falls on the Girondins who had roused the faubourgs, the first movement was due to the Jacobins. The 20th of June, when a Parisian populace, numbered by thousands, and aided by a faithless soldiery, marched to insult one poor weak family, one man and one woman, in their home, was the contemptible triumph of such men as Danton and Santerre. The narrative of the next six weeks is the most bloody in a country where blood has never been spared to ambition.

At last arrived the 10th of August, the crisis of the whole movement, and the long-desired democracy was established. What did it bring to its instigators? A petty triumph, a new struggle, and then—death. Of these events Madame Roland was only a spectator. Doubtless she rejoiced over the fall of the monarchy, and perhaps her enthusiasm blinded her to the excesses of the conquerors. She received the chiefs of the movement at dinner as before; and so completely was she recognized as the centre of the Girondins, that those who had no personal friendship for her were glad to be among her guests. After the triumph of Dumouriez over the Prussians, he dined at her house. Madame Roland had forgotten all their differences, and he sat between her and Vergniaud, and received the congratulations of the "patriots." After dinner he went to the opera, where he was received with acclamations. Danton was at his side, for Danton was now his friend for a time. Madame Roland arrived with Vergniaud. She opened the door of the box, but seeing Danton there retreated in horror. She could never forgive this man the sinister hideousness of his wicked face.

The Girondins, terrified at the effusion of blood which their own scheme had brought about, were yet overwhelmed with joy at the proclamation of the Republic. On the evening of that announcement they met in force at Madame Roland's. There were present twelve out of the twenty-one leaders of the party—Brissot, Vergniaud, Condorcet, Pétion, Guadet, Gensonné, and Barbaroux were among them. They supped and drank with a kind of philosophic worship to the success of the great movement. Roland himself looked at his wife, whose enthusiasm was displayed in the brilliancy of her beautiful face, as if to ask if their ambition were not now complete, and nothing remained but to enjoy the realization of their dreams. All eyes turned on Vergniaud, the hero of the day. After supper he filled his glass, and proposed to drink to the eternity of the Republic. Madame Roland, always ready to invest great moments with the poetry of her fancy, bade him

THE INAUGURATION OF THE REPUBLIC.

pluck some rose leaves from her nosegay and scatter them on the wine. Vergniaud obeyed, but with a saddened look. "Barbaroux," said he, turning to the young man, "it is not rose leaves, but cypress leaves we should quaff in our wine to-night. In drinking to a republic, stained at its birth with the blood of September, who knows that we do not drink to our death? No matter; were this wine my blood, I would drain it to liberty and equality." A cry of *Vive la République* answered this toast.

The words of Vergniaud contained a terrible truth. No sooner was the Republic proclaimed than the real motives of so many of its institutors appeared in their true light. Popularity and power for themselves was what they desired, and the liberty of the people was only a cry to insure it. The Girondins and Jacobins began to tear one another to pieces. The lion and tiger fought over the body of the elephant they had combined to kill. Robespierre, the cunning jackal, quietly devoured the prey while they were fighting, and looked forward to feasting on their very carcasses. A system of mutual accusation was established, and each party watched for the slightest pretext to assail the other.

Madame Roland, mere woman as she was, did not escape. One Achille Viard, a worthless adventurer, accused her in the Convention of a secret correspondence with the constitutional party who had taken refuge in London, for the purpose of saving the life of the king, an object which the Girondins, who saw how his execution would disgrace the Republic, eagerly desired. She was called to the bar of the Assembly. Her beauty, her calm modest dignity, and the clear innocence on her face already extracted a verdict in her favor from the whole body. They listened in silence and admiration, while in a clear voice she asserted her innocence; and when she had done, a general murmur of approbation rose from each and all, except her accuser, who stood silent with shame. She left the Assembly acquitted by acclamation.

But though she acquitted herself thus publicly, private calumny, circulated by her husband's enemies, continued to assail her. The long-desired Republic brought her nothing but misery. A conspiracy to assassinate the Girondins had been discovered only just in time to save them; but the life of that husband whom she regarded as the grand pillar of liberty, was in perpetual danger, and she wished to leave Paris with him and her daughter for her country-house at Beaujolais, but was prevented by the pressure of the time. The Girondins, who represented moderation, were still supported by all the middle classes, and by the departments. Their assailants were the inhabitants of the low faubourgs of Paris, people who, scarcely worthy to be called men and women, longed only for blood and excitement, and were readily roused by the Jacobins and Cordeliers to denounce the lovers of moderation.

Conspiracy followed conspiracy against the lives of the detested party, who, though unpopular with the terrorist mob of Paris, which thronging into the Assembly, by their threats and presence made moderation and rational deliberation impossible, were thus supported by the respectable part of the community. These conspiracies, however, failed. They were one after another revealed to the Girondins, who were thus enabled to prepare themselves.

At last a well-organized plot for their assassination and secret burial was proposed in a meeting at the Archevêché, of which the infamous Marat was captain. They were to be arrested in the night singly, taken to a house in the Rue St. Jacques, subjected to a mock trial, and then buried in the garden behind, while it would be reported that they had fled the country. A young Breton happened to pass the door of the Archevêché when the conspirators were assembling, and noticing that they were admitted on showing a private copper medal, he had the audacity to pull out a *pièce de deux sous*, showed it carelessly, and was admitted. The plot which he thus learned he reported at once to the deputy of his department, who was a Girondin. He was persuaded to go again the next night in the same way, and did so successfully. But he was this time noticed and followed, and the next day his body was found floating down the Seine.

The failure of these plots at assassination decided the Montagne, and the whole insurrectionary party, to unite in a *coup d'état*, and force the Girondins to quit office in the presence of an armed force. They might now have been excused if they had fled to seek safety; but conscious that their strength could alone avert the anarchy and terrorism which would succeed their downfall, they resolved to be firm to the last. They met in silence in a small apartment in the Rue de la Harpe, and one woman, of whom Danton had said, "Why do they not choose a man for their leader? This woman will destroy them; she is the Circe of the Republic;" this woman was among them, encouraging them with her bold words, making each ashamed in the presence of his fellow-men of any desire for personal safety at the sacrifice of their principles. Courageous to the last, they prepared not for deliberation but for death.

The first step taken by the Insurrectionists was to arrest Roland. Six armed men presented themselves in his apartment, and read an order for his arrest from the revolutionary committee. Roland replied that he did not recognize the authority of that body, and refused to follow them. The men had no orders to employ force, and their chief, leaving them to watch Roland, went to report his reply. It was now for Madame Roland's courage to display itself. She wrote a letter to the Convention, announcing the attempted arrest of her husband, and set off in a fiacre for the Tuileries, where that body sat, more tyrannical by far than its former inhabitants. The Rolands were detested by the "people" of Paris, the frantic savages who thronged the streets, thirsting for blood. She knew it, yet did not shudder at the risk she ran. The Place du Carrousel was full of the armed populace, whom Henriot had collected for the grand *coup*. She passed through them boldly, and made her way to the Tuileries. At the doors of the Convention the sentinels forbade her to enter; but she insisted in such strong terms, that they allowed her to pass into the room set apart for petitioners. Through the closed doors she heard the contest going on, which was to end in the defeat of the Girondins. At last, after waiting an hour, she managed to get hold of Vergniaud, to whom she told all. He persuaded her to give up the idea of reading her letter and to return to her husband.

Meanwhile Roland had continued to protest against the presence of the five armed men, who had at last consented to leave him. When Madame Roland reached home she found her husband gone, but soon discovered that he was taking refuge in the house of a friend in the same court. She found him out, embraced him, and then returned once more to the Tuileries. This time the Carrousel was quiet, but the cannon remained pointed at the palace, and groups of *sans-culottes* were collected around them. She found that the sitting of the Convention was over, talked a while to some of the ragged loiterers, and mounted the fiacre again. A little dog claimed her protection by nestling in her gown. She took it with her, and thought that she, too, wanted protection now. She thought of the fable of an old man who, wearied with the persecutions of his own fellow-creatures, retired to a wood to cultivate the friendship of animals. At the post of La Samaritaine the cab was stopped by the guard, who expressed astonishment at a woman being alone so late at night. "Alone!" replied Madame Roland, "I am accompanied by innocence and truth, what more would you have?" The guard allowed her to pass.

There was not room for her in the house where her husband had taken refuge, and she was compelled to return to her own apartment. Weary with the excitements of the day, she threw herself on her bed, but had scarcely done so when she was roused by a deputation from the Commune asking for Roland. She told them he had left her, and refused to say where he was. The deputation retired, and for an hour she slept well. She was roused by her maid, who told her that some gentlemen wished to speak to her. It was one o'clock in the morning, and she therefore guessed their errand easily. She came out of her room and listened while a *mandat* was read for her arrest and imprisonment in the Abbaye. She refused to recognize the authority of the Commune, and deliberated with herself whether resistance would be of any avail. She resolved to sacrifice herself to her husband's safety, hoping that while she was being taken, he would have time to escape. A *juge de paix* arrived and put seals on all her effects. One of the armed men wanted to have them put on her piano. He was told that it was only a musical instrument, and thereupon pulled out a rule and measured it, evidently with a view to appropriation. She sat down to write a note to a friend to beg his protection for her daughter; but as the officer insisted on seeing the letter, she tore it to bits, which he scrupulously picked up and put under seal.

At seven in the morning she was forced to leave her home and her child. An inquisitive crowd had meanwhile poured into her rooms, and they now surrounded the fiacre in which she was placed, and shouted "A la guillotine!" "Would you like to have the windows closed?" asked her guard, politely. "No," she replied, "oppressed innocence must never take the attitude of guilt. I fear no one's looks." "You have more courage than many men," said the guard, unable to repress their admiration. "I groan for my country," she answered; "I regret the error which made me think it worthy of liberty and happiness. I appreciate life, but despise injustice and death."

At the prison she was fortunate in a worthy and kind-hearted jailer, who, with his wife, did every thing in his power to soften the misery of confinement to her. But those of my readers—let me trust they are few—who know what it is to be in prison, if only for one day, will understand that no comforts or attentions can make up for the want of personal liberty, nothing can remove the degradation of being in the power of others, often, too, at the mercy of those who have none. No wonder, then, at the suggestion of Grandpré, she wrote a letter to the Convention, not indeed complaining or succumbing, but protesting boldly against the illegality of her arrest, and demanding that an investigation should be made into it. The letter, of course, brought no results.

It is curious now to note the spirit of this woman. She said to herself, "Death must come, but I will live till the last moment." She had brought in her pocket a volume of Thomson's poems, a work she was very partial to. She was allowed to have books, and selected "Plutarch's Lives," which had first made her a Republican, and Hume's "History of England," with Sheridan's dictionary, *that she might improve her knowledge of English.* Even in the cell, and in the very shadow of death, she was resolved to make the most of her mind. Her jailer granted her many little alleviations. She was allowed to have flowers in her cell, and to receive visits from a few particular friends, from whom she learned that her husband was in hiding in the neighborhood of Rouen; and assured of his safety, she was the more ready to die in his place. She was enabled, too, through their medium, to place her daughter with a Madame Creuzé la Touche, in whom she could confide. From these friends, too, she learned that one after another of her party had been condemned and executed, and lastly that her own name was written on the black list of Fouquier-Tinville. This list was signed by Robespierre, the man who in urging the execution of the king had protested his hatred of capital punishment, and affected disgust at the shedding of blood, and simulated grief at being forced by the most weighty considerations to insist on Louis's death. This man had been one of the earliest of Madame Roland's political friends; she had brought him forward in the political world, convinced that he was a well-meaning man. She had defended him in spite of the affectation of his manner, which disgusted her. She had tried on one occasion to save his life. He had been her guest time and again; her correspondent; her friend. He had enthusiastically entered into her aspirations for liberty, he had imparted to her his own. He was the man who signed her death-warrant.

Once during her imprisonment she was visited by a physician, who turned out to be a friend of Robespierre's, and as he offered to take a letter from her to that man, she wrote one. She reminded him in it of the fickleness of fortune, and bade him take warning by the evil reputation of Sylla and Marius, who had enjoyed popularity in their day. The letter was dignified and touching, yet she feared it might look like a prayer for mercy, and she would not receive that at the hands of Robespierre. She tore it up.

When all hope of justice was dead, she determined that posterity at least should acquit her, and began to write her life. A friend named Bosc visited her frequently, and she confided to him the sheets of those Memoirs from which this one has been chiefly drawn. He carried them out under his cloak, and two years after her death he published them under the title she had given them, "Appeal to Impartial Posterity." From time to time during the six months she was thus employed, she received hints which led her to believe that her hour was come: yet she wrote on hurriedly but brilliantly, with all the eloquence of oppressed innocence. It consoled her to recall the days of her quiet girlhood, and to contrast them with the short checkered career of her political life, and the gloomy end that was put to it.

But the weariness of captivity, added to ill health, broke her spirit at last; and she obtained some poison, and prepared to put an end to her misery. She wrote then to her husband. "Forgive me, excellent man, for taking upon myself to dispose of a life I had consecrated to you. Believe me, I could have loved it and you the better for your misfortunes, had I but been permitted to share it with you. Now you are merely freed from a useless object of unavailing anguish to you." To her daughter she wrote, "Forgive me, dear child, young and tender girl, whose sweet image penetrates my mother's heart, and shakes my resolution. Ah! never indeed would I have removed your guide from you, had they but left me to you. Cruel hearts! have they no pity for innocence? Let them do; my example will be with you, and I feel, I may confess, at the doors of the tomb, that that is a rich legacy."

At this moment she felt keenly the want of that Christian faith which she had thrown away for worthless philosophy, which could give her no strength, tell her of no future, and assure her of no relief. Yet she believed in God. Those who have called her an Atheist can not have read her own words. At this moment her thoughts turned from the world which had so deceived her, where all was disappointment, all hollow rottenness, up to that God whom she had learned to see and to love in nature. "Divinity, Supreme Being," she prayed, "Soul of the world, principle of all that I feel to be great, good, and happy, thou whose existence I believe in, because I must have sprung from something better than what I see, I come to join thy Spirit." But that is all. How cold this half-doubtful belief, so scantily accorded. Is it not almost equal to the despairing infidelity of the dying soldier who exclaimed, "Oh! my God, if there be a God, save my soul, if I have a soul?" We must pass in silence over this fearful doubting, we must be content to believe that, in these her last days, she did look forward to immortality, did feel that somewhere there was a better world than that which around her flowed with blood in the name of outraged freedom. She recalled, then, her friends and servants, and wrote her last words. "Farewell, thou sun whose bright rays brought calm into my soul, as they recalled it to heaven; farewell, lovely lands, whose view has so often moved me; and you, simple inhabitants of Thézèe, who were wont to bless my presence, whose brows I wiped, whose poverty I softened, and whom I nursed in sickness; farewell, farewell, quiet little rooms where I fed my soul with truth, charmed my fancies with study, and learned, in the silence of meditation, to command my feelings and to despise vanity."

But she had still a duty to do, and to write a separate letter to her child.

"I know not, my little friend, if it will be granted me to see or write to you again. Remember your mother. These few words comprise all the best I can say to you. You have seen me happy in fulfilling my duties and making myself useful to the suffering. There is no other way of being happy. You have seen me calm in misfortune and captivity, because I had no remorse, and retained the memory and the pleasure which good actions leave behind them. There is no other way than this to support the ills of life and the changes of fortune. Perhaps, and I trust so, you are not reserved for trials like mine; but there are others against which you will need as much to battle. A strict and busy life is the only preservative against all dangers, and necessity as well as wisdom compels you to work seriously. Be worthy of your parents: they leave you a high example, and if you profit by it, your life will not be useless. Adieu, loved child, whom I nourished at my breast, and strove to imbue with my principles. A time will come when you will be able to judge of the effort I make at this moment not to be melted by the thought of you. I press you to my bosom. Adieu, my Eudora."

But Stoic as she was, she was still a woman. The thought of this one being, who had been more her own than any other, was too much for her, and for her daughter's sake she resolved to live. She threw the poison from her.

She was at this time at the prison of St. Pélagie. She had been set at liberty one day, and mad with joy had rushed to find her daughter and clasp her to her bosom. But it was only a cruel snare. At the very door of the house where her child was she was rearrested, and her prayers to be allowed to see her were unavailing. She was taken back again, not to the Abbaye, but to St. Pélagie.

At length, after an imprisonment of nearly six months, she was taken, in November, 1793, to that fatal Conciergerie from whence in those days no prisoner issued but for the guillotine.

Here she was placed in a wretched cell, next to that in which poor Marie Antoinette had been lodged. She who had rejoiced over the fall of that unhappy queen was now seen in private moments to weep bitterly. Yet her courage did not give way. In the cells were lodged many of the Girondins who were yet to be executed; and when they were let out into the passage for exercise, she talked to them across the grating of her door, and encouraged them to look on death as a martyrdom. She rose now to the level of an orator, and in her misery and despair poured out bitter reproaches against the very men who, in the hall above, were holding the mock trials of her friends. One by one she saw them depart never to return, and felt that her turn must be at hand.

It came at last. Before David, the judge, and Fouquier-Tinville, the public prosecutor, she was accused of being the wife of Roland, and the friend of his accomplices. She stood before them proudly. She was dressed simply, in white, and her long rich hair flowed in curls over her shoulders. Her face, while it had lost all its freshness from long confinement, was still beautiful in expression. This beauty had once melted a whole Assembly, before which she was arraigned, but it served only to enrage her present accusers. That very morning Brissot, the founder of her party, had been executed. She could not hope to escape, yet was resolved to speak out, and defend herself to the country.

The court was at that time open, and the trials were attended by the dregs of the populace, who interfered with them at pleasure, and mingled coarse invectives with the impatient questions of the public prosecutor. The interrogatory was at first of little importance, consisting of questions about her early life and first connection with Roland. It then passed to inquiries about his colleagues, and, lastly, to such gross imputations on her character that she burst into tears. After three hours of this public torture she was dismissed, and returned to her cell.

Two days later she was again called up, and the interrogatory proceeded as before. When called on to tell what she knew of Roland's concealment, she steadfastly refused to say a word. "There is no law," she exclaimed, "in the name of which one can insist on a betrayal of the dearest feelings in nature."

"With such a talker we shall never have done," cried Fouquier-Tinville, furiously; "close the interrogatory."

She turned on him a look of withering pity. "How I pity you!" she said; "you can send me to the scaffold, but can not take from me the joy of a good conscience, and the conviction that posterity will acquit Roland and me, and devote our persecutors to infamy." She was told to choose a pleader. She chose Chanveau, and retired, crying merrily as she went, "I only wish you, in return for the harm you wish me, peace of mind equal to what I feel, whatever price you attach to it." She ran down the steps eagerly. Her friends were waiting to receive her in the passage, and as she passed through them, she drew her finger across her delicate throat to show that she was condemned.

The tumbril had come and gone incessantly on the fatal day. It was in its last journey for that day that it took up Madame Roland and an old trembling man named Lamarche. The mob, reveling in blood, shouted "A la guillotine!" "I am going there," she answered; "but those who send me thither will not be long ere they follow. I go innocent; but they will come stained with blood, and you who applaud our execution will then applaud theirs." The mob answered her with the vilest insults and grossest epithets. Youth and beauty could no more excite admiration in their ferocious hearts than the sight of trembling old age by her side could draw forth pity. Lamarche wept bitterly; but Madame Roland, proud of her fate, was unnaturally gay, and strove to cheer and encourage him. When they arrived at the Place de la Concorde, where beneath a huge clay statue of Liberty stood the guillotine, reeking still with the blood of her friends, she leaped lightly from the cart. The executioner pulled her by the arm toward the scaffold. "Stay," said she, feeling sympathy for her companion even at this moment. "I have a favor to ask, though not for myself." She then explained that the sight of her death would redouble the poor old man's misery, and begged that he might be allowed to die first. She heard the knife fall on his neck without a shudder, then bowing to the great statue, she cried, "Oh! Liberty, Liberty! how many crimes are committed in thy name!" and mounted the scaffold firmly. In a few seconds her head, fair as it was, rolled into the basket prepared to receive it.

Thus at nine-and-thirty died this strange woman. There is more of warning than of example in her story.

Some days later some shepherds trudging along a Norman highway with their flocks before them spied in a ditch the body of a man. They raised it up, found it to be that of an old man, tall, thin, stern even in death. In his heart was yet the stiletto which belonged to yonder sword-stick lying by, and on his breast was pinned a paper with these words on it: "Whoever thou art that findest these remains, respect them as those of a virtuous man. After my wife's death I would not remain another day upon this earth so stained with crimes." This was Roland, who had thus destroyed himself.

What a fitting end to the lives of two "Apostles of Liberty!" The one to die at the guillotine, the other to end his own life in an act of cowardice. Such be the end of all those who think to besiege liberty by a tyranny far worse than the power they overthrow—a tyranny of might and terror.

How different are these two deaths to the glorious ends of the apostles of Christianity! Where is hope in the last days of Madame Roland or her husband? where is the true courage of faith? the one, in despair, venting invectives from her cell, brazen to the world, yet weeping in private; the other talking of a "world stained with crimes," when he himself had first raised the criminals, first urged them on to acts of rebellion and anarchy. How different this conceit, too, with which he proclaims himself a "virtuous man" to the humility with which a Christian martyr passed away! how different his wife's unrelenting hatred to the forgiveness the other sheds on his persecutors in the midst of his torments! How blank these deaths without a future to look to! How utterly despairing these lives where all had turned out rotten, when there was no trust in a perfect life elsewhere, no longing for the land of that pure government, those public virtues, that perfect organization, which in their arrogance they had hoped to set up on earth! How truly consistent is the cowardice of suicide with such a cheerless creed! How naturally adapted is such an end to the arrogance which rejected revelation and sought to raise men into gods! Well might Roland take care that his suicide should be known to the world, and well might his wife write an appeal to posterity. What else, poor creatures, had they to look to? What comfort, what hope in the hour of death? None, but the cold justice of time, the acquittal of posterity. And posterity has given them their due. Yes, it is quite enough meed of praise for either Roland or his wife to say that they were better than any of their celebrated contemporaries; that their moral characters were irreproachable; that they did not abuse power when they gained it, nor seek it selfishly; that they were moved by pure principles, and took even their most mischievous measures in the belief that they were acting aright. Compared with Marat and Robespierre they were saints: compared with the obscurest Christian who does his duty humbly in faith and hope, they stand out as demons. But their own age must judge them, for their faults were its own. Let them go.

LADY MARY WORTLEY MONTAGU.

This liveliest, wittiest, severest, and—if we believed Horace Walpole, which we do not—*dirtiest* woman of her time, is celebrated for her charming letters, her Oriental travels, for being first the idol and then the abomination of Pope, and, lastly, but by no means least, as a public benefactress, by introducing into this country, in spite of the most vehement opposition, the operation of inoculating for the small-pox. As a female humorist moving in all kinds of society, admired by all, abused by many, but whether with admiration or dislike talked of by every body, Lady Mary claims her niche in this work.

Her father was, when she was born, the fifth Earl of Kingston. Her mother, Lady Mary Fielding, was first cousin to the father of Henry Fielding, the author of "Tom Jones," so that two humorists, male and female, are to be found in the same family at the same time. It is always troublesome, when one is reading the life of one person, to go back two or three generations to others who gave them little more than their name. Suffice it then to say of Lady Mary's mother, that she was daughter to William Fielding, Earl of Desmond, whose fourth brother, John Fielding, was the grandfather of Richardson's rival. Her father, Evelyn Pierrepont, of Thoresby, was grandson to a certain William Pierrepont of the same place, who supported the party of Cromwell in the civil war, and was commonly known as *Wise William*. In 1706 this father was created, by Queen Anne, Marquis of Dorchester; and in 1715 George I. made him Duke of Kingston. By his first wife, Lady Mary Fielding, he had three daughters and one son. The eldest of these was Lady Mary herself, born in 1690; the next was Frances, who married the Earl of Mar, who took so prominent a part in the movement of 1715; the next Evelyn, who married John Lord Gower. After giving birth to her only son, William, in 1694, the Countess of Kingston died, and thus Lady Mary Pierrepont was left in childhood without a mother. In reviewing her life and character, this fact must be taken into consideration and proportionate allowance made for her.

Her father, the Earl of Kingston, was a fine gentleman and a bad father, the friend of beaux and wits, but not over-affectionate to his children. This, too, must be considered.

Her first *début* in society was rather illustrious. She was eight years old, a pretty, fair-haired child, with a good deal of spirit and not a little vanity. Her father was amused with the pertness, and proud of the pretty face of his little daughter. He was a member of the famous Kit-Kat Club, which was then held in Shire Lane (now Lower Searle's Place), which lies between Lincoln's Inn Fields and Fleet Street. This little street, so called because it divided the city from the shire, was always a nest for wits. Here lived old Isaac Bickerstaff, the Tatler, who met his club at the "Trumpet" Tavern, which still stands, and here assembled the Kit-Kat Club. It was composed of thirty-nine noblemen and gentlemen who were devoted to the Hanoverian succession, and all strong Whigs. Its curious name was the subject of much discussion. Some said that the house in which it met was kept by one Kit or Christopher Katt, who concocted those incomparable mutton pies which always formed a part of the supper of the members, and which from him were called Kit-Kats. Others maintained that the maker of the pies was named Christopher, and his house had the sign of the Cat and Fiddle. Pope (or it may be Arbuthnot) found another derivation for the name in the following well-known verses:

"Whence deathless Kit-Kat took its name
Few critics can unriddle,
Some say from pastry-cook it came,
And some from Cat and Fiddle.
From no trim beaux its name it boasts,
Gray statesmen or green wits;
But from the pell-mell pack of toasts
Of old cats and young kits,"

referring to the then fashionable system of toasting some celebrated beauty after dinner. The ladies approved of had the honor of having verses to them engraved on the glasses, and, in some cases, of their portraits hung up in the club-room. The members at the time of which we speak were all more or less distinguished. There was Marlborough himself; there were Sir Robert Walpole, the minister of George I. and George II.; Vanbrugh, known for bad plays and worse architecture; Addison; Congreve; Dr. Garth, who could run as well as prescribe, and beat the Duke of Grafton in a foot-match of two hundred yards in the Mall; the Dukes of Somerset, Richmond, Grafton, Devonshire; the Earls of Dorset, Sunderland, Manchester, and Wharton; Lords Halifax and Somers; Maynwaring, Stepney, and Walsh, and the Earl of Kingston, Lady Mary's father. Jacob Tonson, the bookseller, was their secretary, and Sir Godfrey Kneller painted all their portraits, of that peculiar size ever since known as a Kit-kat.

It must have been difficult for thirty-nine men to find thirty-nine uncontestable beauties whenever they might be called on to do so, and in such a dilemma, or perhaps to indulge a whim, the Earl of Kingston one day proposed his daughter as his toast. The company demurred, on the plea that they had never seen her. "Then you shall see her," cried the father, ready to carry out the joke. She was sent for, and received with acclamations, acknowledged to be a beauty, and even an incipient wit, and handed, like a pretty doll as she was, from lap to lap among poets, wits, statesmen, and rakes. The omen was auspicious, and the bon-bons and kisses with which she was overwhelmed were only the types of that admiration she was destined to receive later. In after life she remembered the incident, and affirmed that it was the happiest moment she had ever known.

How the next ten years of her life were passed we have no accurate information. She lived at the dull house at Thoresby, in the "plains of Nottingham," or at Acton, near London, and seems to have been mainly occupied in cultivating her mind. She herself tells us that her education was "one of the worst in the world," from which, as from other passages in her letters, we may infer that Lord Kingston gave her little or none. This deficiency her own energy supplied. Fond of reading more than any thing else, she eagerly devoured such books as were then to be found in country libraries, many of them ponderous folios of serious writing, among which we may perhaps include the romances of Mademoiselle de Scudery, ponderous enough surely, and certainly a serious undertaking, and the other so-called novels then in vogue, and translated into English. These twelve-volume works were no light reading, though the lightest of the day. They took a six-month or so to get through; and being full of high-flown sentiment must have had a far more powerful effect on the young reader's mind than the three-volume novels, of which a young lady boasted to me the other day that she could read two a day and four on Sunday. Reading was then decidedly more profitable than it is now. It was, in fact, a study, not a mere indulgence. With her brother William's tutor, she is said to have studied French and Latin, but it is more probable that she taught herself the latter. Her diligence, her thirst for knowledge, and her intrepidity in tackling any branch of it, added to her wonderful memory, enabled her to acquire what other young ladies of her day, content with tapestry-work and tittle-tattle, never thought of attempting, and in after years the same spirit made of her a very decent Turkish scholar. It is possible that in these more masculine studies she may have received some aid from her uncle, William Fielding; but it is certain that Bishop

Burnet, the author of the "History of the Reformation" and Bishop of Salisbury, inspected and assisted her classical studies. At the age of nineteen she translated from the Latin (for her acquaintance with Greek seems to have been too limited to admit of her using the version in that language) the "Enchiridion" of Epictetus. This translation, made in a single week, shows considerable proficiency in Latin, and, as the work of a girl who was perhaps self-taught in that language, deserves to stand very high. She forwarded it to the bishop with a long letter, in which several quotations prove that she had even then read Erasmus carefully, requesting him to correct her errors in the translation, which he did. This letter is perhaps more remarkable than its inclosure, and shows that at that age the young girl had already acquired no small amount of useful wisdom, better still than her Latin and Greek. She speaks thus of the education of women in her day, and I fear that what she says applies pretty nearly to that of many of our own fair contemporaries:

"We are permitted no books but such as tend to the weakening and effeminating of the mind. Our natural defects are every way indulged, and it is looked upon as in a degree criminal to improve our reason or fancy we have any. We are taught to place all our art in adorning our outward forms, and permitted, without reproach, to carry that custom even to extravagancy, while our minds are entirely neglected, and, by disuse of reflections, filled with nothing but the trifling objects our eyes are daily entertained with. This custom, so long established and industriously upheld, makes it even ridiculous to go out of the common road, and forces one to find many excuses, as if it were a thing altogether criminal not to play the fool in concert with other women of quality, whose birth and leisure only serve to make them the most useless and worthless part of the creation. There is hardly a character in the world more despicable or more liable to universal ridicule, than that of a learned woman: those words imply, according to the received sense, a talking, impertinent, vain, and conceited creature. I believe nobody will deny that learning may have that effect, but it must be a very superficial degree of it."

The name of Burnet reminds us of an anecdote of his son Thomas, for a long time the scapegrace of the family. The bishop, observing him one day to be unusually grave, asked him what he was meditating. "A greater work," replied the young man, "than your lordship's 'History of the Reformation.'" "Indeed! what is that?" "My own reformation." "I am delighted to hear it," quoth the bishop, "though I almost despair of it." The young man's meditation was not fruitless, and he lived to be Chief Justice of Common Pleas, and, what was better, a respectable man.

In such studies, industriously pursued, were the younger years of Lady Mary's life passed; but when her father resided at Thoresby, and surrounded himself with his jovial companions, it was her duty to entertain them at his table. According to the custom of the day, she had the arduous task of carving for the whole party, while the earl at the other end pressed his guests, if indeed they required pressing, to drink and be merry. This undertaking, which the etiquette of the day made imperative on the lady of the house, was so considerable that she was obliged to take her own dinner in private beforehand. We can well understand the nausea of such banquets to the young lady.

Though Lady Mary had none of the young-ladyism or sentimentality of girls of her age, we are not to suppose her either hard or masculine. Her mind, indeed, had a manly vigor which she had developed by books rarely read, and thoughts rarely indulged, by others of her sex; but her character and her tastes were perfectly feminine. On the one hand we find her not only devoted to, but even composing poetry; on the other, cultivating the tenderest and most affectionate friendships with young women of her own age.

Of her verses there is not much to say, except that they are free from sentimentality; so free, indeed, that they never once speak to the heart, and therefore fail to fix themselves on our minds. They have the epigrammatic turn and love of antithesis which seem inseparable to the poetry of her day, their fair share of classical allusions, and an easy gracefulness of style. To this they unite strong sense and some satire, though not nearly so witty as that in her letters. She began to make verses early. At the age of twelve she composed a fair imitation of Ovid's Epistles, entitled "Julia to Ovid;" at fourteen, again, she penned some verses to Truth. But the most celebrated of her metrical pieces are the "Town Eclogues," and the various addresses and ballads, of which we shall speak in the proper place. It may suffice to say that, in spite of the temporary popularity of these, Lady Mary has no claim to be considered a poetess. Her verses are only pretty and neat. They show no inspiration, no power, no loftiness of thought; but they are sufficient to prove the elegance of her tastes.

Her early friendships were among those of her own station. She had some intimacy with Lady Anne Vaughan, the only child of the Earl of Carberry, and, therefore, an heiress. This young lady was very unfortunate in her marriage with Lord Winchester, afterward the third Duke of Bolton, who married her only for her money, and soon threw her over for the celebrated actress Polly Peachum (Miss Lavinia Bestwick), whom he married after the death of his wife. The most respectable of the maids of honor of Queen Anne, Mistress (that is, Miss) Jane Smith, the third daughter of the Whig Speaker Smith, and an intimate friend of Lady Suffolk, was another of her intimates. Then there came the volatile Dolly Walpole, the sister of Sir Robert, the minister. Dorothy was a merry, harmless Norfolk girl, one of a family of nineteen, and with no fortune but her face, which proved one in time, and which made her the belle of her native county. Bred up at Houghton, she was brought by her brother, then Mr. Walpole, to London, with a view of finding a husband. Her brother's wife is described as an intriguing and not very amiable woman, who was determined that Dolly should make a good match. She was surrounded by admirers, of whom one, every way desirable, presently declared himself. His relations, however, little thinking that Mr. Walpole would one day be the right hand of two sovereigns, and have more in his power than the richest peer of the realm, inquired about the young lady's portion. Like most mercenary people, they were destined to be cheated. They found that she was dowerless, and therefore forbade a connection which some years later would have been worth thousands to them and theirs. Dolly, who was in love, was miserable. Mrs. Walpole was unkind to her; and so when Lady Wharton offered her a shelter in her own house, she readily accepted it. She was too ignorant of the scandals of town to know what an infamous character Lord Wharton bore, and that this step would be ruinous to her. Sir Robert happened to be out of town; but when on his return he learned where his sister was, he went to Lord Wharton's with his usual irascibility and utter want of tact, and thundered for admittance, claiming his sister in no very polite terms. When admitted, he assailed Lady Wharton in "Anglo-Saxon" language, carried off his sister, and took her down to Houghton, to pass her time in penitence for her mistake. The incident furnished a pretty story for the scandal-mongers of the town, and poor Dolly's name was hawked about in no very agreeable manner. For three years she mourned at Houghton her lost love and her tarnished fame. At that time, however, Charles, second Viscount Townshend, who had been away as embassador at the Hague, and was now a widower, returned to Raynham Hall, in the neighborhood of Houghton, saw Miss Dorothy Walpole's pretty face, and, ignorant of the little story about Lord Wharton, fell in love with it, and proposed to the owner. He was accepted, and they were married in 1713.

The match was ample compensation for the lost love. Lord Townshend afterward became a minister, and played a conspicuous part under George the First.

It is said that Lady Mary took some part in this affair, opposing Mrs. Walpole, defending the simple Dolly, and making herself obnoxious to her sister-in-law; and it is also hinted that this part may account for the animosity which Horace Walpole, Dolly's nephew, felt toward Lady Mary. Horace was always much attached to his mother, and he never forgave a foe of his family. There is no doubt that, for one cause or another, he never spoke well of the subject of this memoir.

But the best and most intimate of Lady Mary's friends was Mistress Anne Wortley, the sister of the man she afterward married. The Wortley-Montagus united in themselves two of the oldest families in England. The Montagus, from whom are descended the ducal families of Manchester and Montagu, and the Earls of Halifax and Sandwich, date their arrival in England from a Norman follower of William the Conqueror with the uncouth name of Drogo de Monte Acuto. The Wortleys were a Saxon family of Yorkshire. The grandfather of Mrs. Anne Wortley and Mr. Edward Wortley Montagu was Sir Edward Montagu, of Hinchinbroke, in Huntingdon, who, being high admiral at the time of the Restoration, influenced the fleet to declare for Charles II., and was, in consequence, created Earl of Sandwich. His eldest son succeeded to the title. His second was Sidney Montagu, who married Anne Wortley, an heiress and daughter of Sir Francis Wortley, of Wortley, in Yorkshire, whose surname thereupon he added to his own. The son and daughter of this Sidney were the husband and bosom-friend of Lady Mary. As for this Sidney himself, he is described as sitting in his ingle-nook, employed in the refined and delicate occupation of swearing at his servants, washing down his oaths with store of canary, while his brother, the dean, meek and mild, sat opposite to him, beseeching Heaven to pardon the blasphemies he had not the courage to reprove.

With Mrs. Anne Wortley Lady Mary corresponded affectionately and even passionately, when she had fallen in love with her brother, and meant for him all the endearments she lavished upon her. The following letter, written in 1709, is a good specimen of Lady Mary's style at nineteen, and of the usual epistolary style of the day, and is interesting as showing what were her studies and interests at that age:

"I shall run mad. With what heart can people write when they believe their letters will never be received? I have already writ you a very long scrawl, but it seems it never came to your hands; I can not bear to be accused of coldness by one whom I shall love all my life. This will, perhaps, miscarry as the last did. How unfortunate I am if it does! You will think I forget you, who are never out of my thoughts. You will fancy me stupid enough to forget your letters, when they are the only pleasures of my solitude. * * * Let me beg you for the future, if you do not receive letters very constantly from me, imagine the post-boy killed, imagine the mail burnt, or some other strange accident; you can imagine nothing so impossible as that I forget you, my dear Mrs. Wortley. * * * I am now so much alone, I have leisure to pass whole days in reading, but am not at all proper for so delicate an employment as chusing you books. Your own fancy will better direct you. My study at present is nothing but dictionaries and grammars. I am trying whether it be possible to learn without a master; I am not certain (and dare hardly hope) I shall make any great progress; but find the study so diverting, I am not only easy, but pleased with the solitude that indulges it. I forget there is such a place as London, and wish for no company but yours. You see, my dear, in making my pleasures consist of these unfashionable diversions, I am not of the number who can not be easy out of the mode. I believe more follies are committed out of complaisance to the world, than in following our own inclinations. Nature is seldom in the wrong, custom always; it is with some regret I follow it in all the impertinencies of dress; the compliance is so trivial, it comforts me; but I am amazed to see it consulted even in the most important occasions of our lives; * * * I call all people who fall in love with furniture, clothes, and equipage of this number, and I look upon them as no less in the wrong than when they were five years old, and doated on shells, pebbles, and hobby-horses. I believe you will expect this letter to be dated from the other world, for sure I am you never heard an inhabitant of this talk so before."

What she here says of dress reminds us that in after years she was described by Walpole, who saw her at Florence, as being very untidy, in a dirty mob, and with uncombed hair. That well-known anecdote, too, is of Lady Mary, which relates how, being once reproached with having dirty hands, she replied (it was at the French opera), "Ah, si vous voyiez mes pieds!" That she was eccentric and indifferent to dress there can be no doubt. It is rather to her praise than otherwise; but that she was dirty in her person we can believe only on the word of Horace Walpole, who hated her, and did not mind what he said about his foes. That she could dress well, when she chose, is no less certain; for her dress at court one evening was so pleasing, that the Prince of Wales, who admired her a little too much, called the princess from her cards to see "how well Lady Mary was dressed." "Lady Mary always dresses well," replied the princess in dudgeon, returning to her basset.

One afternoon when Lady Mary went to call on her friend Mrs. Wortley, she found in her room a gentleman, some thirty years old, leaning familiarly by the fireplace, and watching her as she entered with a keen critical eye. His face, in spite of the huge full-bottomed wig, then in fashion, was handsome and expressive, a shade thoughtful, but cold and terribly sensible. In his manner there was a mixture of Yorkshire bluntness and *méfiance*, with something of Norman dignity. He talked like a man of the world, with a touch of the scholar, which delighted her. He had evidently mingled with the humorists of London clubs, but he preferred classics. Keen observer as she was, she at once entered on that subject. Accustomed rather to despise women, and particularly young ladies, he was amazed and charmed to find one of so much sense and such unusual reading. He improved the occasion, and lingered in his sister's room longer than he had ever done before. Nor did he leave it willingly. Here were beauty, wit, and strong sense united in one person. He was not a philosopher, but he was not susceptible. It required fascinations as great as these to move him, and he was moved. This man was Edward Wortley-Montagu, commonly called Mr. Wortley, the brother of Lady Mary's bosom friend.

They talked of Roman heroes. Fancy a young lady and young man of to-day flirting over the classics! He mentioned an author, and she regretted she had never read his works. Some days after she received an edition of this author, in the fly-leaf of which were written the following verses:

"Beauty like this had vanquished Persia shown,
The Macedon had laid his empire down,
And polished Greece obeyed a barb'rous throne.
Had wit so bright adorned a Grecian dame,
The am'rous youth had lost his thirst for fame,
Nor distant India sought through Syria's plain;
But to the muses' stream with her had run,
And thought her lover more than Ammon's son."

We perceive from this very clear declaration that Mr. Wortley had not much facility of rhyming, whatever his classical attainments. But he was not without his attractions in the eyes of an intellectual woman. He had been well educated, if we mistake not, at Cambridge; had made the grand tour in 1703, and even extended his foreign experience beyond the usual limits by a residence of two years in Venice. Like most young men of family in that day he had entered Parliament early.

There he sat at different times for the city of Westminster, the city of Peterborough—both very influential constituencies—and the boroughs of Huntingdon and Bossiney. He was a Liberal and a progressionist, two very good qualities in this day, though then sullied by a necessary adherence to the Hanoverian succession. About the time of his meeting with Lady Mary, he had brought in a bill for the naturalization of foreign Protestants. Later he entered one for limiting the number of the officers of the House, and securing the freedom of Parliament; and this bill, which nearly affected the interests of the members, was agitated for five years, and eventually lost in 1713. In the same year, 1709, he obtained leave for a bill to encourage learning and secure copyrights of books to the authors. Thus we can judge that he was a sensible, well-meaning man, as different from his father as gold from tinsel. He had other recommendations. His tastes or his Whiggism brought him in contact with the humorists of those days. Addison was his intimate friend. Garth, Congreve, Maynwaring, and even Steele, were among his associates. Perhaps he had not much wit or humor himself; he seems even to have dreaded it; but it is certain he had much sound sense, and was not altogether a common man. On the other hand, he had just as much heart as was wanted for his career, a strong feeling of honor, and no romance.

The events that followed upon this interview form the real romance of Lady Mary's life; and, whatever else may be said of her, her conduct in them attaches us to her. A romance, indeed, this love affair was, quiet, and apparently cold as it may have been. It was the old romance of a woman loving fondly a man who disapproved of her, and of her efforts to attach him in spite of natural modesty and a consciousness of his indifference.

That Mr. Wortley was much in love there is no doubt, but he set his own judgment against his own heart; he doubted if this girl, who appeared to be coquettish, vain, fond of the world and society, would be a suitable companion for a man of his quiet and serious tastes, or take sufficient interest in his political ambitions. He not only felt this, but openly told her what he felt in the matter, and treated her with a nonchalance which only increased her affection for him.

For some time after he had offered and been accepted, their intercourse was carried on through the medium of letters to and from his sister; and it is impossible not to see that a great deal of the affection expressed in Lady Mary's letters is meant for the brother. But about 1711 Mrs. Anne Wortley died in the flower of her youth. Some time after this, Lady Mary wrote her first letter to Mr. Wortley—"the first," she says, "I ever wrote to one of your sex, and shall be the last." She begins by excusing her boldness in writing to him at all, and then defends herself against a charge of frivolous tastes, which he seems to have made, and while endeavoring to conceal her love for him, pleads for his affection. "You distrust me; I can neither be easy, nor loved, where I am distrusted. Nor do I believe your passion for me is what you pretend it; at least I am sure, was I in love, I could not talk as you do. * * * I wished I loved you enough to devote myself to be forever miserable for the pleasure of a day or two's happiness. I can not resolve upon it. You must think otherwise of me, or not at all."

His complaints, doubts, and accusations continued, and at last she writes: "I resolved to make no answer to your letter; it was something very ungrateful, and I resolved to give over all thoughts of you. I could easily have performed that resolve some time ago, but then you took pains to please me; now you have brought me to esteem you, you make use of that esteem to give me uneasiness; and I have the displeasure of seeing I esteem a man that dislikes me. Farewell, then; since you will have it so, I renounce all the ideas I have so long flattered myself with, and will entertain my fancy no longer with the imaginary pleasure of pleasing you. * * * You think me all that is detestable; you accuse me of want of sincerity and generosity. * * * There is no condition of life I could not have been happy in with you, so very much I liked you, I might say loved, since it is the last thing I'll ever say to you. This is telling you sincerely my greatest weakness; and now I will oblige you with a new proof of my generosity; I'll never see you more."

But in his answer to this he says: "I would die to be secure of your heart, though but for a moment;" and, seizing on this expression, she again attempts to exonerate herself, and the letters that follow are much in the same strain, defending their writer from charges of coquetry, of inconstancy, of a love of society, and even of interested views. Yet he could not make up his mind to give her up. "I see what is best for me," he writes; "I condemn what I do, and yet I fear I must do it." In this letter he asks for an interview, and gives us some insight into the manner of their meetings. He proposes that it should take place at the house of Mrs. Steele, the wife of Sir Richard, who was then Mr. Steele. "You may call upon her or send for her, to-morrow or next day. Let her dine with you, or go to visit shops or Hyde Park, or other diversions. You may bring her home, I can be in the house, reading, as I often am, though the master is abroad." Hyde Park, it may be noticed in passing, was then, as now, the great promenade of London. Horse-races and foot-races were often held in the ring, and in the afternoon the ladies drove round and round it in a cloud of dust; "some," says a writer in 1700, "singing, others laughing, others tickling one another, and all of them toying and devouring cheese-cakes, marchpane, and China oranges." The lodge there was celebrated for its milk, tarts, and syllabub, to taste which was the regular accompaniment of the drive. At that time the Serpentine, which was not made till 1730, was represented by a couple of ponds, and the lodge in question was close to these.

But whatever doubts he had, Mr. Wortley at last made open proposals to Lady Mary's father, then Lord Dorchester. They were favorably received, and all went well till the settlements came to be discussed. Mr. Wortley disapproved of the foolish practice of settling property on a son unborn, who might turn out a spendthrift or a fool. Lord Dorchester replied, that no grandchild of his should risk being a beggar, and would have nothing more to say to his proposals of marriage. The wisdom of this precaution on Mr. Wortley's part was shown in the sequel. His son turned out both fool and spendthrift and something worse, and the Wortley estates, if settled on him, would soon have been squandered upon the wretched creatures who from time to time passed as his wives.

Lord Dorchester, however, did not leave his daughter alone, and when a more complaisant suitor with a handsomer income offered himself, briefly commanded her to marry him. To disobey such an order was then the height of undutiful conduct; yet so great was the disgust which Lady Mary entertained for the gentleman proposed that she ventured to write to her father, offering not to marry at all rather than to unite with him. The furious parent sent for his daughter, and told her that she must marry him at once, or consent to pass the rest of her days, while he lived, in retirement in a remote part of the country. Her relations all encouraged the match, and seemed to think her mad for wishing to love her future husband, assuring her she would be just as happy after marriage whether she loved him or not. What was a vow, taken at the altar before God in the most solemn manner, compared with a settlement on an unborn baby, a jointure for herself, and plenty of pin-money? What, indeed, in that day, and, we fear, with too many parents even in our own quasi-religious times? She replied to her father that she detested the man proposed, but was in his power, and must leave him to dispose of her. Lord Dorchester took this as a consent, made the settlements, and even ordered the trousseau.

Lady Mary was in despair, and Mr. Wortley, now that his prize was likely to be snatched from him, closed his hands on it eagerly. He proposed that they should be privately married; Lady Mary was delighted, and at once consented, though not without fears at such a step. "I tremble for what we are doing," she writes. "Are you sure you shall love me forever? Shall we never repent? I fear and I hope." Yet delay would be fatal, and so she quietly walked out of the house one day, and was married to him by special license in August, 1712. Of course the father was furious, and of course, I hear some worldly people say, the marriage turned out ill. This is not exactly the case, as we shall see. It was as happy, perhaps, as the majority of matches—for many years it was enviably so—and the fact that it ended in a very amicable separation late in life only proves that this couple had more sense than some, who, though continuing to live together, do so only to quarrel and make the separation of heart and feeling far greater than one of mere abode.

After their marriage, Mr. and Lady Mary Wortley resided in different parts of the country, but not much in London. Sometimes they were at Hinchinbroke, the seat of Mr. Wortley's grandfather, Lord Sandwich, sometimes in Huntingdon, for which Mr. Wortley was the member at that period, sometimes in Yorkshire, occasionally at Wharncliffe, one of the houses there belonging to the Wortley family, as it now does to their descendants. The scenery round the last place is said to be very fine after a Yorkshire model; and because Lady Mary does not fall into raptures about it she is accused of a want of love of nature. We are not inclined to defend Lady Mary's tastes and character of mind in every particular, though we are disposed to think she was a much better woman than some of her contemporaries, especially Walpole, made out; but this complaint is sheer nonsense. That she had an eye for beauty, and could appreciate it, we may see from many of her foreign letters; that she did not care for that of Yorkshire is no great sin: other people have been and are indifferent to that not very comfortable county; and it may be allowed to prefer shady lanes, wooded ground, and rich pastures to the bleak hills near Sheffield. After all, her expression is merely that "Wharncliffe had something in it which she owned she did not dislike, odd as her fancy might be."

Her letters to her husband, who frequently left her a long time alone at this period, are among the best proofs that she was not that vile, worldly creature which Walpole, who invented freely when he could not find legitimate abuse for those he disliked, tries to make her out. We here see the simplicity of her character. She is evidently weary without her husband, and is thrown among dull people, yet she makes the best of it, and is content to talk of her walks on the terrace, and friendship with a robin redbreast. Later she is anxious about her boy, who is ill, and later still she makes a complaint, for the justice of which we have no direct evidence, but which is written in a touching manner. She reminds her husband that he has been absent from July to November: that he writes seldom and then coldly; that he never asks after his child; and that when she was ill he expressed no sympathy and no sorrow. As all this is written without affectation or show of misery—a luxury to some women—we may believe that there was cause for her complaint. The letter having no date, had been dated by Mr. Wortley himself. Does not this tell a tale? The passionless man was smitten in his conscience: he was willing to note the time when such complaints were made against him, he may even have been touched by them.

Her letters of this period, though far less spirited and less clever than those written from abroad, are interesting, as giving us glimpses into the then state of affairs. Thus in 1714 she describes how the king was proclaimed in York, and an effigy of the Pretender dragged about the streets and burned, and how the young ladies of the neighborhood were in constant fear of the threatened invasion. Another letter gives us a hint of how Parliament was "elected" in those days—perhaps, we may add, in these too—"I believe there is hardly a borough vacant * * * Perhaps it will be the best way to deposit a certain sum in some friend's hands, and *buy some little Cornish borough.*" In another she amuses us by the description of a love affair between a very high-church young lady of forty and a curate with a "spungy nose" and a squint. She points out the curate going about in a dirty "night-gown" (dressing-gown) to the happy spinster, who blushes and looks prim, but quotes "a passage from Herodotus, in which it is said that the Persians wore long night-gowns." Fancy consoling one's self for a lover's appearance by comparing him to a Persian!

But Lady Mary was not always engaged in such rural observations. On the accession of George I., her husband was made a Commissioner of the Treasury, and she came up from Yorkshire to stay in London. She was introduced at court, and her wit and—if we may call it so—her beauty made a great impression there. The coarse, heavy king was struck with her; the brutal, vulgar Prince of Wales polluted her with his leers, and disgusted her with his admiration. She was at the age of her prime, four-and-twenty, and married.

Her face, though not absolutely beautiful, had something most attractive in it. Pope, who had seen her as a girl and was in love with her, wrote verses to "Wortley's eyes;" and if her portraits are not the basest flatterers, her expression was precisely that to captivate and enthrall a man of mind. There was no languor, no weakness, and yet no boldness in it. It betrayed an independent spirit, where a lofty self-respect, which was not vanity, united with a contempt for the follies and vices of the world, as she knew it. There were thought, dignity, eminence in her look, and her bitter, unflinching wit did not give it the lie. The face was a pure oval, the head freely set on a neck which might have been longer. The nose was sharp and very slightly *retroussé*, the mouth small, well formed, and firm set. The celebrated eyes, if not very large, were very bright, and the fair, fresh complexion added somewhat to their brilliance. She was beautiful by youth and expression; in old age she is described as a hideous hag, and the fire of the "Wortley's eyes" had become too keen and bitter to redeem the wreck of the face. After all, if we look up the women whose beauty has gone hand-in-hand with their wit, and made tempests in many hearts, we shall find that they have rarely possessed perfect features, and that the mind has indeed been the real beauty of the body. So it should be.

The court of George I. was the worst in the history of England: it was every whit as vicious as that of Charles II., without the redeeming quality of elegance. All was gross and vulgar, from the heavy German monarch, who could pass whole evenings cutting out paper, to his minister, Sir Robert Walpole—almost the vulgarest man ever in a British ministry—and down to the wretched German underlings who had followed the Hanoverian to England. Not content with mere vice, the whole court was a kind of speculation. Those in power bought and sold the places of confidence they ought to have carefully distributed, and that unblushingly. Every one sought to make his or her fortune out of the miserable nation upon which the Hanoverian had been foisted. The king's mistresses amassed wealth by the sale of their depraved influence; the king's ministers were little better; women were given appointments which could only belong to men; ladies at their birth were made cornets or ensigns in the army, and received pay up to a marriageable age. There was not even the semblance of religion which invested the court of Louis XIV., where preachers could at least speak freely, and did speak freely; the clergy, especially the bishops, were little less corrupt than the courtiers.

The king was surrounded by Germans, who looked upon

England as a rich windfall, out of which they would make the most they could. They themselves had not wit enough to laugh at their dupes, but their English *protégés* did it for them; and Walpole treated poor old Marlborough with insolence, from which his fame as a soldier, if nothing more, should have protected him. The king spoke no English, and never tried to learn either our language or our institutions. He left all to his ministers—*tant mieux*—and amused himself in the company of Madame Schulenberg, whom he created Duchess of Kendal, and who was nearly sixty when he brought her over. It was then that England saw the representatives of her so-called "noblest" families catering for the favor of this low person, and even marrying the illegitimate offspring of the king for the sake of court grace. Lord Chesterfield, the greatest beau and wit of his day, was not ashamed to ally the blood of Stanhope, which he affirmed was the surname of our first parents, *Adam de Stanhope and Eve de Stanhope*, with that of the Countess of Schulenberg; while Lord Howe, the father of the celebrated admiral, was quite delighted to secure the daughter of the other "lady," the Countess of Kielmansegg.

The best of this was that Chesterfield was duped, and very rightly punished. The old friend of his majesty had not come to England to make money for an English earl, and the douceurs which she had received for a royal smile or a promise of a place were carefully dispatched to her Vaterland, that the noble race of Schulenberg might forever bless the sacrifice she had made of her virtue. Chesterfield, disgusted, got rid of his wife as soon as possible, and thanked Heaven that the fair Melosina—such was her name—presented him with no heir to sully the line of Adam de Stanhope and Eve de Stanhope with a bar sinister.

The Duchess of Kendal, though thus antique, very ugly, and very thin—in fact, a witch—possessed immense influence over the heavy mind of the King of England. Fortunately for this country she was too stupid to use this influence on her own responsibility. She contented herself with turning it in that direction from which the highest bribe was forthcoming; and so well known was this supremacy, and the mode of commanding it, that even foreign embassadors recommended their governments to treat with her; and Count Broglio, the French minister here in 1724, openly hints in his dispatches that "the Schulenberg" must be bribed. The king was easily managed. He had not much conversation, and did not like to be bothered. He passed his evenings from five till eight in the charming society of this ancient Laïs, engaged in the intellectual pastime of cutting up paper. Except when an obstinate fit came over him, he readily gave in to his "friend's" suggestions. The other follower of his majesty, the Countess of Kielmansegg, who was created Countess of Darlington, was many years younger than the favorite, and as overpoweringly stout as the other was painfully thin. She did not make a rival of the Schulenberg, being persuaded that such influence as she possessed was sufficient to make her fortune. She was, moreover, much cleverer than the other person, and much connected with the Whig ministry. She had wonderful powers of conversation for a German, and could be very agreeable when she chose. The king was indifferent to her, and only lounged in her apartments for the pleasure of smoking his pipe at ease. He was essentially the man for a German beer-garden, and would have made a good figure in the faubourgs of Vienna, but he was scarcely suited for the throne of such a country as Great Britain. But we English are a strange people; and while we dread a French invasion as the end of all things, we are quite content to invite a dirty and vicious band of vulgar Germans to come and rule over us and rifle our pockets.

The king was surrounded by Hanoverian creatures, who lorded it finely over the English nobility, who were obliged to kiss their feet. There were Baron Bothmar, who had been an agent in London for the elector during the last reign; Bernstorf, who had come over with him, and possessed considerable influence, and, in conjunction with Walpole, managed to get large sums of money into his hands; Goritz, another baron, but more respectable than the rest; Robethon, a French adventurer, to whom Lord Townshend was indebted for his place; and even a couple of Turks, Mahomet and Mustapha, who had been taken prisoners in the war in Hungary, and were now very useful in guarding the king's person and assisting him in affairs in which none but infidels (or Hanoverians) accustomed to the idea of a seraglio would have consented to take a part. To complete this virtuous and charming court, there was young Craggs, an Englishman, the son of a footman, risen into power by the lowest services rendered to the Duke of Marlborough. Young Craggs had got into the elector's favor through the influence of a *third* mistress of his majesty, who did not accompany him to England, the Countess Platen, who was pleased by the handsome face of the youthful John Thomas. It was Craggs senior who confessed that, when getting into his carriage, he had always an effort to prevent himself getting up *behind*.

To manage such a band, all of them engaged in making the most possible money out of England, a rich bully like Sir Robert Walpole was indispensable. His character is well known;

and it is a comfort to find that his colleagues in the ministry, with only two exceptions, Pulteney and Stanhope, all despised and hated, while they could not but fear him. But it is horrible to find Englishmen and English ministers joining with these rapacious foreigners in spoiling the country, selling places and receiving bribes; still more horrible to find that English ladies of high rank were ready to sell their honor to such people, as the Countess of Suffolk did to the Prince of Wales—a brute who, as Lady Mary tells us, "looked on all men and women he saw as creatures he might kick or kiss for his diversion." It certainly makes us smile at the gullibility of John Bull to find that, after denouncing the vices of the Stuarts, he invited over a yet more corrupt set to take their place, and that the main recommendation to the Hanoverian succession should have been the "religion" of that family.

To this atrocious court was Lady Mary introduced at the age of four-and-twenty, a wit and a beauty. Now surely it is something to her praise that while half the court ladies of her own station were following the example of their august master, though often without the temptations which she must have had, Lady Mary, this monster of corruption, as she appears in Walpole's letters, should never have succumbed to them. In the present day it is indeed no praise to a woman to be virtuous, because it is simply what we expect of her, and to be the reverse excludes her from the society of all classes. But when vice was the fashion, and a *liaison*, as it was charitably called, rather exalted than debased a woman, we may at least think passably of one on whom the peculiar smiles of royalty and the attentions of an heir to the throne had no effect but nausea. Lady Mary has left us an account of the court she frequented, which shows, if we take into account the tone of her day, how completely she despised its wickedness; and had she written novels à la Thackeray instead of simple letters, Lady Mary would be hailed, as "Michael Angelo" is, as the bold satirist of the follies, if not the reformer of the vices of society.

One work she did produce about this period, which, though poor compared with the satires of Pope, entitles her quite to rank near him. This was the "Town Eclogues," written in 1715, and published in the following year. They consisted of six poems, one for each day of the week, entitled respectively, "Roxana, or the Drawing-room;" "St. James's Coffee-house;" "The Tête-à-tête;" "The Bassette-table;" "The Toilette;" and "The Small-pox." These poems excited a great deal of attention, as the characters portrayed in them were traced to well-known living personages; but reading them, now that all the personal interest is passed, we can only say that they are clever, well turned, somewhat rough, and almost too plain to be finely satirical. The coarseness with which they are replete was a common fault of the day, and was almost refined by the side of Pope and Swift, while, to judge from the letters of other ladies of rank, her contemporaries, Lady Mary did not exceed the license allowed, even to women, in writing.

An anecdote, which she has related of her court days at this period, has been so often repeated that perhaps it would be wrong to omit it here. On one evening passed at court she wished to escape in order to keep some important engagement. She explained her reasons to the Schulenberg, who told them to the king, but his majesty was too much charmed with Lady Mary's wit—and well the heavy German may have been so—to allow her to depart. At last, however, she contrived to run away. At the bottom of the stairs she met Craggs, the footman's son, who asked her why she was decamping so early. She told him how the king had pressed her to stay, and without replying he lifted her in his arms and carried her up the stairs into the antechamber, there kissed her hands respectfully and left her. The page hastily threw open the door and re-announced her. She was so confused by this sudden transportation, that she told the king, who was delighted to see her come back, the whole story. She had just finished when in came Craggs. "Mais comment, Monsieur Cragg," cried the king, "est-ce que c'est l'usage de ce pays de porter les belles dames comme un sac de froment?" The secretary, confused, could say nothing for a minute or two, but at last recovering himself, muttered, "There is nothing I would not do for your majesty's satisfaction," an answer which was well received.

From this corrupt court Lady Mary escaped to one where there was less corruption, because there was less pretense of either honesty or morality. The Turk had few vices, because his easy religion allowed him many indulgences. The Protestant monarch had many, because his religion, which he cared little for, allowed him none. The Turk could go to the mosque with a free conscience; Madame Schulenberg went regularly to her Lutheran chapel in the Savoy, but we may question whether the reading of the seventh commandment was not trying to her ears.

In 1716 the embassy to the Porte became vacant, by the removal of Sir Robert Sutton to Vienna. The post was a very important one at that epoch, as it was to England that the Continent looked to settle the differences between Turkey and the Imperialists. That the mission was intrusted to Wortley may be taken as some proof that his talents had recommended him to the ministry. He resigned his situation in the Treasury, and set out in August on a journey which was then hazardous and difficult. It was daring in his wife to accompany him, and shows that she was still much attached to her husband. Few ladies ventured upon Eastern travel, and she was even supposed for a long time to have been the first Englishwoman who had done so; but this was not the case, Ladies Paget and Winchelsea having both accompanied their lords in their respective embassies. However, Lady Mary was the first woman who wrote any account of her travels in those regions, and her letters from the East attained great celebrity. At first, indeed, they were looked upon as exaggerated and replete with "travelers' tales;" but Mr. Dallaway, who traveled the same route and lived in the same palace at Pera, has vindicated them from this imputation. They were first published in 1763, without the cognizance of her relations, edited, it is supposed, by a Mr. Cleland. She had given a copy of them to Mr. Sowden, the English chaplain at Rotterdam, and it appears that two English gentlemen whom he did not know called upon him one day, and requested to see the letters. They had contrived that he should be called away; and when he came back, he found that they had decamped with the books, which, however, they returned the next day with many apologies. To that edition a preface was appended, written in 1724 by a Mrs. Astell, a strong-minded lady, who upheld the "rights of woman," and was delighted to have a person of so much wit as Lady Mary belonging to her own sex. The letters are addressed chiefly to the Countess of Mar, her sister, to Mrs. Thistletwaite, Mrs. Skerrett, Lady Rich, other ladies belonging to the court, and to Pope. She appears to have traveled from Rotterdam to the Hague, Nimueguen, Cologne, where she writes, "I own that I was wicked enough to covet St. Ursula's pearl necklaces," "and wished she herself converted into dressing-plate;" to Nürnberg, after passing Frankfort and Würtzburg. Here she makes an observation which is probably made by every English traveler, with much satisfaction, contrasting the cleanliness and order of the Free Protestant towns with the shabby finery of the rest; and tells us that in a Roman Catholic church at Nürnberg, she had actually seen an image of our Savior in "a fair full-bottomed wig very well powdered." From Nürnberg they passed on to Ratisbon, whence taking boat they proceeded down the Danube to Vienna. Here she received one of Pope's extravagant love-letters, which, rather than lose a friend, she allowed him to write to her, replying in a jocose strain, which did not show much reciprocity of feeling. In this letter Pope says: "I think I love you as well as King Herod could Herodias (though I never had so much as one dance with you)"—fancy Pope dancing!—"and would as freely give you my heart in a dish, as he did another's head." He bears a high testimony to her wit and mind. "Books have lost their effect upon me; and I was convinced since I saw you that there is something more powerful than philosophy, and since I heard you that there is one alive wiser than all the sages."

In all her letters Lady Mary shows the same powers of observation, mingled with a keen sense of the ridiculous. She sees every thing and describes all she sees; but like a good traveler she takes more notice of the people than of the country, and does not weary her reader with a description of hotels they are not likely ever to enter, and dinners they have not eaten. Many touches here and there prove how little change 150 years make in the character of a nation. Thus she describes the extravagant dressing of the Viennese ladies, their hair piled up over a roll of stuff to an enormous height, and "their whalebone petticoats of several yards' circumference, covering some acres of ground." Surely the latter part of this description might have been written just as well in the month of January, 1860. At Vienna a German count made Lady Mary a declaration, and when she replied somewhat indignantly, added with perfect *sang-froid*, "Since I am not worthy of entertaining you myself, do me the honor of letting me know whom you like best among us, and I'll engage to manage the affair entirely to your satisfaction." So much for Viennese morals, which have not altered in a century and a half any more than Viennese petticoats.

Mr. Wortley's instructions delayed him about two months at Vienna, and the travelers thence proceeded to Prague, and thence through Dresden, Leipsic, and Brunswick to Hanover, where they made a halt, to return to Vienna in January, 1717.

At last, at the end of January, the couple started on their perilous journey eastward. However, its perils proved to have been much exaggerated. The terrible Tartar soldiers who ravaged Hungary, killing every thing, down to innocent cocks and hens, that they came across, did not molest our travelers. The weather, indeed, was bitter, but sables, and the fur of Muscovite foxes, kept out the cold. Inns there were none; but it is one thing to travel as an embassador, and another to voyage as a nobody: so the envoy extraordinary and his wife were every where well received; and all went on smoothly enough for her ladyship, though probably the Turks, who talked to her, may have been uneasy, and wondered if the women of England were not all men.

Lady Mary's letters during this period are very amusing, and her naïve description of things, as she found them, are really the best ever written about the East, not even excepting Eliot Warburton's. Thus, when she goes to the bath, she not only uses her eyes, but her mind. She finds that the frequent contemplation of the nude figure destroys the interest we feel in the human face. Judging from the way we examine the beauties of animals, this is quite comprehensible; and we quite forgive Lady Mary for adding a sigh over the natural sensuality of mankind, which she believes would be twice as great, if civilization had not introduced clothing—an argument which will not readily be admitted. Near Belgrade, again, she passes the field of Carlowitz, still reeking with the blood of the Turks, defeated by Prince Eugene. She looks with horror on the mangled corpses strewn about the field, and without bursting—as is the modern fashion—into a storm of declamation, quietly deplores the evils, and laughs at the "necessity" of war. "Nothing seems to be plainer proof of the *irrationability* of mankind (whatever fine claims we pretend to reason) than the rage with which they contend for a small spot of ground, when such vast parts of fruitful earth lie quite uninhabited. It is true, custom has made it unavoidable; but can there be a greater demonstration of want of reason, than a custom being firmly established so contrary to the interest of man in general? I am a good deal inclined to believe Mr. Hobbes, that the *state of nature is a state of war;* but thence I conclude human nature not rational, if the word means common sense, as I suppose it does."

The grand-seignior, as the sultan was then called, was at that time at Adrianopol. At Sophia, on her way, she visited a Turkish bath, which she describes in full—the ladies reclining on the sofas, unencumbered with any costume, while attendants combed and dressed their hair and so forth; and how they were quite satisfied, on seeing one stiff hideous portion of her dress, so hated by men, and known only to civilization, that her husband had locked her up in iron in a fit of jealousy.

Her letters from Adrianopol are full of most interesting descriptions, written in the easiest and most unpretending style, and, inasmuch as she was a woman, and therefore admitted where men are excluded, more interesting than any Eastern travels ever written. The belief, so general in England, that she was admitted to the seraglio, has been clearly disproved by Lady Louisa Stuart, the writer of the "Anecdotes" appended to Lord Wharncliffe's edition of Lady Mary's works; but wherever she could go, Lady Mary doubtless went, with plenty of courage and yet more curiosity.

At Adrianopol and elsewhere Mr. Wortley lived in the greatest possible magnificence, the English government being quite alive to the value of *effect* upon the Turks. He traveled with three hundred horses and a retinue of one hundred and sixty persons besides his guards. These last were janissaries; and Lady Mary's letters contain many interesting notices of those now extinct functionaries. The grand-seignior and his ministers, she tells us, were quite in their power: "No huzzaing mobs, senseless pamphlets, and tavern disputes about politics," influenced the Ottoman government; but when a minister displeased the soldiery, in three hours' time his head, hands, and feet would be thrown at the palace door, while the sultan sat trembling within.

Of the Turkish ladies—their dress, their habits, and their morals—Lady Mary had many opportunities of judging, and pronounces them the most free, rather than the most enthralled, women of the world. At Adrianopol she visited the Sultana Hafiten, the widow of Mustapha II., and Fatima, the wife of the Kyhaïa, or deputy to the grand vizier. The latter she affirms to have been far more lovely than any woman she had ever seen at home or abroad. "I was so struck with admiration," she writes, "that I could not for some time speak to her, being wholly taken up in gazing. That surprising harmony of features! that charming result of the whole! that exact proportion of body! that lovely bloom of complexion, unsullied by art! that unutterable enchantment of her smile! But her eyes! large and black, with all the soft languishment of the blue! * * * After my first surprise was over, I endeavored, by nicely examining her face, to find out some imperfection, without any fruit of my search but my being convinced of the error of that vulgar notion that a face exactly proportioned, and perfectly beautiful, would not be agreeable; nature having done for her with more success what Appelles is said to have essayed by a collection of the most exact features to form a perfect face. * * * To say all in a word, our most celebrated English beauties would vanish near her."

At length, in the month of May, 1717, the embassy left Adrianopol, after a residence there of about six weeks, and proceeded to Constantinople, where it was lodged in a palace in Pera. Here, wrapped closely in her *ferigee* and *asmack*, the adventurous Englishwoman rambled about the city of minarets, seeing all its wonders, and observing narrowly the manners of its inhabitants. Its mosques, its baths, its palaces, its Babel of foreigners, all were described in an easy, lively style; and at a time when there were so few books of Eastern travel, and those mostly of a very formal character, it will be understood that these letters were read in England with avidity. Her position, as wife of the embassador of Great Britain, admitted her into the highest native society, as far as a woman could enter it at all; while her knowledge of Turkish, which she learned from one of the dragomans of the embassy, and her interest in classical antiquities, enabled her to give a literary value to her letters. On the other hand, the reader of them will be shocked by what he will perhaps consider their occasional coarseness; but it must be remembered that the manners of her day permitted even a woman to speak openly of many things now passed over in silence; and certainly her descriptions, if sometimes too graphic, give us a more thorough knowledge of the people and the scenes she painted than the more delicate productions of modern days.

In the month of October, however, Mr. Wortley received letters of recall, countersigned by his friend Addison; and her stay in Constantinople was therefore limited to about a year.

On the 6th of June, 1718, Mr. Wortley and his suite prepared to return to England, but not by the route they had formerly traveled. They now took ship through the Levant round to Tunis, and Lady Mary was delighted by the sight of all the celebrated haunts of Greek lore. After a short stay at Tunis they sailed for Genoa, passed through Piedmont, stopping at Turin, crossed Mont Cenis into France, and, after short halts at Lyons and Paris, reached England in October, 1718.

Lady Mary brought back with her a great reputation as a traveler, and the valuable knowledge of inoculation, which she was determined to introduce into England. She had observed the practice in the villages of Turkey, where it was generally performed by an old woman with a good-sized needle. She had a very natural horror of the small-pox, which had carried off her only brother, to whom she was tenderly attached, and had visited herself in a very severe manner. Of the effects of this attack she wrote a description in one of her "Town Eclogues," in which Flavia laments the destruction of her beauty. Fortunately, however, the disease left few traces on her face; but one of its effects was to destroy her eyelashes, thus impairing the softness of the expression, and giving her eyes that fierce look which worked such a spell over Pope, who has immortalized them.

Her first trial of the cure which she had thus discovered was made, with great magnanimity, on her own son, with whom it succeeded admirably; and, with a patriotism which entitled her to the gratitude of the country, she determined, on her return, to introduce it into England. This was no quiet, no pleasant task, for, instead of a national benefactress, she was hailed as a demon. The faculty prophesied disastrous consequences; the clergy preached against "the impiety of thus seeking to take events out of the hands of Providence;" and the ignorant and foolish declaimed against her. Yet the repeated success of the operation brought it, though gradually, into favor; and Lady Mary had the courage and the patriotism to persevere. A commission of four physicians was deputed by government to watch the effect of it upon her own daughter; and, when this was found satisfactory, poor Lady Mary had to endure the fresh persecution of too much popularity, and her house was turned into a species of consulting-place for every one who could claim the slightest acquaintance with her, until, in the course of four or five years, the safety and advantages of the operation were firmly established. Certainly, this zeal of Lady Mary's shows a better heart than the partisans of Pope and Walpole will allow her; and whatever her character may have been, she deserves a high place as the introducer of an operation which, until the discovery of vaccination, was the rescue of many thousands of lives, and which, but for her courage, might have remained untried to this day.

On her return Lady Mary became a great favorite at court, especially with the Princess of Wales, afterward Queen Caroline; but she had not been long in England when, at the persuasion of Pope, she retired to a house at Twickenham, where he was then decorating his well-known villa, making, among other things, a subterranean grotto, decorated with looking-glasses—surely the last piece of furniture the hideous little man should have coveted. Lady Mary gives a curious reason for her retirement from London. Mr. Hervey, afterward Lord Hervey, celebrated for his effeminate character and some mediocre poetry, was then recently married to the beautiful Mary Lepell, whose life, under the title of Lady Hervey, is given in these volumes. "They visited me," writes Lady Mary, "twice or thrice a day, and were perpetually cooing in my rooms. I was complaisant a great while, but (as you know) my talent has never lain much that way: I grew at last so weary of those birds of Paradise I fled to Twick'nam, as much to avoid their persecutions as for my own health, which is still in a declining way." Yet it was in after years these very people, her partiality for whom brought about her quarrel with the author of the "Dunciad."

Mr. Wortley bought the house that Pope had recommended to them, and Lady Mary was chiefly occupied in the alterations they were making in it, the education of her little daughter, and the society of Pope, Gay, and Swift, who were all at Twickenham.

It was here that Pope induced her to sit, or rather stand, to Sir Godfrey Kneller for her portrait in her Turkish costume, which she describes in one of her letters. This dress was truly magnificent, and became her figure *à merveille.* The trowsers were of thin rose-colored damask, brocaded with silver flowers; the slippers of white kid, embroidered with gold. "Over this hangs my smock of a fine white gauze, edged with embroidery. This smock has wide sleeves, hanging half way down the arm, and is closed at the neck with a diamond button; but the shape and color of the bosom are very well to be distinguished through it. The *antery* is a waistcoat made close to the shape, of white and gold damask, with very long sleeves falling back, and fringed with deep gold fringe, and should have diamond or pearl buttons." Then came a *caftan*, of the same stuff as the trowsers, and reaching to the feet. It was confined by a broad girdle, studded with precious stones; and in this was stuck the dagger with a splendid jeweled hilt. The *talpac*, or head-dress, of fine velvet, was, again, covered with pearls or diamonds, and beneath it the hair, drawn up from the face, hung down behind at full length, braided with copious ribbons. The attitude of queenly dignity which Lady Mary assumed in this costume is very graceful; and her fine figure is set off by it far more than it could have been by the stiff fashions of her day.

Little Pope was in raptures as Sir Godfrey drew the portrait in crayon, to finish it off at his leisure; and we may imagine him hovering about the artist, gazing first at the original and then at the likeness, and already jotting down the following verses, which he gave to his idol, on this occasion:

"The playful smiles around the dimpled mouth,
The happy air of majesty and truth,
So would I draw (but oh! 'tis vain to try,
My narrow genius does the power deny),
The equal lustre of the heavenly mind,
Where every grace with every virtue's joined,
Learning not vain and wisdom not severe,
With greatness easy, and with wit sincere,
With just description show the soul divine,
And the whole princess in my work should shine."

Very different these lines to the brutal satires he afterward vented on this "princess."

To all gifted with a fine vein of satire, let Lady Mary's quarrels be a warning. She not only lost friends by her uncontrollable wit, but by the bitterness with which she attacked her foes has left posterity in doubt which party was to blame. It was the custom of her day to write ballads on every occurrence in society; and Lady Mary was by no means singular in this indulgence. These productions were hawked and sung about the streets, but seldom traced to their authors, though Lord Hervey and Lady Mary, known to be both poets and satirists, had much of the odium attached to them. It was one of these squibs which gave rise to the first of her many quarrels. A certain Mrs. Murray, for a long time one of her most intimate friends, had had a most disagreeable adventure, which, for a time, was the talk of the town. One of her father's footmen, named Arthur Grey, had, in a drunken fit, one night entered her room, presented a pistol at her head, and declared his solemn intention to gratify the passion he felt for her. Her cries roused the household, the man was seized, tried at the Old Bailey (where Mrs. Murray was compelled to appear as a witness), and condemned, on the charge of attempted burglary, to transportation. Two ballads, if not more, appeared on the occasion. As Mrs. Murray was very pretty, and of winning manners, it was possible to take a romantic view of the incident, and this Lady Mary did in a poem entitled "An Epistle from Arthur Grey, the footman, to Mrs. Murray;" describing the passion which he had hopelessly entertained for his mistress, and the despair in which he had had recourse to violence. There was nothing in these verses to offend Mrs. Murray, except the mere fact of their giving additional popularity to an event which ought to have been forgotten. To say the least, it was bad taste on Lady Mary's part to write them. But side by side with these appeared a ballad, which was in every way infamous. Mrs. Murray, believing Lady Mary to be the author of both poems, withdrew from her society. The ballad-writer was foolish enough to ask for an explanation, and stoutly denied the authorship of the second piece. Mrs. Murray was not satisfied with this denial, and at a masquerade singled out Lady Mary, attacked her grossly, and hinted at impropriety in her conduct. According to her own account, Lady Mary did not retort, but met this attack with gentleness. However this may have been, the acquaintance could not continue, and Lady Mary had the public odium of scurrility.

Lord Hervey was by no means the best friend Lady Mary could have. His effeminacy and fastidiousness were so well known that she herself said of him that "this world consisted of men, women, and Herveys;" and it is related that, when once asked to take beef at dinner, he replied, "Beef! oh no—faugh. Don't you know that I never eat beef, or *horse*, or any of those things?"

In addition to this Lord Hervey professed to be a skeptic,

and he was certainly a man of bad moral character even for that age. On the other hand he had a fascinating manner, plenty of natural wit, the advantages of a polished education, and—what, perhaps, had more influence with Lady Mary than all the rest—some acquaintance with the Continent. He was already known as a poet; and his "Four Epistles after the manner of Ovid" were much admired. Gay, and a pleasure-seeker, he appears still to have been capable of serious thought, at least sufficient to compose a deistical pamphlet. At Richmond he had met his wife, among the rather brilliant than respectable ladies who thronged about the Princess of Wales, such as Mrs. Howard, Mrs. Selwyn, Miss Bellenden, and Miss Howe. With these ladies Pope,

"The ladies' plaything and the muses' pride,"

as Aaron Hill wrote of him, was a great favorite. The Herveys became intimate with him at Richmond, and thus with Lady Mary herself.

Probably this set of wits at Twickenham exemplified the proverb of our copy-books about familiarity and contempt. Certainly they appear to have indulged the first in far too great a degree, and certainly the second came in its wake sooner or later. Lady Mary especially laughed at both Pope and Hervey. She was at Twickenham what the princess was at Richmond, the centre of the same circle when it moved a little farther up the Thames, and she was surrounded by Gay and Swift, Chesterfield, Bathurst, and Bolingbroke, besides Pope and Hervey. Pope's temper was none of the best. Like all satirists, he could not stand being made a butt, however good-naturedly. His mean appearance made him very lonely and morbid with any woman whose affection he wished for, as well as esteem. There is no doubt that Pope was in love with Lady Mary. Though his letters are almost too extravagant to be called love-letters, of which they are sometimes the parodies, at least as coming from a man with a keen sense of the ridiculous, yet many touches in them betray that the fancy he had entertained for her, when a girl, had ripened into something like passion when she was a married woman. Lady Mary allowed him to write these declarations to her, perhaps thinking that neither he could be vain enough nor the world so silly, as to believe she would return them; but what man is not vain when he finds the slightest possible encouragement? It is said that, at last, he made her a declaration in person, which she, unable to control herself, received with a burst of laughter, rude enough though well deserved. Pope never forgave it, and ceased to visit her. This is one story told to account for their subsequent quarrel.

On the other hand it is related that Pope was jealous of Lord Hervey, with whom Lady Mary became very intimate, and who, though so effeminate, was very handsome in face; and as for effeminacy, there is scarcely a man of any note of that day who may not be charged with it more or less; unless, like Beau Nash and Sir Robert Walpole, he were a mannerless bully. That Pope, with his morbid character, was jealous of John Lord Hervey, is possible enough; nevertheless, it is only fair to give his own version of the story, which is that he cut his old acquaintance "because they had too much wit for him." The subterfuge is too evident. Did Pope, would Pope, ever admit that any one had too much wit for *him?* or, admitting it, would not his vanity have prompted him to accept the fight? On another occasion that great poet—for such even his enemies confess him—ascribed the quarrel to a wish on the part of Lord Hervey and Lady Mary to get him to write a satire on certain persons, of whom he did not think ill enough to accept their propositions. Very good, Mr. Alexander Pope! but was this excuse of thine any thing more than an excuse? Strong, terrible as thou wert, we know thee a liar, all the world knows it, and Johnson confesses that before Lady Mary Wortley thou retreatedst with ignominy. There are, however, few tasks less thankful than raking up the embers of a dead poet's life. There are always plenty of people to defend the poet on the strength of his poetry; and perhaps it is best so. In seeking for the cause of this quarrel, we only seek to exonerate a woman, who really, as women go, was a great deal too good for the bitter, peevish, unannealed author of the "Dunciad." Look through the case as we will, we can find little or no blame attaching to Lady Mary; and, knowing the morbidness of Pope's character, we are not at all disinclined to attribute all the blame to him. At any rate, Lady Mary asserts that their quarrel was "without any reason that she knew of;" but there was clearly no love lost between them, at least on her part; since, on the publication of "Gulliver's Travels," she writes, "Here is a book come out that all our people of taste run mad about; 'tis no less than the united work of a dignified clergyman (Swift), an eminent physician (Dr. Arbuthnot), and the first poet of the age (Pope), and very wonderful it is, God knows; great eloquence have they employed *to prove themselves beasts*, and show such a veneration for horses, etc." This was written in 1726, and, we think, is sufficient and very satisfactory proof that at that time Lady Mary and Pope were at variance.

These quarrels of authors, however, can yield us little profit. These two never made it up. They "flayed" one another in the most disgraceful manner. Pope began it in his "Miscellanies" (1727), where he attacked Hervey; but it was not till 1732 that he published his great satire, "An Imitation of the Second Satire of the First Book of Horace," and certainly as good as, if not superior to, the original. In this Lord Hervey was well ridiculed as "Lord Fanny," and Lady Mary was bantered under the title of "Sappho."

The "Imitation of Horace" will probably live, but who cared for it in those days? Great as Pope was, it was personality that then won the day; and there was more personality in the answer to these verses than in the verses themselves. In short, the "Verses to the Imitator of Horace" made more sensation, inasmuch as they revealed the secret of a quarrel between the Wortleys and Herveys on the one side, and the most avaricious man of his day on the other. Now, as to the authorship of these verses there is much doubt. One says 'twas Lord Hervey, another, 'twas Lady Mary, wrote them. Wilson Croker, the serpent of critics, and ring-nose of dilettants—a man, therefore, to "go upon"—has pronounced that they are more Hervey's than Wortley's, and more Wortley's than Hervey's—no paradox, meaning withal, that Hervey wrote them and Wortley made them her own. Certainly they are too good for the lord and too bad for the lady; whether fathered by the one or mothered by the other, they are a disgrace to both parents and god-parents. Pope was not only not spared in them, but those physical defects which he could not help, and about which he was morbidly sensitive, were attacked in a ruthless and cruel manner. Thus they begin:

"In two large columns on thy motley page,
Where Roman wit is striped with English rage;
Where ribaldry to satire makes pretense,
And modern scandal rolls with ancient sense.

* * * * *

Thine is just such an image of *his* pen,
As thou thyself art of the sons of men,
Where our own species in burlesque we trace,
A sign-post likeness of the human race,
That is at once resemblance and disgrace.

* * * * *

Hard as thy heart, and as thy birth obscure."

This last line was disgraceful, and Hervey or Wortley, whichever wrote it, ought to have blushed to taunt the poet with his origin; yet, probably, he heeded no such sneer. Then come allusions to his appearance—

"But how should'st thou by beauty's face be moved,
No more for loving made than to be loved?

It was the equity of righteous Heav'n,
That such a soul to such a form was giv'n."

A sneering threat, equally ungenerous, follows:

"But oh! the sequel of the sentence dread,
And whilst you bruise their heel, *beware your head.*
* * * * *
And if thou draw'st thy pen to aid the law,
Others a cudgel, or a rod, may draw.
* * * * *
If limbs unbroken, skin without a stain,
Unwhipt, unblanketed, unkick'd, unslain,
That wretched little carcass you retain;
The reason is, not that the world wants eyes,
But thou'rt so mean, they see, and they despise."

Yet there was some truth in the last lines, for Pope *was* hated.

"But as thou hat'st be hated of mankind,
And with the emblem of thy crooked mind
Mark'd on thy back, like Cain by God's own hand,
Wander, like him, accursed through the land."

To these odious verses Pope replied in prose and again in verse, yet more cruel than Hervey's or Wortley's. Lord Hervey was a valetudinarian, and almost supported his existence by means of asses' milk, and Pope accordingly calls him

"—— that mere white curd of ass's milk."

So the quarrel went on. Doubtless Pope's genius and bitterness won the day, but what a poor triumph it was! The man who ridiculed mankind had not strength of mind himself to despise the effusions of poetasters like Hervey and Lady Mary, and retorted in even a vulgarer tone than theirs. But perhaps the worst part of the business was, that Pope, with mean cowardice, tried to get out of the scrape by lies. Even Johnson, his admirer and biographer, admits that in his retreat before Lady Mary Wortley he was mean. He soon after attached himself to the opposite party in politics, of which he now became an ardent upholder, and could therefore never forgive Hervey for being his opponent. He attacked him under the name of *Sporus*, and that ably; but while we admire Pope's wit, we can not but regret that a man of such noble genius should have been guilty of such petty spite.

Of Lady Mary's position during this period little need be said, because any reader of any memoirs of those days must have met her name frequently as a leader of society. Besides her house at Twickenham, she had one in Cavendish Square, where she received on Sundays the whole court society of London, keeping those whom she liked to supper. Among her intimates were Sarah, Duchess of Marlborough, and Henry Fielding. She naturally thought more of the former than of the latter, though she was too little a truckler to the spirit of the time to care much for rank. There was rather a certain exclusiveness of caste, a pride of superior understanding and acknowledgment of things, which made the line so marked between the "upper" and "lower." Every body, more or less, could say with Lady ——, when looking at her lady's maid—"Regardez cet animal, considérez ce néant, violà une belle ame pour être immortelle." If this was the pride of the day—and its stupid blindness, for so it is—we wonder there was not an English revolution in 1789 or even before; but we may still wonder: there are people who think like this to-day, and there is no revolution.

For twenty years Lady Mary Wortley Montagu held court in Cavendish Square or at Twickenham. Her keen sense of right and wrong disgusted her for English manners of that day, and no wonder. Her plain speech, which certainly spared neither affectation nor pretense, made her many enemies among people who were, in addition to their vices, both affected and pretentious. She longed to be away from this world of folly, and sought for peace. She believed she should find it on the Continent, and tried to persuade her husband to live abroad.

Whether Mr. Wortley really intended to follow his wife or not, can not be ascertained; though, from an expression in a letter he wrote to her shortly after her departure, it would seem not; for he there says: "I wish you would be exact and clear in your facts, because I shall lay by carefully what you write of your travels." It is, however, probable that neither of them at this time contemplated more than a temporary separation, which Lady Mary's ill health and Mr. Wortley's advanced years tended to make permanent. But there seems not the slightest cause for ascribing their separation to incompatibility of temper, or any other estrangement. She wrote to him from her first stage in England and again from Dover, and from that time they continued to correspond very frequently, and quite as affectionately as two sensible people, of whom the one was more than sixty and the other just fifty, could be expected to do.

Lady Mary left England, then, on July 26, 1739; reached Calais; traversed France, which she found vastly improved in twenty years; and passing through Piedmont and Lombardy, reached Venice in September. She had wished for her comfort to travel incognito, but found this impossible. Wherever she went, she was received as a great celebrity, and writes: "I verily believe, if one of the pyramids of Egypt had traveled it could not have been more followed." At Venice she pitched her tent, living in a palazzo on the Grand Canal, and mingling with the highest society of the place, until the following August, when she made a tour through Italy. At Florence she met Horace Walpole, then a young man of three-and-twenty, traveling through Europe. His description of her, though as exaggerated as all his remarks about her, is too amusing to be omitted. "Did I tell you Lady Mary Wortley is here? She laughs at my Lady Walpole, scolds my Lady Pomfret, and is laughed at by the whole town. Her dress, her avarice, and her impudence must amaze any one that never heard her name. She wears a foul mob that does not cover her greasy black locks, that hang loose, never combed or curled; an old mazarine blue wrapper that gapes open and discovers a canvas petticoat. Her face swelled violently on one side, * * * partly covered with a plaster and partly with white paint, which for cheapness she has bought so coarse that you would not use it to wash a chimney."

When we add that we have left out one part of this description, as too indelicate to reprint, the coarseness of this account will be admitted. The words left out contain an imputation which could not in any probability have been true, which inclines us to doubt the veracity of the whole. Of her dress we have spoken before. Of her "impudence," we can only say that Lady Mary was always very plain-spoken, and her candor in condemning affectation to its face may have offended Walpole, who was not always quite free from it. The accusation of avarice, which Walpole repeats in other letters, seems to have been generally credited at the time, though we have no proofs of it. Mr. Wortley was probably very careful of his money, as he left at his death a very large fortune; and Pope, after his quarrel with Lady Mary, speaks of him as "old Avidien," in reference to his parsimony. It is probable that his wife's eccentric habits and indifference to dress may have brought the character given to her husband upon her. At Lady Walpole she might well laugh; but as for scolding Lady Pomfret, who was her intimate friend and correspondent, she can only have done so in a most friendly manner, to judge from her own letters.

But we may offer, as a contrast to this description, one given by a clergyman who met the original shortly afterward, namely, the Rev. Mr. Spence, the author of "Spence's Anecdotes."

"Lady Mary is one of the most shining characters in the world, but shines like a comet; she is all irregularity, and always wandering; the most wise, the most imprudent; loveliest, most disagreeable; best-natured, cruelest woman in the world, 'all things by turns, but nothing long.'"

Whatever Walpole thought of this celebrated woman, he was "particularly civil to her," as Lady Mary herself confesses, which he had no other reason to be than that he found her agreeable. The truth is, that Horace, in his letters, would say almost any thing of those of whom he could do so without danger, for the sake of appearing witty, and Lady Mary is not the only person who has been wrongfully held up by him to the world in a most atrocious light.

After wandering from Florence to Rome, Naples, and Genoa, Lady Mary settled at last, in 1742, at Avignon. This place she left in 1746 on account, she tells us, of the number of "Scotch and Irish rebels" (meaning the supporters of Prince Charles Edward in 1745) who were crowding there, and who, as Lady Mary was a stanch Hanoverian, made the place very unpleasant to her. A perilous journey through the north of Italy, where the Spanish army met the travelers on their route, brought her to Brescia in Lombardy; and for the next twelve years she lived chiefly at the little watering-place of Louvere, on the Lake of Isco, in Austrian Lombardy, and at the foot of the Tyrolese mountains. In this charming, and at that time retired spot, the waters of which seem to have done her good, she lived away from the world, with which she kept up no more connection than that of letters, addressed chiefly to her husband and daughter, who also sent her out parcels of the new English books. She seems to have passed her life chiefly in reading and writing. She commenced a history of her times, but foolishly burned all but a fragment sufficient to make us regret the loss of the rest, as it gives a most amusing and authentic account of the court of George I. But even in this calm retirement she was not without her cares. The reckless, disgraceful conduct of her son, who appears to have been guilty of every enormity he could conveniently commit, caused her great anxiety. While at Avignon, his mother had seen him, and endeavored to make a good impression on him, but in vain, as he insisted on returning to Paris, where his conduct had been so bad that he was even imprisoned with a Mr. Taaffe, a disreputable Irish member of Parliament, and devoted friend of Madame de Pompadour, for robbing and cheating a Jew at cards, which, to say the least, showed an amount of sharpness that he was not generally celebrated for. In fact, his mind was very weak, and it is evident, from Lady Mary's letters, that she was afraid he would become insane. He was frivolous and almost childish in his extravagance. In 1751, Walpole, writing from London, says of him: "Our greatest miracle is Lady M. Wortley's son, whose adventures have made so much noise; his parts are not proportionate, but his expense is incredible. His father scarcely allows him any thing" (this is not true, as may be seen from a letter of Lady Mary's, vol. ii., p. 325, of Wharncliffe's edition), "yet he plays, dresses, diamonds himself, even to distinct shoe-buckles for a frock, and has more snuff-boxes than would suffice a Chinese idol with a hundred noses. But the most curious part of his dress, which he has brought from Paris, is an iron wig; you literally would not know it from hair. I believe it is on this account that the Royal Society have just chosen him of their body." Lady Mary's letters on the subject of her son show an amount of feeling which the "cruelest woman" of her day had often been denied to possess.

At Louvere Lady Mary entered more into Italian society than she had ever done before, and this was the more possible, as it was not sufficiently gay to interfere with her retirement. Her letters are full of descriptions of Italian life at that period; and most interesting are her accounts, most amusing her adventures. We regret that we have not space to give extracts from her letters written at this period, but we must notice one adventure, which has been most libelously interpreted by Walpole. For some time she was kept a prisoner by an Italian count in his own house, where she had gone to make a visit. Probably he expected to obtain a ransom from her relations; but as she does not mention the subject in any of her letters or papers, it is difficult to arrive at the real state of the case. To show how shamefully Walpole could malign those whom he did not like, we must mention that he accounted for this detention by an improper *liaison* between the count and Lady Mary. Unfortunately for his character for veracity, the lady was at that time sixty-one years of age; and it may well be asked, if such a connection was at all within the bounds of probability.

In 1758 Lady Mary finally settled at Venice. In 1761 Mr. Wortley died, leaving, says Walpole, a fortune of half a million, of which a thousand a year was left to his son for life and twelve hundred a year to his widow. The main part of the property descended to the daughter, Lady Bute, the wife of the then minister. The conduct of Mr. Wortley and his wife to their son has been aspersed; but, considering his disgraceful behavior, it appears that they acted very well in leaving the bulk of the fortune to his sister.

Lady Mary now returned to England, and took an apartment in George Street, Hanover Square. This was in a house, the rooms of which were shaped like a harpsichord. She writes: "I am most handsomely lodged. I have two very decent closets and a cupboard on each floor." She was re-

F

ceived enthusiastically and with much curiosity, for her fame was established. Walpole gives the following account of her. "I went last night to visit her. * * * I found her in a little miserable bed-chamber of a ready-furnished house, with two tallow candles and a bureau furnished with pots and pans. On her head, in full of all accounts, she had an old black-laced hood, wrapped entirely round, so as to conceal all hair or want of hair. No handkerchief, but up to her chin a kind of horseman's riding-coat, calling itself a *pet-en-l'air*, made of a dark green (green I think it had been) brocade, with colored and silver flowers and lined with furs, bodice laced; a foul dimity petticoat sprigged, velvet muffeteens on her arms, gray stockings and slippers. 'Her face less changed in twenty years than I could have imagined. I told her so, and she was not so tolerable twenty years ago that she needed have taken it for flattery, but she did, and literally gave me a box on the ears.' She was very lively, all her senses perfect, her languages as imperfect as ever, her avarice greater. She entertained me at first with nothing but the dearness of provisions at Helvoet, with nothing but an Italian, a French, and a Prussian, all men-servants, and something she calls an *old* secretary, but whose age, till he appears, will be doubtful. She receives all the world, who go to homage her as queen-mother" (Lord Bute was at that time prime minister), "and crams them into this kennel. * * * She says she has left all her clothes at Venice."

But Lady Mary was suffering from that most terrible disease, cancer in the breast. For a short time she contrived to receive her many friends, and many of the curious, who were not her friends, but anxious to get a view of the famous wit and Oriental traveler. The disease had been rendered dangerous by her journey, and, after some ten months' residence in England, she died at the age of seventy-two, on the 21st of August, 1762.

She is said to have left *one guinea* to her worthless son. She also left her letters behind her. Walpole says: "I doubt not they are an olio of lies and scandal." They have turned out not to be the former; and as to scandal, they contain, perhaps, less than any letters of that day, which was, in every sense, a scandalous one.

Lady Mary filled a useful place in this life. In spite of her enemies, no improper conduct has ever been brought home to her. She hated and despised the vices of her age, and her plain speaking may have done some good in making them ridiculous. She was eminently a satirist, and perhaps the greatest female satirist that has ever been. She attacked things evil fearlessly. Some people are cursed by too great readiness for hate. These are evil, and their natures demoniacal. Others, with less passion and more sense of justice, are cursed —for in this world it is a curse—with too quick a perception of evil. They detect the fiend at once, and can see only with bleared gaze the angel struggling with him. They attack the evil, but can not join in the purer triumph of the good. Pure enough themselves, they yet want sympathy with the pure. Their interest is not in the enjoyment of good, but the assault of evil. Warlike spirits, they almost despise the Christian humility of the patient and the hopeful. They would see the world perfect, yet when perfect they would not enjoy it, because there would be no more imperfection to assail. They rarely love, never praise. Such spirits are useful, are almost necessary in an evil world, where it is important to rouse the indignation of the passively good. But they are not lovable, and they often degenerate into mere cynics. The isolation in which their contempt of hypocrisy—the commonest vice of mankind—leaves them at last, sinks into a morbid selfishness. They have few friends, and even of these they can not help seeing the faults. People like these are happy only in complete solitude or in the company of the utterly harmless; and it is often touching to see with what tenderness your bitter satirist will caress a child, seeking from its ignorance the love he has cut off from himself in the world.

There are many such characters among the great men of this world, and most great characters have a touch of dogmatism. It is in the nature of genius to assert itself strongly. In some it takes the form of vanity; in others of bitterness. But this character is rare among women, who, as a rule, would rather be loved though all the world were damned, than save one soul by making themselves disagreeable. Lady Mary was an exception to this rule of womankind. She showed at an early age how thoroughly she despised the meaner qualities of mankind. Her love of her husband was founded in conviction that he was free from all affectation and hypocrisy—his very openness in telling her of her faults endeared him to her. She always knew her own faults, though she would not always confess them. Her so-called cruelty, especially to Pope, was based on the same grounds. A vainer woman might have been flattered by the love of the greatest poet of his age. Lady Mary could not help seeing his weak points, and despised him for them. Say what we will of Pope, we must own him a coward. His very satire wanted elevation. It was that of despair, of bitterness, rather than of indignant justice. He did not write as one that would thrust down evil proudly, but as the viper which wriggles to the heel it hates, to poison it. He left his venom in many a conscience, but he was neither feared nor admired, only hated. After all, there was much to love in Pope, much to pity, much to excuse. But Lady Mary would not see it; and that the scourge of society, the man who said that those who did not fear God should at least fear *him*, should be guilty of the evil passion he entertained for her, may well have made her despise him. It is something to say for her that whatever she may have written in verse, and with his own weapons, she seldom spoke ill of him in her letters. She seems to have forgotten, if not forgiven him.

In Lady Mary herself there is much to love. Though married to a man of no very lovable character, she was a faithful wife. She was an excellent mother to her daughter, Lady Bute, and tried to be so to her worthless son. Walpole's assertion that she ill treated her sister, Lady Mar, has not been proved, and her affectionate letters to her scarcely permit us to credit the possibility of her doing so. With all her contempt for littleness, she was a warm friend, though an unsparing enemy. Her introduction of inoculation under much opposition is some proof of the general benevolence that was in her, and we can not read her letters without seeing that she could appreciate the good as well as detect the evil in mankind. There is something very attractive in her eccentricity; and her contempt of her own appearance certainly exonerates her from all charges of vanity. But perhaps there are two portraits which do her more justice than any review we can now take of her character—the one painted in a few words by Mr. Spence, as we have already quoted it, and the other in miniature prefixed to Lord Wharncliffe's edition of her letters. The latter especially, the writer confesses, has made a very favorable impression on him.

GEORGIANA, DUCHESS OF DEVONSHIRE.

Notwithstanding the purity of morals enjoined by the court of George III., the early period of his reign presents a picture of dissolute manners as well as of furious party spirit. The most fashionable of our ladies of rank were immersed in play or devoted to politics: the same spirit carried them into both. The Sabbath was disregarded, spent often in cards, or desecrated by the meetings of partisans of both factions; moral duties were neglected and decorum outraged.

The fact was that a minor court had become the centre of all the bad passions and reprehensible pursuits in vogue. Carlton House, in Pall Mall, which even the oldest of us can barely remember, with its elegant screen, open, with pillars in front, its low exterior, its many small rooms, the vulgar taste of its decorations, and, to crown the whole, the associations of a corrupting revelry with the whole place—Carlton House was, in the days of good King George, almost as great a scandal to the country as Whitehall in the time of improper King Charles II.

The influence which the example of a young prince, of manners eminently popular, produced upon the young nobility of the realm must be taken into account in the narrative of that life which was so brilliant and so misspent; so blessed at its onset, so dreary in its close—the life of Georgiana, Duchess of Devonshire. Descended in the third degree from Sarah, Duchess of Marlborough, Georgiana Spencer is said to have resembled her celebrated ancestress in the style of her beauty. She was born in 1757. Her father, John, created Earl of Spencer in 1765, was the son of the reprobate "Jack Spencer," as he was styled, the misery at once and the darling of his grandmother, Sarah, who idolized her Torrismond, as she called him, and left him a considerable portion of her property. While the loveliness of Sarah descended to Georgiana Spencer, she certainly inherited somewhat of the talent, the reckless spirits, and the imprudence of her grandfather, "Jack;" neither could a careful education eradicate these hereditary characteristics.

Her mother was the daughter of a commoner, the right honorable Stephen Poyntz, of Midgham, in Berkshire. This lady was long remembered both by friends and neighbors with veneration. She was sensible and intelligent, polite, agreeable, and of unbounded charity; but Miss Burney, who knew her, depicts her as ostentatious in her exertions, and somewhat self-righteous and vain-glorious. She was, however, fervently beloved by her daughter, who afterward made several pecuniary sacrifices to insure her mother's comfort. The earliest years of Lady Georgiana (as she became after her father was created an earl) were passed in the large house at Holywell, close to St. Albans, built by the famous Duke of Marlborough on his wife's patrimonial estate. Aged people, some fifteen years ago, especially a certain neighboring clergyman, remembered going to play at cards in this house; and the neighborly qualities of Lady Spencer, as much as her benevolence to the poor, endeared her much to the gentry around. She exercised not only the duties of charity, but the scarcely minor ones of hospitality and courtesy to her neighbors. Before the opening of railroads, such duties were more especially requisite to keep together the scattered members of country society. Good feelings were engendered, good manners promoted, and the attachment then felt for old families had a deeper foundation than servility or even custom. As Lady Georgiana grew up, she displayed a warm, impressionable nature, a passion for all that was beautiful in art, strong affections, and an early disposition to coquetry. Her character spoke out in her face, which was the most eloquent of all faces; yet it was by no means beautiful if we look upon beauty critically. There were persons who said that her face would have been ordinary but for its transcendent loveliness of expression. Unlike the fair Gunnings, she was neither regular in features nor faultless in form, yet theirs was baby beauty compared with hers. True, her hair inclined to red, her mouth was wide, but her complexion was exquisite; and the lips, ever laughing, were parted over a splendid set of teeth, an attribute rare in those days when the teeth were often decayed in youth. She had, too, a charm of manner natural to her, and a playfulness of conversation, which, springing from a cultivated mind, rendered her society most fascinating. "Her heart, too," writes Wraxall, her contemporary, "might be considered as the seat of those emotions which sweeten human life, adorn our nature, and diffuse a nameless charm over existence."

A younger sister, Henrietta Frances, afterward Lady Duncannon, and eventually Countess of Besborough, was also the object of Lady Georgiana's warm affection; and, although Lady Duncannon was very inferior to her in elegance of mind and personal attractions, she equaled her in sisterly love.

During the middle of the last century literature was again

the fashion among the higher classes. Dr. Johnson and the Thrales, Miss Burney, Hannah More, still clustered at Streatham: many of our politicians were, if not poets, poetasters. It is true, if we except the heart-touching poems of Cowper, the Muses were silent: the verses which were the delight of polished drawing-rooms were of little value, and have been swept away from our memories of the present day as waste-paper; but a taste for what is refined was thus prevalent, and thus affected the then rising generation favorably.

Lady Georgiana Spencer had, however, a very few years allotted her for improvement or for the enjoyment of her youth, for in her seventeenth year she married.

William, the fifth Duke of Devonshire, at the time when he was united to Lady Georgiana, was twenty-seven years of age. He was one of the most apathetic of men. Tall, yet not even stately, calm to a fault, he had inherited from the Cavendish family a stern probity of character, which always has a certain influence in society. *Weight* he wanted not, for a heavier man never led to the altar a wife full of generous impulses and of sensibility. He was wholly incapable of strong emotion, and could only be roused by whist or faro from a sort of moral lethargy. He was, nevertheless, crammed with a learning that caused him to be a sort of oracle at Brookes's, when disputes arose about passages from Roman poets or historians. With all these qualities, he was capable of being, in a certain sense, in love, though not always with his lovely and engaging first wife.

Miss Burney relates a characteristic trait of this nobleman: it was related to her by Miss Monckton. The duke was standing near a very fine glass lustre in a corner of a room in the house of people who were not possessed of means sufficient to consider expense as immaterial; by carelessly lolling back, he threw the lustre back, and it was broken. He was not, however, in the least disturbed by the accident, but coolly said, "I wonder how I did that!" He then removed to the opposite corner, and to show, it was supposed, that he had forgotten what he had done, leaned his head in the same manner, and down came the second lustre. He looked at it with philosophical composure, and merely said, "This is singular enough," and walked to another part of the room without either distress or apology. To this automaton was the young Lady Georgiana consigned; and the marriage was, in the estimation of society, a splendid alliance.

Her animal spirits were excessive, and enabled her to cope with the misfortune of being linked to a noble expletive. Her good-humor was unceasing, and her countenance was as open as her heart. Fitted as she was by the sweetest of dispositions for domestic life, one can hardly wonder at her plunging into the excitements of politics when at home there was no sympathy. Hence her bitterest misfortunes originated; but one can not, with all her indiscretions, suffer a comparison between her and the Duchess de Longueville, which Wraxall has instituted. The Duchess of Devonshire scarcely merits the covert censure: except in beauty and talents, there was no similitude.

Buoyant with health and happiness, the young duchess was introduced into the highest circles of London as a matter of course. Her husband represented one of the most influential families of the Whig aristocracy, and his name and fortune made him important.

Three West End *palaces*, as they might well be termed, Carlton House, Devonshire House, and Burlington House, were open to every parliamentary adherent of the famous *coalition*—the alliance between Lord North and Charles James Fox. Devonshire House, standing opposite to the Green Park, and placed upon an eminence, seemed to look down upon the Queen's House, as Buckingham Palace was then called. Piccadilly then, though no longer, as in Queen Anne's time, infested with highwaymen, was almost at the extremity of the West End.

In right of his descent on his mother's side from the Boyle family, the Duke of Devonshire was also the owner of Burlington House, situated near Devonshire House, and inhabited by his brother-in-law, the Duke of Portland.

Thus a complete Whig colony existed in that part of London, the head and front of their party being no less a person than George, Prince of Wales. He was at this time in the very height of his short-lived health and youth, and still more short-lived popularity; a man who possessed all the exterior qualities in which his father was deficient—grace as well as good-nature, the attribute of George III., a certain degree of cultivation, as well as of natural talent, a tall handsome person, with a face less German in type than those of his brothers, some generosity of character—witness his kindness to Prince Charles Stuart and his brother, whom he pensioned—an *appearance*, at all events, of an extremely good heart, and a great capacity for social enjoyments.

Dr. Burney states that he was surprised, on meeting the prince at Lord Melbourne's, to find him, amid the constant dissipation of his life, possessed of "much learning, wit, knowledge of books in general, discrimination of character, and original humor." He spoke with Dr. Charles Burney, the distinguished scholar, quoting Homer in Greek with fluency; he was a first-rate critic in music, and a capital mimic. "Had we been in the dark," said Dr. Burney, "I should have sworn that Dr. Parr and Kemble were in the room." Hence, the same judge thought "he might be said to have as much wit as Charles II., with much more learning, for his merry majesty could spell no better than the *bourgeois gentilhomme.*" Such was the partial description of the prince by a flattered and grateful contemporary, who wrote in 1805. Twenty years later Sir Walter Scott, after dining with the then Prince Regent, paid all justice to *manners;* but pronounced his mind to be of no high order, and his taste, in so far as wit was concerned, to be condemned.

The prince was, however, just the man to be the centre of a spirited Opposition. In his heart he was Conservative; but the Whigs were his partisans against a father who strongly, and perhaps not too sternly, disapproved of his mode of life and his politics.

The circle around them was as remarkable for their talents, and, in some respects, as infamous for their vices as any Lord Rochester, or Sedley, or Etherege of the time of the second Charles. In that day, a Protestant Duke of Norfolk took an active part in political affairs, and formed one of the chief supporters of the Whigs. Carlton House, Devonshire House, often received in their state rooms "Jock of Norfolk," as he was called, whose large muscular person, more like that of a grazier or a butcher, was hailed there with delight, for his grace commanded numerous boroughs. He was one of the most strenuous supporters of Fox, and had displayed in the House of Lords a sort of rude eloquence, characteristic of his mind and body. Nothing, however, but his rank, his wealth, his influences, his Whig opinions, could have rendered this profligate, revolting man, endurable. Drunkenness is said to have been inherent in his constitution, and to have been inherited from the Plantagenets. He was known in his youth to have been found sleeping in the streets, intoxicated, on a block of wood; yet he is related to have been so capable of resisting the effects of wine, that, after laying his father, a drunkard like himself, under the table at the Thatched House, St. James's, he has been stated to have repaired to another party, there to finish the convivial rites. He was often under the influence of wine when, as Lord Surrey, he sat in the House of Commons; but was wise enough, on such occasions, to hold his tongue. He was so dirty in person, that his servants used to take advantage of his fits of intoxication to wash him; when they stripped him as they would have done a corpse, and performed ablutions which were somewhat necessary, as he never

F 2

made use of water: he was equally averse to a change of linen. One day, complaining to Dudley North that he was a prey to rheumatism, "Pray," cried North, "did your grace ever try a clean shirt?"

This uncleanly form constituted a great feature of the Whig assemblies. At that time every man wore a queue, every man had his hair powdered; yet "Jock" renounced powder, which he never wore except at court, and cut his hair short. His appearance, therefore, must have been a strange contrast with that of the Prince of Wales, curled and powdered, with faultless ruffles, and an ample, snow-white cravat, to say nothing of the coat which looked as if it were sewn on his back. It is to the Duke of Norfolk that the suggestion of putting a tax on hair-powder has been ascribed. His life was one series of profligacy. Yet, such was the perverted judgment of the day, that this unworthy descendant of the Plantagenets was as popular as any peer of his time. When sober, he was accessible, conversable, and devoid of pride. When intoxicated, he used half to confess he was still a Catholic at heart. His conversion to the reformed faith was held not to be very sincere; and his perpetual blue coat of a peculiar shade—a dress he never varied—was said to be a penance imposed on him by his confessor. He did no credit to any Christian Church, and the Church of Rome is welcome to his memory.

Richard Brinsley Sheridan, at this period in his thirty-third year, was not then wholly degraded by drinking, debt, and, as far as money was concerned, dishonesty. His countenance at this age was full of intelligence, humor, and gayety: all these characteristics played around his mouth, and aided the effect of his oratory to the ear. His voice was singularly melodious, and a sort of fascination attended all he did and said. His face, as Milton says of the form of the fallen angel,

> "Had not yet lost
> All her original brightness."

Yet he lived to be known by the name of "Bardolph"—to have every fine expression lost in traces of drunkenness. No one could have perceived, in after days, the once joyous spirit of Sheridan in a face covered with eruptions, and beaming no longer with intelligence. He resembled, says Wraxall, at sixty, one of the companions of Ulysses, who, having tasted of Circe's "charmed cup,"

> "Lost his upright shape,
> And downward fell into a groveling swine."

This extraordinary man was the husband of one of the most beautiful, and, in being his wife, one of of the most unfortunate of women. Miss Linley, the daughter of a celebrated musical composer, and called, for her loveliness, the "Maid of Bath," had the calamity of being wooed and won by Sheridan. Never was there a more touching and instructive history than hers. Her beauty was rare, even amid the belles of a period rich in attractive women. Dark masses of hair, drawn back on her brow, fell in curls on a neck of alabaster. Her features were delicate and regular; the expression of her eyes was exquisitely soft and pensive. Her charms have been transmitted to her female descendants, Mrs. Norton, the Duchess of Somerset, and Lady Dufferin, while they have also inherited her musical talents, and the wit and ability of their grandfather. Mrs. Sheridan, after a life of alternate splendor and privation, died at Clifton, of consumption, before middle age. Her death was saddened, if not hastened, by her carriage, as she was preparing to drive out on the Downs, being seized for her husband's debts. While united to this young and lovely wife, Sheridan was one of the brightest stars in the dissolute sphere of Carlton House; but for domestic life he had neither time nor disposition. His fame was at its climax, when, during the trial of Warren Hastings, he spoke for hours in Westminster Hall, with an eloquence never to be forgotten; then, going to the House of Commons, exhibited there powers of unrivaled oratory. Meantime the theatres were ringing with applause, and his name went from mouth to mouth while the "Duenna" was acted at one house, the "School for Scandal" at another. He was, in truth, the most highly gifted man of his time; and he died in the fear of bailiffs taking his bed from under him—an awe-struck, forlorn, despised drunkard!

But of all the party men to whom the young Duchess of Devonshire was introduced, the most able and the most dissolute was Fox. The coloring of political friends, which concealed his vices, or rather which gave them a false hue, has long since faded away. We now know Fox as he *was*. In the latest journals of Horace Walpole, his inveterate gambling, his open profligacy, his utter want of honor, is disclosed by one of his own opinions. Corrupted ere yet he had left his home, while in age a boy, there is, however, the comfort of reflecting that he outlived his vices. Fox, with a green apron tied round his waist, pruning and nailing up his fruit-trees at St. Ann's Hill, or amusing himself innocently with a few friends, is a pleasing object to remember, even while his early career recurs forcibly to the mind.

Unhappily he formed one of the most intimate of those whom Georgiana, Duchess of Devonshire, admitted to her home. He was soon enthralled among her votaries, yet he was by no means a pleasing object to look at as he advanced in life. He had dark saturnine features, thought by some to resemble those of Charles II., from whom he was descended in the female line: when they relaxed into a smile they were, it is said, irresistible. Black shaggy eyebrows concealed the workings of his mind, but gave immense expression to his countenance. His figure was broad, and only graceful when his wonderful intellect threw even over that the power of genius and produced, when in declamation, the most impassioned gestures. Having been a coxcomb in his youth, Fox was now degenerating into a sloven. The blue frock-coat and buff waistcoat with which he appeared in the House of Commons were worn and shabby. Like the white rose which distinguished the Stuarts, so were the blue and buff the badge of the American insurgents, and of Washington, their chief.

Having ceased to be the head of the Maccaronis, as the *beau-monde* were then called, Fox had devoted himself to play. Whist, quinze, and horse-racing were his passion, and he threw away a thousand pounds as if they had been a guinea; and he lost his whole fortune at the gaming-table. Before thirty he was reduced to distress, even in the common affairs of life. He could not pay the chairmen who carried him to the House. He was known to borrow money from the waiters at Brookes's, which was the rallying-point of the Opposition. There the night was spent in whist, faro, suppers, and political consultations. Dissolute as he was, there was a kindness, a generosity of disposition that made his influence over man or woman most perilous to both. Then he was one of the most accomplished of students in history and general letters; and to his studies he could even devote himself after irretrievable losses at play. Topham Beauclerk, after having passed the whole night with Fox at faro, saw him leave the club in desperation. He had lost enormously. Fearful of the consequences, Beauclerk followed him to his lodgings. Fox was in the drawing-room, intently engaged over a Greek "Herodotus." Beauclerk expressed his surprise. "What would you have me do? I have lost my last shilling," was the reply. So great was the elasticity of his disposition, sometimes, after losing all the money he could manage to borrow at faro, he used to lay his head on the table, and, instead of railing at fortune, fall fast asleep. For some years after the Duchess of Devonshire's marriage, Fox had continued to represent Westminster. So long as he retained that position, Pitt's triumph could not be considered as complete, nor the Tory party as firmly established in the administration. Three candidates appeared on the hustings in April, 1784—Lord Hood, Sir Cecil Wray, and Fox. So late as the twenty-sixth of the month, Wray, who had sat for some time for West-

THE BEAUTIFUL DUCHESS OF DEVONSHIRE: A KISS FOR A VOTE.

minster in Parliament, maintained a small numerical advantage over Fox. The election, which began on the first of the month, had now gone on more than three weeks: ten thousand voters had polled; and it was even expected that, since the voters were exhausted, the books would be closed, and Wray, who was second on the poll, Lord Hood being first, would carry the day.

Happily we have now no adequate notion of the terrors of such an election: it was a scene of fun and malice, spirit and baseness, alternately. Englishmen seemed hardly men: while they one hour blustered, the next they took the bribe, and were civil. Fox went down to Westminster in a carriage with Colonel North, Lord North's son, behind as a footman, and the well-known Colonel Hanger—one of the reprobate associates of George IV. (when Prince Regent), and long remembered on a white horse in the Park, after being deserted by the prince and out of vogue—driving, in the coat, hat, and wig of a coachman. When Queen Charlotte heard of this exploit of Colonel North's she dismissed him from his office of comptroller of her household, saying she did not covet another man's servant.

As the month drew to a close, every hour became precious, and Fox gained at this critical juncture two new and potent allies. Dressed in garter-blue and buff, in compliment to Fox and his principles, forth came the young Duchess of Devonshire and her sister, now Lady Duncannon, and solicited votes for their candidate. The mob were gratified by the aspect of so much rank, so great beauty, cringing for their support. Never, it was said, had two "such lovely *portraits* appeared before on a *canvass*."

It required, indeed, no ordinary courage to undertake collecting votes, for a strong disposition to rioting now manifested itself. Nevertheless, being provided with lists of the outlying voters, these two young women drove to their dwellings. In their enterprise they had to face butchers, tailors, every craft, low or high, and to pass through the lowest, the dirtiest, and the most degraded parts of London. But Fox was a hundred votes below Wray, and his fair friends were indefatigable: they forgot their dignity, their womanhood, and "party" was their watchword. They were opposed by the Marchioness of Salisbury, whom the Tories brought forward. She was beautiful, but haughty; and her age, for she was thirty-four, whereas the Duchess of Devonshire was only twenty-six, deteriorated from the effect of her appearance.

Forgetting her rank, which Lady Salisbury always remembered, and throwing all her powers of fascination into the scale, the young duchess alighted during one of her canvassing days at a butcher's shop. The owner, in his apron and sleeves, stoutly refused his vote, except on one condition—"Would her grace give him a kiss?" The request was granted. This was one of the votes which swelled the number of two hundred and thirty-five above Sir Cecil Wray, and Fox stood second on the poll. Of course much stupid poetry was written on the occasion.

"Condemn not, prudes, fair Devon's plan,
In giving *Steel* a kiss;
In such a cause, for such a man,
She could not do amiss."

Even the Prince of Wales took an active interest in this memorable election; and George III. is said to have also interfered. Never was political rancor so high, nor conscience so low, as at that period. The hustings resembled the stand at Newmarket. "An even bet that he comes in second," cried one: "five to four on this day's poll," screamed another. Amid all these shouts, gazed at by the lowest of all human beings, the low, not only in rank but in feeling, the drunken, paid-for voters, stood the duchess and a band of fair titled friends supporting Fox, who was called the "Man of the People."

It was on the 17th of May when Fox, over whose head a scrutiny hung on the part of Sir Cecil Wray, and who was not thought even then returned as member, was chaired. This procession took place as the poll closed. Fox was carried through the streets on a chair decorated with laurel, the ladies in blue and buff forming part of the *cortège*. Before him was displayed the prince's plume: those three ostrich feathers, the sight of which might bring back to our minds the field of Cressy, where they were won, and henceforth worn for four successive centuries. A flag, on which was inscribed, "Sacred to Female Patriotism," was waved by a horseman in the triumphant cavalcade. The carriages of the Duke of Devonshire and the Duke of Portland attracted even less attention than that of Fox, on the box of which were Colonel North and other friends, partisans of Lord North's, who now mingled with their former opponents. As the procession turned into Pall Mall, it was observed that the gates of Carlton House were open: it passed in, therefore, and saluted, in veering round, the Prince of Wales, who, with a number of ladies and gentlemen, stood in the balustrade in front. Fox then addressed the crowd, and attempted to disperse them; but at night the mob broke out into acts of fury, illuminated, and attacked those houses which were in sullen darkness.

The next day the prince invited all the rank, beauty, and fashion of the Coalition party to a fête on his lawn. It was a bright day that 18th of May; and under the delicious shade of the trees the young and gay forgot, perhaps, in the enchantments of the scene, politics and elections. Lord North, dressed in blue and buff—his new livery—strutted about amid those who only fifteen months before had execrated and denounced him, until, by the Coalition with Fox, he had made himself their idol. Every one, on this occasion, crowded round the minister, whose wit was as inexhaustible as his *sang-froid*, and whose conversation in its playfulness resembled that of our great premier of 1859. Blue and buff pervaded the garden. Colonel North (afterward Lord Guildford) and George Byng, hitherto bitter enemies, were seen, dressed alike, walking together familiarly. The prince was irresistibly fascinating, and nothing could be more splendid than the fête given by royalty overwhelmed by debt.

As the party were thus enjoying themselves, by a strange coincidence the famous cream-colored horses of George III. were beheld proceeding in solemn state down St. James's Park. His majesty was going to Westminster to open Parliament. Nothing but a low wall separated Carlton Gardens from the park, so that the king could not forbear seeing his former minister, his son, and the successful candidate disporting themselves in all the elation of success.

In the evening Lower Grosvenor Street was blocked up with carriages, out of which gentlemen and ladies all in blue and buff descended to visit the famous Mrs. Crewe, whose husband, then member for Chester, was created, in 1806, Lord Crewe. This lady was as remarkable for her accomplishments and her worth as for her beauty; nevertheless, she permitted the affection of Fox, who was in the rank of her admirers. The lines he wrote on her were not exaggerated. They began thus:

"Where the loveliest expression to features is join'd,
By Nature's most delicate pencil design'd;
Where blushes unbidden, and smiles without art,
Speak the softness and feeling that dwelt in the heart;
Where in manners enchanting, no blemish we trace,
But the soul keeps the promise we had from the face;
Sure philosophy, reason, and coldness must prove
Defenses unequal to shield us from love."

Nearly eight years after the famous election at Westminster, Mrs. Crewe was still in perfection, with a son of one-and-twenty, who looked like her brother. The form of her face was exquisitely lovely, her complexion radiant. "I know not," Miss Burney writes, "any female in her first youth who could bear the comparison. She uglifies every one near her."

This charming partisan of Fox had been active in his cause; and her originality of character, her good-humor, her recklessness of consequences, made her a capital canvasser.

The same company that had assembled in the morning at Carlton House now crowded into Grosvenor Street. Blue and buff were the order of the evening, the Prince of Wales wearing those colors. After supper he gave a toast—"True blue, and Mrs. Crewe." The room rang with applause. The hostess rose to return thanks. "True blue, and all of you," was her toast. Nor did the festivities end here. Carlton House some days afterward received all the great world, the "true blues" of London. The fête, which was of the most varied kind, and of the most magnificent description, began at noon, went on all night, and was not ended till the next day. Nothing could exceed its splendor. A costly banquet was prepared for the ladies, on whom his royal highness and the gentlemen waited while they were seated at table. Nothing could exceed the grace, the courtesy, the *tact*, of the prince on these occasions, when he forgot his two hundred thousand pounds of debts, and added to them. Louis XIV., said an eye-witness, could not have eclipsed him.

This was probably the brightest era in the life of the Duchess of Devonshire. She was the lady paramount of the aristocratic Whig circles, in which rank and literature were blended with political characters. Slander soon coupled her name with that of Fox; and that name, though never wholly blighted, was sullied. Miss Burney, meeting her at Bath, some years afterward, describes her as no longer beautiful, but with manners exquisitely polite, and "with a gentle quiet" of demeanor. Yet there was an expression of melancholy. "I thought she looked oppressed within," was Miss Burney's remark. On another occasion she found her more lively, and consequently more lovely, vivacity being so much her characteristic that her style of beauty required it. "She was quite gay, easy, and charming; indeed that last word might have been coined for her:" and Miss Burney soon perceived that it was the sweetness of her smile, her open, ingenuous countenance, that had won her the celebrity which had attended her career of fashion.

But even then there was a canker in the duchess's felicity. Lady Elizabeth Foster, the daughter of the Earl of Bristol, and a contrast to her in person—large, dark, and handsome—had attracted the duke, her husband, and the coldest of men had become deeply enamored of this woman, whom he eventually married. Gibbon said of Lady Elizabeth that she was the most alluring of women. Strange to say, a sort of friendship existed between the duchess and Lady Elizabeth, who was with her at Bath, when Miss Burney saw them together. Even then a cloud hung over these two ladies of rank; and Mrs. Ord, Miss Burney's cautious friend, reproved her for making their acquaintance.

Three children of rare promise were given to occupy the affections which were so little reciprocated by the duke. The elder of the three, Georgiana Dorothy, afterward married to the Earl of Carlisle, and the mother of the present Duchess of Sutherland, is described by Miss Burney, at eight years of age, as having a fine, sweet, and handsome countenance, and with the form and figure of a girl of twelve. She, as well as her sister, were at that time under the care of Miss Trimmer, the daughter of Mrs. Trimmer, one of the most admirable writers for children that has ever delighted our infancy. Miss Trimmer is described as a "pleasing, not pretty" young lady, with great serenity of manner.

Lady Henrietta Elizabeth, married to the Earl of Granville, so long embassador at Paris, was, at six years of age, by "no means handsome, but had an open and pleasing countenance, and a look of the most happy disposition;" a tribute borne out by the many virtues of that admirable lady in after life. The Marquis of Hartington, afterward Duke of Devonshire, then only fourteen months old (this was in 1791), had already a house, and a carriage to himself, almost in the style of royalty. He lived near his father, while the duchess was staying with her mother, Lady Spencer. To persons of domestic notions this seems a singular arrangement.

This apparently happy family party had, however, some trials to obscure their supposed felicity. Scandal not only pointed at Lady Elizabeth Foster as possessing an undue influence over the duke, but attacked the duchess in the most sacred relations of her life. The little marquis was reputed to be illegitimate; the report assumed several shapes; of course rancorous political partisans pointed to the intimacy with Fox; others to the intimacy at Carlton House. Another story also obtained credit, and never died away. This was that at the time when the duchess was confined, Lady Elizabeth gave birth to a son, the duchess to a daughter, and that the children were changed; that the late duke entered into a contract with his uncle, the late Lord George Cavendish, never to marry, in order that his lordship's children might have an undisputed succession at his grace's death.

There was another source of disquiet to Lady Spencer and the duchess at this time, in the deep depression of Lady Duncannon. This lady, the mother of Lady Caroline Lamb, so conspicuous for her eccentricity in our own time, seems to have been affectionately beloved by her brother the Lord Spencer, the grandfather of the present earl. "He made up to her," says Miss Burney, "with every mark of pitying affection, she receiving him with the most expressive pleasure, though nearly silent." This afflicted woman lived, nevertheless, to a great age, and survived her gay, spirited sister, the Duchess of Devonshire.

Lady Spencer belonged to that class whom we now call evangelical; a class earnest in feeling, originating in a sincere desire to renovate the almost dead faith of the period, to set an example of piety and decorum, and also "to let their light shine before men." Miss Burney describes her as too desirous of a reputation for charity and devotion. Nevertheless, Lady Spencer could not detach her daughter from the gay world.

The duchess continued to take an active part in politics, and to mingle with the tumult of elections, faro, and party triumphs, love, poetry, and the fine arts. Her son was born in the dawn of that Revolution in France which shook the foundations of all social life. At this very period a serious calamity befell their country in the first fit of insanity that attacked George III. Up to the very time when France was plunged into commotion, his majesty, apparently in perfect health, had held his weekly levees at St. James's until the last week of October, 1788. Early in November the first paroxysms of his disordered intellect occurred at the Queen's Lodge, after dinner, her majesty and the princesses being present. The gates of the Lodge were closed that night; no answers were given to persons making inquiries; and it was rumored that his majesty was dead.

The state of the public mind may readily be conceived: the capital exhibited a scene of confusion and excitement only exceeded by that displayed four years afterward, when the decapitation of Louis XVI. was announced in London.

A regency was proposed; and six physicians were called in to act in consultation. Dr. Warren was considered to hold the first place in this learned junto. Dr. Addington, the father of the late Lord Sidmouth, Sir Lucas Pepys, and Dr. Willis, were among the rest. Warren was disposed to Whiggism, and thought the king's recovery doubtful; Willis was a Tory, and pronounced it possible, and, indeed, probable: his dictum was believed at St. James's and at Kew Palace; Warren was credited at Carlton House and Devonshire House. If the first was the oracle of White's, the second was trusted at Brookes's. The famous Duchess of Gordon, the partisan of Pitt and Dundas, supported Willis and his views, and was the whipper-in of the Tory party. The Duchess of Devonshire was the firm and powerful supporter of the prince in his claims to the regency. The Tories were for the power not only over the royal household, but over the council, being vested in Queen Charlotte. A caricature was circulated representing the Lord Chancellor, Pitt, and Dundas, as the three "weird sisters" gazing at the full moon. Her orb was half enlightened, half eclipsed. The part in darkness contained the king's profile; on the other side was a head, resplendent in light, graciously gazing at the weird sisters; that was the queen. In the February of the ensuing year, nevertheless, to the great joy of the nation, the king showed signs of amendment. One day Mr. Greville, brother to the Earl of Warwick, was standing near the king's bed, and relating to Dr. Willis that Lord North had made inquiries after the king's health. "Has he?" said the king. "Where did he make them, at St. James's or here?" An answer being given, "Lord North," said his majesty, "is a good man, unlike the others: he is a good man." The party at Carlton House, among whom the Duchess of Devonshire must ever be ranked, were disappointed at this timely recovery, while the honest-hearted middle and lower classes of England were unfeignedly rejoiced; but there was too much party rancor existing for any better spirit to arise and show itself. Even in society, the venom of party was suffered to intrude. Lord Mountnorris being one evening at a ball given by the French embassador, canvassed the whole room for a partner, but in vain. He begged Miss Vernon to interfere, and to procure him a partner for a country dance. She complied, and presented him to a very elegant young lady, with whom his lordship danced, and conversed some time. Soon afterward a gentleman said to him, "Pray, my lord, do you know with whom you have been dancing?" "No," he replied; "pray, who is she?" "Coalitions," said the gentleman, "will never end; why, it is Miss Fox, the niece of Charles, and sister of Lord Holland." The noble lord was thunderstruck. Had Pitt seen him? If so, he was undone. He ran up to reproach Miss Vernon. "True," was the reply; "she *is* the niece of Fox, but since she has twenty thousand pounds to her fortune, I thought I had not acted improperly in introducing you."

In the famous quarrel between Burke and Fox, the Duchess of Devonshire took the office of mediator. Burke thus attacked Fox in the House of Commons.

"Mr. Fox," he said, "has treated me with harshness and malignity. After harassing with his light troops in the skirmishes of 'order,' he has brought the heavy artillery of his own great abilities to bear on me. There have," he added, "been many differences between Mr. Fox and myself, but there has been no loss of friendship between us. There is something in this cursed French constitution which envenoms every thing."

Fox whispered, "There is no loss of friendship between us." Burke replied, "There *is*. I know the price of my conduct: our friendship is at an end."

Fox was overwhelmed with grief at these words. He rose to reply, but his feelings deprived him of utterance. Relieved by a burst of tears, while a deep silence pervaded the house, he at last spoke.

"However events," he said, in deep emotion, "may have altered the mind of my honorable friend—for so I must still call him—I can not so easily consent to relinquish and dissolve that intimate connection which has for twenty-five years subsisted between us. I hope that Mr. Burke will think on past times, and whatever conduct of mine has caused the offense, he will at least believe that I did not intend to offend." But the quarrel was never reconciled, notwithstanding the good offices of the Duchess of Devonshire, the friend of both parties.

Soon after the commencement of the eighteenth century, this party spirit was, as it were, rebuked, first by the death of Pitt, and afterward by that of Fox, who was long in a declining state. When he heard that Pitt had expired, he said, "Pitt has died in January, perhaps I may go off in June. I feel my constitution dissolving." When asked by a friend, during the month of August, to make one of a party in the country, at Christmas, he declined.

"It will be a new scene," said his friend.

"I shall indeed be in a new scene by Christmas next," Mr. Fox replied. On that occasion he expressed his belief in the immortality of the soul; "but how," he added, "it acts as separated from the body, is beyond my capacity of judgment." Mr. Fox took his hand and wept. "I am happy," he added, "full of confidence; I may say of certainty."

One of his greatest desires was to be removed to St. Ann's Hill, near Chertsey, the scene of his later, his reformed, his happier life. His physicians hesitated, and recommended his being carried first to the Duke of Devonshire's house at Chiswick. Here, for a time, he seemed to recover health and spirits. Mrs. Fox, Lady Holland, his niece, and Lady Elizabeth Foster, were around his death-bed. Many times did he take leave of those dearest to him; many times did death hover over him; yet we find no record that the Duchess of Devonshire was among those who received his last sigh. His last words to Mrs. Fox and Lord Holland were, "God bless you, bless you, and you all! I die happy—I pity you!"

"Oh! my country!" were Pitt's last words; those of Fox were equally characteristic. His nature was tender and sympathetic, and, had he lived in other times, he would have been probably as good as he was great.

His remains were removed from Chiswick to his own apartments in St. James's, and conveyed under a splendid canopy to Westminster Abbey. As the gorgeous procession passed Carlton House, a band of music, consisting of thirty, played the "Dead March in Saul." The Prince of Wales had wished to follow his friend on foot to the grave, but such a tribute was forbidden by etiquette.

It is to be regretted that princes must be exempted from so many of the scenes in this sublunary life calculated to touch the heart, to chasten and elevate the spirit. As the funeral entered the Abbey, and those solemn words, "I am the Resurrection and the Life," were chanted, the deepest emotion affected those who had known and loved him whose pall they bore.

Among other tributes to the memory of Fox were the following lines from the pen of the Duchess of Devonshire. The visitor to Woburn Abbey will find them underneath the bust of the great statesman in a temple dedicated to Liberty by the late Duke of Bedford.

"Here, near the friends he lov'd, the man behold,
In truth unshaken, and in virtue bold,
Whose patriot zeal and uncorrupted mind
Dared to assert the freedom of mankind;
And, while extending desolation far,
Ambition spread the hateful flames of war:
Fearless to blame, and eloquent to save,
'Twas he—'twas Fox—the warning counsel gave;
Midst jarring conflicts stemm'd the tide of blood,
And to the menac'd world a sea-mark stood!
Oh! had his voice in mercy's cause prevailed,
What grateful millions had the statesman hail'd:
Whose wisdom made the broils of nations cease,
And taught the world humanity and peace!
But, though he fail'd, succeeding ages here
The vain, yet pious efforts shall revere;
Boast in their annals his illustrious name,
Uphold his greatness, and confirm his fame."

The duchess only survived Fox a year: she died in 1806, beloved, charitable, penitent. Her disease was an abscess of the liver, which was detected rather suddenly, and which proved fatal some months after it was first suspected. When the Prince of Wales heard of her death, he remarked: "Then the best-natured and best-bred woman in England is gone." Her remains were conveyed to the family vault of the Cavendish family in All Saints' Church, Derby; and over that sepulchre one fond heart, at all events, sorrowed. Her sister, Lady Duncannon, though far inferior to the duchess in elegance both of mind and person, had the same warm heart and strong affection for her family. During the month of July, 1811, a short time before the death of the Duke of Devonshire (the husband of the duchess), Sir Nathaniel Wraxall visited the vault of All Saints' Church. As he stood admiring the coffin in which the remains of the once lovely Georgiana lay mouldering, the woman who had accompanied him showed him the shreds of a bouquet which lay on the coffin. Like the mortal coil of that frame within, the bouquet was now reduced almost to dust. "That nosegay," said the woman, "was brought here by the Countess of Bessborough, who had intended to place it herself upon the coffin of her sister; but as she approached the steps of the vault, her agony became too great to permit her to proceed. She knelt down on the stones of the church, as nearly over the place where the coffin stood in the vault below as I could direct, and there deposited the flowers, enjoining me to perform an office to which she was unequal. I fulfilled her wishes."

By others the poor duchess was not so faithfully remembered. Her friend Lady Elizabeth Foster had long since become her rival, yet one common secret, it was believed, kept them from a rupture. Both had, it was understood, much to conceal. The story of the late Duke of Devonshire's supposed birth has been referred to: he is supposed to have been the son of the duke, but not of Georgiana, Duchess of Devonshire, but of her who *afterward* bore that title, Lady Elizabeth Foster. The inflexible determination of the late duke to remain single, according, it is said, to an agreement between him and his uncle, then Lord George Cavendish, always seemed to imply, in a man of such pure and domestic tastes, so affectionate a disposition, and so princely a fortune, some dire impediment.

In 1824 Lady Elizabeth Foster, then the second Duchess of Devonshire, expired at Rome, where she had lived many years in almost regal splendor. Among her most intimate friends were the Cardinal Consalvi and Madame Récamier, who were cognizant of the report, which was confirmed in their minds by the late duke's conduct at her death. Lady Elizabeth, as we shall still by way of distinction call her, was then so emaciated as to resemble a living spectre; but the lines of a rare and commanding beauty still remained. Her features were regular and noble, her eyes magnificent, and her attenuated figure was upright and dignified, with the step of an empress. Her complexion of marble paleness completed this portrait. Her beautiful arms and hands were still as white as ivory, though almost like a skeleton's from their thinness. She used in vain to attempt to disguise their emaciation by wearing bracelets and rings. Though surrounded by every object of art in which she delighted, by the society, both of the English, Italian, and French persons of distinction whom she preferred, there was a shade of sadness on this fascinating woman's brow, as if remembrance forbade her usual calm of life's decline.

Her stepson (so reported), the late duke, treated her with respect and even affection, but there was an evident reserve between them. At her death he carefully excluded all friends to whom she could in her last moments confide what might perhaps, at that hour, trouble her conscience. Her friends, Madame Récamier and the Duc de Laval, were only admitted to bid her farewell when she was speechless, and a few minutes before she breathed her last.

The circumstance struck them forcibly as confirmatory of the report alluded to; but, it must in candor be stated, that the duke's precautions may have originated in another source. His stepmother was disposed to Romanism, and he may have feared that the zeal of her Catholic friends should prompt them, if opportunity occurred, to speak to her on the subject of her faith, and to suggest the adoption of such consolations as their own notions would have thought indispensable at that awful moment. The point is one that can not be settled. It may, however, be remarked, that in disposition, in his wide benevolence and courteous manners, the late duke greatly resembled the subject of this memoir—the beautiful, the gifted, but the worldly Georgiana, Duchess of Devonshire.

LETITIA ELIZABETH LANDON. (L. E. L.)

It is now more than forty years ago since an eminent writer and journalist, looking from the window of his house in Old Brompton, was attracted by the appearance of a little girl who was trundling a hoop with one hand, and holding in the other a book of poems, of which she was catching a glimpse between the agitating course of her evolutions. It was literally "run and read." The gentleman was William Jerdan; the girl was Letitia Elizabeth Landon.

The scene must have been a pleasing one; the matured, successful man of letters, full of criticism and politics, Canning's last *mot*, Normanby's first novel; besieged by authors with attentions, fêted by nobles—the then prince of weekly journalists had so much still of truth in his heart, of benevolence and fatherly interest, that he paused in the intervals of his work to look at the studious yet playful child and her hoop.

She was then, in spite of adverse circumstances, a round-faced, rosy little creature, blithe as any lark, active as a butterfly, but pensive and poetic as a nightingale. Take also into your mind's picture the localities: Brompton was out of town then; haymaking went on in Brompton Crescent; monthly roses and honeysuckles flourished in Brompton Row; Michael's Grove *was* a grove, though one might count its trees; and, beyond, there were lanes that penetrated beyond Old Brompton and terminated at once in the country. Vegetation there was early and rapid, and the place had an almost village-like simplicity about it. There was no Brompton Square, no Alexander Square—neither terraces nor crescents with grander names than the mere designation, Michael's, the patron saint or building sinner, wherefore one knows not, and the humble name, Brompton. Yet stay; let me look into my inestimable friend Peter Cunningham's valuable "Handbook for London," in which we are told how Amelia Place, now Pelham Crescent, was once a pleasant row of houses looking over a nursery garden (in L. E. L.'s time); how the churchyard, on the first grave of which she wrote one of her most beautiful poems, was, in *her* childhood, a blooming garden; nay, more, how famed the "hamlet," as Cunningham calls it, of Brompton had been as the grave of authors, actors, and singers. How Beloe, the sexagenarian, and Count Rumford—

strange anomaly!—had died in the same house, 45 Brompton Row; how here George Colman had succumbed to fate; then Curran; here again, Miss Pope, the lady actress *par excellence*, who taught our grandmothers how to enter a room, how to go to court, and how to contract their mouths by repeating the words "niminy piminy" (*vide* some old play in which she used to convulse the audience by these syllables). He tells us all this; so let us realize that Letitia Landon was reared amid flowers, and near the imaginative and dramatic personages in whom she ever found great interest.

She was not, however, born at Brompton, but in the adjacent parish of Chelsea, in the genteel inclosure of Hans Place, number twenty-five. Since poverty is next to a crime in some classes of English society, the lowly circumstances of her family were for some years adduced as a proof that they were of mean origin. She was descended, nevertheless, from an ancient and honorable race, the Landons of Crednell, in Herefordshire, and flourished on their own estate until Sir William Landon, Knight, rashly ventured his luck in the South Sea bubble, and his estates were absorbed in the general wreck. After that time, adieu to opulence, or, indeed, to prosperity of any stable kind for that branch of the family from which Letitia was descended.

Still they were able to keep up a position in the world, and to enter those professions which hold so good a place in England. From generation to generation the Landons were beneficed clergymen: John Landon, Rector of Nursted and Ilsted, in Kent, the great-grandfather of Letitia, was noted for his literary abilities, which were directed against his son, the Rector of Tedstone Delamere. He was, however, encumbered with eight children, the eldest of whom was another John Landon, the father of L. E. L., who, eschewing a clerical life, quitted his home, went off to sea, made a voyage to the coast of Africa, that very south coast where his daughter afterward perished, and came home again, quitting the service on the death of his friend and patron, Admiral Bowyer.

His younger brother, meanwhile, Whittington, had entered the church, and obtained considerable distinction at Oxford. Aided by his own scholastic knowledge, by his agreeable manners—which are said by those who remember him to have been both dignified and urbane—he became eventually Provost of Worcester College, the patronage of the Duke of Portland having been extended, in this instance, to his elevation. The provost was also endowed with the deanery of Exeter, and his flourishing circumstances operated favorably in those of his elder brothers. Through the kindness of a mutual friend, named Churchill, John Landon became a partner in the house of Adair, then a prosperous army agent in Pall Mall.

His next piece of success was to find a wife with a good fortune—Miss Catharine Jane Bishop, of a Welsh extraction, who began life, as those who knew her formerly have asserted, when unmarried, with fourteen thousand pounds to her fortune, "her horse, and her groom." On the 14th of August, 1802, the eldest child of this apparently happy couple, Letitia Elizabeth, was born. They were then living in Hans Place, in a house built by Holland, the great architect of those days and those parts, and long inhabited by his son, Captain Holland. It is situated to the west, the southwest side of the quiet little square, and is a charming house of its *genre*, with two pleasant drawing-rooms, and a third, forming a sort of conservatory boudoir, and looking into a strip of garden. Beyond, in L. E. L.'s time, were the gardens of the late Peter Kemp, Esq., then residing at the Pavilion, a house also built by Holland for his own residence. The gardens were since tenanted by a market gardener, famous for his salads and asparagus.

Beyond these gardens there were only detached houses, skirting a strip of land then called Chelsea Common, but more like a large field than a common. The little garden of number twenty-five was full of roses. Umbrageous trees on the left denoted the beautiful pavilion gardens, exquisitely planted with appropriate shrubs, with a miniature lake, to which sloped a lawn, broken here and there by parterres. All this scene was familiar to L. E. L. in her infancy, and in the dawn of her childhood; and she always retained a fondness of Hans Place. A racket-ground has usurped the space whereon the market gardener (the well-known Catleugh, a frequent exhibitor of geraniums) raised his salads, or gathered for his customers the earliest strawberries with the dew still on them. The pavilion gardens are divided; lands and rents have risen since the days when Letitia looked out from her nursery window on gooseberry bushes and cherry trees; yet the repose of Hans Place is still unbroken.

One beloved companion shared the small pleasures of the little Letitia, and that was her brother Whittington, some years younger than herself. They were inseparable, except when Letitia went to learn to read, taught by an invalid neighbor, who used to scatter large letters over the floor, and tell her pupil to name them, and form them into words. When she was good, the child was rewarded, and her recompense, whatever it might be, was taken home and shared with her brother. "She must have been very quick," Mr. Landon years afterward remarked, "for she used to bring home many rewards;

and I began to look eagerly for her coming back." When, unsuccessful or inattentive, she had brought home nothing, the future poetess crept up stairs to her nurse, to whom she was much attached, to be consoled.

At five years of age, she went as a day-scholar to an admirable school, at that time established at number twenty-two in Hans Place. This house, for many years in after life, was the residence of L. E. L. through sickness, in happiness, in good report and bad report: and it had other associations beside those connected with L. E. L. to arrest the attention of the passer-by. It is the next house to the pavilion gates on the east side of the square; and has a kind of off-shoot, of one story, containing a long, low room, half-overshadowed with plane-trees of the pavilion, half with the elms of a close, small garden in the back, in which half of L. E. L.'s life was passed.

It happened that Miss, or, as she styled herself, Mrs. Rowden, was a lady of singular acquirements and energy: more especially she cultivated, what is now so greatly neglected, the committing to memory the English classics, and the reciting before an audience the best passages, as they do at Harrow and Eton on prize days. She was herself a poetess, and quite a character in her way; clean, lively, full of energy, kind, devoted to what she esteemed the highest of all professions, that of education. Such women are now rare. Then French was taught in Miss Rowden's school by an emigrant, the Comte St. Quentin, whose accent and idiom were very different from those of the modern French teacher, taken from a far lower class than formerly, when the noble exiles from Paris gave lessons. Hence L. E. L. acquired two things which she never lost —a love of poetry, and a pure French accent: a fair intellectual stock in trade to begin her youth with. Mary Mitford was another gifted pupil of Mrs. Rowden's, and remained for years the friend and correspondent of her instructress, who marrying the Comte St. Quentin, removed eventually to Paris. L. E. L. was not, however, very long a regular pupil of Mrs. Rowden's, but used, in after days, to attend classes there, so as to derive advantage from her plans. Among other celebrated persons who knew and respected Mrs. Rowden, was Lady Caroline Lamb, who was an inmate of number twenty-two for some time. Lady Caroline used to give out the prizes on breaking-up days; and for several years her graceful form was seen entering the long, low room which has been described, leading by the hand her little boy, whom she was destined to lose. "After the business of the day was over," writes a former pupil of Mrs. Rowden's, "Master Lamb used to be set on a high table to recite Shakspeare, which he did with wonderful emphasis for such a child. I well remember his giving the 'Seven Ages of Man.'" No wonder the poor boy died early. How little could Lady Caroline imagine that, amid the smiling, eager faces then uplifted toward her, there was one for which many an eye would afterward turn with intense eagerness as the three magic letters L. E. L. were uttered; that, in that very room, should be decided the tragical fate of that child, the youngest in the school, who could then, it was her only fault her teacher said, never walk steadily from joyousness of spirit, there suffer sickness, anxiety, and the hard unkindness from an unsparing world!

Scarcely was L. E. L. seven years old when her father removed to Trevor Park, East Barnet, and for some time her education was superintended by her excellent cousin, Miss Elizabeth Landon, who survives her intelligent little pupil. Her imagination, and more especially her memory, were now plainly apparent to her family. At night she would amuse her parents by their fireside by the wonderful castles her fancy pictured. She was perfectly happy in the garden, talking to herself, and walking with what she called her "measuring-stick" in her hand. When spoken to at such times she used to say, "Oh! don't talk to me; I have such a delightful idea in my mind." During all this period of her life, the education of L. E. L. was carefully attended to. It was not by an impulse of genius alone that she became a poetess, but by long mental culture of a generous kind; by reading works of sound history, travels, biography—wading through books—not skimming them, and mastering each as she went on. In music, however, although she had the advantage of being taught by Miss Bissett, a lady of first-rate powers, she never attained any proficiency, although all her life fond of vocal music. Neither could she ever be made to write a good hand. Her writing was cramped, as if she had used her left hand only, and was always a matter of difficulty to her. Her affections developed with her intellect. She was so full of faults, and yet so fond of her brother, that it was found expedient when one was guilty of an offense to punish the other for it. "Nothing," her brother said, "could subdue her will except it was done through her affections." The system adopted with her was a stern one; but it prepared her for that life of work and of self-dependence which she afterward encountered. Even at this early age the disinterested, self-denying character of her maturer years was apparent. "I had," writes her brother, "petitioned my father for three shillings, when he offered me, by way of compromise, a new eighteen-penny piece if I would learn the ballad,

'Gentle river, gentle river,
Lo! thy streams are stained with gore.'"

Alas! it was thirty verses long, and flesh and blood in the boy revolted. But Letitia, seeing his dilemma, offered to learn the verses herself, repeated them perfectly, and got the three shillings. She then persuaded her brother to learn it, teaching him verse by verse. "I don't," says Mr. Landon, "remember whether I ever said it; but I do remember that she gave me the three shillings."

One of her early exploits was teaching her father's gardener, thirty years of age, to read: this was her first good deed. The man rose to be a milkman; and eventually, enabled by Letitia's tuition to keep his own books, he prospered so well as to settle down in a respectable public-house at Barnet.

At Trevor Park, L. E. L.'s happiest, perhaps her only *really* happy days were passed. Imagination is an infinite source of delight to children. She found in her brother a ready listener to her "travels"—all supposititious rambles—to her "desert island." Happily for her, the pure, high-toned works of Walter Scott were the reading of the day. Well does every parent judge who has them in his library. It was an inestimable advantage to the young people of that time. All in *his* works has a tendency to elevate: his poetry, which is so far inferior to his prose, is devoid of the passionate gloom of Byron, free from the poisonous casuistry of Shelley. L. E. L. knew the "Lady of the Lake" by heart, and lived on Scott's poetry, as she has said in her poem on the Great Unknown.

"I peopled all the walks and shades
With images of thine;
This lime-tree was a lady's bower,
The yew-tree was a shrine;
Almost I deem'd each sunbeam shone
O'er bonnet, spear, and morion."

The mental appetite of the young at that age is not *difficile;* and she forgot, in the enchanting interest of the story, the defects in Scott as a versifier: "Marmion" was her favorite; and she sometimes in after life repeated in low, almost tremulous accents, and very impressively, those lines descriptive of Constance when brought before the conclave of monks to receive sentence. She was always touched by the recital of every valiant action: and one of her earliest pieces were stanzas on "Sir John Doyle," that brave old soldier (the uncle of Lady Bulwer Lytton), whom L. E. L. afterward personally knew.

During the course of years, her character was thus formed. As it developed itself, an impressionable, hasty, honest nature appeared: tears and smiles, long after the age of infancy, came easily, and quickly succeeded each other. The sweetness of her temper in after life was remarkable. As a child, she was passionate; but she acquired afterward one of the best sort of tempers—that which is naturally impulsive, but which is regulated by principle and firm regard for the feelings of others.

To her cousin L. E. L. owed much: from her mother she inherited much. Mrs. Landon resembled her daughter greatly. A thin, small woman, with a countenance full of animation, it was evident, from the expression of her eyes, whence the talents of L. E. L. were derived. Short as L. E. L. was, her mother was somewhat shorter; quick as were L. E. L.'s movements, those of her mother were quicker still. In voice, in native vivacity of character, they greatly resembled each other. Mrs. Landon was a person of cultivated mind, warm feelings, great penetration, considerable wit.

During the season of the prosperity of Mr. and Mrs. Landon, another daughter was born—a fragile being, who died of consumption at thirteen years of age. Mrs. Landon was devoted to this poor child, in whom, from difference of age, L. E. L. found no companionship: so that, while her brother was at school, she still lived, as it were, undisturbed in her own little world, and her imagination became the ascendant power of her mind.

Until the age of thirteen, L. E. L. was a healthy, blooming girl, full of spirits—a romp, as girls should be at that age; and her childhood, in spite of her melancholy account of it in several of her compositions, was a joyous one. But clouds were lowering over her home, and from henceforth the struggles, which were scarcely closed until her death, began. Mr. Landon—an amiable man, of an easy and sanguine temper—had encumbered himself with a farm, and lost large sums from the mismanagement of his bailiff. Business was not prosperous, and the failure, eventually, of Adair's House plunged him into difficulties which he never retrieved. Trevor Park was given up: and he took his wife and children to Old Brompton, where the first dawnings of L. E. L.'s genius were discovered, encouraged, and finally introduced to the world by Mr. Jerdan. It was about the year 1818 that some of L. E. L.'s poetical efforts were printed in the "Literary Gazette," which at that time was almost the only purely literary weekly journal, and a periodical of great influence and extended circulation.

She was only fifteen when, a year before, she had published a little volume entitled "The Fate of Adelaide," a poem which she dedicated to her mother's intimate friend, Mrs. Siddons. "The Fate of Adelaide" was involved in the failure of its publisher, Mr. Warren, of Bond Street, and, though it sold well, L. E. L. never received any profit for her production. She next appeared under the shelter of her famous initials in a series of "Poetical Sketches" in the "Literary Gazette." These sketches are eminently beautiful, and were deservedly successful: the initials became, as Laman Blanchard expresses it, a *name*. That was not an age of poetry; and the strong utilitarian tendencies of the times would, one might suppose, have frozen the current of a young and unknown poetical genius. Malthus and Senior flourished; Miss Martineau was not far off; Byron was "improper;" Scott was "feeble;" Tennyson, a boy at college; and poetry was a thing appertaining to a long past century, not to ours. Yet passion, fancy, feeling, in all the freshness of an original mind, spoke to the heart, and had a response. When, in 1831, Sir Edward Bulwer Lytton (then Mr. Bulwer only) edited the "New Monthly," in his review of "Romance and Reality"—L. E. L.'s first novel—he thus alluded to the effect produced by her poetry, and by the mystery that hung over her identity.

"We were," he says, "at that time more capable than we now are of poetic enthusiasm; and certainly that enthusiasm we not only felt ourselves, but we shared with every second person we then met. We were young, and at college, lavishing our golden years, not so much on the Greek verse and mystic character to which we ought, perhaps, to have been rigidly devoted, as

"'Our heart in passion and our head in rhyme.'

"At that time poetry was not yet out of fashion, at least with us of the cloister, and there was always in the reading-room of the Union a rush every Saturday afternoon for the 'Literary Gazette,' and an impatient anxiety to hasten at once to that corner of the sheet which contained the three magical letters L. E. L. And all of us praised the verse, and all of us guessed at the author. We soon learned it was a female, and our admiration was doubled, and our conjectures tripled. Was she young? Was she pretty? And—for there were some embryo fortune-hunters among us—was she rich? We ourselves who, now staid critics and sober gentlemen, are about coldly to measure to a prose work" (what is here quoted is introductory to a review of "Romance and Reality") "the due quantum of laud and censure, then only thought of homage, and in verse only we condescended to use it. But the other day, in looking over some of our boyish effusions, we found a paper superscribed to L. E. L., and beginning with 'Fair Spirit.'"

While she was thus almost unconsciously exciting a strong curiosity about herself, the young poetess was experiencing a great calamity, which certainly overshadowed all her life with its consequences. Her father died. It was not only that she

it appeared, the beautiful and gifted Rosina Wheeler. Miss Spence was of Scottish origin, somehow related to Fordyce and his sermons, whom she always managed to bring out in a couplet with Lady Isabella Spence. L. E. L. was gratified by a call from Miss Spence, who, in those days of leo-hunting, was proud to be the first to present to a select circle in little rooms, in Little Quebec Street, Mayfair, the veritable L. E. L., fresh caught for their amusement. Here L. E. L. first met Sir Lytton Bulwer, then a fair young man, of aristocratic elegance, full of wit and fancy, and then passionately attached to her whom he since made his wife. The *petits comités* in Little Quebec Street were often attended by Lady Caroline Lamb, who soon evinced an interest in L. E. L. which ended only with Lady Caroline's life. Miss Wheeler, to a perfect beauty of face, with her magnificent figure, united great wit, great liveliness, and a power of appreciating the genius of L. E. L. Their friendship was afterward painfully terminated; but in Sir Bulwer Lytton L. E. L. ever found a constant, sensible, and sincere friend, whose regard for her survived her death.

Her descriptions of these social literary meetings, these *bas bleus réunions* up three pairs of stairs—Miss Spence in a blue toque doing the honors — were very graphic; and Moore, who heard them sometimes, thought that the powers of Miss Austen were vested, as well as great poetical gifts, in L. E. L. But when her novels appeared it was seen that he was mistaken.

Literary and intellectual society were not, however, wholly new to L. E. L., though not in the *bas-bleu* system. Mrs. Siddons's friendship for Mrs. Landon lasted their lives, and was of an intimate character. "Sally Siddons," Mrs. Landon used to say, "worked the first cap ever put on my Letitia's head when a baby." She referred to that charming, doomed daughter of Mrs. Siddons who died of consumption while her mother was the star of Ireland's provincial towns. Campbell, in his "Life of Mrs. Siddons," has depicted the mother's agony when her darling was taken from her. Sally was engaged, it is believed, to be married to Sir Thomas Lawrence.

Accustomed also to mingle with a small number of friends of good position whom Mrs. Landon ever retained—for her adverse circumstances never lowered her in *any way*—the manners of L. E. L. were gentle and very agreeable. She had no shyness. She had great, very great *tact*, a natural gift, as well as the result of good early society. She was willing to be pleased, and desirous, perhaps too desirous, to please; for that, which is a virtue, sometimes induced her to say things far too flattering to be always thoroughly *meant*. She was led into it from imitation. Her nature was a sincere one; but the *bas-bleu* buttering system was then at its height.

She was at this time from eighteen to twenty-two or three, a comely girl with a blooming complexion, small, with very beautiful deep gray eyes, with dark eyelashes: her hair, never very thick, was of a deep brown, and fine as silk: her forehead and eyebrows were perfect; the one white and clear, the other arched and well defined. She was inclined rather to be fat; too healthy looking; and then her other features were defective; her nose was *retroussé*. Her mouth, however, without being particularly good, was expressive, and proportioned to her small and delicate face. Her hands and feet were perfect; and in time her figure, which had a girlish redundance of form in it, became slighter, and ended by being neat and easy, if not strictly graceful. She had a charming voice; and one could not but wonder that with that, and with so much soul, she did not sing—as a sort of necessity of her nature. Few persons have had their songs set so often to music; and few persons wrote songs so adapted to society, and to the graceful performance of amateurs, as she did. Her "I know not when I loved thee first," and her "Constance," have been set by clever composers, and are deservedly popular. Her verses have always been liked by composers.

Her success brought hope to her excitable mind. Good luck she owned surpassed her expectations. "I am convinced," she wrote to her cousin, "that a kind of curse hangs over us all." Some lines which she composed at this time, when visiting an aunt in Gloucestershire, addressed to her mother, show a fondness that seems to render the after separation inexplicable.

In 1824, when Letitia was twenty-two years old, "The Improvisatrice" was published. Its success was immediate. "The stamp of originality," as Mr. Blanchard writes, "was on this work. There was a power in the pages that no carelessness could mar, no obscurity own—and the power was the writer's own." "The Improvisatrice" was identified with the writer whose soul had been for some years poured forth in songs that had all the *verve* of being improvised. Although at this period of her life it is asserted that L. E. L. had never loved, never sorrowed, her new poem, like her contributions to the "Literary Gazette," was full of forlorn hope and blighted affection, so given that it required some strength of reasoning not to believe them real.

"It was my evil star above,
 Not my sweet lute that wrought me wrong;
It was not song that taught me love,
 But it was love that taught me song."

But the instant L. E. L. was known, the circle surrounding her was disenchanted. She pleaded guilty to no sentiment; she abjured the idea of writing from her own feelings. She was so lively, so girlish; so fond of a dance, or a play, or a gay walk; so full of pleasantry, so ready with her shafts of wit, that one felt half angry with her for being so blithe and so real. Still those who knew her well did comprehend her: they knew what deep feelings lay beneath all that froth of manner which did her so much injustice. They knew that many of her sallies were drawn forth by the tiresome flattery of some, the *fade* observations of others. A successful author has much to undergo from society: the continual repetition even of the most gratifying tributes becomes wearisome beyond expression, and most of our noted authors put an embargo on it. But L. E. L. was too good-natured to do this: she assured each admirer of her works that his or her tribute was just what she wished for. She always listened—always answered with courteous respect to the well-intended observations: it was only those conversant with the expressions of her varying face that could know what she felt.

When she said, however, that she had never been in love she spoke, at that time, the truth; and indeed it is probable that she never experienced the passion as she described it: if she did so, the emotion was transient and produced no effect on the circumstances of her life.

She was now to be found by the numerous and fashionable visitors who were proud of her acquaintance in a small apartment in Sloane Street, where she lived under the protection of her grandmother, Mrs. Bishop, to whom she was affectionately attached. The drawing-room of these lodgings was sometimes filled with gay ladies of rank in the morning, and with men of letters and literary ladies in the evening. L. E. L. was a social being; and young as she then was—little more than twenty-three—had the gift, so perfect in France, so rare in England, of receiving well. Nothing could be more lively than these little social meetings, and nothing more unexceptionable. It is true that among men of letters, great diversities of character are to be found; but, in the society of her own sex, L. E. L. was very careful how to steer her way. It was at this period that she was seized by her first severe attack of illness, inflammation of the lungs. She suffered much, and her constitution never perfectly rallied afterward. It was about this time, also, that the first attempt to injure her character was made in the "Sun" newspaper.

The paragraph coupled her name with that of the friend to whom she owed so much: consultations were then held by her friends as to the steps to be pursued. Mr. Jerdan advised an action being threatened if an instant contradiction did not appear, and he was *right:* a threat of that kind would probably have produced far more important consequences than the silencing an ephemeral report. It would have intimidated a host of almost invisible slanderers who found delight in bringing down to the vulgar level of their own minds one all genius and purity. Even had an action been necessary, there would have been nothing to fear. Every action of L. E. L.'s life was open as daylight. From first to last she was always in the sight of friends, many of them married; her mornings were passed in incessant writing; her evenings in society; while her grandmother never left the house.

Well might she write these exquisite lines at the close of her second poem, "The Troubadour," to her father's memory:

"My heart said, no name but thine
Should be on this last page of mine.
My father! though no more thine ear
Censure or praise of mine can hear,
It soothes me to embalm thy name
With all my hope, my pride, my fame!

* * * *

My own dear father, time may bring
Chance, change, upon his rainbow wing,
But never will thy name depart—
The household god of thy child's heart—
Until thy orphan child may share
The grave where her best feelings are.
Never, dear father, love can be
Like the dear love I had for thee."

It was during the height of her fame also, raised to its climax by the publication of "The Troubadour," that her young sister sank away, happy in being taken from the adversity which she had never had physical strength to bear. L. E. L. was not aware of her danger till all hope was gone; then she hastened to her mother's. Never can her description be forgotten of her feelings on gazing on the living skeleton before her. At this period, and ever afterward, she began to contribute regularly to her mother's means of subsistence. This was one of the greatest sources of satisfaction in her independence; and the generous-hearted girl felt it to be so.

She was plunged into the full career of London society when her grandmother died, and her plans were again unsettled. Perhaps in not returning to her mother, L. E. L., as an authoress, was right; as a member of society, she was wrong. As an authoress, she required quiet; entire freedom from irritation; absence from small worries incidental to a home of privation. Advice that she could not always follow, yet dared not, lest altercation should arise, dispute. After a lapse of years these considerations seem valid, and constitute a plea for that which was constantly urged against her—her absence from her mother's protection. It was, in point of fact, all that could be urged to her detriment. In referring to the reports against her she thus wrote in the bitterness of her soul—

"I have not written so soon as I intended, first, because I wished to be able to tell you I had taken some steps toward change; and I also wished, if possible, to subdue the bitterness and irritation of feelings not to be expressed to one so kind as yourself. I have succeeded better in the first than the last. I think of the treatment I have received till my soul writhes under the powerlessness of its anger. It is only because I am poor, unprotected, and dependent on popularity, that I am a mark for all the gratuitous insolence and malice of idleness and ill-nature. And I can not but feel deeply that had I been possessed of rank and opulence, either these remarks had never been made, or, if they had, how trivial would their consequence have been to me! I must begin with the only subject —the only thing in the world I really feel an interest in—my writings." * * * "When my 'Improvisatrice' came out, nobody discovered what is alleged against it. I did not take up a review, a magazine, a newspaper, but if it named my book it was to praise 'the delicacy,' 'the grace,' 'the purity of feminine feeling' it displayed." * * * "With regard to the immoral and improper tendency of my productions, I can only say it is not my fault if there are minds, which, like negroes, cast a dark shadow on a mirror, however clear and pure in itself." * * * "As to the report you named, I know not which is greatest—the absurdity or the malice. Circumstances have made me very much indebted to the gentleman [whose name was coupled with hers] for much of kindness. I have not a friend in the world but himself to manage any thing of business, whether literary or pecuniary." * * * "Place yourself in my situation. Could you have hunted London for a publisher; endured all the alternate hot and cold water thrown on your exertions; bargained for what sum they might be pleased to give; and after all canvassed, examined, nay, quarreled over accounts the most intricate in the world? And again, after success had procured money, what was I to do with it? Though ignorant of business, I must know I could not lock it up in a box." * * * "Who was to undertake this—I can only call it drudgery—but some one to whom my literary exertions could in return be as valuable as theirs to me? But it is not on this ground that I express my surprise at so cruel a calumny, but actually on that of our slight intercourse. He is in the habit of calling on his way into town, and unless it is on a Sunday afternoon, which is almost his only leisure time for looking over letters, manuscripts, etc., five or ten minutes is the usual time of his visit. We visit in such different circles, that if I except the evening he took Agnes and myself to Miss B——'s, I can not recall our ever meeting in any one of the round of winter parties. The more I think of my past life and of my future prospects, the more dreary do they seem. I have known little else than privation, disappointment, unkindness, and harassment. From the time I was fifteen, my life has been one continual struggle in some shape or another against absolute poverty, and I must say not a tithe of my profits have I ever expended on myself." "No one knows but myself what I have had to contend with."

She might well exclaim, as she did: "Oh for oblivion and five hundred a year!"

She had now removed into Hans Place, to the very number, twenty-two, where her childish gayety had put the whole propriety of a range of girls out. Mrs. Rowden had now left, and the school was under the guidance of three ladies, named Lance, whose aged father lived with them. No residence could be more unobjectionable. Hans Place was, and it still is, the quietest nook in London. The school not being large, the Misses Lance received two or three ladies of strict respectability as inmates; and gladly retained L. E. L., from the great consideration she ever showed them, from the absence of all self-indulgence in her nature, and from a general esteem and regard for her, on far lower terms than the rest. It was, indeed, requisite, for the labor of the pen is precarious, and may be suspended at any time by ill health, or blasted altogether by the failure of a publisher.

L. E. L. established herself in a small attic looking out into the square, with its small, well-guarded circles of shrubs and turf, and there slept and wrote, often till the depth of winter, without a fire. She dined with the school, drank tea in the parlor with old Mr. Lance and his daughters, and received her visitors in the long, low room in which in her careless infancy she had seen Lady Caroline Lamb deliver the prizes. The chief trouble she gave was in the continual opening of the door to coroneted carriages, or loungers from the clubs, or those killers of one's morning, intimate friends, who think they are privileged to look in early, and ruin their hosts with the interruption. Then, at night, some lady would often call and take the poetess to some gay fête; L. E. L. all this time retaining the freshness of her clear fair complexion, and improving in form, in manner, and in *style*, that all-important ingredient for success; yet, as she once bitterly said when comments were made on her dress (which was somewhat fanciful), "It is very easy for those whose only trouble on that head is to change, to find fault with one who never knew in her life what it was to have two new dresses at a time." Yet those were precisely the critics who gave no quarter to the poor and hard-worked writer.

Visits to her two uncles, the Dean of Exeter and the Rev. James Landon, the Rector of Aberford, in Yorkshire, varied her brilliant, toilsome life. She spoke of Oxford with rapture. One may, indeed, well conceive how gladly she would ramble in the delicious gardens of Worcester College, with its glassy water, its ancestral trees, and the cloistral-looking old portion of the college over which her uncle presided.

Poetry was not at that time so fashionable among the young Oxonians as now, when every undergraduate has a Tennyson, so that she never achieved the exploit of captivating a fellow nor of breaking the heart of any student.

At Aberford she spent the Christmas of 1825, where it was properly disseminated that she was the "London author." The consequence, she said in one of her letters, was that, "seated by the only young man I had beheld, I acted upon him like an air-pump, suspending his very breath and motion; and my asking him for a mince-pie, a dish of which I had for some time been surveying with longing eyes, acted like an electric shock, and his start not a little discomposed a no-age-at-all, silk-vested spinster, whose plate was thereby deposited in her lap; and last, not least, in the hurry he forgot to help me!"

"I grant," she adds, "that in the country nothing seems easier than to become the golden calf of a circle; but I never envied Miss Seward."

Meantime, while slanders lay dormant, other reports were circulated. It was said that she had had two hundred offers; but it was, she said, very unfortunate that her offers should be so much like the passage to the North Pole and Wordsworth's cuckoo—talked of but never seen. It is undoubted that she had a proposal from a rich American, and that several young men were her votaries, though without, perhaps, much hope of success; but still she had then met no one to whom she could give her whole affections. She was rather unimpressionable in that particular, as the favorites of society usually are. Whatsoever the reports against her, they never affected her reception in the gay, and, indeed, in the great world. From Sir Edward and Lady Bulwer, and Mrs. Windham Lewis (Mrs. Disraeli), she found a constant welcome; and the friends formed in these somewhat similar coteries were not lost. The late Lady Emmeline Stuart Wortley sought her out, and introduced her to the Marchioness of Londonderry, at whose splendid assemblies the youthful poetess was the star of the evening.

Lady Caroline Lamb was dead, but many of the individuals whom L. E. L. had met under her roof were still delighted to lionize her: the late Lord Munster was one of her kindest and most partial friends.

It is invidious to mention a host of great names, as if high-sounding titles could add to the lustre of true genius. But, in treating of L. E. L. as a social being, while she may hardly be deemed in strict parlance a "Queen of Society," it must be allowed that brilliant and exciting scenes were for many years her appointed sphere.

In her own little home, however, she had her votaries and her throne. It is now long since forgotten, how, in the long, low room, papered as it was with one of those dim papers of the last forty years, which make "darkness visible," L. E. L. gave a fancy ball, which was attended in fancy dresses by Sir E. and Lady Bulwer, and other friends—some proportion of whom were editors and publishers, for L. E. L. never forgot that she had to depend on the press for support. Sometimes she received a small *réunion* of all her regiment of authors and journalists, the Misses Lance her chaperons, or some lady of consequence and often of rank. Lady Stepney was one of her most indulgent friends; Mr. and Mrs. Hall also gave her their support. Not even Hannah More brought to life could have found any thing to challenge censure in these agreeable and irreproachable evenings; but while this may be called the sunshiny day of her brief and unquiet maturity, she was often sad at heart. "Let any one," she wrote to a friend, "look their own past experience steadily in the face, and what a dark and discouraging aspect it will present! How many enjoyments have passed away forever! how much warmth and kindliness of feeling! how many generous beliefs! * * * As to love—does it dare to treasure its deepest feelings in the presence of what we call the world? As to friendship—how many would weigh your dearest interests for one instant against the very lightest of their own? And as to fame, of what avail is it in the grave?—and during life it will be denied or dealt forth grudgingly. No, no; to be as indifferent as you can possibly contrive, to aim only at present amusement and passing popularity, is the best system for a steam-coach along the railroad of life; let who will break the stones and keep up the fire!"

This is the language of a mind and body overworked; for all L. E. L.'s efforts of the muse were not always spontaneous.

Mr. Jerdan, who arranged her affairs with publishers, gives a statement of all that she accomplished, and all that she received for her writings during the whole of her literary career. He puts it thus:

For "The Easter Offering" she received		....	£30
"The Improvisatrice"	"	....	300
"The Troubadour"	"	....	600
"The Golden Violet"	"	....	200
"The Venetian Bracelet"	"	....	150
"Romance and Reality"	"	....	300
"Heath's Book of Beauty"	"	....	300
"Francesca Carrara"	"	....	300
And certainly for Annuals, Magazines, and Periodicals, not less in ten or twelve years than		....	300
			£2480

Mr. Jerdan has not, however, mentioned "Ethel Churchill," the best of L. E. L.'s three novels. Those who are not in the habit of writing can not conceive the exhaustion, the effort, the dejection of mind and lassitude of body which exertions of this nature, when continual, produce. Often has L. E. L. started from her bed, after spending an evening in society, and, in the morning, when the printer's boy was waiting, written on her knees a sonnet, or the remaining lines of a poem. She wrote with wonderful facility; but the mental excitement was unceasing, and much of her now constant ill health was ascribed to that incessant wear and tear of every faculty. She was also disappointed about this time in the property which she expected to receive from her grandmother, who had, as some ladies are obliged to do, sunk the greater part in an annuity. She bequeathed, however, the rest to L. E. L., and this sum, three hundred and fifty pounds, was every farthing she ever received after the age of seventeen, independently of her own exertions. This fact proves what women *can* do, with industry and ability: it ought to be an incentive to parents to educate the intellect, not merely to promote mechanical accomplishments.

Her annual income may, therefore, be estimated at two hundred and fifty pounds. Out of this sum she reserved for her own use one hundred and twenty pounds; the rest she devoted to her mother, and to the aid of her brother, who had passed through Oxford, and had taken holy orders. She never owed a sixpence; but she never had a farthing to spend over the necessaries of life. "In truth," she was, as Mr. Jerdan remarks, "the most unselfish of human beings." In 1834, L. E. L. visited Paris. She was happy in finding a most desirable escort in Miss Tarns, a lady some years older than herself. Her letters from France are charming—so natural, at times so poetical, so *young*, and so fresh.

Every thing delighted her — the caps of the women, the Tuileries, the shops, and the civil people in them; and even the exquisite dinners. But she was disappointed in finding all the *beau monde* out of Paris; and perceived, as most foreigners do, that being in that gay city in June is not seeing Paris. Mr. and Mrs. Gore, however, welcomed her, and several French and German *litterateurs.* Amable Tastu and his wife, Odillon Barrot, Heine, and others, called upon her, and commiserated her for being in that enchanting city when every one was out of town. Not even the charms of the Boulevards, where her hotel was situated, could prevent L. E. L. from feeling that her visit, as far as seeing Parisian society was concerned, was a failure. She was not aware that it is only the *demi-monde* who are seen in Paris in the summer, for if not absent, the French are then invisible. L. E. L. was essentially, with all her poetic genius, a lover of society. "Excepting the visits that are paid me," she writes, "I can see nothing of the people; as to sights, you know me too well to suppose that I care about them two straws. I would sooner have a morning visit from an amusing person than see the Tuileries or the Louvre ten times over." Like most English people, she fell into the error of supposing it necessary to have a gentleman to accompany a lady to sights, not being aware that a young lady, accompanied by another lady of *un age décent*, may go to any *respéctable* public place in Paris. She had, however, some alleviations to her disappointment; Madame Tastu presented her to Madame Récamier, at whose house she met Chateaubriand, and Prosper Mérimée paid her much attention. But L. E. L. did not enjoy herself in what it requires almost an apprenticeship to enjoy —French society. She was unconquerably shy, although few persons would have discovered it; and the utmost she could do was to conceal her embarrassment, which, however, varied according to the manners and dispositions of those with whom she conversed, as is generally the case.

We have referred to the calumny which followed L. E. L. through life. It was about this time that its shafts, which had affected first her peace of mind, now influenced her destiny.

She was in the zenith of her fame when Mr. Forster, then a young barrister, and, at the same time, the editor of the "Examiner," made her an offer of marriage. Mr. Forster's personal character was unexceptionable — an honorable, warmhearted, and highly-talented man. He was sincerely attached to L. E. L.; but no sooner was he accepted, than *friends* stepped forward to tell him a thousand tales of her supposed imprudencies and even criminalities. Mr. Forster did not believe these imputations; but, desiring that they should be cleared away, he mentioned them to L. E. L. as statements that ought to be refuted. Her answer was: "Go to my female friends, the married, the respectable, the trustworthy friends whom I see almost daily. Make every inquiry in your power." Her injunctions were followed: all were unanimous in expressing their horror at the slanders against one whom they both loved and respected. Mr. Forster was satisfied. He urged L. E. L. to give him a right to protect her by instantly consenting to a marriage. "No," she answered firmly; "I will never marry a man who has distrusted me." The marriage was definitively broken off, and L. E. L. lost a prospect of being domesticated with a man whose abilities she almost reverenced, and of living in that scene and that society which she always preferred to any other—the literary society of London.

It is possible that if L. E. L. had been devotedly attached to Mr. Forster, she would not have suffered this painful occurrence to have separated her forever from him. *But she was not.* Mr. Blanchard, wishing to spare the feelings that were, on one side, most genuine, has represented the rupture of the engagement as a high-minded act of self-sacrifice, from a principle of wounded honor, on the part of L. E. L. A friend, a gentleman who knew her well, probed the matter to the quick. He urged her for her own happiness not to persist in this, as he thought, needless separation. She promptly assured him that her affections were *not* interested in the brief engagement, and she spoke in a tone that convinced him that she meant what she said. Yet, that the act cost her much, no one who reads the letters here inserted (taken from Mr. Blanchard's Memoir) can entertain a doubt. She did ample justice to the generous heart that had never really doubted her; and the struggle produced a severe, and at one time dangerous illness, which long left its traces on her delicate frame. If those who calumniated her be still living, no monitions are needful to touch the conscience of the false witness. Here is the reproof. Here is L. E. L.'s fate read to you: the chance of protection, of home happiness, of an existence of comparative ease, is before her; here she flings it from her, and the close of her life's brief tragedy soon follows.

After the deed was done, as is almost always the case, her sentiments somewhat changed—a state of exasperation came on. Alas! was it not augmented by the wanton hints of the careless or the mischievous? She became irritated against him who, of all that ever paid her the attentions of a lover, perhaps most truly loved her. Upon being told that the late Allan Cunningham, whom she appreciated, as all who knew him must have done, as a noble specimen of mankind, stated to a friend of hers the circumstance here related, adding that the engagement was likely to be renewed, she repelled the idea with great vehemence, and, in a tone and manner very unusual to one of so gentle a nature, begged that the subject might never be mentioned to her again.

Let the letter, accompanied with this explanation, now interpret her feelings at the moment when it was written. It is expressed with all the kindliness, the impulsiveness, and the true sincerity of her noble nature. Nor can those who knew her peruse it without a pang.

"I have already written to you two notes which I fear you could scarcely read or understand. I am to-day sitting up for an hour, and, though strictly forbidden to write, it will be the least evil. I wish I could send you my inmost soul to read, for I feel at this moment the utter powerlessness of words. I have suffered for the last three days a degree of torture that made Dr. Thomson say, 'You have an idea of what the rack is now.' It was nothing to what I suffered from my own feelings.

* * * * * *

"Again I repeat that I will not allow you to consider yourself bound to me by any possible tie. To any friend to whom you may have stated our engagement, I can not object to your stating the truth. Do every justice to your own kind and generous conduct. I am placed in a most cruel and difficult position. Give me the satisfaction of, as far as rests with myself, having nothing to reproach myself with. The more I think, the more I feel I ought not—I can not—allow you to unite yourself with one accused of— I can not write it. The mere suspicion is dreadful as death. Were it stated as a fact, that might be disproved. Were it a difficulty of any other kind, I might say, Look back at every action of my life, ask every friend I have. But what answer can I give, or what security have I against the assertion of a man's vanity, or the slander of a vulgar woman's tongue? I feel that to give up all idea of a near and dear connection is as much my duty to myself as to you. Why should you be exposed to the annoyance, the mortification of having the name of the woman you honor with your regard coupled with insolent insinuations? You never would bear it.

"I have just received your notes. God bless you! but—After Monday I shall, I hope, be visible; at present it is impossible. My complaint is inflammation of the liver, and I am ordered complete repose—as if it were possible! Can you read this? Under any circumstances, the

"Most grateful and affectionate of your friends,

"L. E. Landon."

Let the poison rest: nothing now can harm her whom it so sharply pained, so deeply injured then.

"She hath no need of tears."

It is, however, remarkable that the slander could never be traced. It was circulated in drawing-rooms, breathing into the atmosphere, tainting with its foul current the minds of those even who hung over L. E. L.'s chair with seeming pleasure, or who gazed on her from some remote corner, wondering at the gayety of her spirits, the gentle sweetness of her deportment. A whisper went round: those who knew her best caught it as it went, but never could the first whisper be detected. The report always stopped short somewhere, and was angrily disclaimed by some one just as one believed that the source was ascertained. It is fruitless, perhaps foolish, to dwell on these remembrances now; for she is long since at rest in heaven, and justified by universal assent here.

She now often talked of marrying any one, and of wishing to get away, far away, from England, and from those who thus misunderstood her. Formerly she had been too indifferent to these reports; now she became too sensitive. To be captious was not in her nature, yet she was becoming morbid, depressed, hopeless: yet never did a revengeful or bitter sentiment pain those who most loved her, and who watched over her with sorrowing care; for her health was now almost constantly variable. Happily her friend, her first friend, Mr. Jerdan, and his daughters did not forsake her on account of the coarse and cruel manner in which the name of L. E. L. had been traduced on his account. They were devoted to her to the last.

To all ordinary observers L. E. L.'s spirits seemed quite to recover the shock just described. She was more sought after in the society of the great than ever; and, to do them justice, the ladies of rank who welcomed her to their houses never lent an ear to the rumors against her: they were, and they still are, in that class, too well accustomed to *on dits* of a calumnious nature to conceive those which were leveled against an unprotected young woman of any moment. Besides, with all their defects as a class, there is a loftiness of feeling in the English aristocracy, and an independence of action, which are not to be found in the middle ranks of society.

It was before her wounded spirit had been perfectly soothed that L. E. L. met one evening, at the house of a mutual friend at Hampstead, the late George Maclean, then governor of Cape Coast Castle. Mr. Maclean had just then distinguished himself by great judgment, and some considerable amount of personal valor, in quelling an insurrection of Ashantees, during which General Turner had perished.

L. E. L. was greatly touched by any thing that approached to heroism. Her fine lines on Sir Walter Manny show her sentiment for the old chivalric gallantry. She heard much of Mr. Maclean from her friend Miss Emma Roberts, who had introduced her to Mr. and Mrs. Matthew Forster, Mr. Maclean's intimate associates. There was to be a party to welcome the hero, and L. E. L. was invited. In her enthusiasm she wore a Scotch tartan scarf over her shoulders. She had a ribbon in her hair, and a sash also, of the Maclean tartan; and she set out for the *soirée* in great spirits, resolved on thus complimenting the hero.

Mr. Maclean was much struck by her appearance. In looks L. E. L. was improved by being more delicate than ever in form and complexion. The rich hues of the tartan over her white muslin dress became her neck. She had at this time every advantage of a comfortable home. The Miss Lances had given up 22 Hans Place; then she lived some time with a friend of theirs (an excellent woman), Mrs. Sheldon; *she* also changed her plans of life; but after the cruel rupture of her engagement with Mr. Forster, a lady of large fortune, living with every luxury in Hyde Park Street, insisted on L. E. L.'s making her house her home, received and treated her as a daughter, and gave her what she could not otherwise have expected—the protection of herself and her husband, persons of the highest respectability and character.

Under these favorable and happy auspices did L. E. L. begin her fatal acquaintance with Mr. Maclean. Never had she been before so serene, so protected, so happy. She had an elegant drawing-room allotted her to receive separately her own friends: a carriage was always ready for her to make visits. Nothing could exceed the almost maternal care that watched over her still frequent illnesses.

Those who so loved, so cared for her, lived to mourn her, but they are now at rest. Honored be their memory—good, pious, generous as they were.

Still L. E. L. felt that she was not independent, and hers was an independent mind. All these circumstances combined made her wish to have a claim, a home somewhere; and Mr. Maclean soon offered to her these sighed-for objects of her heart.

He was accepted, and introduced to her friends as her betrothed. Many approved her choice. Mr. Maclean was of an ancient Scottish family, the son of the Rev. James Maclean of

Urquhart, Elgin, and the nephew of General Sir John Maclean. In early youth he had been sent out to Africa as Colonial Secretary at Cape Coast Castle: he was scarcely of age when he was made governor of the colony. He was a grave, spare man, between thirty and forty when he became engaged to L. E. L., but he looked very much older. His face, without being very plain, was not agreeable. It was pallid: and his dark hair fell upon a brow by no means of an elevated or intellectual cast. His dark-gray eyes were seldom raised to meet those of another. He was very taciturn, and still spoke his native Scotch, when he did speak, which was seldom: never, if he could help it. A practical man, he seemed to look upon all sentiment as folly, wit as superfluous, taste and fancy as weakness of mind, the softer passions as a waste of time. Still, he was L. E. L.'s choice—her mature choice. His position was good; and, except the necessity of going to Africa, there was nothing to be said against the marriage.

Most mysteriously, the engagement was suddenly interrupted by Mr. Maclean's leaving London, and ceasing all correspondence. L. E. L. hoped for the best, wrote to him—no answer; wrote again—no answer again. Then her health became affected: she had an attack of nervous fever. She explained all: the calumnies had reached him also. Her depression was extreme; and her attachment for Mr. Maclean appeared to be deeper than it had ever before been to any of her many suitors. After some time, during which Mr. Maclean maintained a rigid silence, he reappeared; entered into no explanations; vouchsafed no apology. But it seems L. E. L. was satisfied, and the engagement went on. She was not, at first, aware that Mr. Maclean was obliged to return to Cape Coast, and probably expected that after so long a service in so dreadful a climate he would have been promoted to some other post. But it was not to be so; and she heard of his resolution to resume his duties at the colony without changing her determination to marry him.

This all took place in the summer of 1837. Mr. Blanchard states, in his "Memoirs of L. E. L.," that the impediment to their union had been on prudential accounts only, and that never did Mr. Maclean for an instant give credit to the reports against her. Still, another obstacle arose. L. E. L. was informed by a friend that Mr. Maclean was already privately married to a woman of color at Cape Coast. The assertion was distinctly denied, however, by Mr. Maclean: no connection of the kind, he said, existed; nor had any connection of *any* kind existed for a considerable time. There existed, nevertheless, a certain degree of anxiety in the mind of L. E. L. A marriage is legal in England if it has been celebrated according to the rites of the colony in which it has taken place. Mr. Maclean, however, explained himself wholly to the satisfaction of Miss Landon; and she never communicated what had passed between them, nor her annoyance on the subject, to her brother until *after* her marriage.

Preparations were then in progress for their immediate union, and L. E. L. felt a perfect confidence in the truth and honor of Mr. Maclean. She believed him to be free: and her convictions may have been correct.

A brief period of happiness was now her lot. Her health was still precarious, but improving. "Perhaps one reason that I am so recovered is," she wrote to Lady Stepney, "that I am so much happier. All the misery I have suffered for the last few months is past like a dream—one which, I trust in God, I shall never know again. Now my own inward feelings are what they used to be. You would not now have to complain of my despondency." And at this time her admirable novel of "Ethel Churchill" having been most successful, her happiness seemed complete.

On the 7th of June, 1837, she was married to Mr. Maclean, the ceremonial taking place in St. Mary's, Bryanston Square. It was, by Mr. Maclean's wish, so strictly private that even the family with whom L. E. L. resided did not know that it had taken place until a fortnight afterward.* Mr. Landon, the bride's brother, performed the ceremony: Sir Edward Bulwer Lytton gave the bride away. After the service, all who were present at the church, except the bride and bridegroom, made their congratulations and went away. Mr. and Mrs. Maclean went to the Sackville Street Hotel; but on the following day L. E. L. returned to her friend's house, and entered into society, as usual, under her maiden name. It is impossible to avoid suspecting that this arrangement was the result of some fear in Mr. Maclean's mind lest the event should be known too soon at Cape Coast; but the reason he alleged was his dislike to congratulations and festivities, and the great amount of business which he still had to transact at the Colonial Office before his return.

It was on the day of the coronation of Queen Victoria that L. E. L. was last seen on any public occasion in this country. Invitations had been sent to her from most of the best clubs in London to occupy a place at their windows. She chose Crockford's, as being nearest to Piccadilly: she wished to leave as soon as the procession had passed to the Abbey. Some who knew her glanced from their carriage as the unparalleled *cortège* passed down St. James's Street. She wore a white bridal bonnet and a simple muslin dress, and with a party of friends stood in a balcony, waving her handkerchief in the enthusiasm of the moment as the troops appeared. As the last regiment of the gorgeous Lancers rode down the street she suddenly withdrew, and those who were watching her from the opposite window saw her no more.

That evening many friends called on her in Hyde Park Street to bid her farewell. The town was blazing with illuminations, the bells were ringing, the populace was hurrying here and there as L. E. L. received for the last time those she had loved so well. In the morning before, hurried to death, she had nevertheless found time to see Dr. Schloss, the publisher of the "Bijou Almanac," to which she had for some years given her name and poems gratuitously. The simple German shed tears as he thanked her for her liberality, her endeavors to serve him, her sympathy for a poor stranger. L. E. L. was truly charitable. She could not give money, but she gave her time, her toil, wherever there was distress.

In the evening the scene was changed. The gay, the literary friends, the lovely daughters of the house—now, alas! gone save two—the early friend of her girlhood, Sir Edward Lytton Bulwer, Mr. Disraeli, and many others, lingered long to wish her happiness and a safe return. It was understood that she was only to remain three years at Cape Coast, and the delicacy of her lungs rendered it, on that account, even desirable for her to go to a warm climate, as she had been threatened with asthma. At supper, Sir E. L. Bulwer, in a graceful speech, proposed the health of "his daughter," alluding to his having acted as a father at her marriage. The vessel did not sail from Portsmouth until the 5th of July, but on the morning of the 28th of June L. E. L. quitted London forever. So painful and protracted was the parting that she and her companions were too late for the first train. She was much excited by this her first journey by a railroad, and said to Mr. Maclean, "Why don't you have them in Africa?" but toward evening she became much depressed, and a sort of terror seemed to possess her mind at the separation from her brother. Poor L. E. L.! When her brother, during their stay at the inn at Portsmouth, said to her, "What shall you do without your friends to talk to?" "Oh!" she replied, "I shall talk to them through my books." She had already planned work which would require just three years to finish. "Every one," her brother wrote, "was full of hopes, and though, perhaps, they sounded more like doubts, there was no want of cheerfulness at dinner, especially on her part. But the brig was all this time getting away from Spithead, and the captain of the cutter which followed to take Mr. Hugh Maclean and myself back, came below and said we could not stay any longer. All our spirits, real or not, dropped at once. The others went out, and I remained some time with my sister. At last they came down, and took her upon deck. I then perceived that Mrs. Bailey, who had not been before observed by us, was in the adjoining cabin, and I took the opportunity of speaking to her, as the only European female who would be near my sister, and the impression which at the time she made on my mind was that of a woman both kind-hearted and trustworthy. We parted again on leaving the vessel, but nothing more was said. My sister continued standing on the deck and looking toward us as long as I could trace her figure against the sky."

The brig "Maclean," in which Mr. Maclean and L. E. L. sailed, had been fitted up, as far as the accommodation for L. E. L. was concerned, with every attention to her comfort. The weather was fair, and the voyage prosperous. There was nothing more than the ordinary discomforts of a sea voyage; but in so saying, a volume of small miseries is implied. Mrs. Bailey, the wife of the steward of the ship, acted as L. E. L.'s maid; no English servant was permitted to accompany her as a permanent attendant—an arrangement which L. E. L. most bitterly regretted, and which must be forever lamented by her surviving friends. After a time, L. E. L. was sufficiently recovered from sea-sickness to write two of the most exquisite poems that she ever composed—"The Polar Star," and the "Night at Sea." They were transmitted to her friends: the last legacy from the warm heart that, when the poems were read with tears in England, had ceased to beat. She still affixed to them her initials, L. E. L. On the 15th of August she thus wrote to her brother: "Cape Coast Castle. Thank goodness I am on land again. Last night we arrived; the lighthouse became visible, and from that time, gun after gun was fired to attract attention, to say nothing of most ingenious fireworks invented on the spur of the moment. A fishing-boat put off, and in that, about two o'clock at night, Mr. Maclean left the ship, taking them all by surprise, no one supposing he would go through the surf on such a foggy and dark night. I can not tell you my anxiety, but he returned safe, though wet to the skin. We found the secretary dead, poor young man! so that every thing was in utter confusion." This was, indeed, an inauspicious beginning; but it was not until long afterward that the friends of L. E. L. attached any importance to this strange conduct on the part of Mr. Maclean; when his thus going ashore in the dead of the night was a source of some suspicions that he had deemed it necessary to send away from the fort, in which his bride was so soon to take up her abode, some persons probably long established there. But no *fact* of the kind has transpired.

When she landed, L. E. L. was in good health. For some time she wrote cheerfully and favorably of her new home. The next letter to Mr. Blanchard describes the castle and her mode of life. That mode of life was changed, it is true, from the half-sorrowful, half-pleasurable existence of London; but L. E. L. was one who could readily adapt herself to every thing. Her own health continued good, but a severe illness of Mr. Maclean's seemed to cause her much anxiety and fatigue. For four nights she scarcely took any rest; still, and with all the inconveniences of having no competent servant, the amiable, unselfish L. E. L. wrote to her dearest friend, "I can not tell you how much better the place is than we supposed. If I had been allowed to bring a good English servant with me, to which there is not one single objection, I could be as comfortable as possible."

She spoke more highly, too, in that letter, of Mr. Maclean's public character, and the reputation he had for strict justice. Allegations had certainly been made against him in England for cruelty by a Captain Burgoyne, who married a daughter of Lady Elizabeth and Sir Murray Macgregor, and who, with his wife, passed two years at Cape Coast; but these had been silenced, if not refuted.

In subsequent letters Mrs. Maclean's tone regarding her husband changed considerably. Mr. Maclean left her the whole day alone, until seven in the evening, and also intrenched himself in a quarter of the huge fort or castle, where he forbade her to follow him. She confessed that she thought him strange, inert beyond description, very reserved, and never speaking a word more than he could avoid. Still her spirits were good. She spoke of no unkindness. He seemed to leave her to write, or to think, or to wander about the fort just as she pleased.

The total solitude, the absence from loved friends, would have tried the courage of one less elastic than herself, but hers stood the shock.

At the close of the year 1838, the brig "Maclean," in which L. E. L. had sailed for Africa, returned, bringing the tidings of her death. She was well and cheerful on the evening of Sunday, the 14th of October, and had occupied herself in writing to her English friends for several days. On the 15th of the month, Emily Bailey, the stewardess, and her only English attendant, was to return in the "Maclean." Between the hours of eight and nine Mrs. Bailey went to Mrs. Maclean's room in order to give her a note addressed to her by an officer in the colony. She attempted to open the door, but was unable to do so for several minutes, owing to some heavy weight on the inside. When she at last succeeded, she perceived Mrs. Maclean lying on the floor with her face against the door, and with a bottle—an empty bottle—in her hand. There was a slight bruise on the cheek of the dead, or dying, L. E. L. Mrs. Bailey fancied she heard a faint sigh as she leaned over her. She went, however, instantly for her husband, to call Mr. Maclean, who came immediately, and sent directly for advice. The surgeon to the fort, Mr. Cobbold, who came promptly, and Mr. Maclean, carried the body to a bed in the room, and efforts were made to resuscitate life, but wholly in vain.

The bottle was then examined: it had evidently contained prussic acid, and was labeled, "Hydrocyanicum Delatum. Pharm. Lond., 1836." The awe-struck persons in that chamber of death then looked around. A letter was on the table, which she, who lay before them unconscious, had been writing. The ink was scarcely dry with which she had penned those last wörds to her friend, Mrs. Fagan: "*Write about yourself; nothing else half so much interests your affectionate* L. E. Maclean." She had even dated her letters, so composed had been her thoughts, "Cape Coast Castle, Oct. 15." These were the last lines she ever traced.

Mr. Maclean had risen from a bed of sickness to rush to his wife's apartment. He was the last person, except Mrs. Bailey, who had seen her alive. She had gone to his room—which seems, at all events during his illness, not to have been *hers*—to give him some arrow-root; and complaining of weariness, had said she would go to bed again for an hour and a half. What he felt, what he said, how he stood the shock of seeing her, whose last act had been one of kindness to him, a corpse, is not recorded, and no one ever read his countenance.

An inquest was summoned, and depositions taken; and every thing seemed more and more mysterious in proportion to what was disclosed. She had been seen in health the night before; yet Mrs. Bailey stated that she had had spasms, and was in the habit of taking prussic acid for spasms; and he concluded that she must have taken an over-dose that day. Nevertheless, no odor of prussic acid was emitted from the mouth; and the learned—among the rest, the late Robert Liston, then in London—on being applied to, declared that, had she died from prussic acid, "she could not have retained the bottle in her hand: that the muscles would have been relaxed." Mr. Cobbold, the surgeon, merely deposed that the pupils were dilated, the heart still weakly beating, and that he had given ammonia, but in vain. He does not say that the ammonia was swallowed; he does not say that it was rejected.

Then the question arose, where could she have got the prussic acid which, according to Mrs. Bailey, she used so freely? Mr. Maclean stated—"in her medicine chest:" and the assertion went down well at Cape Coast; but when the matter transpired in England, Mr. Squires, of Oxford Street, the chemist, who had prepared and supplied the medicine chest, affirmed that no prussic acid had been supplied in it; and on hunting up all the prescriptions written for L. E. L. by Dr. Thomson, who had alone attended her for fourteen years, it was discovered that prussic acid had never been ordered for L. E. L. either for spasms or for any other disorder.

No post-mortem examination was proposed, or made: the inquest and funeral were all ended in six hours after the lamented L. E. L. had ceased to exist. The verdict of the coroner's inquest was, that the death of Letitia Elizabeth Maclean was "caused by her having incautiously taken an over-dose of prussic acid, which, from evidence, it appears she had been in the habit of taking as a remedy for spasmodic affections to which she was liable."

The names of the coroner and jury are given in Mr. Blanchard's Memoir. All that is put down accurately; but one important fact was omitted, that after her leaving Mr. Maclean's room, a cup of coffee had been handed in to L. E. L. by a little native boy, whose office it was to attend in the gallery or corridor in which her room was situated. Why was this boy not called in evidence? Why was not the cup found, and any portion of its contents, if still in it, analyzed? That cup must have been in the room in which this fatal mishap, or secret poisoning, took place; yet no mention was made of it on the inquest. Whichever it may be set down to—whether to accident or to a dark, designing act—can never now be known, till we stand *there*, where all things are known. The truth has never transpired. Reports even prevailed that the cause of death was suicide; but there was the undried letter—that effusion of affection, to Mrs. Fagan, to give that—the *last* reproach to one so calumniated—the lie. By some, and especially by Mrs. Maclean's afflicted mother, who long survived the blow, it was believed to be an accident. By others it has been suspected that the repudiated wife, or mistress, whose claims so nearly prevented this ill-omened marriage, was in some remote corner of the fortress still; and, as the natives of that coast are wonderful adepts in the art of poisoning, it has been thought that L. E. L. fell a victim to jealousy: and that Mr.

Maclean was anxious, by the hurried and irregular proceedings adopted, to screen her from the consequences, and to prevent disclosures ruinous to himself.

Some years afterward the governor of Cape Coast came to England. He must then have been made fully aware of all that the press had published—the public had said about his wife's mysterious death. Yet he was wise enough never to enter into any justification. The secretary of the colonies, at the time of L. E. L.'s death, was equally forbearing. Lord Normanby and Lord John Russell, successively in office in that department, found, as they wrote to the afflicted brother, "so many difficulties in the way, that they were obliged, with great regret, to abandon their original intention of inquiry." The "difficulties" arose, it is suspected, in the strenuous exertions and promised vote of an active M.P. who had interposed to save his absent friend the annoyance of an inquiry; but the people of England, who look upon L. E. L. as a child of genius all their own, will ever regret that some measures were not taken, in spite of "difficulties," to clear up this dark story.

After Mr. Maclean's death, which happened about six years after that of L. E. L., two young English officers visited Cape Coast: they landed, indeed, chiefly for the purpose of learning all they could about the young poetess, whose name was still remembered, when they were at Cape Coast, as of one to whom all felt respect during her brief sojourn. They tried to gain particulars of Mr. Maclean's last illness. It was long: but never, during that weary journey through the valley of the shadow of death, except once did he breathe *her* name—never did he refer to what must have pained him, the reports about the manner of that death! He requested his secretary to take especial care of a box of papers which he always kept under his bed, and to destroy them after his death, of the certainty of which he was aware.

Mr. Blanchard, in 1841, wrote: "A handsome marblet is on its way, it appears, to Cape Coast Castle, to be erected in the castle, bearing the following inscription:

"Hic jacet sepultum
Omne quod mortale fuit
LETITIÆ ELIZABETHÆ MACLEAN.
Quam egregiâ ornatam indole
Musis præcipue amatam
Omniumque amores secum trahentem
In ipso ætatis flore
Die Octobris XV. A.D. M.D.CCC.XXXVIII.,
Ætat. XXXVI.

Quod spectas, viator, marmor,
Vanum heu doloris monumentum
Conjux mœrens erexit."

"Here lies interred
All that was mortal
Of LETITIA ELIZABETH MACLEAN.
Adorned with a lofty mind,
Singularly favored of the Muses,
And dearly beloved by all,
She was prematurely snatched away
By death, in the flower of her age,
On the 15th of October, 1838,
Aged 36 years.

The marble which you behold, O traveler,
A sorrowing husband has erected:
Vain emblem of his grief!"

Mr. Maclean's body was interred, by his own direction, by that of his wife: and that was the only reference made to L. E. L. by her husband. It was proposed to erect a tablet to the memory of L. E. L. by subscription in that church at Brompton on which she wrote her poem—"The First Grave." But Mrs. Landon's circumstances after her gifted child's death were found to be so indigent, that it was thought better to raise a subscription to support her than to erect a tablet. The late Mrs. Bulwer Lytton and Sir Edward Bulwer Lytton came forward to aid in this last act of respect to L. E. L.'s memory: and Sir E. B. Lytton continued a handsome annual subscription till the death of Mrs. Landon in 1854. Sir Robert Peel assigned to her a small pension of fifteen pounds, all that he had then to bestow out of a fund at the disposal of the prime minister's wife: and these resources, with the aid of her son, who, then a curate only, could only assist, not wholly maintain his poor mother, made her tolerably comfortable during her life. It had been a life of trial; and long before it was the will of God that her spirit should be at rest, she had "longed to be dissolved, and be with God." At length she sank to rest, full of faith and hope, and piously nursed by the niece who had educated L. E. L., and who had sustained her in her many sorrows. Mrs. Landon survived her daughter nearly twenty years: during that wearisome period she was never known either to touch upon the subject of her differences with L. E. L., nor, latterly, to refer to her death.

It will naturally be asked why Mr. Maclean left the mother of his wife to the generosity of friends, to support her after she, who had ever cared for her mother's wants first, was gone.

Mrs. Landon was a woman of an independent spirit. She could not be insensible to the convictions in the mind of others, that her gifted child had not had justice done her *after* death. The hurried inquest, the careless garbled evidence, the pretext of the bottle—all raised suspicions which may have been wholly groundless, but which can not be condemned as unlikely or unnatural. By the brig "Maclean," Mr. Maclean wrote to her, and, referring to the allowance of fifty pounds a year which Mrs. Maclean always made her (though adding to it often considerable sums), he engaged to double that provision, and to give her a hundred pounds a year for her life. Mrs. Landon, in reply, said that, "could she be assured her daughter was *happy* with him, she would thankfully accept that annuity." No answer was returned, nor did Mr. Maclean ever communicate with Mrs. Landon again. When he came to England he did not attempt to see her: nothing that had belonged to L. E. L. was even sent, as is usual in such cases, to her mother, or to any friend or relative.

Such are the unsatisfactory facts appertaining to the sudden close of a life so cherished. Time has not contributed one gleam of light upon an event which is still deplored, for surviving friends: and which even now and then seems to recur to the memory of the public like a painful but half-forgotten dream. We shall never be more enlightened than we are now; but of this, let those who delight in L. E. L.'s exquisite verses be assured, that it was not *suicide* that took her, not, we trust, unprepared from a world she loved well, with all its thorny cares. Had such an idea as that of self-destruction crossed her mind, she would have written to her brother, whom she so fondly loved, in explanation, in extenuation—a farewell, a plea, would have been found in her writing somewhere. But, to show the state of her mind, calm, though pensive, as that of an exile might incline to be, she penned this last letter to a beautiful and intelligent friend, long since, as well as her husband, Colonel Fagan, also deceased.

"My dearest Maria,—I can not but write you a brief account, how I enact the part of a feminine Robinson Crusoe. I must say, it itself, the place is infinitely superior to all I ever even dreamed of. The castle is a fine building; the rooms excellent. I do not suffer from heat; insects there are few or none; and I am in excellent health. The solitude, except an occasional dinner, is absolute: from seven in the morning till seven, when we dine, I never see Mr. Maclean, and rarely any one else. We were welcomed by a series of dinners which I am glad are over, for it is very awkward to be the only lady; still the great kindness with which I have been treated, and the very pleasant manners of many of the gentlemen, make me feel it as little as possible. Last week we had a visit from Captain Castle, of the 'Pylades.' His story is very melancholy. He married, six months before he left England, one of the Miss Hills, Sir John Hill's daughter, and she died just as he received orders to return home. We had also a visit from Colonel Bosch, the Dutch governor, a most gentlemanlike man. But fancy how awkward the next morning: I can not induce Mr. Maclean to rise, and I have to make breakfast, and do the honors of adieu to him and his officers; white plumes, mustaches, and all. I think I never felt more embarrassed. I have not yet felt the want of society in the least. I do not wish to form new friends, and never does a day pass without thinking most affectionately of my old ones. On three sides we are surrounded by the sea. I like the perpetual dash upon the rocks; one wave comes up after another, and is forever dashed in pieces, like human hopes that only swell to be disappointed. We advance—up springs the shining froth of love or hope, a moment white, and gone forever! The land view, with its cocoa and palm trees, is very striking; it is like a scene in the 'Arabian Nights.' Of a night the beauty is very remarkable; the sea is of a silvery purple, and the moon deserves all that has been said in her favor. I have only once been out of the fort by daylight, and then was delighted. The salt lakes were first dyed a deep crimson by the setting sun, and as we returned they seemed a faint violet in the twilight, just broken by a thousand stars, while before us was the red beacon-light. The chance of sending this letter is a very sudden one, or I should have ventured to write to General Fagan, to whom I beg the very kindest regards. Dearest, do not forget me. Pray write to me, 'Mrs. George Maclean, Cape Coast Castle, care of Messrs. Foster and Smith, 5 New City Chambers, Bishopsgate Street.' Write about yourself—nothing else half so much interests

"Your very affectionate L. E. Maclean.

"Cape Coast Castle, Oct. 15th."

No one who reads this letter can doubt the collected mind, the clear memory, the reasonable emotion with which it was written. There is not a single exaggerated expression in the whole composition. She even gives her direction to her friend, as if she contemplated the certainty of a continued correspondence.

To conclude with her own exquisite lines:

"The future never renders to the past
The young beliefs intrusted to its keeping;
Inscribe one sentence—life's first truth and last—
On the pale marble where our dust is sleeping:
We might have been."

THE POET'S EXILE: L. E. L. AT CAPE COAST CASTLE.

MADAME DE SEVIGNÉ.

A Frenchwoman with none of the vices and little of the frivolity of Frenchwomen, a true Louis-Quatorzienne, without the prejudices of that reign, a woman of society, and one of its leaders, yet a prodigy of domestic affections, a frequenter of the court but a lover of the fields, a wit without attempting it, and a great writer without knowing it, Marie de Sévigné has justly won the admiration of every great man who appreciates wit and honors virtue. Even the satirical Saint-Simon can find nothing to say against her, but praises her ease, her natural graces, her goodness, and her knowledge. Horace Walpole, himself the prince of letter-writers, made an idol of her, and tried to copy her style, which he considered as his finest model. Of her very portrait he says, enthusiastically: "I am going to build an altar for it, under the title of Notre Dame des Rochers," in allusion to her country-house in Brittany, Les Rochers. Mackintosh is loud in her praises. He read her letters while in India, and his journal has frequent notices of them. "She has so filled my heart," he says, "with affectionate interest in her, as a living friend, that I can scarcely bring myself to think of her as being a writer, or having a style; but she has become a celebrated, probably an immortal writer, without expecting it." Of her easy yet forcible style, he says, in speaking of a passage in one of her letters, "Tacitus and Machiavel could have said nothing better." But Lamartine, one of her latest biographers, is perhaps her greatest admirer. He views her with a poet's eyes, and calls her "almost a poetess," and "the Petrarch of French prose." He sees in her the one great instance, that has come down to us in literature, of maternal devotion, and, as an embodiment of this idea, has not hesitated to count her among the great civilizers of the world, and to place her name side by side with those of Socrates, Homer, Milton, Bossuet, and Fénelon. To a less romantic vision this excessive devotion to a daughter, "*qui ne la méritait que médiocrement*," says Saint-Simon, may appear like a weakness, still more so when contrasted with her indifference to her son; and it is perhaps rather as a woman of the world, standing out virtuous and sensible in an age of universal vice and extravagance of opinions, that the English reader will prefer to contemplate Madame de Sévigné.

Her life has indeed two sides, the romantic and the practical. Her early life, her devotion to her husband, and her absorbing passion for her daughter, belong to the former. The rest is so sober, that some have called her cold, and even her greatest admirers confessed her lukewarm.

In the old abbey-house of Livry, in the forest of Bondi, near Paris, there lived, about the year 1642, an old man and a young girl, like a dusty, black-letter folio lit up by a stray sunbeam, when the bookcase is opened. Christophe de Coulanges is the Abbé of Livry, a worthy old man, visited from time to time by men of learning, and, though of severe piety, not quite separated from the outer world. His niece, Marie de Rabutin, is an orphan of fifteen, his charge and his pupil. This young girl is indeed a joy in his quiet house. Her face alone is beautiful. The fresh delicate complexion, the oval form, the features regular if not classical, the rich abundance of fair hair, are all in themselves enough for beauty. La Fontaine wrote of her—

> "With bandaged eyes you seem the God of Love;
> His mother, when those eyes illume the face."

But those large blue eyes, dreamy one moment with falling lids, and the next lit up with thought and mirth, are the centre-fires of the whole, and in them the expression is forever changing. Add to this a slight and graceful figure, and it is easy to understand that even her beauty dazzled the world of Paris at her first appearance. And this girl, beautiful and gay as she is, is now studying Greek and Latin with her old uncle, now receiving learned lessons from Ménage and Chapelain, and collecting a stock of erudition which was to fit her in after life for the companionship of men whose names are classical.

It is remarkable that a woman, who, if she had nothing further to distinguish her, would remain to the world as the type of a mother's devotion, should not only have been left motherless when six years old, but have had a grandmother so little aware of maternal duty, that she could abandon her young children to enter a convent, though her son threw himself across the threshold of her house to prevent her departure, for which act, and the building eighty convents, the Church of Rome thought fit to canonize her. The husband of this infatuated woman was Christophe de Rabutin, Baron de Chantal and Seigneur de Bourbilly, which lies near Semur, in the department of the Côte d'Or, and between thirty and forty miles from Dijon. The family was old and respectable, but not one of the great families of France. The son of this Christophe married a Mademoiselle Coulanges, daughter of an influential house. Their only child was Marie, afterward Madame de Sévigné. She was born at Paris on the 5th of February, 1626, and brought up at the Château de Bourbilly. In 1628, her father died in the defense of the Ile de Rhé against the English; and not long after his widow followed him, leaving the little child of six years old with no nearer relative, on her father's side, than her grandmother, who, as indifferent to her grandchild as she had been to her own children, left her to the care of a maternal uncle, the Abbé de Coulanges. At Livry, of which she so often speaks in her letters, she passed the next nine years of her life, under the protection of this uncle, thus escaping that education of the convent to which young girls were then subjected, and of which she afterward herself expressed her disapproval.

At fifteen the beautiful Mademoiselle de Rabutin-Chantal, sole heiress to an estate of three hundred thousand francs, was introduced by the De Coulanges to the court and court circles of Paris, and was at once pronounced fascinating. She had indeed qualities which made such a verdict universal. It was not only the gay and light who were charmed with her mirth and beauty; the more serious found in her a fund of solid learning after the fashion of those times, and a power and taste for reflection. And these qualities were set in the yet more valuable attributes of a rare modesty free from all prudery, and a good heart ready for the cultivation of friendship.

The young girl was beset with candidates for her hand, among whom were members of the noblest families in France. Her choice was unfettered. She was an orphan, an only child, and an heiress; and there is therefore every reason to believe that the choice she made was that of her own heart. It does but add one instance more to the hundreds that might be quoted of women actuated in this most solemn matter purely by fancy. Young as she was, for she was married at seventeen, Marie de Rabutin had sufficient perception of character already not to be misled by mere appearances, or dazzled by external attractions. Yet the Marquis de Sévigné was a man who had little but these to offer. Handsome, dashing, and courageous, he was at the same time selfish, sensual, and incapable of a sincere attachment. He accepted the devotion she offered him with careless indifference; and, insensible alike to her superiority of mind and integrity of character, threw her over for acquaintances utterly unworthy of comparison with his young wife. He was of an old Breton family, and a *maréchal de camp*, and held a good position at court. To add to this, he was a relation and favorite of the Cardinal de Retz, then coadjuteur to the Archbishop of Paris; and the Abbé de Coulanges, influenced by these considerations, favored rather than opposed the match.

The Cardinal de Retz was at that time the rising star in

France. Richelieu had been dead about two years: his mantle had descended on the shoulders of Mazarin; but there was already a party formed against the crafty Italian, and Paul de Gondy, then about thirty years old, was on the look-out for an opportunity of putting himself forward. Richelieu had already pronounced him a "dangerous spirit," on reading his book, "The Conjuration de Fiesque," which De Gondy had written when eighteen years of age. On the death of his uncle, in 1643, he was made Archbishop of Paris. Like his predecessors, he had been destined for a courtier or a soldier, rather than a priest. Richelieu was educated for the army, Mazarin served in it: De Gondy was forced to take orders against his will, and had passed his early days in duels and gallantries. Like his predecessors, again, he was a man of ambition, but, unlike them, he had no definite purpose in view. He caballed and plotted more for the pleasure of being in the opposition than to gain a step toward an end. The power he obtained was immense, but he trifled with it. Wavering and hot-headed, he rushed into new intrigues while the old ones were yet incomplete; and while for a time he was more popular than either Richelieu or Mazarin had ever been, he failed to make use of the advantage, and wasted his energies in petty enterprises. Yet he seems to have been a lovable character, and in after years Madame de Sévigné, who saw more of him than any one else, was much attached to her "dear cardinal." Her intimacy with him was afterward fatal to her favor at court. Louis XIV. hated nothing so much as the recollection of the *Fronde*, in which De Retz had taken so prominent a part, and this dislike he extended even to the cardinal's friends.

Monsieur de Sévigné then might be considered certain of promotion from his connection with the cardinal, and the marriage was therefore looked upon as a good one. It was destined to prove very different.

The life of a Frenchwoman then, as much as in the present day, began with marriage; and Madame de Sévigné entered upon hers in an age of great promise, the forerunner of the Augustan age of France. The turbulent ministry of Richelieu was followed by a reaction in favor of letters, learning, and the measures of peace. Anne of Austria was guided by the wily but conciliating Mazarin; and the factions which had disturbed France so long were reduced for a time to mere intrigues of court. The society of Paris had at length breathing space from stormy politics, and turned to the softer allurements of wit and letters. This society, circling round the court, influenced and controlled by it, yet possessed a freedom of thought which has been little known in France since those days. The

THE HÔTEL DE RAMBOUILLET.

great men of the age of Louis Quatorze were still young, but the Cid of Corneille and the Maxims of La Rochefoucauld were already in the mouths of all readers. On the other hand, vice was rampant, encouraged by the example of the court, and religion was reduced to bigotry or asceticism. Priests ruled the court, and were foremost in its luxurious sensuality. When repentance came, as it often did with the decline of power or the decay of beauty, the penitent rushed from a world where all was so hollow, and where their attraction was no longer felt, and hid their heads in convents or monasteries, which rivaled one another in the severity of their asceticism. Port Royal and La Trappe were living sepulchres, where elegant courtiers and gallant reprobates mortified the flesh they had spared nothing to indulge, and thought to pacify Heaven by the torture of their long-pampered bodies. It was an age of extravagance in feeling, and prejudice in thought. The people were despised, "the country" identified with the king. France was the court, Paris the small circle of courtiers who hovered round it.

The chief centre of this circle at this period was the Hôtel de Rambouillet: Madame de Rambouillet, a Florentine by birth, and connected with the Medici, had brought with her to Paris a love of Italian poetry and a pardon for Italian licentiousness. She gathered round her all the lovers of literature, and admitted, at the same time, the lovers of life who crowded in from the court. They talked of the virtues of Greece and Rome, and exemplified in themselves the vices of France. Hither came Mazarin to play cards and talk bad French; De Retz and a whole host of love-making abbés in his wake. Here La Rochefoucauld observed human nature in the narrow sphere which is the "world" in his Maxims, and made love to *les beaux yeux* of the Duchesse de Longueville, politician and authoress. Here came the great magistrates and dignitaries of state, headed by the magnificent swindler Fouquet the financier, whose acquaintance Madame de Sévigné probably made in these salons. The "dignity of wit," which was then as high, if not higher, a title than office to the popularity of these circles, was represented by all the talkers of the day, among them being conspicuous two near relations of Madame de Sévigné. Monsieur de Coulanges, a cousin on her mother's side, was a merry little man, celebrated for telling, or rather acting, a good story, which always set the company in a roar of laughter. De Bussy-Rabutin, a connection on her father's side, was almost as popular a letter-writer as Madame de Sévigné herself. He was a gallant of the first water, always pushing intrigues, always repulsed, and always visiting his repellers with the lash of satire, and the yet more cowardly weapon of calumny. Vain to excess, he was also contemptibly servile, and when sent into exile by Louis Quatorze, he could not endure his fate with noble resignation, but attacked the monarch with slavish entreaties and nauseous flattery.

But the cream of the society at the Hôtel de Rambouillet was that knot of absurd blue-stockings, whom Molière annihilated in his "Précieuses Ridicules"—a name derived from a habit which these classical ladies had of addressing one another as "*ma précieuse.*" Of these female pedants Mademoiselle Scudéry, the authoress of terrible romances in ten or twelve volumes, in which Cyrus or Ibrahim was the hero, and warriors of the ancient world talked and acted much in the same strain as the ornaments of the Regency, was *facile princeps.* Around the "incomparable Sappho," as this lady was called, in her set, were gathered a number of learned individuals of the same cast: Julie, the daughter of Madame de Rambouillet, christened by the "*précieuses*" "the incomparable Artemis," and Pellisson, the ugliest man of his day, of whom Boileau wrote

"L'or même a Pellisson donne un teint de beauté;"

and who, after having tamed spiders in the Bastile for five years, was rewarded by Mademoiselle de Scudéry with the character of Acante in her novels, were among the most celebrated. The "*précieuses*" and their male admirers talked classics, composed and (cruel torture!) read sonnets and epigrams, exchanged compliments with elaborate allusions to Augustus, Alcibiades, Artaxerxes, or any other hero of antiquity, and believed themselves to be the only really educated and truly gifted people in France. In later days Mademoiselle de Scudéry transferred the same society to her own house; but at this time the "*précieuses*" thronged the Hôtel de Rambouillet in great numbers, where Madame de Rambouillet, to save herself the trouble of accompanying every visitor through the antechamber, often received them in bed, as Mazarin afterward did his own guests. This troublesome custom of going a certain length with your guest, according to his or her rank, was at that time imperative, and is still kept up in some old-fashioned circles in Paris. Saint-Simon relates an anecdote of some nobleman who was very precise on this point, and annoyed his visitors with it so much, that at last one of them locked the door upon him as he went out; but the polite host was not to be so eluded, and positively got out of the window in order to make his guest the proper farewell bow at the front door.

Into this mixed coterie of pedants and prudes on the one

hand, and unprincipled pleasure-seekers on the other, the young Marquise de Sévigné was introduced, with wit enough to make her an object with the one, and beauty enough to render her a victim of the other set. Sense and modesty contrived to triumph over the temptations of both. Though she is sometimes included in the lists of "*les précieuses*," she had quite good taste enough to laugh at their rhapsodical absurdities; and, on the other hand, her strong principle, which her enemies designated coldness, enabled her to overcome the allurements of the other extreme.

Nor was she exempt from trials. Already her worthless husband had proved his indifference to her in a series of intrigues for which there was no excuse. She was left very much alone in her domestic life; and yet in an age when vice was the rule, virtue the exception, she maintained the high purity of her reputation. It is a curious proof of the feeling of that age, that Madame de Sévigné could accept as friends the very men whom she rejected as lovers. Among these the principal were the magnificent Fouquet, of whom Boileau wrote—

"Jamais surintendant ne trouva de cruelles;"

Madame de Sévigné making an exception to his successes; the Prince de Conti, the Comte du Lude, a noted lady-killer, and Bussy-Rabutin, of whom we have spoken, and who, when his fair cousin rejected his vile suit, revenged himself by calumnies which no one, fortunately for her, would believe.

Yet in after years Madame de Sévigné was a devoted friend to Fouquet, and corresponded on easy terms with Bussy-Rabutin. What a story does this tell of the depravity of that age! Nay, she even went further, and appears to have herself agreed to the verdict of her age which pronounced her virtue to be mere insensibility. Far from being proud of having rejected these suitors, she seems sorry that she was compelled to offend them in so doing, and excuses rather than glories in their rejection. Certainly her correctness, from whatever cause it arose, is much to her honor. Temptation, encouragement, and example surrounded her on every side. Propriety of conduct was not only an exception in those circles, but an odious exception. The woman who would not be as bad as her neighbors drew upon herself their envy and hatred. She was denounced as a prude, a prig, one who set herself up to be superior, and so forth. Such humors, so they were regarded, were fit, not for society, but for the cloister. Thither let her carry her virtue, if she chose, but not intrude it where it could only suggest disagreeable comparisons. Such was the feeling of the day, and for such judgments it was but poor consolation to be compared by "*les précieuses*" of the Hôtel Rambouillet to some high-featured Lucretia of classical history.

Then, again, Madame de Sévigné's admirers were not men of ordinary stamp. Fouquet's ill-gotten wealth, De Conti's rank, Du Lude's handsome face, and Bussy's insolence, were such high recommendations among the ladies of the court, that it was an honor, rather than a disgrace, to be singled out by them, and Madame de Sévigné's rejection of these lady-killers was set down to pride or obstinacy.

No one could imagine all the time—for it was too strange an idea to enter into any body's head—that Madame de Sévigné, gay, charming, and beautiful as she was, was still in love with her husband; and had any one supposed it for a moment, the cruel conduct of this man would have made such a devotion appear extravagant in their eyes. Madame de Sévigné did not reproach him, but secretly mourned over his inconstancy, and hoped for an ultimate improvement. To effect this, she, with much difficulty, persuaded him about two years after their marriage to quit the temptations of Paris and retire with her to their château at "Les Rochers," in Brittany, in the neighborhood of Vitré. We can well understand that this step was dictated by nothing but the desire of recalling to herself her estranged husband. To quit Paris at nineteen, in the zenith of her success, when her beauty was fresher and fuller than it could ever be again, would have been to any Frenchwoman like a voluntary entrance of purgatory; but to quit it for a lonely château, in a dark, foggy, ungenial country; to leave all the wit, mind, and spirit of the Place Royale for the heavy platitudes of half-drunken hunters, or the tittle-tattle of rustics who had never emerged from their narrow district, and, Chinese-like, recognized no world beyond it, must have been trying to any woman of mind. Yet Madame de Sévigné seems to have been quite happy in here enjoying for a time the careless affection of a man to whom she was passionately attached. The young wife was satisfied if she could only have him to herself; she did not ask for much love, knowing that he could not and would not give it her.

Here, then, the young couple, he twenty-four and she only twenty, passed the succeeding three years with just so much society as the neighborhood afforded, which, if any comparison can be made between Brittany of the present day and Brittany of two centuries ago, was very little. In March, 1647, her first child was born, that only son, of whom, in after days, she wrote so amusingly, and who seems to have mingled a very small share of his mother's good sense with the extravagant love of dissipation which he inherited from his father. But the following year was yet more blessed by the birth of that daughter, afterward Madame de Grignan, to whom she addressed her famous letters, and for whom she felt—if indeed there is no affectation in her style—an affection which has been extolled as the *ne plus ultra* of maternal tenderness.

Her happiness, however, was not to be long-lived. In 1648, not long after the birth of this second child, there broke out in France that incomprehensible and apparently most useless revolt, which goes by the name of "La Fronde." At the head of the movement was Madame de Sévigné's friend and her husband's relative, the Cardinal de Retz. The rise of De Gondy, the cardinal, had been rapid. Vincent de Paul had been his tutor, yet how little had he profited by the lessons of that great man—if we may not say, great saint? Little more, indeed, than to acquire the art of conversion. De Gondy used it to turn a Huguenot into a Romanist; and Louis XIII., delighted with his success, appointed him the coadjuteur of the Archbishop of Paris. In 1643, at the age of twenty-nine, the young schemer was raised to the archiepiscopal chair. No longer able with dignity to indulge in the extravagances of vice, he had recourse to those of political intrigue. Mazarin was his main point of attack. He courted and gained the affections of the people; and unable openly, from his position, to wage war against his rival, he encouraged the popular discontent, seized the opportunity of an *émeute* in 1648, and using the Duc de Beaufort as his lay instrument, to carry out his own machinations, developed it speedily into a civil war.

This was now raging, and the Marquis de Sévigné, as a soldier in the royal service, was recalled from his retirement in Brittany to his duties in the capital. This was unfortunate for his poor wife. At his request she returned to Paris with her children, but only to experience fresh slights, and endure new insults from her inconstant husband. Among the famous women of Paris—famous for beauty, wit, and want of modesty—Ninon de l'Enclos was at that time the most notorious. Though openly depraved, she was not entirely excluded from the higher ranks of society: Madame de Maintenon, herself irreproachable, was not ashamed to be her intimate friend and companion; and it is curious to find Madame de Sévigné speaking of her familiarly as "Ninon." With this person Monsieur de Sévigné fell, or affected to fall, in love, and dissipated his fortune for her worthless smiles. It was in vain that his neglected wife sought to recall him; and at last she yielded to the advice of her former guardian, the Abbé de Coulanges, and after making an arrangement for a separate maintenance, retired with her children to Les Rochers, leaving her husband to his profligate life in Paris. We have no means of ascertaining what efforts the wife did really make to save her wretched husband; but if these seem to have been slight, insufficient, and unworthy of the deep attachment she felt for him, we must remember, in palliation, how much the ideas of that age differed from our own on these subjects. As we shall afterward see, in speaking of her son, Madame de Sévigné, like the rest of the then world, looked on such attachments as follies rather than vices, and perhaps the danger of her husband's *soul* was the last thought that entered her mind. As to her attachment, there can be little doubt that, constant only in inconstancy, the Marquis de Sévigné had at last chilled it by his conduct. But whatever she may have felt, the punishment that followed to her and to him disarms us of all reproaches.

She had not been long in retirement at Les Rochers when she received a letter which felled her to the ground. Her husband, she was told, was desperately wounded. In the course of a scandalous intrigue he had run athwart the ambition of the young Chevalier d'Albret, another dissolute courtier; a quarrel had arisen; a duel had followed, and this was the result. Madame de Sévigné wrote to her husband a letter of tender reproaches and woman-like forgiveness. The news was false. The quarrel had indeed taken place—the duel had been arranged—but it had not yet come off. The letter of his wife may have brought some remorse into the profligate's heart, but could not avert the catastrophe. The misnamed "honor" of the age demanded the blood of one or other of the foes. They met and fought, and De Sévigné fell. He was in his twenty-seventh year, and left behind him a wife of twenty-three and two young children.

Thus closed the first romance of Marie de Rabutin's life. She had loved and chosen this man from her heart. She had forgiven his inconstancy, and endured his neglect. He was now taken from her, slain in a quarrel for a woman unfit to be her rival. So completely had he neglected her, that she had nothing of his to cherish as a relic; and in her grief and love was fain to demand, from the very woman for whom he had abandoned her, his portrait and a lock of his hair. Her grief, indeed, was so intense that we are told that in after years she could never meet his antagonist (if we may not say his murderer) without falling into a swoon. He had absorbed all her love, and she was one of those women whose passion has but one centre. When that was gone, and grief, after long years, had calmed down, the passion still survived in a maturer form, and the deep love of the wife passed into a calmer yet as powerful attachment for her—and his—child; and it is only thus that we can account for her devotion to her daughter, Madame de Grignan.

The reckless Marquis de Sévigné had squandered his own fortune and his wife's on worthless objects, and Madame de Sévigné found it necessary to retrench for several years. She now devoted herself to the education of her children, and passed her time chiefly at the house of the old Abbé de Coulanges, her first protector. But she well knew that her son would require that personal interest at the court through which alone came fortune and promotion, and she resolved to return to Paris. Some four or five years after her husband's death she again entered the salons of Paris, a young widow of seven-and-twenty, as beautiful as ever, and celebrated for her wit and *abandon*.

The court of Louis Quatorze was now in its highest glory. The great men of every tone and taste who had been young ten years before were now risen into eminence; and Madame de Sévigné could soon count the best of them among her friends and correspondents. Corneille, Racine, Molière, La Fontaine, and Boileau were the poets and satirists with whom she talked and laughed. Her more serious thoughts were imparted to or drawn out by the two Arnaulds, the founders of Port-Royal and fathers of Jansenism, with their pupil, the suffering, patient, and delicate Pascal; and by the grandest preachers of the century, Bourdaloue, Mascaron, and Bossuet. Among her heroes were the restless De Retz; the heroic Scotchman Montrose, then an exile; La Rochefoucauld, the author of the "Maxims;" Marshal Turenne; Le Grand Colbert; Condé; and more of the great and pseudo-great men of the Augustan age of France. The ladies with whom she mixed have names scarcely less historic. There were the Duchess de Longueville, the political intriguant of the Fronde; the penitent La Vallière; the heartless, but respectable Madame de Maintenon; Madame de Montespan; the Countess d'Olonne, daughter of Madame de Rambouillet; and another star of the *précieuses*, Madame de La Fayette, the authoress of "Zaïde" and other novels, but more celebrated as the devoted friend of La Rochefoucauld, of whom she said, "Il m'a donné son esprit, mais j'ai reformé son cœur," which, if a true boast, was not an insignificant one. As Madame de Sévigné was a woman of no little perception, her opinions of some of these contemporaries, as we find them in her letters, will not be without interest.

With regard to the poets, the French have found fault with her for setting Corneille so far above Racine. This was undoubtedly the fashion of the day, as she herself tells us, and

Madame de Sévigné may have been influenced by it; but, whatever the common taste in France, there are eminent judges in England who find more nature and truer passion in the older tragedian. She admired Racine extremely, especially his "Bajazet" and "Esther." Of the former she says: "The character of Bajazet is frigid; the customs of the Turks are not correctly observed; they don't make so much fuss about marrying; the crisis is not well prepared, and one can not enter into the causes of this great butchery; however, there are some good things in it, but nothing perfectly good, nothing to elevate, none of those bursts which make us shudder in Corneille's pieces." Again she says of Racine, "He composes plays for La Champmêlé" (an actress with whom he was in love, and to whom he taught her parts), "but not for future ages. Long life, then, to our old friend Corneille; let us forgive him a few bad verses in consideration of the divine bursts which carry us away; they are master-strokes which can not be imitated. Boileau says even more of him than I do."

As an instance of the flattery to which even genius stooped in speaking to a monarch who loved adulation more than any thing, she relates an answer made by Racine to Louis Quatorze, when the sovereign expressed his regret that the poet had not accompanied the army in its last campaign. "Sire," said Racine, "we had none but town clothes, and had ordered others to be made, but the places you attacked were all taken before they could be finished." "This," adds Madame de Sévigné, "was pleasantly received."

Boileau and La Fontaine were both great favorites with Madame de Sévigné. The fables of the latter were even then learned by heart and recited in society, as they still are among old-fashioned people in France. Of the famous satirist Boileau she said to his face that "he was tender in prose, but cruel in verse;" a very true verdict, for he was as amiable in private life as he was bitter on paper.

All the Arnaulds were friends of Madame de Sévigné, but she was most intimate with Arnauld d'Andilly and his son the Marquis de Pomponne. The family of Arnaulds—the most respectable, most learned, and most religious in France at that period—has been identified with the famous Society of Port-Royal, and this, again, with the anti-Jesuit doctrines of Jansenism. The progress of that society was, in fact, owing to them. In 1625 the nuns of a convent called Port-Royal des Champs, near Paris, found that the site, owing to the marshes, was too pestilential to remain in, and were forced to quit their establishment. Madame Arnauld, a rich widow, and the mother of the commissary-general, Arnauld d'Andilly, and the famous Bishop of Angers, bought for them the Hôtel de Clugny in Paris, and with her daughter as abbess, gave to the new establishment the name of Port-Royal of Paris. She herself and six of her daughters, besides her granddaughter, La Mère Angélique, who was the abbess of Port-Royal, were all inmates of this convent, and were noted for their austere virtues and unparalleled learning. Richelieu said of them that they were as pure as angels, but as proud as demons.

In 1637 two young men, M. Lemaitre, a lawyer, and M. de Serricourt, an officer in the army, agreed that the world was all vanity, and that happiness was only to be found in pious solitude. Such was, indeed, the religion of the day, and such it always is when society reaches that point of civilization where vice and luxury take the place of manly exertion. It was the spirit of the early Christians, who saw with disgust the profligacy and effeminacy of Greece and Rome; and it was almost the spirit of our own Puritans who recoiled from the license of the courts of James and Charles. Asceticism is a feature peculiar to civilization. It is a reaction in favor of manliness. Unknown to rude ages in stirring life, and unnecessary to ages of purer and really higher civilization, it seems to mark those which are distinguished for their extravagance, luxury, and profligacy. It is an indignant rebound from effeminate vices into a simplicity of life which, whatever else may be said of it, appears to be manly from the very courage and self-denial which it exacts. But it is no less extravagant than that which it flees; it is no less an unnatural and even diseased condition, and it is only such an age as those in which it occurs that can mistake it for religion. "The greater the sinner, the greater," indeed, "the saint." The ascetics of all ages have been generally the worst of men before their change; they only exchange one luxury for another, and in the intensity of self-torture they find a comfort, almost, one may say, an ease (for habit makes it so), which exempts them from the far more trying exercise of true religion. It requires little discernment to perceive that it is far easier to live on bread and water in an obscure cell, tearing one's flesh with knotted cords, than to meet temptation in an open field and there resist it.

But an extravagant age naturally confounds an extravagance with religion, and the ascetics of the days of Louis Quatorze were admired by the court, whose members probably intended, when youth, beauty, and fashion had left them, to follow in their steps, and pacify an evil conscience by almost childish severities. At the time that Madame de Sévigné wrote, a noted instance of sudden conversion had taken place. The young and handsome De Rancé was the most dissipated of all the dissipated abbés of that priest-haunted court. His excesses were the talk even of people who were too accustomed to excesses to notice them. In 1657 the small-pox was raging in Paris, and about the same time the abbé was desperately in love with Madame de Montbazon, a celebrated beauty. Calling on her one day, he found the servants away and the doors open, and walked up to her room without waiting to be announced. He opened the door, and in a leaden coffin beheld the headless form of the lady he had loved so passionately. On the ground by its side was the once beautiful head itself, now a hideous mask. The small-pox had attacked her in its most violent form, and in a few hours she was dead. Her servants, dreading the contagion, had sent for the first coffin that could be found. It was too short, and they had resorted to the horrid expedient of decapitation to meet the difficulty. Her lover had come in at the very moment that they were gone to fetch a hearse to carry the body away. He staggered back from the awful sight, and escaping from the house, vowed to bury himself alive for the rest of his days. And he did so.

In the centre of a dense huge forest near Evreux, in Normandy, is a close narrow valley, still as a grave and dark as a pit. Around it the jealous cliffs rise high and steep, and the forest itself penetrates into the abyss, as if to add to its gloomy darkness. In the bottom of it eleven foul and stagnant pools load the heavy air with sickness, and in the middle of these there stood the once famous monastery of La Trappe. It was a den of thieves. The monks, secure in their foul pit, far from the world, and protected by the pathless forest, issued in lawless bands at night, armed to the teeth, and, concealing themselves along the highway, rushed out to plunder the unsuspecting traveler. They were known in the province as "The bandits of La Trappe."

Among these men De Rancé went alone, unarmed, and little by little gained an ascendency over their minds, till he brought them, one after another, to quit their lawless life, and return to one of asceticism. But the rules he enjoined could not but be severe, and he made them more and more so. Bread, water, and vegetables was all their food. The furniture of their cells was replaced by a truckle-bed of rope, a rug, and a human skull. The silence of the gloomy valley was doubled by the terrible silence imposed for the sake of security on its half-dead inhabitants. The stalwart but now wasting figures of the once lawless monks passed one another without a word. Their sealed tongues were loosed only for one hour on Sunday, and then it was to speak on matters of faith and doctrine. The world was, or seemed to be, forgotten; shut out, foregone forever. None knew his fellow's name, except the abbot himself. Each new-comer took a new name when he renounced the world, and once a father and a son lived there together unknown to each other till the latter died. It was then that on his tombstone the father read the young man's name, and recognized his son. Pain and self-torture were courted as redemptives, and De Rancé once turned away a novice because he noticed that, while weeding, he pushed aside the nettles, to prevent being stung!

In such a grave did De Rancé bury himself, and the Trappists were the wonder and the admiration of the age.

It is not therefore surprising that the example of Lemaitre and Serricourt should have been eagerly followed by the courtiers and gallants whose consciences were pricked. In a short time they had a large band of companions, renouncing the world, and bent on learning and good works, and these men called themselves the Society of Port-Royal. They differed from monks in being bound by no vows, and wearing no peculiar dress. Their clothing was plain; their lives simple and penitential; their time given to study and the care of the poor. They soon increased in such numbers that, finding their house in Paris too small, they retired to the convent of Port-Royal des Champs, which had been abandoned by its nuns. Here they set to work to drain and cultivate the valley, and the once gay courtiers were transformed to laborers and mechanics, gardeners and carpenters, and had to wield spade and mattock in the delicate white hands which had hitherto handled only the sword or played with a lady's fan. They soon became fashionable saints. The court ladies poured out their sorrows and sins to them, and received very blunt wholesome advice in return; and parents of all ranks sent their children to be educated by them. Their system of tuition, and the grammars they prepared, are still upheld and even employed in France and Switzerland. Madame de Sévigné, who visited Port-Royal des Champs in 1674, when the nuns had returned there once more, calls it a paradise, and says that "holiness extends for a league all round it." "The nuns are angels on earth," she adds, with a touch of her usual levity; "it is a hideous valley, just fitted to inspire a taste for working out one's salvation;" a truly Louis-Quatorzian idea.

Arnauld d'Andilly entered the *confrèrie* at the age of fifty-five, after passing his life in court and camp, holding the appointment of commissary-general. When Madame de Sévigné knew him, in 1671, he was a very old man. She relates an interview which she had with him at Pomponne, his son's house. Her "*bon homme*," as she affectionately calls him, proved his good sense in the serious conversation that followed. "He said that I was a pretty heathen; that I made an idol of you in my heart; that this kind of idolatry was as dangerous as any other, although it might seem to me less heinous; and that, in short, I should look to myself." He talked to her for six hours, but does not seem to have cured her, though what he said is precisely what any modern reader must think when he reads her extravagant phrases of affection for her indifferent daughter. Arnauld d'Andilly had two sons and five nephews, all members of the Society of Port-Royal.

Among these the chief friend of Madame de Sévigné was the Marquis de Pomponne, one of his sons. He was a man of great capabilities, and an honorable, dignified character. He held the post of secretary of state for foreign affairs from 1671 to 1679, when he was dismissed, and retired to Pomponne, where Madame de Sévigné and his friends constantly visited him. Pascal, the disciple of the Arnaulds, the mathematician, philosopher, and saint, was another of Madame de Sévigné's heroes. A paralytic stroke at eighteen deprived him of the use of his limbs, and from that time he was never free from suffering: yet not contented with this, he became a recluse, and, to complete his torments, wore a belt of pointed iron. His "Pensées" were the admiration of every reader, and Boileau thought them better than any thing ancient or modern. Madame de Sévigné gives an anecdote on this subject. Boileau was dining with a Jesuit, and the Jesuits, as is known, detested the Jansenists, among whom Pascal was counted. The conversation turned on ancient authors, when Boileau exclaimed that he knew of a modern one superior to them all. The Jesuit asked him who it was. Boileau did not like to say. "You have read his book, I am sure," said he. The Jesuit pressed him to reveal the name, and the company joining with them, Boileau at last exclaimed—"M. Pascal." "Pascal!" cried the Jesuit, red with rage; "oh! Pascal is as good as any thing false can be." "False!" cried Boileau; "false, *mon père*, he is as true as inimitable. He has been translated into three languages." "That does not make him true." Boileau grew warm. "What!" he cried; "do you talk of the false? Dare you deny that one of your own writers has said that a Christian is not obliged to love God?" "Sir," said the Jesuit, trying to calm him, "we must make distinctions." "Distinctions! *Morbleu!* Distinctions about loving God!" And so saying, Boileau jumped up, ran to the other end of the room, and refused to speak to the Jesuit for the rest of the evening.

The influence of the Arnaulds on Madame de Sévigné was

perceptible in after years; but it is remarkable that the powerful sermons of men who were not such enthusiasts, but viewed religion in a truer light; men like Bossuet, Bourdaloue, Mascaron, and Fléchier, the greatest preachers of their day, and among the greatest ever heard in France, should not have moved her as much as the private conversation of a family of ascetics. The fact was, that to hear sermons, and comment on them, was then, as now, a fashion; and then, as now, the style was admired or criticised; the words were declared powerful, searching, and so forth, but the matter was not taken to the heart. The warnings, the entreaties, the thunders of men who were sincere in their condemnation of the vices of the court were listened to as a piece of well-studied oratory to be talked of in their salons, in the same tone as one talked of the eloquence of Demosthenes and Cicero; and because they were regarded in this light, because the power of a sermon led only to a calculation how soon the preacher would be raised to a bishopric, or what reception he would get at court after it, the most solemn warnings took no effect. Courtiers looked forward to redeeming the present by an old age of penance; but in the mean time the king's commands must be attended to, the king's vices imitated, and there was no time to think of the King of all kings.

It is somewhat in this spirit that Madame de Sévigné speaks of the celebrated sermons, or rather discourses, of her day. Of Bossuet, indeed, she speaks little, but about Bourdaloue, the court preacher, and an intrepid thunderer against the court vices, she is always enthusiastic. Bourdaloue was the Knox of the French court, and spared neither king nor courtiers. Madame de Sévigné tells us that he even described people in his sermons, though reserving their names. Such a license was permitted and even defended by Louis XIV. As an instance of it, we have the anecdote of Fénelon, who once being asleep during a sermon in the chapel at Versailles—what must laymen have done, if even Fénelon could sleep in church?—was suddenly awakened by the voice of the preacher, dropping from its lofty tone to a very practical one, and exclaiming—"Awaken that sleeping abbé, who comes to church only to pay court to his majesty!" Such apostrophes remind us of Baptist Noel pointing out to his congregation the ladies who wore flowers in their bonnets. But even in Madame de Sévigné's highest praise of Bourdaloue, we see the feeling of the age with respect to sermons. "He preached divinely." "You would have been enchanted." "How can one love God when one hears none but bad sermons?" and so forth. The religion of the day was a purely formal one, and the sermon was admired but rarely felt. Madame de Sévigné passes with ease from extolling the finest tirades of Bourdaloue or Mascaron to an easy smile about the depravity of her own son. That Bourdaloue, however, was no ordinary preacher, we can understand from the fact that she and Boileau, who both cordially hated the Jesuits, could not help admiring him, Jesuit though he was.

Among the other great men of the day, those she most admired were the Cardinal de Retz and La Rochefoucauld. She was intimate with the former for thirty years. She says of him at one time: "His soul is of so superior an order that one can not expect for him a mere common end, as for others." At another, she anticipates that he will yet effect something remarkable, and even be made pope. "He lives," she writes in 1675, after his retirement, "a very pious life, goes to all the services, and dines at the refectory on fast days:" not a very great stretch of religion for a cardinal forsooth, but for a courtier in surplice, such as De Retz really was, a great change for the better. At this period, however, he was employed, not on pious reflections, but rather worldly recollections, for he was writing his Memoirs, as every body of any mind did in those days. At another time she says: "I love and honor his eminence in a manner which makes the thought" (of his illness) "a torment to me: time can not diminish my feelings for him." There is no doubt that, with all his faults, De Retz was a lovable man, and Madame de Sévigné would doubtless have been louder in her praises of him had she not been writing to a daughter who detested him. One thing the cardinal did which, considering his age, claims our esteem for him—he paid his debts. They amounted to more than a million francs (forty thousand pounds), which would be equal to fully seventy thousand in the present day. Madame de Sévigné says: "He copied no one in this, and no one will copy him." No courtier, still more, no cardinal, ever thought of such an act of honesty in those days, and De Retz stood alone in this respect.

It is pleasant to read her account of La Rochefoucauld's warm domestic affections; and we may ask whether the man who reduced vice and virtue alike to the principle of self-love, did not prove something higher in his own case. Madame de Sévigné says: "As for M. de la Rochefoucauld, he was going, like a child, to revisit Verteuil, and the spots where he has shot and hunted with so much pleasure. I do not say 'where he has fallen in love,' for I do not believe that he has ever been in love." He appears to have profited himself by his maxims, and to have endured the terrible attacks of gout, under which he at last succumbed, with a firmness worthy of the author of the "Maxims." Of those reflections, Madame de Sévigné says, what we probably all feel on reading them: "There are some of them which are divine, and to my shame, some, too, which I can not understand;" with this difference, that we are not ashamed of our impossibility to comprehend them.

Both De Retz and La Rochefoucauld were of the Fronde party, and Madame de Sévigné, though she took no active share in it, as the Duchesses de Longueville and de Chevreuse did, had to bear Louis's ill-will on account of her friendship for these two men. To add to this, when the papers of the finance minister, Fouquet, were examined, some letters from her were found among those of his particular friends, and the dislike of the monarch was assured. In days when a sovereign's frown was the prelude to total disgrace, this was no slight danger; but every one agrees in acquitting this worthy woman of any of that servility to which even the most independent descended before Louis XIV., and she remained true to her friend, who had also aspired to be her lover. That Fouquet embezzled the funds of the state to an extent unparalleled in the annals of swindling, there can be little doubt, and that he even plotted against the crown itself appears no less certain; but whether Madame de Sévigné believed these accusations or not, she continued true in her friendship, and always spoke of the financier as unfortunate rather than criminal. Her letters were perfectly innocent in every respect; but their discovery seems to have caused some suspicions among her acquaintance, and to have drawn forth an exculpation of herself in writing to M. de Pomponne. "I assure you," she says, "no matter how much credit I may gain from those who do me the justice of believing that I had no other intercourse with him than this, I can not help feeling deeply distressed at being compelled to justify myself, and very probably without success, in the estimation of a thousand people who will never believe the simple truth." Fouquet had fortified the island of Belle-Isle as a place of refuge, and in the last moment, when warned of the king's suspicions by the Duchesse de Chevreuse, had set out to Nantes with a view to retiring to his fortress. Louis, for his own reasons, allowed him to depart; but the moment he had done so, he summoned an officer of his guard and commissioned him to arrest the fugitive. It is said that he had only delayed this measure as a prudential precaution; but that when Fouquet's guest at an entertainment of unusual magnificence, given by the minister at his Château de Vaux, the king had seen in his cabinet a portrait of Madlle. de la Vallière, with whom he was then in love, and incensed at finding a rival as well as a thief in his surintendant, had wished to have him arrested in the middle of the fête, but was deterred from doing so by Anne of Austria. Fouquet was, at any rate, brought back to Paris, underwent a long trial before the Parliament, where Madame de Sévigné, disguised by a mask, watched the bearing of her friend on his defense, and was eventually condemned to imprisonment for life at Pignerol, where he lingered for nineteen years, and died in 1680. Madame de Sévigné's letters, during the period of his trial, are full of the most tender anxiety for her friend, and are sufficient proof that her virtue can not be ascribed, as it has been, to mere insensibility. Her friendship for Fouquet partakes, indeed, of the character of attachment, and we need not be surprised that by this time the widow had forgotten a husband so completely unworthy of her. Fouquet was a man who inspired attachment, and the many friends who shared his disgrace, La Fontaine and the two Arnaulds among them, seem to have been moved by such a feeling. Madame de Sévigné, at least, never forgot the prisoner at Pignerol, as his other friends did; but if she had any sentiment for Fouquet, it was the only one she felt after the death of her husband.

During the fourteen or fifteen years that followed that event, she was occupied partly with the education of her children and partly with the society of Paris. In the prime of her life, her wit, and her beauty, she was every where sought for and enthusiastically welcomed. She was suited to all the kinds of society that then circled round the court. Her learning made her a fit companion for *les précieuses*, though she did not go along with their absurdities. Her wit and still pretty face gave her the power of shining among the gayer sets, and her good sense and womanlike hero-worship recommended her to the political intriguers, of whom so many were her intimate friends; while her strict propriety of conduct did not exclude her from the society of the more serious men of the age. She was every where a favorite, and when she left Paris, Paris unanimously implored her to return.

Meanwhile she was devoted to her children, especially to her daughter. She gave them the education which was then thought a good one, prepared them for this world rather than the next, taught them classics more than Christianity, and gave them polish rather than principle. Her beloved daughter was in due time introduced, and excited the most marked sensation. The Comte de Tréville, then an oracle at court, said of her, "This beauty will set the world on fire." Ménage called her "The miracle of our days," and De Bussy-Rabutin, who had been in love with her mother, named her "*La plus jolie fille de France*"—a name which stuck to her for years. It is difficult to understand all this admiration when we look at the portraits that have come down to us of Madame de Grignan. We are at once inclined to give the preference to her mother. The daughter's features were neither very regular nor very pleasing, as far as we can judge. The complexion appears to have been brilliant and delicate, and the rich hair, though a shade darker than Madame de Sévigné's, was even more luxuriant and beautiful. But the expression is cold and uninteresting. The dark eyes want that life and changefulness which was such a charm in her mother's face, and the general air is one of languor. She wanted, in fact, that cheerfulness which had made Madame de Sévigné so universal a favorite. She herself wrote to her mother: "At first sight people think me adorable, but on further acquaintance they love me no longer;" and if we can judge from letters, her character was not one to elicit sympathy or affection. Her beauty was not sufficient to make up for the smallness of her fortune and her mother's ill-favor at court; and, much as she was admired, the adored daughter was not sought by any of those desirable young men on whom Madame de Sévigné, with a mother's ambition, fixed her desiring eyes.

Angry at this, mother and daughter both agreed to quit Paris, and spent a whole winter at Les Rochers. When they returned to Paris, the beauty of Madlle. de Sévigné is said to have made some impression on the king, but her coldness still repelled the young men of great families. She had already arrived at, and almost passed, the age at which a "*jeune fille*" was expected in those days to "form an alliance." She was nineteen, and that was a terrible age. A year passed, and she was still Madlle. de Sévigné; another, and then both mother and daughter gave up the hope of a brilliant marriage and arranged one which was positively bad.

The Comte de Grignan was a lieutenant-general in Languedoc; of good descent and excellent reputation. On the other hand, he was forty years old, had been twice married already, was a heavy, stolid, uninteresting man, and was not, apparently, very deeply devoted to Mdlle. de Sévigné. Nevertheless, when he proposed, he was readily accepted. An extract from a letter of Madame de Sévigné shows what could be thought of the sacred tie of matrimony in those days. "His former wives," she writes, "have died in order to make room for my daughter, and destiny, in a moment of unwonted kindness, has also removed his father and his son; so that, possessing greater riches than ever, and uniting by birth, connection, and excellent qualities, all that we could desire, we made no hesitating terms, as it is usually the custom to do, and we feel much indebted to the two families which have passed away before us. The world seems satisfied, which is much. * * * He has fortune, rank, office, esteem, and consideration in society. What more should we expect? I think we come well out of the scrape." A scrape it was, in those days, to be single at twenty!

This indifferent pair was united on the 29th of January, 1669, and for a short time Madame de Sévigné's desire of keeping her daughter by her was granted. But the separation she dreaded came at last. M. de Grignan was appointed Vice-governor of Provence, and was compelled to leave Paris for the south of France. Madame de Sévigné induced him to leave his wife behind for her confinement. She gave birth to a daughter, Marie, who was called Mdlle. d'Adhémar, and who some years afterward was sent, according to a custom of the day, which sacrificed the daughters to make up the fortune of the sons, to a convent, from which she never emerged. Her other daughter, Pauline, "*cette jeune Pauline*," afterward became Madame de Simiane, the friend of Massillon and a letter-writer, like her grandmother, but of inferior merit.

The separation of Madame de Sévigné and her beloved daughter, which took place in 1670, was a terrible blow to the former; but we are indebted to it for a collection of the most curious and interesting letters ever written, which have the advantage of having been penned in perfect simplicity, with no thought of publication, and no desire, as those of Walpole evince, of being read with admiration in a circle of clever acquaintance. From this period Madame de Sévigné seems to have lived only for her daughter. Madame de Grignan returned this devotion with something like indifference. Her letters to her mother have been lost. It is said that her daughter Madame de Simiane destroyed them on religious grounds. Madame de Grignan was a devoted admirer of Descartes, whom she called her "*père*;" and she not only studied his works with assiduity, but seems to have enlarged on philosophy in her letters. It is said, too, that in some of them she turned into ridicule the absurd religious, or rather superstitious processions of La Provence, processions at which Massillon was afterward so much disgusted that he put an end to them. But this ridicule was enough to shock the prejudices of her daughter. From the few letters that remain, the character of Madame de Grignan appears to have been frigid and reasonable, rather than warm and joyous like that of her mother. Even from Madame de Sévigné's letters we gather that she wearied of the extravagant devotion of her parent, who seems at times almost to make excuses for her affection. On the other hand, Madame de Grignan's moral character was irreproachable. Wedded to a husband to whom she was indifferent, she espoused philosophy rather than court admiration; and however cold her letters may have been, we may gather from Madame de Sévigné's remarks that they contained matter worthy of the consideration of thinkers. On the whole, it may be well regretted that they are lost to us.

While thus devoted to her daughter, Madame de Sévigné cared too little for her son.

This young man was of a weak character, vacillating between the best and the worst impulses. He had received an excellent education, but not sufficient principle to enable him to meet the temptations of Parisian life in days when the monarch himself set the example of depravity. He was devoted to classical literature, and great in Homer, Virgil, and Horace, and even printed a dissertation on a passage of the last about which he and Dacier had a dispute. He was educated for the army, and at the age of twenty took part in an expedition to Crete. The Turks had been besieging Candia for twenty-four years. France was their ally, but her sympathies naturally went with the Venetians, who held the capital of the island. Louis could not therefore send a regular expedition to their relief, but he authorized the Comte de la Feuillade to raise a corps of gentlemen-volunteers to aid the Venetians, and among them the sons of all the greatest French families enrolled themselves. The young Comte de St. Paul, the son of the Duchesse de Longueville, raised a squadron of one hundred and fifty young cavaliers, all eager to fight in the cause of Christianity. By the advice of Turenne, who was a friend of Madame de Sévigné's, her son joined this corps, and set out for Crete. The French volunteers did, however, more harm than good by their rashness and folly, making repeated sorties against the Turks, in which their numbers were soon terribly reduced. The survivors quarreled with the Venetian defenders of the town, and set sail before it was taken, returning to France with little glory, though they made the most of it.

M. de Sévigné returned to Paris, and, while waiting for promotion, followed in the common stream and wasted his fortune upon actresses. He was at one time the rival of Racine in his admiration of La Champmêlé, at another he was devoted to Ninon de l'Enclos, who had before ruined his father, and was now no less than fifty-four years of age, yet still lovely and attractive. She is said to have preserved her beauty and appearance of youth to the last. The part played by Madame Sévigné on this occasion is very remarkable. Her son, who had a great affection for her and great confidence in her good sense, actually confided these amours to his mother. Madame de

Sévigné was too much imbued with the spirit of her age to be very much shocked, but had too much sense not to wish to reform him. Not only was he dissipating his fortune—"his hand is a crucible in which money melts away," she writes—but he was, she feared, following in the steps of his unfortunate father, and might come to as bad an end. Like him he was very handsome and a great favorite, but he had inherited from his mother an inclination to better things, which showed itself from time to time in fits of deep contrition. Madame de Sévigné did not, as some mothers would have done, thrust him away from her and leave him to sink deeper in the mire. She listened to his confidences, and even laughed at his amusing adventures, but attempted to show him reasonably the folly of his conduct; and when she saw that a change had come over him, seized the moment and drew him back gently to the contemplation of a better life. Yet, strange to say, she talks lightly of all this to her daughter, narrates his gallantries and adventures, his successes and repulses, with a light pen, and passes in the next sentence to praises of the divine eloquence of Bourdaloue or Mascaron! Nothing could more completely show the feeling of her age. Fortunately perhaps for her son, he had a strong satiric vein: he was a warm admirer of Boileau. His letters, some of which remain, are written in an amusing, clever style. He saw the absurdity of his own conduct. Madame de Sévigné tells us that he even read to her some of his letters to the actress La Champmêlé. They were full of the most extravagant passion, she says, and M. de Sévigné laughed at them as merrily as she did herself. This consciousness of his own absurdity, mingled with his mother's reproaches, had the effect of curing him for a time. Madame de Sévigné took him down to Brittany, and the country, that panacea for all the diseases, mental and bodily, of the city, worked a salutary effect on him. In 1677 he bought the post of second lieutenant of the Gendarmes-Dauphins, and from his account of himself to his sister, he was now very steady and living under his mother's roof. In the following year he distinguished himself at the siege of Mons, and his squadron, in covering a battery, endured a fire of nine guns for two hours with such pertinacity as to draw forth the admiration even of the enemy. In 1683 Madame de Sévigné succeeded in finding a wife for him, Mdlle. de Bréhan, the daughter of a rich *Conseiller du Parlement*, of excellent family, and having a fortune of two hundred thousand francs; "a great marriage in these days," says Madame de Sévigné. His marriage saved him. He became a respectable member of society, occupied himself with literature, and showed a tendency to become *dévot*, which after his mother's death he developed very strongly. His wife had a like propensity, and they bought a house in the Rue St. Jacques at Paris, in order to be near their religious counselors.

The last ties of Madame de Sévigné's life were broken at the marriage of her daughter, as the first had been at the death of her husband. From that period, 1669, to her death in 1696, a space of twenty-seven years, she seems to have lived for letter-writing. If we except Corbinelli, an Italian who had come with Mazarin to France, and been employed diplomatically by him in Italy, and who, says Lamartine, "was an Italian Saint-Evremond, able to compete with the greatest minds, but shrinking from an encounter with the difficulties which lie in the path of fame, and assuming, as much through idleness as want of ambition, the character of an amateur"—with the exception of this man, who was devoted to her as a friend, called on her every day when she was in Paris, and even followed her to Livry and Les Rochers, we do not find that she felt any attachment to man or woman, except her daughter, up to the time of her death. Her friendships for De Retz, for La Rochefoucauld, and others, had more of admiration than sentiment in them. Thus her life became wrapped up in her daughter, to whom she wrote three or four times a week, and even oftener, sometimes even twice a day. At the same time, the necessity of getting promotion for her son, and perhaps a natural love of society, kept her, whenever in Paris, in the circles of the gay and intellectual. In 1679 she took a long lease of the Hôtel de Carnavalet, a fine old house in the Rue Culture Sainte-Catherine; and here she received those celebrated friends of whom an account has already been given. Though now far past her fiftieth year, and no longer a beauty, her wit and the friendship which the leading men and women felt for her, kept her still a popular favorite in the court society, though to the court itself she went rarely, owing to the coldness with which Louis XIV. treated her, as a former friend of Fouquet and La Fronde. With the gossip of this society her letters are full; but we can not accuse her of being a mere gossip, as some letter-writers have been. She is less so, for instance, than Horace Walpole. Her letters contain just as much talk on books, religion, philosophy, and general politics, as on the frowns and smiles of the great monarch, the favor accorded to this courtier, the disgrace of another, the marriages contracted, the *bon mots* pronounced and circulated, and so forth; and the oddity of it is, that she passes without a second's hesitation from the lightest to the gravest subject, and back again.

But though it is in society that she shines most, and is most interesting in her judgments of men and measures and her anecdotes of the court, there is a soft and romantic touch, a touch almost of poetry, throughout her letters, that redeems the worldliness of the rest. She was a thorough Frenchwoman, but not a thorough Parisian. When she went to see the old "*bien bon*" (her uncle the abbé) at Livry, or when she was far away in the inaccessible solitudes of Brittany, she does not repine, nor regret the metropolis as a more vulgar mind would. She rejoices in the song of the nightingale, in the change of the leaf, in the glad freshness of the air, and in her own simple way becomes a poet without meaning it.

Madame de Sévigné was not ambitious. Unlike most of her lady friends, she could admire her heroes without joining in their political schemes. Thus it is, that those twenty-seven years of her life, during which she wrote her letters, are full, not of her own doings, or cares, or hopes, or projects, but of the private history of the court of Louis XIV., and, what in its way is as interesting and certainly more sunny to look upon, the private history of a mother's heart. We, the calm readers of to-day, fret and are half indignant when she breaks away from a narration that throws, or seems to throw, a new light on the character of one of the great men or women of the day, or even to illustrate history in a valuable manner, to cover her cold philosophizing daughter with tender phrases; but to a poetical mind this very fault is a beauty. It shows how profound was the mother's pride she felt, and proves that these expressions of affection to which, perhaps, the French of to-day would apply the epithet *banale*—hackneyed—were not neatly turned for admiration, but positively sprang from a heart absorbed with a single interest. Even her gossip is intended to give pleasure to her daughter; and when she speaks of her own friends, she is careful not to say too much of those whom she knows her child dislikes.

The charm of her letters is, that they were written only to be read by that one centre of all her affections. When she writes to Bussy, or to Madame La Fayette, there is indeed the same glowing wit and neatness, the same mark of a clever observer of all that goes on around her; but there is less of that peculiar natural grace which is the real secret of her artless style. She is again and again an instance of the old truth, that nature and the heart are the best masters of composition, and that if men and women would write as they feel and think, they would always write readably, if not absolutely well.

To write letters was indeed the great accomplishment of women of that day, for they had nothing to do with music, and very little with any other art. All the lady-wits wrote letters by the hundred. Madame de Coulanges, Madame La Fayette, Madame de Grignan, Madame de Simiane, and others, have left more or less of their epistolary productions; and certainly for ease, elegance, and refinement, they surpass any thing of the kind that has appeared in any other day or country. The letters of Madame de Sévigné may not have that distinct interest which we find in those of Lady Mary Wortley Montagu and others of our own country; but they are far superior to them in taste and refinement. There is little coarseness in her letters. There is certainly a little now and then, but such as the open expression of the age warranted. In Lady Mary's there is a downright disregard of all decency at times, and such as the custom of no age could warrant.

For thirty years after her death Madame de Sévigné's letters were unknown to any but Madame de Grignan and a few friends. A selection was made from them in 1724, and published. They are said to have been written rapidly, with little respect for caligraphy, in a thin, careless hand. Like all the letters of the time, they were tied round with a string of floss silk and sealed on either side.

The letter-writing years of Madame de Sévigné's life passed calmly and pleasantly. She had few or no real anxieties, and few events in her life, beyond the trifling ones with which her letters are replete. She lived at her Hôtel du Carnavalet in Paris, or at Livry, or at Les Rochers, and every where she recalled her daughter's presence. As Arnauld told her, she made an idol of that daughter, but that was all. In her latter years she too, like all the rest, became *dévote*, a word to be translated by "pious" rather than "religious." A *dévote* went to mass twice a day, and made an intimate friend of her confessor. Madame de Sévigné gives a good reason for the love that ladies have of frequent confession. They like, she tells us, to talk of themselves, and would rather talk ill of themselves than not at all. The *dévotes* did much good in a systematic way, and as a salve for a poor conscience, but they did not necessarily give up society, nor even bad society. "Bless the man," said one of them at a dinner party, when a servant filled her glass with wine, "does he not know that I am *dévote?*" The servant's mistake was very excusable.

Madame de Sévigné died, as she had lived, for her daughter. While at Les Rochers she learned that Madame de Grignan was attacked by an internal disease, lingering but not dangerous. She set off, though it was winter, on the long and, at that time, hazardous journey to Provence, and there she tended her daughter day and night for three months. She was nearly seventy years of age, and this exertion was too much for her.

Madame de Grignan recovered, but her mother succumbed to the fatigues of nursing her. She was seized with malignant small-pox, and died on the 16th of April, 1696, in her seventieth year. She was buried in the Château de Grignan. Her daughter survived her only nine years, dying in 1705, from grief for the loss of her only son, the young Marquis de Grignan.

Her letters, as Lamartine says, are her real tomb. In them her soul is to be found. They are worth reading for many reasons. They are a truer history of the reign of Louis XIV. than any that has been written. They are the purest outburst of an excellent heart. They are free from any spiteful or evil spirit; they breathe a calm, which in this world of worry is most refreshing; they are a monument of motherly affection. Madame de Sévigné is not entitled to the name a "great woman;" she has worked, or helped to work, no great change in the human race. She was a *woman* in every sense, and did not emerge from a woman's natural sphere. She was a Frenchwoman in every sense, yet she is perhaps the very best instance we can find of Frenchwomen. In short, we can not read her letters without admiring her for her mind, and loving her for her heart.

SYDNEY LADY MORGAN.

SYDNEY LADY MORGAN, as she latterly styled herself; but I remember her first as Lady Morgan merely, with a respectable-looking husband, a large, light, heavy man, in spectacles, who at once worshiped and admonished her as we do a child.

It was in what she used to call the out-of-the-way regions of North Marylebone that I had stood near a piano the whole evening endeavoring to make out who could be that short personage who sat behind a small table (though in the circle), on which was set one of those dark-green circular shades which spring up out of a stand! yet even this protection to her poor eyes was not thought enough, for the lady held before her face a green fan, so that a deep shade was cast upon the diminutive figure behind; and even in a well-lighted room she was as much in retreat as if she had been taking her pleasure on a sunless day in an arbor.

I soon perceived that she was a centre of attraction even in that room where Agnes Strickland at one time, Campbell at another, Rogers, and, in the course of the evening, numberless scientific celebrities had come and gone. Sheil, even then partially bald, sat down near her, and relapsed into his beloved brogue; and there was such a play of wit between them, such brilliant attacks on his part, such pungent yet good-natured retorts on hers, that I felt sure she was from the dear Emerald Isle: one of a race that has always its joke and its reply, even at death's door.

I said to a grim-looking gentleman near, "I am a stranger, sir; pray, who is that?"

I turned my eyes toward the green fan.

"That lady? do you mean that very nice-looking person near the screen? A fair, comely lady, with light hair? Well, you remember hearing of Miss O'Neil—before you were born, it must have been; that is she; she is now Lady Becher."

"Oh yes, I know; I did not mean her. There is a lady—see, Lady Becher is bending now to talk to her: she holds a fan."

"Oh! don't you know? Lady Morgan, of course."

"Lady Morgan! but—"

"I don't mean Lady Morgan of Tredegar, but the authoress of "The Princess," of "Florence Macarthy;" don't you remember?"

"Certainly."

"Every one knows her," pursued my informant, who, I found afterward, was a toured reviewer; "you will find her agreeable: she makes herself pleasant."

And, indeed, so I thought; for it was some time before I could get a cool post of observation. Having at last intrenched myself near a folding door, behind a fat dowager, I took a calm survey of Sydney Lady Morgan. She appeared to me then on the wrong side of the half century: no, one, however, even now, knows the year of her birth, for she had the tact to keep it to herself; but it is conjectured to have been 1777, or thereabouts; but no one could have supposed it possible who knew her, even at the last, that she could be eighty. She was then a very small and very slight woman, with an easy drooping figure, that looked as if Nature had been careless when she put it together; and then she was somewhat crooked, though not strikingly, even when, as she used to say, she "circulated" through the room at her own soirées; and this defect, good woman as she was, as a plea she used to attribute to having practiced the harp too much in her youth. But I believe that there were few women of the period in which Lady Morgan figured as a girl, that were straight, thanks to stiff stays and backboards.

Her face, though never more than agreeable, had a great charm in its feminine contour. She wore at that time her own hair. I will not swear that it was *all* her own, for there were suspicious-looking curls dripping down upon the slight throat; but it was evidently partly natural, for it was thin, and drawn across her wide forehead with a sort of tasteful negligence. It was, however, of a lighter hue than the bands with which, in her last days, she attempted to restore the venerable ruin of Sydney Lady Morgan.

Her eyes were large, and of a bluish gray, in early life probably blue. One of them had a slight cast, and went off at a tangent to the right; but this did not spoil the expression, which was very sweet and very thoughtful, without, at any time that I knew her, being brilliant or searching. She always looked like a person who saw imperfectly; and she always spoke of herself as half blind, and talked of visits from Alexander and dark rooms, leeches and shades; and I never saw her without that green fan in her hand. It became an antiquity like herself. Yet I believe she saw more than any one else did; nothing escaped her. She knew every *nuance* of feeling that passed in the minds of others: she remarked dress, and she never *un*intentionally forgot or mistook a person.

Her other features were neither prominent nor beautiful, yet peculiar—Lady Morgan's own mouth and nose. I never saw any one that resembled her; and if our grandmothers were here to say it, they would declare that Lady Morgan had been a pretty woman.

She had the manner of a woman who had been attractive, and that supplies the want of a chronicle. Besides, the face was soft, agreeable, kindly—somewhat wrinkled even then, but harmoniously tinted with a *soupçon* of rouge. I remember her dress perfectly. It was juvenile to a fault—white muslin, short sleeves, and a broad green sash tied behind; something dropping and light about her head; and a lace scarf over her shoulders. She was still the wild Irish girl in fancy, though rather an old Irish girl.

She soon, however, changed this style; and though I never saw her what is called well dressed, if one were to take her and measure her by the yard, yet she had an intuitive notion of the becoming, combined, at that period of her life, with a close attention to economy.

This remarkable woman was born, then (let us concede it), in the year 1777, on shipboard, between Ireland and England. Her father, Mr. Macowen, was an actor, a singer, the manager of a theatre, and a man of talent and local celebrity. It is said that he was handsome and dashing, and had the reputation of being more successful with the ladies than with the public as an actor. His good looks he transmitted partially only to Sydney, but in full splendor to her sister, the late Lady Clarke, who was extremely handsome.

Abjuring the Mac, as there was then a strong prejudice against the sons of Erin, this lady-slayer came over to London, and appeared in Rowe's heavy play as Tamerlane. Theatrical critics were in those days as much guided by party views as the House of Commons: there were persons who could not tolerate Kemble, but who idolized Young; and Garrick, in whose wake Mr. Owenson must have followed, had his detractors, who adored Betterton. And so, while some praised, others decried Mr. Owenson's Tamerlane; and the unsuccessful player was obliged to leave London and start for the provinces. While "starring" at Shrewsbury, the handsome Irishman captivated a certain Miss Hill, a "single woman of a certain age," just old enough, happily for him, to be foolish on matrimonial points. She eloped with him, and they were married; and their first child was a daughter, the gifted, charming Sydney, so called, as well as many of her female contemporaries in the west country of Ireland, in grateful remembrance to Sir Henry Sydney, who was Lord Deputy of Ireland in the time of Elizabeth.

Such was the origin of one whose life presents an instance of what unassisted women can do, to raise themselves in the scale of society, upon even a slender stock of education, with energy and talent. Who would have predicted that the small, fragile child, bred up amid actors, learning first her letters, probably, upon a play-bill—conversant with properties—the pet of the green-room—whose loud merry laugh might be heard, before the drop-scene was drawn up, behind the foot-lights—who would suppose that she would have lived to eighty-two, to figure in the most polite neighborhood of London, among the most lettered, the most famous, and the most aristocratic society in the world?

Her father had all the qualities which were afterward developed, under more favorable circumstances, in her. He was fond of the arts, to which she always professed devotion, though no judge of art. He was immensely convivial—hence her hereditary taste for society, and her aptitude for conversation. His companionship in his own way was delightful; so was hers in a more refined and genial form. He sang excellently: she also sang and played on the harp. He was a man who delighted to bring forward young poets: here was a grand point of resemblance. Nothing delighted Lady Morgan more than to have a pet poet, whose fame she wished to nurture: whose work, sent bound, and with a copy of verses to *her* specially, she used to lay on her table—that little table near her; and to show, only to *show* to her visitors, saying, "The gentleman you met on the stairs with that wild-looking hair is an enthusiastic young poet; see, this is his last. I don't offer to lend it to you, you can get it for seven-and-sixpence at Pickering's."

Upon scraps of education Sydney throve mentally, as girls do upon an unsystematic bringing up. It is Miss Austen, I think, who says that reading to one's self *is* an education to girls. I dare say it was the only one *she* had; but then her reading would be solid works—Bowdler, Hannah More, who flourished in Bath in her time, Russell's "Modern Europe," and a few proper novels. But Sydney's studies were, as she grew up, at once more desultory and ambitious. She learned Italian, and read the "Natural History" of Lord Bacon. More especially she devoured the history of her native land, which Ireland undoubtedly was; and she mixed up all these pursuits with music and poetry, sang to her harp, wrote a volume of poems, and published them by subscription, dedicated to Lady Moira, whose lord was then lord lieutenant, and wrote in periodicals. She used to relate how enchanted she was when for some tale the editor sent her two guineas, her first-earned money, and those two guineas, she said, were the source of all my scribbling; the encouragement was worth hundreds. It seems almost like a lesson to editors not *too* sternly to crush young hopes, lest, with the chaff often first put out, good seed is destroyed. It is well known that Mrs. Gaskell, whose novels are classics in their way, vainly tried many years ago to get a volume of poems published, though they had much of the fancy and grandeur of thought observable in "Ruth;" and it is also true that Charlotte Brontë's first work was sent to every publisher in London, until it excited, by its veteran exterior, the curiosity of Mr. Williams, the able literary adviser of Smith and Elder, who read it and refused it, but suggested that the authoress should try a fresh subject, and "Jane Eyre" was produced.

Armed with her two guineas, a large sum for the little harpist, Sydney wrote her "Wild Irish Girl," original, romantic, and absurd. Far better was her "Novice of St. Dominick," the effort of her maturer years, of which the story is interesting, although the incidents are improbable, and there is in it a tone of truer feeling than her later novels display. All these avocations were interspersed with poetic flights. Lady Morgan was the writer of "Kate Kearney." She published, also, a collection of Irish melodies antecedent to Moore's: she played and sang to her harp in every society into which her precocious talents brought her; yet still she was but "Miss Owenson" the "Wild Irish Girl." Single women can do little to form a circle, they can but adorn one when formed: Lady Morgan, as "Miss Owenson," was a delightful and a popular member of society, but a member only; young, without influence, devoid of aristocratic connection, and poor.

There was one feature in her destinies: she was early appropriated by the Liberal party as their own. She was of that day when Irish wrongs were rife, and the wounds inflicted on an oppressed country during the rebellion were unhealed. She grew up in the politics of the Emmetts and of Lord Edward Fitzgerald; and though her large amount of common sense modified, in after life, the convictions of her youth, she was consistent to the last, and perfectly aware of the errors of her countrymen. When she had fully emerged into literary eminence, and her works were popular in England, Mr. Wilson Croker, the last of the exploded race of political bigots, attacked her personally and cruelly. He pretended to start a commission of inquiry on her age, her parentage, her early position. "Have we not seen this lady on stages and at fairs?" he asked in the pages of the "Quarterly Review." He turned upon her that which a gentlewoman can least stand—the laugh. We may dispute facts, but no one deprecate a laugh. And his taunts, his stinging criticisms, his private influence, his party importance as the great organ of the spiteful, amused the world for a time, and alarmed the steady-going aristocrats of Grosvenor Square, who drew back in haste from what they believed to be a mingled mass of false pretensions, bad singing, reprehensible politics, and questionable religious convictions. In those days the passions even of good men predisposed them to credit that which assimilated to their own prejudices. A man used to be thought, as in the days of the "Spectator," of no principles who did not believe a certain amount of falsehoods. "Party lies" were at their acmé. In the words of Addison: "the coffee-houses were supported by them; the press was choked by them: eminent authors lived upon them." "Our bottle-conversation," he says, "is so infected by them, that a party lie is grown as fashionable an entertainment as a lively catch or a merry story." And, in the same way, the exaggerations of "John Bull," in the days of Theodore Hook, of the "Satirist," the "Age," and, I am sorry to add, of the "Quarterly Review," furnished all the great talkers of the time with subjects for after-dinner discourse. Nor were those the days in which "lies were discharged in the air, and began to hurt nobody."* The West End of London was then all Tory, and small people thought it fashionable to belong to that *clique* which ate with silver forks and abhorred Russell Square. Whiggism and *mauvais ton* were thought to go together; as in France, the old Legitimists despise the Liberal party not so much for their opinions as for their alleged vulgarity; and these convictions had their influence in crushing Lady Morgan at first, and for some time. Her gayety, her real kindness of heart, and her talents won, however, the heart of Dr. Morgan, a physician of good family, and a widower, of moderate but comfortable income; and being eventually knighted (it is said, partly from compliment to *her*), at Dublin, she assumed, as his wife, a position at once eminently respectable and agreeable. Meantime her pen had been in active requisition. "Ida of Athens" and "The Missionary," though popular at the time of their appearance, are now forgotten; they are manifestly the work of a young and original author. As a writer, Lady Morgan gained much by her marriage. The poetry of her life was perhaps gone; but the cultivated taste and logical mind of her husband rectified her exuberant fancies; and, as a married woman, her best novels were produced: "O'Donnel" was considered by herself to be her mas-

* See Addison on Party Lying: a capital paper. No. 507, Saturday, October 10.

terpiece: it placed her on a literary eminence, as the first novelist that advocated the Irish cause, and fearlessly she wrote. It is true that Miss Edgeworth's "Castle Rackrent" had then appeared (her delightful tale "The Absentee" was of later date); but while she assailed the defective habits and principles of the people, pointing out also the effects of the false and ancient system that England had pursued toward Ireland, Lady Morgan took up the more romantic features of the cause. The works of Miss Edgeworth tend to reform, to instruct; her story is subservient to her purpose. The novels of Lady Morgan excite the passions and enlist the sympathies. The one is the disciple of reason and truth—the other the organ of fancy, political convictions, and romance.

It was in 1818, when the sprightly authoress must have been forty-one years of age, that Lady Morgan engaged to write her book on France. She had by that time seen enough of society in this country and in Ireland, to prepare her for the task: for it is of little avail to send out individuals to judge of foreign circles who have seen no good company in their own nation; and, although with the brand of the "Quarterly" upon her, Lady Morgan had even then tasted largely of the pleasures afforded by those aristocratic circles which she even loved "not wisely, but too well." Her "Book of the Boudoir" gives an animated picture of Irish noblesse and their provincial life: in depicting that in England she is less fortunate. As L. E. L. said of Mr. Galt: "He is like Antæus; never strong except when he touches his native land," so may it be said of Lady Morgan, that she was never so humorous in thought, so felicitous in expression, so brilliant in fancy, as when her conversation or her writings turned on her country, and the "Paddies," as she irreverently styled them, formed her theme.

Her journeys to France, to Italy, and to Spain constituted the different epochs of her uneventful life. Let us, before we start with her on those tours, look for an instant into her interior life at home, and see how in her mature age she shone as a domestic companion, sister, wife.

People who assert that Lady Morgan was a mere woman of society, "pleasant but wrong," caring for no one, devoid of genuine feeling, content with all that the world offers, knew her but little. It is too much the custom to assign that description of character to persons of a lively, social nature. Lady Morgan was a woman of the warmest affections; devoted to her family ties. Her sister, Lady Clarke, had married an eminent surgeon in Dublin, and was the mother of several daughters when Lady Morgan meditated her first Continental journey. These children were the objects of a tenderness perfectly maternal. In one of her letters to Lady Clarke, Lady Morgan thus refers to them—

"Dear little toddles! I am sure that nepotism is an organic affection in single and childless women. It is a maternal instinct gone astray. In popes and princes it is a frustrated ambition—a substitute for paternity. It is a dangerous tendency; aunts and uncles never love 'wisely, but too well;' besides, it brings with it responsibilities without authority, and imposes duties without giving rights: and so by-by, babies."

There was not a word of exaggeration in all this. These "babies" grew up to be elegant, handsome, and accomplished women, in whose dawn of life their aunt Sydney found deep interest: they were the delight of her middle life, and one of them the solace of her age. In the fullness of her success as a "Queen of Society," Lady Morgan was rarely to be seen without one of her nieces, whose musical powers, whose love of art, reminded her of the days when she was, as she used to say, a sort of show-girl, with her harp and her Irish melodies. Upon the death of one of her nieces, the first Mrs. Marmion Savage, Lady Morgan sorrowed as a mother would have done. Every tie she had was dear to her: the warm Irish heart was never choked by the cares and deceitfulness of life. In her "nepotism" she reminded one of a Frenchwoman, to whom the ties of relationship, which we English are too prone to cast away from us, are stronger in our Continental neighbors than in any other European country.

As a wife she was pre-eminently happy, from similarity of tastes. Sir Charles soon participated in her literary objects, and became the writer of the grave articles in the "Monthly Magazine," published by Colburn, and at one time edited by Thomas Campbell, and later by Sir Edward Bulwer Lytton. Sir Charles had a dignified, calm manner, which well supported the gay, though always gentle, Sydney in society. He was still and ever devoted to that profession which, above all others, settles itself in the mind of man, forms that mind, applies itself to almost every circumstance in life, and is reverenced by the mature intellect because it is useful, enlarged, and true. Sir Charles Morgan was a physician of that period when the *gentleman* was necessary to the profession. He ceased, with his marriage, to practice, but devoted himself to philosophy and literature. As a writer, his works have not lived: as a philosopher, there was one vital canker in his code. He was skeptical: there have been those who have declared that he was even an unbeliever; but it is generally thought that his notions were those of Cuvier: those that Lawrence once advocated, but which he has long since nobly recanted—of Materialism and Deism, not of bold Atheism. And the fact that even the opinions of Sir Charles Morgan went to this extent is dubious. But, unhappily, it is but too true that his influence had a serious effect on the mind of his wife.

That "party lie" which, diffused among thousands, is "as a drop of the blackest tincture, wears away and vanishes when mixed and confused in a considerable body of water." Yet "the blot is still in it, but is not able to discover itself:"* that falsehood represented her as scoffing at every form of faith. Yet such was not the case: unfortunately, the term *liberal* had in her mind been confounded with incredulity. Her faith was not that of the Church of England, but had its own form, independent of creeds. How far her heterodoxy went, whether to the very confines of unbelief or merely to externals, was obvious to those who intimately knew her. In her later years, she was dazzled by the cleverness of the book styled "Vestiges of Creation," and adopted many of its arguments. Yet an eminent scientific man who conversed with her expressed an opinion that her convictions were unsound, though not wholly skeptical. Her house was the resort of many clergymen: her favorite niece was married to a clergyman of great worth and piety, who was on the happiest terms with her: no one ever went to her large parties without seeing there the Dean of St. Pauls, Dr. Milman, and many others who would have turned away with horror from a female Atheist, even in all the radiance of talent and success. She belonged, indeed, in her youth to that period when all faith, all observances, had been but recently overthrown, and were slowly reasserting themselves after the shock of the French Revolution. In her first work on France, Lady Morgan has described the reorganization of society under the Bourbons, after the Restoration in 1816. It is still thought, in some circles of Parisian *littérateurs*, that to be incredulous, or, as they term it, philosophic, is a proof of the *esprit fort*, to which distinction some women make the fatal mistake of aspiring. But in Lady Morgan's days the notion was in full force. She thirsted for that society in which she could meet with responsive liberalism of all kinds, and received with delight an offer from the late Henry Colburn, that enterprising and liberal publisher, to set off for Italy, and to write a work upon it of the same description as her (still unequaled) book on France. Her own words must impart the offer, and its reception:

"This morning as I was on my knees, all dust and dowdiness,

* Addison.

comes the English post—old Colburn—no, not old Colburn, but young, enthusiastic Colburn, in love with 'Florence Macarthy,' and a little *épris* with the author! 'Italy, by Lady Morgan!' He is not touched, but rapt, and makes a dashing offer of two thousand pounds, to be printed in quarto, like 'France;' but we are to start off immediately, and I have immediately answered him in the words of Sileno in 'Midas:'

"'Done! Strike hands!
I take your offer:
Farther on I may fare worse.'"

Lady Morgan set off instantly *viâ* London for France. Over that country the mistaken policy of Louis XVIII. had even then cast a gloom, but the lively Sydney was happy in the society of La Fayette, of Humboldt, then in Paris, of Dénon, Lacroix, and last, not least, of the Princess Jablonsky. Her portraits are wonderfully graphic, and, though true, not ill-natured. Witness, in her diary, an admirable description of Louis XVIII.: "A fine gentleman, an elegant scholar; graceful (if not grateful), as the Bourbons always are; gracious, as the French princes have been, though their courtesies meant nothing."

While Lady Morgan had much to allege against those whom she styles "the Tory detractors of England," at the head of them "The Quarterly," she owed to her success as a partisan the introduction to Château la Grange. Her "France," which had gone through three editions in one year, was proscribed by *Louis aux Huitres*, as Louis XVIII. was then styled. A sort of interdict to her entering France had also been placed by the government of that country; nevertheless, tempted by La Fayette, who had assured her that it was chiefly a matter of form, she resolved to go, and the result was one of the most delightful visits that she had ever enjoyed.

In the month of August, 1818, Lady Morgan quitted the "darling dusty old Fabrique," as she calls it, the *Hôtel d'Espagne*, in the Faubourg St. Germain, for the Château la Grange, situated in the Department de la Brie. During the whole of her stay in Paris this indefatigable woman had been "cramming" for her journey to Italy, and reading all that she could collect on the subject at the Bibliothèque Royale.

She now prepared to set off on her journey with all the spirits of eighteen; bought herself a "*chapeau de soliel*" in the *Marché des Innocents*, with a bunch of corn-flowers stuck in the midst of it; made a tour of calls and sights; dined in a little public-house under the heights of Montmorenci, on the door of which was inscribed "*Ici on danse tous les jours;*" admired the practice, and remarked what misery and murder it would spare if such prevailed in England, instead of drinking gin and porter;

THE COUNTERFEIT LADY MORGAN.

passed the evening at Baron Dénon's, where she met Ségur and Humboldt. The separation between Bonaparte and Josephine was still the theme of Parisien soireés, and Humboldt told some pleasing anecdotes in mitigation of the supposed hardness of Napoleon's character. Then Lady Morgan departed for La Grange; on her journey to which a curious incident showed her the conspicuous place which she then occupied in the minds of the French; for her liberal principles had met with a responsive voice among a certain class in France as far removed from the doctrines of the Rouge Republican as from the absolutism of the despot: these were the "*Industriels*"—a class to be distinguished from the "*Ouvriers*," of whom they are the aristocracy, the higher orders of mechanics.

Delighted with France, she always declared that there was then twenty times more liberality and public spirit than in Ireland, and that pamphlets were published there which would have been prosecuted in England. Perhaps her opinion was warped by the favorable manner in which her work on France had been received. As she was proceeding to visit General La Fayette—whose part in the first French Revolution is familiar to every one—she met with a curious compliment to herself. Waiting at Grandeville for La Fayette's carriage, which was to meet her there, she and Sir Charles joined a group who were standing outside the inn watching some one at the window. "What is it?" asked the unconscious Sydney. "What does it mean?" "Oh!" cried the man, "c'est Miladi Morgan, who has spoken so well of us workmen in her book about France. She is waiting for General La Fayette's carriage." "At that moment," writes the heroine of the story, "'the Lady Morgan' came to the window. It is impossible to describe any thing so grotesque, though such figures are still seen in France. A head, powdered and *crêpée*, two feet high; several *couches* of rouge on her cheek, and more than one on her chin; black patches *à discrétion;* a dress of damask silk with scarlet flowers." This venerable lady, above seventy, received the homage of the assembled admirers with the utmost complaisance, and, coming out, entered her vehicle; it was called a *désobligeante*, corresponding probably to our antique *vis-à-vis* of the days of "old Q." and Queen Charlotte; a coachman in "a livery as ancient and dusty as if he had served in the Fronde," drove this grand *dame de province* away from the *real* Lady Morgan and her husband, who were enchanted to see the gracious bows and smiles with which the old lady received the homage intended elsewhere. Lady Morgan, nevertheless, was dying to come out with the secret.

"Hitherto," she writes to her sister, "Morgan had kept me

quiet, but my vanity at last broke bounds: my charming *chapeau de paille*, with its poppy flowers; my French cashmere; and my coquetry, which, young or old, will go with me to my grave, would stand it no longer.

"'Odious! in woolen! 'twould a saint provoke!'
Were the last words that poor Narcissa spoke.

"As I was stepping into the La Grange carriage, I bowed to the nice 'young man' who handed me in, '*Je suis, moi, la véritable Lady Morgan.*' He said he guessed as much."

Lady Morgan and her husband arrived at La Grange on a fine September evening. The old castle tower, with the mantling ivy over it planted by Charles James Fox, the glowing sunset and the dark woods beyond, formed a scene not to be forgotten. At the castle gate stood the noble and venerable La Fayette, the "Cromwell-Grandison" to whom poor Marie Antoinette had turned for help, and whom she had innocently admired. He was surrounded by his grandchildren, then twelve in number; and conducting with all the grace of his country the welcome strangers to the *salon*, presented them to Ary Scheffer, since famed in art, and to Auguste Thierry. Carbonel the composer, who set Béranger's songs to music, and two Americans, formed the party, with the exception of two English gentlemen, one of whom told Lady Morgan that he had expected to find La Fayette eighty years old. "Where have you picked up such a notion?" was the reply. "Why, in your ladyship's work on France reviewed by the 'Quarterly.' The 'Quarterly' said that the general was a dotard." Lady Morgan's own description of this truly hospitable household is a true but somewhat sad picture of what a French château afforded before the insane law of partition cut up every thing like substantial prosperity in France. Few of the nobles of that country can now afford to live as La Fayette did, with twenty or thirty guests dining daily under the groined roof of the old stone hall, at a table where each dropped into his place without ceremony; where all ostentation was banished; no plate allowed for ornament; an excellent plain French dinner and delightful conversation forming the entertainment. Yet among those who sat round that board were the descendants of some of the most renowned families of France. "I never," Lady Morgan wrote to her sister, her beloved Olivia, "saw such a beautiful picture of domestic happiness, virtue, and talent." What increased the enjoyment of the warm-hearted little Irishwoman was that "Morgan was happy." Seated under the towers of La Grange, by the side of a pond, fishing, or listening to Carbonel singing Béranger's vaudeville, "*Il est passé le bon vieux temps*," the *ci-devant* physician forgot the delights of the Paris hospitals, in which he took a deep interest.

As the host and his guests strolled through the woods of La Grange, Lady Morgan ventured to ask the general whether it was true that he had gone with Marie Antoinette to a masked ball in Paris, the queen leaning on his arm. "I am afraid," he answered in that low emphatic voice peculiar to him, "that it was so. She was," he added, "so indiscreet, and, I can conscientiously say, so innocent."

Poor Marie Antoinette! Years after her doom thus was her fame justified by one whose good opinion she valued; and when Lady Morgan, with some hesitation, resumed: "The world said, general, that she favored the young champion, '*le héros des deux mondes!*'"

"*Cancan de salon!*" he briefly answered, and the subject was dropped.

Sunday was a day of rest as well as a festival at La Grange. At eight the great hall, perforated by Turenne's bullets during the war of the Fronde, was filled with peasantry, the servants, one or two *gens-d'armes* who looked in, and all the company; peers of France, artists, writers, the general and his twelve grandchildren; the concierge being the musician. As he struck up a *ronde*, the whole company formed themselves into that popular dance, at which Louis Philippe, when at Eu, often delighted to look on, especially when words were sung, as the dance went round. It is the national country dance of France. While the party were footing it, a party consisting of a young man in deep mourning, followed by his servants and portmanteau, passed behind the dancers into the interior of the castle. This proved to be Auguste de Staël, the favorite and only surviving son of the celebrated authoress.

After "charming days, more charming evenings," listening alternately to Carbonel's compositions and to Thierry's anecdotes, sitting to Scheffer for her portrait, walking *sur la pelouse* till sunset, and talking to the general about Bonaparte till bedtime, Lady Morgan returned to Paris. She left La Grange with deep regret. "All the clever men from Paris come here constantly," she wrote to her sister. "My little harp (which some Frenchwoman had mistaken for a dead child in its coffin) has the greatest success."

At the Château la Grange, Lady Morgan enjoyed those rich delights which society such as she met there affords, when coupled with the contemplation of virtue and domestic happiness. La Fayette, after a stirring life, was closing his days in peace among his family; Lady Morgan fully appreciated the unanimity of a French home *de province*. The perfect system that pervades families; the obedience of the young; the rapt devotion of the old to the younger members; the art and part the old servants take in every thing; the unaffected freedom which never dispenses with politeness, but abhors ostentation; this she could fully comprehend. But there was one want ungratified, she desired to see Béranger. Why was the lyric artist not there?

"Because," said La Fayette, "he won't come. I have asked him and he has refused, on the same principle that he declined to dine with Talleyrand and the Rochefoucaulds; because I am *trop grand seigneur*." His answer to La Fayette was: "My instinct leads me to the *caveau*, and not to the *château*." Béranger was not tempted to the drawing-rooms of the great—a distinction which might have fettered his verses, and which certainly would have diluted the strength of his genius.

In the midst of all her felicity she never forgot the absent. To her sister she wrote: "I am quite delighted you have a boy; he will be easily provided for. We will educate him among us, and he will be a protection to his sisters. What I would give to have you all here!"

She spent some time in Paris after her visit to La Grange; and in that gay capital learned that art of society which she never lost. Great names crowded to her Wednesday evenings in the Rue St. Augustin, in which central situation she had fixed herself, Talma reciting "coldly but finely" Shakspeare in French (Ducie's translation). Jouy, the "*Hermite de la Chaussée d'Antin*," complaining that his new play was prohibited by the censor of the press; the beautiful Comtesse de Rochefoucauld; the Princesse de Beauveau and her daughters; and the Duchesse de Broglie, were among the French notabilities who adorned her *salon*. Lady Morgan had always her degrees of welcome. Some she received "with acclamation;" any one who, as she pronounced of Thierry and Ary Scheffer, "bid fair for posterity," were always well received. About others she had her caprices: no one could sooner throw people just at the distance she liked than Lady Morgan. Though she professed, after the French fashion, that people were always to be let in, those who came without invitation on nights when the party had been invited were sure to find out their mistake. "I saw your windows lighted up, and, dear Lady Morgan, I came in, and here I am," said a lady to her, under this predicament, one evening.

"So I see," was the dry answer, and Sydney turned from her. This was in London.

Lady Morgan, during the winter of 1818, was still preparing for Italy, at that time a journey of some risk. She must have been in her true element in Paris. Christmas came, and with it the dismissal of De Cazes, and the establishment of an ultra ministry. Benjamin Constant was her frequent visitor, and read with real or feigned delight her "Florence Macarthy." She was beginning to find her popularity a burden; yet she undertook the journey to Geneva with "fears if not with misgivings." Even Colburn's two thousand pounds could not make her think it otherwise than awful. Nevertheless, at last, with a sort of ecstasy, she wrote "Geneva" on the top of her letters. At that striking city she was received with great cordiality both by Dumont and Sismondi; but she had, she avowed, no antecedents or impressions about the "City of Calvin." It contrasted strangely with the fantastic and historical Paris, that city of pleasant memories, which she had left. By a sort of instinct, as it seemed, she selected the Hôtel de la Balance as her abode, and inhabited the very rooms in which Madame de Staël held her famous literary receptions when she visited Geneva from Copet. At the Baron de Bonstetten's Lady Morgan met De Candolle, M. Betanist, and Pictet; but Dumont, who had been tutor to the present Lord Lansdowne, and spoke English perfectly, was her favorite *littérateur*. The conversation in such society she describes as the perfection of enjoyment; light though literary, desultory, but interspersed with personal anecdote, and therefore piquant. "It was at Geneva," adds this indomitable partisan, "that we first breathed the air of a republic." She must have had enough of republics since that time, after the failure in France, and its results.

In the spring of April, 1819, Lady Morgan announced to her sister that she was "all Italy's." It could not have been easy to return to task-work after all the holiday time in Paris and Geneva. In the former capital Lady Morgan had avoided her countrywomen, who played at hazard, and were not respectable. She now begged Lady Clarke, her "dear Livy," not to send any of the "Crawleys" *trapesing* after her; "not to give any one her Italian address except the O'Conor Don.' She went, feeling that she had a great vocation, but very little confidence in being able to do any thing in the regeneration of Italy. This was "sixty years ago;" alas! what has been done since?

In Italy she formed the acquaintance of Lord Byron, of whom her reminiscences were vivid even to her latest days. Lady Morgan was a lenient judge of those errors which the world, properly, visits severely. Bitter, like all the Irish when offended, her moral decisions were generally fair. When she knew Byron, he was under a deserved cloud of reprobation, even by that exalted society which overlooked George IV.

and ignored his connection with Lady Conyngham. Byron was just then finally separated from his wife. That story which got abroad that Dr. Lushington, who was the great adviser of the separation, knew of circumstances too dreadful to be disclosed, which feeling justified that step—a step which, as usual, drove the husband to desperation, without insuring the wife's peace—was generally circulated. Those exquisite lines—

> "Fare thee well, and if forever,
> Still forever fare thee well,"

were in every one's mouth, in every one's heart, when Lady Morgan saw Lord Byron. She always espoused his cause. An exquisite miniature of the ill-starred poet remained till her death in her drawing-room, bequeathed to her by Lady Caroline Lamb. The noble brow; the blue, clear speaking eyes; the fine classic nose; and, above all, the beautiful mouth, full of sweetness, yet firm and sensible, are evidence of the likeness being faithful. It is just such a head as one would wish a poet to be endowed with: it does not give the impression of an "imagination of fire playing round a heart of ice," as Southey would have us think of Byron, but of a genial, thoughtful nature—of a man born to be loved, though forcing into evil his destiny. This was, above all, the picture in her possession to which Lady Morgan always drew the attention of strangers, and it hung near the sofa on which she usually sat.

The ignorance and indolence of the Italian ladies struck this active woman forcibly. Yet she defends them in her work on Italy from the general charge of pervading immorality, and contends that there are families as pure, as well-principled, and as domestic as in England.

She returned to England to form that circle in which she lived, and in which she delighted ever after. The fierceness of parties was subsiding when she took up her temporary abode in James Street, Buckingham Gate, in a house belonging to Sir Henry Bulwer, with whom, as with his celebrated brother, Lady Morgan was intimate. Her "Florence Macarthy" appeared, and her fame as a novelist was high: she ventured, also, into the paths which even she was glad to illumine by her imagination. Full of Italy, she wrote a very interesting life or, rather, sketch of the life of Salvator Rosa. She published, also, her "O'Briens and O'Flahertys," but the greatest of her works of fiction, "The Princess," was yet to come.

Lady Morgan after a time removed to William Street, Knightsbridge, where, in the immediate proximity of all the *beau monde* of London, she established her quarters. Having been much abroad, Lady Morgan did not deem it necessary to give large, expensive dinners in order to keep "her world" together. She seldom received dinner company; and when she did so, her table was never thronged; six or eight formed its fullest complement of guests; and, indeed, her means did not permit the extravagance of a proper London dinner. During Lord Melbourne's administration she received a pension of three hundred pounds a year for her services as the supporter of the liberal party in Ireland. Sir Charles Morgan had also a tolerable income; so that, to the end of her days, Lady Morgan could not have known pecuniary anxiety. She was by nature hospitable, though not extravagant, and assembled some of the best company in London upon Lady Cork's principle of "plenty of tea and wax lights." "The world," she used to say, "is a very good world, but you must seek it; it will not do to neglect it.'

Early in life Lady Morgan had been intimate with the Abercorn family. The Dowager Lady Cork—the Miss Monckton of Miss Burney's days—was one of her friends. Lady Cork was eccentric, and had an absent way of putting into her pocket any thing that lay before her. It is related of her that being one day at the house of a noble earl in —— Square, some very ancient and valuable watches belonging to the family of her host were shown. "I tremble," whispered a fashionable divine, to whose extemporary sermons half the west end of London thronged, "to see those watches in Lady Cork's hands."

"They are as safe, sir, with me as with you," was her reply (having overheard him), and time proved that she was right. The earl, by no means a type of "absolute wisdom," was gathered to his fathers. His countess succeeded to all the personalty; among them to these same watches. After a few months of weeds—one can not say of mourning—she married the Rev. Dr. ——, and the watches, of course, came into his possession.

The Countess of Charleville, whose rare qualities have been well described in her "Diary" by Lady Morgan, was one of her most prized friends. The letters of this lady to Lady Morgan give, indeed, an insight into a character of singular good sense and gentleness. Of a cultivated mind, this venerable lady, with her singular charm of manner and of person, attracted around her most of the eminent men and women of letters of the day: Tom Moore, "who would not sing until a large audience of pretty women were collected to hear him;" William Spencer, whose verses, airy, polished, graceful like his person, made him the idol of society, while the charm of his manner and of his character converted the acquaintance of an evening into the friends of a lifetime; Captain Morris, the lyrist—these were among the lions of those drawing-rooms in which Lady Charleville, wheeled from one room to another by her handsome son, then Lord Tullamore, formed a picture of no ordinary interest. The good sense and good spirit of this lady's letters to Lady Morgan, her gentle sincerity and excellent criticisms, denote a superiority of intellect very rare, because it was combined with the greatest humility.

This beloved and respected lady had lost the use of her lower limbs before she had passed middle life, yet she survived till the age of ninety, and died, a short time previously to Lady Morgan, in 1858. Their friendship was the friendship of half a century. They were both Irishwomen, Lady Charleville being one of the Cremorne family; both witty; though perhaps Lady Charleville's wit had the greater refinement of the two; both women of society, yet not in the disparaging sense. Had Lady Charleville been a Frenchwoman, and lived in France, "she would have been assigned a place in social history with the Sévignés and Du Deffands."

One can not but confess that Lady Charleville shows her *tact* in her avowal that she could not comprehend Sir Charles Morgan's work on the "Philosophy of Life," the principles of which were attacked by Reynolds, the Christian advocate at Cambridge. Lady Cork disapproved of Sir Charles's philosophy, and therefore sheltered herself under the plea of being "overwhelmed by the detail and quantity of the physical knowledge" it contained. Yet the work was praised by Humboldt, and translated into French by Lacroix. It was accused of materialism.

Then at Lady Cork's, Lady Morgan added to her now increasing circle of society. It seems, indeed, like speaking of another age to recall, as she does in her "Diary," Lady Ameland, the insulted wife of the late Duke of Sussex, and the mother of the Prince and Princess D'Este. "Oh, these men and their laws!" exclaims Lady Morgan; "so lightly made, so lightly broken, as passion or expediency suggests; from Henry VIII. and his pope—before, and after!" This was on Lady Cork's pink night: the next was her blue evening, when editors and reviewers went to meet people of science.

Lady Morgan, in her selections from her "host of friends," showed better taste than to separate classes or to have pink or blue nights. Those who have been much in London during the last five-and-twenty years can not forget the assemblage of noble if not royal authors; of beauty, and fashion, and science, and musical skill, which rendered her drawing-room so remarkable.

That room was in itself a picture. Ascending a not very wide staircase, you entered a small *salon*, opening with folding doors into another, which terminated in a veranda. The furniture was red: and, without any attempt at splendor, the room had a comfortable aspect. The walls were crowded with pictures of great interest, but no value. Lady Morgan's own portraits—the earlier ones, in a scanty, *décolleté* dress—a girdle—a bodice two inches in length—curled locks—a pen in one hand, the other supporting her head—formed a main feature. During the latter years of her life, a small likeness was painted of her in her widow's cap, and in black, which gave her all the kindly expressions of her character. Near her seat Lord Byron's face riveted those who sat opposite to it. Around the room were portraits of Madame de Pompadour, La Belle Jennings, and one or two likenesses painted by Lady Morgan's beloved niece. A variety of small pictures, to each of which "*une histoire*" was attached, filled up every corner; articles of *virtù* of all sorts; memorials of the great and the lettered, dead and living, always elicited some rapid anecdote, so promptly told as scarcely to interrupt the conversation which was passing through the circle. Then you were always invited to walk into the back drawing-room, and take a survey of her "shrine," which had a curtain drawn before its precious contents—miniatures, relics, rare books. A large *portière* hanging over the folding doors divided the rooms when Lady Morgan had a large reception. On a little sofa in the corner sat the lady paramount of the *salon*, always in the shade—always with the green fan, either to shade her from the fire or from the light.

Lady Morgan was rarely from home in the afternoons, and that was one secret of her popularity in London and Paris. People like best to knock at a door where they know they shall be let in. London is too large to call on absentees. In Paris no one likes to mount the stairs and to go down again—the sport of the *concierges*, who often choose to be ignorant as to the lady "*au second*" being at home or not. Then Lady Morgan was "there and then" ready to say something pleasant as soon as you came in. On Sunday afternoons her little rooms were crowded. On Sunday evenings she often collected a few intimates, who walked in *sans façon*. Her round of society was, indeed, transiently interrupted by the death of Sir Charles Morgan, in 1847. He was carried off by a fever, to her deep affliction. Yet, in the course of a month, her rooms were again opened to those she best knew and most liked. Though she survived him nearly twenty years, those who had long remembered Lady Morgan saw that for some time she was a changed person. Her Irish drollery, her cherished vanity, so amusing and so really natural, was quenched. Yet still she paused not, she retired not, and many blamed her for want of feeling. "I take to company," she said one day, with a deep sigh, "as others take to drinking—to drown sorrow." Let it be remembered she had no family, few home cares to console or employ her. Whatever were Sir Charles's religious convictions, he died in them, and died happy, and his widow was happy about his eternal fate. That latitudinarianism is the only cloud that rests on Lady Morgan's memory.

Before Sir Charles's death she had visited Belgium and written "The Princess," by far the ablest of her novels. In it she draws a picture of fashionable life. It is the life, however, of Holland House, rather than of the large class she portrays in general. Her princess is an improbable, an impossible being; but so great is the skill with which each incident is dovetailed into the others that one's common sense is beguiled. In her opinions of Belgium, Lady Morgan's judgment has been confirmed by the happy results of a long and liberal rule over that country. As a "Queen of Society" her reputation was now at its acme. Lord Brougham, the Earl of Carlisle (then Lord Morpeth), Sheil (whose death she deeply lamented), and many other political characters, were visitors. Her heart beat with pleasure when her two favorites, Sir Henry Bulwer and Sir Edward Bulwer Lytton, sat by her sofa. She lived, perhaps, to feel that they had forgotten her, and before her death mentioned that it was several years since she had seen the great author of "Pelham." "He always expresses himself kindly when on any occasion he writes to me, but that is *all.* My house is not what it was," she added, sadly.

A younger tribe of aspirants first found themselves in that *salon* before the year 1848. Eliot Warburton—gifted, openhearted—the very type of a true Irish gentleman, was her especial favorite. We saw him at one of her latest *déjeûners*, with that bright eye, that gay smile, which won every heart. His brother, too, the accomplished author of "Hochelaga" and the "History of Canada," the manly, intellectual soldier—as a man, beloved, respected, and mourned—he, too, was almost always one of her most cherished guests. Both are gone hence in their prime: their lives sunshine—their deaths tragedies.

Many foreigners of distinction or of notoriety crowded near that *portière*, and listened to professional music, which always varied Lady Morgan's *soirées*. Malibran, of whom she hoped much, too much, has been seen in her house. Lady Morgan spoke French with facility, though with accent. Her notes, her conversation, were objectionably interlarded with French idioms.

As age advanced Lady Morgan became more and more rigid in the ladies whom she admitted to her house. A change in her ideas as to the tone of society certainly marked the decline of her life. She was speaking one day of two ladies not without the pale of respectability, but somewhat disposed to overstep it. "I never see them now," she said, gravely. "My house is a dull house for that sort of people."

Her last literary project was the publication of her own "Memoirs." Strange to say, she still writhed under the lash of the departed Croker, and wished to rescue her family and herself from his contemptuous assertions.

In 1854 her brother-in-law, Sir Arthur Clarke, wrote to her, strongly urging her to put this idea into execution, and offering to be her amanuensis. It was still her frequent theme when her decline of health made it appear almost impossible. Croker was dead: she would never have attempted it while he held the knout, and held it with a cruel, unsparing hand. She made a compromise between wishes, which stimulated her to the task, and time, which said no; for the dark shadows of the tomb were even gathering round her when, on Christmas day, 1858, she wrote the last words in which she ever addressed her "dear public." She gave some portion of her autobiography to the world in an "odd volume, which at some future day may drop into a more important series, where I may yet be able to wind up the confessions of my life and errors, as the old Puritans phrased it, and obtain absolution without going into the confessional."

This sanguine idea, which was expressed after Lady Morgan had had "all but a fatal illness," to use her own words, was not realized.

During the last three years of her existence it hung on a thread. She continued to receive, and rather to urge, the visits of friends whom she liked, in the evening. But she was scarcely equal to the exertion. "I am so tired," she said one evening to her niece; "I feel so low." What a change from the gay spirits of the wild Irish girl! Yet to the last she was full of life—in its best sense—its affections to some strong, its interests in all undying. She was even eloquent at times; but the flashes that used to irradiate died away from physical not from mental weakness. Her memory was spared, her hearing remained, and her sight seemed never to have failed much more than at eighty-two all things fail.

She died on the 16th of April, 1859: and with her ends one of those few remaining literary cliques, easy, when once formed, to maintain, but difficult ever to bring together again. She belonged, it has truly been said, to another age, another world—that of Rogers, Byron, Moore; yet she was not out of date in this: her feelings as well as her manners had wonderful youth in them. All the young liked her; none felt that they had, in visiting Lady Morgan, been seeing an old woman—her sympathies were so fresh, her manners so genial. Let not the world speak of her as solely one of themselves. While of the world, while, perhaps, judging it not rightly, her heart was benevolent, her affections ever in the right source.

JANE, DUCHESS OF GORDON.

"Few women," says Sir Nathaniel Wraxall, "have performed a more conspicuous part, or occupied a higher place on the public theatre of fashion, politics, and dissipation, than the Duchess of Gordon."

Jane, afterward Duchess of Gordon, the rival in beauty and talent to Georgiana, Duchess of Devonshire, was born in Wigtonshire, in Scotland. Her father, Sir William Maxwell of Monreith (anciently Mureith), represented one of the numerous families who branched off from the original stock—Herbert of Caerlaverock, first Lord Maxwell, the ancestor of the famous Earl of Nithsdale, whose countess, Winifred, played so noble a part when her husband was in prison during the Jacobite insurrection. From this honorable house descended, in our own time, the gallant Sir Murray Maxwell, whose daughter, Mrs. Carew, became the wife of the too well-known Colonel Waugh: the events which followed are still fresh in the public mind. Until that blemish, loyalty, honor, and prosperity marked out the Maxwells of Monreith for "their own." In 1681 William Maxwell was created a baronet of Nova Scotia. Various marriages and intermarriages with old and noble families kept the blood *pure*—a circumstance as much prized by the Scotch as by the Germans. Sir William, the father of the Duchess of Gordon, married Magdalene, the daughter of William Blair, of Blair, and had by her six children—three sons and three daughters—of whom the youngest but one was Jane, the subject of this memoir.

This celebrated woman was a true Scotchwoman—stanch to her principles, proud of her birth, energetic, and determined. Her energy might have died away like a flash in the pan had it not been for her determination. She carried through every thing that she attempted; and great personal charms accelerated her influence in that state of society in which, as in the French capital, women had, at that period, an astonishing though transient degree of ascendency.

The attractions of Jane Maxwell appeared to have been developed early, for before she entered on the gay world, a song, "Jenny of Monreith," was composed in her honor, which her son, the Duke of Gordon, used to sing, long after the charms, which were thus celebrated, had vanished. Her features were regular; the contour of her face was truly noble; her hair was dark, as well as her eyes and eyebrows; her face long and beautifully oval; the chin somewhat too long; the upper lip was short, and the mouth, notwithstanding a certain expression of determination, sweet and well defined. Nothing can be more becoming to features of this stamp, that require softening, than the mode of dressing the hair then general. Sir Joshua Reynolds has painted the Duchess of Gordon with her dark hair drawn back, in front, over a cushion, or some support that gave it waviness; round and round the head, between each rich mass, were two rows of large pearls, until, at the top, they were lost in the folds of a ribbon; a double row of pearls round the fair neck: a ruff, opening low in front, a tight bodice, and sleeves full to an extreme at the top, tighter toward the wrists, seem to indicate that the dress of the period of Charles I. had even been selected for this most lovely portrait. The head is turned aside—with great judgment—probably to mitigate the decided expression of the face when in a front view.

As she grew up, however, the young lady was found to be deficient in one especial grace—she was not feminine; her person, her mind, her manners, all, in this respect, corresponded. "She might," says one who knew her, "have aptly represented Homer's Juno." Always animated, with features that were constantly in play, one great charm was wanting—that of sensibility. Sometimes her beautiful face was overclouded with anger; more frequently was it irradiated with smiles. Her conversation, too, annihilated much of the impression made by her commanding beauty. She despised the usages of the world, and, believing herself exempted from them by her rank, after she became a duchess, she dispensed with them, and sacrificed to her venal ambition some of the most lovable qualities of her sex. One of her speeches, when honors became, as she thought, too common at court, betrays her pride and her coarseness. "Upon my word," she used to say, "one can not look out of one's coach window without spitting on a knight." Whatever were her defects, her beauty captivated the fancy of Alexander, the fourth Duke of Gordon, a young man of twenty-four years of age, whom she married on the 28th of October, 1767. The family she entered, as well as the family whence she sprang, were devoted adherents of the exiled Stuarts, and carried to a great extent the hereditary Toryism of their exalted lineage. The great-grandmother of the duke was that singular Duchess of Gordon who sent a medal to the Faculty of Advocates in Edinburgh, with the head of James Stuart the Chevalier on one side, and on the other the British

Isles, with the word *Reddite* inscribed underneath. The Faculty were highly gratified by this present. After a debate, they accepted the medal, and sent two of their body to thank the duchess, and to say that they hoped she would soon be enabled to favor the society with a second medal on the *Restoration.* Duke Alexander, the husband of Jane Maxwell, showed in his calm and inert character no evidence of being descended from this courageous partisan. He was a man of no energy, except in his love of country pursuits, and left the advancement of the family interests wholly to his spirited and ambitious wife. They were married only six years after George III. had succeeded to the throne. Never was a court more destitute of amusements than that of the then youthful sovereign of England. Until his latter days, George II. had enjoyed revelries, though of a slow, formal, German character; but his grandson confined himself, from the age of twenty-two, to his public and private duties. He neither frequented masquerades, nor joined in play. The splendors of a court were reserved for birthdays, and for those alone; neither did the king usually sit down to table with the nobility or with his courtiers. Never was he known to be guilty of the slightest excess at table, and his repasts were simple, if not frugal. At a levee, or on the terrace at Windsor, or in the circle of Hyde Park, this model of a worthy English gentleman might be seen, either with his plain-featured queen on his arm, or driven in his well-known coach with his old and famous cream-colored horses. Junius derided the court "where," he said, "prayers are morality and kneeling is religion." But although wanting in animation, it was far less reprehensible than that which preceded or that which followed it. The Duchess of Gordon, irreproachable in conduct, with her high Tory principles, was well suited to a court over which Lord Bute exercised a strong influence. She had naturally a calculating turn of mind. Fame, admiration, fashion, were agreeable trifles, but wealth and rank were the solid aims to which every effort was directed. Unlike her future rival, the Duchess of Devonshire, who impoverished herself in her boundless charities, the Duchess of Gordon kept in view the main chance, and resolved from her early youth to aggrandize the family into which she had entered.

Her empire as a wit was undisputed, for the Duchess of Devonshire was then a mere girl at her mother's knee; but that for beauty was disputed by Mary, Duchess of Rutland, so well remembered in our own time, as she survived till 1831.

This exquisite specimen of English loveliness, compared by

some to Musidora, as described by Thomson, was the most beautiful woman of rank in the kingdom. Every turn of her features, every form of her limbs was perfect, and grace accompanied every movement. She was tall, of the just height; slender, but not thin; her features were delicate and noble; and her ancestors, the Plantagenets, were in her represented by a faultless sample of personal attributes. She was the daughter of a race which has given to the world many heroes, one philosopher, and several celebrated beauties—that of Somerset; and as the descendant of the defenders of Raglan Castle, might be expected to combine various noble qualities with personal gifts. But she was cold, although a coquette. In the Duchess of Devonshire it was the *besoin d'aimer*, the cordial nature recoiled into itself from being linked to an expletive that betrayed her into an encouragement of what offered her the semblance of affection—into the temptation of being beloved. To the Duchess of Gordon her conquests were enhanced by the remembrance of what they might bring; but the Duchess of Rutland viewed her admirers in the light of offering tributes to a goddess. She was destitute of the smiles, the intelligence, and sweetness of the Duchess of Devonshire; and conscious of charms, received adoration as her due. "In truth," Sir Nathaniel Wraxall, who knew her well, writes, "I never contemplated her except as an enchanting statue, formed to excite admiration rather than to awaken love, this superb production of nature not being lighted up by corresponding mental attractions."

This lady was united to one of the most attractive and popular of men, but one of the most imprudent and convivial. The son of that celebrated Marquis of Granby whom Junius attacked, the young Duke of Rutland was a firm partisan of Pitt, whom he first brought into the House of Commons, and at whose wish he accepted the government of Ireland in 1784. Never was there such splendor at the vice-regal court as in his time. Vessels laden with the expensive luxuries from England were seen in the Bay of Dublin at short intervals; the banquets given were most costly; the evenings at the castle were divided between play and drinking; and yet the mornings found the young duke breakfasting on six or seven turkey's eggs. He then, when on his progress, rode forty or fifty miles, returned to dinner at seven, and sat up to a late hour, supping before he retired to rest.

The duchess had little place in his heart, and the syren, Mrs. Billington, held it in temporary thraldom; but constancy was to a man of such a calibre impossible. Nevertheless, when the duke saw his wife surrounded by admirers, whom her levity of manner encouraged, he became jealous, and they parted, for the last time as it proved, on bad terms. One evening, seeing him engaged in play, the duchess approached the window of the room in which he sat, and tapped at it. He was highly incensed by this interference with his amusements. She returned to England an invalid, in order to consult Dr. Warren, the father of the late physician of that name. While residing with her mother in Berkeley Square, she heard that the duke was attacked with fever. She sent off Dr. Warren to see him, and was preparing to follow him when the physician returned. At Holyhead he had heard that the duke was no more. He died at the early age of thirty-three, his blood having been inflamed by his intemperance, which, however, never affected his reason, and was, therefore, the more destructive to his health. His widow, in spite of their alienation, mourned long and deeply. Never did she appear more beautiful than when, in 1788, she reappeared after her seclusion. Like Diana of Poictiers, she retained her wonderful loveliness to an advanced age. Latterly, she covered her wrinkles with enamel, and when she appeared in public, always quitted a room in which the windows, which might admit the dampness, were opened. She never married again, notwithstanding the various suitors who desired to obtain her hand.

For a long time the Duchess of Gordon continued to reign over the Tory party almost without a rival. When, at last, the Duchess of Devonshire came forward as the female champion of the Foxites, Pitt and Dundas, afterward Lord Melville, opposed to her the Duchess of Gordon. At that time she lived in the splendid mansion of the then Marquis of Buckingham in Pall Mall. Every evening numerous assemblies of persons attached to the administration gathered in those stately saloons, built upon, or near the terrace whereon Nell Gwynne used to chat with Charles II. on the grass below, as he was going to feed his birds in his gardens. Presuming on her rank, her influence, her beauty, the Duchess of Gordon used to act in the most determined manner as a government *whipper-in.* When a member on whom she counted was wanting, she did not scruple to send for him, to remonstrate, to persuade, to *fix* him by a thousand arts. Strange must have been the scene—more strange than attractive. Every thing was forgotten but the one grand object of the evening, the theme of all talk—the next debate and its supporters. In the year 1780, events took place which for some time appeared likely to shake the prosperity of the Gordon family almost to its fall.

The duke had two brothers, the elder of whom, Lord William, was the Ranger of Windsor Park, and survived to a great age. The younger, Lord George, holds a very conspicuous but not a very creditable place in the annals of his country. No event in our history bears any analogy with that styled the "Gordon Riots," excepting the Fire of London in the reign of Charles II.; and even that calamity did not exhibit the mournful spectacle which attended the conflagrations of 1780. In the former instance, the miserable sufferers had to contend only with a devouring element; in the latter, they had to seek protection, and to seek it in vain, from a populace of the lowest description and the vilest purposes, who carried with them destruction wherever they went. Even during the French Revolution, revolting and degrading as it was, the firebrand was not employed in the work of destruction; the public and private buildings of Paris were spared.

The author of all these calamities, Lord George Gordon, was a young man of gentle, agreeable manners, and delicate, highbred appearance. His features were regular and pleasing: he was thin and pale, but with a cunning, sinister expression in his face that indicated wrong-headedness. He was dependent on his elder brother, the duke, for his maintenance; six hundred pounds a year being allowed him by his grace. Such was the exterior, such the circumstances of an incendiary who has been classed with Wat Tyler and Jack Cade, or with Kett, the delinquent in the time of Edward VI.

It was during the administration of Lord North that the Gordon Riots took place, excited by the harangues and speeches of Lord George. On the 2d of June he harangued the people; on the 7th these memorable disturbances broke out: Bloomsbury Square was the first point of attack. In Pope's time this now-neglected square was fashionable:

"In Palace Yard, at nine, you'll find me there;
At ten, for certain, sir, in Bloomsbury Square."

Baxter, the Nonconformist, and Sir Hans Sloane, once inhabited what was, in their time, called Southampton Square, from Southampton House, which occupied one whole side of Bloomsbury Square, and was long the abode of Lady Rachel Russell, after the execution of her lord. Like every other part of what may be called "Old London," it is almost sanctified by the memories of the lettered and the unfortunate. But the glory of Bloomsbury Square was, in those days, the house of Lord Mansfield, at the north end of the east side; in which that judge had collected many valuables, among which his library was the dearest to his heart: it was the finest legal library of his time. As soon as the long summer's day had closed, and darkness permitted the acts of violence to be fully recognized, Hart Street and Great Russell Street were illuminated by large fires, composed of the furniture taken from the houses of certain magistrates. Walking into Bloomsbury, the astounded observer of that night's horrors saw, with consternation, the hall door of Lord Mansfield's house broken open; and instantly all the contents of the various apartments were thrown into the square, and set on fire. In vain did a small body of foot-soldiers attempt to intimidate the rioters. The whole of the house was consumed, and vengeance would have fallen on Lord Mansfield and his lady had they not escaped by a back door a few minutes before the hall was broken into: such was that memorable act of destruction—so prompt, so complete. Let us follow the mob in fancy, and leaving the burning pile in Bloomsbury Square, trace the steps of the crowd into Holborn. We remember, as we are hurried along, with a bitter feeling, that Holborn was the appointed road for criminals from Newgate to Tyburn. It is now one blaze of light: in the hollow near Fleet Market, the house and warehouses of Mr. Langdale, a Catholic—a Christian like ourselves, though not one of our own blessed and reformed Church—is blazing: a pinnacle of flame, like a volcano, is sent up into the air. St. Andrew's Church is almost scorched with the heat; while the figures of the clock—that annalist which numbers, as it stands, the hours of guilt—are plain as at noonday. The gutters beneath, catching here and there gleams of the fiery heavens, run with spirituous liquors from the plundered distilleries; the night is calm, as if no deeds of persecution sullied its beauty; at times it is obscured by volumes of smoke, but they pass away, and the appalled spectators of the street below are plainly visible. Here stands a mother, with an infant in her arms, looking on; there, a father, leading his boy to the safest point of observation. We wonder at their boldness; but it is the direst sign of affright—in their homes they are insecure—every where, any where, the ruthless unseen hand may cast the brand, and all may perish. At this early hour there seemed to be no ringleader—no pillage; it appeared difficult to conceive who could be the wretch who instigated, who directed this awful riot: but, at the windows, men were seen calmly tearing away pictures from the walls; furniture, books, plate, from their places, and throwing them into the flames. As midnight drew near, the ferocious passions of the multitude were heightened by ardent spirits: not a soldier, either horse or foot, is visible. "While we stood," says an eye-witness, "by the wall of St. Andrew's church-yard, a watchman, with his lantern in his hand, passed on, calling the hour as if in a time of profound security."

Meantime the King's Bench Prison was enveloped in flames;

the Mansion House and the Bank were attacked. But the troops were killing and dispersing the rioters on Blackfriars' Bridge; a desperate conflict between the horse and the mob was going on near the Bank. What a night! The whole city seemed to be abandoned to pillage—to destruction. Shouts, yells, the shrieks of women, the crackling of the burning houses, the firing of platoons toward St. George's Fields, combined to show that no horrors, no foes are equal to those of domestic treachery, domestic persecution, domestic fury and infatuation.

It was not alone the Roman Catholics who were threatened. Sir George Savile's house in Leicester Square—once the peaceful locality in which Dorothy Sydney, Waller's "Sacharissa" bloomed—was plundered and burned. Then the Duchess of Devonshire took fright, and did not venture to stay at Devonshire House for many nights after dusk, but took refuge at Lord Clermont's in Berkeley Square, sleeping on a sofa in the drawing-room. In Downing Street, Lord North was dining with a party; his brother, Colonel North, Mr. Eden, afterward Lord Auckland, the Honorable John St. John, General Fraser, and Count Malzen, the Prussian minister. The little square then surrounding Downing Street was filled with the mob. "Who commands the upper story?" said Lord North. "I do," answered Colonel North; "and I have twenty or thirty grenadiers well armed, who are ready to fire on the first notice."

"If your grenadiers fire," said Mr. Eden, calmly, "they will probably fire into my house just opposite."

The mob was now threatening; every moment the peril was increasing. Mr. St. John held a pistol in his hand; and Lord North, who never could forbear cutting a joke, said, "I am not half so much afraid of the mob as of Jack St. John's pistol." By degrees, however, the crowd, seeing that the house was well guarded, dispersed, and the gentlemen quietly sat down again to their wine until late in the evening, when they all ascended to the top of the house, and beheld the capital blazing. It was here that the first suggestion of a coalition between Lord North and Fox, to save the country and themselves, was started, and afterward perfected behind the scenes of the Opera House in the Haymarket. During this memorable night George III. behaved with the courage which, whatever their failings, has ever highly distinguished the Hanoverian family. By the vigorous measures, late indeed, but not too late, which he acceded to at the Council, London was saved. But the popular fury had extended to other towns. Bath was in tumult: a new Roman Catholic chapel there was burned. Mrs. Thrale, hearing that her house at Streatham had been threatened, caused it to be emptied of its furniture. Three times was Mrs. Thrale's town house attacked; her valuables and furniture were removed thence also; and she deemed it prudent to leave Bath, into which coaches, chalked over with "No Popery," were hourly driving. The composure with which the rioters did their work seemed to render the scene more fearful, as they performed these acts of violence as if they were carrying out a religious duty rather than deeds of execrable hatred.

It was not until two or three days after tranquillity had been restored that Lord George Gordon was apprehended. Ministers were justly reproached for not having sent him to the Tower on the 2d of June, when he had assembled and excited the mob to extort compliance with their wishes from the House of Commons. Such a step, when the House was surrounded by multitudes, and when, every moment, it was expected that the door would be broken open, would have been hazardous: had that occurred, Lord George would have suffered instant death. General Murray, afterward Duke of Atholl, held his sword ready to pass it through Lord George's body the instant the mob rushed in. The Earl of Carnarvon, the grandfather of the present earl, followed him closely with the same intent.

The indignation of the insulted Commons was extreme, and the distress and displeasure of Lord George's own family doubtless excessive. The House of Commons have never been thus insulted before. It is difficult to determine what could be Lord George's motives for the conduct which led to these awful results, during the whole of which he preserved a composure that bordered on insensibility: he was a perfect master of himself while the city was in flames. Much may be laid to fanaticism, and the mental derangement which it either produced or evinced. When too late he tried in vain to abate the fury he had excited, and offered to take his stand by Lord Rodney's* side when the Bank was attacked, to aid that officer, who commanded the Guards, in its defense.

Lord George then lived in Welbeck Street, Cavendish Square, and tradition assigns as his house that now occupied by Mr. Newby the publisher, No. 30, and for many years the house of Count Woronzoff, the Russian embassador, who died there. Lord George there prepared for his defense, which was intrusted to the great Erskine, then in his prime, or, as he was called in caricatures, with which the shops were full, from his

* Second Baron Rodney, son of the admiral, then a captain in the guards.

extreme vanity, *Counselor Ego.* In February, 1781, the trial took place, and Lord George was acquitted. He retired to Birmingham, became a Jew, and lived in that faith, or under the delusion that he did so. The hundreds who perished from his folly or insanity were avenged in his subsequent imprisonment in Newgate for a libel on Marie Antoinette, of which he was convicted. He died a very few years after the riots of 1780, in Newgate, generally condemned, and but little compassionated.

It appears from the letters addressed by Dr. Beattie to the Duchess of Gordon, that she was not in London during the riots of June, 1780. The poet had been introduced to her by Sir William Forbes, and frequently visited Gordon Castle. We find him, while London was blazing, sending thither a parcel of "Mirrors," the fashionable journal, "Count Fathom," "The Tale of a Tub," and the fanciful, forgotten romance by Bishop Berkeley, "Gaudentio di Lucca," to amuse her solitude. "Gaudentio," he writes, "will amuse you, though there are tedious passages in it. The whole description of passing the deserts of Africa is particularly excellent." It is singular that this dream of Bishop Berkeley's of a country fertile and delicious in the centre of Africa should have been almost realized in our own time by the discoveries of Dr. Livingstone.

To his present of books Dr. Beattie added a flask of whisky, which he sealed with his usual seal—"The three graces, whom I take to be your *grace's near* relations, as they have the honor, not only to bear one of your titles, but also to resemble you exceedingly in form, feature, and manner. If you had lived three thousand years ago, which I am very glad you did not, there would have been four of them, and you the first. May all happiness attend your grace!"

This graceful piece of adulation was followed by a tender concern for "her grace's" health. A sportive benediction was offered while the duchess was at Glenfiddick, a hunting seat in the heart of the Grampian Hills—a wild, sequestered spot, of which Dr. Beattie was particularly fond.

"I rejoice in the good weather, in the belief that it extends to Glenfiddick, where I pray that your grace may enjoy all the health and happiness that good air, goats' whey, romantic solitude, and the society of the loveliest children in the world can bestow. May your days be clear sunshine; and may a gentle rain give balm to your nights, that the flowers and birch-trees may salute you in the morning with all their fragrance! May the kids frisk and play tricks before you with unusual sprightliness; and may the song of birds, the hum of bees, and the distant waterfall, with now and then the shepherd's horn resounding from the mountains, entertain you with a full chorus of Highland music! My imagination had parceled out the lovely little glen into a thousand little paradises; in the hope of being there, and seeing every day in that solitude, what is

"'Fairer than famed of old, or fabled since,
Of fairy damsels, met in forest wide
By errant knights.'

But the information you received at Cluny gave a check to my fancy, and was indeed a great disappointment to Mrs. Beattie and me; not on account of the goats' whey, but because it keeps us so long at such a distance from your grace."

When at Gordon Castle, the duchess occupied herself with pursuits that elevated while they refreshed her mind. She promised Dr. Beattie to send him the history of a *day*. Her day seems to have been partly engaged in the instruction of her five daughters, and in an active correspondence and reading. It is difficult to imagine this busy, flattered woman reading Blair's Sermons, which had then been recently published, to her family on Sundays; or the duke, whom Dr. Beattie describes as "more astronomical than ever," engrossed from morning to night in making calculations with Mr. Copeland, Professor of Astronomy in Marischal College, Aberdeen. Beattie's letters to the duchess, although too adulatory, were those of a man who respects the understanding of the woman to whom he writes. The following anecdotes, the one relating to Hume, the other to Handel, are in his letters to the Duchess of Gordon, and they can not be read without interest.

"Mr. Hume was boasting to the doctor (Gregory) that among his disciples he had the honor to reckon many of the fair sex. 'Now tell me,' said the doctor, 'whether, if you had a wife or a daughter, you would *wish* them to be your disciples? Think well before you answer me; for I assure you that whatever your answer is, I will not conceal it.' Mr. Hume, with a smile and some hesitation, made this reply: 'No; I believe skepticism may be too sturdy a virtue for a woman.' Miss Gregory will certainly remember she has heard her father tell this story."

Again, about Handel:

"I lately heard two anecdotes, which deserve to be put in writing, and which you will be glad to hear. When Handel's Messiah was first performed, the audience were exceedingly struck and affected by the music in general; but when the chorus struck up, "For the Lord God Omnipotent reigneth," they were so transported that they all, together with the king (who happened to be present), started up, and remained standing till the chorus ended; and hence it became the fashion in

England for the audience to stand while that part of the music is performing. Some days after the first exhibition of the same divine oratorio, Mr. Handel came to pay his respects to Lord Kinnoul, with whom he was particularly acquainted. His lordship, as was natural, paid him some compliments on the notable entertainment which he had lately given the town. 'My lord,' said Handel, "I should be sorry if I only entertained them—I wish to make them better.'"

Beattie's happiest hours are said to have been passed at Gordon Castle, with those whose tastes, in some respects differing from his own, he contributed to form; while he was charmed with the beauty, the wit, the cultivated intellect of the duchess, and he justly appreciated her talents and virtues. Throughout a friendship of years her kindness was unvaried;

"Ne'er ruffled by those cataracts and breaks
Which humor interposed too often makes."

The duchess felt sincerely for poor Beattie's domestic sorrows; for the peculiarities of his wife, whom he designated as "nervous;" for the early death of his son, in whom all the poet's affections were bound up, and to whose welfare every thought of his was directed.

One would gladly take one's impressions of the Duchess of Gordon's character from Beattie rather than from the pen of political writers, who knew her but as a partisan. The duchess, according to Beattie, was feelingly alive to every fine impulse: demonstrative herself, detesting coldness in others; the life of every party; the consoling friend of every scene of sorrow; a compound of sensibility and vivacity, of strength and softness. This is not the view that the world took of her character. Beattie always quitted Gordon Castle "with sighs and tears." It is much to have added to the transient gleams of happiness enjoyed by so good and so afflicted a man. "I can not think," he wrote, when under the pressure of dreaded calamity—that of seeing his wife insane; "I am too much agitated and *distrait* (as Lord Chesterfield would say) to read any thing that is not very desultory; I can not play at cards; I could never learn to smoke; and my musical days are over: my first excursion, if ever I make any, must be to Gordon Castle."

There he found what is indispensable to such a man—congeniality. Amusement was not what he required; it was soothing. It was in the duchess's presence that he wrote the following "Lines to a Pen—"

"Go, and be guided by the brightest eyes,
And to the softest hand thine aid impart;
To trace the fair ideas as they rise,
Warm from the purest, gentlest, noblest heart;"

lines in which the praise is worth more than the poetry. The duchess sent him a copy by Smith of her portrait by Sir Joshua Reynolds, a picture to which reference has been already made.

In 1782 the duchess grieved for the death of Lord Kaimes, for whom she had a sincere friendship, although the religious opinions of that celebrated man differed greatly from those of Beattie. Lord Kaimes was fifty-six years an author, in company with the eccentric Lord Monboddo, the author of the theory that men have had tails. Lord Kaimes passed some days at Gordon Castle shortly before his death. Monboddo and he detested each other, and squabbled incessantly. Lord Kaimes understood no Greek: and Monboddo, who was as mad and as tiresome about Greek and Aristotle, and as absurd and peculiar on that score as Don Quixote was about chivalry, told him that without understanding Greek he could not write a page of good English. Their arguments must have been highly diverting. Lord Kaimes, on his death-bed, left a remembrance to the Duchess of Gordon, who had justly appreciated him, and defended him from the charge of skepticism. Lord Monboddo compared the duchess to Helen of Troy, whom he asserted to have been seven feet high; but whether in stature, in beauty, or in the circumstances of her life, does not appear.

The happiness of the duchess was perfected by the blessings granted to her in her family. In 1770 the birth of her eldest son George, long beloved in Scotland while the Marquis of Huntley, took place. Dr. Beattie describes him as "the best and most beautiful boy that ever was born;" he proved to be one of the most popular of the young nobility of that period. Dr. Beattie strongly advised the duchess to engage an English tutor, a clergyman, for him, recommended either by the Archbishop of York, or by the Provost of Eton. When it afterward became a question whether the young heir should go to Oxford or to Cambridge, the doctor, who seems to have been a universal authority, allowed that Cambridge was the best for a man of study, while Oxford had more dash and spirit in it: so little are matters altered since that time.

Fifteen years appear to have elapsed before the birth of a second son, Alexander. Both these scions of this ducal house became military men: the young marquis was colonel of the Scots Fusileer Guards, and served in the Peninsular war, and was eventually Governor of Edinburgh Castle. Long was he remembered by many a brother officer, many an old soldier, as a gallant, courteous, gay-hearted man; with some of the faults and all the virtues of the military character. He married late in life Elizabeth, daughter of Alexander Brodie, Esq., of Arnhall, N.B., who survived him. Lord Alexander Gordon died unmarried; but five daughters added to the family lustre by noble and wealthy alliances.

Wraxall remarks "that the conjugal duties of the Duchess of Gordon pressed on her heart with less force than did her maternal solicitudes." For their elevation she thought, indeed, no sacrifice too great, and no efforts too laborious. In the success of her matrimonial speculations she has been compared to Sarah, Duchess of Marlborough, who numbered among her sons-in-law two dukes and three earls. But the daughters of the proud Sarah were, it has been observed, the children of John Churchill, and on them were settled, successively, Blenheim and the dukedom. The ladies Gordon were portionless, and far less beautiful than their mother. To her skillful diplomacy alone were these brilliant fortunes owing.

Lady Charlotte, the eldest, was eighteen years of age when her mother first entertained matrimonial projects for her, and chose for their object no less a personage than Pitt, then prime minister. Her schemes might have proved successful had not Pitt had that sure impediment to maternal management—a friend. This friend was the subtle Henry Dundas, afterward Lord Melville; one of those men who, under the semblance of unguarded manners and a free open bearing, conceal the deepest designs of personal aggrandizement. Governing India, governing Scotland, the vicegerent in Edinburgh for places and pensions, Dundas was looking forward to a peerage; and kept his eye steadily on Pitt, whom he guided in many matters, adapting his conduct and conversation to the peculiar tone of the minister's mind. Flattery he never used —dictation he carefully avoided: both would have been detrimental to his influence with the reserved statesman.

Pitt was by no means calculated to win the affection of a blooming girl of eighteen, who, whatever Wraxall may have thought, lived to be one of the most beautiful and graceful women of her time. Many years ago, during the life of Sir Thomas Lawrence, his portrait of the Duchess of Richmond, formerly Lady Charlotte Gordon, was exhibited at Somerset House. So exquisite were the feminine charms of that lovely face, so elegant the form he had portrayed, that all crowded to look upon that delineation of a woman no longer young; while beauties in the bloom of youth were passed by as they hung on the walls in all the glowing colors of girlhood.

On most intimate terms with the duchess, Pitt seems to have been touched with the attractions of Lady Charlotte, and to have paid her some attentions. He was one of the stiffest and shyest of men: finely formed in figure, but plain in face; the last man to be fascinated, the last to fascinate. Drives to Dundas's house at Wimbledon when Pitt was there; evenings at home, in easy converse with these two politicians; suppers, at which the premier always finished his bottle, as well as the hardier Scotchman, failed to bring forward the reserved William Pitt. The fact was, that Dundas could not permit any one, far less the Duchess of Gordon, to have the ascendency over the prime minister that so near a relationship would occasion. He trembled for his own influence. A widower at that time—his wife, a Miss Rennie of Melville, who had been divorced from him, being dead—he affected to lay his *own* person and fortune at Lady Charlotte's feet. Pitt instantly retired, and the sacrifice cost him little: and Dundas's object being answered, *his* pretensions also dropped through. Two years afterward, Lady Charlotte became the wife of Colonel Lennox, afterward Duke of Richmond, and in the course of years the mother of fourteen children; one of whom, Henry Adam, a midshipman, fell overboard from the "Blake" in 1812 and was drowned. According to Wraxall, the Duke of Richmond had to pay the penalty of what he calls "this imprudent, if not unfortunate marriage," being banished to the snowy banks of St. Lawrence under the name of governor.

In modern times, our young nobility of promise have learned the important truth ably enforced by Thomas Carlyle, that *work* is not only man's appointed lot, but his highest blessing and safeguard. The rising members of various noble families have laid this axiom to heart; and, when not engaged in public business, have come grandly forward to protect the unhappy, to provide for the young, to solace the old. The name of Shaftesbury carries with it gratitude and comfort in its sound; while that of him who figured of old in the cabal, the Shaftesbury of Charles II.'s time, is, indeed, not forgotten, but remembered with detestation. Ragged schools; provident schools; asylums for the aged governess; homes in which the consumptive may lay their heads in peace and die; asylums for the penitent; asylums for the idiot; homes where the homeless may repose; these are the monuments to our Shaftesbury, to our younger sons. The mere political ascendency—the garter or the coronet—are distinctions which pale before these as does the moon when dawn has touched the mountains' tops with floods of light. As lecturers amid their own people, as the best friends and counselors of the indigent, as man bound to man by community of interests, our noblemen in many instances stand before us—Catholic and Protestant zealous alike. "Jock of Norfolk" is represented by a descendant of noble impulses. Elgin, Carlisle, Stanley—the Bruce, the Howard, the Stanley of former days—are our true heroes of society, men of great aims and great powers.

The Duchess of Gordon was indefatigable in her ambition, but she could not always entangle dukes. Her second daughter, Madelina, was married first to Sir Robert Sinclair; and, secondly, to Charles Fyshe Palmer, Esq., of Luckley Hall, Berkshire. Lady Madelina was not handsome, but extremely agreeable, animated, and intellectual. Among her other conquests was the famous Samuel Parr, of Hatton, who used to delight in sounding her praises, and recording her perfections with much of that eloquence which is now fast dying out of remembrance, but which was a thing *à part* in that celebrated Grecian. Susan, the third daughter of the duke and duchess, married William, Duke of Manchester, thus becoming connected with a descendant of John, Duke of Marlborough.

Louisa, the fourth daughter, married Charles, second Marquis Cornwallis, and son of the justly celebrated Governor of India; and Georgiana, the fifth and youngest, became the wife of John, the late Duke of Bedford.

Such alliances might have satisfied the ambition of most mothers; but for her youngest and most beautiful daughter, the Duchess of Bedford, the Duchess of Gordon had even entertained what she thought higher views. In 1802, while Bonaparte was first consul, and anticipating an imperial crown, the Duchess of Gordon visited Paris, and received there such distinctions from Napoleon Bonaparte, then first consul, as excited hopes in her mind of an alliance with that man whom, but a few years previously, she would probably have termed an adventurer!

Paris was then, during the short peace, engrossed with fêtes, reviews, and dramatic amusements, the account of which makes one almost fancy one's self in the year 1852, that of the *coup d'état*, instead of the period of 1802. The whirlwinds of revolution seemed then, as now, to have left all unchanged: the character of the people, who were still devoted to pleasure, and sanguine, was, on the surface, gay and buoyant as ever. Bonaparte holding his levées at the Tuileries, with all the splendor of majesty, reminds one of his nephew performing similar ceremonies at the Elysée, previously to his assuming the purple. All republican simplicity was abandoned, and the richest taste displayed on public occasions in both eras.

Let us picture to ourselves the old, quaint palace of the Tuileries on a reception-day *then;* and the impression made on the senses will serve for the modern drama; be it comedy, or be it tragedy, which is to be played out in those stately rooms wherein so many actors have passed and repassed to their doom.

It is noon, and the first consul is receiving a host of embassadors within the consular apartment, answering probably to the "*Salle des Maréchaux*" of Napoleon III. Therein the envoys from every European state are attempting to comprehend, what none could ever fathom, the consul's mind. Let us not intermeddle with their conference, but look around us, and view the gallery in which we are waiting until he, who was yesterday so small, and who is to-day so great, should come forth among us.

How gorgeous is the old gallery, with its many windows, its rich roof, and gilded panels! The footmen of the first consul, in splendid liveries, are bringing chairs for the ladies who are awaiting the approach of that schoolmaster's son: they are waiting until the weighty conference within is terminated. Peace-officers, superbly bedizened, are walking up and down to keep ladies to their seats and gentlemen to the ranks, so as to form a passage for the first consul to pass down. Pages of the back stairs, dressed in black, and with gold chains hanging round their necks, are standing by the door to guard it, or to open it when *he* on whom all thoughts are fixed should come forth.

But what is beyond every thing striking is the array of Bonaparte's aides-de-camp—fine fellows—war-worn—men such as he, and he alone, would choose: and so gorgeous, so radiant are their uniforms that all else seem as if in shadow in comparison.

The gardens of the Tuileries meantime are filling with troops whom the first consul is going to review. There are now Zouaves there; but these are men whom the suns of the tropics have embrowned; little fellows, many of them, of all heights, such as we might make drummers of in our stalwart ranks: but see how muscular, active, full of fire they are; fierce as hawks, relentless as tigers. See the horse-soldiers on their scraggy steeds; watch their evolutions, and you will own, with a young guardsman who stood gazing fifty years afterward on the troops which followed Napoleon III. into Paris, that "they are worth looking at."

The long hour is past; the pages in black are evidently on the watch; the double door which leads into the *Salle des Maréchaux* is opened from within; a stricter line is instantly kept by the officers in the gallery. Fair faces, many an English one among them, are flushed. Anon he appears, while an officer at the door, with one hand raised above his head and the other extended, exclaims "*Le Premier Consul.*"

Forth he walks, a firm, short, stolid form, with falling shoulders beneath his tight, deep-blue frock. His tread is heavy rather than majestic—that of a man who has a purpose in walking, not merely to show himself as a parade. His head is large, and formed with a perfection which we call classic: his features are noble, modeled by that hand of Nature which framed this man "fearfully," indeed, and "wonderfully." Nothing was ever finer than his mouth—nothing more disappointing than his eye: it is heavy, almost mournful. His face is pale, almost sallow, while—let one speak who beheld him—"not only in the eye, but in every feature, care, thought, melancholy, and meditation are so strongly marked with so much of character, nay, genius, and so penetrating a seriousness, or rather sadness, as powerfully to sink into an observer's mind."

It is the countenance of a student, not of a warrior; of one deep in unpractical meditation, not of one whose every act and plan had then been but a tissue of successes. It is the face of a man wedded to deep thought, not of the hero of the battle-field, the ruler of assemblies; and, as if to perfect the contrast, while all around is gorgeous and blazing, he passes along without a single decoration on his plain dress, not even a star to mark out the first consul. It is well: there can but be one Napoleon in the world, and he wants no distinction.

He is followed by diplomatists of every European power, vassals, all, more or less, save England; and to England, and to her sons and daughters, are the most cherished courtesies directed. Does not *that* recall the present policy?

By his side walks a handsome youth whom he has just been presenting to the Bavarian minister—that envoy from a strange, wild country, little known save by the dogged valor of its mountaineers. The ruler of that land, until now an elector, has been saluted king by Napoleon the powerful.

On the youth, who addresses him as *mon père*, a slight glance is allowed even from those downcast eyes which none may ever look into too full. Eugène Beauharnais, his stepson, the son of his ever-loved Josephine, has a place in that remorseless heart. "All are not evil." Is it some inkling of the parental love, is it ambition, that causes the first consul to be always accompanied by that handsome youth, fascinating as his mother, libertine as his step-father, but destitute at once of the sensibilities of the former and of the powerful intelligence of the latter?

It is on him—on *Eugène Beauharnais*—that the hopes of the proud Duchess of Gordon rest. Happily for her whom she would willingly have given to him as a bride, her scheme was frustrated. Such a sacrifice was incomplete.

Look now from the windows of that gallery; let your gaze rest on the parade below, in the Rue de Rivoli, through which Bonaparte is riding at the head of his staff to the review. He has mounted a beautiful white horse; his aides-de-camp are by his side, followed by his generals. He rides on so carelessly that an ordinary judge would call him an indifferent equestrian. He holds his bridle first in one hand, then in another, yet he has the animal in perfect control: he can master it by a single movement. As he presents some swords of honor, the whole bearing and aspect of the man change. He is no longer the melancholy student; stretching out his arm, the severe, scholastic mien assumes instantly a military and commanding air.

Then the consular band strike up a march, and the troops follow in grand succession toward the Champs Elysées. The crowds within the gallery disappear: I look around me: the hedges of human beings, who had been standing back to let the hero pass, are broken, and all are hurrying away. The pages are lounging; the aides-de-camp are gone; already is silence creeping over that vast gallery of old historic remembrances. Do not our hearts sink? Here, in this centre window, Marie Antoinette showed her little son to the infuriated mob below. She stood before unpitying eyes. Happier had it been for him, for her, had they died then. Will those scenes, we thought, ever recur? They have—they *have!* mercifully mitigated, it is true: yet ruthless hands have torn from those walls their rich hangings. By yon door did the son of Egalité escape. Twice has that venerable pile been desecrated. Even in 1852, when crowds hastened to the first ball given by Napoleon III., the traces of the *last* Revolution were pointed out to the dancers. They have darkened the floors; all is, it is true, not only renovated, but embellished, so as to constitute the most gorgeous of modern palaces; yet for how long?

It is, indeed, in mercy that many of our wishes are denied us. Eugene Beauharnais was, even then, destined to a bride whom he had never seen, the eldest daughter of that Elector of Bavaria to whom Bonaparte had given royalty; and the sister of Ludwig, the ex-King of Bavaria, was the destined fair one. They were married; and she, at all events, was fond, faithful, nay, even devoted. He was created Duke of Leuchtenberg, and Marie of Leuchtenberg was beautiful, majestic, pious, graceful; but she could not keep his heart. So fair was she, with those sweet blue eyes, that pearl-like skin, that fine form, made to show off the *parures* of jewels which poor Josephine bequeathed to her—so fair was she, that when

Bonaparte saw her before her bridal, he uttered these few words, "Had I *known*, I would have married her myself." Still she was but *second*, perhaps third, perhaps fourth ('tis a way they have in France) in his affections; nevertheless, when he died, and it was in his youth, and Thorwaldsen has executed a noble monument of him in the Dom Kirche at Munich—when that last separation came, preceded by many a one that had been voluntary on his part—his widow mourned, and no second bridal ever tempted her to cancel the remembrance of Eugène Beauharnais.

For Lady Georgiana Gordon a happier fate was reserved. She married, in 1803, John, the sixth Duke of Bedford, a nobleman whose character would have appeared in a more resplendent light had he not succeeded a brother singularly endowed, and whose death was considered to be a public calamity. Of Francis, Duke of Bedford, who was summoned away in his thirty-seventh year, Fox said: "In his friendships, not only was he disinterested and sincere, but in him were to be found united all the characteristic excellencies that have ever distinguished the men most renowned for that virtue. Some are warm, but volatile and inconstant; he was warm too, but steady and unchangeable. Where his attachment was placed, there it remained, or rather there it grew." * * * "If he loved you at the beginning of the year, and you did nothing to lose his esteem, he would love you more at the end of it; such was the uniformly progressive state of his affections, no less than of his virtue and friendship.

John, Duke of Bedford, was a widower of thirty-seven when he married Georgiana, remembered as the most graceful, accomplished, and charming of women. The duke had then five sons, the youngest of whom was Lord John Russell, and the eldest Francis, the present duke. By his second duchess, Georgiana, the duke had also a numerous family. She survived until 1853. The designs formed by the duchess to marry Lady Georgiana to Pitt first, and then to Eugène Beauharnais, rest on the authority of Wraxall, who knew the family of the Duke of Gordon personally; but he does not state them as coming from his own knowledge. "I have good reason," he says, "for believing them to be founded in truth. They come from very high authority."

Notwithstanding the preference evinced by the Prince of Wales for the Duchess of Devonshire, he was at this time on very intimate terms with her rival in the sphere of fashion, and passed a part of almost every evening in the society of the Duchess of Gordon. She treated him with the utmost familiarity, and even on points of great delicacy expressed herself very freely. The attention of the public had been for some time directed toward the complicated difficulties of the Prince of Wales' situation. His debts had now become an intolerable burden; and all applications to his royal father being unavailing, it was determined by his friends to throw his royal highness on the generosity of the House of Commons. At the head of those who hoped to relieve the prince of his embarrassments were Lord Loughborough, Fox, and Sheridan. The ministerial party were under the guidance of Pitt, who avowed his determination to let the subject come to a strict investigation.

This investigation referred chiefly to the prince's marriage with Mrs. Fitzherbert, who, being a Roman Catholic, was peculiarly obnoxious both to the court and to the country, notwithstanding her virtues, her salutary influence over the prince, and her injuries.

During this conjuncture the Duchess of Gordon acted as mediator between the two conflicting parties, alternately ad vising, consoling, and even reproving the prince, who threw himself on her kindness. Nothing could be more hopeless than the prince's affairs if an investigation into the source of his difficulties took place; nothing could be less desired by his royal parents than a public exposure of his life and habits. The world already knew enough and too much, and were satisfied that he was actually married to Mrs. Fitzherbert. At this crisis, the base falsehood which denied that union was authorized by the prince, connived at by Sheridan, who partly gave it out in the house, and consummated by Fox. A mem orable, a melancholy scene was enacted in the House of Commons on the 8th April, 1787—a day that the admirers of the Whig leaders would gladly blot out from the annals of the country. Rolle, afterward Lord Rolle, having referred to the marriage, Fox adverted to his allusion, stating it to be a low, malicious calumny. Rolle, in reply, admitted the *legal* impossibility of the marriage, but maintained "that there were modes in which it might have taken place." Fox replied that he denied it in point of *fact*, as well as of *law*, the thing never having been done in *any* way. Rolle then asked if he spoke from authority. Fox answered in the affirmative, and here the dialogue ended, a profound silence reigning throughout the house and the galleries, which were crowded to excess. This body of English gentlemen expressed their contempt more fully by that ominous stillness, so unusual in that assembly, than any eloquence could have done. Pitt stood aloof; dignified, contemptuous, and silent. Sheridan challenged from Rolle some token of satisfaction at the information; but Rolle merely returned that he had indeed received an answer, but that the house must form their own opinion on it. In the discussions which ensued a channel was nevertheless opened for mutual concessions—which ended eventually in the relief of the prince from pecuniary embarrassments, part of which were ascribed to the king's having appropriated to his own use the revenues of the Duchy of Cornwall, and refusing to render any account of them on the prince's coming of age. It was the mediation of the Duchess of Gordon that brought the matter promptly to a conclusion; and through her representations, Dundas was sent to Carlton House, to ascertain from the prince the extent of his liabilities; an assurance was given that immediate steps would be taken to relieve his royal highness. The interview was enlivened by a considerable quantity of wine; and after a pretty long flow of the generous bowl, Dundas's promises were energetically ratified. Never was there a man more "malleable," to use Wraxall's expression, than Harry Dundas. Pitt soon afterward had an audience equally amicable with the prince.

From this period until after the death of Pitt, in 1805, the Duchess of Gordon's influence remained in the ascendant. The last years of the man whom she had destined for her son-in-law, and who had ever been on terms of the greatest intimacy with her, were clouded. Pitt had the misfortune not only of being a public man—for to say that is to imply a sacrifice of happiness—but to be a public man solely. He would turn neither to marriage, nor to books, nor to agriculture, nor even to friendship, for the repose of a mind that could not, from insatiable ambition, find rest. He died involved in debt—in terror and grief for his country. He is said never to have been in love. At twenty-four he had the sagacity, the prudence, the reserve of a man of fifty. His excess in wine undermined his constitution, but was a source of few comments when his companions drank more freely than men in office had ever been known to do since the time of Charles II. Unloved he lived; and alone, uncared for, unwept, he died. That he was nobly indifferent to money, that he had a contempt for every thing mean, or venal, or false, was in those days no ordinary merit.

During the whirl of gayety, politics, and match-making, the Duchess of Gordon continued to read, and to correspond with Beattie upon topics of less perishable interest than the factions of the hour. Beattie sent her his "Essay on Beauty" to read in manuscript; he wrote to her about Petrarch, about Lord Monboddo's works, and Burke's book on the French Revolution; works which the duchess found time to read and wished to analyze. Their friendship, so honored to *her*, continued until his death in 1803.

The years of life that remained to the Duchess of Gordon must have been gladdened by the birth of her grandchildren, and by the promise of her sons George, afterward Duke of Gordon, and Alexander. The illness of George III., the trials of Hastings and Lord Melville, the general war, were the events that most varied the political world, in which she ever took a keen interest. She died in 1812, and the duke married soon afterward Mrs. Christie, by whom he had no children.

The Dukedom of Gordon became extinct at his death, and the present representative of this great family is the Marquis of Huntley.

MADAME RÉCAMIER.

There is no flirt so bad as a French flirt, and no fool so ridiculous as a French fool. The life of Madame Récamier is the life of a flirt surrounded by fools. Its interest is derived from the fact that the latter, while fools in connection with her, were great men apart from her—the Bonapartes and Chateaubriands. The amusement of her life is derived from the fact that her beauty made fools of them.

The idol of a Montmorency was the daughter of a notary at Lyons named Bernard, who gave her the imposing prænomina, Jeanne Francoise Julie Adelaïde. Of these she used the third, and her admirers turned it into that of Shakspeare's heroine, whom she resembled about as much as Lucien Bonaparte did Romeo, in whose character he addressed her. She was born on the 4th of December, 1777. In 1784 M. Bernard succeeded in obtaining the post of receveur des finances at Paris, and his daughter was therefore sent to the Convent of La Déserte at Lyons, but in due course rejoined her parents at Paris. Though still quite a child, she was already remarkable for her beauty; and her foolish mother, very proud of it, increased her natural vanity by dressing the little girl up elaborately, and taking her to places of public amusement, when her proper sphere was the schoolroom. It was thus that she was once brought to Versailles, and made a *début* at court which was a fitting omen of her future successes. At that time, 1789, poor Louis was already the slave of his people, and made any sacrifice to appease them. The public was even admitted to the king's dining-room, to stare at royalty while it ate; and the Bernards entered among the crowd. Marie Antoinette, struck with the little girl's beauty, sent for her after dinner, to have her measured with her daughter, who was of about the same age.

At the age of fifteen Juliette Bernard was married to a man of forty-three, and we are asked to believe that this was by her own will. We are more inclined to credit, what we are also assured was the case, that this unequal marriage, though actually performed, was never consummated, and that M. Récamier behaved to his child-wife only in the character of a father. Such is the manner in which the sacred tie of matrimony may be desecrated in France; and her niece and biographer, Madame Le Normant, can tell us this without a blush, or the slightest excuse for either party.

M. Récamier was a rich banker, the son of a merchant of Lyons. He was generous and good-natured to a fault, and, at the same time, utterly without feeling. To-day he would lend a friend any amount of money; to-morrow, if the same friend died, he would coolly murmur, "Another drawer shut," and forget him. Like George Selwyn, he was devotedly fond of executions; but Selwyn enjoyed the sight of suffering as a keen pleasure: M. Récamier, too insensible to be impressed by it at all, could only appreciate the show. At the time of his marriage the Reign of Terror had been inaugurated, and M. Récamier could indulge his peculiar taste to his heart's content. He repaired every day, by way of a cheerful walk, to the Place de la Concorde, where the guillotine was being fed with human prey, beneath a colossal statue of Liberty, and thus, he said, accustomed himself to the idea of a death, which sooner or later he fully expected to suffer in his turn. Happy times, when one could look calmly forward to the blow of the knife, and know that in that same basket the head one wore would have to fall; that the horrid cries, with which you pursued the wretched victim to the scaffold, might to-morrow greet you too as you sat huddled in the tumbrel.

But the guillotine, which demanded so many a better head, left that of M. Récamier on his broad shoulders, only an act of gratitude on its part for the regularity with which he attended its levées. The Terror passed: the people, weary of blood, opened the churches again, to exchange the excitement of wholesale murder for that of retail "religion;" crowded to the theatres, the promenades, the public amusements; and danced as merrily as if none of them had lost a friend for years. It was now that Juliette Récamier began to cause that sensation which gave her at a later period such wonderful influence over the society of the consulate.

Arrived at a womanly age, though only twenty, and looking younger still in contrast to her husband of forty-eight, she had come to the full of her beauty. At this period it seems to have been a sensuous beauty, where worth rather than mind gave the expression. Her white glistening shoulders were its especial glory; her whole figure, including the feet, was classically moulded. The face was short and round rather than oval: the hair and eyes were brown; the complexion most brilliant, almost, one might say, dazzling; the features neat, regular, French rather than classical; and the head set easily upon the shoulders. The look, while it showed a consciousness of superiority, too grand, perhaps, to be called vanity, was alluring from a certain kindness and sympathy about it. You could tell at once that she was a woman and no more, nay, something less, a Frenchwoman. Of the angel she had certainly nothing, for the face was earthly, though one of the most beautiful on earth. She was rather a goddess, with all the pride, and much of the sensuality of one, though that sensuality was as refined as one imagines the pleasures of Queen Juno.

The writer remembers to have seen at the house of her biographer, Madame Le Normant, the famous portrait of her by Gérard, which she gave to the most successful of her admirers, Prince Augustus of Prussia, and which by his will he left again to her. She is there depicted in a vapor bath, reclining rather than sitting on a species of classical couch, with the beautiful feet bare and her hair and dress arranged after the model of the statues of Diana.

Perhaps her complexion was more striking than any other of her charms, and when she appeared in public, it more than once drew round her an awkward crowd of admirers. Thus on one occasion she was deputed to hold the plate at St. Roch, for some charitable *quête*, and knelt, as is usual in these cases, in the middle of the church. Two gentlemen remained at her side to protect her, but found the office on this occasion no sinecure. The crowd became enormous; the people stood on the chairs, benches, even on the altars, climbed the pillars, and pushed about, only to catch a glimpse of the lovely *quêteuse*. The money collected amounted to the enormous sum of twenty thousand francs. The French will do any thing and give any thing to gaze upon a beautiful woman. The writer remembers a curious instance of this in Paris. A small café in the Rue Richelieu had been fortunate enough, some years ago, to obtain the services of a very handsome Italian girl. The very first night that she appeared at the *comptoir*, the café was soon filled to overflowing, and in a few hours a crowd was collected round the door. The second night, when the fame of the fair attendant's beauty had spread abroad, this crowd was increased to such an extent that the neighboring *garde* of soldiers was called in to keep order. The writer remembers well the excited state of the mob. The whole of the Rue Richelieu near the Boulevards was thronged with the curious. The *garde* was placed at the door of the café and admitted only a few at a time. They entered in high expectation, and returned in disgust. The writer happened to be among those admitted, and in the café he saw no one of more interest than an elderly, dark-tinted Frenchwoman, who was making a handsome sum out of the *éclat* thus produced. It proved that on the previous night the phenomenon of beauty had been offered, and accepted, an enormous sum to appear elsewhere, and in a very different character, and the owners of the café were reaping the benefit of her mere reputation. On issuing from it, the writer and others were drenched in a shower of water thrown from the windows above. This and the disappointment produced a tumult which forced the *garde* to use their bayonets, and was not even then calmed down till a small force of cuirassiers appeared on the scene and drove back the incensed mob. This took place in 1854; and it can therefore well be imagined what enthusiasm the pleasure-seekers of 1796 evinced when Madame Récamier appeared among them, dazzling all eyes with her loveliness.

Among the earliest tributes to this beauty were those of two of the Bonapartes, the emperor himself and his brother Lucien. The first she met twice only. On the 10th December, 1797, the Directoire gave a fête in honor of the conqueror of Italy. It took place in the large court of the Luxembourg, where an altar to, and statue of, Liberty had been erected. Talleyrand, the turn-coat, read to the future emperor an address of praise. Madame Récamier, who could not from her seat see him well, rose to obtain a better view of the hero of the day. The crowd which had been staring at him, turned to admire the beauty of the day, and hailed her with a murmur of approbation. Napoleon's vanity was hurt; he showed his impatience and bent upon her one of his chilling condemnatory looks. She sat down at once. Thus in the outset of her life she had the satisfaction of rivaling Napoleon himself in popular admiration.

The next meeting took place in the winter of 1799. Lucien Bonaparte, whose admiration of Madame Récamier was then the talk of Paris, was giving a fête, at which she appeared. Soon after her arrival, she saw near the fireplace of the principal room a man whom she took to be Joseph Bonaparte, whom she had often met at the house of their common friend, Madame de Staël, and bowed to him. Her greeting was returned, but the next moment she discovered her mistake, and found that she had been salaaming to the first consul himself. She had heard of him as so severe and cold, that she was astonished at the mildness of his look toward her. Later, Fouché came up to her and whispered, "The first consul thinks you charming."

In the course of the evening the great man was holding by the hand a daughter of Lucien's, a child of four years old. Talking to his flatterers he forgot it, and the little thing began to cry. "*Ah, pauvre petite,*" said he, "I forgot you."

Madame Récamier, afterward the victim of this man, remembered to his advantage the tenderness with which he uttered these words.

When dinner was announced, Napoleon gave proof of his pride and vulgarity—for he was, perhaps, one of the vulgarest men who ever sat on a throne—and without offering his arm to any one, stalked out first. Cambacérès, the second consul, placed himself next to Madame Récamier at table, when Napoleon cried out to him, "Ah! ah! citizen consul, close to the prettiest, eh?"

The dinner was soon over. Bonaparte, the great man there, ate, as usual, very fast. This bad habit lost him in after years the battle of Leipsic, and even then spoiled his temper. Before the battle he breakfasted off a leg of mutton stuffed with sage and onions—no bad dish; but he ate so fast, in his hurry to be on the field, that the meal was followed by a violent attack of indigestion: his head was affected by it, and in his agony he could not give proper attention to the details of the fight.

After dinner, on the previous occasion, he rose, without waiting for any one. The rest, of course, followed his illustrious example. As he went out, he said to Madame Récamier, "Why did you not sit next me at dinner?" It turned out that he had told Bacciocchi to place her near him. In the salon he took his stand near the piano: the instrumental music bothered him, and he thumped on the piano and called loudly for Garat, who sang in his best strain. After the song he came up to Madame Récamier, who had been listening enrapt, and said, "So you like music, madame." He would have gone on, but Lucien joined them, and the first consul, who knew his brother's admiration for the beauty, retired. Such were the manners of the consulate, and such Madame Recamier's place in its vulgar court.

Lucien Bonaparte, who interrupted this conversation, was her most devoted admirer. He was then four-and-twenty, taller and more graceful than his brother, but far less great. He met his idol at a dinner given by M. Sapey, and soon after sent her a collection of letters, entitled "Letters from Romeo to Juliette," in which he expressed his devotion in very ordinary un-Romeic language, though passionate enough. He must have looked very foolish when Madame Récamier, who had never been addressed in this strain before, handed him back his first love-letter in the midst of a party, told him it was very pretty, but advised him to cultivate politics, in which he might succeed, rather than literature, in which he might, perhaps, fail.

Here we catch another glimpse of French morals under the consulate. Juliette confided the addresses of the first consul's brother to her husband. He was far from indignant, and begged her not to repulse them too harshly. He knew that his success in business depended much on his good standing with the rising family, and he was quite willing to sacrifice the honor of his wife to his own prospects. She, however, had virtue enough to be captivated neither by the handsome face nor by the high position of her admirer, and met his advances with merry laughter. He persisted for a time and then withdrew, thoroughly wounded by her contempt, and—we might hope in vain—ashamed of himself. Some months after he sent M. Sapey to obtain his letters of Romeo to Juliet from the heroine. She declined to give them up. French morals again. She knew that if she did so they might be used against her, and she resisted all attempts to obtain them.

M. Récamier's position as a wealthy banker gave him in those days an importance which he would not have held under the empire. Madame Récamier's renown as a beauty added to the reputation of the house, and in their hotel in the Chaussée d'Antin, then Rue du Mont Blanc, they received all the planets who revolved round their sun—Napoleon. The generals of the consulate were there, Bernadotte, Masséna, and Moreau; the ministers and others, Lucien Bonaparte, Eugène Beauharnais, and Fouché; M. de Narbonne, M. de Lamoignon, and Adrien and Matthieu Montmorency. Then there came Madame de Staël, Camille Jordan, La Harpe, Lemontez, Legouvé, and Emmanuel Dupaty.

The two Montmorencys were her especial friends. Both had been in exile; the one returned from England, the other from America. They were first cousins, and great friends. Adrien, who was afterward the Duc de Laval, was about thirty-one at this period. He was afterward embassador at Madrid, Rome, Vienna, and London. He was proud of his old name, and a royalist by predilection. He is said to have been clever, but had an unfortunate stutter, which militated against his success.

His cousin, Matthieu, was a much better man. He served in the army in America, and for a long time was gay and dissipated. The death of a beloved brother, the Abbé de Laval, who was a victim to the Revolution, cured him. Matthieu, although belonging to the oldest family in France, had espoused liberal ideas, and even supported the Revolution. He accused himself of being indirectly the cause of his brother's death. This idea weighed upon him, and in time he became, under the influence of his intimate friend, Madame de Staël, a well-minded and religious man. The proof of this is that he did his utmost to impress Madame Récamier with religious feelings. He was very intimate with her, and used his friendship in the best possible manner, by way of making her better than he found her. His letters to her prove that he had doubts, not of her character at that time, but of her power to resist the many temptations of the gay society in which she mixed; and he was right.

Another of these friends, the celebrated La Harpe, had also been wild at one time, and changed his mode of life. There is a touching anecdote of him in Madame La Normant's life of our heroine. Madame Récamier had invited him to her country-house at Clichy: a number of young blades were there assembled, and a doubt was raised as to the sincerity of La Harpe's conversion. It was resolved to test it. It was known that he had always been a great admirer of woman; and one of M. Récamier's nephews, a pretty, beardless youth, dressed himself in woman's clothes, and quietly took his place near the fire in La Harpe's bedroom. The guests, being let into the secret, placed themselves behind a screen, and waited the arrival of the convert. He came at last, and, walking straight to his bed, fell on his knees and said his prayers. The whole company was shamed. He prayed long and earnestly, and at last, rising, perceived the would-be lady at his fireside. He took her by the hand, led her to the door, and told her, kindly but decisively, that whatever she might have to say to him he would hear the next day. The boy, utterly ashamed of himself, forgot his part, and could say nothing: the spectators made their escape, quite convinced of the sincerity of the old man, and the circumstance was never again alluded to.

Poor simple La Harpe was destined to be made a victim. He was dragged into a marriage with a girl who, three weeks after they were wedded, sued for a divorce, on the ground that she hated him. The divorce took place, but the old man freely forgave his young wife, and thought himself well rid of such an absurd connection.

In 1802 an affair took place which put an end to the relation between Madame Récamier and the Bonapartes. Her father, M. Bernard, had been made one of the heads of the post-office. A secret royalist correspondence had been circulated in the south of France, and the postmaster had been accused—as it would seem rightly—of countenancing it. He was arrested. On the night of his capture, Madame Bacciocchi, the consul's sister, was dining with Madame Récamier: the rest of the party consisted of Madame de Staël, La Harpe, Matthieu de Montmorency, M. de Narbonne, and Madame Bernard. A letter was brought in to the last, who on reading it fainted. It turned out to contain the news of her husband's arrest. Madame Récamier instantly applied to Madame Bacciocchi, to obtain for her an interview with Napoleon, and the latter gave her a rendezvous at the opera. Thither Madame Récamier went, when all other resources failed, but Madame Bacciocchi now openly showed her indisposition to help her. Bernadotte, who was present, came to her aid, and through his means the *mis en accusation* was canceled. On this Madame Récamier hastened to the Temple, where her father was confined, and induced one of the jailers to admit her to his cell. She had scarcely imparted the good news to the old gentleman, when the jailer came in, dragged her out by the arms, and thrust her into a dark cell, where she had to endure imprisonment for two hours, which seemed like two years. She was released at last, and it was then explained that the authorities had come, at the moment of her entrance, to take her father to the *préfecture*, and that the jailer, fearing discovery, had used this means to conceal her. It was a strange situation for the greatest beauty and almost the first leader of fashion then in the French capital. Bernadotte, whose conduct on this occasion was very generous, saved M. Bernard from a trial, which might, like some that took place not long after, have ended in condemnation to death. As it was, Bernard, though set at liberty, was disgraced and deprived of his appointment.

The first eight years of the present century were the period of Madame Récamier's reign as a social sovereign. Her husband's banking-house had become one of the first in France, so that their wealth was enormous. Besides the splendid apartments in the Rue du Mont Blanc, they had a charming country-seat at Clichy, and at both places received the first society, political, literary, and general, of the metropolis.

We now find the beautiful woman of five-and-twenty in the zenith of her popularity. Her manners and her heart were both as good as her beauty; and though a desperate coquette —far more so than English ideas could countenance—she does not appear, from any thing that we know, to have passed the bounds of innocent flirtation. The age, the indifference, and the stolid character of her husband, added to the peculiarity of their connection, to which we have already referred, may be some excuse for a succession of flirtations, which arose, less from a love of admiration, than from a desire to be loved by some one. At least, they do not appear to have spoiled her heart, which remained good to the last; and before we condemn her, we must take into consideration the great difference of French ideas on this subject from our own. We have already shown how she treated the advances of Lucien Bonaparte, but she does not seem to have been so indifferent to a succession of celebrated men, who admired her no less ardently. Yet, lest any of our readers should suspect that these flirtations were really carried too far, let us give the testimony of a contemporary who was certainly not the man to ascribe virtue to any woman who had not shown ample proof of it—Charles James Fox. He pronounced her to be "the only woman who united the attractions of pleasure to those of modesty."

Fox was in Paris in 1802: it is said that he went there in order to make researches at the Scotch college, as an addition to his materials for a projected history of the Stuarts; but, however this may be, he turned the excursion into a wedding-tour; and before he set out was privately married to Mrs. Armistead, who should have been his wife many years before. His fame was great in France. He had come forward in England as "the Man of the People," and was quite prepared to receive from the Republicans of France the full honors of the character he had assumed. He was every where hailed as a great patriot; and Napoleon, always anxious to conciliate the English Whigs, and form, if possible, a Bonapartist faction in this country, received him with marked interest. His portrait was to be seen in every shop window, and the young beaux of Paris, who had heard of his fame as a dandy, were all eager to imitate his style of dress.

Among other celebrities to whom he was introduced was of course Madame Récamier. One afternoon she called for him in her carriage, and insisted that he should accompany her in it along the Boulevards; "for," said she, "before you came, I was the fashion; it is a point of honor, therefore, that I should not appear jealous of you." We are told that some days after this drive, while Fox was sitting with Madame Récamier in her box at the opera, a Frenchman entered and placed in the hands of each a copy of an ode, in which the English statesman was eulogized under the title of Jupiter, and his companion under the name of Venus! On glancing at this impertinent effusion, Fox was somewhat confused; but Madame Récamier only laughed at it, and assured him that she cared nothing for the opinion of the good people of Paris. She was, indeed, a little too careless of her reputation, and it is no wonder that many of her friendships should have been construed into intrigues.

At that time the masked balls at the opera were attended by respectable people, which is not now the case. Ladies went to them in mask and domino, but gentlemen in simple evening dress: there was little or no dancing; and the amusement of the evening depended on the mystery which surrounded the fair portion of the assembly, who were permitted to accost freely and even attach themselves to any gentleman present. It was then that a lady could satisfy a long-cherished grudge by plain truths spoken to an enemy's face under protection of her incognito, or even declare a secret passion, while the ugly little mask concealed her modest blushes. The astonished or disgusted individual thus addressed applied himself to a study of the voice, the eyes, flashing brightly from their oval caverns, the walk, the manner, and the half-concealed figure of the person who addressed him, with more or less success; and strange adventures followed on these interviews; strange acquaintances were often formed at the balls of the opera. In Germany this custom is still preserved even among the upper classes; and the writer, who has frequented many a masked ball in that country, can testify to the excitement of these mysterious addresses, and the amusement or disappointment which ensues on the revelation or discovery which takes place, if the lady can be induced to remove her mask.

Under the protection of her brother-in-law, M. Laurent Récamier, Juliette frequented these balls, and there made several acquaintances, which she afterward pursued. Among these was the young prince, afterward King of Würtemberg, who, enchanted by the voice and manner of the mask who accosted him, went so far as to force a ring from her finger. Madame Récamier resented this liberty, and spoke with such dignity, that, having discovered who she was, the prince returned it to her the next day with a letter of humble apology.

Metternich, who was in Paris about this time, was another opera acquaintance of Juliette's. She met and talked to him there for a whole season; but though the prince, who was then first secretary of the Austrian embassy, knew who she was, he was deterred for a long time from following up the acquaintance, on account of the known hostility of Napoleon to Madame Récamier.

She seems to have attacked princes and royalties with particular energy; and the balls at the opera-house made her acquainted with many heads which have been since crowned. The most devoted of these was the Grand-duke of Mecklenburg-Strelitz, who is still living, and whom she met at the opera in 1807 or 1808. On discovering who she was, he was very anxious to visit at her house; but Madame Récamier, knowing Napoleon's sentiments toward herself, refused at first to allow him, by visiting her, to draw down any ill-will on his own head. He insisted, however, so pertinaciously, that she consented to receive him one evening, and the grand-duke, to avoid recognition, left his carriage some doors off, and proceeded on foot to her hotel. Finding the door open, he at-

THE GRAND-DUKE'S VISIT TO MADAME RÉCAMIER.

tempted to glide past the porter's lodge without being seen; but the wary Cerberus was on the alert, and the grand-duke had not gone far, before he darted out after him, suspecting a thief or trespasser of some sort. The grand-duke, anxious not to be known, even to the porter, heard him call after him, but instead of replying, hastened on. The concierge followed. The grand-duke ran. The porter ran after him. The grand-duke reached the main staircase and rushed up; the porter followed, three steps at a time, calling angrily after the intruder. They reached the ante-room of the apartment together; and the incensed concierge seized the young prince by the collar. He resisted, and a loud and angry scuffle ensued, the noise of which reached Madame Récamier, who came out, and was highly amused at seeing the state of affairs. Of course the grand-duke was released, and the porter, who had made such an unpleasant mistake, retired "with his tail between his legs."

The admiration of the prince for Madame Récamier was not merely the fleeting fancy of a young man. It took such hold upon him that in 1843, thirty-six years after this event, he wrote to her from Strelitz, to ask her to send him the portrait which we have already described, and which, on the death of Prince August of Prussia, had returned to the possession of its original. The request was very prudently refused, and the portrait, which was considered Gérard's *chef-d'œuvre*, and excited so much attention that the painter, pestered with visits to his studio to see it, threatened to destroy it if another came, still hangs in the boudoir of Madame le Normant; but the letter of the grand-duke is remarkable, as containing proof that Napoleon regarded Madame Récamier's salon, where so many great men met, with not only suspicion, but the hatred of a rival. It appears from this letter that he declared openly in Josephine's drawing-room that "he should regard as a personal enemy every foreigner who frequented Madame Récamier's parties." He was, in fact, jealous of the popularity of the fair Parisians. Like Louis XIV. he wished to monopolize the admiration of all France, and could not forgive any one—even a woman—who enjoyed any share of it, unless openly attached to himself or his government. Like the same monarch, he was intensely jealous of superiority of mind; and, like his present successor, longed to be considered a thinker, though his real talents lay, as the present emperor's do also, in action and administration. As Louis XIV. hated Madame de Sévigné because of her wit, Napoleon persecuted Madame de Staël for hers, when he found that she refused to join him, and chose to remain independent. The salons of

Paris were, in fact, his chief opponents. Europe might bow before him, but he could not prevent his own subjects talking against his ambition in their own drawing-rooms; he could not prevent it, that is, without extreme measures, and these he finally took. In the exile into which he drove Madame de Staël, and afterward Madame Récamier too, Napoleon has proved his weakness. It is not the part of a *soi disant* "conqueror of the world" to war against women. Louis XIV., though equally vain, was too well-bred to go so far. Napoleon added to his intense vanity the overbearing pride of an upstart, and the vulgarity which is a distinguishing feature of all his family. To none are Shakspeare's words so applicable as to him and his successors—

"The beggar mounted rides his horse to death."

But to return to Madame Récamier's princely admirers. Germany yielded her one more in the person of Prince Ludwig of Bavaria, now the ex-king. This celebrated monarch was then quite a young man, probably only in his twenty-first year; and it is therefore interesting to note that his intimacy with Madame Récamier arose from the very points in his character which have since placed him so high among European sovereigns, while in conduct he is almost their acknowledged buffoon—his love of art, and his admiration of womanly beauty. Indulging the first, he raised Munich from a small insignificant commercial town to the noblest capital—as far as artistic beauty goes—in Europe; while his liberal patronage has revived in Germany a peculiarly Teutonic school of painting and architecture, at a time when that country threatened to fall in these respects far to the rear of England and France. Indulging the latter, or perhaps we may say unable to resist it, he has given to his court an example of immorality, which the whole society of Bavaria has been too ready to follow, and brought his country to a revolution, the most ludicrous and most disgraceful of any that followed the volcano of February, 1848, and his own head crownless toward the grave. Who has not heard of Lola Montez and the German kingdom which this Irish dancer, with her terrible eyes, had power to upset? Who has not been told of the gallery of beauties which Ludwig of Bavaria collected in his palace; some from among the heroines of his own amours, others from the more respectable beauties of his court, with an English minister's wife among them?

Ludwig is the Charles II., perhaps we may say the Haroun al-Raschid of Germany. Now an old man, with one foot in the grave, he is still beloved by the very subjects who forced him to abdicate. This is owing, not to the sovereign, but to the man. Never was monarch so thoroughly fitted to be the friend of his subjects; while, in letting himself down to their level, he exacted their respect. Many an anecdote is told of him at Munich to prove his homely, easy, yet royal character. On one occasion, walking jauntily up the Ludwig's Strasse, and talking familiarly with every one he met, he spied a man who did not take off his hat to the king. He walked up to him, knocked his hat off his head, and then lectured him in terms that the man could not forget. On another, he was carrying privately under his cloak a bundle of game to, report says, some damsel, whose graces he wished to win—let us hope, rather, to some starving family (for he is capable of both), when one of the birds happened to fall on the pavement. An old woman who recognized the king, picked it up and shuffled after him, crying at the top of her harsh voice, "*Ihre Majestät—Ihre Majestät hat was fallen lassen.*" The king was seen to hurry on in despair, leaving the *spiel-hahn* to the old woman; but he had been recognized, and the story went the round of the capital.

Ludwig can never have been a handsome man, though tall, slight, and gay in manner. He is ready with an answer, kind, yet dogmatic, and often unsparing in his remarks. At the age of seventy-three, with no teeth and very little hair, he can now be nothing but the parody of the dashing young prince, who, at Paris, tried to make love to Madame Récamier in 1807. But he is still, what Madame de Staël then pronounced him—"*un bon homme qui a de l'esprit et de l'âme.*"

He was among those royalties who implored Madame Récamier, the mere banker's wife, to be allowed to visit her. But she cared little for the Prince of Bavaria, and there were the same reasons for excluding him from her salon as she had given to the Grand-duke of Mecklenburg-Strelitz. He insisted, however, under the plea of a wish to see her portrait by Gérard; but whether it was the artist or the woman the young prince admired the more on this occasion, remains, perhaps, to be proved. He was, at any rate, admitted; and in after years (1824) when he had become King of Bavaria, and was traveling with a view to collecting pictures for his famous Pinakothek, he again met Madame Récamier at Rome, and there renewed his acquaintance with her.

We thus see this beautiful woman filling the part which, of all others, must most captivate a Frenchwoman, attaching to herself all the young sprigs of royalty in Europe, and assembling in her salon all the men of mark in France. Nay, more, we find her provoking unconsciously the jealousy of an emperor, and sympathizing with the woman, Madame de Staël, of whose talents he was the most envious, and whom he could not forgive for being cleverer than himself. In her person he banished talent in 1803, and he was only waiting for a fit opportunity to send beauty after it. In after years, when he coveted the glory of Louis XIV.'s court, he regretted these measures, and wished to have as much mind and loveliness around his throne as France could supply. Unfortunately he had sent the best of both out of his country, and except for such splendor as money could furnish, and for such eccentricities as the emperor himself gave out, this imperial court at the Tuileries had nothing very brilliant about it at any time.

The brilliance of the court held in the Rue du Mont Blanc, on the other hand, in the hotel of Madame Récamier, had certainly something better than money to support it. Both face and brain were there. But, alas! for the degenerate days of the consulate, money made all the difference, and without *écus*, Madame Récamier might keep a few true friends, but could not be a leader of society. In 1806 the trial came. It was the old story—*the bank broke.*

Too many banks have done the same thing since to make the story of this failure at all interesting. There are only two peculiar points connected with it. One is, that a million of francs from the Bank of France would have saved Récamier, and was refused, less, it is thought, for commercial than for political or even personal reasons; the other, that the loan was refused, although the failure of Récamier seems to have involved the whole credit of Paris. Napoleon, who made bank, bourse, and exchange his toys as much as army and navy, may or may not have countenanced this refusal. It matters little now. He had invited, had even pressed Madame Récamier, through Fouché, to attach herself to his household, and her refusal doubtless irritated a man who could not bear to be slighted.

The result only remains. Récamier, though not quite ruined, had to sell every thing, even to his wife's jewels. There is a difference to be noticed here between English and French society. The friends of Madame Récamier not only did not desert her at this crisis, but became more her friends than ever. Junot, among others, tried to impress the emperor with commiseration for this catastrophe. He replied coldly, "You would not show more regard to the widow of a marshal of France, dead on the field of battle." It is certainly reassuring in human nature, to find that all her *best* acquaintances remained steadfast to the fallen Queen of Society. Bernadotte, Matthieu de Montmorency, and Madame de Staël, all expressed their thorough sympathy with her; and when, to increase her misfortunes, there came the death of her mother, Madame Bernard, these assurances were actively renewed.

In looking back over this period of her first glory, which thus came to an end, we have only one more episode to relate —that of her visit to England during the peace of Amiens. Well introduced by the Duc de Guignes, who had been formerly embassador at St. James's, and still more recommended by her reputation and beauty, she was received in the highest circles in London. The Duchess of Devonshire, whose life is given in a former part of this volume, was among those at whose receptions she made a prominent figure; and at Devonshire House she made the acquaintance of the future duchess, Lady E. Foster, whom she met again in 1824 at Rome, where the then duchess figured as the patroness of arts and literature. Madame Récamier's short visit to London was as brilliant as that of a foreigner could be in our jealous capital. She was *fêtée*, and made more of than most French beauties. Probbly her beauty was less striking in England than in France; yet Englishmen, and Englishwomen of the day, which is more, paid her a noble tribute of admiration. The wife of the Paris banker had the extreme honor (?) of being admired by the Prince of Wales (George IV.), and her doings and sayings were recorded in the papers. On the whole, her transit of the Channel was not ill repaid, and she suffered less than Madame de Staël, who, when a celebrated but awkward wit sat between her and Madame Récamier, was hurt by his gaucherie in saying, "Here I am between wit and beauty." If Madame de Staël was really pained by the remark, it proves her vainer and less sensible than we had thought.

The failure of M. Récamier introduces us to another phase of his wife's existence, which, we must confess, is less agreeable. In 1807 she visited her intimate friend Madame de Staël in her retreat at the Château de Coppet, near Geneva. Among the illustrious personages at this period living in Geneva was the Prince August of Prussia. A weak, yet amiable youth of four-and-twenty, he made and cultivated the friendship of the author of "Corinne." He was handsome after a German model, and felt deeply the dishonor of his country, which had made him a quasi prisoner at Geneva.

At Coppet he met Madame Récamier, and conceived a passion for this woman, who was six years older than himself. Madame Récamier, without wishing to do her injustice, was always, we must confess, very eager to entrap princes, and readily improved the present occasion. For three months she flirted with him inexorably, and succeeded in capturing him.

The banks of the lake of Geneva aided her in her designs. She taught the young man the art of love, and in return he, very handsomely, we must own, offered her his hand as well as his heart. This was a strange proposal to a married woman, but it does not appear to have disconcerted Madame Récamier. How could she act? She was married; what could she do? She could not give up a prince of the blood, yet, being married, she could not become his wife. She took a measure which, if not disgusting to French ideas, is certainly so to ours. She accepted his love and agreed to be his wife; and to make this possible, she actually *wrote to her husband and proposed a divorce!* One can imagine the reply of an Englishman to such a request; but M. Récamier was not at all surprised. His fortune was broken; he was reduced to very limited means; he had never been more than a father to his wife, in spite of his vows, and St. Paul's rule for marriage. He agreed to the proposal willingly, probably reflecting that his wife, as the consort of a Prussian prince, would be more useful to him than as simply his own. At the same time he showed an amount of feeling, or pride, which raises him a little in our estimation. He consented, but put before his wife the bitter loss and estrangement it would be to himself. Madame Récamier felt that this letter was not a complete concession, yet she would have thrown over her husband had it been judicious. The offer of the prince was made in the heat of admiration, but in his cooler moments he saw what a fool he should appear in Prussia if he married the ex-wife of a Paris banker. He did not press the matter farther, and Madame Récamier did not press a divorce, for which there was no ground but ambition. She returned in the autumn to Paris, and as she could not give the prince herself, she sent him her portrait by Gérard, to which we have already alluded.

Whatever we may feel toward Madame Récamier, we can not deny that in this affair she comes before us in a very worldly light. She was to annul her marriage, which her religion proclaimed indissoluble; she was to wed a Protestant, which her Church, if it did not forbid, at least highly disapproved; and all for the sake of the title and position of princess. Nay more, the fact that she offered to do so within a few months of her husband's failure gives the affair a still more interested coloring; and the age of the young man—a boy compared to herself—completes its disgraceful character. The only thing we can say for her, after regarding these considerations, is, that she herself seemed ashamed of what she was doing, and did not proceed farther than making the proposal. She returned to Paris, however, without setting the young prince free, and perhaps had not yet made up her mind to relinquish him. They corresponded for some time in a manner which proves that the prince was afraid of his offer to Madame Récamier becoming known; and for four years she kept him in suspense. Many propositions to meet on the frontier were made, but the prince was, or pretended to be, always prevented from carrying out his plans, until, in 1811, an appointment was made for Schaffhausen; the prince went; the lady set out, but a blow came to prevent her arrival at the place of rendezvous, a sentence of exile being pronounced against her.

To conclude here this somewhat disgraceful episode: the prince again met Madame Récamier at Paris in 1815, entering with the allied armies, and he saw her for the last time in 1825 at the Abbaye-aux-Bois.

From 1808 the life of Madame Récamier is intimately mixed up with that of Madame de Staël; the first beauty, with the first wit, of Paris. With the life of Madame de Staël during this period we are not now occupied; but we find her friend often with her at Coppet, consoling her in her exile, and taking part in the amusements with which she beguiled it. Thus in 1809 Madame Récamier joined the private theatricals at Coppet, and in Racine's "Phèdre" took the part of Aricie. In the following year Madame de Staël was installed in a house near Blois, lent to her by M. de Salaberry, and here her friend joined her again. The house had long been deserted, and the peasants were amazed to hear a sound of much music within its old walls. Madame de Staël's daughter was playing the harp, her music-master the guitar, and Madame Récamier singing very prettily to this accompaniment. The astonished clods surrounded the house, and listened quite bewitched. The account of this residence is given at more length in the memoir of Madame de Staël.

About this time, it is worth noticing, Madame Récamier, childless and almost, one may say, husbandless, adopted the biographer, whose memoirs of her have recently appeared, Madame Le Normant. She was her niece, the daughter of M. de Cyvoct, and she remained with her for many years till the period of her marriage. Her husband, M. Charles Le Normant, is now the curator of the coins and medals, including the cameos, which are preserved at the Bibliothèque Impériale at Paris. M. Le Normant has an apartment attached to this great library, where his wife, whom the writer has had the pleasure of knowing personally, receives the first literary society of Paris. The son of this couple, M. François Le Normant, is already coming before the world as an antiquary, although quite a young man.

However peaceful may have been the life which Madame Récamier, now a woman of three-and-thirty, and though not at all too old to flirt, thrown out of the sphere of coquetry by the failure of flirtation, proposed to herself, it was interrupted by the ridiculous cowardice of a man who has been represented as the most courageous of the whole Christian era. Napoleon was not only not secure upon his usurped throne, but feeling that the friends of liberty were naturally his enemies, imagined himself surrounded by foes who really cared little or nothing for him. The same cowardice, which he had shown first in the banishment of Madame de Staël, then in the murder—for it was nothing else—of the poor little Duc d'Enghien, now displayed itself in two other orders of exile. It was not sufficient to proscribe the authoress of "L'Allemagne;" her very visitors must be put under a ban. Matthieu de Montmorency, her most attached friend, received his order of exile after paying a short visit to Coppet; and Madame Récamier, who staid there a single night on her way to Aix, in Savoy, where she was to drink the waters, was soon after commanded not to return to Paris. Perhaps the cruelest feature of these measures was that the banishment was *not* from France. It was limited to a circle of a hundred miles round Paris. Any one who knows what a Frenchwoman is, and how Paris is her world, without which the rest of France is only a huge void, will understand that such a sentence was worse, to one like Madame Récamier, than complete exile. Privately we may entertain the idea—which may also have been Napoleon's—that a forced residence in the provinces would be good for the character of a thorough Parisienne; but there was no doubt an intentional cruelty and unworthy spite in the emperor in pronouncing such a sentence. To understand this, we must remember that under a despotic government the friend of an exile becomes as criminal as the exile himself; and Madame Récamier was by this decree cut off from all her ties, except those with persons as unfortunate as herself.

She was for some time destined to a hotel life, that most uncomfortable of existences. Her first residence was at the *Pomme d'Or* at Chalons. In 1812 she repaired to Lyons, where she found the Duchesse de Chevreuse, an old acquaintance, in the same position as herself; and here she formed a friendship which lasted for many years. M. Ballanche was the son of a printer of Lyons. She had visited his father's press with the Duchesse de Luynes, an eccentric, clever woman, who preferred male to female attire, and had a private press of her own. On this occasion, the duchesse, while passing through the compositors' room at the Ballanches', set herself quietly at a case, tucked up her dress—she was that day, for a change, in woman's clothes—and with astonishing quickness, imitating even the movement of body peculiar to compositors, set up the type for a whole page.

Ballanche was a philosopher as well as a printer. Few men could rival him in ugliness, which, however, was the work of accident rather than nature. A portion of his jaw, attacked by disease, had been removed, and one cheek was thus, as it were, wanting. His profile remained handsome, but the face was horrible to look at. He was presented to Madame Récamier by Camille Jordan, and at his first visit his boots, from some unexplained cause, had as disagreeable a smell about them as those of Sir Roger Williams, to whom Queen Elizabeth, with more sincerity than politeness, exclaimed, "Williams, how your boots stink!" "Tut, madam," replied the Welshman, who was presenting an unfavored petition, "'tis my *suit*, not my boots, that stinketh." However, Madame Récamier, though better bred than the English sovereign, could not bear the noxious odor, and allowed the worthy printer to perceive the cause of her nausea. He behaved very charmingly on the occasion. Instead of retiring offended, he went into the hall, took off his boots, and returned without them. Unhappily some visitors arrived soon after, and M. Ballanche had to explain with some nervousness the cause of this peculiar and rather suspicious appearance.

During her residence at Lyons, Madame Récamier received much company of every kind. As an instance of this, we have an anecdote of Talma, the actor, and the Bishop of Troyes, whom fate one day brought together unexpectedly at her table. The bishop was too much a man of the world to be shocked at meeting a dignitary of the stage—that counterpart, let us not say parody, of the pulpit. Talma was introduced to him, an acquaintance struck up, and the bishop induced to recite a part of one of his sermons. "Good! good!" cried the actor, touching him lightly on the chest; "good down to here! But how about your legs?" It was evident the bishop had acted only in the pulpit.

In 1813, Madame Récamier, accompanied by her little niece, then seven years old, left Lyons for Rome. Here she took an apartment, determined to reside in the Holy City for some time. One of the first visits she made was to the studio of Canova. In a series of rooms the great sculptor had his works displayed as they were finished, and the public was admitted to look at them. He himself worked away in a separate room, and thus insured peace and freedom from interruption. Madame Récamier, always a flirt, was not satified with the works;

she wanted to see, and, perhaps, to impress, the workman, and therefore sent in her name. Canova came out in his working dress, holding his paper cap in his hand, and very gracefully invited her into his own studio, where she found his younger brother, the Abbé Canova, who was so devoted to him that he followed him about like his shadow. Canova's was a charming character. Gay, simple, easily pleased, but fonder of peace and quiet than of society, he spent his great wealth, not in tawdry show and splendor, but in assisting fellow-sculptors and doing kindnesses to poor authors. The acquaintance thus formed with Madame Récamier ripened into friendship. He passed most of his evenings at her house, and was not insensible to the charm of her beauty. When the summer heats drove her from Rome, the sculptor offered her the loan of his *locanda* at Albano, an offer she readily accepted. In this lovely spot, with the beautiful lake on one side and a view of the sea on the other, the ex-leader of fashion was quite happy with no more company than that of her niece. As an instance of her good-nature, we may mention that on one occasion, when an Italian fisherman was brought in by the French, being accused of giving information to the English, and was condemned to be shot the next morning, Madame Récamier, on hearing of it, and seeing the fearful state of terror in which the poor wretch was, at once took post to Rome, and went round to the chief French authorities to implore them to let the man off. Her prayers, however, were unheeded, and the fisherman was shot. Up to the last moment he had hoped, turning his bandaged eyes in the direction of Rome, and expecting to hear the sweet voice of the *Signora Francese* returning with his pardon.

In December, 1813, Madame Récamier left Rome for Naples. By way of escort, she had Sir J. Coghill, the well-known antiquary, who was traveling in Italy in quest of Etruscan vases and ancient inscriptions. The Englishman was in his own carriage in front, and with true British imperiousness managed to secure the post-horses, which had been retained for some great unknown personage who was to arrive that evening. In this manner they reached Terracina early, but had not been there long when Madame Récamier heard in the court-yard a loud, indignant voice exclaiming, "Where are the rascals who have robbed me of my post-horses from Rome to here?" She recognized the voice, put her head out of the window, and cried, "Here they are; I am the culprit." It was Fouché, the minister of police, who was traveling in all possible haste to Naples on a political errand to Murat. But Fouché was too much of the policeman to be joked, and took the occasion to warn Madame Récamier against going to Naples.

At this period Murat was assailed by English and Austrians to join the coalition against Napoleon. The insults with which the upstart had treated him, an upstart of his own creation, and the fear which the worthy—somewhat vulgar—man had of being drawn into the ruin of the emperor, which he saw plainly enough, as every one did, was imminent, induced him to accept the English proposition and sign the coalition. A very French scene took place on this occasion. Madame Récamier happened to be with Caroline Murat, the Queen of Naples, when her husband entered in great agitation, and asked their old friend—for Madame Récamier had known the Murats for years—what course she advised. "Sire," she answered, "you are a Frenchman. To France you must be true." Murat, who had not the sense—he had never much sense—to see that he might be true to France, though false to the emperor, exclaimed, "I am a traitor!" opened a window, walked out upon the balcony, pointed to Madame Récamier the English fleet sailing calmly and grandly into the Bay of Naples, and then laid his face in his hands and sobbed. If this story be true—and Madame Le Normant is the best authority we can have—we do not wonder that those who remembered the weak, stout, good-natured Murats, as the writer remembers their children, should have cared little to set them up in the place of Bomba, who, with all his faults, had the dignity of a sovereign.

But to return to Rome and the Canovas, as Madame Récamier did in the spring: the sculptor invited her to come and see the works he had commenced in her absence. She went with pleasure, but was surprised to find little or nothing new, and certainly nothing worth coming to see. At last he brought her to his private room, made her sit down, and then, with his brother, drew aside a green curtain at the end of the room and displayed to her sight two busts, both modeled after her likeness.

"See whether I have been thinking of you," cried the enthusiastic sculptor, in Italian, delighted with his long-concocted surprise. But he was destined to be disappointed by the vain Frenchwoman. Even the beautiful work of Canova was not good enough for her. She was so annoyed at the truthfulness of the portraits—doubtless imagining herself to be much lovelier—that she could not conceal her feelings even before the admiring artist. He dropped back the curtain, and said no more about the busts. Soon after, one of them, done in marble, was displayed in his rooms, crowned with bays, and entitled "Beatrice." After Canova's death, his brother sent it to Madame Récamier, with the quotation from Dante:

"Sovra candido vel, cinta d'oliva
Donna m'apparve." . . . .

To which was added: "Rittrato di Giulietta Récamier, modellato di memoria da Canova nel 1813, e poi consacrato in marmo col nome di Beatrice." Perhaps this incident is even less in Madame Récamier's favor than her flirtation with Prince August. Worldliness was natural, and a part of her education almost; but, as a lovely woman, she ought to have known that personal vanity half destroys the charm of beauty.

However, 1814 brought a change of affairs. Napoleon fell, and France was free again. The exiles every where hastened to Paris, and Madame Récamier found herself once more in the midst of the De Staëls, Montmorencys, etc., and resumed at last, after an absence of three years, her character of a Queen of Society. It is amusing to see how the weak now exulted after the fall of the strong man who had kept them in awe. Nothing was good enough for these poor restored exiles. Paris, France itself, was theirs. They had been kept out of their own; they re-entered their possessions triumphantly; and so rejoiced were they at the ruin of their oppressor, that they received with glee and open arms the enemy against whom they had so long inveighed. With the De Staëls and Récamiers, the English were the mode, and Wellington the hero of the day. Madame Récamier returned to flirtation as well as to wealth—for her husband had gradually recovered from his failure in the interval—determined to add the hero of a hundred fights to the number of her slaves. In a sketch which she wrote out for a long memoir of these glorious days, we find Wellington *facile princeps* in her heart, and, if we may credit her, quite in love with this woman of seven-and-thirty. Here is a specimen of her flirtation given by herself in these notes: "Dinner at the Queen of Sweden's, with her and the Duke of Wellington, whom I met again. His coldness to me; his attention to the young Englishwoman. I am seated at dinner between him and the Duc de Broglie. He is glum at the beginning of the dinner, but revives and ends by being very agreeable. I notice the displeasure of the young Englishwoman opposite to us, and cease talking to him and devote myself entirely to the Duc de Broglie."

What magnanimity, and what vanity! On the morrow of Waterloo, the duke, still her captive, repairs to her apartment. Between patriotism and coquetry, she is confused. The duke mistakes her emotion for joy at the downfall of Napoleon, and exclaims: "*Je l'ai bien battu.*" After this, Madame Récamier—to believe her biographer—shut her doors against the duke in disgust.

These pretty stories—sure to find favor with the French—may or may not be true. The Duke of Wellington, great man as he was, was far from immaculate. At any rate the following note, in bad French, is quite characteristic, and, according to Madame Le Normant, is only one of a number he sent to her, "all alike."

"Paris, le 20 Octobre, 1814.

"J'etais tout hier à la chasse, madame, et je n'ai reçu votre billet et les livres qu'à la nuit, quand c'était trop tard pour vous répondre. J'espérais que mon jugement serait guidé par le votre dans ma lecture des lettres de Mademoiselle Espinasse, et je desespère de pouvoir le former moi-même. Je vous suis bien obligé pour *la pamphlète* de Madame de Staël.

"Votre très obéissant et *fidel* serviteur, WELLINGTON."

But dukes and princes were nothing to the beautiful banker's wife, and during the winter of 1814 we find her intimate with half-queens and ex-empresses; in other words Hortense, Joséphine, and Caroline Murat. She added now to the list of her slaves that weak, bombastic weathercock, Benjamin Constant, who was among those who triumphed most loudly over the downfall of the despot, and who, when he started up from Elba to flash gloriously over France and Europe for a moment, was one of the first to lick the dust before him. The return of the bugbear, sudden and triumphant, scattered the exulting exiles with their tails between their legs. There was a rush and escape from Paris, like that of naughty schoolboys when the master's step is heard in the passage returning to the schoolroom. The generals whom Napoleon had crowned—the greatest mistake in his policy—and who had turned against him in the hour of need—as, of course, they would, and as he ought to have foreseen—ran off helter-skelter to be out of the way of his re-risen wrath. Murat, always a coward, turned round once more, and left Naples to return only to meet a just fate, the proper death of a turn-coat. There was a general end of these half-kings, and Wellington had the honor, not only of capturing the ringleader of the band of housebreakers, but of throwing down almost all the thrones his accomplices had so pleasantly enjoyed for a time. It was amusing to see these mushroom-monarchs retire to private life in America or England, and drop the "king" for the "Mr."

Madame Récamier was among the few of the returned exiles who remained in Paris, and had now to mix in a yet more curious society than any of which she had had experience. Madame Krüdner, at that time the keeper of the Emperor Alexander's conscience, and a very remarkable woman, was much sought after by the gayest Parisians from a knowledge of the influence she possessed over the emperor, who visited her incognito for the purpose of conversing on religious subjects. She opened her parties with prayer; and it was remarkable to see the courtiers, who flocked there either from curiosity or interest, fall on their knees while the hostess herself extemporized the prayer. Among the number was even Constant, who believed in nothing, not even in himself, though perhaps there was some excuse for that, as nobody else believed in him either. He admitted that he felt himself an arch hypocrite when he knelt down on these occasions.

In Paris Madame Récamier now saw most of her old friends reassemble; but the most intimate of them, Madame de Staël, returned from Italy only to die. Her friend's grief was great, but even by the side of her death-bed, she was able to form another friendship with a person no less distinguished—Chateaubriand.

Sir James Mackintosh, who a year previously met the author of "Le Génie du Christianisme" at Paris, and who, by the way, says of Madame Récamier that she was still very pretty at that period, and had pleasing manners, and describes her coming into a party followed by two or three adorers, says of him: "He is a mild and somewhat melancholy person, and more interesting than his works." He was at this time about middle-aged, still handsome, and very attractive in his gentle, delicate manners. His travels had given him a far more extended knowledge of the world than most Frenchmen possess, and increased the natural liberality of his sentiments. He was free from the narrowness of French prejudices against England; and when Mackintosh was about to leave Paris for this country, told him to carry with him his prayers "*pour toute sorte de prospérité pour la vieille Angleterre,*" whereof the idea was Chateaubriand's, but the French probably Sir James's. But Chateaubriand was a man who aspired to more than he gained: he was not satisfied with his own aspirations. A disappointment, which came from within rather than from external circumstances—over which a truly great man can rise indifferent—left him morbid and bitter. His friendship with Madame Récamier was, as he professes, a relief to his spirits. She seems to have understood this melancholy man more than the world did. She cheered him, not, perhaps, entering so much into his feelings, as flattering imperceptibly his vanity, which was naturally soothed by the friendship of a beautiful woman, who had been such a star in the world of society. Often, indeed, the recluse, the bitter philosopher, verging on misanthropy, is drawn back to the world—at least to humanity

—by the delicate allurements of a mere flirt. Madame Récamier was little more. She was not a woman of profound mind. Her companionship with thinkers like Ballanche and Chateaubriand was not spiritual, or metaphysical, or philosophic, or speculative; such men did not want such companionship. They had run into superhumanity (if the term be permitted), and they wanted more humanity. They found it in its pleasantest, least offensive, most attractive form in this amiable, agreeable, pretty woman, who had lived to enjoy life, and enjoyed, and even prized it still. Madame Récamier won back these morbid thinkers by the strength of her very reality. She was their medium between a world "*d'outre tombe*," and a living world, to which they felt, or professed, such hostility. Far from angelic, she was a kind of angel to them, who was able to throw a halo of common beauty over the world they detested. The fact that she was a woman, still beautiful, still gay, still full of life, gave her this power. In this respect a woman, however commonplace, is more than a poet, and Madame Récamier was, though a flirt, not commonplace.

In 1819, the husband of Madame Récamier—for among these numerous flirtations we no longer think of M. Récamier himself—experienced fresh losses. An English wife might now have devoted herself, and sacrificed her love of gayety to the consolation of her unfortunate spouse. Madame Récamier was a Frenchwoman, her place was in society, and to that she must be true. She took the other alternative, and securing for herself a portion of the fortune which her husband had dissipated in fruitless speculations, separated from him and took a small apartment in the Convent of L'Abbaye-aux-Bois, in the Rue de Sèvres. Her room was almost as poor as the cell of a real nun; but here she received the whole world of Paris, and the receptions at the Abbaye-aux-Bois became celebrated. Chateaubriand has described her apartment in his "Mémoires d'outre Tombe," and this retreat has since been raised to a level with that of St. Joseph, where Madame de Montespan retired from the embraces of a monarch, and Madame du Deffand held a long rule; but at the period at which Madame Récamier took up her lodging there, it was so little known, that Madame Moreau, who was asked by her to dinner, thought it necessary to set off an hour before, in order to accomplish the journey. Hither Chateaubriand came day after day, and here were found the old friends, the Montmorencys, Simonard, Ballanche, and a mass of acquaintance, among whom were the Duchess of Devonshire, the Earl of Bristol, the Duke of Hamilton, Sir Humphry and Lady Davy, Maria Edgeworth, and Alexander von Humboldt, as foreigners; Chateaubriand, Benjamin Constant, and, later, Villemain, Montalembert, Tocqueville, Guizot, Thierry, Sainte-Beuve, and Prosper Mérimée. Surely Madame Récamier's fame must have reached a great height when men of such different colors and principles could crowd together in her little room. Here, too, Delphine Gay, as a young girl, made her début in reciting a poem of her own, which was afterward crowned by the Academy. M. Ampère, the younger, then one-and-twenty, was introduced to Madame Récamier, and afterward became an *ami de la maison;* and Miss Berry, more celebrated as the friend of Horace Walpole's old age than for her talents as an authoress, made a ludicrous and rather awkward mistake about the Queen of Sweden, of whom she related an anecdote in her very presence.

Thus we see that Madame Récamier's society at this period was composed as much of literary and political celebrities, French and foreign, as of the merely fashionable people of Paris. To collect them, and still more to keep them, she must have had something more than her reputation for beauty, which was now declining, for she was forty-three years of age. We hear little of her own wit amid anecdotes of that of her friends, and her fortune was too much reduced to make that her attraction. The secret lay probably in that charm of manner, that perfect ease and grace in conversation, matured in some five-and-twenty years of continual good society, and that sympathy for the opinions and feelings of others, which brought her so many friends, even among men and women vastly superior to her in intellect.

The attraction she possessed for these friends, and which she heightened by a certain show of *affection*, which, as a flirt, she did not hesitate to offer, was so strong that all her friendships, innocent in other respects, took the form of love-affairs. In England she will not be acquitted of infidelity to a husband still living, and from whom she had separated herself in his misfortunes, simply because these *liaisons* did not extend to criminality; nor can we, as doubtless the French can, read without disgust the passionate letters of Chateaubriand, a married and middle-aged man, to Madame Récamier, a married and middle-aged woman. We may well wonder, too, that people, keenly alive to the ridiculous in others, should have seen nothing ludicrous in their expressions of devotion. Thus, in November, 1820, Chateaubriand is sent on a diplomatic mission to Berlin. He wishes to throw it up because it will separate him from Madame Récamier. He writes, "*Je ne vis que quand je crois que je ne vous quitterai de ma vie.*" Again: "I fear I shall not be able to see you at half past five, and yet I have but this happiness in the whole world." "I shall pass my life near you in loving you." "You only fill my whole life." When he is gone, she writes him part of her letter in invisible ink, which becomes legible on being held to the fire. Was this a political or an amatory precaution? He writes like a young lover mourning over his separation. He throws out hints of positive jealousy of Matthieu de Montmorency, and is in rapture when he obtains leave to return. With all allowance for Gallic ardor of expression, we can not think that these letters are merely the outpourings of a platonic attachment; and as in after years Chateaubriand declared roundly his devotion to Madame Récamier, we can not, at least in England, acquit him of having, as a married man, made love to a married woman. Knowing, too, Madame Récamier's confessed coquetry, we can not acquit her, on the other hand, of having encouraged him.

Chateaubriand returned after a few months' absence, but in the following April had again to quit her, being sent on an embassy to England, the country "where," he says, "I was so unhappy and so young." Here he wrote to his idol three or four times a week, and much in the same strain; but Madame Récamier, true to her character of flirt, appears, in his absence, to have encouraged his rival, Matthieu de Montmorency—a far better friend for her in every way—and to have replied rarely enough to these effusions.

We have, however, no need to be surprised that Chateaubriand should have expressed more than a platonic affection for Madame Récamier. He had once before, if not oftener, forsaken his wife, and on one occasion with so much dishonor, that we can not omit the story which Madame Récamier gives in full, and the first part of which Chateaubriand unblushingly relates in the "Mémoires d'outre Tombe."

Four-and-twenty years before the embassy to England, Chateaubriand, an exile, an orphan, and almost penniless, had found in this country sympathizing and benevolent friends, among whom was the Rev. Mr. Ives, of Bungay, in Suffolk. This gentleman had a daughter, a beautiful charming girl of fifteen, whose modesty must have contrasted powerfully with the prudery and coquetry of the émigré's countrywomen. Chateaubriand fell in love with her. He was handsome, clever, and even fascinating. The poor girl gave him her whole heart frankly; and he was dishonorable enough to encourage her attachment; in short, to amuse himself at her expense. Her parents saw how the matter was. The young man was about to leave them, and they feared for their child's heart. With much frankness and delicacy—to which he has, in his "Mémoires," given a ridiculous turn—Mrs. Ives, on the eve of his departure, offered the young exile, whose position, she thought, made him too timid to come forward himself, the hand of her daughter, and a home under their own roof. Nothing could have been more disinterested.

"I fell on my knees," he writes, "and covered her hands with kisses and tears. She thought I was weeping from joy, and sobbed with pleasure. She put out her hand to ring the bell, and called her husband and her daughter. 'Stop,' I cried, 'I am married!' She fell into a swoon."

Time did not efface from the poor victim's heart the memory of her first love, and we can imagine the agony which his cruelty brought into this kind English family that had so warmly sheltered him. Many years passed, and Charlotte Ives accepted at last the hand of a naval officer, who in due time rose to the rank of admiral. When Chateaubriand, now a famous author and embassador, returned to England four-and-twenty years later, he met Charlotte again, as the wife of Admiral Sutton, and mother of two fine young men, who had to be put forward in the world. Chateaubriand offered her his aid, and she accepted it in favor of her sons. She wrote to him two letters, asking him to exert his interest for them, and full of dignity and modesty, yet betraying the depth of a feeling which she had never been able to conquer. She concludes the last with these words:

"But I will not presume further to detain your attention. Let it be permitted me only to say, my lord, that feelings too keen to be controlled rendered the first few minutes I passed under your roof most acutely painful. The events of seven-and-twenty previous years all rushed to my recollection; from the early period when you crossed my path like a meteor, to leave me in darkness when you disappeared, to that inexpressibly bitter moment when I stood in your house an uninvited stranger, and in a character as new to myself as perhaps unwelcome to you."

Madame Récamier now held a proud political position. Her best friend, Matthieu de Montmorency, was minister for foreign affairs, and Chateaubriand embassador at London. The main ambition of the latter was to be nominated for the Congress of 1822, and it was through Madame Récamier that he pushed his claims. His frequent letters are uninteresting, full of himself, of vanity, and ambition; but they give clear indications of the influence which Madame Récamier possessed at this period. She succeeded in obtaining his wish for him, though not in the manner he desired it; for the two rivals both went to the Congress, and Chateaubriand naturally had to take the second place.

However, he agreed wonderfully with Montmorency until their return from Paris, where, as there was no longer work for two in the government, it devolved on one or other to give up his ambitious prospects. The rivals were not pitted only in the arena of love, or friendship, whichever you choose to consider it; they were divided in politics, yet by so slight a shade of opinion, as made them far more bitter foes than direct opponents would have been. The one, a Revolutionist at heart, was a Royalist by tradition, and out of the two had grown into a Liberal Royalist; the other, whom tradition attached to the *ancien régime*, while ambition induced him to put up with a constitution, was still a Conservative Royalist. The king naturally favored the latter; and thus, when the opportunity presented itself, and Matthieu de Montmorency, the Liberal, was compelled to retire, Chateaubriand, the Conservative, was at once invited to accept the vacant portfolio. According to his own account, he refused it again and again till forced to take it; but, however this may be, we can understand that this measure would have raised up a bitter feeling between the two men. Montmorency, indeed, was too good a man to indulge this sentiment; but, as we always hate more those we have injured than those who injure us, Chateaubriand could no longer bear the man over whom he had triumphed.

Let us leave these great-little men to their jealousies, and return to their common idol. In 1823, the health of her niece had become so delicate that the doctors advised for her a warmer climate, and Madame Récamier set out for Italy.

It is a curious phase in the history of this flirt, that the older she grew the more devoted became her adorers. She had the uncommon art, too, of keeping as well as making them. A Frenchman generally loves more with his mind than with his eyes, and the dignity of his attachment seems to be enhanced by the age of its object. At any rate Madame Récamier may have now made the consoling reflection, that the admirers of her middle age—for she was now six-and-forty—were men of a far superior stamp to those of her youth. The Bonapartes and German princes, who had been enslaved by her beauty, were inferior to the great thinkers who now surrounded her. There was youth and poetry in the person of the young Ampère; philosophy in that of quaint, simple, awkward, but good-hearted Ballanche; power and religion united in the graceful Montmorency; and ambition and fame in vain, morbid, melancholy Chateaubriand.

The first two accompanied her to Italy, the third was soon to join her there, and Chateaubriand would certainly have gone, if ambition had allowed him to do so. Thus we see that

Madame Récamier, no longer young, no longer very beautiful, had the art of disposing of the fates of her adorers.

At Rome Madame Récamier took a position only second to that she held in Paris. The Duchess of Devonshire, with whom she was intimate, was the leader of society in the Holy City, and, endowed with fine tastes and high accomplishments, had surrounded herself with the celebrated painters and sculptors of all nations then in Italy. Into this society Madame Récamier entered enthusiastically, and assembled its members in her own salon. But death broke up these circles. The Duchess of Devonshire was no longer a young woman; the death of her most intimate friend, the Cardinal Gonsalvi, overwhelmed her, and in the following year, 1824, she succumbed.

Madame Récamier, now that her chief attraction was gone, left Rome for Naples. At the former place, however, she had renewed a forgotten acquaintance of early days. Rome was full of a wretched, shabby herd of ex-kings and ex-queens of the empire, and their hangers-on. Among these were Lucien, her old admirer; Jerome, ex-king of Westphalia; and Queen Hortense. Sedulously avoided by all the other French in Rome, they dragged on a wretched existence, very different to their former mushroom grandeur, content with less ambitious titles than "king and queen," and truly grateful to any body who would notice them. Madame Récamier met Hortense, then called "Duchesse de St. Leu," at St. Peter's; and though she would not openly renew her acquaintance with her, she condescended to meet the "queen" from time to time in her rambles among the ruins. It was on one of these occasions that Hortense entered into a long explanation of her own conduct in accepting the title of Duchesse de St. Leu from the Royalists, while Napoleon was, as she thought, secure for life at Elba. The prisoner, however, escaped, and turned up at Paris to vent his wrath on the heads of his apostate family. He sent for his step-daughter, and demanded what she meant by accepting a title from his enemies. Hortense, terrified by his sternness, explained that she had done so out of consideration for her children. The emperor, pacing the room, sternly spoke of the law, and seemed to enjoy the terror he inspired. The queen pleaded her feelings as a mother, following him about with supplication. "Then," replied the emperor, severely, "they should have told you, madame, that when one has shared the prosperity of a family, one must know how to bear its reverses." Unconsciously he had approached the window of the Tuileries, followed by his step-daughter, who had burst into tears. An immense mob had assembled in the court, watching for him, and a grand shout of welcome greeted the returned prisoner. Napoleon bowed quietly; but the queen had also been seen, and the papers of the day, in relating the appearance of the emperor at the window, added, that the applause of the multitude had so affected Hortense that she had to shed tears!

The death of the Duchess of Devonshire was not the only blow to Madame Récamier at this period. Chateaubriand, for whom, doubtless, she felt more than for any of her devoted friends, was dismissed from office without a word of explanation. True to his character, ambitious and vain, he was not content to retire with dignity, but commenced in his own paper, the "Journal des Débats," a series of attacks upon the government he had recently belonged to, the untempered bitterness of which proved, beyond doubt, that it was Chateaubriand, not France, he desired to advance, and gave the true measure to his professed patriotism.

From Naples Madame Récamier returned to Rome, where she passed the winter of 1824–25. Thence she again proceeded to Naples, accompanied by her friends, to the number of whom was now added M. Charles Le Normant, who afterward married her niece. At last, in May, 1825, she returned to Paris, after an absence of eighteen months. She now occupied again her little room at the Abbaye-aux-Bois, and once more received the chief society of Paris. Her visitors were mostly the same, and, of course, the devoted Chateaubriand was constantly there. His rival, Matthieu, did not long trouble him. On Good-Friday, 1825, death removed him forever. He died while praying in the Church of St. Thomas Aquinas, at Paris.

From a French point of view Matthieu de Montmorency was little less than a saint. He had passed his later years in a strict observance of the rites and ceremonies of his Church and the practice of active charity. He had attempted, and not in vain, to exercise a proper influence over the minds of his friends. To him it is probably owing that Madame Récamier, though a flirt, has never been proved to be worse. His friendship was her safeguard. But what shall we say of a man who, professing all this religion, and probably feeling it, can separate himself from a wife "whose piety and virtues rendered her worthy of his respect;" and only resume his connection with her when a series of deaths in his family made it probable that the great name of Montmorency would become extinct, unless he had an heir to hold it? Making due allowance for a difference of ideas on the subject of marriage, we can not accord to Matthieu de Montmorency, who passed his life away from his wedded wife and in the continual company of the wife of another man, the crown of a saint.

On the death of his rival, Chateaubriand *composed* a prayer for a dead friend, for the use of Madame Récamier, full of French sentiment: this prayer, which he probably did not even *feel*, gives the measure of the religion of the author of the "Génie du Christianisme." If we do not here give a translation of it, it is because a prayer has always seemed to us too private and sacred an outpouring of the heart to be printed among mere worldly thoughts. Suffice it to say, that it raises worldly friendship to the level of our love to God, or even above it!

During the next four years, Madame Récamier continued to inhabit the little room in the convent, and passed much the same life as hitherto. No particular events are recorded during this period, but the death of her father, M. Bernard, and the departure of Chateaubriand to Rome, where he was named embassador, and where he remained from September, 1828, till May, 1829, when he returned to Paris.

In 1830, M. Récamier, who had long been a cipher in the life of his wife, and had, in spite of all his troubles, reached the ripe age of eighty, had the good taste to die. We read a great deal in Madame Récamier's life of her desolation at the loss of her friends, Madame de Staël and Matthieu de Montmorency, but we find no expressions of grief at the death of her husband. This is at least consistent. Her friends took little notice of this trifling affair, and she had probably too long forgotten that she was married at all, to care for the freedom that her husband's death gave her.

Whatever she may have thought, more important events happened to drive it out of her mind. In July, 1830, came the second great revolution that Madame Récamier was to witness. She was at Dieppe at the time, but returned to Paris while the streets were full of barricades. With it fell the friends of Madame Récamier. A Legitimist movement took place in La Vendée, and Chateaubriand and other royalist chiefs were arrested. In the following year the cholera broke out in Paris, and Madame Récamier, to avoid it, fled to Switzerland, there to join Chateaubriand, who had gone thither on being set at liberty. Here she visited the Queen Hortense at Arenenberg, and made the acquaintance of that taciturn son, who even at home assumed, as of right, the airs of a prince, and who is now on the throne of France. In 1833 she took up her residence at Passy, and was again surrounded by her usual coterie.

For the next five years her life presents little incident, and was chiefly passed in Paris. At the Abbaye-aux-Bois she extended the circle of her acquaintance, which was now chiefly literary and *dilettante*. Among the men of celebrity who were frequent in their visits to her little room, are several whose names are well known in England, Alexis de Tocqueville, Louis de Loménie, Sainte-Beuve, and so forth. Chateaubriand was always there, and always devoted to her. He had finally given up politics, and was employed in literature alone.

In 1840, Madame Récamier's health obliged her to leave Paris for Ems. On her return, Louis Napoleon was being tried for his ridiculous attempt at Strasburg, and Madame Récamier was examined as a witness. She was afterward permitted to visit him at the Conciergerie. Two years later he wrote to thank her for this visit; and it is strange to find this ape of his uncle writing in terms of the politest regard to this woman, whom thirty years before his predecessor had exiled as a nuisance. As a proof of Madame Récamier's celebrity at this period, we may cite the soirée she gave by subscription for the sufferers by the inundations at Lyons. The tickets were nominally sold at twenty francs, but as much as a hundred was readily given for the opportunity of seeing this famous leader of society in her "cellule" at the Abbaye-aux-Bois. The sale realized no less than four thousand three hundred and ninety francs. Rachel, Viardot-Garcia, Rubini, and Lablache sang or recited gratuitously, and the rooms were crowded to overflowing with the *élite* of Paris, including most of the embassadors.

Madame Récamier has an especial title to be called a "Queen of Society." She lived in it and for it to the last. In 1845, she lost the use of her eyes by cataract, but still continued to receive, though not less than sixty-eight years of age. With the exception of short journeys into the country, she remained almost always at the Abbaye-aux-Bois, and her life became monotonous in its habits. Regularly every day at half past two she received a visit from M. de Chateaubriand, in spite of his great age—he was nearly eighty, and in very bad health. After an hour's *tête-à-tête* between this aged but still devoted couple, visitors were admitted, among whom came regularly old M. Ballanche, now a distinguished member of the Institute; and from then till the hour of rest she lived for her friends. In the morning she had the newspapers and new books read to her, and took a short drive.

But one can not live forever; and one by one this circle of old friends dropped off to a world where society, good or bad, is of little account. Madame de Chateaubriand was the first to go, and worthy Ballanche followed in 1847. The lasting friendship of these people of a former age, nay, indeed, of a former century, would be very touching, if it had not wound up with a very ridiculous *pose*. His wife had been dead only a few months when Chateaubriand, verging on eighty, infirm, tottering, and with one foot in the grave, offered his hand, as he had long given his heart, to Madame Récamier, blind and verging on seventy. She had the good sense to refuse him; and the following year, in July, 1848, the grave closed upon him too. Madame Récamier attended by his bedside to the last, and her grief at his death was that of a widow rather than a friend.

Madame Récamier was left alone, the last of all her set. She had no further interest in life. A third great revolution was raging round her, who was a remnant of the first. The world was busy with new theories, new follies, new crimes. There remained nothing for her but to quit it. Yet she lingered on. In the house of her niece, this woman of society still received visits for a time, and still, perhaps, flirted with M. Ampère, the last and youngest of her adorers. But in 1849, the cholera, which in younger days she had fled from Paris to avoid, returned with terrible malignity. She was too old to escape now, and among the many victims of the scourge, this famous woman was counted on the 11th May, 1849. It is said that after her death her features assumed a peculiar beauty. Death, content, paid this little tribute to the body of a woman who had been the most celebrated beauty of her age.

THE OFFER: CHATEAUBRIAND AND MADAME RÉCAMIER.

LADY HERVEY.

The subject of this memoir is not held up as a model nor exhibited as a warning. As a woman of the world she can not be esteemed an object for imitation. As one who, in the midst of great temptations, escaped great perils, she ought not to be pointed out as a delinquent. She was born in 1700, and was the daughter and heiress of Brigadier-General Nicholas Lepell, a name since restored, or corrupted, to Lepple, one of those ancient native families of Sark, whose descent is unquestioned, whose pride is avowed, who are French in manner and in language, and English in their government.

Mary Lepell, afterward Lady Hervey, being an only daughter, enjoyed all the advantages of education then bestowed on well-born and well-endowed young ladies, and on them only. She had for her marriage portion the whole of the little Channel Island of Sark; and no pains were spared to render her, what she afterward became, "a perfect model of the finely-polished, highly-bred, genuine woman of fashion." Thus did Horace Walpole describe her.

As she grew up, and displayed not only considerable intelligence, but very great attractions of face and form, her father, in compliance with the received notions of the day, sent her to court, and at the age of fourteen, the age at which Sarah Duchess of Marlborough and her sister began their court life, she became maid of honor to Caroline, then Princess of Wales, and afterward queen-consort of George II.

Mary Lepell was, in some respects, eminently fortunate in the character of the princess whom she served. Queen Caroline had a masculine understanding, and, as Dr. Alured Clarke terms it, "a large compass of thought." Nevertheless, she had a lively imagination, and great vivacity, even wit. Her repulses were good, and she could take as well as give a joke. She had quite a royal memory; such a memory as confers popularity on sovereigns; such a memory as endowed George III. with the semblance of mind. She was an excellent historian of great and small matters; knew the genealogy of most illustrious English families; could bring, at a moment's notice, anecdotes to illustrate her point; and she enjoyed also, what is so seldom enjoyed by royalty, invariably high spirits, which rendered her the life of her court circle, and drew out from her courtiers the best efforts cf their wit and fancy, in which she greatly delighted.

To all these social qualities the queen added great penetration of character, and a most sympathetic, indulgent nature. She was charitable and kind in the extreme.

Still she was German, and, as such, was deficient in delicacy of feeling, and in nicety as to the morals of those around her. She had been accustomed, also, from her youth, to the system of German courts, in which the queen tolerates the mistress, or even mistresses, of the reigning prince, and receives them in her court; and hence the example set by Caroline tainted that region which had, under Anne's rule, or, rather, under that of that fierce dragon of society, "Queen Sarah," attained to a perfection of decorum.

When Mary Lepell became maid of honor to this princess, there existed the usual animosity between the monarch and the heir-apparent which has marked the House of Hanover with littleness of character. The separation of parties was favorable to those who clustered round the Princess Caroline at Richmond, where she then lived with her consort; for she could with safety avoid, and even discountenance the vulgar as well as immoral ladies of the court of George I.; adopt as her adviser and intimate friend the gay Sir Robert Walpole, whose boisterous and not very decorous mirth she learned to tolerate; and escape the petulance and arrogance of Sunderland, who played the first part at St. James's. She could also indulge in her taste for letters and for literary conversation, for which George I. had about as much fondness and capacity as he had delicacy or morality. She could talk divinity with Hoadley; sentiment with Lord Hervey; and of the world—the great world which he knew so well, with Chesterfield; and she could assemble around her beauties with minds, and delight in seeing them rise above the dull frivolities of an ordinary court.

Among the beauties of Richmond Palace, which the princess then inhabited, the three Marys carried away the meed of admiration—Lady Mary Wortley Montagu, Mary Bellenden, and Mary Lepell.

All these three ladies of rank were distinguished not only for their beauty, but for their intelligence, their wit, and their *savoir faire;* a quality without which their wit would have been indiscreet, their beauty perilous, their intelligence pedantic.

Lady Mary stands at the head of this famous trio. She was very handsome, very lively, very quick, very well informed; but she wanted heart; and one great source of attraction to womankind was therefore deficient. Miss Bellenden was beautiful, gay, spirited, and so unspotted by a court as to marry a poor man, though addressed by half the fashionable fops of the day. Though of more decided beauty, she was deficient in the sound sense and cultivation of the third Mary, the lovely Mrs. Lepell, as she was styled. Those who looked only at the exterior admired Mary Bellenden the most of the three; those who sought underneath the exquisite graces of form and face for more valuable qualities were entranced by the sweetness, the truth, the thoughtful mind, and real superiority of Mary Lepell. "Her manners had," says Lord Wharncliffe, "a foreign tinge, which some called affected, but they were easy, gentle, and altogether exquisitely pleasing." Her good sense was so prominent a feature of her character, that it became, as life went on, almost proverbial.

Like Sarah Jennings, Mary Lepell "loved but once," and married before the spring of her summer-like life was over. At court, when in waiting, she encountered, among other loungers, John, afterward Lord Hervey, the second son of John, first Earl of Bristol, by Elizabeth Felton, his second wife. He had an elder brother, then alive—Carr, Lord Hervey, a young man of great abilities, but of a most profligate life, and the reputed father, according to Lady Mary Wortley Montagu, of Horace Walpole. There was a great eccentricity of character and manner in the Hervey family—witness the well-known division of mankind by Lady Mary into "*Men, women, and Herveys!*"—a race full of mental and personal peculiarities, which were not likely to be lessened by the marriage between the Earl of Bristol and Elizabeth Felton, who was more singular even than a "Hervey." John Hervey, the first and last object of Mary Lepell's affections, was educated at Westminster, and afterward at Clare Hall, Cambridge, where he graduated (as a nobleman) in 1715. During the vacations, his father, wishing to make him a man of the world, used to take him to Newmarket, in order to give his delicate and somewhat effeminate son a taste for jockeyism and a love for manly pursuits; and it is said that "Lord Fanny," as he was afterward called, actually undertook to ride a match, but the fears of his fond mother overruled the wishes of his father and his own, and the dear treasure was not allowed by Lady Bristol to run that risk. He grew up a valetudinarian; and all that a pious, intellectual, and sensible father could do to strengthen his mind and body was counteracted by a flighty, self-willed, and excitable mother. Only once was he let loose from what is metaphorically called "her apron-string," and that signal flight was merely to Hanover and back, to pay his respects to George

I., then Elector of Hanover, as his brother Carr had done before him. Here he formed the acquaintance and gained the favor of Frederick, Prince of Wales, a circumstance which decided the current of his after life.

He was now thrown on his own tastes for a pursuit, for his father, Lord Bristol, opposed his entering the army, and literature or politics were the only other resources for a young man of family. He passed, however, much of his time at Richmond, while his mother, the countess, was in waiting on the Princess Caroline; and, doubtless, the old precincts long known as Maid of Honor Row, often saw his elegant, handsome, but languid form pacing with the "three Marys" in the shade of the old trees on Palace Green; while in the evenings, chatting with Pope or with Chesterfield, the young man drank deeply of that potion, the ingredients of which were, in those days, skepticism and worldly knowledge, which were thought to compose the proper elixir for a young nobleman to strengthen and prepare him for life.

Meantime, while the intimacy between him and Mary Lepell was thus ripening, such accusations as these were leveled against the fair maid of honor:

"What I am going to say," writes the Duchess of Marlborough, "I am sure is as true as if I had been a transactor in it myself, and I will begin with the relation with Mr. Lepell, my Lord Fanny's wife's father, having made her a cornet in his regiment as soon as she was born, which is no more wrong to the design of a regiment than if she had been a son; and she was paid many years after she was a maid of honor.

"She was extreme forward and pert, and my Lord Sunderland got her a pension from George I., it being too ridiculous to continue her any longer an officer in the army. And into the bargain she was a spy; but what she could tell to deserve a pension I can not comprehend. However, the king used to talk to her very much, and this encouraged my Lord Fanny and her to undertake a very extraordinary project. And she went to the drawing-room every night, and publicly attacked his majesty in a most vehement manner, insomuch that it was the diversion of all the town, which alarmed the Duchess of Kendal and the ministry that governed her to that degree, lest the king should be put into the opposer's hands, that they determined to buy my Lady H—— off; and they gave her four thousand pounds to desist; which she did, and my Lord Fanny bought a good house with it, and furnished it well."

This malicious effusion must, however, be taken with much reservation. Sir Robert Walpole was at that time an admirer of Lady Hervey's, and there existed not a human being whom, in her later days, the duchess hated with more intensity than Sir Robert, whom she and the duke had at first patronized. It was saying much: for she was a hater *par excellence;* and afterward she assigned to Lord Hervey a pre-eminence in her dislike only second to that she had allotted to the detested minister of George II.

At all events, the Duchess of Marlborough stood alone in her opinion of Mary Lepell, for never has there been so beautiful a woman so little maligned.

It was in apartments of the women of the bedchamber to the Princess of Wales that Miss Lepell mingled with the only agreeable coterie of a dull court. Sir Robert Walpole, of course, was one of those most conspicuous amid a clique, of which Chesterfield, Hervey, and Colonel Selwyn, the father of George Selwyn, formed the chief attractions among the gentlemen. Walpole, though dashing and confident, was not the man to fascinate a young woman of a refined and thoughtful character. Sir Robert, though the most distinguished statesman of his age, since St. John had quitted the scene of political life in England, was a coarse, immoral man. He was at that time a widower, and his conduct as a husband to his first wife had been any thing but exemplary. Nothing can be more bitter than Swift's lines upon him, yet they can never be repudiated as wholly inapplicable. Their malevolence does not neutralize their truth.

"With favor and fortune fastidiously bless'd,
He's loud in his laugh and he's coarse in his jest;
Of favor and fortune unmerited, vain,
A sharper in trifles, a dupe in the main;
Achieving of nothing, still promising wonders,
By dint of experience, improving in blunders;
Oppressing true merit, exalting the base,
And selling his country to purchase his place;
A jobber of stocks by retailing false news;
A prater at court in the style of the stews;
Of virtue and worth by profession a jiber;
Of juries and senates the bully and briber;
Though I name not the wretch, you'll all know who I mean,
'Tis the cur-dog of Britain and spaniel of Spain."

Not only had Sir Robert been notorious in his own gallantries, but he had neglected his beautiful and accomplished wife, Catharine Shorter: had left her to withstand the attention, if she could, of the most fashionable and dissipated men in the gay world; and allowed her reputation, if not her character, to suffer from that pernicious contact. Sir Robert was also no longer young, being born in 1676, in the same year which is notable for giving birth also to Bolingbroke.

His pretensions to the hand of Mary Lepell were therefore soon set on one side; but that he assisted her with advice how to persevere till she had obtained her pension is most probable: and that she was by no means unwilling to avail herself of any method of procuring it, is—in those days when honor seemed to have died out altogether—also very likely.

Perhaps the attentions of Walpole stimulated the ardor of John Hervey, who was already, though not in office, a great favorite both with the Princess of Wales and with Mrs. Howard, which was almost the same thing. His elegant figure, in all the modishness of dress, which was at that period at its height —in flowing peruke, dainty ruffles, diamond buttons on his fine blotting-paper-colored coat—was there contrasted with Pope's deformity; his good-humor, and the refined courtesy which had been perfected in France, with Pope's essential bitterness, which was so awkwardly glossed over with affectation and professions. Many a laugh, probably, had the three gay Marys at the little poet's expense. They treated *him*, and suffered the poet to treat *them*, in return, with a familiarity which we should greatly censure in the present day, and which ended, in the case of Lady Mary Wortley Montagu, in a fierce, unreconciled quarrel. The seeds of jealousy of Hervey in Pope—that smallest of men, and greatest of modern libelers—were doubtless laid in that pleasant time when

"Tuneful Alexis on the Thames' fair side,
The ladies' plaything and the Muses' pride,"

was wafted along the *then* pure stream, amid delicious meadows and glades, to Twickenham, to call for Lady Mary, who was living there; or to the old house at Ham, there to alight and walk, little Pope and tall Hervey escorting up and down the grand avenues the three charming Marys.

Sometimes, too, there came with them a less safe companion in their suburban pleasures. This was Frederick, Prince of Wales, to whose service John Hervey was attached, who had fallen in love with Mary Bellenden. This beautiful girl, the youngest daughter of John, second Lord Bellenden, had just the manners which fascinate by their gayety, and mislead the designing by their levity. Never was any one so agreeable; and all who ever knew her spoke of Mary Bellenden as the *most perfect creature ever seen.* The prince thought so too, for he paid her attentions which she returned with disdain, crossing her arms in his presence, and then saying "she was not cold." And when, one evening, sitting by her, Frederick took out his purse, and began counting out his money, the high-spirited young lady, in disgust—for she hated him, and his money, and his addresses—by a sudden movement, either of hand or foot, sent his royal highness's guineas rolling about the floor, and, while he was gathering them up, ran out of the room.

We can fancy Prince Frederick, therefore, a small man, with eyes of extraordinary brightness, not then married, young and silly, with his face so strongly resembling that of a sheep, one hand in his coat, the other holding the lovely Bellenden's nosegay, or carrying her Blenheim or her fan—how well can we picture him picking his way in silk stockings and diamond-buckled shoes, underneath those ancestral elms, Mary all the while scarce deigning him a look!

Behind come Mistress Lepell and Lord Hervey; she blushing with delight; touched, but still sensible; in love, but not madly so; for her nature is sedate, though of a cheerful turn: her feelings are too sound, too deep, to come to the surface easily.

And he? Is he what the Duchess of Marlborough would have it—painted, and not a tooth in his head? or, as Pope describes him, "Fop at the toilet, flatterer at the board," in respect to his demeanor; while he declares that he had "a cherub's face—a reptile all the rest."

Can this wretched courtier, so described, it is true, some years afterward, have been the object of the lovely Mary Lepell's choice? Nay more, could she attach herself so entirely to a man

> "Whose wit all see-saw between *that* and *this;*
> Now high, now low; now *master* up, now miss;
> And he himself one vile antithesis?"

The only trait, according to the late John Wilson Croker, in the celebrated libel from which those lines are taken, that is strictly true, is Hervey's love for *antithesis*, which he inherited from his mother, and which was conspicuous both in speaking and in writing.

Pertness, frivolity, foppery, were the vices of the young then as now, and Hervey no doubt displayed his full share of them: but the ridicule of Pope becomes cruelty when his delicacy of health and valetudinarian habits were attacked; and the invidious name of "Sporus," or of "Lord Fanny," betrayed the diabolical malice of the Minister Pulteney, by whom the substance of the libel was written, and of Pope, by whom it was turned into verse, as brilliant as any ever written by him or any other modern poet.

Lord Hailes, in his notes on "The Opinions of the Duchess of Marlborough," explains the case. Lord Hervey was threatened in youth with epilepsy, and he could only repel the attacks of that disease by abstemious diet. Hence he took to the use of tea, which was then, as still it is in some parts of the Continent, used in England more frequently as a *tisane* in illness than as a refreshment in health. In vain did his father urge him to discontinue the custom of drinking that "detestable and poisonous plant," as he called it, which had, he said, once brought his son to death's door, and which would carry him through it if he did not give it up. Lord Hervey's daily food was asses' milk, and once a week he allowed himself an apple. He used emetics daily; and, Lord Hailes admits, was in the habit of painting to conceal his ghastly appearance. These habits certainly were not calculated to propitiate the romantic attachment of a young and admired girl; nevertheless, in spite of them, in spite of a life of reprehensible immorality, in spite of a court routine, which usually banishes youth long before even middle age has arrived, Lord Hervey was then, and even in the decline of life, a singularly handsome man, as a portrait of him demonstrates. It was painted in his latter days, and is, Mr. Croker affirms, neither "ghastly nor forbidding."

At the time of his courtship with Miss Lepell he was still, however, though in what the French would call *petite santé*, not condemned to live by rule, as in later times.

Even Lord Hervey's enemies, however, went out of their way to extol Mary Lepell; and even Pope complimented one so admirable.

For what reason it has not been ascertained, the marriage between Hervey and Mary Lepell was for some time kept secret. It is believed to have taken place on the 20th of May, 1720, but was not proclaimed until the 20th of October, although she had visited Ickworth, the seat of Lord Bristol, twice during the summer of that year, still retaining her maiden name; while her father-in-law wrote to her under the "endearing name of daughter," as his lordship himself expressed it. Their supposed union was, however, alluded to by Gay in his poem called "Mr. Pope's Welcome from Greece," in this couplet—

"Now Hervey, fair of face, I mark full well,
With thee, youth's youngest daughter, sweet Lepell."

This mystery was explained thus. When Mary Bellenden rejected the addresses of Prince Frederick, she owned to him that her affections were engaged. Frederick had, he told her, suspected that this was the case; but he added with the generosity of his nature—for he had that quality in a far more eminent degree than any of his race—that if she would tell him the object of her choice, and not marry without his knowledge, he would consent to the match, and be kind to her husband. Both the single Marys were, be it remembered, somewhat in his power from their position as maids of honor to his mother. Miss Bellenden gave him her promise, but without disclosing the name of her betrothed; and then, fearful of any obstacle being thrown in the way, she was privately married to Colonel Campbell, one of the grooms of the prince's chamber, and, many years afterward, Duke of Argyll. It is conjectured by Mr. Croker that Mary Lepell and Hervey took a similar course, fearing lest their union should be disapproved of by their royal patrons. The marriage of both the Marys was announced nearly at the same time. They had probably resolved to brave the storm—if storm there was—together, and to announce the step they had taken, and to give in their resignation as maids of honor at the same time, just a few days previous to the birthday, the 30th of October, when two other young ladies were appointed in their place.

The family into which Mary Lepell now entered were willing, and indeed rejoiced to receive one so endowed with beauty and fortune. Yet she had a difficult part to play, for they were all peculiar though clever—all at variance; all, in short, stranger than other human beings: to sum up the whole, they were "*Herveys.*" Lady Mary's definition applied too well.

Never was there a more respectable nobleman than the first Lord Bristol, descended from one of the heroes of the Armada, and ennobled by George I. He was just enough of an original to be agreeable: he was a fine scholar, and wrote verses after the manner of Cowley, who had been patronized by his grandfather, and whose "Elegy on Hervey," his benefactor, is considered by some as approaching in merit to Milton's "Lycidas." With all the polish of a fine gentleman, Lord Bristol, in his mode of life, was a specimen of the good English squire: he was also unfashionable enough to be a good husband, an indulgent father, and a sincere Christian.

It was the lot of this exemplary man to be united to a woman of most uncertain temper, to whom he was passionately devoted, but whose eccentricity, whose love of pleasure, and love of play, were the talk of the court circle, of which, in her capacity of bedchamber lady to the Princess Caroline, she formed a member. From her Lord Hervey is said to have inherited his wit and his turn for versification.

From the first days of their union, Lady Hervey and her husband led a very gay and fashionable life, rather on the French than the English system of conjugal domesticity; but on one point they both after a time agreed; this was to doubt the truth of revelation. The Princess Caroline, although herself, as we have seen, an earnest believer, encouraged free discussion: and Lord Hervey, setting aside the example of his father, cherished a prejudice against creed, and churches, and churchmen, which was fostered by the conversation of such men as

Tindal, Collins, and Woolston, whose works were then as widely circulated as is now the able but fallacious treatise "On the Vestiges of Creation."

In 1732, Lord Hervey wrote a deistical defense of Mandeville's "Fable of the Bees," in reply to Bishop Berkeley's "Minute Philosopher;" signing the work "By a Country Clergyman," and, unfortunately, his intimacy with Conyers Middleton, who had been his tutor, produced a result still more distressing; it led to free-thinking tendencies in the mind of Lady Hervey. Perhaps, as Croker says, "free-thinking is too lenient a word to apply to her opinions."

Some years after her marriage, we find her recommending Tindal's works to Lady Suffolk. "I beg in my turn," she writes, "I may recommend a book to you; it is writ by Tindal: the title of it, 'Christianity as old as the Creation,' etc." Happily the work is forgotten, and the race of "free-thinking" women—invariably superficial, and generally conceited specimens of their sex—has become extinct on this side of the Channel, and rarely to be met with in France, since the Restoration. Yet her laxity of faith produced no laxity of morals, as it did in her husband. Women are happy in being guarded by a hundred barriers from temptations which environ man, and which, at the period, and in the rank of life in which Lord Hervey moved, it required strong faith to resist. He soon, however, became one of the most notable libertines of a reprobate age; and even the early death of his brother Carr, brought on by a dissolute life, failed to warn him. That event happened in 1723, and, of course, made a material difference in Lord Hervey's fortune and expectations. Henceforth he was no longer the Honorable John, but Lord Hervey; and he was returned for Bury St. Edmunds. Yet it is remarkable that while Sir Robert Walpole professed to like him, Lord Hervey never held any appointment under government; a source of mortification to this otherwise successful courtier.

He continued at court, excepting when, unaccompanied by his wife, he traveled to Italy; while she passed much of her time at Bath, or at Ickworth, where she was beloved by her father-in-law, and even by the eccentric countess, who quarreled with every one else. As a wife, as a daughter-in-law, and as a mother, she was equally estimable, equally valuable and beloved. And perhaps with all the noted inconstancy of her husband, she was happier in her married state than in that of a maid of honor—a kind of slavery which Pope thus wittily described:—"We all agreed," he says, after relating how he had met Mrs. Howard, Mrs. Bellenden, and Mrs. Lepell, at Hampton Court, "that the life of a maid of honor was of all things the most miserable, and wished that every woman who envied it had a specimen of it. To eat Westphalia ham in a morning, ride over hedges and ditches on borrowed hacks, come home in the heat of the day with a fever, and (what is worse a hundred times) with a red mark on the forehead from an uneasy hat; all this may qualify them to make excellent wives for fox-hunters, and bear abundance of ruddy-complexioned children. As soon as they can wipe off the sweat of the day, they must simper for an hour, and catch cold in the princess's apartment; from thence (as Shakspeare has it) to dinner, with what appetite they may—and after that, till midnight, walk, work, or think, which they please. I can easily believe no lone house in Wales, with a mountain or a rookery, is more contemplative than this court; and as a proof of it, I need only tell you, Miss Lepell walked with me three or four hours by moonlight, and we met no creature of any quality but the king, who gave audience to the vice-chamberlain, all alone, under the garden wall."

Nevertheless, the giddy Mary Bellenden, shortly after her marriage, regretted this sauntering, half-private, half-public existence, and wrote pleadingly to Mrs. Howard to let her go back to court; but her more rational friend, Miss Lepell, found her enjoyment in the cultivated society, the literary and political interests of which Lord Hervey and his friend, at that time, William Pulteney, formed a sort of centre: and her letters are full of expressions of contentment, and are descriptive of the varied scenes in which she mixed. It was just the difference between a mere belle and a woman of cultivated understanding.

During her whole life, Lady Hervey evinced a great respect for Lord Hervey's critical judgment, although it seems to have been scarcely superior to her own, and cherished a fond attachment to him; yet there were many drawbacks to her happiness. Lord Hervey's malady increased, and in 1729 he was advised to travel to Italy for his health: Lady Hervey, on account of her children, was unable to accompany him. On his lordship's return, he resumed his attendance at St. James's, where his former patroness, Caroline, now reigned paramount as queen-consort, after the death of George I. At court, there must be no imperfections, no sickness, no sorrow: at the German courts, especially, no one must appear till the period of mourning is over. Those who "hedge" a monarch or his queen must be free from all mortal ills. Lord Hervey, therefore, found it essential to conceal from all eyes, except those of trusted friends, his distressing epileptic complaint. Stephen Fox, who had traveled with him in order to take care of him, and who must have been aware of his disease, and Lady Hervey, were his sole confidants.

"I have been so very much out of order," Lord Hervey writes to the former, "since I writ last, that going into the drawing-room before the king, I was taken with one of those disorders with the odious name that you know happened to me once at Lincoln's-Inn Fields play-house. I had just warning enough to catch hold of somebody (God knows who) in one side of the lane made for the king to pass through, and stopped till he was gone by. I recovered my senses enough immediately to say, when people came up to me asking what was the matter, that it was a *cramp* took me suddenly in my leg, and (that *cramp* excepted) that I was as well as ever I was in my life. I was far from it; for I saw every thing in a mist, was so giddy, I could hardly walk, which I said was owing to my *cramp* not quite gone off. To avoid giving suspicion, I staid and talked with people about ten minutes, and then (the Duke of Grafton being there to light the king) came down to my lodgings where * * * I am now far from well, but better, and prodigiously pleased, since I was to feel this disorder, that I contrived to do it *à l'insu de tout le monde.* Mr. Churchill was close by me when it happened, and takes it all for a *cramp.* The king, queen, etc., inquired about my *cramp* this morning, and laughed at it; I joined in the laugh, said how foolish an accident it was, and so it has passed off: nobody but Lady Hervey (from whom it was impossible to conceal what followed) knows any thing of it."

His lordship, with all his love for gallantry, seems to have justly appreciated a wife at once kind and discreet. To her might be applied those lines of Pope's which were addressed to Mrs. Howard—

"I know a thing that's most uncommon,
(Envy be silent, and attend),
I know a reasonable woman,
Handsome and witty, yet a friend."

While Lord Hervey visited Italy without his wife, Lady Hervey passed much of her time in Paris. In 1731, Mrs. Howard, whom both she and Miss Bellenden flattered, and perhaps really liked, although they were perfectly aware of her real character and position in the court, became mistress of the robes to Queen Caroline. To her many of Lady Hervey's most charming letters were addressed—to that "dearest of Howards" as she sometimes called her.

In the present day, women amuse and edify themselves and sometimes others by works of history, or biography, or poetry, or fiction. We even find a lady writing a capital work on navigation: another is the astronomer of her age: a third immortalizes every English queen, bringing each royal consort so much *en evidence* that one can hardly avoid fancying that we have known the long defunct in some older time. A fourth introduces to our most intimate acquaintance each Prince of Wales that is to be had: a host of lively authoresses take us into France: we are transported even to Bengal and back by two giddy girls: we have not, in short, a taste, a wish, a want, a deficiency that the press does not, through an angelic host of delicate pen-women, supply. We go down as low as needlework—not to mention cookery or gardening, both high-art.

In the seventeenth century all this was cramped into letters. Few women of rank and talent thought of publishing, which was generally done by inferior personages, such as tutors, parsons, half-pay captains, secretaries, or "your very humble servants"—a class of which happily, where there is now a battalion, there was then a regiment. But a lady, with a vocation for scribbling, took out a sheet of letter-paper—*such* paper! coarse, rough, small in size—and dipped her goose-quill into ink—such ink! so brown, so perishable—and, in a hand not *much* inferior to that of your lady's-maid when she makes out the washing-bill, indited a missive on politics, scandal, literature, or religion, which was dispatched to some noted person who could circulate the composition favorably. It is worthy of remark, that in few of the letters of the Augustan period are private feelings, secret sorrows, or heartfelt joys, or the ordinary anxieties of life, dwelt on: it is all for and of the public that they write.

Lady Hervey was an authoress of this description, and her letters are very lively, full of good sense, and as refined as those of Lord Hervey's wife and of Mrs. Howard's friend can be expected to be. While Mrs. Bellenden begins one of her letters with "My Gad!" those of Lady Hervey are always couched in polite terms. When at Ickworth, her epistles turn upon the books she reads; but she still longs to hear something of her old haunts; of the companions she is severed from, and of those, more especially, who surround Mrs. Howard, then Lady Suffolk, whom she calls her "Swiss Countess," in allusion to the liberal opinions of the Mistress of the Robes, the Swiss being then the representatives of the liberal principles in Europe, while the apartments of Lady Suffolk were termed "our Swiss cantons."

Sometimes Lady Hervey writes from Goodwood, where a great deal of company was expected. "I believe," she says, "we shall not be much the better for it; for ciphers in company do not, like ciphers in arithmetic, add to the figures and increase their value; unless it be by comparison." At one time she is visiting the Duke of Richmond at Aubigné, in Berri, a seat formerly belonging to Louise de la Querouaille, Duchess of Portsmouth, and the grandmother of the Duke of Richmond in Lady Hervey's time. Berri had been raised into a duchy by Louis XIV., in honor of Louise de la Querouaille (those being the days when characters like hers *were* honored). The Duke of Richmond was received in such a manner, on taking possession of this estate of equivocal inheritance, that Lady Hervey wrote: it "would fill a newspaper" to tell it. She was always very partial to France. "As for the French," she said, "we must either love or hate them; there is no mean."

"But," she adds, "I shall send you no account of the Duke and Duchess of Richmond's entrance into this town, nor of their reception; it would fill a newspaper. But if you have a great mind to be informed of it, look into the English History for the account of King Charles II.'s entrance into London on his restoration, and that will pretty well answer it; adding a few more harangues, larger bonfires, greater illuminations, more rockets, finer presents, louder drums, shriller trumpets, finer colors, and stronger *huzzas;* which last (as a French servant told me) is in English, '*Live the Duke and Duchess of Aubigné!*' I questioned it a little at first; but a second servant confirmed it, and I am convinced."

From Paris her letters were still more lively; and, indeed, nothing could be more attractive to a person of intelligence than the materials of which society there was then composed; and Lady Hervey's previous life, under the very lax influence of Lady Suffolk, must naturally have led her to think lightly of all that *honnête galanterie* which, to most Englishwomen, is so revolting.

Several English noblemen at that time resided occasionally in Paris. The fortunes of the French noblesse were not then, as now, irretrievably injured, while their modes of life were simple. Suppers were in vogue: those fine old hotels, of which here and there one sees a specimen in the Faubourg St. Germain, were in all their picturesque splendor when Lady Hervey visited the French capital.

"Lord, madam!" writes Horace Walpole, speaking of the banker La Borde's house to Lady Suffolk, "how poor all your houses in London after his! In the first place, you must have a garden half as long as the Mall, and then you must have fourteen windows, each as long as the other half, looking into it; and each window must consist of only eight panes of looking-

THE FAIR LEPELL

Surrounded in the Pump-room at Bath by many notable Characters of the Day, mingling in social Chat: Lord Chesterfield, Beau Nash, Horace Walpole, Lord Chatham, the Duchess of Queensberry, Lady Suffolk, etc.

glass. You must have a first and second ante-chamber, and they must have nothing in them but dirty servants. Next must be the grand cabinet, hung with red damask, in gold frames, and covered with eight large and very bad pictures, that cost four thousand pounds. I can not afford them you a farthing cheaper. Under these, to give an air of lightness, must be hung bas-reliefs in marble!"

Much of Lady Hervey's time was also spent at Bath, in a vain endeavor to eradicate an hereditary predisposition to gout from her constitution. She bore this painful malady with great patience; and with similar sweetness of character she sustained those other troubles which, though not mentioned in her letters, can not fail to have vexed her: the devotion which Lord Hervey expressed, and perhaps felt, for Lady Mary Wortley Montagu, could not have been particularly agreeable to an attached wife. While abroad, though it is asserted that most affectionate letters were addressed to Lady Hervey by his lordship, none have been found; while the lines he wrote to Lady Mary Wortley Montagu, more like the tender effusions, as even Mr. Croker admits, of a lover of twenty, than of a friend of thirty-three—these remain in all their sentimental elegance.

"Oh! would kind Heaven, these tedious sufferings past,
Permit me, Ickworth, rest and health at last,
In that lov'd shade, my youth's delightful seat,
My early pleasure and my late retreat.
* * * * *
There might I trifle carelessly away
The milder evening of life's clouded day;
From business and the world's intrusion free,
With books, with love, with beauty, and with thee.
* * * * *
But if the gods, sinister still, deny
To live in Ickworth, let me there but die;
Thy hands to close my eyes in death's long night,
Thy image to attract their latest sight;
Then to the grave attend thy poet's hearse,
And love his memory as you loved his verse."

Then came a duel with Pulteney and a quarrel with Pope, both of which events were the talk of the town for many weeks; while Lady Hervey sometimes took refuge in the quiet duties of a country life at Ickworth, or the gossiping circles of Bath, or in the enchantments of Paris.

Lord Hervey's time, too, was incessantly occupied in those ridiculous court cabals which he has himself described with so much humor, notwithstanding his dissipated character, his painted face, his deistical principles, and his valetudinarian habits; his vegetable diet, his bread-sauce, his "milk tea," his breakfast of dry biscuit, and all those precautions which a hypochondriac adopts, but which an unbelieving healthy friend laughs at. Notwithstanding his premature decay, and the "ridicule made upon him," as he expresses it, by "ignorance, impertinence, and gluttony," Lord Hervey unwittingly, and perhaps unwillingly, captivated the heart of the Princess Caroline, the daughter of George II. Horace Walpole, who knew every thing, found this out; and there are many passages in Lord Hervey's own Memoirs that confirm the fact. There was something, doubtless, soothing in his courtier-like devotion both to the wife and daughter of a monarch who would have been, if not a king, a subject, of the most favorable description, for Sir Cresswell Cresswell and his Divorce Court in these days. Among other anecdotes, one related by Lord Hervey is highly characteristic of his majesty's vulgarity and temper. The queen had ventured, during the king's absence, to take away some very bad pictures out of Kensington Palace, and to substitute some very good ones. There was a certain fat Venus, painted like a sign-post, that his majesty preferred to all the Vandykes in the world, and especially to "three nasty children," as he styled them (probably those of Charles I.), that the queen had hung up near a door, and he ordered them to be taken away. While the queen, her daughter, and Lord Hervey were talking about this the next morning, the king came into the gallery, and staid about five minutes. He "snubbed the queen, who was drinking chocolate, for being always stuffing; the Princess Emily for not hearing him; the Princess Caroline for being grown fat; the Duke (of Cumberland) for standing awkwardly; Lord Hervey for not knowing what relation the Prince of Sultzbach was to the elector palatine: and then carried the queen to walk, and be re-snubbed in the garden. The pictures were altered according to the king's direction soon after: the excuse Lord Hervey made for their not being done that morning, was the man's being out of the way who was always employed on these occasions."

It appears, however, that the Princess Caroline was not only the object of Lord Hervey's regard but of that of his wife, which was continued to her royal highness many years after the death of Hervey; and with respect to Lady Mary Wortley Montagu, that their correspondence, which was returned to her by Lord Hervey's son, George, showed that a long and steady friendship between two persons of different sexes might exist for many years *without love.* Lord Hervey professed to admire women who were no longer young; and Lady Mary was, during his gallant attentions to her, past forty-seven:

"Just in the noon of life, those golden days
When the mind ripens ere the form decays."

She was six years his senior.

The decline and death of her husband may therefore be supposed to have given Lady Hervey far greater concern than these platonic attachments, toward which she seems to have entertained no aversion. During the year 1742 Lord Hervey's health continued to decline. "When I say that I am still alive, and am still privy seal," he wrote to Lady Mary Wortley at Avignon, "it is all I can say for the pleasures of the one or the honor of the other." He next complains that he had been three weeks ill of a fever, "an annual tax that his detestable constitution paid to this detestable climate every spring." He was then, he wrote, in easy circumstances; Lepell, his second daughter, was recently married to the Hon. Constantine Phipps, afterward Earl of Mulgrave. The Duchess of Buckingham had left him (Lord Hervey) Buckingham House and all the furniture and plate for his life—but that life was rapidly waning away. "The last stages of a mournful life," he wrote in June, 1743, "are filthy roads, and, like all other roads, I find the farther one goes from the capital the more tedious the miles grow, and the more rough and disagreeable the way." Yet he was then at Ickworth: "I know," he adds, "of no turnpikes to mend them; but doctors who have the management of it, like the commissioners for most other turnpikes, seldom execute what they undertake; they only put the toll of the poor cheated passenger in their pockets, and leave every jolt at least half as bad as they find it, if not worse." This sentence formed a part of his last letter to his distant friend. Lord Hervey died on the 8th of August, 1743. Lady Hervey remained with Lord Bristol till his death, which took place in 1751. She acted toward him with the duty and affection of a daughter. In the October of the same year in which he died, writing to the Rev. Edward Morris, who had been tutor to her sons, in a strain of mingled sorrow and philosophy—

"They," she writes, "are insensible who do not feel their own misfortunes; but they are weak who do not struggle with them; and true philosophy consists in making life worth our care, not in thinking it below it. The misfortunes Mrs. P. can have met with are few and slight compared to those I have experienced: I see and feel the greatness of this last in every light, but I will struggle to the utmost; and though I know—at least I think—I can never be happy again, yet I will be as little miserable as possible, and will make use of the reason I have to soften, not to aggravate my affliction. I hope she will do the same, for I wish her happiness as sincerely, as warmly as I do my own."

Many sources of interest, however, in some measure supplied the place of a husband who was unworthy of so much regret. Four sons—George, Augustus, Frederick, William, successively Earls of Bristol—and four daughters, Lady Mulgrave, Lady Mary Fitzgerald, and two who died unmarried, survived their father. On the youngest, Lady Caroline, Churchill wrote these lines, which seem to indicate that the graces of Lady Hervey descended to this her youngest daughter:

"That face, that form, that dignity, that ease,
Those powers of pleasing, with that will to please,
By which Lepell, when in her youthful days,
Even from the currish Pope extorted praise,
We see transmitted in her daughter shine,
And view a new Lepell in Caroline!"

Lady Hervey appears afterward to have returned in some measure to the world, for in 1765, only three years before her death, Horace Walpole writes the most amusing apology to her for his absence from some reception at her house. He complains that it was scandalous at his age to be carried backward and forward to balls and suppers and parties as he was; his resolutions of growing old were admirable; he always awoke with a sober plan, and ended the day in dissipation. But he promises his old friends to begin to be between forty and fifty by the time he was fourscore; and he believed he should keep to his resolution, not having chalked out any business that would take him above forty years more; "so that if he did not get acquainted with the grandchildren of all the present age, he hoped still to lead a sober life before he died." We find him also talking of two new fashions brought by Lady Hervey from Paris; the one a tin funnel covered with green ribbon, holding water, in which the ladies kept their bouquets fresh: he feared they would take frequent colds in overturning this reservoir. The other he half playfully, half angrily insists on, since Marshal Saxe was victorious in Flanders over our troops, and declares we must step out of the high pantoufles that were made for us by those cunning shoemakers at Ramilies and Poitiers, and go clumping about, perhaps, in wooden shoes. "My Lady Hervey, who, you know, dotes upon every thing French, is charmed with the hopes of these new shoes, and has already ordered herself a pair of pigeon-wood." This letter was written shortly after one of Lady Hervey's last visits to Paris, where, among other agreeable visits, she had passed some days at L'Isle Adam, in the Valley of Montmorenci, with the Prince and Princesse de Conti. Her description of the kindness of the French (in the classes superior in intelligence and character) may be echoed in the heart of every one well acquainted with the people but little understood and much libeled by us.

"I am sure I have reason to praise the friendly as well as agreeable disposition of these people: it is not possible to have found more friendly, attentive, essential marks of kindness, even in the midst of the most affectionate relations and friends, than I have found here during my illness and on my recovery. My acquaintance called at my door every day, and sometimes twice in a day, to know how I did, and if there was nothing I wanted they could help me to. Three or four of my more particular acquaintances, I may say friends, passed an hour or two every day in my ante-chamber to hear from my physician and women what symptoms and changes appeared in me. I had light quilts, couches, easy-chairs, and all sorts of things to contribute to my ease sent in to me; and on my recovery the best sort of wines of several kinds, lest what I bought should be adulterated. Little chickens out of the country, new-laid eggs warm from the hen, and a thousand other little delicacies to please a difficult palate and not load a weak stomach. If you could guess at all the proofs of kindness I meet with, and all the agreeableness of my way of living here, you would neither blame nor wonder at my reluctance to quit this delightful place and most agreeable people. Adieu, sir; I have neither paper nor time to add any thing more."

Historical and critical reading, visits, journeys to Paris and to London diversified Lady Hervey's life until she became too infirm to move from home. She died on the 2d of September, 1768, in the sixty-eighth year of her age. Horace Walpole, to whom she left a small remembrance in her will, refers to her decease with more feeling than was his usual strain.

"I have had another misfortune as I had last year in poor Lady Suffolk. Lady Hervey, one of my great friends, died in my absence. She is a great loss to several persons; her house was one of the most agreeable in London; and her own friendliness, good-breeding, and amiable temper had attached all that knew her. Her sufferings with the gout and rheumatism were terrible, and never could affect her patience or divert her attention from her friends."

It is some merit or good fortune to be eulogized by a man who loved so few, and to have escaped the sarcasm of Horace seems almost a miracle. Lady Hervey was a woman after his own heart—a moral and amiable woman of the world. Although her letters in the latter part of her life are serious and thoughtful, they do not evince the faith, the hope, the childlike love to our Creator that appear in Mrs. Elizabeth Montagu's last epistolary productions. Yet Lady Hervey *acted* well, and, we may hope, on a basis of principle that she did not choose to manifest. Her beauty in early life has been greatly praised: from a miniature in middle age it seems to have been owing to a sweet and intelligent expression rather than to symmetry of feature. In the portrait referred to, one of the treasures of Strawberry Hill, she is painted in a hood drawn partially back from her light hair, which is dressed in the rococo style; a small bow of very narrow ribbon confines the hood underneath the chin. The dress is laced in front, with an ample fichu of thin muslin over the neck and shoulders; the sleeves fall in long folds over the arms, but are drawn up at the elbows. Such was probably her ordinary costume; it was simple, convenient, and suitable; and both the costume and the age for sitting were probably selected by Horace as calculated to perpetuate her remembrance, not as she looked in courts and festivities, but in the intimate circle of every-day life, of which her wit, her gentleness, her good sense, and her patience under suffering, must have constituted her the charm and the resource.

MADAME DE STAËL.

Of the many Frenchwomen who have ruled society for good or ill—and when does a Frenchwoman fail to rule if she have beauty, wit, or vice enough?—there is none we can so thoroughly admire as the authoress of "Corinne." Not that our admiration can be unmixed. Few men, perhaps *no* women, have had their lives thoroughly ventilated by an inquisitive public without the discovery of some littleness that marred their greatness, adding nothing to the attractiveness of their personal characters. The men and women we adore in print and in public, to whom we pour out freely the riches of our praise, the fullness of our admiration, are often disliked in their families or hated by their friends. One drives economy to niggardliness; another is found perking his or her head in enviable cômplacency before a private looking-glass; another torments his servants; another destroys, with a Spartan virtue, all the hopes and happiness of her children; another is secretly covetous; another adulatory; another servile; another pompous; another, wise as he speaks or acts before the world, an arrant fool in his household. In truth, if one were to look *au dessous des cartes*, as Madame de Sévigné advises, not Carlyle or Emerson could find a hero in the world. "No man is a hero to his valet," and *certes, certissime*, no woman is a heroine to her lady's-maid.

But there is this grand difference between Madame de Staël and the other French leaders of society—they had contemptible, she pardonable faults; or, rather, they had faults where she had foibles. Looking at her only as a woman of society, we may perhaps assign four principal causes to her superiority: she had much mind; she had little beauty; she was educated in such a manner that the former supplied the want, but did not usurp the office of the latter; and, lastly, she was a Protestant. In most celebrated Frenchwomen, beauty has been a great temptation: where this was wanting, wit, ill-directed, has been no less so. If they have had any education at all, it has been a bad one; and if they have had any religion at all, it has been confined to that late-sought devotion which is a quiet salve for the conscience, but can take no one to heaven.

Madame de Staël owed much to her parents; and as her earlier years were entirely mixed up in the events of their later ones, it may be well to give sketches of them. All our readers know that Necker was the great finance minister of that unfortunate, threadbare sovereign, Louis XVI. Do they all know that he began his career as a *commis*, or clerk, in a banking-house? or, knowing this, can they see something of the man already? Not that every man who rises from insignificance to eminence, or from penury to opulence, is either an admirable or a lovable man. Nine tenths of such men have had no object in view but self; and too often the long devotion to their own desires makes them, when they reach the summit of their own ascent, incapable of broad views, generous measures, or noble sacrifices. Necker was not one of these. But they and he had one valuable quality in common — energy. This quality his daughter inherited.

Necker was born in 1734, in that town which can boast more heroes than any of its size, Geneva. It had cherished Calvin and Voltaire, the greatest revolutionists of religion and philosophy. It was now to send forth an honester man than either in the person of Jacques Necker. The son of the Genevan professor of civil law, he received as good an education as his native town could give a young boy, but at fifteen had to begin life. He was sent to Paris and placed in the banking-house of Vernet as a clerk. Another man, under his circumstances, backed by no interest, might have been clerk there forever. Young Necker worked with that steady application which eventually wins the hard-fought day, and rose to be first cashier, and in time a partner of Thelusson's bank. Perseverance lifted him so far, but might not have done much more for him. He had reached a landing where his natural capabilities were to come into play. A few wisely-made, happy speculations brought him in time wealth. Wealth recommended him to the worthy Genevans. They made him their minister at Paris. Soon after Thelusson died, and Necker set up a bank of his own. Wealth brought wealth. Many men make it, few know how to keep it. Necker, being neither covetous nor extravagant, knew this and prospered. The king's advisers saw a man who could make the most and the best of his own money, and in their straits—for the Bourbons were always in want of funds, and Louis XVI. most of them all—thought he would be a proper man to take care of theirs.

In 1776 they made him director, and soon after comptroller-general of the finance department. He was the first Protestant who had held any great post in the government since the terrible day of St. Bartholomew. Necker found the finances in the worst possible condition: reform, economy, prudence, were his great principles. He nobly refused all emolument for the

Herculean labor before him. The people applauded, but the court disliked his restrictive measures. The difficulty of his position induced him to resign in 1781. He had, however, already published his "Compte Rendu," or account of his administration. This was attacked by his successor, M. de Calonne. Necker prepared a reply, which he sent to Louis, who, while convinced of its veracity, implored him not to publish it. The ex-minister felt that the nation was his judge, that his character was at stake, and determined to put his defense before the people. The consequence of this act was an order of exile to a distance of forty leagues from Paris. So great was his popularity at this moment that the citizens accompanied him in large numbers out of Paris. This word "exile" fell like a thunderbolt on his daughter. Thirty years later, it had rung too loud in her own ears to make any impression. During his retirement, instead of attacking his enemies, as a less Christianly man might have done, he employed himself in the composition of a work entitled "De l'Importance des Opinions Religieuses."

It would be out of place to sum up the political history of the next seven years, when Europe watched with awe the great struggle between an excited, disgusted people, and its obstinate, incompetent rulers. Minister after minister was tried and dismissed. The people, disappointed, put off, and cheated with a stone when they clamored for bread, prepared for a grand outburst. The storm-cloud grew and grew, and had nearly covered the heavens, ready to break in lightnings, when Necker, more on account of his popularity than of his supposed ability, was invited to take the helm of government once more in 1788. As he did so, the funds rose thirty per cent., and the hopes of the nation even higher. But he was not the man for a great emergency. He needed time and patience, and neither were allowed him. His admiration for the English form of government induced him to hope that he could introduce it into France. In modeling the constitution, he claimed acknowledgment for the existence of that large class, of which he was a member, and which had hitherto been overlooked by the government—the *tiers état*, the *bourgeoisie*, the mercantile, trading, and artisan class, in short, the *middle* class of France. He claimed for it an equal strength in the Assembly with that of the nobility and clergy together. He desired to convert the absolute government of France into a limited monarchy. At another time he might have succeeded; as it was he failed. The very strength which he gave to the popular party, while it irritated the court and the nobility more than ever, hastened the revolution which none but excessive measures on one side or the other could have averted.

The folly and obstinacy of Louis brought the matter to a crisis in June, 1789. Relying on the hope of foreign support, he resolved to make one last struggle to recover every thing, and destroy with one blow the work that had been slowly progressing so long. One step in this direction was to dismiss the popular minister and get him well out of the country. Necker might have raised his voice, and the people would have risen to protect him; but he was too moderate a man to wish such a rescue. He was at dinner when the order of exile came. He was in the habit of driving out after that early meal. Without either changing their dress or taking a particle of luggage, he and his wife mounted their carriage as usual and drove away from Paris, not knowing when they might return. The moment his departure was known the theatres were closed, though it was on Sunday evening, and barricades were run up in every direction. The Revolution had begun.

The Assembly canceled his exile, and he returned to enjoy the applause of the people for a space. Fool, indeed, is he whom the voice of a throng can fascinate. Necker was too moderate a man to deal with Girondins, Jacobins, and Cordeliers, with an infuriated people, abusing the liberty that it had gained at last and clamoring now for license. Marat abused him in the "Ami du Peuple." Others called him "aristocrat." His attempt to shield the monarch, while he struggled to bring him round to sensible measures, incensed the revolutionists against him. Worthy and well-meaning as he was, he had neither the courage nor the abilities to stand the brunt of the raging waves of popular discord, and in September, 1790, he sent in his resignation. It was accepted with perfect indifference. His popularity was long since over. Disheartened, disappointed, disgusted at the result of his labors and the ingratitude of the people for whom he had worked, he retired to Coppet (of which we shall speak later), and attempted to console himself with literature. In 1804 he died at a ripe old age.

Such was, briefly, the life of Madame de Staël's father. His character may be pretty well seen through it—moderate, sensible, honest, and straightforward. There are some other points, to discover which we must know more of his private life. His daughter, who was devoted to him, and thought him one of the greatest statesmen of the world, has given one or two hints of his good heart, his sensibility, and his aspirations after public usefulness. Probably she inherited from him the softer parts of her character; but these may also be owing to a reaction against the puritanical hardness of her mother.

This mother was Gibbon's love, if that historian ever was in love, which may well be doubted. Susanne Curchod was the daughter of the Protestant pastor of Crassy in Switzerland, who educated her in all the stern morality of a rigid Calvinist. Gibbon was a young man at Lausanne, the place he loved more than any other, when he met and fell in love with her. Her parents were poor, and readily agreed to the marriage he proposed; but the stern old gentleman at home refused to allow his son to marry a girl without a penny. "After a painful struggle," he says, "I yielded to my fate. I sighed as a lover: I obeyed as a son. My wound was insensibly healed by time, absence, and the habits of a new life." In other words, he was *not* in love.

The rejected damsel was too much of a Spartan to let this first love blight her life. She was thoroughly a "good girl," with as little romance as Calvinism leaves to its devotees. On the death of her father she resolved to support herself, and entered a school at Geneva as a teacher. Here Necker, returning to his native town, after twenty years of hard up-hill work, found, admired, wooed, and easily won her. She made him an excellent wife. Duty was her grand guide. And he was, perhaps, too much wrapped up in ambition to care for more. Nay, the father of the greatest French authoress had a horror of lady-writers; and when he discovered in his wife an inclination to wield the pen, he showed such displeasure that henceforth she wrote her "Mélanges" only in odd moments and almost by stealth.

The only fruit of this union was Anne-Marie-Louise-Germaine Necker, born in Paris in 1766. If Madame Necker had had her way she would have made a Quakeress of this child. But the very same disposition which was at that time preparing France for revolution, made of the young girl a highly imaginative authoress instead of a strict dry Puritan. It was in vain that Madame Necker applied rule and compass to a human soul. It would not be cut into straight lines, nor come out in dull, ugly, yet highly respectable forms. The little girl was soon cutting out paper figures and making them act their part in mimic life. The mother came down on her. The paper men and women were hurriedly thrust into the child's bosom, only to be drawn out again when mamma was gone.

Yet Madame Necker did much for her. She directed her reading, and gave her a stock of valuable knowledge which she used liberally in after years. The child, too, loved her parents. As an instance of this we may quote an anecdote relating to Gibbon. The historian, though he had recovered his passion for Susanne Curchod, was quite alive to the charms of

Madame Necker's well-balanced, sternly-upright mind. He visited the Neckers constantly in Paris. Perhaps the little girl of ten, with her acute powers of observation, discovered the pleasure which her mother took in the society of her former lover. Be this as it may, she noticed that Gibbon was a favorite guest, and that the grief of her parents at his departure was great. An idea gets into her head and there matures. She steals quietly to her mother, and proposes that she herself shall marry Mr. Gibbon, in order that he may never again be taken from them! Poor little thing! she could not then guess that in after years Gibbon and she would represent almost the antipodes of the intellectual globe.

At the age of eleven she was a forward child. Her father's guests, who were some of the most distinguished men of the day, such as Marmontel and the Baron de Grimm, historians of another generation, took great notice of her. On one occasion the Abbé Raynal held her little hands for a long time and talked to her as if she had been a woman; and, little doubt, she answered him in the same strain. She amused herself, even at this age, with writing comedies and tragedies, and, like every great writer, began her vocation very early in life.

But the girl grew into a woman. In England, she might have come out early as an authoress, have captivated a man worthy of her mind, and been happy or unhappy according to the measure of her dreams. In France she was spared the necessity of choosing. Probably, as Necker's only daughter, she might have had an *embarras de choix.* Anyhow, she was not allowed to interfere in the matter. A Protestant, a respectable man of good means, of good position, and so on, was the desideratum for a husband in the eyes of those worthy parents.

Now Paris or France contained scores of men of good means and good position—nay, if the Neckers had cared for it, of rank—who would have been happy to offer their hands to the minister's daughter. Will any one doubt it, when he is told that her *dot* was the enormous sum of eighty thousand pounds, and reminded that the tenth part of that is considered a good marriage portion for a French girl even in the present day? But it was not equally easy to find a young French Protestant combining these advantages—for such the Neckers, with all their Calvinism, considered them; and indeed it may be observed that worldliness and other-worldliness often unite in the same individual. One would have hoped from Necker, with his love of English institutions, and from Madame Necker, with her high Spartan principles, that they, at least, would have regarded marriage in some nobler light than as a mere contract of mutual commercial benefit; and if any one plead that this view of the sacred tie was so completely that of the whole French nation, that to take any other would have been considered as ultra-romantic, it must be remembered that whatever the general ideas on the subject, the changes which preceded the Revolution introduced a greater freedom even in the matter of marriage, and that about this time it was much more customary than it had ever been to allow girls when of a reasonable age to make a choice among their suitors.

These thronged around Mdlle. Necker with her eighty thousand pounds in cash and large expectations; but, as we have said, the religion was an obstacle with most. Among the Protestant members of the corps diplomatique was a young Swede, named Eric Magnus, Baron de Staël-Holstein. He was secretary to the Swedish embassy; he was a great favorite with Gustavus III. of Sweden, who encouraged his suit, and promised to make him his embassador on the first vacancy, if he succeeded in winning the hand of the daughter of a powerful minister like Necker; farther, he was young and handsome; and, farther, he had no quality, but an easy—too easy—temper to recommend him. When we remember the romantic, one may say sentimental, character of the author of "Corinne" and "Delphine;" when we find in her works an almost *English* tone of feeling in regard to domestic matters, we may well wonder that she should have consented so easily to the proposition of her father to marry a young man for whom she felt no kind of affection. But, though some people have called Madame de Staël more than half English, looking at her works, we have only to examine her life to be persuaded that she was perfectly French. She took a French view of the sacred bond of matrimony. Filial love has always held a higher place in France than conjugal affection. Mdlle. Necker was wrapped up in her father, whom she regarded as the greatest man of his day, and she accepted the husband he proposed as a matter of course. There was only one condition to be made—he was never to ask her to leave France. To this the young baron readily consented, and the marriage took place in 1786.

From this period this convenient husband figures little in the life of Madame de Staël. He appears to have been prodigal or generous to a most alarming extent; and his first act was to convey to his intimate friend Count Fersen, on his marriage-day, the whole of his ministerial salary. It is not certain, but may be suspected, that this act was in consequence of an agreement between the friends, in virtue of which the count undertook to secure the heiress's hand for his friend.

The baron was, we are told, a spendthrift; but this is not sufficient excuse for Madame de Staël's having separated from him not many years after their marriage. There is, however, in France, a very convenient law for ladies who make *mariages de convenance;* the wife may at any time withdraw from her husband on the plea of saving her fortune for her children. Thus, not only the filial, but also the parental virtues are encouraged to nullify the conjugal; and when a girl has married for the sake of position, rank, wealth, or what not, and finds that her husband is but a dull companion for her, she has only to allow him to grow extravagant—an easy measure with Frenchmen—to raise a cry of improvidence, separate, and, if she is unprincipled enough, console herself with some one whose society she prefers.

Madame de Staël was sufficiently French to do all but the last. She had sufficient principle and too little beauty to become *galante* after the separation. The baron betook himself betimes to his fatherland, and betimes returned to Paris, but did not interfere with his spouse. It was only in 1802, when he was lying on his death-bed, that his wife rejoined him, nursed him through a severe illness, insisted on his accompanying her to Coppet, and had the satisfaction of seeing him die at Poligny on the way thither, leaving her an eligible widow.

Yet we must not be hard on Madame de Staël for making this match, whatever we may think of her afterward unmaking it. A young lady of twenty, who should even demur at her parents' choice for her, would in France be considered guilty of utter want of filial respect. Doubtless, Madame Roland, whom we English admire for her independence in this respect, is strongly condemned by her fellow-countrywomen, and by the mammas especially. Madame de Staël did not approve of such unions. "I will oblige my daughters to marry for love," she used to say, though she did not act up to the resolution; and later in life she herself made a species of marriage of affection, or one at least in which there was great admiration on the one hand. It is amusing to read Madame de Necker-Saussure's comment on this act. "The inconvenience," she writes, "of love-matches is, that they do not originate from choice." To appreciate this paradox one must be thoroughly imbued with the ideas of French morality, in which the innocent love of a young man and young woman in the hope of marriage is regarded as immodest on the one hand, and an indulgence of passion on the other almost criminal.

As a leader of society, Madame de Staël does not come out in any remarkable degree till many years after her marriage.

Nevertheless, she opened her salons at this period, and her position as Necker's daughter, her wealth, and her wit attracted to them most of the people worth knowing at that time in Paris. Still she had no celebrity; and, on the other hand, people complained that she was too much of a genius to shine in society. She was always ready to fire off on any subject of interest to herself, however little suited to her interlocutor. Necker was fond of relating, with a hearty laugh, how she had once attacked a stiff old lady of the court, known as the essence of propriety personified, with, "Pray, madame, what do you think of love?" She was above etiquette, and would sometimes appear with a torn flounce, or at others without a cap. These terrible crimes made Madame Necker very cross and M. Necker laugh delightedly, but they may have militated against the success of the young married woman in society.

Yet she was quite happy—she was in Paris. To her, as to every real Frenchwoman, Paris was the navel of the world. The Hindoo says the same of Delhi; the Chinaman of Pekin; and we are certain many a true John Bull thinks it of London. But this narrowness, which none but a fool will confound with either patriotism or the true love of country, but which partakes of the same localism which makes Farmer Jones regard the parish he lives in as the only spot of earth "fit for a Christian," surprises us in a woman of Madame de Staël's wide experience and general absence of prejudice. At Coppet, one day, her friends drew her attention to the magnificent scenery of the shores of Lake Leman. "Show me the Rue du Bac," said she, turning her head away. "I would willingly live in Paris on a hundred a year in a lodging up four pairs of stairs."

Madame de Staël took no share in the events of the Revolution, and had little interest in them when her father resigned for the last time. As his daughter, her political opinions can be easily guessed. She felt no sympathy with, but, we may be sure, much horror at, the terrible cost of liberty in those terrible days, for her heart was always touched by suffering; but she could not regret the fall of the monarchy. Her chief anxiety was less political than personal; and the fate of her friends, many of whom belonged to the court, was a matter of great concern to her. At the final outbreak in August, 1792, she might easily have secured her own safety by a flight to Switzerland; she was, in fact, provided with passports; but she could not leave Paris while her friends were all in danger, and she might be of use to them. Moreover, her position as wife of the Swedish minister gave her some security, which she even used for their good. Soon after the outbreak, she harbored M. de Narbonne, the ex-minister of war, for whom she was reported to entertain too strong an attachment. A domiciliary visit was made at her house while he was there. She mustered all her courage, and used such dignity to the gens-d'armes, that they retired without making a search. De Narbonne was afterward supplied with a passport by another friend, and escaped to England.

Another of her friends, M. de Jaucourt, had actually been arrested and consigned to the fatal prison of the Abbaye, when she courageously undertook to save him. She found that among the members of the Commune was a literary man, named Manuel, and sought and obtained an interview with him. She could only appeal to his feelings. "In six months," she said to him, "you too may have no power. Save my friend and reserve for yourself one sweet remembrance for the period when you, in your turn, may be proscribed." The eloquence of the young woman of six-and-twenty succeeded with the Republican; De Jaucourt was set at liberty, and in six months Manuel may have recalled that one act of mercy when on his road to the guillotine.

But her kindness for her friends involved herself in very imminent danger. Little guessing what that day was to be, she had fixed the 2d of September for her departure from Paris. In order to save the Abbé de Montesquiou, she had given him the passport of one of her servants, and appointed to meet and take him up on the road. The 2d of September was the first of those fearful days of blood when the name of Liberty was befouled forever in France by the most terrible assassinations which are to be found in the world's history. Assassins, male and female, had been hired to clear the prisons, and they did it. Before the evening of that day, the court of every prison was filled with corpses reeking with blood, and thronged with the vilest of the people, drinking now brandy mixed with gunpowder, now goblets of blood itself. Paris, nor the world, knew no such awful days as those of September, and the stench of blood mounted to Heaven with the cries of the tortured victims, to call for judgment on the instigators of this villainy. That judgment came in time. Nay, that judgment is still being executed, and France, enslaved by an ambitious man, is paying for the insults she offered to humanity in the outraged name of Liberty.

On the morning of that day Madame de Staël set out in a carriage and six. It was a foolish display, and might well have been dispensed with. She was scarcely half way down the street, when a crowd of those wretched female demons, who proved in the Revolution that woman can be worse than man when once let loose, surrounded her carriage with cries "*A bas l'aristocrate.*" Very little sufficed to raise a disturbance on that day, and in a few minutes the coach was stopped, the servants overpowered, and Madame de Staël compelled to drive to the Hôtel de Ville, to give an account of herself. The last time she had been there was three years before, when she had listened to the cheers that welcomed her father back to Paris. Who would be fool enough to care for the *vox populi?* who blasphemous enough to repeat that it is *vox Dei?*

When she reached the Hôtel de Ville, and alighted, she had to walk through ranks of pikes pointed at her. One brute made a thrust at her, and she was only saved from death by the gendarme who accompanied the prisoner. She was taken before Robespierre, whom she had known at her father's house; but that was nothing to him. She pleaded the right of the Swedish embassador's wife; but all her eloquence might have been in vain, had not Manuel, of whom we have already spoken, appeared at that moment on the scene. He took her to a private cabinet which looked upon the Place de la Grève before the Hôtel de Ville. Here she saw the terrible bands of assassins, returning from the prisons, to be paid in money for their reckless murders, and in the midst of the crowd stood her own carriage. The people were about to tear it to pieces, when a man mounted the box and defended it by voice and gesture. She was astonished at this piece of unasked kindness, but in the evening the defender entered her cabinet with Manuel, and turned out to be the wretch Santerre. When she asked him why he had defended her property, he explained that in the days of the famine he had witnessed and shared the distribution of wheat ordered by her father, M. Necker, and could not allow his daughter's property to be destroyed. There was gratitude even in this butcher of his countrymen.

At night her friend Manuel conducted her to her carriage, took his seat beside her, and thus escorted her in safety to her house. The next day he sent her a gendarme to assist her in escaping from Paris. This official turned out to be the famous Tallien, who, in less than two years after, brought Robespierre to the guillotine. In this manner Madame de Staël escaped to Coppet.

In the following year she went to England. No one has been able to assign any reason for this journey; but it may perhaps be attributed to a lurking affection for M. de Narbonne, the ex-minister, whom, as we have seen, she had rescued, and whom, it is said, she loved. De Narbonne was now in England. A little colony of *émigrés* had planted themselves at Mickleham, near Richmond, in Surrey. Among them were Talleyrand, the Duc de Guignes, who had been the French minister at London some years before, Madame de la Châtre, the daughter of Montmorin, who had perished fighting among the pikes of the assassins on the 2d September; and M. d'Arblay, who afterward married Miss Burney, of whom an account is given in this volume, under the notice of Madame Piozzi.

Some of these *émigrés* were entirely without means, though belonging to the oldest and wealthiest families in France. Others had succeeded in saving a few hundred pounds, and all shared together in the same friendly house at Mickleham. M. de Narbonne was the richest of them, and paid for all. They managed to buy one small carriage, and, as there was only room for two in it, the ex-ministers took their turn to mount behind as footman, when the inmates of the colony wished to drive out to see the country. In the immediate neighborhood of Mickleham was Norbury Park, belonging to a Mr. Phillips, whose wife was the sister of Miss Burney. A great friendship soon struck up between the unfortunate *émigrés* and the inmates of the park, and this ended, *en passant*, in the marriage of Miss Burney to M. d'Arblay, who undertook to teach her French.

Miss Burney's conduct in the matter of Madame de Staël is not without reproach; but it is quite consistent with her well-known worldliness. She became intimate with the great Frenchwoman, so much so that they wrote numerous little notes to one another, of which we give one as a specimen of Madame de Staël's English at this period.

"When J learned to read english, J begun by milton, to know all or renounce at all in once. J follow the same system in writing my first english letter to Miss burney; after such an enterprize nothing can affright me. J feel for her so tender a friendship that it melts my admiration, inspires my heart with hope of her indulgence, and impresses me with the idea that in a tongue even unknown, I could express sentiments so deeply felt. my servant will return for a french answer. J entreat Miss burney to correct the words, but to preserve the sense of that card. best compliments to my dear protectress, Madame Philippe."

In the next letter she invites Miss Burney to spend a *large* week with her at Juniper Hall.

As most of our readers well know the charming scenery of Richmond, and Mickleham hard by, it is unnecessary for us to describe those beauties of England which these poor emigrants delighted to visit. They certainly deserved some favor of the

English people, who were shocked and disgusted at the atrocities of the Revolution, to that extent that even the name of liberty was ostracized for a time in this country. They received little notice or hospitality. Had they come in the days of their glory, with pockets full of louis, and titles well recognized at home, they would have been fêted as "distinguished foreigners." They came poor and naked, and the nation of shopkeepers—vulgar to the last—despised them. It was no wonder, then, that the kind inmates of Norbury Park won the affection of these outcasts by their little attentions. But even Miss Burney, who eventually married one of their number, was not free from worldliness. She was told that reports were circulated that Madame de Staël had, in her house in Paris, entertained the leaders of the Revolution. There is no doubt that some of them were there, such as Robespierre himself, but they were there among a crowd of Constitutionalists, all more or less of Necker's opinions, and only on sufferance. Nevertheless, after an intimate friendship for a short time, Miss Burney thought fit to withdraw. Later, when she was in Paris, Madame de Staël, pure from any vindictive feeling, wrote to offer to renew her acquaintance, and Miss Burney returned a letter, which she considered a perfect specimen of diplomatic refusal, but which we can now calmly call extremely vulgar. But then Miss Burney *was* a vulgar woman, and if any one doubts it let them read her Diary and Letters.

But the friendship or enmity of that vain little creature, whose much-lauded Diary is after all nothing but a series of the most egotistical sketches, made little difference to the bulk of the French colony, among whom were M. Lally Tollendal, La Fayette, the Princesse d'Henin, the Princesse de Poix, and Guibert, the author, who, Madame de Staël confessed to Mrs. Phillips, had been very much in love with her before she was married. The whole party lived on most amicable terms, as fellows in misfortune, and amused themselves very well in spite of their want of means, which obliged them to sell their jewels and lace, to teach their native language, or even, later, to take menial offices. They engaged a gentleman to teach them English, made excursions together, and invited their English neighbors to Mickleham, with more hospitality, perhaps, than economic prudence.

On all these occasions, Madame de Staël was the leader, in virtue of her wit and good spirits, and the portion of Miss Burney's correspondence which refers to the French colony, is divided between her and M. d'Arblay. Yet the refugees were not to be left in peace at Mickleham. England, which now boasts itself the refuge of political destitutes, sent Talleyrand to America, with a very peremptory order. De Narbonne also left, and Madame de Staël returned to Coppet.

With great energy she now devoted herself to the succor of the many unfortunate exiles who crowded Switzerland, like the ghosts of former glory, and to the vague hope of reconciling France and England, with which she published two pamphlets on the questions of the day.

Many a great reputation or great success results from a disheartening check. Napoleon Bonaparte, a young, unknown, and insignificant soldier, lost his appointment in the army on the overthrow of Robespierre. This loss made him Emperor of the French, when he might otherwise have been nothing but an obscure soldier. It brought him up to Paris, to get another post. He saw Barras, Barras saw him. Barras saw not the mere soldier, but the future Emperor of the French, the conqueror of Europe. He kept him in Paris, and the young Bonaparte's fame was secured.

It was not probable that the daughter of Necker, the friend of constitutional liberty, should adhere very ardently to the encroaching policy of General Bonaparte, as year after year his brief, brilliant campaigns raised him a step higher in influence at Paris. Still, Madame de Staël had returned to Paris, had opened her salon and her mouth, and not only could not avoid the first man of the day, but even sought him out to tackle him with her wit. She found her match in the blunt, rude soldier. "Whom do you think the greatest woman, dead or alive?" she asked him, with that direct mode of attack which was her peculiar characteristic, and made her society often, as Byron thought it, rather oppressive. "Her, madame," replied the general, "who has borne the most sons." "They say you are not very friendly to the sex," she resumed. "I am passionately fond of my wife," said he, and off he walked.

Still Napoleon was justly afraid of her bitter truths. "She has shafts," he said, some years later, "which would hit a man if he were seated on a rainbow." Madame de Staël had more than one occasion of testing her powers with the great man. Thus, when he was preparing for the invasion of Switzerland, which was almost to her as a native country, she sought an interview with him, and in a *tête-à-tête* of an hour, attempted to dissuade him from such an unjustifiable step. He listened attentively, but was, of course, by no means convinced; and Madame de Staël could have known very little of this man, or been very confident of her own powers, to suppose for a moment that she could turn him from any fixed purpose.

Necker was still living at Coppet, and, as a proscribed *émi-*

gré, would have been involved in the fate of the Swiss. His wife was dead, and his daughter hastened to him and attempted in vain to induce him to leave the château and fly to a securer spot. The event proved that he was right to remain there. The French troops entered by the Canton Vaud, and passed close to Coppet; but a message from the Directoire informed M. Necker that his life and freedom would be respected during the invasion. The inhabitants of Coppet listened to the sound of the cannon which was borne to them through Alpine echoes from Berne, a distance of nearly eighty miles, and the old Genevan knew well enough that his native land was destined to become an appanage of his adopted country.

Madame de Staël returned to Paris about the same time that Napoleon came back in triumph from Egypt, and made his first great steps toward absolute power, backed by the army. She reopened her salon, which was now crowded with all that party which, like herself, dreaded the increasing influence of this new man, and looked with regret on the decay of the republic, which they had imagined to be well and firmly established. Among her guests was Joseph Bonaparte, for whom she entertained a sincere regard. The first consul gathered from his brother something of the principles of the most popular drawing-room in Paris, and felt that here was a rival to his own popularity among the educated classes of the metropolis. The great-little man was not above jealousy of such a woman, and tried to attach her to himself.

"What does she want?" he said to Joseph. "Her father's two millions? She shall have them. Leave to stay in Paris? She shall remain. What *does* she want? Why does she not join *us?*"

When Joseph reported this to his friend, in the hope of bringing her round to his brother's party, she replied, "The difficulty, monsieur, is not what I want, but what I *think*."

The popularity of her salon was not increased by the speech in the Senate of Benjamin Constant, the famous journalist, who there denounced the first consul, without specifying him by name, as aspiring to arbitrary power. Madame de Staël was suspected of having prompted this speech, and the next day her salon was empty, and she was recommended by the minister, Fouché, to "retire for a few days to the country." At this period, both Lucien and Joseph Bonaparte were as frequent visitors at Madame de Staël's as at her intimate friend, Madame Récamier's. Joseph was her especial favorite, and it will well be understood how completely the conqueror of Switzerland, Egypt, and Italy dreaded the tongue and independent spirit of this one woman, when it is known that he even warned his brother, soon after the speech of Constant, to desist from his visits, which of course he did. It was from the day on which this speech was made that Madame de Staël dates the hostility of the future emperor. Constant was known to be her intimate friend. It was known that he had apprised her of his intention; and she confesses that she had encouraged him strenuously to deliver the speech which created so much sensation.

From this period, therefore, Madame de Staël's life has as great a political as literary importance, and her salons may be regarded in the light of Napoleon's *cauchemar*. There is no doubt that this independent woman, who looked with natural apprehension on his increasing power, was one of the few people who withstood it by all the means in her reach. As the wife of the Swedish embassador, she collected in her salons the leading politicians of all colors; but as the Revolution had driven out of France all but its own adherents, the parties now in Paris were reduced to those who saw the power of the first consul on the increase and bowed to it, whether from fear or motives of interest, and those who, seeing it, longed in vain to oppose it.

The latter was by no means a large party. Every one was weary of the Revolution, and despised the Directoire. The most zealous Republicans regarded Napoleon as the restorer of order: even Madame de Staël herself, at this period, dreaded his future rather than objected to his present measures. His great enemies were the remnant of the aristocratic party, who still hoped for the restoration of the Bourbons; but this party was in exile; and they destroyed all sympathy felt for them in France, while they only strengthened the power and increased the popularity of the first consul, by the disgraceful attempt to assassinate him by an infernal machine.

But whether to Napoleonists or Republicans, Madame de Staël expressed her political opinions openly and with all the force for which she was celebrated in conversation. As the Tribunal was still a free body, any such influence in Paris, as would encourage the opposition to him in that house, was naturally dreaded by the ambitious tyrant, and the salon of this clever and independent woman became virtually a rival establishment to the Tuileries.

In this political atmosphere Madame de Staël passed the first two or three years of the century, varied only by visits to her father at Coppet, and her own literary labors, which added greatly to her celebrity, although attacked by the press. In the mean while the first consul, though busied with his projected invasion of England, was on the watch for an opportunity to get rid of so influential a foe; but as liberty of speech was not then denied to the talkers of Paris, there was for a long time nothing that he could take hold of. At length, however, Necker, who had been long working in retirement at Coppet, published the result of his labors in a work entitled "Last Views of Politics and Finance," which gave great umbrage to the first consul. It was somewhat cowardly on his part to visit the sin of the father, whom he could not safely touch, on the daughter's head; yet this he did, and Necker was warned that Madame de Staël would no longer be tolerated in Paris. She was at Coppet at this time; and though about to return to Paris, she preferred to take up her abode at a small country house about ten leagues from the capital. Here she was visited by the few friends who could find time to come so far. But though thus in retirement, she was not allowed to remain in peace. Some woman, from some private motive, reported to the first consul that the road to her house was positively covered with her numerous visitors. Though this was perfectly false, Napoleon was delighted to find a pretext for banishing his clever opponent; and with her began the warfare which he was not ashamed to make upon the women of France, as he had upon the armies of her enemies. Toward the end of September she received by a commandant of gendarmerie an order to retire to a distance of forty leagues from Paris, and not approach the capital within a circle of that radius. This was the fashionable mode of exile at that day, when the offense was not sufficiently marked to justify a banishment from the country. It gratified the spite of the tyrant, who well knew that a Parisian is miserable out of Paris; and as the distance is too great to allow the exile to enjoy frequent personal communication with friends in the metropolis, the sentence destroyed her influence without appearing to the public to be very severe.

To Madame de Staël this was the commencement of an exile which lasted ten years. To the woman who preferred a small room in the Rue du Bac to a château in the lovely scenery of Lake Leman, this was indeed a terrible hardship. "You see," she said to the gendarme, "the consequences of being a *femme d'esprit;* and I would recommend you, if there is occasion, to dissuade any females of your family from attempting it." It was true enough: the great Napoleon, to some people the greatest hero of the modern world, had banished this woman because she was clever. He lived to regret it. He not only made an enemy of one of the best authors of France, but in after years, when he had established a court, and wished to surround himself with wit and talent, as he had already done with rank, he would have given any thing to have conciliated the exile.

He could create dukes, counts, and marquises, but there his power ceased. He could not create minds, make wits, and dub authors.

The exile was a terrible blow to Madame de Staël. She was essentially the woman of society, and Paris was the only place where it could be found. She was undoubtedly vain of her intellectual powers. It can not be denied that to hear herself talk was a keen enjoyment to her; that is, if she had a masterly mind to cope with; for as for the stupid, she held them low indeed. The society of thinkers was the only atmosphere in which she could breathe freely. She declared that exile, which kept her from it, was simply death to her.

With this feeling she looked about for a refuge where she could enjoy the commerce of men of intellect. The capital which, of all others, contained at this period the most remarkable was Weimar. The three greatest thinkers of Germany were residents there—Goethe, Schiller, and Wieland. The duke, celebrated as the Mæcenas of modern Europe, was only too glad to have the author of "Delphine" among the lights of his capital, and received her enthusiastically. She studied German diligently; she talked to Goethe and Wieland in French, which they spoke well, and to Schiller, who could scarcely speak it at all, in broken phrases; in short, she made the first of those notes and observations which were afterward to appear in her celebrated work "De L'Allemagne."

From Weimar she repaired to Berlin, where she became very intimate with the Prince Louis-Ferdinand of Prussia. It was he who first informed her of Napoleon's murder of the poor young Duc d'Enghien, the descendant of the great Condé. The whole circumstances of this heartless affair are too well known to need recapitulation here. Suffice it to say, that this act made Napoleon more enemies than all his despotism, or all the bayonets of all his armies. In the "Moniteur" of the following day the assassination was coolly announced as the judicial execution of "the person called Louis d'Enghien." The next note which the Prince Louis-Ferdinand sent to Madame de Staël began, in parody of this: "The person called Louis de Prusse begs Madame de Staël," etc. This murder made Madame de Staël more than ever the foe of Bonaparte.

Another friendship which she first formed in Berlin was more worth having than that of the prince. We refer to old August-Wilhelm von Schlegel. This man was of the old school of German erudition, which was somewhat less pedantic, less narrow, and more polished than that of modern men of learning in Germany. He was by no means wrapped up in the dead world, though he went as deeply, if not more deeply, into its ashes than any contemporary scholar, adding to his classical attainments a profound knowledge of Sanscrit, then the most difficult Oriental language to acquire, owing to the absence of grammars and the small number of texts published; yet in spite of these obstacles Schlegel made one of the earliest translations of a Sanscrit work, and published an edition of the original which still holds the first place. But he had sufficient enlargement of mind to appreciate the excellence of modern literature; his acquaintance with modern languages was great; he wrote French just with the same facility as his native tongue, and had a thorough knowledge of English and Italian, and of the whole literature of Europe. To these acquirements—common, perhaps, in the present day, but at that time very rare—he added great critical ability, and a love of art as well as of literature.

Madame de Staël seized the opportunity which her acquaintance with this eminent man afforded her to place her son under his tuition; but Auguste de Staël seems to have inherited his father's Swedish solidity rather than his mother's brilliant talents; and the grandson of Necker, the son of the author of "Corinne," and the pupil of Schlegel, passed in society, when he grew up, as an ordinary mortal. We can not wonder: it is a rare thing to find genius and high intellect in three successive generations of the same family: it seems as if the mental energy exhausted itself after arriving at its prime in a parent. How many a wise man begets fools; how many a clever brain is succeeded by a dullard; and how often, as in the case of Chesterfield, the utmost care and anxiety in a parent fail to make a child what its father has been!

The death of Necker, in 1804, recalled Madame de Staël to Coppet. She was too late to witness the last moments of her idolized parent; and her desolation was complete. In this father and his fame her early life had been wrapped up. The tenderness between this parent and this daughter is often touching. In his later years she had been his adviser and aider; and in his last illness he had written—in vain of course—to the first consul to assure him that his daughter had no share in his own obnoxious work, and to implore, in mercy, the canceling of her sentence. She testified her love and reverence in a manner which was the best in her power, and soon after his death wrote the story of the well-finished life, raising him on the highest pedestal of her admiration.

Madame de Staël was now nearly forty years of age; but

years with her increased her charms, which were those of intellect and conversation. Her beauty, if we may so call it, was of a kind which improves with time. All depended on the expression, and this seemed to gather animation as her mind developed, and the events of her varied life gave fresh fire to the soul within. Every thing fitted her at this time to shine in the society of her beloved Paris, but this she was denied. She was not only an exile, but alone in the world. Her mother had gone first, then her husband, and, lastly, the one relation whom she loved best. All that was left to her was France; and as Paris was forbidden ground, that country was shut up to her.

Under these circumstances she set out for Italy accompanied by Schlegel, her son's tutor, whose antiquarian knowledge made him a most valuable companion in that land which is a tomb beneath a palace. Her romantic character was fitted to receive all the impressions which that land can give, sad and solemn as they are; her health needed the soft air of the south: the warmth and enthusiasm of the Italian character charmed her after the stolid cogitativeness of the Germans; and as she had before done among the latter, she now among the former made those keen observations which were to give to her best novel the charm that delighted all Europe on its appearance.

In the following year she returned to France; but, not willing to brook a fresh struggle with the master of a hundred legions, she remained in quiet obscurity at Auxerre, where her son Auguste, then a boy of sixteen, was put to school. She even ventured, now that she thought she was forgotten by her persecutor, to within twelve leagues of the proscribed city. She then published "Corinne," a book of travel in the guise of a novel, of which she herself was the heroine. It made the greatest sensation all over Europe. As an instance of this, we are told that in Edinburgh the professors of the university used to stop one another in the street to ask how far each had read of the great new work.

Though politics were scarcely touched upon in this novel, Napoleon was annoyed by its success. "No matter what she writes," said he, "political or not; after reading her, people hate me." Perhaps he was jealous of his enemy's intellectual powers, just as Louis Quatorze was of those of Madame de Sévigné. She must be a partisan of his or nobody. It was not easy to quench Madame de Staël, but the great man did what he could, and on the 9th of April, 1807, the anniversary of her father's death, she received a fresh order of exile.

This decided her to go to Vienna that she might complete

MADAME DE STAËL'S "PENNY POST."

her observations on Germany. Here she passed about a year, well received, in spite of her proscription, by both the court and "the society." But she could not put up with the stolid Teutons, heavy even in their vices, their tedious etiquette, their everlasting dinners, their elaborate dressings, their stupid pride, and their utter want of wit and all that refinement of mind, which, even more than wit, characterizes the better class of French society.

She passed the next two years at Coppet, completing her work on Germany, in tranquil retirement, and shunned by all those neighbors who dreaded to draw down the wrath of the great man in the gray coat at Paris. When the work was ready, she drew nearer to Paris, and pitched her tent this time in the beautiful historical château of Chaumont-sur-Loire, the proprietor of which, a friend and connection of her family, was in America. His return obliged her, with her sons and daughter, to move to a little farm called Le Fossé, which was lent to her by her friend M. de Salaberry.

Here, as we have mentioned in the memoir of Madame Récamier, she was joined by that celebrated beauty, who had for many years been her intimate friend. She also collected round her some few others of her oldest and best friends, Adrien and Matthieu de Montmorency, who afterward figured so prominently under the Restoration; Benjamin Constant, true to his name with her, though not with politics; M. de Barante, and others. The society of these old friends, whose political sentiments and common hostility to the empire united them in a bond of sympathy, was easy enough, and their conversation must have been brilliant. All of them except Madame Récamier were authors; all had taken a prominent part in the events of their day; all were thinkers and talkers.

A strange fancy took them, however, for the manner of passing their afternoons. After dinner they seated themselves round a table, and, in complete silence, wrote to each other charming little notes containing the ideas that were passing in their minds. The "Penny Post" as they called it, so completely absorbed them, that they did not interrupt it, even when strangers came in. Thus, on one occasion a gentleman of the neighborhood, a sturdy hunting man, who passed his life in the woods, entered from the chase in his usual costume, with his huge horn wound round his body, as it is worn to this day in France. He stared in amazement at the silent literary party and could make nothing of it. Madame Récamier good-naturedly thought to set him at his ease, and wrote him a little note, such as a Parisian would have died to possess from the celebrated beauty. The sportsman, however, shook his head, declined to receive it, and excused himself on the plea that he could never read writing by daylight. "We laughed a little," says Madame de Staël, "at the disappointment which the benevolent coquetry of our beautiful friend had met with, and thought that a billet from her hand would not always have met with the same fate."

But even this harmless party was soon to be broken up by the hatred of Napoleon. Madame de Staël had a most fatal celebrity. One evening she went to see a little opera at the small theatre at Blois. As she left it on foot, she was followed by a crowd of curious people anxious to get a good sight of the celebrated exile. The stupid police wrote that she was "surrounded by a court." Soon after this she put the last line to her work on Germany, which had taken her six years to write, and was in high spirits at the thought of its appearance. She had made arrangements with a publisher in Paris; the book had passed with a few corrections through the hands of the public censor; its popularity was expected to be so great, that no less than ten thousand copies were printed for the first edition; all seemed to be going on well, when the persecutor again pounced down upon her, the whole of the edition was destroyed by the police, and to put the *comble* upon it all, the author was ordered *to quit France in three days forever.*

Miserable, and in despair, she returned once more to Coppet. In what spot could the broken spirit of genius, silenced in its greatest work by a vulgar, jealous hand, find better rest? Coppet, the retreat of Necker, later the home of troops of exiles—later again, the gay scene where Madame de Staël collected her best friends, where the young Prince August of Prussia had made love to the beautiful Récamier—Coppet was on the banks of Lake Leman.

Leman is the haunt of genius. Every corner of this lovely lake has nestled a poet or a philosopher. Here are the white walls of Chillon, here the one green island,

"A little isle,
Which in my very face did smile,
The only one in view."

Here Byron, broken down by "home desolation," spread in vain the broad lateen sail of his boat from shore to shore, unable to rise from his misery. Here Gibbon, in his garden summer-house, had put the last line to his magnificent history, and strolled alone in the long covered acacia-walk, nursing a dream of fame. Here even Shelley had a cottage; and the city which harbored the Deist, had heard the stern fierce voice of fanatic Calvin. Lastly, the souls of the Revolution were here, Rousseau and Voltaire. Yes; Voltaire is here in his best light, in the little colony of Ferney, which he founded himself and attempted to civilize. Here is the little theatre in which his own plays were acted, and opposite to it the church —yes, the church—which he himself erected, and which bore the inscription—erased by some blind fools—"Deo erexit Voltaire." For Voltaire, cynic, satirist, sneerer, mass of vanity, mocker of Christianity, was not an Atheist. He believed in God, and more—he, who saw the evils of Romanism, the darkness of its superstitions, the narrowing tyranny of its exactions, yet admitted that religion, even the observance of religion, nay, even public worship, was necessary to the well-being of a community, and for his own pet colony erected a *church*. Can we justly blame Voltaire, if those who set him up as their model of belief, in later years proclaimed Atheism by an edict and shut up the churches of France?

Surely, then, Leman, with all these associations, and all that beauty which Byron has immortalized in the lines we quote, should have sufficed to calm her spirit.

"Clear placid Leman! thy contrasted lake
With the wild world I dwell in is a thing
Which warns me with its stillness to forsake
Earth's troubled waters for a purer spring.
This quiet sail is as a noiseless wing
To waft me from destruction: once I loved
The ocean's roar, but thy soft murmuring
Sounds sweet, as if a sister's voice reproved,
That I with stern delights should e'er have been so moved.

"It is the hush of night, and all between
Thy margin and the mountains dusk yet clear,
Mellowed and mingled, yet distinctly seen,
Save darkened Jura, whose capt heights appear
Precipitously steep; and drawing near,
There breathes a living fragrance from the shore
Of flowers yet fresh with childhood; on the ear
Drops the light drip of the suspended oar,
Or chirps the grasshopper one good-night carol more."

The village of Coppet is a mere nothing; the château a plain building, interesting chiefly for its associations. But let us be permitted to quote the description given of it by that charming writer, Sir E. Lytton, in "The Student."

"The road to Coppet from Ferney is pretty but monotonous. You approach the house by a field or paddock, which reminds you of England. To the left, in a thick copse, is the tomb of Madame de Staël. As I saw it, how many of her eloquent thoughts on the weariness of life rushed to my memory. No one perhaps ever felt more palpably the stirrings of the soul within, than her whose dust lay there. Few had ever longed more intently for the wings to flee away and be at rest. She wanted precisely that which Voltaire had—common sense. She had precisely that which Voltaire wanted—sentiment. * * * * And now the house is before you. Opposite the entrance, iron gates admit a glimpse of grounds laid out in the English fashion. The library opens at once from the hall, a long and handsome room containing a statue of Necker; the forehead of the minister is low, and the face has in it more of *bonhommie* than *esprit.* In fact that very respectable man was a little too dull for his position. The windows look out on a gravel walk or terrace; the library communicates with a bedroom hung with old tapestry.

"In the *salle à manger* on the first floor is a bust of A. W. Schlegel and a print of La Fayette. Out of the billiard-room, the largest room in the suite, is the room where Madame de Staël usually slept, and frequently wrote, though the good woman who did the honors declared "she wrote in *all* the rooms." Her writing, indeed, was but an episode of her conversation. * * * On the other side of the billiard-room is a small salon, in which there is a fine bust of Necker, a picture of Baron de Staël, and one of herself in a turban. Every one knows that countenance full of power if not of beauty, with deep dark eyes. Here is still shown her writing-book and inkstand. Throughout the whole house is an air of English comfort and quiet opulence. The furniture is plain and simple; nothing overpowers the charm of the place; and no undue magnificence diverts you from the main thought of the genius to which it is consecrated. The grounds are natural, but not remarkable. A very narrow but fresh streamlet borders them to the right."

The château is now the property of Madame de Staël-Vernet. This description is not very attractive, and when we add that the château is so placed as *not* to command a view of the lake, we may perhaps forgive Madame de Staël for preferring the Rue du Bac.

Here the exile was subject to a series of annoyances unworthy of her great foe, and cruelly aggravating her banishment. One préfet of Geneva was dismissed as being too civil to her; the next took care to exceed his duty in the opposite direction. She was forbidden to travel. She consoled herself with the society of Schlegel, who for eight years had been educating her son. It was discovered that the friendship of this great man was some consolation to her, and he was ordered summarily to quit Coppet. No offense was imputed to him, except that in an essay he had given the preference to the "Phædra" of Euripides over the "Phèdre" of Racine!

But the vengeance of Bonaparte was not satisfied with these persecutions. He determined that the poor woman, whose chief crime lay in having refused to join his party, should be bereft of all her friends. Matthieu de Montmorency visited her at Coppet. The day of his arrival the préfet of Geneva wrote to Paris to announce it. The return of the mail brought him an order of exile. Madame Récamier, on her way to the baths of Aix, would not be persuaded not to enter the doomed house, but had scarcely set her foot in it when she too was condemned to the same fate. Saint-Priest, the ex-minister of Louis XVI., and an old man of seventy-eight, was living at Geneva. In spite of Madame de Staël's entreaties, he insisted on visiting her in her infliction. In the depth of winter, he was banished from Switzerland for this act of friendship. As the climax to all this, a gendarme was set to watch Madame de Staël in all her movements, and thus even her home was made wretched to her.

Thus robbed of all her friends, and reduced to almost complete solitude, she claims some indulgence for an extraordinary step which she now took.

In 1810, when she first returned to Coppet, there was staying in Geneva a young soldier of the name of Rocca. He had been in the Spanish campaign, and received wounds which prostrated him, and which, indeed, eventually hastened his death. His tottering walk, his pale hollow cheeks, his look of suffering, contrasted with his youth and handsome face, made him an object of interest to the good people of Geneva. Madame de Staël's tender heart was touched by the sight of his misery, and she felt that in her own she had a fellow-feeling for him. She attempted to cheer him, and her kindness and the charm of her conversation appear to have had such effect on the invalid that he told one of his friends that "he would love her so, that she would at length marry him." How the courtship proceeded we know not, but, if he was grateful for a little compassion, Madame de Staël was melted by the attachment of this stranger at a time when old friends even deserted her. He succeeded at last, and she married him. She was at this period in her forty-fifth year; she was old enough to be his mother; the match was no doubt an extraordinary, but by no means an admirable one. But here our blame would cease, if it were not for what followed. She consented to marry him, on condition that the union should remain secret. Her motive for this can not be known. Whether she desired to preserve the name by which she was celebrated; whether she feared that her great foe would take even her husband from her; or whether, as is quite as probable, she felt that there was something ridiculous in the union of a woman of nearly fifty with a boy but little older than her own children, we can not tell. To conceal a marriage is to tell society a lie. We can not acquit Madame de Staël in this matter, and her warmest admirers have blamed her. Yet we are rather inclined to pity the persecuted woman, and to remember that society had thrown her aside, and that she owed but little to it now.

This union brought her some little happiness, but the almost incomprehensible oppression of the emperor left her no rest. She was assailed by the pettiest and most unworthy persecutions, the only object of which could be to render her life, even in its retirement, utterly miserable and unbearable. They nearly succeeded in this end, and at one moment the unhappy woman meditated suicide. The consequence presents a curious example of the conquest that a strong and well-biased mind can gain over the deepest depression of the spirit. Madame Roland, when in a similar position, *prepared for* suicide. Madame de Staël never did more than meditate upon it. She put before herself the arguments on both sides of the question; she sought undoubtedly for some palliative for this unpunishable crime. But her mind was too well balanced to admit the existence of any; and the only consequence of her meditations was an essay against suicide. Madame Roland had rejected the idea for the sake of her daughter. Madame de Staël rejected it for the sake of her God. The comparison holds good. Both were Frenchwomen, and educated about the same period, surrounded with the same public opinions on the subject. At the period of the Revolution, the act

"Which Cato practiced, Addison approved,"

was considered a deed worthy of a hero. It was at least held that when a man found himself in a position of degradation from external and inevitable causes, he had the right to leave the world; and the courage (so it was called) which the deed required ennobled him in his last moments. Unhappily, this erroneous idea is not yet exploded in France; and when we find M. Lamartine praising Roland for his suicide, and claiming a hero's niche for him for that one act alone, we may well appreciate the superior principle which deterred Madame de Staël from attempting it. We may well believe that her Protestant education, and her deep religious feeling, aided her in these terrible moments.

She took a much more sensible course. She fled beyond the power of the man who tried to weary her of her life. This flight was not accomplished without imminent dangers. Its story is almost romantic, but we have not space to go into its details. Suffice it to say that she was aided by M. Schlegel, and accompanied by her son, daughter, and husband. She fled through the Tyrol to Vienna, and so through Poland to Russia. The moment her departure was discovered, orders were sent after her for her arrest. The stupidity of German officials alone preserved the party. M. Rocca was even compelled to adopt a disguise; and on one occasion they were shackled by the attendance of a police official, who would not allow them to stay more than a specified time at any place, and ate immoderately. The Hegira was, however, effected after many alarms and perils; and the party reached Russia, which was the only country, besides England, in which, at that time, they could be free from their oppressor.

At St. Petersburg, Madame de Staël was well received by the emperor and the nobility. Her hostility to Napoleon was well known. She was, in fact, almost the only French subject of any note who stood out against him. All her old friends had given in to his rule, and even sought employment under him.

But Russia was not the destination she longed to reach. Her wishes were centred on free England, where she had once tasted the charms of perfect liberty combined with order, and where she was sure to find so many valuable and faithful friends. England, which had been Necker's Utopia, was now her dream, and she only waited till her health was recruited to set out for this country.

She arrived here in June, 1813, and took up her abode at No. 30 Argyll Street, Regent Street, a locality which may then have been more fashionable than it is at present. The house she lived in was afterward converted into an establishment for medicated vapor baths.

Now began those last four years of her life which were its most brilliant period. Her reputation was far greater now than it had been in the days of Juniper Hall. Politically she was celebrated for the persecutions she had endured, and as the only person of any importance who had stood firm against Napoleon to the last. This would have been title enough to the esteem of English politicians; but her two greatest works, "Corinne" and "De l'Allemagne," landed her in the thick of thinkers and literary men.

She was the lioness of that season, and seems to have known it, for she says, in reference to the supposed coldness of the English: "They are like the Albanian dogs sent by Porus to Alexander, which disdained to fight any animal but a lion." Certainly the lioness found plenty of English mastiffs of the noblest breed to fight with her in amicable discussion.

The first of these was Mackintosh, "the brightest constellation of the North," as Lord Byron calls him, one of the most amiable, accomplished, and agreeable men of his day, whose only fault, perhaps, was that he could never be severe. Madame de Staël had translated his celebrated speech in defense of Peltier some years before, and she felt that he was the friend of those whom Napoleon persecuted. He became her most intimate friend, and thus writes of her:

"On my return I found the whole fashionable and literary world occupied with Madame de Staël * * * the most celebrated woman of this, or perhaps any age. * * * She treats me as the person she most delights to honor. I am generally ordered with her to dinner, as one orders beans and bacon." This was quite true, as we learn from Byron's letters, where "the Staëls and Mackintoshes" are always mentioned together; but which was the beans and which the bacon we can not pretend to decide. "I have, in consequence," he continues, "dined with her at the houses of almost all the cabinet ministers. She is one of the few persons who surpass expectation. She has every sort of talent, and would be universally popular if in society she were to confine herself to her inferior talents—pleasantry, anecdote, and literature, which are so much more suited to conversation than her eloquence and genius."

This is perfectly just, and Madame de Staël's chief fault in society was undoubtedly that of declaiming with too much enthusiasm on political or even philosophical questions. She had a mode, too, of direct attack, which the calm English could not always relish, and which Byron, as we shall see, particularly disliked.

"I saw Lord Wellesley fight a very good battle with her," continues Mackintosh, "at Holland House, on the Swedish treaty; indeed, he had the advantage of her, by the politeness, vivacity, and grace with which he parried her eloquent declamations and unseasonable discussions."

Tact, the button on the foil of conversation, seems, in Madame de Staël's case, to have been whipped off by her enthusiasm.

In the previous July, Byron writes to Moore: "The Staël last night attacked me most furiously; said I had 'no right' to make love; that I had used —— most barbarously; that I had no feeling, and was totally insensible to *la belle passion*, and *had* been all my life. I am very glad to hear it, but did not know it before."

She was the most popular guest at Lansdowne House and Holland House. Lords Grey, Harrowby, Erskine, and Jersey were alternately her hosts and guests. At Rogers's literary dinners she always had her seat; and Byron and Mackintosh, nay, all the leading men of the day in politics or literature, were her intimates. We are told that to the houses of these celebrities people were invited on purpose to see the authoress of "Corinne;" that they mounted on chairs and tables to get a view of her; and that, in short, she was as great a curiosity in London as Napoleon himself could have been.

Her vanity—of which she had, we must own, a fair share—must have been flattered to the utmost by these attentions; but in the midst of her success came a blow which destroyed all her enjoyment. Her elder son and daughter were with her, the former popular on account of his excellent English, the latter admired for her musical powers; but the younger son was in Germany. He had joined the army banded against his mother's persecutor; but his fiery temper led him into a quarrel, a duel ensued, and the young Albert de Staël was laid low. Lord Byron, in his usual playful manner, alludes characteristically to this event.

"Madame de Staël-Holstein has lost one of her young barons, who has been carbonadoed by a vile Teutonic adjutant—kilt and killed at a coffee-house at Scrawsenhawsen. Corinne is, of course, what all mothers must be, but will, I venture to prophesy, do what few mothers could, *write an essay upon it.* She can not exist without a grievance, and somebody to see or read how much grief becomes her."

This may have contained some truth; but Byron was the last person who ought to have raised the sneer. He was, of all others, the man who most loved a grievance—especially a domestic one—and was always ready to write and publish a poem upon his misery. Yet we may doubt if the remark was made in an ill-natured spirit, for he rather liked "De l'Allemagne," as he calls her, in spite of her want of tact. His subsequent notices are much in the same strain; but some of them are so characteristic, and, allowing for a little exaggeration, so just, that we can not help giving a few of them from his journal.

"*Nov.* 17th, 1813. Last night at Lord H——'s: Mackintosh, the Ossulstones, Puységur, etc., there. I was trying to recollect a quotation (as *I* think) of Staël's from some Teutonic sophist about architecture. 'Architecture,' says this Macaronico Tedescho, 'reminds one of frozen music.' It is somewhere; but where?—the demon of perplexity must know, and won't tell. I asked M——, and he said it was not in her; but

P—— r said it must be *hers;* it was so *like*. H—— laughed, as he does at all 'De l'Allemagne,' in which, however, I think he goes a little too far. But there are fine passages; and, after all, what is a work, any—or every work—but a desert with fountains, and perhaps a grove or two, every day's journey? To be sure, in madame, what we often mistake and 'pant for,' as the 'cooling stream,' turns out to be a *mirage* (criticè, *verbiage*); but we do, at last, get to something like the temple of Jove Ammon, and then the waste we have passed is only remembered to gladden the contrast."

"*Nov.* 30th. To-day (Tuesday) a very pretty billet from Madame la Baronne de Staël-Holstein. She is pleased to be much pleased with my mention of her and her last works in my notes. I spoke as I thought. Her works are my delight, and so is she herself—for half an hour. * * * But she is a woman by herself, and has done more than all the rest of them together, intellectually. She ought to have been a man. She *flatters* me very prettily in her note; but I *know* it."

"She ought to have been a man" reminds us of the anecdote of Talleyrand. Madame de Staël asked him if he had read her "Delphine." "Non," he replied, "mais on m'a dit que nous y sommes tous les deux déguisés en femmes." She had described herself in "Delphine," with a plentiful addition of personal beauty, wanting in the original, and Talleyrand in the old countess. The reply must have been too much even for Madame de Staël.

Her admiration of Byron was unlimited. Thus, on December 5th, he writes: "Asked for Wednesday to dine and meet the Staël—asked particularly, I believe, out of mischief, to see the first interview after the *note*, with which Corinne professes herself to be much taken. I don't much like it; she always talks of *myself* and *herself*, and I am not (except in soliloquy) much enamored of either subject—especially one's works. What the devil shall I say about 'De l'Allemagne?' I like it prodigiously; but unless I can twist my admiration into some fantastical expression, she won't believe me; and I know, by experience, I shall be overwhelmed with fine things about rhyme, etc., etc. The lover, Mr.——, was there to-night, and C—— said 'it was the only proof *he* had seen of her good taste.' Monsieur l'Amant is remarkably handsome; but I don't think more so than her book." This, we presume, refers to Rocca, whom she had not yet acknowledged as her husband; nor did she do so until on her death-bed, even to her own children. Byron goes on in this place to praise her book, which he confesses he read again and again.

In another place he calls her "a very good-natured creature," which undoubtedly she was. On December 10th he writes, after meeting her at a most distinguished dinner at Lord H——'s: "The Staël was at the other end of the table, and less loquacious than heretofore. We are now very good friends, though she asked Lady Melbourne whether I had really any *bonhommie*. She might as well have asked that question before she told C. L., 'C'est un démon.' True enough, but rather premature, for *she* could not have found it out, and so—she wants me to dine there next Sunday."

"*Jan.* 16, 1814. I saw Lewis to-day, who is just returned from Oatlands, where he has been squabbling with Madame de Staël about himself, Clarissa Harlow, Mackintosh, and me. My homage has never been paid in that quarter, or he would have agreed still worse. I don't talk, I can't flatter, and won't listen, except to a pretty or foolish woman. She bored Lewis with praises of himself till he sickened—found out that Clarissa was perfection, and Mackintosh the first man in England. * * * She told Lewis wisely, he being my friend, that I was affected, in the first place, and that, in the next place, I committed the heinous offense of sitting at dinner with my *eyes* shut, or half shut. * * * I wonder if I really have this trick. I must cure myself of it, if true. * * * It would not so much signify if one was always to be checkmated by a plain woman; but one may as well see some of one's neighbors as well as the plate on the table." He calls her "obstinate, clever, odd, garrulous and shrill," and adds, "Poor Corinne! she will find that some of her fine sayings won't suit our fine ladies and gentlemen."

Her love of talking, especially with men, was well known. Byron says, in speaking of a dinner-party he was at: "We got up too soon after the women, and Mrs. Corinne always lingers so long after dinner, that we wish her in—the drawing-room."

Her society in London was too mixed to suit the ideas of our proud grandees. Madame de Staël had no such humbug about her, and, besides, her knowledge of the restrictions of English society was, of necessity, limited. Talent, mind, celebrity of any kind, were the passports to her salon; it could scarcely be expected of a foreigner, resident among us only for a season, that she should be able to seize those delicate shades of caste, in which our exclusives, with true vulgarity, delight to display their silly pride. Still, she was accredited by her works to the great Mæcenases of the day, of whom Lord Lansdowne was, perhaps, the first. She passed the winter in the country houses of these noblemen at Bowood—Lord Lansdowne's, and at Middleton—Lord Jersey's.

In the spring of 1814 her enemy fell, and she rushed back triumphantly to Paris, more celebrated and far more popular than when she left it. Here she set up her brilliant throne for a space, and opened her drawing-room to those crowds of mighty men of mind who now flocked to the city which had so long been closed to them. The Restoration hailed, with eagerness, the talented daughter of the minister of the last of the Bourbons; the newspapers were delighted to have a few words from her pen; her rooms were thronged with all the representatives of political and literary liberty. Wellington and Blücher, Chateaubriand, La Fayette, and young Guizot came to her as to the centre of political movement. Humboldt, Sismondi, the Schlegels, and her old friend, Benjamin Constant, rallied round her as the axle of the literary wheel. Canova represented art; and Madame Récamier, still radiant at six-and-thirty, beauty. Could any private court be more brilliant, with a queen of fifty, the most brilliant, almost the most celebrated of them all? Brilliant, indeed, but like most brilliancies, and many a better one than the salon of a Frenchwoman, fleeting and short-lived.

Her old enemy was not slain. The caged lion was to break the bars of his prison and burst on Europe in a fit of fury. The return of Napoleon from Elba was perhaps the finest stroke of all his policy; certainly the most comic incident in the history of the last century. He came upon his feasting foes like a shower of rain on a picnic party, or a policeman on a prize-fight—these similes are sadly commonplace—like a ghost upon the revelers over his coffin. Strong as they were, he routed them in a moment. They, who had gloried in their security while the tyrant was away, fled like servants who had been drinking their master's wine in his absence, or stood cowed and trembling to receive their sentence. The turn-coats had no time to turn their coats once more. He cleared his inconstant court in a few hours. The army and the people hailed him, and he spared no courtier, not even his own relations who had taken any part in the Restoration. Perhaps Madame de Staël was the only French person then in Paris who felt that she, at least, had been true to her colors. But the re-risen man was her foe, as he had always been, and she fled like the rest, only with a better conscience.

She retired once more to Coppet, the refuge of the routed; but she did not long remain here. M. Rocca's health, which had never been good since his wounds in Spain, became worse than ever, and she determined, for her husband's sake, to seek the milder climate of Italy. The change was successful, and Rocca gained such strength that he was able to survive his wife.

In 1816 she returned to Coppet. Her persecutor was now fallen forever, and she might have re-entered Paris in safety, but Italy and Switzerland were full of the great men of the day, and she preferred to remain in their neighborhood. Among others, Byron, who in the mean time had married and *unmarried*, had settled not far from her. He visited her at Coppet, and found in her a good, kind friend. Her courageous spirit induced her to attack the poet boldly on the subject of his separation. He was, indeed, most wretched; and his poems —as morbid at this time as at any other, if not more so—prove what his misery in this unhappy marriage must have been. She took him to task roundly, and so prevailed with him that, on the strength of her persuasion, he wrote to England to offer a reconciliation with his wife. That wife belonged to one of the coldest families in England, which is saying much. She refused the offer. Byron, with all his faults, behaved nobly in this transaction, and his conduct under embarrassed pecuniary affairs raises him in our estimation, when we find him declining to receive the handsome remuneration offered by Murray for the "Siege of Corinth" and "Parisina," and afterward distributing the money pressed upon him among authors, who, less fortunate than himself, were in a condition to need his aid. It is due to Madame de Staël to state that he wrote from Diodati in 1816: "Madame de Staël has made Coppet as agreeable to me as kindness and pleasant society can make a place." There is no doubt that she had an excellent heart, and that, allowing for all his faults, she saw much good in that most unhappy but most lovable man. Poor Byron, the plaything of circumstances! With less vanity and more religion he might have been the finest character of his day.

But Madame de Staël was never satisfied with the seclusion of Coppet. She yearned after the "life" of Paris and the generous interchange of active minds. She returned to her native city only to die. For a time she kept up her active spirit, though her health was growing worse and worse. She wrote, she talked, she received. Yet time and age brought out more fully those religious feelings which had been wisely instilled in her childhood. Late in life, when talking of metaphysics, she said: "I prefer the Lord's Prayer to it all," and we can quite believe it. Yet her affections were, of necessity, for the world. "I should be sorry," she said in her last days, "if every thing were at an end between Albertine (her daughter, the Duchesse de Broglie) and me in another world." Hard as life had been to her, though she had longed at one time to escape from it, she passed from it with regret.

In February, 1817, she was seized by a violent fever. It attacked her limbs first, and they were soon, like those of Socrates under the effect of the poison, immovable. Still her mind, like his, remained unaltered, unimpaired. Her house was besieged by inquirers after her health, among whom Wellington came himself every day to her door to ask how she fared. The day before her death she read some of Byron's "Manfred." An English young lady, Miss Randall, who had been with her for some years, watched her last moments. She died in peace —and a religious peace too—on the 14th of July, 1817, at the age of fifty-one. She will be remembered as the first woman of her age, if not, as Mackintosh says, of *any* age. Certainly she was the first leader of society both during and after the Empire, and we are inclined to think that society owed much to her, and to thank Heaven that it found so respectable and so philosophic a leader.

There is nothing to say against Madame de Staël. There is no doubt of her vanity, but she had something to be vain of. There is no doubt that her interest was, after her father's death, mainly centred in herself, yet she was a very interesting, as well as a very admirable woman. There is no doubt that her concealment of her second marriage was foolish. She confessed it on her death-bed to her children, and recommended to their protection the young child that had been its fruit. Her husband died soon after her, still a young man.

Yet blame her as we will, for this fault or that, we must still admire her; first, as a Frenchwoman who, though leading society, was free from all its vices; second, as the first authoress of her day; thirdly, as a woman of great and good heart, and one whom, were she alive, many a young man of feeling would perhaps love as well as young Rocca adored her.

There is no Queen of Society of whom we can say so much.

MRS. THRALE-PIOZZI.

The village of Streatham has little now of antiquity to recommend it to the mediæval taste of the day. Its very name is vulgar Saxon instead of elegant Norman—*Strete* signifying a highway, and *ham* a dwelling; though the Normans, with little regard to its derivation, called it in Doomsday Book "*Estratham*." Lysons, unwillingly enough, consents, after fifty years had established the orthography, to spell it *Streatham*, though the needless *e* went, good man, to his heart.

But what matters it? What matters it that, in the time of the Conqueror, certain manors were held by certain canons of Waltham? that Earl Harold had another? Earl Morton another? and that there was, doubtless, mighty quarreling among them all for any spare corner they could ravish from the poor? What matters it that in the parish church of St. Leonard, in the centre of Streatham, reposes the mutilated figure of an armed knight, with pointed helmet, mail-gorget, and plated cuirasses? and there, as he rests underneath a canopy ornamented with quatrefoils, the vulgar point to his tomb, and say "John of Gaunt," whereas that doughty warrior lies entombed in St. Paul's? Near this tomb is another far more interesting to sensible readers of modern days, although, we will grant it, less romantic. That of Henry Thrale, brewer, and of his mother-in-law, Mrs. Salusbury, recall the true legitimate associations which ought to haunt the imaginative visitant to the now commonplace locality of Streatham. Let him walk on to the small common between Tooting and the village, and view the large solid house, which was formerly called a villa, in which Thrale's memory, and that of all who belonged to him, may be said really to be entombed: and so, probably, thought his widow, when she left it to her second husband, Gabriel Piozzi, the singer, for his life.

Here the glories of Streatham are centred: Doomsday Book, Earl Harold, Earl Morton, and, with reverence be it spoken, the canons of Waltham Abbey, are all dim, if not fairly wiped out from our mental vision, when we see, in the places of those same rapacious earls and grasping canons, the shades of Thrale and his wife, of "little Burney" and Sir Joshua Reynolds, of David Garrick and Edmund Burke, of Oliver Goldsmith and Arthur Murphy, and Topham Beauclerk, and hear them, in fancy, all calling each other by their Christian names; nay, picture them to ourselves sitting round the hospitable board of the worthy Thrale, best of men and brewers, and drinking his excellent claret and still better beer. And if we could really have looked in, even after all we have named, or most of them, had gone to their rest, we might have seen their portraits, limned by the great Reynolds, hanging round, and gazing, perhaps, benignantly at those of the master and mistress of the house, at the top of the room.

But it is time to discard the pleasures of imagination, and to turn to biography.

Dr. Johnson, who, as Horace Walpole observes, "was good-natured at bottom but ill-natured at top," has dealt unjustly with the origin of Henry Thrale, to whose memory he devoted a page of Latin on his tombstone in the church of St. Leonard. "Thrale," he says, "worked at six shillings a week for twenty years in the great brewery which was afterward his own." The brewery then belonged to Edmund Halsey, whose family still flourish in Hertfordshire, and own Gaddesden Park. The concern was situated at St. Albans, and was highly profitable; it was the foundation of the provincial greatness of the Halseys. But Mr. Wilson Croker, never famous for good-nature, or for making people out to be wiser or better than they are, declares that Johnson has done the parentage of Henry Thrale injustice in this account, for which he gives the authority of Blakeway. Now the clerk of St. Albans told Blakeway that Thrale's father had married a sister of Halsey's; that in other respects his family was not to be despised; and pointed out to him a handsome monument in the noble abbey to the memory of Mr. John Thrale, merchant, who died in 1704, with the family arms and crest on the monument; the "crest on a ducal coronet, a tree vert." Nevertheless, Mr. Halsey, after the fashion of old commercial men in those days, was somewhat hard-hearted, and kept his nephew at work for the six shillings weekly, without remorse, until his death. It happened, however, that Lord Cobham, the uncle of the Marquis of Buckingham, became a suitor to his daughter, and married her. The brewery, therefore, at Mr. Halsey's death, became his property in right of his wife. As a peer could not in those days continue the business, it was determined to sell it. For some time it was difficult to find a purchaser for so large a concern; it was therefore decided that Thrale should be applied to. He was an active, honest man, well versed in the ways of the house, and the brewery was therefore offered to him for the sum of thirty thousand pounds. In eleven years, having given good security, he paid the purchase-money. He accumulated a large fortune, was high sheriff of Surrey, and member for Southwark. He spent his money like a prince, or rather as most English commercial men do, for they are often princely in their ideas. His son, Henry Thrale, was sent to Oxford, and *after* he had left that college, not when there—for it was not the notion of those days that men required a fortune to be spent on their education—had a thousand a year allowed him by his father, who used to say: "If this young dog does not find so much after I am gone as he expects, let him remember that he has had a great deal in my time." Johnson truly said, "An English merchant is a new species of gentleman."

The "young dog," although he had associated with peers and country gentlemen at college, continued to carry on his father's business, which, he told Boswell, was so lucrative that he would not give it up even for an annuity of ten thousand a year. "Not," he said, "that I get ten thousand a year for it, but it is an estate to a family." As Henry Thrale left no son, the brewery was sold for a hundred and thirty-five thousand pounds, which was reputed to be an immense sum at the time.

Like most of our great capitalists, Henry Thrale expected, in his marriage, what is called a "good connection." He was united, and most happily, to Hesther, the daughter of John Lynch Salusbury, a gentleman of Flintshire; her mother, the daughter of Sir Thomas Cotton, of Combermere, was also of that descent to which we now assign, with infinite stress, the word "aristocratic." Nor let it be supposed that it was otherwise when Henry Thrale, brewer, led to the altar this descendant of a noble house. The notion that a merchant, or a mercantile man of any *métier* could be a gentleman, was only then creeping into society. The classes, before the Hanoverian dynasty, were as much separated as they still are on the Continent. The generous Steele had written in favor of an abolition of those invidious distinctions. The odious Boswell clamored, in his petty way, in behalf of their continuance.

"Give me leave to say," Mr. Lealand, in addressing Sir John Bevil in "The Conscious Lovers," remarks, "that we merchants are a species of gentry that have grown into the world this last century, and are as honorable, and almost as useful as you landed folks, that have always thought yourselves so much above us; for your trading, forsooth, is extended no farther than a load of hay or a fat ox. You are pleasant people indeed! because you are generally brought up to be lazy; therefore, I warrant you, industry is dishonorable."

So far Richard Steele—so far a liberal, courtly, kindly gentleman. Now for Boswell.

After stating the question whether a new system of gentility should be established, by which knowledge, skill, and the spirited hazards of trade should be entitled to give distinctions such as are granted to military exploits, political superiority, or mere birth, he says: "Such are the specious but false arguments for a proposition which will always find numerous advocates in a nation where men are every day starting up from obscurity to wealth. To refute them is needless. The general sense of mankind cries out with irresistible force, '*Un gentilhomme est toujours gentilhomme.*'" Without pursuing the subject farther, or knocking Boswell and his argument on the head, we may assert that every attribute of a gentleman was centred in Mr. Henry Thrale. He was tall, to begin with, and a good stature is no bad inheritance: his figure was well proportioned, his carriage stately. So far he must have satisfied Boswell's idea of *un vrai gentilhomme.* He was a man of excellent principles, an excellent scholar, of considerable literary attainments: to these characteristics he added a great knowledge of trade, sound sense, and plain independent manners, such as well become an English squire. In spite of being married to a lady of great pretensions to letters, and of unbounded loquacity, no man was more a master of his own family than Henry Thrale. "If he but holds up a finger," says his sturdy friend Johnson (who truly loved him), "he is obeyed." Wise man! for those whom he thus commanded were far happier under that despotic but kindly rule than if they had constituted a family democracy. Mrs. Thrale, on the other hand, was short, plump, and brisk in her manners. Johnson's speech to her, when she appeared before him in a dark-colored gown, is characteristic of this bustling, energetic little *précieuse.* We think we see her before us, as we hear the old dogmatist say, "You little creatures should never wear those sort of clothes, however. They are unsuitable in every way. What! have not all insects gay colors?" (He must have forgotten all his small scraps of entomology.)

By Miss Burney, however, who, when she wrote characters, wrote them generally with discrimination, Mrs. Thrale was by no means regarded, in any way, as "an insect." "She had a great deal both of good, and of not good, in common with Madame de Staël-Holstein," she says; and she goes on to draw a comparison between the two, exalting her friend to the level of that extraordinary woman: "Their conversation," she declares, "was equally luminous, from the sources of their own fertile minds, and from their splendid acquisitions from the works and acquirements of others."

In this respect no one had a fairer chance of literary superiority than Mrs. Thrale. "Her mother was a woman," as Dr. Johnson, in his epitaph on Mrs. Salusbury affirmed, "blessed in personal appearance; of an open cheerful temper, strong domestic affections; an accomplished linguist, fluent in speech; whose wisdom was tempered with the softer qualities of the mind; who gave to the pleasures of literature such portion of her time as she could well spare from her home duties; to her home duties as much care and attention as she devoted to letters."

With such a husband, and such a mother, Mrs. Thrale could scarcely fail to be in some way eminent. Even Johnson, when he was angry with her, and after her second marriage, allowed that "if she was not the wisest woman in the world she was certainly one of the wittiest."

There is no doubt also, from her portrait, that, short and plump as she was, Mrs. Thrale possessed great personal beauty. She was twenty-five years of age when Arthur Murphy, who had long been an intimate friend of her husband's, brought Samuel Johnson, in the year 1764, to Mr. Thrale's house in the Borough, where the pair then lived. Murphy had long been extolling Johnson's conversation, and wishing that the Thrales would invite him; for, which, indeed, they only wanted a pretext. There was a certain shoemaker, named Woodhouse, whose poems were then the theme of general commendation; and, upon the plea of meeting him, Murphy took Johnson to Mr. Thrale's hospitable house. Mr. Woodhouse and his verses have long since descended into oblivion, yet his name lives as the immediate instrument of bringing about this celebrated friendship.

Murphy, before he introduced Johnson, warned Mrs. Thrale not to be suprised at his appearance. The hint was certainly not superfluous. Poor Johnson was no favorite of Nature's. His face is said to have been originally well formed; his contemporaries so asserted: if true, our taste in beauty must be strangely altered. His unfortunate visage was seamed and disfigured with the scrofula—that fearful disease which as an infant, put out to nurse, he had contracted; and which good Queen Anne, in her diamonds and long black hood—unconscious, as she stretched out her round arm, on whose head her fair hand rested—had failed to cure. He was very dirty and very shabby, for which Mrs. Thrale was doubtless prepared by the following circumstance. One evening, when invited with Reynolds to the Miss Cotterells', in Newport Street, Soho, then the centre of the fashionable world, an indiscreet servant-maid had passed an affront upon him. Seeing Johnson's beggarly-looking figure following Sir Joshua and his sister Frances into

P 2

the room, she could not conceive that he was one of the company, and just as he was going up stairs, she pulled him back, and cried out, "You fellow! what is your business here? I suppose you intend to rob the house." Poor Johnson was thrown into such a paroxysm of shame and anger that he roared out like a bull, and cried, "What have I done? What have I done?" Nor could he recover the whole evening from this affront.

Mrs. Thrale might well, therefore, expect to see a man of revolting appearance; and certainly she was not disappointed. If the original form of the face had been good, it was now utterly distorted; one eye was nearly sightless from disease; a scratch wig hid the best part of his face—his forehead; he had an almost convulsive movement either of his hands, lips, feet, or knees, and sometimes of all together; a most uncomfortable neighbor either at one's side at dinner, or perhaps still worse, if opposite.

To the kind and intellectual inmates of Thrale's house these defects were, however, only a source of pity. Dr. Johnson made himself so agreeable, and found his host and hostess so charming, that he dined with them every Thursday that winter, until he was so ill that he could not stir out of the room in Bolt Court which he occupied, for months.

Such was the commencement of an intimacy which is said, by its general effect upon the learned and blameless hypochondriac, to have saved him from insanity. He was respected, listened to, flattered, when he laid down the law at table; when he spoke of his malady, of his visionary fears and religious despondency in private, he was soothed by the kind Thrale, and cheered by the spirits of the "insect." Often must he, we may be assured, have trespassed on the patience of his hosts without perceiving that he did so. Johnson had persecuted Richardson with his visits till he had persisted in making the novelist first endure, and then like him. He had persevered in his evening calls on Reynolds till he had almost made the great painter dislike him. He staid very late. One evening Sir Joshua, having been harassed by professional business, saw him enter with dismay. He immediately took up his hat, and went out of the house. But the hint was quite useless; Johnson still went on calling: the words *de trop* were not in his Dictionary, and he would have pooh-pooh'd any remark that had implied his company at any time not being wanted. This was not from self-esteem, but from the total absence of *tact*.

When Mr. Thrale removed to Streatham, they persuaded Johnson to leave Bolt Court, and to live with them almost wholly at Streatham; "where," says Mrs. Thrale, "I undertook the care of his health, and had the honor and happiness of contributing to its restoration."

Nothing ought to be more satisfactory to the rich than the power they have of giving ease, cheerfulness, and even the sources of health to the *educated* poor. The great, the excellent, but the disagreeable Johnson owned to Goldsmith that he owed his recovery to Mrs. Thrale's attentions.

He delighted in carriage exercise: at Streatham there was a coach at his service. When Mrs. Piozzi asked him why he doted on a coach so, he answered that, "in the first place, the company were shut in with him there, and could not escape as out of a room; and, in the next place, he heard all that was said in a carriage." Riding, on the contrary, seemed to give him little pleasure. It neither raised his spirits, nor did he otherwise derive that benefit from it that it generally confers. He was heard to relate how he had once fallen asleep on horseback when performing a journey in that manner. Yet, notwithstanding this distaste, he was occasionally persuaded to hunt by his friend Mr. Thrale, and would then display no want of courage, leaping and even breaking through hedges, and this, as he himself stated, from no excess of eagerness in the chase, but merely to avoid the trouble of mounting and dismounting. Boswell's statement that he *once hunted*, would lead us to infer that it was more an occasional than an habitual practice; and on this subject he has himself said, "I have now learned by hunting, to perceive that it is no diversion at all, nor ever takes a man out of himself for a moment: the dogs have less sagacity than I could have prevailed on myself to suppose; and the gentlemen often called out to me not to ride over them. It is very strange and very melancholy that the paucity of human pleasures should persuade us ever to call hunting one of them." And yet he was said to have been proud of being called a sportsman; and Mrs. Piozzi declares he was never so much gratified by praise as when once upon the Brighton downs Mr. Hamilton exclaimed, "Why, Johnson rides as well, for aught I see, as the most illiterate fellow." He would ride Mr. Thrale's old hunter very presentably, and would follow the hounds for fifty miles, and end, at times, without allowing that he was either amused or fatigued.

What a change must all this have been to a man whose relaxation had been a tavern; whose home was either a den in the Temple or a dungeon in Bolt Court; who was in the habit of staying out till two every morning, and coming down the next day, unbrushed, perhaps unwashed, sometimes unfed, and always sick at heart and ill at ease.

Henceforth we must picture to ourselves the party at Streatham, which had hitherto been always remarkable for eminent and literary persons—now invariably marked by one object—that of the great Samuel in scratch wig and black single-breasted coat; both, however, considerably renovated and brushed up by the care of his kind hostess.

Boswell is near him; a young man under thirty, with a comic-serious face, and with an imperturbable good-humor which may by the stern be thought sycophantic. Johnson had known him two years when he became acquainted with the Thrales. They had met in the back parlor of Davies, the bookseller's shop in Great Russell Street, where Boswell, "*toujours un gentilhomme*," according to his own account, had condescended to drink tea. Boswell saw Johnson through a glass door communicating with the shop, and had time to whisper to Davies, "Don't tell where I come from," recollecting the doctor's hatred of the Scotch. "Mr. Boswell from Scotland," cried the bookseller and actor, archly. Let Boswell tell the rest himself, for no one but himself can do his own meanness justice.

"'Mr. Johnson,' said I, 'I do indeed come from Scotland, but I can not help it.' I am willing to flatter myself that I meant this as light pleasantry to soothe and conciliate him, and not as any humiliating abasement at the expense of my country. But however that might be, this speech was somewhat unlucky, for, with that quickness of wit for which he was so remarkable, he seized the expression 'come from Scotland,' which I used in the sense of being of that country; and, as if I had said that I had come away from it or left it, retorted, 'That, sir, I find is what a very great many of your countrymen can not help.' This stroke stunned me a good deal; and when we sat down I felt myself not a little embarrassed and apprehensive of what might come next."

Having thus forsworn his country, the young Scot soon found his way to No. 1 Inner Temple Lane, where Johnson then lived in chambers; and thus began that acquaintance to which the world owes the most *telling* piece of biography ever given to an English public. Let us, then, behold Johnson, in his old rusty black coat, with his little shriveled, unpowdered wig, too small for his head; his shirt-neck loose, his knee-bands loose, his black worsted stockings "ill drawn up," his feet in unbuckled shoes, instead of slippers; let us see him thus as all the fine company that drive down from London to Streatham come in and out, or stay to dinner. Boswell was then, be it remarked, a man about town, whose father had wanted to buy him a commission in the Guards, but who now preferred following Johnson as a household dog follows his master and picks up the crumbs which he drops.

Near, often, to Johnson, his trumpet to his ear, sits Reynolds, whose mild countenance and gentle manners are strongly contrasted with Johnson's pugnacious demeanor and convulsive movements; Oliver Goldsmith, recommended to Johnson from his being "poor and honest," in a laced coat and darned stockings, endeavoring to shine, but put down, though leniently, by Johnson; Bennet Langton and Topham Beauclerk, the fine gentlemen of the party, form the group whose shades haunt the now antiquated house, which once rang with their repartees or resounded to their solemn arguments.

But about ten years after Johnson had been almost domesticated at Streatham, another "insect," in the shape of Fanny Burney, came to vary the scene. She was at this time twenty-six years of age; and as the authoress of "Evelina," was "taken" to Mrs. Thrale's, which was a sort of show-fair for such specimens as "little Burney"—sensitive and simple, though somewhat fond of great people, and worldly withal; who had been in a state of apprehension when first her acquaintance with Mrs. Thrale began lest that lady should infer, from her describing vulgar characters in "Evelina," that she had been accustomed to associate with them. "But if you do tell Mrs. Thrale," she wrote to her father, alluding to the secret of her own authorship, "won't she think it strange where I can have kept company to describe such a family as the Branghtons, Mr. Brown, and some others?" With this fear of being accused of an *innate vulgarity*, she had first entered into Mrs. Thrale's presence. But no sooner did she know her than Mrs. Thrale was the "goddess of her idolatry," whose praise could not be too highly valued. Johnson, too, had read *the* book, the only book at that time in little Burney's thoughts, and had said there were passages in it that were worthy of Richardson. "My dear, dear Doctor Johnson, what a charming man you are!" writes the young authoress; and away through dusty roads she sets off to Streatham, where Mrs. Thrale's house then stood pleasantly in a paddock. Mrs. Thrale was strolling about, and as the chaise stopped heard the voice of Dr. Burney, whom she knew. "And you have brought your daughter; now you are good;" and with these words, and extending both her hands, the hostess of Streatham led "Evelina" into the house, talking for some time to her father in order to give Fanny an opportunity of recovering her composure.

Mrs. Thrale, with great delicacy, never alluded to "the book," nor was it named, until Mr. Seward, coming in, ran "on to speak of the work with which she had lately *favored the world.*"

Dinner came in due time; a dinner, the profusion of which was in those times its merit. Sir Joshua Reynolds, speaking of the dessert, thought it a compliment to say that if all the company were helped out of one dish there would be enough for all. How the Thrales would have despised the thimblefuls of sweetmeats which are ranged on our modern plateaux in the form of dessert! That day the dinner, little Fanny thought, was noble; the dessert most elegant. Dr. Johnson, who did not come till this "noble dinner" was on the table, took his place. "Sitting by Miss Burney," he vouchsafed to say, "made him very proud." Mr. Thrale, the shrewd young *bleue* observed, did not seem "a happy man; but I think," she added, "I have seldom seen a rich man with a light heart and light spirits."

Thus began the holiday of Fanny Burney's life—that period which she passed at Streatham. Mrs. Thrale was all gayety and drollery, and amused her with descriptions of the *natives* of Streatham. Dinner was sumptuous: tea was social. Even a supper concluded the day of heavy eating, when Johnson would in jest challenge Thrale to get drunk. Breakfast was occupied in joking "Evelina" about her "Holborn beau," when Johnson declared that even Harry Fielding never drew so good a character as the "fine gentleman *manqué*;" Fanny, in all the "delicate confusion" of which she writes so incessantly, being as happy as a queen in spite of her blushes.

In all these scenes Mrs. Thrale appeared to the utmost advantage—hospitable, well-bred, and, with what is an attribute of good breeding, a forgetfulness of self quite surprising in a pretty, flattered, talented woman.

Sometimes the company was astounded by a profound silence, when any thing had offended him, on the part of Johnson. Sometimes he undertook to lecture the ladies on their dress—the last subject, one would suppose, on which he had any right to give advice. Poor Mrs. Burney had been "bothered out of her life" about going to church in a linen jacket that had offended the doctor; she had succumbed and changed it; nevertheless nothing pleased him. He then had found fault with her wearing a black hat and cloak in summer; next time she went to Streatham, Mrs. Burney meekly told him she had got her old white cloak scoured to please him. "Scoured!" says he, "have you, madam?" (thus writes Fanny), "so he seesawed," his usual way when irritated, "for he could not for shame find fault, but he did not seem to like the scouring." Poor Fanny, therefore, was even more rejoiced that he approved of her dress than that he praised her novel; "for if he disliked," she with much *naïveté* said, "alackaday! how *could*

iarly susceptible. So her heart bounded when the agreeable Lord Mulgrave stood near her, or when she was driven up by the crowded assembly close to Lord Althorpe, afterward Earl Spencer, leaning against a folding-door. But compliments from *Beau* Travell, who gave the *ton* to all the world, and set up young ladies in the *beau monde;* attentions from Mr. Tyson, the popular master of the ceremonies; sermons from the Bishop of Peterborough, who insisted on their forming a party with him to Spring Gardens, and giving them tea there; grave interviews with Mrs. Elizabeth Carter and Harriet Bowdler, were at once both pleasant and edifying: the attentions of Captain Bouchier, the praise of Beau Travell, and all other pleasures were interrupted by the Gordon Riots, which broke up the delightful cliques of Bath Easton and the Belvidere, and drove Mrs. Thrale and her *protégée* and daughters from a city which was so disturbed by the fanatic acts of bigots.

Even Streatham was divested of all furniture from fear of conflagration; and Mrs. Thrale, in great agitation, decided to travel about the country. A large party of fashionables had walked from the parades that very day, to see the Roman Catholic chapel consuming: all was then quiet; but it was like the quiet after a thunderstorm.

Some malignant foe having stated in the papers that Mr. Thrale was a Papist, his property, and it was feared his person, were marked out for destruction by the "pious mob." It was, Miss Burney believed, "a Hothamite" report, to inflame Mr. Thrale's constituents against him.

For a time the greatest peril attended Mrs. Thrale's steps in *any* direction. In June, 1780, she and her friend fled from Bath, leaving it full of dragoons, and well protected by a band of chairmen, powerful beings, who were sworn in as constables, and armed with bludgeons. Mrs. Thrale and her dear Fanny now separated, and the former, with her daughters, Susan and Sophy, joined her husband at Brighton. The mutual epistles of the friends at this time were full of tenderness.

"Ah! my sweet girl," writes Mrs. Thrale; "all this stuff written, and not one word of the loss I feel in your leaving me! But, upon my honor, I forbear only to save you fretting; for I do think you would vex if you saw how sadly I looked about for you ever since I came home."

"Nobody does write such sweet letters," Fanny wrote in reply, "as my dear Mrs. Thrale; and I would rather give up my month's allowance of meat than my week's allowance of an epistle."

Fanny Burney was now at home in St. Martin's Lane. The house once belonged to Sir Isaac Newton, and the Burneys thence received from their Streatham friends the name of "Newtonians." While Fanny Burney was drinking tea with Dr. Johnson, and "only one brass-headed-cane gentleman" in Bolt Court, Mrs. Thrale was still gaining health with her "Susy and Sophy at Brighton, where the girls bathed and grew, and rioted her out of her senses."

Soon after this we find Fanny Burney's journal resumed at Streatham. But trial was then impending over that favored spot. Fanny was ill: was tenderly nursed by Mrs. Thrale, kind to all; but fears were excited for the kind, the generous Henry Thrale, whose state, she plainly saw, augured proximate danger.

"Your letters, my love," she wrote at this time to her sister, "have been more than usually welcome to me of late; their contents have been very entertaining and satisfactory, and their arrival has been particularly seasonable; not on account of my illness—that alone never yet lowered my spirits as they are now lowered, because I know I must ere long, in all probability, be again well; but oh, Susy! I am—I have been—and I fear must always be, alarmed indeed for Mr. Thrale; and the more I see and know him, the more alarmed, because the more I love and dread to lose him."

They had then just been passing a few happy days at Brighton, where the charming Lady Hesketh, the friend of Cowper, had become, as Miss Burney said, "quite enchanted with Mrs. Thrale;" while she had made Fanny talk with her very copiously, by looking at her, and remarking that nothing was so formidable as to be in company with silent observers; on which Fanny gathered courage, and entered the lists with her ladyship. After this, followed in Evelina's "Diary" a list of visits, compliments, and characters, cleverly though slightly dashed off by the young and happy authoress.

"And now, my dear Susy," she at last begins, "to tragedy, for all I have yet writ is farce to what I must now add." Mr. Thrale had been ill with the influenza, or what was so termed. He was returning to Streatham, when a violent shivering fit came on. Two servants were sent on to order dinner and good fires to be prepared at Reigate, unhappily with no success. The town was full of militia, and the poor fever-stricken man was shown into a comfortless room; one of those large, cheerless, frigid apartments that are still to be met with in old-fashioned country towns, if not much frequented except for electioneering committees or county assemblies. The opulent Henry Thrale, who could command thousands, could not now insure the commonest and perhaps the best comfort of ordinary life—a good fire. The circulation of his frame, frozen by the cold, did not return, and consciousness was suspended. He tried to articulate, but in vain.

"Poor Mrs. Thrale," wrote Fanny Burney, "worked like a servant. She lighted the fire with her own hands; took the bellows, and made such a one as might have roasted an ox in ten minutes. * * * After dinner Mr. Thrale grew better, and for the rest of our journey was sleepy, and mostly silent."

They reached Streatham, nevertheless, that night, and the next day Dr. Herberden and Mr. Seward came; and in a few days the invalid became so much better that Dr. Johnson was also admitted; and Fanny Burney and Miss Thrale, who were learning Latin under his solemn auspices, resumed their lessons, and gained much praise from the awful pedagogue for their aptitude.

It must have been touching, on this occasion, to have seen Dr. Johnson's attention to his friend Thrale, whom he never left when he was ill and in low spirits; but, trying to cheer him, nursed him like a brother.

Arthur Murphy arrived soon afterward, and was in "high flash;" took Fanny's reluctant hand, and kissed it; and then entered into a "mighty gay conversation," and put them all into spirits. Even Mr. Thrale was well enough then to adjourn with the rest of the party to little Burney's dressing-room, as she was not exactly ill, but *en petite santé* that evening.

For some time all went on smoothly. Mr. Thrale began again "to dine below, play at cards, and make," as Mrs. Thrale wrote to her Fanny, when she had returned to St. Martin's Lane, "as much haste to be well as mortal man can do." The accounts of "my master," as Mrs. Thrale playfully called her husband, continued to improve, and Streatham was as cheerful as ever. Dr. Burney had been *ordered* by Mr. Thrale to sit to Reynolds for his picture: so these two favorites were secured for the day. "Merlin," Mrs. Thrale wrote word, had been here to tune the piano, and had told her friend Mrs. Davenant and her that he had invented a particular mill to grind old ladies young, as he was so particularly fond of their company. "I suppose," she adds, "he thought we should bring *grist*. Was that the way to keep people in *tune*, I asked him?"

For a while Streatham preserved its charming aspect of hospitality and social superiority. Mrs. Thrale, fascinating, still young and flattered, was received, in virtue of her own birth, it may be presumed, at court; and had a court dress woven from a pattern of Owyhee manufacture, brought by Captain Burney, Fanny's brother, from the island. It was trimmed with gold "to the tune of sixty-five pounds," and was the source of much talk. Then her engagements, she still wrote, were complicated between business and "*flash*" (a slang word long sent down to the lower classes). Then she had a *conversazione*, at which Mrs. Montagu glistened with diamonds: "Sophy" (her daughter) "smiled; Johnson was good-humored; Lord John Clinton attentive; Dr. Bowdler tame; my master not asleep;" and at which, she carelessly adds, "*Piozzi sang.*" "Then," she gayly remarks, "Mrs. Byron rejoices that her admiral and I agree so well. The way to win his heart is connoisseurship, it seems; and for a back-ground and contour, who comes up to Mrs. Thrale, you know?"

Admiral Byron, to whom this allusion was made, was that gallant ancestor whose name and exploits were honored by his grandson, Lord Byron. His well-known history gave him all the attributes that Lord Byron most cherished—romantic deeds. While only a midshipman on board Lord Anson's ship the "Wager," which was in a circumnavigating squadron, young Byron was cast away on a desolate island in the South Seas. There he endured, with all the elasticity of a young and gallant man, five years of extreme hardship. He returned to England to rise to the highest ranks of his profession, and to figure in a *conversazione* at Streatham. His wife, one of the Cornish Trevannions, was an intimate friend of Mrs. Thrale's; while his daughter Augusta, who married Colonel Leigh, was one of the beauties of the time. The admiral's only son, John, was the father of Lord Byron. In him the noble characteristics of the race seemed to be suspended; and his marriage with Catherine Gordon (notwithstanding her descent from James II. of Scotland) was a real calamity to the honorable and gifted family of Byron.

This was the last *conversazione* at Streatham during Mr. Thrale's life. Fanny Burney was now almost ill from vexation; for Mr. Thrale, whose mind seems to have suffered from his malady, suddenly resolved to go to Spa, thence to Italy, and thence wherever his fancy led him. Mrs. Thrale and Dr. Johnson were to accompany him. This plan was, however, disapproved of both by Sir Richard Jebb, then the fashionable physician, and by Dr. Pepys; and it was settled that a body of friends should encircle Mr. Thrale, and entreat him to relinquish so arduous a journey. But the counsel was needless.

Early in the morning of the 4th of April, 1781, Mr. Thrale, who had appeared for some time very lethargic, expired. Dr. Johnson was by him when he expired, and thus, in his "Prayers and Meditations," refers to the event: "I felt almost the last flutter of his pulse, and looked for the last time upon the face that for fifteen years had never been turned on me but with respect and benignity." It was much to say of any friend in this inconsistent world; *much*, very much to say of a rich man toward a poor though not dependent friend.

Johnson was made one of Thrale's executors: but the Literary Club, which met the evening of the good brewer's death, were disappointed in their hopes that he had rendered the hard-working Johnson independent of his own exertions. He left him, in common with his other three executors, two hundred pounds. Johnson was then, be it remembered, in the enjoyment of a pension of three hundred a year; and it is observable that those persons who have most to spend themselves are always of opinion that their indigent friends can live upon little. It was very diverting to see Johnson now for the first time in his life acting in a capacity which, from his having had but little concern in the real business of life, appeared to him one of vast consequence. He gave up his time and thoughts zealously to the matter. It was Johnson still—still the pedagogue, when, with an air of importance, he appeared bustling about as an executor with his pen and ink-horn in his button-hole, like an exciseman; and when, eventually, the brewery was sold, on being asked what he considered to be the real value of the property, he answered in true Johnsonian style: "We are not here to sell a parcel of boilers and vats, but the potentiality of growing rich beyond the dreams of avarice."

Mr. Thrale's death was thus alluded to by his widow in writing to Miss Burney, to whom she penned these few but telling words: "Write to me—pray for me." That hurried note was thus endorsed in Fanny Burney's "Diary"—"Written a few hours after the death of Mr. Thrale, which happened by a sudden stroke of apoplexy on the morning of a day on which half the fashion of London had been invited to an intended assembly at their house in Grosvenor Square."

That memorandum relates the sad fact: the bereavement appears to have crushed Mrs. Thrale, who was stricken down as if never to recover; but she *did* recover to marry, if not unworthily, unwisely, a second time. "You bid me pray for you," wrote Fanny Burney, "and so indeed I do, for the restoration of your sweet peace of mind. I pray for your resignation to this hard blow; for the continued union and exertion of your virtues with your talents; and for the happiest reward their exertion can meet with, in the gratitude and prosperity of your children. These are my prayers for my beloved Mrs.

Thrale." Farther on she adds: "Nothing but kindness did I ever meet with from Mr. Thrale: he ever loved to have me, not merely with his family, but with himself; and gratefully shall I ever remember a thousand kind expressions of esteem and good opinion which are now crowding upon my memory."

Mrs. Thrale after this misfortune fled to Brighton, to be consoled by her aged friend, Mr. Scrase, her "Daddy Crisp," and rejected, until her return to Streatham, even the society of Fanny Burney. It was at first decided by Mr. Thrale's four executors that this gay "Queen of Society," Mrs. Thrale, was to carry on the business with their aid, Dr. Johnson being one of the quartette; and the rich widow, as might be expected, was "sadly worried," and in "continual fevers" about her affairs, which were greatly complicated, so that sometimes, after her visits to the Borough, Mrs. Thrale alarmed her friends by fainting away. Streatham, nevertheless, was crowded by titled and episcopal condolers: and, in the course of May, the widow's spirits seemed to be tolerably recovered, if one may judge by the following anecdote from Evelina's "Diary." Mr. Crutchley, be it observed, was one of the four executors, and a man whom little Burney from hating, had begun to like. He was young, and probably rich. But perhaps he read her thoughts, and checked her opening designs, and the raillery of Mrs. Thrale, by an act of impertinence which no one can so well relate as its victim.

"Sunday morning nobody went to church but Mr. Crutchley, Miss Thrale, and myself; and some time after, when I was sauntering upon the lawn, before the house, Mr. Crutchley joined me. We were returning together to the house, when Mrs. Thrale, popping her head out of her dressing-room window, called out, 'How nicely these men domesticate among us, Miss Burney! Why, they take to us as natural as life!'

"'Well, well,' cried Mr. Crutchley, 'I have sent for my horse, and I shall release you early to-morrow morning. I think yonder comes Sir Philip.'

"'Oh! you'll have enough to do with *him*,' cried she, laughing; 'he is well prepared to plague you, I assure you.'

"'Is he?—and what about?'

"'Why, about Miss Burney. He asked me the other day what was my present establishment. "Mr. Crutchley and Miss Burney," I answered. "How well those two names go together," cried he; "I think they can't do better than make a match of it. *I* will consent, I am sure!" he added; and to-day, I dare say, you will hear enough of it.'

"I leave you to judge if I was pleased at this stuff thus communicated.

"'I am very much obliged to him indeed!' cried I, dryly; and Mr. Crutchley called out—

"'*Thank him! thank him!*' in a voice of pride and of pique that spoke him mortally angry.

"I instantly went into the house, leaving him to talk it out with Mrs. Thrale, to whom I heard him add, 'So this is Sir Philip's kindness!' and her answer, 'I wish you no worse luck.'"

Nevertheless Fanny's heart still clung to surly Mr. Crutchley, who was, in her opinion, "generous, amiable, and delicate;" but who does not appear to have "come forward," nor, to our notions, to have justified her encomiums by his conduct.

We now find the dining-room at Streatham thronged with Irish ladies, whom Mrs. Thrale was obliged to put up with on "account of connection;" and the names of Perkins and of Barclay begin to succeed those of Byron and Mulgrave, Clinton and Montague, in Fanny's now sobered "Diary." We are not, therefore, surprised that the brewery was to be sold, Mr. Barclay, the Quaker, being the bidder. On the eventful day when the sale was to be agreed upon, Mrs. Thrale went to the Borough to meet the executors. It was an agitating occasion to all at Streatham, and the wealthy widow was much excited as she got into her coach, telling Miss Burney that, if all went well, she would on her return wave a white handkerchief out of the coach window.

Four o'clock came, dinner was ready, and no Mrs. Thrale. Five o'clock came: no Mrs. Thrale. So Fanny went out on the lawn, where she loitered in eager expectation till near six, when a coach appeared, and a white pocket handkerchief was waved from it.

Fanny ran to the door to meet her friend. Mutual embraces and kind expressions followed, and then dinner was ordered. The *difficile* Mr. Crutchley and Dr. Johnson—now deaf, but softened by his friend Thrale's death into being always amiable—were the sole guests.

From the moment of his friend's death Dr. Johnson's intimacy with his family declined. Mrs. Thrale still professed to esteem him: nay, even more; she had said once to Boswell, "There are many who admire and *respect* Mr. Johnson, but you and I *love* him." But the noble-hearted old man now found that he was to give place to a very different order of persons to any before whom he had ever quailed. He could have met the learned on their own grounds: he would have defied the fashionable; but deaf, solemn, and grieved Johnson was pushed out of Streatham by singers and music-masters. Sacchini, about whom every one raved, was even in July singing before a party at Streatham with Piozzi, "the music-master." Piozzi, on that occasion, "sang his very best:" and no doubt with a zeal that was amply repaid by the rich widow's hand. Mr. Thrale left no son: his three daughters were almost grown up. "Queeney," as the eldest was called, in reference to her name being Esther, was a fine girl, now introduced every where; but there was too great a degree of levity in Mrs. Thrale's character for her to perceive what a cruel injustice she did her daughters in giving them, as it soon appeared she intended to do, so unsuitable a step-father. Poor Johnson had once written to a friend: "You and I should now naturally cling to one another. We have outlived most of those who could pretend to rival us in each other's kindness. In our walk through life we have dropped our companions, and are now to pick up such as chance may offer us or to travel on alone." He soon found that, as far as Mrs. Thrale was concerned, he was to "travel on alone." Various reasons for the alienation that took place between them have been alleged: by some, that Johnson was jealous of Mrs. Thrale's affections; by others, that he was mortified by the loss of his accustomed enjoyments at Streatham—so long open to him during Mr. Thrale's life. It was, however, no selfish or absurd reason that made Johnson bitter when he beheld the place of his friend supplied by an Italian singer. It was wounded affection acting upon a noble, guileless nature, that could not adopt prudence when it implied the sacrifice of sincerity. Well, indeed, might he grieve: well might Dr. Beattie have thought Mrs. Thrale "incapable of acting so unwise a part as she afterward did:" for after Mr. Thrale's death, all sense of decorum, all tributes of sorrow to his memory seem to have gone to the grave with him whom she scarcely pretended, after the first few weeks, to mourn.

The first time that Boswell saw Mrs. Thrale after her husband's death, all seemed as usual, and she even said she was glad that Mr. Boswell was come, as she was going to Bath, and did not like to leave Dr. Johnson before he came, and her manner was kind and attentive. Johnson appeared depressed and silent, but was as brilliant after his after-dinner's nap as ever.

"'Talking of conversation,' he said, 'there must, in the first place, be knowledge, there must be materials; in the second place, there must be a command of words; in the third place, there must be imagination, to place things in such views as they are not commonly seen in; and in the fourth place, there must be presence of mind, and a resolution that is not to be overcome by failures: this last is an essential requisite; for want of it many people do not excel in conversation. Now *I* want it, I throw up the game upon losing a trick.' I wondered to hear him talk thus of himself, and said: 'I don't know, sir, how this may be, but I am sure you beat other people's cards out of their hands.' I doubt whether he heard this remark. While he went on talking triumphantly, I was fixed in admiration, and said to Mrs. Thrale, 'Oh for short-hand to take this down.' 'You'll carry it all in your head,' said she; 'a long head is as good as a short hand.'"

He continued, his biographer states, his friendship for Mrs. Thrale and her family as long as it was acceptable. What a touching letter he wrote to her after his first stroke of palsy in 1783, when he was seventy-four years of age!

"On Monday, the 16th, I sat for my picture, and walked a considerable way with little inconvenience. In the afternoon and evening I felt myself light and easy, and began to plan schemes of life. Thus I went to bed, and in a short time waked and sat up, as has long been my custom, when I felt a confusion and indistinctness in my head, which lasted, I suppose, about half a minute. I was alarmed, and prayed God that, however he might afflict my body, he would spare my understanding. This prayer, that I might try the integrity of my faculties, I made in Latin verse. The lines were not very good; I made them easily, and concluded myself to be unimpaired in my faculties.

"Soon after I perceived I had suffered a paralytic stroke, and that my speech was taken from me. I had no pain, and so little dejection in this dreadful state, that I wondered at my own apathy, and considered that perhaps death itself, when it should come, would excite less horror than seems now to attend it. In order to rouse the vocal organs, I took two drams. Wine has been celebrated for the production of eloquence. I put myself into violent motion, and I think repeated it, but all in vain. I then went to bed, and, strange as it may seem, I think, slept. When I saw light it was time to contrive what I should do. Though God stopped my speech, he left my hand. I enjoyed a mercy which was not granted to my dear friend, Lawrence, who now perhaps overlooks me as I am writing, and rejoices that I have what he wanted.

"I have so far recovered my vocal powers as to repeat the Lord's Prayer with no very imperfect articulation."

Yet he once said of Mrs. Thrale, when alone with Boswell, "Sir, she has done every thing wrong since Thrale's bridle was off her neck;" and in this opinion he was supported by the common censure of all who knew her. To her choice of intimate acquaintance, Johnson might now have applied the remark which he made in the house of a gentleman who had not been particular in his associates—

"Rags, sir, will always make their appearance where they have a right to do it."

It was not, however, long before Mrs. Thrale returned to her house in London, where again she received the *beau monde*. Miss Burney, a second time successful in her "Cecilia," over which Mrs. Thrale, according to her own account, shed tears and stopped to kiss the book at times, in her enthusiasm, was again the centre of attraction. Here, in addition to the usual half-literary, half-fashionable set, were "Cottons and Swinnertons," beaux who never "ceased laughing" at the "loud salute" given by Dr. Johnson to little Burney on her arrival in the room. Among all the gayeties which ensued, the name of Paccherrotti, the singer, appears frequently; but that of Piozzi, whether from accident or design, is completely dropped. Great names, in their line, however, were called out before Mrs. Thrale's door. Sir Ashton Lever, Nollekens, Reynolds, Burke, Erskine, Selwyn, are resounded in mingled chorus with those of Johnson and of Samuel Parr. Parr was introduced by Mr. Twining, and was asked to dinner to meet Johnson, who was his model in manners and style. The renowned rector of Hatton was then at Norwich. The encounter must have been interesting; but Miss Burney was far too much taken up with herself and the compliments to her "Cecilia," to give any sustained account of the conversation of these two notable doctors. Johnson was, however, extremely pleased with Dr. Parr's conversational powers, which consisted, as those who remember him can certify, not in the battledore-and-shuttlecock rebound, not in the give-and-take style, but in an impressive conversational eloquence that burst forth when any especial theme called out his admiration or excited his wrath. Dr. Parr, in his benevolent mood, was a glorious creature; his praise was discriminating, though highly colored; his language perfect; his manner most dramatic. When indignant, the eloquence of those lisping accents was something marvelous; but it was often, indeed almost always, vitiated by coarseness.

When Dr. Parr left, Johnson thus expressed himself: "Sir, I am obliged to you for having asked me this evening. Parr is a fair man: I do not know when I have had an occasion of such free controversy. It is remarkable how much of a man's life may pass without meeting with any instance of the kind of open discussion." Parr was, be it remembered, a stern Whig, the pet of the Foxites; Johnson as stern a Tory and Jacobite as ever wielded a pen. After he died, and one of his foes was "snarling at his fame," Dr. Parr, with great animation, exclaimed, "Aye, now the old lion is dead, every ass thinks he may kick at him."

In the simplicity of their ideas, and in their love for good homely old English fashions, these two great scholars agreed wonderfully. Dr. Parr revived at Hatton the fashion of keeping May-day, against which the Puritans had preached, and which the finery of modern England had exploded, lest grandeur should mix with plebianism. He used to crown the prettiest villager among the farmers' daughters at Hatton with a wreath of May flowers: for a day before, he had employed his young lady friends to decorate a tall May-pole, over which swung garlands of cowslips and blue-bells, mixed with ribbons. Around it danced high and low, rich and poor. He chose old May-day, the 12th, as being more mediæval, and often quoted that pretty little poem called the "Tears of Old May-day."

Such were his notions. Dr. Johnson was as primitive as the excellent Rector of Hatton. His description of his marriage was in itself at once a proof of his early notions and of the simplicity with which he avowed them. He used to relate the following particulars of his marriage (in 1755 to Mrs. Porter) with all the *naïveté* possible:—"Sir, it was a love marriage on both sides. Sir, she had a notion that a woman of spirit should use her lover like a dog." They were, it seems, to ride on horseback to Derby, and set out in very good humor.

"So, sir, at first she told me that I rode too fast, and she could not keep up with me; and when I rode a little slower she passed me, and complained that I lagged behind. I was not to be made the slave of caprice; and I resolved to begin as I meant to end. I therefore pushed on briskly, till I was fairly out of her sight. The road lay between two hedges, and I was sure that she could not miss it; and I conceived that she should soon come up to me. When she did, I observed her to be in tears."

There is no doubt that Johnson owed the happiness he enjoyed at Streatham chiefly to the steady friendship of Mr. Thrale, and that his want of politeness, in an age of ceremony, was often offensive to Mrs. Thrale. For instance, having argued for a long time with a very pertinacious gentleman, who had talked in a very puzzling manner, his opponent said: "I don't understand you, sir;" upon which Johnson replied, "Sir, I have found you an argument, but I am not obliged to find you an understanding."

In the same spirit was his answer, according to Mrs. Thrale's account, when she was lamenting the death of a first cousin who was killed in America.

DR. JOHNSON'S WEDDING.

"Pry'thee, my dear," Johnson cried, "have done with canting. How would the world be the worse for it, I may ask, if all your relations were at once spitted like larks, and roasted for Presto's supper?" Presto was the dog that lay under the table at the time.

But this anecdote was distorted by the venom of the narrator. It seems, from an eye-witness, that Mrs. Thrale, while supping very heartily on larks, laid down her fork, and exclaimed abruptly: "Oh, my dear Mr. Johnson! do you know what has happened? The last letters from abroad have brought us an account that our poor cousin's head was taken off by a cannon-ball." Johnson, shocked at her unfeeling manner, replied: "Madam, it would give you very little concern if all your relations were spitted like larks, and dressed for Presto's supper."

When, in 1784, Dr. Johnson had the mortification of being apprised by Mrs. Thrale that "what she supposed he had never believed" was true, namely, that she was going to marry Signor Piozzi, his exclamation carries with it our sincere sympathy:

"Poor Thrale! I thought that either her virtue or her vice would have restrained her from such a marriage. She is now become a subject for her enemies to exult over, and for her friends, if she has any left, to pity and forget."

About this time, also, Dr. Johnson's spirits were much dejected by the death of his friend Topham Beauclerk. "Poor, dear Beauclerk," he wrote, "*nec, ut soles, dabis joca.* His wit and his folly, his acuteness and merriment, his merriment and reasoning are now over. Such another will not often be found among mankind."

Dr. Johnson was himself sometimes the object of his gay friend's satirical propensities. Beauclerk used to relate, in an irresistible manner, the following incident which occurred when the famous Madame de Boufflers was in England.

"When Madame de Boufflers was first in England," said Beauclerk, "she was desirous to see Johnson. I accordingly went with her to his chambers in the Temple, where she was entertained with his conversation for some time. When our visit was over, she and I left him, and were got into Inner Temple Lane, when all at once I heard a noise like thunder. This was occasioned by Johnson, who, it seems, upon a little recollection, had taken it into his head that he ought to have done the honors of his literary residence to a foreign lady of quality; and, eager to show himself a man of gallantry, was hurrying down the staircase in violent agitation. He overtook us before we reached the Temple gate, and, brushing in between me and Madame de Boufflers, seized her hand, and conducted her to her coach. His dress was a rusty-brown morning suit, a pair of old shoes by way of slippers, a little shriveled wig sticking on the top of his head, and the sleeves of his shirt and the knees of his breeches hanging loose. A considerable crowd of people gathered round, and were not a little struck by this singular appearance."

The far-famed friendship between Johnson and Mrs. Thrale was now brought to a painful termination. He who had been the friend of her first husband was not likely to be tolerated by the second. Poor Johnson! All the heart was on his side; and with a pang he withdrew from his beloved Streatham. On the 6th of October, 1782, he took leave of the library there, recording "his last use of it." Since no act of his life was believed by him to be performed without the Divine will; since no era in that existence was even commenced without a reference to an overruling Providence, his wounded feelings sought solace from Him who was ever Johnson's stay and help. The following prayer, composed on his leaving Mr. Thrale's family, can not be read without emotion:

"Almighty God, Father of all mercy, help me by thy grace, that I may, with humble and sincere thankfulness, remember the comforts and conveniences which I have enjoyed at this place; equally trusting in thy protection when thou givest and when thou takest away. Have mercy upon me, O Lord, have mercy upon me! To thy fatherly protection, O Lord, I commend this family. Bless, guide, and defend them, that they may so pass through this world, as finally to enjoy in thy presence everlasting happiness, for Jesus Christ's sake. Amen."

After his departure from Streatham, Mrs. Thrale and Johnson met but seldom. During his long illness she paid him no attention. In the autumn of 1784 his death was evidently approaching. "Write to me often, and write like a man," were his words to Boswell. He would not desire expressions of grief or condolence. "My dear friend, life is very short and uncertain: let us spend it as well as we can." Again: "Love me as well as you can." Still, though a martyr to dropsy and asthma, he wished to recover. He died on the 13th of December, 1784, his last words being those of blessing, his last prayers for support in the hour of weakness.

Mrs. Thrale's marriage with Mr. Piozzi deprived her of another friend, poor little Burney, who, as Queen Charlotte said, "was as true as gold."

Probably this friendship might have continued had it not been finally broken up by the publication of Dr. Johnson's letters to her, and those of Mrs. Piozzi to the doctor, in 1788. A

A SCENE IN THE TEMPLE: JOHNSON'S GALLANTRY.

thousand painful associations were revived in the remembrance of poor "Evelina:" but these were not the worst results of the injudicious publication; for the anecdotes of Dr. Johnson, afterward given to the world, imparted a bitter pang to all who loved the memory of the excellent author of "Rasselas."

Two years afterward, the friends once so dear to each other met again, but on very different terms to those formerly subsisting between them. "This morning," wrote Miss Burney, who was then domiciled at Windsor, "in my way to church, just as I arrived at the iron gate of our court-yard, a well-known voice called out, 'Ah! there's Miss Burney!'

"I started, and looked round, and saw—Mrs. Piozzi.

"I hastened up to her: she met my held-out hand with both hers. Mr. Piozzi and Cecilia were with her, all smiling and good-humored.

"'You are going,' she cried, 'to church? so am I. I must run first to the inn. I suppose one may sit—any where one pleases?'

"This was all; she hurried on—so did I.

"I received exceeding great satisfaction in this little and unexpected meeting. She had been upon the Terrace, and was going to change her hat; and haste on both sides prevented awkwardness on either."

Such was the rencounter between friends once apparently so attached. Then there seems to have been a blank, and a cold reconciliation. The last letters that Mrs. Thrale wrote to her friend began "Dear Madam," and expressed thanks for being so "kindly remembered." She refers to her first husband in the *léger* manner in which all her ties, all her hopes and regrets were expressed. "Old Jacob" (her servant) "and his red nightcap," she says, writing to her former friend, "are the only two creatures that come about me of those you remember, and death alone will part us. He and I both lived longer with Mr. Piozzi than we had done with Mr. Thrale." She regretted the change in the times, in literature especially, "since *le bon vieux temps*, dear madam," and styles herself "poor H. Le P." Why poor, we can not comprehend. No one, no thing was more changed than herself. The once blooming Hetty Thrale was now a lively old woman, with one foot in the grave but her heart still in the world. She had now been obliged to dismantle and forsake "poor Streatham Park;" the expenses of "these times being treble what they were;" and, having given up an estate in Wales, she lived almost entirely at Clifton. Her health and spirits were still wonderful, and she died at last from the effects of an accident. On her eightieth birthday, being at Bath, she gave a grand ball, supper, and concert in the rooms there to two hundred people, and *opened the ball herself*. Her decease took place in consequence of the effects of a fall in a journey from Penzance to Clifton.

Mrs. Thrale-Piozzi was, no doubt, a woman of extraordinary imagination and intelligence. Her wit, her memory, her power of allusion and quotation were wonderful, even among the highly-cultured set in which she moved. Her vivacity, even to the last days of her life, was unexampled. She had, as Madame d'Arblay wrote, "a great deal of good and not good, in common with Madame de Staël." She was generous and graceful in conferring kindnesses, but neither delicate nor polished, although flattering and caressing. She was sarcastic and fearless, and therefore feared. Her second marriage brought her contempt: whether it brought felicity or not is never to be ascertained. She was not a person either to sink under unkindness or to brook it—if a husband like Piozzi *could* be undutiful to a wife with a large independent fortune.

In the anecdotes of Dr. Johnson which she published, she comprised all that she knew of him during the course of twenty years into the compass of a small volume; and those, as it has been truly said, who read the book in *two hours*, naturally suppose that *all* his conversation was such as she described. She has, therefore, done him injustice, and her inaccuracy in many of her statements has been severely censured. To her misrepresentations the false views of Johnson's character which have obtained are assignable. Horace Walpole, who was, he declared, "nauseated by Madame Piozzi," talks of the horrid vulgarisms with which she stuffed her travels in Italy. One might, he says, imagine that the writer had never "stirred out of St. Giles's." Her Latin, French, and Italian were so "miserably spelt" that he thought she had better have studied her own language before she "floundered" into foreign tongues. The work to which he refers, "Observations and Reflections made in the course of a Journey through France, Italy, and Germany," was honored with a couplet in the "Baviad:"

> "See Thrale's gray widow with a satchel roam,
> And bring in pomp laborious nothings home."

"If," writes Horace Walpole to Miss Berry, "you could wade through two octavos of Dame Piozzi's *though's*, and *so's*, and *I trow's*, and can not listen to seven volumes of Scheherezade's narrations, I will sue for a divorce *in foro Parnassi*, and Boccalini shall be my proctor."

Such was the sneer of one whose dictum, in that day, might condemn or raise any work, but whose satire could not injure, as a Queen of Society, one so rich, so gay, so comely, so witty, and so intellectual as the "gray widow," Mrs. or Madame Thrale-Piozzi.

One little incident, during her last days, evinces the kindness of her nature; and such a quality pleads so much.

Those who knew the theatres in the days of Vestris in her youth, of Liston, and of the elder Mathews, will call to mind a tall, gentlemanly young man, who began his theatrical career in the highest parts of tragedy, and closed it as a "walking gentleman." Even in that *rôle* he was too enormous for the Haymarket Theatre, and he had the unhappiness to be what old Fuller compares to a "great house with a small cockloft," deficient in the high mental powers which we exact in performers. The "Examiner" was then the great dramatic oracle; it fell on poor Augustus Conway, and demolished him and his prospects. He was compared to Gog, and so maltreated that, from Hamlet and Macbeth, he came down to the office and post of prompter. He was, indeed, the child of shame and of misfortune. He was the natural son of Lord William Conway, by the daughter of a farmer. The poor girl, to avoid exposure, had been sent to the West Indies, where Augustus was born. He was thus descended from a family famed, if for nothing else, for their almost gigantic stature, and thus, hereditarily, he was unlucky in two ways. His history reminds one of that of Savage. He hunted up his father, and at one time nearly succeeded in finding him, but no relief came. His parentage was acknowledged, but a family of unbounded wealth refused the least assistance. Driven almost to despair, he found at this crisis a friend in Mrs. Piozzi. It is true the most absurd constructions have been put on her admiration of Conway; but, at all events, the interest she took in his welfare lessened his misery. It is to be regretted that she did not permanently assist him. He was still pursued by the press; still unable to get relief from his relations. In despair, he resolved to try his fortune in America, and therefore embarked at Liverpool. During the voyage he was seized with temporary insanity, and in that state threw himself into the sea. Such was the fate of an honorable, sensitive, gentlemanly being, the last known object of Mrs. Piozzi's regard. In his pocket was found a bill of exchange endorsed by his mother.

Among his effects were found a number of manuscript letters from Mrs. Piozzi, which were published, edited by J. Russell Smith, under the title of "Love-letters addressed to Augustus Conway, Esq., by Mrs. Piozzi when she was eighty." But it appears that her expressions were those of the Dellacruscan school, romantic and enthusiastic, without any aim but kindness, any meaning but a romantic interest in one unfortunate and yet deserving.

LADY CAROLINE LAMB.

"With a fanciful head and a warm heart," the subject of this memoir represents the head of a clique which flourished during the time of Byron's brief career in society; but which, for some years after his departure to Italy, continued to form one section of the *beau monde* in London. The daughter of Henrietta Frances, Countess of Bessborough, and consequently the great-granddaughter of Sarah, Duchess of Marlborough, and the niece of the celebrated Duchess of Devonshire, Lady Caroline derived some portion of her distinction from those connections; but for her celebrity she was indebted to another source. Her lustre was borrowed. With considerable natural talent, her works, had they been the production of one unknown to fashion, would have excited perhaps a transient attention: from the wife of William Lamb, afterward Lord Melbourne, and from the enthusiastic admirer of Byron, almost any literary effort must have been thought worthy, at least, of a *sensation*. That they were not worthy of more, is evident from the obscurity into which "Glenarvon" and its successor have dropped, in our own days of literary revivals and reprints.

Born during the latter part of the last century, Lady Caroline Ponsonby was reared amid the fading memories of Mrs. Montagu and the Burneys. Her mother had lived as much in an atmosphere of literature as in that of exclusiveness, and her children were brought up with an hereditary respect for genius. Most ladies of rank dabbled in verse: strong political and weak religious convictions were in vogue: the great world has since then been tamed down, and its eccentricities smoothed into uniformity. In the youth of Lady Caroline, the shadow of revolutionary France still hung over society—still darkened, still misled it; and women thought their glory consisted in being romantic and peculiar.

The family whence Lady Caroline sprang were of Whig principles, and her grandfather, Lord Bessborough, was a member of Brookes's. But, with all his liberalism, the earl disliked Sheridan; and an anecdote of his daughter-in-law, Lady Duncannon, Lady Caroline's mother, is told, showing to what lengths female politicians will go on certain occasions. When Sheridan's name was put up as a candidate at Brookes's, two persons resolved to get it blackballed. These were Lord Bess-

Q 2

borough and George Selwyn. They succeeded several times: the matter was to be put to the test again. The two foes resolved not to absent themselves during the time allowed by the regulations of the club for the ballot. In order to defeat them, Sheridan's friends agreed to try stratagem, and enlisted into their scheme the fearless Lady Duncannon. Seeing the adverse couple at their posts one evening when Sheridan's name was again put to the vote, they sent a chairman into the coffee-room with a note to Lord Bessborough, written in the name of Lady Duncannon, saying that a fire had broken out in his house in Cavendish Square, and begging him to return home. Off started my lord, and getting into a sedan-chair freed the club from his presence. He doubted not the cause for alarm, since Lady Duncannon lived in the same house with himself. Nearly at that precise moment came a verbal message to Selwyn, to request his presence at home, "Miss Fagniani" (his adopted daughter, who afterward married Lord Yarmouth) "being seized with an alarming illness." No sooner had he made his exit than Sheridan was proposed and elected. The two enemies returned without delay on discovering the trick played on them, but the ballot was closed.

By so eager a partisan, so complete a woman of the world, was Lady Caroline reared. Under the influence of her charming aunt, the Duchess of Devonshire, did she receive her first impressions of the life she was to enter upon. As she grew up, the amiable, popular manners, the love of poetry, the taste and talent which distinguished her aunt, gradually opened in Lady Caroline; but they were all weakened in their effect by peculiarity, and the absence of strong natural sense. It is almost a misfortune to have a desire to shine without the qualities to insure that end. Neither had Lady Caroline the beauty which, in her aunt and mother, set off every thing they chose to do. She was delicate; with a small, pensive face; never plain, yet not beautiful.

In 1805, a year before the death of the Duchess of Devonshire, Lady Caroline was married to the Hon. William Lamb, afterward Viscount Melbourne. This nobleman was then a rising member of the lower house, and already noted for his talents as a debater. He was handsome and witty, with a singular placidity of character, almost amounting to apathy. As a statesman, his administration was marked by many notable legislative enactments; as a man, his moral character was far from being defensible. At the period of his marriage with Lady Caroline Mr. Lamb was one of the most agreeable of men. In his later years, either oppressed with business, or suffering from repletion, or from the effects of indulgence, he contracted a habit of sleeping, almost in society, and, it is said, even in the presence of the queen, who graciously insisted on his not being disturbed. Whatsoever may have been the want of congeniality that soon exhibited itself between Lady Caroline and her husband, it never broke out into an open contest. He was wholly immersed in his career; and never, although he was the friend of most of the famous Edinburgh wits, appreciated modern literature. Late in life, when prime minister, it was suggested to him by a certain literary baronet that men of letters should be noticed, invited, and brought forward. "Who are they? Where do they live? What have they all written?" was his answer. The editors of the leading journals were specified. "In France journalists are raised by being made important—sometimes ennobled even," was also the remark. "Pray invite them, dear B——," was Lord Melbourne's reply. They were invited, and they came. The august rulers of public opinion were ushered in, and specially introduced by their patron, the baronet. So much wit, so much criticism had never before sat round the dinner-table at Melbourne House. All were prepared, were primed to shine; but, before dinner was half over, his lordship was fast asleep: and soon after the repast was over, though not before the wine had gone freely round, the army of editors took their departure in some disgust.

In all her enthusiasm for what has been well called "*maccaroni* literature," Lady Caroline's clever, witty, handsome husband did not, therefore, sympathize. The fashionable pair lived as much apart as decorum permitted; though Lady Caroline seems to have continued always on good terms with Lady Melbourne, her mother-in-law. Her time was passed between Brockett Hall and St. James's Square, in all the luxurious delights of a youth without care, yet Lady Caroline was far from being happy; and the lady in "Ernest Maltravers, entitled "*La Femme incomprise*," may certainly convey a notion of her character.

It was in the year 1813 that Lord Byron in his Diary refers to a friendship that probably had an unhappy interest on Lady Caroline's existence. This was between Lord Byron and Lady Melbourne, her mother-in-law, of whom the poet speaks as "the best friend he ever had, and the cleverest of women." "To Lady Melbourne I write with most pleasure; and her answers are so sensible, so *tactique*. I never met with half her talent. If she had been a few years younger, what a fool she would have made of me, had she thought it worth her while; and I should have lost a valuable and most agreeable *friend*. Mem. A mistress can never be a friend; while you agree, you are lovers; and when it is over, any thing but friends." To Lady

Melbourne his works, and any thing painful or agreeable that was said of them, were shown and confided. She was, like Lady Caroline, a neglected wife, treated externally with respect. Ladies of those days were well broken-in to the position. There was no Judge Cresswell to release them at short notice. In November, 1813, a few lines written by Byron in his Diary appear to refer to Lady Caroline Lamb. "Two letters, one from ——, the other from Lady Melbourne, both excellent in their respective styles; —— contained also a very pretty lyric on 'concealed griefs'—if not her own, yet very like hers. Why did she not say that the stanzas were, or were not, of her own composition? I do not know whether to wish them hers or not. I have no esteem for poetical persons, especially women; they have so much of the ideal in practice as well as *ethics*."

On the 10th of January, 1815, Byron wrote to Moore: "I was married this day week. The parson has pronounced it; Perry has announced it; and the 'Morning Post,' also, under the head of 'Lord Byron's Marriage,' as if it were a fabrication, or the puff-direct of a new staymaker."

Such was his announcement of that infelicitous union, the *dis*-union of which formed the topic of society for many a long day after the bond was forever broken.

Miss Milbanke was the niece of Lady Melbourne, and must, of course, have frequently been in the society of Lady Caroline Lamb. Lord Byron, heart-sick, in debt, weary of a vicious life, and eager to form ties to which a disposition naturally affectionate impelled him, as it were, anticipated much felicity. Miss Milbanke was "the paragon of only daughters," to use his own words, and had been for some time attached to him, which he had not known, and had, indeed, thought her of a cold disposition, which he then found she was not. When he offered, he had not seen her for ten months; perhaps when he did see her, especially with all the odious preliminary of settlements on his hands, the charm was broken. The day of his marriage, he described himself as awaking with a heavy heart, and becoming more deeply dejected on glancing at his wedding-suit laid out before him. His feelings at the ceremony have been described by himself.

"I saw him stand
Before an altar with a gentle bride;
Her face was fair, but was not that which made
The starlight of his boyhood."

Nevertheless, in the very early days of that inauspicious marriage, Byron wrote: "Swift says, no wise man ever married; but, for a fool, I think it is the most ambrosial of all possible future states. I still think one ought to marry upon *lease*;

but am very sure I should renew mine at the expiration, though next term were for ninety-and-nine years."

Alas! his term was soon ended. A year afterward we find Byron "at war with all the world and my wife;" and begging his friend Moore neither to believe all he heard of him nor to defend him.

While these events were going on, the peace of Lady Caroline Lamb was destroyed by one of those infatuations to which bereaved women, whose affections can not turn into the one great natural channel, and neglected wives, are liable. Many were the rumors on the state of Lady Caroline's feelings for Lord Byron; and it was even reported that, being wounded by his indifference, she had attempted to stab herself in phrensy during a large evening party. A romantic predilection, indulged to the extent of monomania, certainly existed. Any other woman's reputation would have been crushed by it; but it was regarded as the result of an eccentric and not wholly accountable mind: and although Lady Caroline, from that time, lost *caste*, she incurred rather ridicule than censure, and the incident was in due time suffered to die away in the public mind. Moore has carefully abstained from a reference to it, or, indeed, to Lady Caroline Lamb at all: so that upon recollection alone the occurrence rests.

The novel of "Glenarvon," in two volumes, is said to be a transcript of Lady Caroline's own mind. It is a powerful tale, verging on the immoral; romantic and improbable. It riveted Lady Caroline to that literary society which she henceforth found more to her taste than the aristocratic sphere in which she was born. Perhaps she thought with Byron, who thus refers to some of the most brilliant of those assemblies in London.

"Last night, *party*" (Tuesday, March 22d, 1814) "at Lansdowne House. To-night, *party* at Lady Charlotte Greville's: deplorable waste of time, and something of temper—nothing imparted—nothing acquired—talking without ideas—if any thing like *thought* in my mind, it was not on the subjects on which we were gabbling. Heigho! and in this way half London pass what is called life."

Lady Caroline's literary circle comprised Holland House, Lady Charleville's, Lord Ward's, Lord Lansdowne's, and others of a similar grade. Of these *réunions* Byron formed the prominent attraction. But the crash had come. As little could be known of the *real* origin of the storm which chased Byron forever from the chances of happiness in life, as of the lurkings of the wind, "which bloweth where it listeth." At the close of January, 1816, Lady Byron left Lord Byron to visit her father: they parted in kindness. On the road she wrote him a letter of playful fondness. A few days after her arrival at Sir Ralph Milbanke's seat, Byron received a letter to say that she would return to him no more.

Nine executions in his house within that year are thought to have accelerated this blow, though they ought to have stayed the hand that dealt it. As usual, Byron referred to its effect in a few but telling words. He had parted with his books when he spoke: his embarrassments were at their climax. "I shall be very glad to see you," he wrote to Rogers, "if you like to call, though I am at present contending with the 'slings and arrows of outrageous fortune,' some of which have struck at me from a quarter I did not expect them. But, no matter, 'there is a world elsewhere,' and I will cut my way through this as I can."

Next we hear of his parting from his sister—his beloved, and in domestic life almost equally unhappy Augusta, to whom he addressed those exquisite lines. She had been his solace—she clung to him when "all the world and his wife" abjured him. So true is Lamartine's description of family ties, of the blood which binds far more strongly than any other human links.

"Though the rock of my last hope is shivered,
And its fragments are sunk in the wave;
Though I feel that my soul is delivered
To pain—it shall not be its slave.
There is many a pang to pursue me;
They may crush, but they shall not contemn;
They may torture, but shall not subdue me—
'Tis of *thee* that I think—not of them."

On the 25th of April he sailed for Ostend; and the dream, the folly, perhaps the sin of Lady Caroline's imagination was removed; and Lord Byron, for the second and the last time, quitted this country.

Henceforth her life was more prosaic, but perhaps more calm than when under the influence of this absorbing enthusiasm. Lady Morgan, who knew her well, does justice to the goodness of a heart that was often mistaken by others, or, as she terms it, the "spontaneous outbreak of a good and kind heart, which, in serving and giving pleasure to others, obeys the instinctive impulse of a sanguine and genial disposition; waiting for no rule or maxim; not opening an account for value expected; doing unto others what you wish them to do unto you. This, in one word, is Lady Caroline Lamb, for if she does not always act wisely for herself, she generally acts only too well for others." Lady Caroline then wrote from Brockett Hall, which she describes as a paradise, full of flowers and fruit: "It stands, indeed, in one of those noble parks peculiar to England, rich in ancestral trees, with green herbage, and picturesque with noble alleys; but the house is heavy, flat in architecture, with a poor entrance, smallish windows, a plain red-brick exterior, all denoting the utilitarian spirit which came in with the last century. It is turned scrupulously away from a view; and overlooks a piece of artificial water, with sloping pleasure-grounds on its brink." In London, Lady Caroline, when Lady Morgan visited her in 1818, received her friends in her bedroom at Melbourne House, at Whitehall, looking over the Park. In the bow-window stood the chair in which Lord Byron sat for his picture to Sanderson: it was fastened to the ground. Lady Caroline reclined on a couch rather than a bed, wrapped in fine muslin. Her manners were always cordial and winning; but she was by no means less singular than in her earlier life. She embraced Lady Morgan with all the cordiality of sisterhood in letters. As the interview went on, an amusing scene occurred. It was the custom among certain fine ladies of that day to have a page, a boy of fifteen or so, always within call: Lady Holland, Lady Cork, and others, each kept this pair of hands and pair of feet for their peculiar use. Lady Cork, who had figured as the "Honorable and charming Miss Monckton," in Miss Burney's Memoirs (in which the original sin of toadyism perpetually appears), was now a dowager advancing in years, wishing to part with a page, whom she now sent for inspection to Lady Caroline, who was reported to have broken the head of her own page with a teapot some time previously. Lady Morgan had already been the vehicle of several attempts on the part of Lady Cork to get rid of her page. Like most ladies of that day, her ladyship had weak eyes: Lady Morgan was her amanuensis. "What! get rid of your page?" cried Sydney. "Don't talk, child, but do as I ask you; first, then, to the Duchess of Leeds: 'My dear duchess, this will be presented to you by my little page, whom you admired so the other night. He is about to leave me: only fancy, he finds my house not religious enough for him! and that he can't get to church twice on Sundays. I am certainly not so good a Christian as your grace, but as to Sundays, it is not true. But I think your situation would just suit him, if you are inclined to take him. Yours, M. Cork and Orrery.'

"Now, my dear, for another note to your friend Lady Caroline." Lady Caroline having been justified by Lady Morgan from the calumny of Lady Cork about breaking the page's head, Sydney began to smile.

"It was a Tory calumny, Lady Cork: and Lady Caroline

was at Brockett, not at Whitehall, where the adventure was said to have happened."

"I don't care whether true or not, my dear. All pages are the better for having their heads broken sometimes. So please write." So a coaxing note was sent off to Lady Caroline, inviting her, after sounding the page's praises, to one of Lady Cork's *blue* parties, and giving her leave to bring any one— Mr. Moore, if she liked—to those famous receptions where "tea and wax lights" in abundance were all that Lady Cork thought of moment. The letter was signed "Yours in all affection," although at the same time the teapot anecdote had been related.

Lady Cork, then in or near her sixtieth year, seemed to belong to another age, even in 1818, than that of Byron and Lady Caroline, beside whose soft muslins she must have come out like an old picture by Houbraken near a modern portrait of Hoppner's or Lawrence's. Her ancient form is still present among us, with her quaint manners, her native insincerity, her passion for society, and her predilection for stolen goods—not from any wish to steal, but from that slight aristocratic tinge of craziness, that "bee in the bonnet" which we find in most old families in every part of the world, in none more so than in Germany and England. Lady Cork having survived the Burneys and their clique, had a way of collecting her friends in detachments. Her pink, that is, her titled guests; her blue, that is, her literary *soirées;* her gray, that is, her religious tea-parties, were the amusement of the town almost until, in 1840, she at last went to the grave of her fathers. She was a very useful member of society in bringing pleasant people together. In England a little title usually dilutes a great deal of dullness; but Lady Cork's parties were more odd than dull. Who could ever regret passing some hours where, before a huge grand piano, a small form, with a broadish Irish face, a blue beaming eye, sat down, and playing, softly, almost a nominal accompaniment, sang one of his own lyrics in a voice of no compass, yet exquisitely musical, the artist of nature? Such was Thomas Moore, amusing when he talked, captivating when he sang. Mrs. Billington was quavering in one room at Lord Ward's, Moore in another, one evening: the professional singer was deserted, the poet's piano was thronged.

Yet there must have been more satisfaction to be found in the salon of the estimable Lady Charleville, another lady eminent in that day for her influence in society, than in that of Lady Cork. A daughter of the house of Cremorne, Lady Charleville had been associated with all that was witty, eloquent, patriotic in Ireland during the infelicitous close of the last century. Lord Clive and Grattan, the opposite poles in politics, were her friends. She stood by Grattan's death-bed when Lord Castlereagh assured him that he should be buried in Westminster Abbey. She had joined her husband in his peril, as one of the district generals, accompanied only by her maid, and armed with pistols, when the whole country was in tumult. Like Charlotte de la Trémouille, Countess of Derby, of old, she remained in her husband's castle when danger threatened, and recurred to those perils of her life with pleasure. Devoted to Protestantism, yet free from uncharitable prejudice, Lady Charleville endeavored, by establishing schools for both persuasions, to benefit alike the Catholic and the Protestant. It was her firm belief at that time that the state provision for the Romanist clergy was indispensable. The result of years has not confirmed her views. Ireland is more Protestant than it was, and the Romish Church there is unendowed.

Before the period of middle life arrived Lady Charleville had lost the use of her lower limbs from rheumatism. When her drawing-rooms were thronged with the *élite* of London it was sad to see this excellent woman wheeled about in a chair, her son, the handsome Lord Tullamore, who married one of the beautiful daughters of Lady Charlotte Bury, performing that office. Yet she still pursued the accomplishment of painting; she still cultivated her comprehensive mind; still enjoyed the society of the good and the lettered, and until her latest hour the power of enjoyment was spared to her. Her fancy, her judgment, her heart were untouched by time. Lady Charleville took a very different position in the world to that occupied by the eccentric Lady Cork, or the kind but injudicious Lady Caroline Lamb. She was as much respected, as beloved. At her *conversaziones* Milman, the Canon of Westminster, at first as a young poet, then in the grave character of an historian, finally in all the sanctity of a "Very Reverend," delighted to converse with the gifted but unaffected hostess. Jekyl, the wit, *par excellence*, of that day, and the personal friend of the prince regent, there laid aside politics, and appeared to Lady Morgan "the most delightful creature she had ever met with." Luttrell formed also one of the clique of Cavendish Square.

The late Marchioness of Hertford, the favorite of the then prince regent, and one of the most courtly and stately of ladies of doubtful conduct, was received by Lady Charleville, and even thought to do honor by her presence! The late Marchioness of Salisbury, famous for her beauty in youth, for her political intrigues, for her gambling, her Sunday parties, her rouge, and her *hauteur*, also looked in, and was "civil." This lady was burnt to death in her old age, at Hatfield, and nothing but the jewels in which she had decked herself for dinner were found to mark out as hers the poor skeleton recognized—a worldly life closed by an awful death. These "Queens of Fashion" had mingled at Lady Charleville's in their youth with the comic muse, Mrs. Abington, and with Miss Farren, afterward Lady Derby—ladies, in their way, of as high *ton* as the stately though fallible Hertford, or the gambling and Sunday-desecrating Lady Salisbury. Old people can remember Manchester Square and the Terrace of Piccadilly thronged with carriages on Sunday evenings; when whist and even faro were fearlessly played at parties to which every one scrambled for invitations. William Spencer, the descendant of Sarah, Duchess of Marlborough, was the fashionable wit, poet, and Adonis of the day, before Byron appeared. His poetry was like himself, polished, gay, slight: his wit enlivened many a country-house, set at ease many a heavy dinner-table. Amid this varied throng attention was changed outwardly into respect when, met at the hall-door by Lord Tullamore, and received on the very landing by Lady Charleville in her arm-chair, Lady de Ameland, who had, in 1794, been obliged to lay down her title of Duchess of Sussex, walked in. Old Dr. Parr over his strange dinners at Hatton used to descant upon the noble qualities of this much-injured woman, who, he affirmed, had more royalty in her port than any of the English princesses. Beautiful as well as majestic, there was in her fine face, it is said, a trace of her ancestral relationship to Mary, Queen of Scots: for she was lineally descended from the Regent Murray. Not far from this courteous and charming woman Mrs. Fitzherbert's marked, high features, and clear blue eyes, serene as if no thunder-cloud hovered over her head, might be recognized. Then, led in, came the graceful Lady Sarah Banbury, with whom George III. had fallen in love as she was hay-making at Holland House, but now blind, aged, yet still displaying traces of former loveliness: she mixed among a generation new to her, and seemed among them like a memorial of past hopes, and interests, and disappointments.

Time rolled away. Lady Cork survived; Lady Charleville survived. Some of those who have thus been briefly enumerated, but whose separate histories would each form a subject of biography, had passed away. A fresh generation of authors, fine gentlemen, wits, poets, churchmen, and politicians waited upon Lady Caroline in her maze of white muslin at Melbourne House, or went to laugh at Lady Cork's gray or pink or blue parties, or visited Lady Charleville in her decline, in respect and regret.

In the early part of the reign of George IV. a sort of resuscitation of literature succeeded a long interval of intellectual darkness. Scott, indeed, had illumined the regency, and never can the effect produced by his "Waverley" be forgotten. Its appearance brought new life into society; new light to the study; a source of pure happiness to the young; a veritable consolation to the old. He was in the wane when "Pelham" was produced. Previous to its appearance, its author, one of the most wonderful men of our time, had circulated among friends a volume of poems, among which was one addressed to "Caroline." This was to Lady Caroline Lamb. Her vicinity when at Brockett Hall to Knebworth; her opportunities of meeting the author of "Pelham" in the society of her husband; or at Lord Cowper's; or among a clique less distinguished for some other qualities than for wit; or at Lord Dacre's, and elsewhere; inspired her with sanguine expectations of that celebrity which has been so complete and so varied. She patronized and she admired the young poet, and she was his confidante in his attachment, his fatal attachment, to her whom he afterward made his wife.

Little coteries were then formed at the house of Miss Benger in the far-off regions of Doughty Street. Miss Benger was among the first of those lady historians who, in spite of the lash of the author in "Fraser's Magazine," "that women should not write history," have contributed much to our knowledge of the past. Without Agnes and Eliza Strickland, without Lucy Aikin, without Miss Freer and Mrs. Everett Green, and even without the humble and half-forgotten Miss Benger, how imperfect would have been our knowledge of female manners and of female influence in the middle ages! To women we owe the most readable biographical works of the day. Men deal better with history, but they are as much at fault in memoirs as in fashionable letter-writing.

Those who remember the reading-room of the British Museum in the days of Sir Henry Ellis—that dingy room, in which one took leave of cleanliness and light when one put off one's clogs at the door—will recall Miss Benger—a thin, worn woman, more than middle-aged, with a sparkling eye, a countenance rather benignant than intelligent—the traces of poverty, but genteel poverty, in her dress, patiently reading through dusty tomes to compile her "Elizabeth of Bohemia;" then, as the clock struck four, folding up her portfolio, and retreating, till, regaining her umbrella, she found herself on the road again to Doughty Street.

Her evenings were, however, enlivened by inexpressive, easy, *willing* company. Of these Lady Caroline Lamb was the pale and pensive star. Her perfect dress, correct in taste, though her fancy was so fantastic in other matters, her gentle, courteous manners, her title, her carriage, and the thunders of her two smart footmen, all gave success to the *petits comités* of Doughty Street. There Dr. Kitchener, a neighbor, dropped in; a useful, conceited man, the precursor of Soyer in his general views, a sort of Combe in cookery, with just and wholesome ideas founded on nature. There L. E. L. was first introduced to the literary circle of Doughty Street by a little woman in a turban, with sparse light locks, and faded gray eyes, and the slightest of all literary pretensions, Miss Spence —poor Miss Spence!—Lady Caroline's shadow and worshiper—the friend of the kind Miss Benger, and of that woman of rare beauty and talent, whose fate the world then coupled with the author of "Pelham."

Sometimes the coterie removed to Little Quebec Street, where, in a small room up three stories, Miss Spence, in her invariable turban, welcomed the noted and the aspiring of the day. L. E. L., then a girl of seventeen; the author of "Pelham;" such other young men as she could entrap to her tea and muffins—reviewers, chiefly, or dilettante authors; sundry old ladies calling themselves "honorable," but with a gone-by demeanor; inferior professional musicians; and Lady Caroline Lamb, ever polite, ever well-bred, and seemingly unconscious that she was not in the circle of Holland House and Brockett —these composed the circle.

These evenings composed the interludes between stately dinners and brilliant *soirées;* and the incense she met with from *littérateurs* probably soothed Lady Caroline for a severe vexation. After the excitement produced by "Glenarvon" had subsided, her friends forbade her to write. Lady Caroline had written a small *brochure* called "Ada Reis," and wished to publish it with Murray. "All I have asked of Murray," she wrote to Lady Morgan, "is a dull sale, or a still birth. This may seem strange, and it is contrary to my own feelings of ambition; but what can I do? I am ordered peremptorily by my own family not to write."

One can not but think that Lady Caroline's family were not far wrong; yet, descended, as she boasted, in a right line from the poet Spenser, from John, Duke of Marlborough, and with all the Cavendish and Ponsonby blood to boot, she thought it excusable to be a little rebellious—since her ancestors were people of spirit; and then to be told to hold her tongue and not write by all her relations united—"what is to happen?"

Certainly poor Lady Caroline's letters displayed at this time a mournful and lonely spirit. We do not cite, in support of this assertion, those touching though unequal verses printed in "Glenarvon," in which these lines seem to refer to her own unhappy attachment—

"Weep for thy fault, in heart and mind degraded,
Weep if thy tears can wash away the stain;
Call back the scenes in which thy soul delighted,
Call back the dream that bless'd thy early youth."

We can not rest on poetry, however wrung from the heart, that pines and moans: a slight fact speaks more plainly. "I am returned from riding alone," she wrote one evening from Melbourne House, "to find myself in these large rooms alone; but I sent for some street minstrels to sing to me." "I would," she wrote to Lady Morgan, "we had staid a few days longer: your head, with far more of genius, has much better sense in it than mine; and besides, you have a better temper, and you have gone through more, formed yourself more, seen the necessity of in some degree considering opinions, although, as for the matter of that, you have got yourself exiled, so that you have not sacrificed your principles to your interest."

The life that had so much of excitement at one time, of melancholy at another, was not destined to be a long one. Four years before Lady Caroline Lamb's death, Lord Byron expired at Missolonghi. One would fain know with what emotions she heard of this event; whether the folly of her youth had passed away; or whether she viewed, in the solemn summons to this gifted man to quit a life he had not well employed, a warning, a call to the worldly, the thoughtless, to seek forgiveness and reconcilement where alone is mercy.

Lady Caroline died in 1828. Her husband became the prime minister of England. He never married again, and his title is extinct. The early death of his only son left no direct representative either of his talent or of her social virtues.

We regard Lady Caroline Lamb as the victim of a mistaken education. She had some talent, great attractiveness, and a gentle nature. But her mind was weakened by the worst sentimentalism; her time was wasted in brooding over her own feelings. The absence of domestic happiness, perhaps, made her more useful to the society which was essential to her than a happier woman would have been. She had good aspirations, but no judgment; literary tastes, but no foundation of careful and accurate study. Her letters are scarcely intelligible from their involved style, but they display kindness, candor, and refinement.

ANNE SEYMOUR DAMER.

The "Emancipation of Women," of which we have had so much nonsensical talk wafted over to us from the other shores of the Atlantic, till a small knot of our own fair spinsters have feebly re-echoed it, has been a fact ever since Christianity, by restricting polygamy, raised the one sex to an apparent equality with the other. Such is the common opinion, and certainly, since the introduction of a religion which placed marriage on so far more noble a footing than it had held either in Greece, Rome, or the East, there has been a large number of celebrated women in every Christian country. That there are more intricate causes to be assigned for it, is proved by the facts that many, if not most, celebrated women have been spinsters, and that every age has had a certain proportion of great female characters in spite of religion, want of education, or the repressive customs of their people. It would seem that every now and then nature adds to beauty, delicacy, tenderness, and all that is feminine and lovable, a proportion of mental energy that we are accustomed to consider the exclusive gift of the stronger sex; whereas, did circumstances draw out or education develop it, we have yet to prove that it might not be as common in the weaker as in the stronger being. Certainly it is to circumstances and to education that we owe the celebrity of the great women of the world; yet when these (which men almost always enjoy) have been granted to women, their recipients invariably stand out as marvels. What proof could we have had of this latent energy in such women as Joan of Arc and Boadicea, but for very peculiar circumstances? Would Novella, the original of Portia, who practiced in the courts at Bologna, and by her woman's tact and ready wit often gained causes which her father despaired of; would poor love-lorn Hëloise have been celebrated for her learning at a period when science was reserved for a few priestly students; would the female preachers of Alexandria, the female doctors, lawyers, painters, sculptors, mathematicians, theologians, essayists, instances of whom are to be found in the annals of Christian Europe; nay, would even the Queens of Society and great lady-wits of the last three centuries—have been what they were, if they had received the ordinary education of women? If we look into the separate instances, we invariably find that either some unusual circumstances have excited their dormant powers, or that their education has been, from some unusual cause, the same as that given to men. Whether we may deduce from this that our present system of education for girls is a bad one, and that we should give them the same tutors and introduce them to the same studies as our boys; or whether it may not be said that the advantages of such an education are counterbalanced by the loss of that softness, delicacy, and complete innocence of mind which are among the greatest charms of women—we need not now discuss. Certainly the *Précieuses* of the reign of Louis Quatorze, whom Molière ridiculed so successfully; the ladies collegiate under our own Queen Bess, whom Ben Jonson satirized in his "Silent Woman;" the blue-stocking set of the last century and our modern "strong-minded women," as they are shamefully called, as if a woman had not as much title to mental vigor as a man—are more admired than loved by men.

But there are some pursuits in which their very physical weakness renders women unfit to cope with men. Though we have had women-soldiers in peculiar cases, we have had no women-builders or female Stephensons. Though we have lady-painters in almost as great a number as lady-writers, so that in a work lately published on women-artists we have counted more than five hundred of some distinction, yet we have had very few female sculptors. Anne Damer is one of those few, and a very uncommon woman in every respect.

The friend of Hume, Fox, and Nelson; the pet of Horace Walpole; a sculptor of no mean merit; an actress with whom Siddons was not ashamed to appear on a private stage; a descendant of two of the noblest and oldest families in England—Anne Damer was nevertheless a most ambitious woman in a way in which ambition becomes not only honorable but lovable. She had the emulation of a man, the beauty of a woman, the courage of a warrior, and the blood of the Normans. This last circumstance, an accident which is the least part of her praise, perhaps recommends her most to our lady readers, to whom "blood" is the worth of blood, and who see in race a palliative of many vices and a high enhancement of a few virtues. In fact, since Norman seigneur sneered at Saxon churl, a Villiers or Montgomery may do with honor what John Thompson or Tom Johnson can only do with ignonimy. But let us take Anne Damer as she was, a Whig, a friend of liberty, an enthusiast after her fashion, a strong-minded woman, perhaps, in the present day, but not a boaster of her family, nor one who, relying on the accident of birth, thinks she may neglect the culture of the individual mind.

Anne Seymour Damer was born in 1748, that is, in the days of the Humorists. Her father was General Henry Seymour Conway, a field-marshal, and a brother of the Marquis of Hertford. Her mother was daughter of a duke and widow of an earl—Caroline Campbell, only daughter of John, Duke of Argyll, and only widow (we hope) of Charles, Earl of Aylesbury and Elgin. Here was nobility enough to satisfy their only offspring, in whom it all centred; but Anne Damer was not to be satisfied with nobility. She wished for nobleness as well. It is certainly a rarity to find a man, to say nothing of a woman, *descending*, as the phrase goes, to art. That it is, indeed, a great *ascent*, the sensible of the present day, like a few of Mrs. Damer's time, will readily admit. Horace Walpole saw nothing degrading in his cousin's handling the hammer and chisel. The sofa-misses of modern Belgravia might perhaps think otherwise.

However, Anne Conway owed something to her birth. She was born "in the society" of that day; that is, her rank at once admitted her to circles to which others climbed with much labor, much patronage, or much genius. They were not purely aristocratic circles. Had they been so, they would not have formed the London Parnassus of really great men; but it happened then, as it does often in the revolving history of the world, that the upper classes held in their hands the main talent of the day, and that the geniuses of classes below them thought it worth their while to work up to those circles. Literature had neither a profession nor a class then. Nobles were wits and wit ennobled. Wit included what we call the profession of letters. Men wrote less to be paid than to be admired. Patrons strove to be Mæcenases and mingled with genius. Genius, with a lingering love of gentility, strove to wear silk stockings, and did not despise, but rather sought, the applause of wealthy nobility. Samuel Johnson, the Tory, is a good specimen of the "literary profession" of that age. He believed in that ambiguous term "a gentleman," and was not ashamed to define it as a "man of extraction."

Anne Conway was too enthusiastic to be a Tory. She was a lover of liberty and progress, and showed samples of both in herself, in the way in which she gave up "society" for the use of the chisel, and in the stern perseverance with which she met the sneer of Hume.

That Anne Conway, a girl of eighteen or twenty years old, should have been walking with David Hume in London streets, would seem strange enough if we were not aware that the historian had about that time been appointed secretary under her father, General Conway. Whether cumbrous David was pouring out upon his fair young listener his last cogitation on humanity, or whether she, in the liveliness of her disposition and her age, was belaying the worthy man with maiden fun, does not appear; but it is said that, meeting an Italian boy with a board of plaster figures on his head, David, in his love of humanity, talked to and tried to draw out the foreign lad, and with true British condescension, having given him a shilling, which doubtless made the boy think the historian as near to Heaven as Oxonians of the day thought him near to the antipodes thereof, walked away. Little Anne Damer, flirting after a fashion with the heavy essayist, rallied him playfully on his good-nature. Hume, not knowing the verse of a then unborn poet—

> "Something God hath to say to thee
> Worth hearing from the lips of all,"

or perhaps, in the height of his Toryism, unable to excuse himself on any such noble basis, made the following rather commonplace speech: "Be less severe, Miss Conway. Those images, at which you smile, were not made without the aid of both science and genius. With all your attainments, now, you can not produce such works."

Anne Conway was not a girl to be "dared." "Dare me," we used to say at school, when we nerved ourselves up to some wonderful feat of courage or dexterity. There certainly is a great incentive in being "dared;" that is, our courage is impunged, our powers are impugned, our talent, wit, readiness, British enterprise are impugned. The boy who jumps over a five-barred gate only because he is "dared," is the same boy who, when later the world silently dares him to make some grand enterprise, to colonize an Australian island, or convert a savage people, or cut a canal through the Isthmus of Panama, or build a bridge across the Menai Straits, or bring in a new Reform Bill, will do these exploits more or less successfully and achieve his fame. But we less expect to find this spirit in a girl of eighteen, a beautiful girl, whom we should suppose to be more taken up with admiration than ambition.

That she received the former no one can doubt who has seen Cosway's portrait of her. The fair face is of a perfect oval; the ample brow not high enough to depart from the rule of Greek proportion; the delicate feature and luxuriant fair hair rising in rebel billows from her brow, and falling carelessly in curls upon her neck, are all beautiful in themselves. The features are marked, and the face is not one to forget easily: the nose is large and aquiline, but delicate: the mouth shows strong decision of character, firmly closed, though turned with merry smile. The head is well set on a long neck: the figure is

ANNE CONWAY (MRS. DAMER) "DARED" BY HUME.

slight and graceful, and is set off by the dress, a light one, with large rosettes and an ample frill round the shoulders—all in that airy, graceful style in which Cosway delighted. But if there were not this beauty, the expression would still entitle the face to be remembered. The eyes, not large enough to be vacant, are full of thought and spirit, looking into you askingly but quietly. All speaks of a highly-cultivated mind and taste—all is refined and intellectual, without the slightest approach to that luxuriance which one may almost call sensuality, and which in some women is irresistible. There was a full-length of her by Cosway at Strawberry Hill, taken evidently at an early age, and of exquisite grace and beauty. She is painted leaning on the pedestal of a bust she had just completed, with the chisel in one, and the mallet in the other hand, and the face, less arch than in the other portrait, here displays more genius and more depth. She is described as gay and witty in society, and, unlike women in general, holding opinions formed by herself on her own view of matters.

Well-read and observant, this charming girl might have been contented with shining in the society of men and women, whose names have even come down to us, though celebrated for nothing but their social successes, if she had had the ordinary ambition of a woman; but being "dared" by Hume to produce a model equal to those she had seen, she gave up the amusement of society, and, locking herself in her own room, prepared to astonish the philosopher. Wax and modeling pencils she of course procured, and, with a large mob-cap over her fair hair and an apron to protect her dress, she worked away till she could present Hume with a head, said to be a portrait of the historian himself.

Always sparing of his praise, and the more so, perhaps, in this instance because the young lady was an arrant Whig, Hume merely remarked that the work was clever for a first attempt, but that it was one thing to work in soft material, and quite another to handle the chisel, and in this he was right. Little or no instruction will enable an observant and ingenious person to model in wax or clay. The potters of Staffordshire, who produce those exquisite marvels in Parian for which Minton is so celebrated, are often self-taught, modeling the clay while soft. But to handle the chisel and mallet with delicacy and finish is only the result of long labor and good primary instruction. Still, Miss Conway, having argued with Hume as to the supposed difficulty of carving, resolved to test it, and in the same private manner procured marble and tools and set to work. In a short time a rough copy of the modeled head appeared in stone from the same long delicate hand, and Hume could no longer withhold either praise or astonishment. He was justly surprised at the energy which undertook, and the talent which completed, an achievement in an art rarely followed by women, and demanding actual manual labor as well as skill.

This first attempt was probably nothing very wonderful; but Miss Conway in making it contracted a taste for sculpture, in which, with her usual energy and perseverance, she determined to excel. As she had ample means at her command, she could procure the best instruction. Cerrachi, who was afterward, in 1802, guillotined for plotting against the life of Napoleon, gave her lessons in modeling; John Bacon, then a young man just coming into fashion as a sculptor, but afterward celebrated for his monument to Lord Chatham in Westminster Abbey, taught her how to use the chisel, and she learned from Cruikshank sufficient anatomy to assist her in drawing her figures.

It was certainly fortunate that Anne Conway thus attached herself to the pursuit of art, for other ties which she now formed turned out far less satisfactorily. The Hon. John Damer, whom she accepted and married in June, 1767, when at the age of nineteen, was the eldest son of the first Lord Milton, and nephew to George, Earl of Dorchester. He was the heir expectant to a fortune of not less than £30,000 a year, and was bent upon squandering it before it came to him. He was one of a wild foolish set in town, whose whole glory was comprised in the curl of a coat collar and the brim of a hat, and who made up for want of wit by extravagant display and ridiculous eccentricity. His chief delight seems to have been to astonish his friends and annoy his amiable wife by appearing three times a day in a new suit. Such folly could only end in ruin. He had the common recourse of spendthrifts, and borrowed largely from the Jews. His wife appears to have borne with his folly, but to the dissipation of all affection toward him, and it is even said that they were at one time separated. However this may be, he went from bad to worse, and ended by blowing his brains out in August, 1776, at the Bedford Arms, Covent Garden, having collected a wardrobe which sold for £15,000, and left behind him a character for folly and recklessness of the most contemptible kind.

Mrs. Damer, a widow, and without children, turned her attention now to the one object which interested her—Art. Young and beautiful as she still was, she seems to have had no thought of making a second marriage. With a view of studying the best models and obtaining the best instruction she traveled through France, Spain, and Italy, and now produced a number of works, which Walpole, with a pardonable partiality for his fair cousin, declared to be equal to the antique. They consisted chiefly of groups of animals and busts, among which was one of herself, carved in 1778, and presented to the gallery at Florence. Cerrachi, her master, took a whole-length of her as the Muse of Sculpture. It has been doubted whether Mrs. Damer did not receive great assistance in these works from her masters and her artist friends; but it is certain that even at this period she had achieved a reputation, enhanced, perhaps, by the peculiarity of a woman devoting herself to such a pursuit, and that woman, too, one of noble family. Darwin, though probably not much of a judge of art, yet gives the common public estimate of her powers when he writes of her:

"Long with soft touch shall Damer's chisel charm,
With grace delight us and with beauty warm;
Forster's fine form shall hearts unborn engage,
And Melbourne's smile enchant another age;"

referring to the busts of Viscountess Melbourne at Pansanger, and of the Duchess of Devonshire.

In every thing which Mrs. Damer undertook we find an amount of daring and spirit which is quite unusual in ordinary women. Her first journey to the Continent afforded an instance of this. The War of Independence was at its height, and the Channel especially was filled with French and American men-of-war. It was really dangerous, as the event showed, to run the gauntlet of these enemies. The packet in which she sailed for Ostend was challenged by a French man-of-war, which it was quite unfitted to engage, yet could not escape. A sailing-match began, enlivened with a brisk exchange of shot, and Mrs. Damer, undaunted as ever, was delighted at an opportunity so rare to women of enjoying the awful excitement of battle. The fight lasted for four hours, ending in the victory of the French, and within sight of Ostend the English packet struck its colors, and its sailors and passengers surrendered themselves prisoners. A more romantic page might now have to be added to the biography of a Queen of Society, but for the gallantry of the French. "La belle Anglaise," who was only in her thirty-first year, and therefore young enough to be still much admired, was liberated, and allowed to proceed on her journey.

As the companions of her studies among the galleries and antiquities of a classic land, she wisely took up classic authors. Homer, Herodotus, Demosthenes, Plutarch, Livy, Virgil, and Cicero, were not too dull nor too hard reading for this spirited woman; and on the margins of these books she wrote her own impressions—rather learned than original—of what she saw. She was certainly an uncommon instance of feminine ambition. The same energy, which had roused her to prove to Hume of what metal she was made, was drawn upon in all that she undertook, supplied her with perseverance to carry out her less extravagant ambitions, and self-reliance sufficient to form others which were utterly unattainable. She certainly conceived that a great name and even great work might be achieved by a woman who despised to be distinguished by her noble descent, and she lost no opportunity of warming and exercising her enthusiasm. This spirit made a very active Whig of her. Progressive in her own life, and in her actions indifferent to the common restraints imposed on woman by the fancies of society, it was no wonder that she should be democratic in her political tendencies. Those were days when party meant something, and politics ran so high throughout the land that women of all classes, from the fruit-seller to the duchess, took an active, vehement part in them. Mrs. Damer, following the example of the beautiful Duchess of Devonshire, of Lady Duncannon, and Mrs. Crewe, was a violent partisan of Charles James Fox, a well-wisher of American independence, and even an admirer of the first French Revolution and the general spirit of popular government.

Whiggism, indeed, meant little less than this at that period. Fox himself declared in favor of the principle of revolution, and the right of the people to choose their own rulers. With a father who had made an enormous fortune with little principle out of a public office—for Lord Holland owed the bulk of his wealth to his appointment of paymaster to the forces—and who spoiled him in his boyhood, Charles James Fox had begun life as a fop of the first water, and squandered £50,000 in debt before he came of age. In succession he indulged recklessly and extravagantly in every course of licentiousness which the profligate society of the day opened to him. At Brookes's and the Thatched House he ate and drank to excess, threw thousands upon the faro-table, mingled with blacklegs, and made himself notorious for his shameless vices. Newmarket supplied another excitement. His back room was so incessantly filled with Jew money-lenders that he called it his Jerusalem Chamber. It was impossible that such a life should not destroy every principle of honor; and there is nothing improbable in the story that he appropriated to himself money which belonged to his dear friend Mrs. Crewe. Of his talents, which were certainly great, he made an affected display; of his learning he was proud, but rather as adding lustre to his celebrity for universal tastes. He was not at all ashamed, but rather gloried in being able to describe himself as a fool, as he does in his verses to Mrs. Crewe.

> "Is't reason? No; that my whole life will belie:
> For who so at variance as reason and I?
> Is't ambition that fills up each chink in my heart,
> Nor allows any softer sensation a part?
> Oh! no; for in this all the world must agree,
> One folly was never sufficient for me."

Sensual and self-indulgent, with a grossness that is even patent on his very portrait, Fox had nevertheless a manner which enchanted the sex; and he was the only politician of the day who thoroughly enlisted the personal sympathies of women of mind and character, as well as of those who might be captivated by his profusion. When he visited Paris in later days, even Madame Récamier, noted for her refinement, and of whom he himself said, with his usual coarse ideas of the sphere of woman, that "she was the only woman who united the attractions of pleasure to those of modesty," delighted to be seen with him. At the time of which we are speaking the most celebrated beauties of England were his most ardent supporters.

The election of 1784, in which Fox stood and was returned for Westminster, was one of the most famous of the old riotous political demonstrations. Fox, inclined by character and education to despotic institutions, had taken up with the democratic cry chiefly from pique. George III., the most respectable of the Hanoverian sovereigns, had always disapproved of him. Fox could never push his way to the ministerial benches, but he could be grand and terrible in the Opposition. Loving hazard of all kinds for its own sake, he had made party hostility a new sphere of gambling, had adopted the character of a demagogue, and at a time when the whole of Europe was undergoing a great revolution in principles, was welcomed gladly as "the man of the people." In the beginning of the year he had been convicted of bribery, but in spite of this his popularity increased. In the House, the Opposition had always the majority, yet the ministry remained in, till, unable to hold out any longer, the king dissolved the Parliament. The general election that ensued was one of the most exciting in a country which has few other excitements than elections to work off the enthusiasm of the populace.

The election for Westminster, in which Fox was opposed by Sir Cecil Wray, was the most tempestuous of all. There were twenty thousand votes to be polled, and the opposing parties resorted to any means of intimidation, or violence, or persuasion which political enthusiasm could suggest. On the eighth day the poll was against the popular member, and he called upon his friends to make a great effort on his behalf. It was then that the "ladies' canvass" began. Lady Duncannon, the Duchess of Devonshire, Mrs. Crewe, and Mrs. Damer dressed themselves in blue and buff—the colors of the American Independents, which Fox had adopted and wore in the House of Commons—and set out to visit the purlieus of Westminster. Here in their enthusiasm they shook the dirty hands of honest workmen, expressed the greatest interest in their wives and families, and even, as in the case of the Duchess of Devonshire and the butcher, submitted their fair cheeks to be kissed by the possessors of votes. Owing to their activity and zeal, the election, after lasting forty-seven days, terminated in favor of Fox, who came in by two hundred and thirty-five votes. From this period Fox became Mrs. Damer's idol, and she afterward induced him to sit to her for his bust.

Mrs. Damer was now thirty-six years of age, and though not so beautiful as the Duchess of Devonshire, and other leaders of society of that day, she seems to have been sought after in the highest circles of the London world for the sake of her talents and her engaging wit. Three years later, in 1787, we find her displaying her powers on a new stage. Amateur theatricals had then come much into fashion, and among their chief patrons was the Duke of Richmond, the friend of Pitt. In the performances which took place at his house, Mrs. Damer was the chief actress, and excited great admiration in the characters of Violante in "The Wonder," Mrs. Lovemore in "The Way to Keep Him," and Lady Freelove in "The Jealous Wife." She is described as "the Thalia of the scene;" and certainly her beaming face was well suited to the demands of comedy at a period when it had not degenerated into farce. This taste and talent for acting she preserved throughout life, and revived in after years at Strawberry Hill, with Siddons and Mrs. Garrick to assist her. But the theatricals at Richmond House were attended by all the "great" of London, who were admitted by cards, on which, to prevent confusion, was the notice "None to be admitted after half an hour past seven." An anecdote is told of Pitt and Fox apropos of this limitation. Pitt had received a card from the duke for the evening on which he was to open the budget, the 20th April, 1787, and knowing that he should be late, wished to return it; but the duke assured him that he should form an exception, and be admitted when he pleased. Fox, who was invited also, heard of this and put off going till the end of the debate, when, following Pitt closely, he arrived at the door of the great saloon at the same time with his opponent. The doorkeeper, who admitted the constitutional leader, wished to exclude the man of the people on the plea that it was half past seven. "Pooh, pooh!" said Fox, "I know that, but to-night I am a 'rider' on Mr. Pitt."

During the next ten years Mrs. Damer continued to shine in society and in sculpture at the same time. Busts from life and imaginary heads were her chief subjects. Among these, the best were one of Sir Joseph Banks and a head of Thalia, both in the British Museum; two colossal heads, supposed to represent the river-gods Thames and Isis, fixed on the middle of the bridge at Henley; and a marble statue of George III. for the Register Office at Edinburgh.

Walpole praises these works highly; but as we have had no opportunity of seeing them, we can not say with how much justice. Perhaps he meant only to turn a pretty compliment, and try how the name of an English lady would fit into a Latin pentameter, when he wrote

"Non me Praxiteles fecit, at Anna Damer,"
("Not me, Praxiteles', but Damer's hand hath formed),"

under an osprey which she modeled for him, and which he set up among the relics which he enshrined at Strawberry Hill, and worshiped, or pretended to worship, as devotedly as ever Romanist worshiped the great toe of a defunct saint. That Walpole, however, whether calculated to judge—which he ought to have been—of statuary, or influenced by other causes, did indeed think very highly of his connection's talents, we know from what he wrote in 1780. "Mrs. Damer's busts are not inferior to the antique; and theirs, we are sure, were not more like. Her shock dog, large as life, and only not alive, has looseness and softness in the curls, that seemed impossible to terra-cotta; it rivals the marble one of Bernini in the royal collection. As the ancients have only left us but five animals of equal merit with their human figures—namely, the Barberini goat, the Tuscan boar, the Mattei eagle, the eagle at Strawberry Hill, and Mr. Jennings', now Mr. Duncombe's dog, the talent of Mrs. Damer must appear in the most distinguished light."

But there were certainly other reasons for Walpole's partiality. In the first place, Mrs. Damer was his connection by marriage. His father, Sir Robert Walpole, the celebrated minister of George I. and George II., and her grandfather, Lord Conway, had married two sisters, the daughters of the wealthy Sir John Shorter, Lord-mayor of London. In the next place, he was a friend and warm admirer of her father, General Conway, whom Mrs. Damer, with her usual enthusiasm, was wont to magnify into a hero. The general had been certainly a very distinguished man. In 1761 he had shown bravery and skill in the command of the British forces in Germany under Prince Ferdinand of Brunswick. He was afterward a groom of the bedchamber; but in 1764 was dismissed from that office and his military commands for voting according to his conscience, and against the ministry, on the question of general warrants. Yet in the following year he was made a secretary of state, and in this capacity distinguished himself on the great American question by his exertions to conciliate the feelings of the nation toward the Americans. Burke afterward described this effort of the general's in glowing terms, and spoke of the trading interest of the country "clinging about him as captives about their redeemer." It was while holding this office that the general made David Hume his under-secretary at the instance of his brother, Lord Hertford, whose secretary the historian had been in his embassy at Paris. It was then that the intimacy commenced between Hume and the general's young daughter, then a girl of eighteen. Mrs. Damer intended to have made a statue of her father and to have published his correspondence, but the one was never begun, and the general's valuable letters were destroyed after her death.

Among others whose faces Mrs. Damer's enthusiastic admiration made her anxious to perpetuate in marble were the two most celebrated men of her day, with whom she was acquainted—Lord Nelson and Napoleon Bonaparte. The former sat to her after his return from the Nile; and of her conversations with the hero of Trafalgar she had some idea of forming a little volume. The bust she carved of him is the one which now stands in the Common Council Room of the City of London. A few days before her death, this active little woman, then seventy-eight years of age, made a copy of this bust in bronze, at the wish of the Duke of Clarence.

Of Napoleon she never had an opportunity of copying the stern, strong-willed features, though he promised to sit to her. Her acquaintance with him was formed in a singular manner. During her first visit to Paris in 1779, she had been introduced to the beautiful and witty Josephine Beauharnais, then a leader of fashion in that city, and their acquaintance had ripened into friendship. She returned, however, to England, and heard nothing more of her old friend, until one day a French gentleman called upon her, and presented her with a fine piece of porcelain, and a letter of invitation from the wife of the first consul, whom she now discovered to be her former friend. Napoleon was always willing and anxious to conciliate the Whigs of England; and it can be easily understood that Josephine found it convenient to recall in this manner a forgotten friendship. After the peace of Amiens, Mrs. Damer set out to Paris, and was presented to the great man, who charmed her with his conversation. She was known to be a friend and warm supporter of Charles Fox, and the first consul expressed his anxiety to have from her hand a bust of the "Man of the People," and to make a present of his own to Fox himself. The former bust Mr. Damer afterward executed, and in later years, when poor Josephine was sacrificed and supplanted, she carried it to Paris and presented it to the emperor. Napoleon, touched perhaps at the sight of a face which recalled happier days, received her with kindness, and gave her his portrait set in diamonds upon a gold snuff-box, which is now in the British Museum.

Other samples of her art are to be found in different parts of England, especially in the houses of her friends, to whom she presented them. Among these were three busts of Mrs. Siddons and the two Kembles at Guy's Cliff, near Warwick. This interesting old place, which takes its name from the cave which Guy, Earl of Warwick, dug out for himself to play hermit in, was at that time in the possession of a wealthy and influential family of the name of Greatheed. Mr. Greatheed was the friend and associate of all the great men and women of his day, and Anne Damer was a frequent visitor at Guy's Cliff.

Those who remember the sale at Strawberry Hill will be able to recall others of her works, and this leads me to speak of her intimacy with its presiding spirit, Horace Walpole. The old age of that little-great man is not one to be despised. Gossip as he was, and trifler as he was, there are points in Walpole's character that command our respect. There is in all his writings, whether memoirs or letters, a spirit of independence and a breadth of view which rarely accompany a taste for archæology, the most conservative of all sciences. He was not a servile though an enthusiastic admirer; he was not a prejudiced though a bitter enemy. His love of art was sincere, and in the present day his archæological tastes would have taken a much wider range, and probably have made of him a man of science. But it is in the constancy of his private friendships that he is most to be admired as a man. Old bachelor as he was, he had still a geniality about him that endeared him to all his friends. It is not surprising that the invalid should have enjoyed most the society of intellectual women; for Walpole was the most refined man of his day, and it was in the women of those days that all the refinement was to be found. We have only to read the private lives of the great men of the last century to see that his almost feminine tastes were quite excusable. That refinement which he cherished was rarely at that time an accompaniment of great intellectual powers in the stronger sex. Strawberry Hill was an abortion of architecture, though not worse than many more celebrated attempts of the last century, and indeed of the present, also, to revive the beauties of Gothic; but it was admirably adapted for the calm winter of such a life as Walpole's. The village of Twickenham, uninvaded at that time by a railway, sat calmly on the banks of a lovely river, which as yet knew nothing of excursion-steamers or London cockneys plying their sculls in bright aquatic costume. At most a quiet barge, noiselessly floating down the stream, raised a ripple on its broad, full waters. In the village itself were stately mansions, surrounded by jealous walls and glorious trees. It had an air of exclusive calm, a purity and peacefulness pleasantly contrasted with the bustle and business of London, from which it was at an easy distance. The old gentleman, printing his own works at a private press with his own hand, looked calmly down on the exciting life of the metropolis, in which he now took so little part, and was able to form a cool judgment of what there passed. In every room he had arranged with taste the relics that he had gathered in many years from the nooks and corners of Europe. The trifling objects which raised a smile on the lips of the modern purchaser some years ago had all a meaning and a history for him. They reminded him of those whom he had most admired during his life, and admiration with Walpole often rose to affection. Here, too, he assembled the small knot of friends whom he really liked, and chief among these were the Miss Berrys and Mrs. Damer. The latter was no longer young, but his junior by many years, and though nearly fifty years of age, she had still all the *verve* and liveliness of five-and-twenty. She was as indefatigable as ever in her sculpture and modeling, and as charming as ever in her conversation. She had none of the cumbrous dignity of a dowager, but loved and delighted in every kind of amusement that offered itself. As he knew so well her taste for art and her respect for antiquities, to which was added a certain archæological acquaintance with them, picked up during her travels, it was only natural that Horace Walpole should have selected her the guardian after his death of the treasures of Strawberry Hill. He left the house and all it contained to her for life, with two thousand a year to keep it up, on condition that she should live there and maintain the dignity of his temple.

In 1797, therefore, on the death of Walpole, Mrs. Damer took possession of Strawberry Hill. Here she collected around her the friends she admired and loved most, and from time to time amused them with private theatricals of a very superior order. Among the pieces selected was one called "Fashionable Friends," a satirical comedy, at one time attributed to the former owner of Strawberry Hill himself. In this Mrs. Damer took the part of Lady Selina Vapor; and whether her acting, which is said to have been admirable, enhanced the amusement of the piece, or the piece itself was really worth the honor, it was thought good enough to appear on the boards of Drury Lane: here, however, the public condemned, and Kemble was forced to withdraw it.

For more than twenty years Mrs. Damer reigned at Strawberry Hill. True to her old plebeian tastes (we use the word in a sense of praise) she would not surround herself only with those aristocratic acquaintance whom she possessed in virtue of her birth, connections, and position, but preferred talent to the last. Her chief friends were the Miss Berrys and Mrs. Garrick, the charming widow of the great actor. This lady had been an opera-dancer at Vienna. In 1744, at the age of nineteen, she came to London, and was taken up very kindly by the Countess of Burlington. On her marriage the earl made her a present of six thousand pounds. "I think," says Dr. Beattie, "I never saw such perfect affection and harmony as subsisted between them" (Garrick and his wife). In 1779 the immortal David died. "No words," continues the same writer, "can paint her woe; and it would be difficult to do justice to the piety, resignation, and dignity of her behavior on this sad occasion." Certainly, too, she must have derived from her husband one of his charms in a social point of view, and the man who was unrivaled in spirited conversation must have imparted some of the same power to his wife. She talked English well, but with a German accent. Miss Burney relates a conversation with her at Mrs. Ord's: Mrs. Garrick was very cordial to the author of "Evelina." "'Do I see you once more before I *tie*, my *tear* little spark!' she exclaimed, embracing me warmly, 'for your father is my flame all my life, and you are a little spark of that flame.' She added how much she had wished to visit me at the queen's house, when she found I no longer came about the world, but that she was too *tiscreet*, and I did not dare say 'Do come,' unauthorized."

Another intimate and particular friend of Mrs. Damer was the great Siddons. And here we may remark that if Mrs. Damer disregarded rank, she was not blinded by talent and merit to moral character, for as to Fox, her admiration was of his political, not his private character. Mrs. Siddons, though an actress, was always irreproachable, and Mrs. Damer could well make her her friend. "In a private company," says Beattie, "Mrs. Siddons is a modest, unassuming, sensible woman, of the gentlest and most elegant manners. Her moral character is not only unblemished but exemplary. She is above the middle size, and I suppose about thirty-four years of age" (this was in 1784). "Her countenance is the most interesting that can be, and, excepting the Duchess of Gordon's, the most beautiful I have ever seen. Her eyes and eyebrows are of the deepest black. She loves music, and is fond of the Scotch tunes, many of which I played to her on the violoncello. One of them ('She rose and let me in,' which you know is a favorite of mine) made the tears start from her eyes. 'Go on,' said she to me, 'and you will soon have your revenge,' meaning that I should draw as many tears from her as she had done from me."

The poetess Joanna Baillie was another of the circle at Strawberry Hill during Mrs. Damer's reign. This lady, herself a writer of tragedies, which, if never acted, still do credit to her good intentions, joined eagerly in the theatricals which Mrs. Damer instituted. In an epilogue which she wrote for one of these performances, she speaks thus of the Gothic villa:

"But in these walls, a once well-known retreat,
Where taste and learning kept a fav'rite seat—
Where Gothic arches, with a solemn shade,
Should o'er the thoughtful mind their influence spread—
Where pictures, vases, busts, and precious things,
Still speak of sages, poets, heroes, kings—
Like foolish children in their mimic play
Confined at grandam's on a rainy day,
With paltry farce and all its bastard train,
Grotesque and broad, such precincts to profane!"

With such and many other intimates of both sexes, Mrs. Damer kept alive the glories of Walpole's "favorite seat." But in 1818 she was persuaded that it would be better to give it up to Lord Waldegrave, on whom it was entailed. She then bought York House, in the same district. Here Clarendon had lived, and here Queen Anne had been born, and it was no great descent from the dignity of the old house to shelter Mrs. Damer and her sculptures.

Though she was now seventy years of age, Mrs. Damer's ambition and enthusiasm were far from being worn out. On the contrary, they seem to have grown with years. Active and energetic to the last, she now contemplated some great work which should raise her name high in the annals of civilization as well as of art. Her relative, Sir Alexander Johnson, held a high legal appointment in the island of Ceylon. On his return to England she conversed with him eagerly about the state of art in the East. From him she learned what influence the wretched images of Krishna, Buddha, Ganesha, and other Hindoo deities, have over the minds of their worshipers. She conceived the idea that by introducing European works of art into India it would be possible to turn this influence to a good account—to replace, in short, the gods of the East by the heroes of Europe. Though this project has been laughed at as Utopian, it is a proof of the far-sightedness of this ambitious woman. Those who know India well, know the place that European art now takes among the educated Hindoos of the three capitals, and are aware how much it is prized. The Rajah of Tanjore, the pupil of Swartz, was at that time engaged in introducing western civilization into his dominions. Mrs. Damer thought to aid him in this excellent design, and sent him a bust of Nelson as a preliminary to her great project. Probably she over-estimated her powers. It was scarcely probable that at her age she could produce works enough, whether good or bad—they would at least be better than common Hindoo art—to effect any great change in the tastes of the natives of India; but we can not but admire the zealous and well-directed ambition of a woman of more than seventy years, who sets to work on such a principle. We can not but hold her up as a fine example to those ladies who long before that age consider their lives as unfit for exertion, and are content to settle down into useless and complaining valetudinarians. With most heroes and heroines it is youth that is appealed to in many a brilliant example, but here we have something for age as well. As Socrates and Cato knew, we are never too old to learn: we are not too old in old age, but too proud: we have passed through the whole experience of life, and believe that, well or ill, we have fulfilled our vocation. Too often this is an idle boast. Mrs. Damer is a proof that we are never too old to aspire. She aspired to civilize India with works from her own hand: she might perhaps have done so, but death cut her off.

We may here introduce an anecdote of the Sir Alexander Johnson of whom we have spoken. We borrow it from Cunningham's "Lives of the Sculptors," in every respect a charming work.

Lord Castlereagh had promised to make Sir Alexander Chief Justice and President of Ceylon: on hearing which, Mrs. Damer, a Whig to the last, exclaimed, "The fellow will cheat you; he is a Tory." "Soon afterward Lord Castlereagh sent express to Sir Alexander, had his commission drawn out, saw the great seal affixed, shook him by the hand, and wished him joy. This was late at night: on the following morning he fought the duel with Canning. Sir Alexander waited on him, when Lord Castlereagh said with a smile, 'You are come to congratulate me on my escape.' 'Yes,' said Sir Alexander, 'and to say that I can not help marveling at your fortitude last night. Who but yourself could have transacted business?' 'Oh, I had a reason for it,' said his lordship; 'had I fallen before the great seal was set to your commission, you would have lost the appointment, and my cousin' (Mrs. Damer) 'would have said, "The fellow, sir, was a cheat; he was a Tory." When Mrs. Damer heard this the tears started in her eyes. 'Go,' she said, 'to my cousin, and say I have wronged him, that I love his manliness, and his regard for honor, and that I wish to renew our intercourse of friendship.'"

Toward her eightieth year Mrs. Damer began to fail in health, and on the 28th of May, 1828, she left her ambitions, her sculptures, and her friends forever, and passed into another life. True to the last to her art, she ordered that her hammers, chisels, drills, and modeling tools should be buried with her in the same coffin. Most unfortunately for posterity she added to this order that her papers should all be burned. There were among them several letters from Horace Walpole, and others as eminent in their day, the loss of which is a great pang to biographers. Perhaps to the last she was afraid of any slur upon her fame as a sculptress, for among her papers were her memoranda upon art, and with these, it may be, she was not satisfied.

Mrs. Damer's is a pleasant life to look back to. In moral character she was irreproachable. In disposition she was fascinating. Her early life, when wedded to a dissolute and ridiculous husband, was not without its thorns; but from the date of his death she seems to have lived in the sunshine of her own making. She was always gay and lively. She was active and energetic to the day of her death. Her ambition was of a kind very rare to women. It was, indeed, worthy of a man. She is one of the few women in the history of the world who have taken up the hammer and chisel, and her success in wielding them is not despicable. Her works are always rough and unfinished. Delicate-handed herself, she imparted little delicacy to her labors. She aspired to masculinity, and seems to have aimed at it even in the roughness of her productions. But she was an ambitious woman, ambitious as few women ever are, and in her ambition, extravagant as it sometimes was, we see a heroism which we may not disregard. We are not inclined to set it down to mere vanity. The only child of so able and honorable a man as General Conway may well be understood to have been inspired by the highest motives, and her early success will excuse what seems undue confidence in her own powers. The intimate friend and ardent admirer of the greatest men of her day may well have felt a craving to be great too in the only sphere that opened to her. It is not indeed the part or even the right of all women to be ambitious. Domestic ties certainly claim the first place; but Mrs. Damer had none of these. Her parents and husband were taken from her while she was yet in the bloom of life, and she had no children. Whatever her place in art, her stand in society was high and excellent. Free and bold in all her opinions, she did not avail herself of the mere privilege of birth and rank, but aspired to assert only her merit, and to encourage that of others. She chose her friends for their talents and character. She was free from pride or obtrusive vanity, and to the last a charming and lively companion. Her society was sought, and her conversation prized by great men; indeed, some of the greatest of her day. She seems to have been free from "envy, hatred, malice, and all uncharitableness," except in the one matter of political party. She could neither trust nor forgive a Tory. On the whole, she is a woman to be admired, and may certainly be held up as a model of energy, activity, and perseverance to all languid ladies who happen to have no "encumbrances."

LA MARQUISE DU DEFFAND.

The lives that we have hitherto set before the reader have been examples, some of virtue, some of energy, some of amiability: in some the social, in others the domestic virtues have been the best points in the characters of the women of whom we have written. All, at least, however frivolous, vain, fond of admiration, or even guilty of the grosser sins, have had some if not many a redeeming point. The life we now write is a *warning*. Madame du Deffand had no redeeming points in her character. Bad-hearted, a bad friend, bad in habits, in morals, even at times in manners, she owed the wonderful empire she possessed solely to her wit. Her life is not only a warning, but perhaps the strongest warning which can be given in this world. Madame du Deffand had no fear of future punishment; she was tried by present calamities. They had no effect on her; she continued her evil indulgences; she was hopeless. And where is the warning? Where was her punishment? *In her own mind.* Never was woman more wretched in her later days; never did conscience pursue a sinner more relentlessly; never was life more hated by its owner. And to modify this misery there was no hope of a future life—of forgiveness at last. No, as if she were not bad enough in every way, Madame du Duffand added the last sin of denying that God whom she had so long and obstinately offended.

Yet this woman was the idol of Walpole, and the intimate of Voltaire, D'Alembert, and many other celebrated men. That they were neither shocked nor disgusted must be referred to the state of the times. Madame du Deffand was a very bad woman, but almost good compared with some of her celebrated contemporaries. No one of any rank, but especially of the higher classes, could in that day cast a stone at her. France has displayed many phases of wickedness in her society, but perhaps she out-Franced herself in the reign of Louis XV.

Any history of the society of that time must necessarily be one of extortion and tyranny on the one hand, and disgraceful intrigues, dignified with the name of "friendships," on the other. To follow Madame du Deffand or any other Frenchwoman of the age through their lives would be simply to retail a list of immoral connections; and we must therefore be content to view her only from a social point, content to show how great was the influence of mind over great men and even great acts.

Madame du Deffand was the daughter of Comte de Vichy Chamrond, or Champrond, as it was also written. She was born in 1697; she was christened Marie, as are perhaps nine tenths of the women of France. Of her relations the following are named: her father was Comte Gaspard de Vichy, of very old and noble family; her mother Mademoiselle Anne Brulart, before her marriage; her eldest brother served for some four years in the French army, and then settled on his estate in Burgundy; a younger brother, the Abbé de Chamrond, became treasurer to the Sainte Chapelle at Paris, and lived at Montrouge in the neighborhood of that city: the Duchesse de Luynes was her aunt, and she had even a cardinal among her relatives, to wit, the celebrated Archbishop of Toulouse, Brienne de Loménie, whom the Parisians, perhaps with good cause, nicknamed *Le Cardinal de l'ignominie.* Lastly, her grandmother was a Choiseul; and when, in after years, Madame du Deffand became very intimate with the Duc and Duchesse of that name, she used to call them her relations, and even her grandpapa and grandmamma, by way of endearment.

The education of Mademoiselle de Chamrond was as bad as that of most French girls of that—perhaps even of this—day. The art of pleasing, which certainly made society very agreeable, was the main study with these demoiselles, if, indeed, not the sole one. Marie was sent to a convent, that of La Madeleine de Trenelle, in the Rue de Charonne at Paris, and the only story of her education is that related by Walpole, namely, that she had, even at that age, doubts upon religion, became in heart and mind a skeptic, and thus induced her relations to send to her the famous Massillon to talk to her. "She was not awed by his character, nor dazzled by his arguments" (writes Walpole), "but defended herself with good sense, and the prelate was more struck by her ingenuity and beauty than shocked at her heresy."

We are not inclined to think that these doubts were maintained in a true spirit of inquiry, such as Madame Roland brought to bear on the question of religion. The same scoffing spirit with which she afterward professed to treat "the philosophers," when offended with D'Alembert, must have given her the first inclination to sneer at religion. She declared a hatred and contempt for the clergy, at which, considering the condition of the Romish Church in that day, we can not be surprised.

At the convent, too, she had probably been introduced "behind the scenes" of so-called "religious" display; and last, but by no means least, to Madame du Deffand, it was the *fashion* to be a skeptic. The wits and thinkers both in England and France laughed at the established faith, and it was therefore a claim to superiority of intellect to be an infidel. Voltaire had turned revelation into ridicule, and Rousseau, in its place, had inaugurated a poetical and most attractive Deism, of which it has been said that "it was Christianity without Christ." Thus it was very natural that Madame du Deffand should have asserted herself an atheist. Probably she remained so in heart all her life, whatever she may have seemed to be. She did, indeed, make one attempt to turn *dévote*, but retreated hastily from it in disgust. As to the sincerity of even this movement we can judge from the fact that, in agreeing to give up the world and her indulgences, she made an exception for "*rouge* and the President Hénault," as indispensable to her comfort.

At the age of twenty-one her father—for her mother was dead—married her to Jean-Baptiste-Jacques du Deffand, Marquis de Lalande, a colonel of a regiment of dragoons, a man of excellent family, whose ancestors had distinguished themselves by their attachment to the dukes of Burgundy, and, we are told, a man of "weak character and a tiresome companion." There is no likelihood that there was, either before or after marriage, the slightest affection between these two. That was an age of bad fashions, and Madame du Deffand seems to have been bent on following the worst of them. It was the fashion, besides being immoral and unbelieving, to separate as soon as possible from your husband. "What has become, madame, of that poor little man I used so often to meet here, and who never opened his mouth?" "Oh, that was my husband; he is dead." This was an actual conversation of the day. Madame du Deffand could not, of course, make herself appear singular, and on the principle—often a very convenient one—of doing at Rome what the Romans do, she managed ere long to relieve herself of the disagreeable encumbrance. As the unfortunate young man is only a cipher in her existence, and will not appear again upon the scene, we may as well at once dispose of him. He lived chiefly with his father in the country, and did not interfere with his wife in any way. Some ten years later, however, she took it into her head to be again united to him. A fortune had been left her, and she had as yet no family to inherit it. She sent, therefore, for the gentleman whose name she bore; complacently enough he came at once; and for six weeks was allowed to take his meals at his wife's house. The sacrifice on her part must be considered a great one, for she actually gave up her *cicisbeo* in order to receive back her wedded mate. The lover was disgusted; and so, in fact, was Madame du Deffand. At the end of the six weeks she found that she could not put up with the marquis, though we are not told that he was any way offensive, except in the misfortune of being her husband. She showed him by her black looks that he bored her, and he had, at least, sense enough to perceive it, and return to his *chasse* in Burgundy. A letter from her friend, the unfortunate Madlle. d'Aïssé, will best describe the rest of the affair. "She takes every imaginable measure to prevent his returning. I have pointed out to her in strong terms the impropriety of her proceedings. She tried to touch me by plaints and pleadings; I was firm, and passed three weeks without seeing her; on which she came to me. There is no kind of ignominy to which she did not descend to induce me not to give her up. * * * She cried a great deal, but could not affect me. The end of this miserable line of conduct is, that she has no one to live with, and that a lover she had before trying to conciliate her husband has left her in disgust; and when he heard that she was getting on well with M. du Deffand wrote her a letter full of reproaches. He returned. Her *amour propre* having roused again the half-extinguished flame, this worthy lady again followed her inclination, and not reflecting upon her position, thought a lover was better than a husband, and dismissed the latter to make room for the former. The consequence is, that she is the talk of society; every body blames her, her lover despises her, her friends abandon her, and she is at a loss to get out of the scrape. She 'throws herself at one's head' in order to show that she is not cut, but without success; pride and confusion influence her by turns."

Doubtful as it is whether the writer of this letter blames her most for having taken back her husband or for having again dismissed him, it is a comfort, in reading it, to learn that her conduct reflected some public reproach upon her, and that the society of Paris—at least that in which Madlle d'Aïssé moved—was not blinded by her social talents to overlook her domestic vices.

We pass over with pleasure the long story of her various "friendships," but there is one which we can not avoid noticing. The President Hénault, of whom mention has already been made, was a standing dish with *La* du Deffand. The president was celebrated in his day, which, thank heaven, is over, for two things—his work called "L'Abrégé Chronologique de l'Histoire de France," and his cook. Voltaire wrote of him—

> "Hénault, fameux pour vos soupers
> Et votre Chronologie." . . .

Walpole thus describes him: "The old President Hénault is the pagod at Madame du Deffand's, an old blind debauchée of wit, where I supped last night" (such are the flattering terms in which this man of society described that woman of society, whom he afterward called his queen and his one idea). "The president is very near deaf, and much nearer superannuated. He sits by the table. The mistress of the house, who formerly" (this letter was written in 1765, when Madame du Deffand was sixty-eight years old) "was his, inquires after every dish on the table, is told who has eaten of which, and then bawls the bill of fare of every individual into the president's ears. In short, every mouthful is proclaimed, and so is every blunder I make against grammar. Some that I make on purpose succeed; and one of them is to be reported to the queen to-day by Hénault, who is her great favorite. I had been at Versailles, and having been much taken notice of by her majesty, I said, alluding to Madame Sévigné, 'La reine est le plus grand roi du monde.'"

Later Walpole says: "The old President Hénault made me a visit yesterday: he is extremely amiable, but has the appearance of a superannuated bacchanal; superannuated, poor soul, indeed he is!" "My press is revived, and is printing a French play written by the old President Hénault. It was damned many years ago at Paris, and yet I think it is better than some that have succeeded, and much better than any of *our* modern tragedies. I print it to please the old man, as he was exceedingly kind to me at Paris; but I doubt whether he will live till it is finished." The play in question was "Cornélie," and the author was at this time eighty-four years of age. He was thirteen years older than Madame du Deffand.

So much for the president; but it is always satisfactory to see people through their own admirers' eyes. Here are extracts from two portraits—the one written by Du Deffand of the president, the other written by the president of Du Deffand. Let us, however, first premise that portrait-writing was the fashion of the age; that it was used often as a means of flattering, oftener still to dissimulate real feelings toward an object; that these portraits were circulated in a certain set, in which both the object and artists were familiars, and that, necessarily, they were, to a certain extent, *varnished*, though with a great pretense of frankness.

Portrait of the President Hénault by Madame du Deffand.

"All the president's qualities, and even his defects, are in favor of society: his vanity gives him a great desire to please; his ease makes all characters his friends; and his weakness seems only to take from his virtues any wildness and boldness they may have in others.

"His feelings are delicate, but his mind is too ready to relieve, or even dispossess them; and as the heart rarely needs an interpreter, one might be sometimes tempted to believe that he only thinks what he pretends to feel; he seems to give the lie to La Rochefoucauld, and would perhaps make him say in the present day that the heart is often the dupe of the head.

"All combines to make him a most agreeable man of society; he pleases some by his good qualities, others by his very defects. He is impetuous in all his actions, his arguments, and his praises; he always seems to be touched to the quick by the sights he views and the subjects he treats; but he passes so rapidly from the greatest vehemence to the most complete indifference, that one can easily perceive that if his spirit is quickly, it is also seldom, affected. This impetuosity, which would be a defect in others, is almost a good quality in him; it gives all his actions an air of meaning and feeling very pleasing to the common herd; every one believes that he has lit up in him a warm interest; and he has gained as many friends by this characteristic as by his really estimable points. * * * Ambition and interest are unknown to him; softer passions move him. * * * He adds to a clever mind much grace and delicacy: he is the best company in the world." (This comes from Madame du Deffand remember.) "His conversation is full of neat and amusing turns, never degenerating into puns or personal remarks. He is rich in talents, and treats every subject with equal ability, whether serious or jocular. In fact, M. de Hénault is one of those men of the world who unite most discordant qualities, and whose mind and agreeableness are generally acknowledged."

Portrait of Madame du Deffand by M. le Président Hénault.

"Madame du Deffand lived at Sceaux, where she passed the greater part of the year. * * * In the winter she resided in a small house in the Rue de Beaune, seeing little society. The moment she was free" (to wit, had sent away her husband), "she made many acquaintances, and in a short time they had so increased that her rooms could not hold them. She gave a supper every evening; and afterward took an apartment in the Convent of Saint Joseph. Her means were increased by the death of her husband, and she had about twenty thousand livres per annum. No woman ever had more friends nor deserved them more. Friendship was with her a passion, in consideration of which you could pardon her extreme fastidiousness: the smallness of her means did not militate against her popularity; and she soon collected around her the best and most brilliant society, the members of which she made her slaves. A good heart, noble and generous, always employed in usefulness, a keen judgment, a pleasant fancy, and a gayety which imparted to her youth (I speak of her later years, for in earlier days she had been attractive in person), a cultivated mind, which did not obtrude itself at a time when she sought only to amuse herself: such were her characteristics. It is much to be desired that her writings should not be lost. Madame de Sévigné would not be the only woman to quote in that case. But who would believe it?—I speak of a blind woman. This misfortune altered neither her wit nor her temper. It might be said that sight was a superfluous sense for her; the sound of the voice sufficed to describe every object; and she was just as *à propos* as if she had had the use of her eyes. Still, not to appear prejudiced in her favor, I must own that age, while it did not destroy her talents, made her jealous and distrustful" (it is the president who says this), "and that she was influenced by first impressions, and had not the art of leading those of whom she had been accustomed to dispose summarily. In short, she had an unequal and virulent temper, though always charming to those whom she cared to please; and, I may say, was the person who has made me at once the happiest and the most unhappy man, for she is the woman I have most loved."

As a key to these two characters, we must cite the words of Marmontel, who asserts that "she played the tyrant over the President Hénault, who, timid by nature, remained the slave of fear when he had ceased to be the slave of love." He corresponded with her regularly whenever absent, which was not often. His letters do not show the same amount of talent as those of most of her correspondents, and are chiefly filled with gossip and details about common friends or common foes. The president doubtless knew that these details were precisely what Madame du Deffand liked most; for Walpole, in the commencement of his acquaintance with her, says that she was "delicious when he could take her fifty years back," but that she was as eager about the current gossip of her day as he himself was about that of a past generation.

The friendship with the president lasted in the firmest manner until his death. Another equally long was not on such affectionate terms. M. Pont de Veyle is thus described by Walpole: "She has an old friend whom I must mention, a Monsieur Pont de Veyle, author of the 'Fat Puni,' and the 'Complaisant,' and of those pretty novels, the 'Comte de Cominges,' the 'Siege of Calais,' and 'Les Malheurs de l'Amour.' Would

"'That may very possibly be the case, madame.'"

Nearly sixty years of Madame du Deffand's life had passed in the reckless pursuit of pleasure, in self-indulgence, and indifference to all the serious claims of this life and terrible prospects of the next, when the hand of God mercifully smote her in a manner which in any other woman would have produced a complete change, if not actual repentance. In 1752 her sight began to fail, and became so weak as to oblige her to employ an amanuensis. For two years it continued to grow worse and worse, and in 1754 she became totally blind. Voltaire speaks thus of the calamity: "What you tell me of Madame du Deffand's eyes gives me great pain. They were formerly very fine and very bright. Why must one always be punished in what one has sinned? and what a rage has Nature for destroying her own fairest works! At any rate, Madame du Deffand retains her wit, which is even more brilliant than her eyes." He also sent her the following pretty little poem, when his own sight began to give way:

"Oui, je perds les deux yeux; vous les avez perdus,
O sage du Deffand! est-ce une grande perte?
Du moins nous ne reverrons plus
Les sots dont la terre est couverte.
Et puis tout est aveugle en cet humain séjour;
On ne va qu'à tâtons sur la terre et sur l'onde;
On a les yeux bouchés à la ville, à la cour;
Plutus, la Fortune, et l'Amour
Sont trois aveugle-nés qui gouvernent le monde."

She appears to have borne the infliction with fortitude at first; but in later years, without the consolation of religion, or even of sensible pursuits, she murmured against this punishment, and felt how helpless it made her life, how completely it left her to the mercy of others, on whom she could not always depend. She managed, however, to make the loss as little felt as possible in society. She always turned her eyes (which remained closed) toward the person to whom she was speaking, and as, in these later years, her mode of life rarely altered, and even her friends and acquaintances were mostly the same, and regular in their daily visits, she became expert in the use of her ears—her sense of hearing being very keen—and was able to mix in the conversation without any marked difference from those who possessed the use of their eyes. In early youth she is described as beautiful, but we can find no traces of beauty in the portrait which was taken of her after her blindness. The features were small and neat, the complexion delicate, but that is all. The face is too long, and the expression, though mild, is by no means interesting.

Madame du Deffand's real life begins, however, at this period. This very infliction was softened to her, by bringing around her more closely all the great thinkers with whom she had before been acquainted, chiefly in virtue of her position among the aristocracy; for thinkers of those days always pressed forward, or were often sought for, into the upper circles of society, in which alone were to be found education and refinement. Indeed it seems to have been no crime to turn toad-eater; and Voltaire himself, the forerunner of a revolution against the aristocracy, was proud and delighted to be admitted into its coteries.

In "the blind old woman," still surrounded by adorers and admirers, the thinking men thought, truly enough, that there must be real wit to allure and keep the same friends in spite of her misfortune; and they were not mistaken. Madame du Deffand, bad in every other point, was as good as any of them in the head. Among these acquaintances, who now became friends, were Voltaire and D'Alembert. Both corresponded with her; and indeed the names of her correspondents would alone suffice as a proof of her popularity among the clever men of the day. Among others were Montesquieu, Madame de Staal, the companion of the Duchesse du Maine, the Chevalier d'Aydie, and the President Hénault. Besides Walpole, too, she had a number of English friends, such as Hume, Wilkes, George Selwyn, and Lords Bath, Bulkeley, and Holdernesse. But the name of D'Alembert introduces a celebrated quarrel, which almost sufficed to divide all these friends into two parties, according as they condemned or approved Madame du Deffand's conduct in the matter. Marmontel in his "Memoirs" does the former; Walpole, naturally, the latter. We confess that, from what we can learn of this lady's character, we are inclined to side with Marmontel.

The blindness with which she was inflicted induced Madame du Deffand to take to herself a companion and amanuensis in the person of Mademoiselle de l'Espinasse, who is celebrated for her letters, which have been published, and for her *liaison* with D'Alembert, which was also published. She was the natural daughter of Madame d'Albon, the mother of the Marquise de Vichy, and was born at Lyons in 1732. She was taken, after the death of her mother, into the house of the Marquis de Vichy, as governess to their children, and humble companion to themselves; but the manner in which they treated her was such as to induce her to leave them and retire to a convent, with no more than the sum of 300 francs (£12) a year, which her mother had left her. An agreeable trait in her character is related by Madame du Deffand herself. It appears that at her death Madame d'Albon had told her of this legacy, and, in addition, given her the key of a chest in which was a very considerable sum of money, which she had kept for her. Immediately after her mother's death, she went to M. d'Albon, the son, placed this key in his hands, and insisted that he should appropriate the contents of the chest, to which she maintained he had a better right than herself; and this generous offer he accepted. Madame du Deffand tried to persuade her to remain with the Vichys at Chamrond, but in vain, and she retired to the convent. After an affectionate correspondence of two years, in letters in which these ladies, after a fashion of the day, style one another "Ma Reine," Madame du Deffand proposed to take her as companion into her own house. The proposal was accepted, and for a while all went well, for the elder lady did not clash with the younger one, who, though only two-and-twenty, and very engaging in manners, was not pretty, and was pitted with the small-pox.

Madame du Deffand had at this time an apartment in the Convent of St. Joseph, in the Rue St. Dominique. This convent had been endowed by Madame de Montespan, who had taken care to have a portion of it separated from the main building in such a manner as to be entered through another court, in order to avoid the restrictions of the convent itself. Here the wretched mistress of Louis XIV. came from time to time during the great festivals of the Church, when it was advisable to have the appearance of penitence; and the character of its foundress made the convent a very suitable retreat for Madame du Deffand. It is curious how the gay Frenchwoman could without shame thus easily play the hypocrite. But in the case of Madame du Deffand, as more recently in that of Madame Récamier, who retired to a "cell" in the same way, and made the Abbaye-aux-Bois celebrated for its society, the motive was probably to save the expense of keeping up a more worldly establishment. Not only were the apartments belonging to the convent let at a cheaper rate than more fashionable ones could have been, but the show of retirement enabled the pretended recluse to adopt a simpler *ménage*, and dispense with carriages and servants.

Here, however, according to Marmontel, the habits of this recluse were the most unnatural and self-indulgent. She passed the night in entertaining her adorers, and the whole day in bed, rising only at six in the evening to receive her guests. Afflicted with sleeplessness, she had no mercy on her humble companion, and forced her to adopt the same mode of life. Thus after the guests were gone, and Madame du Deffand, at daybreak, retired to her bed, she obliged Mademoiselle de l'Espinasse, weary as she was, to read to her for hours. She appears to have treated her in every thing after the same fashion, consulting only her own comfort, and indifferent to that of her companion. Certainly her treatment must have been very bad, as at last Mademoiselle de l'Espinasse swallowed sixty grains of opium, in the hope of ridding herself of a life which was made so miserable. The dose had not the desired effect, though it made her very ill. La Harpe has said of Madame du Deffand, that "it were difficult to have less sensibility or more selfishness;" and as an instance of this, it is related that on the death of M. Pont de Veyle, who had, as we have seen, been her friend for fifty years, she went the same evening to a gay supper-party, and when asked after her friend, exclaimed, "Alas! he died at six this evening; otherwise, you would not have seen me here."

It is said again that on hearing of the death of Mademoiselle de l'Espinasse, she only remarked: "She might have died fifteen years sooner, and then I should not have lost D'Alembert." Even Walpole, who was so devoted to her, gives, involuntarily, little hints of her jealous and spiteful character.

How great was this robbery of D'Alembert may be judged from the admiration she expresses for him in the following portrait, probably written before their breach of friendship.

"D'Alembert was born without relations, interest, or fortune, and had only the ordinary education of most children: no one took the trouble to cultivate his mind, or form his character. The first thing he discovered, when he began to think for himself, was that he cared for nothing. He consoled himself for this indifference by the independence it gave him; but, as his mind developed, he found the inconvenience of this state, and looked within himself for some cure for this unhappiness. He said to himself, that he was the child of Nature, and should consult and obey none but her (to which principle he has remained true); that his rank, his title in the universe, was that of being a man; that nothing was above him nor beneath him; that there is nothing but virtue and vice, mind or stupidity, which merits our respect or contempt; that liberty was the true fortune of the wise; and that it could be acquired and enjoyed by any one, by avoiding the passions and every occasion which might prompt them.

"The safest preservative against them he believed to be study; and the activity of his mind could not limit itself to studies of one kind; every species of science, every branch of knowledge, occupied him by turns; he formed his taste by classical reading, and soon found himself in a position to imitate what he read. In short, his genius developed, and he appeared before the world in the character of a prodigy. His simple manners, upright character, look of youth, and frank address, united with his talents, at first astonished those who met him; but he was not equally well judged by all. Some saw in him nothing more than an awkward youth. His simplicity and frankness struck them as mere loutishness. The only merit they discovered in him was the singular talent he has for mimicking every thing he sees. This amused them, but that was all.

"Such an entrance into society was calculated to disgust him with it; and he soon escaped from it, giving himself up more closely than ever to study and philosophy. It was then that he published his 'Essai sur les Gens de Lettres,' a work which had not the success that he looked for. The nobility thought he was robbing them of their rights by advising authors not to seek their protection; and the authors could not applaud advice so contrary to their interests; so that both patrons and patronized were equally opposed to him. All he had said in favor of liberty seemed to recommend license. An equally bad interpretation was put upon his love of truth; but his disinterestedness, the contempt he had for such criticism, the silence he kept, the prudence of his conduct, and in a word, that real merit which sooner or later triumphs over envy, forced his enemies to do him justice, or at least hold their tongues; they dared no longer oppose the public voice.

"D'Alembert enjoys the reputation due to the highest talents, and the constant practice of the noblest virtues. Disinterestedness and truth compose his character. Generous and feeling, he has every essential quality, but has not all those required by society; he wants that softness and amenity which give it its charm; his heart does not seem to be very susceptible, and one is inclined to think that there is more virtue in him than feeling. He does not give one the pleasure of feeling that you are necessary to him; he asks nothing of his friends, and prefers attending to them than being attended to. Gratitude is too much of a duty to him, and would shackle his liberty. All constraint, all annoyance of every possible kind is insupportable to him: and he has been admirably described as the *slave of liberty*."

We have given this sketch in full, as a very good specimen of Madame du Deffand's literary powers. The style of her letters is very different. The intellectual worth of Madlle. de l'Espinasse soon became apparent to the friends of her protectress, whose house and society were not calculated in any way to improve her moral character. She was in the habit of rising an hour before Madame du Deffand, in order to prepare the rooms; and some of the intimates of the house discovering this, used to arrive privately at that hour to enjoy her society without exciting the jealousy of the old lady of sixty up stairs. Among the number was the great mathematician, who, though more than fifty years of age, gradually contracted a positive passion for this young and clever person. Though she could not return, she accepted it, and even went farther. In an illness with which he was prostrated, she attended him as nurse, and thus commenced a disreputable connection which afterward became publicly known.

Meanwhile, Madame du Deffand discovered the partiality of her friends for her "humble companion," and was furious. Jealousy and selfishness combined were at last too much to be endured, and in a moment of indignation the young lady poured out to her protectress those feelings which her conduct had long been maturing. She then left her, took, in the Rue de Belle-Chasse, an apartment, which was furnished for her by the Duchesse de Luxembourg, and in a humbler way set up, as it were, a rival salon to that of her late mistress. The friends of Madame du Deffand were now divided, and while some continued to frequent the convent, others flew to the Rue de Belle-Chasse. D'Alembert would have remained true to both, but Madame du Deffand imperiously told him that he must either break with Madlle. de l'Espinasse or with herself. He at once chose the latter alternative.

The rival salon succeeded admirably. Mackintosh writes: "Without rank, fortune, or even acknowledged name, she collected around her at her humble apartment the most brilliant and illustrious society of Europe. From the account of La Harpe and Marmontel, it appears that she presided in this society with equal skill and grace; that she guided conversation without appearing to do so. She moderated or increased its ardor as occasion required; Turgot and Cordillac were among those who submitted to her guidance. Turgot admitted her to long and confidential conversations, even when he was minister. Those who knew her, considered her as an extraordinary compound of discretion and decorum, with the most excited imagination and the most fiercely burning sensibility."

Whatever may have been her fault in this quarrel, Madame du Deffand did not behave well after it. A month later, Madlle. de l'Espinasse wrote to her, asking for an interview, in which "to renew, myself," she writes, "the assurance of a respect and attachment which will end only with my life." To this Madame du Deffand returned a cold reply, declining to see or be reconciled to her. Nor did her jealousy abate. Ten years later, in 1675, Walpole thus writes to Conway, who was in Paris: "There is at Paris a Madlle. de l'Espinasse, a pretended *bel-esprit*, who was formerly a humble companion of Madame du Deffand, and betrayed her, and used her very ill. I beg of you not to let any body carry you thither. It would disoblige my friend of all things in the world, and she would never tell you a syllable. * * * Pray, do not mention it; it might look simple in me, and yet I owe it to her, as I know it would hurt her. * * * I dwell upon it, because she has some enemies so spiteful that they try to carry all English to Madlle. de l'Espinasse." The end of the "humble companion" was very unsatisfactory. Her *liaison* with D'Alembert was not the only one of the kind to which she gave way. She became deeply attached to a Marquis de Mora, a young and handsome Spaniard, and for four years lived with him. His family recalled him to Spain; but the separation affected him so deeply that he became dangerously ill, and his relations consented to his returning to marry her. He did so, but before he was sufficiently recovered to travel, and died on the road. Two years later she herself died of fever at the age of forty. Mackintosh says: "Her letters are, in my opinion, the truest picture of deep passion ever traced by a human being."

This quarrel took place in 1764. In the autumn of the following year Horace Walpole, then a man of eight-and-forty, came to Paris. French society was at this time in the worst possible condition. Two characteristics suffice to describe it—vice and wit—with the understanding that the one was as bad as the other. The vicious were all witty, the wit as openly indelicate as the vice. Two classes of persons composed all the chief sets, courtesans and so-called philosophers. The former were the wives and daughters of the "noblest" families of France. A profligate king gave encouragement to a profligate court, and the chief ambition of a woman of rank and fashion was to be the mistress of the monarch. The exceptions to this rule of profligacy were so few that a virtuous woman in those days stood out as an inexplicable phenomenon. Even ugliness was no safeguard, and a *bel-esprit* was expected to be *galante*, however hideous her face might be.

The society of such women was shared chiefly by men who called themselves philosophers, and were certainly thinkers. Voltaire, Rousseau, Diderot, D'Alembert, Helvetius, Hume, and Wilkes were the pets of these great ladies, the constant frequenters of the *petits soupers*, at which they held revel night after night. The conversation here was of a freedom and coarseness which shocked even Walpole. Atheism was openly proclaimed, and it was considered a "blasphemy against reason" to believe in God. "*Il est bigot, c'est un déiste,*" was said by one of these ladies of Voltaire, who was not Atheist enough for them. "Laugh!" wrote Walpole, "they have no time to laugh; there is God and the king to be pulled down first, and men and women, one and all, are all devoutly employed in the demolition. They think me quite profane, for having any belief left."

The wit was in fact of a terribly serious nature. Bon-mots were the business of the day, but the bitterest, most blasphemous, and most indelicate were always the most popular; and their coiners cared rather to be admired as audacious thinkers, than to amuse the company, knowing that what they said to-night would be repeated to-morrow in a thousand letters and at a hundred supper-tables. "The *savants*," writes Walpole, "I beg their pardon, the philosophers, are insupportable, superficial, overbearing, and fanatic; they preach incessantly, and their avowed doctrine is atheism." In fact, as Warburton remarks, Parisian society was a perpetual Belshazzar's feast, and one can not wonder that thirty years later the earth should have opened beneath them all in the form of a Revolution, nor think the punishment too severe.

It was a peculiarity of the highest French society of that day, that the amusements it offered were purely intellectual. The men and women who saw nothing disgusting in coarse wit despised such natural enjoyments as music and dancing. The consequence was, that when they sought to vary the conversation which was the staple object of their meeting, they became either tedious or ridiculous. On the one hand they read out epigrams, or prose characters such as those of which we have given specimens, or even recited verses in that fierce French bombast, which is only tolerable when refined by the talent or heightened by the power of a Rachel; on the other they got up childish little scenes, of the character of which an idea may be gathered from an amusing anecdote of David Hume, at a time when he was quite the pet of the fair Parisians. On one occasion he was to represent an Eastern sultan, who was to beguile two lovely captives, seated on either side of him on a sofa. We can imagine the historian's unwieldy form in Oriental costume; and the contrast formed by the two beautiful Aspasias, who were waiting to be fascinated. But David had no idea of the character—more praise to him—and thumping his knees, he could only look from one to the other, exclaiming, "Eh bien! mes demoiselles; eh bien; vous voilà donc; eh bien! vous voilà, vous voilà ici." It is scarcely necessary to add that the author of the Essay on Human Nature was deposed, and a more gallant monarch raised in his place.

Such was the character of this society of pseudo-philoso-

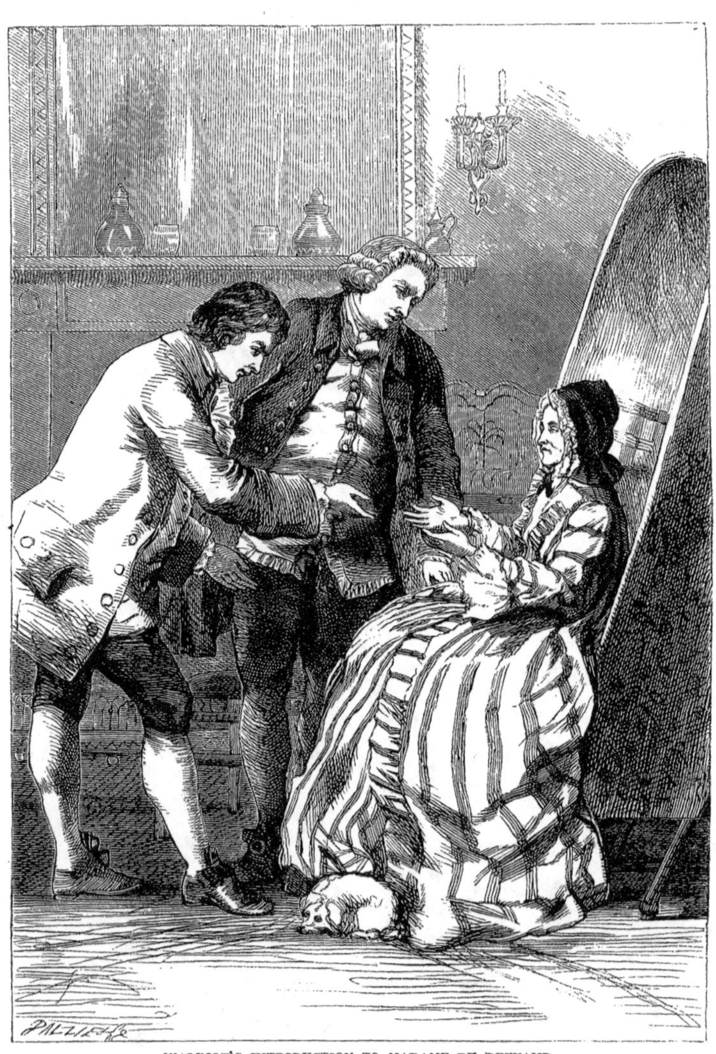

WALPOLE'S INTRODUCTION TO MADAME DU DEFFAND.

phers and honorless women. The salons, which were generally open on specified days, twice a week, sometimes oftener, and especially on Sundays, and where conversation (*i. e.* satirical gossip), cards, and supper were the bill of fare, were very numerous. At this period, however, there were two great rival centres, the salon of Madame de Geoffrin and that of Madame du Deffand. Both were thronged with wits, Aspasias of the highest rank, and so-called philosophers. There was, however, some difference between them. After the desertion by D'Alembert, Madame du Deffand affected to despise all philosophers, and accordingly lost some of them. She also detested professional literary men, and her salon never admitted that much-maligned class. Birth, or the pretension to it, was the great ticket to her favor; but, again, her society was too *spirituel* to admit those who had nothing more than birth to recommend them. These restrictions sufficed to weed her company pretty well. The great families of France contributed their quota; the De Choiseuls, for instance, were among her most intimate friends, as, also, the Maréchale de Luxembourg. Vice was plenteously represented; there were Madame de Mirepoix, who, besides other vices, loved gambling to excess; Madame de Boufflers, who will be remembered in connection with Samuel Johnson; Madame de Rochfort, a *savante*, Madame de Forcalquier and Madame de Talmond, all ladies of the tightest prejudices and loosest morals, and all of the high aristocracy of France. The last mentioned was said to have been the mistress of Charles Edward Stuart, commonly called "the Young Pretender." She had been, as Walpole says, religious to please the queen, and *galante* (*i. e.* wicked) to please herself, and she wore on one arm a bracelet with a portrait of Charles Edward, on the other one with a picture of our Lord. When asked what connection there was between them, she replied, with the then much admired blasphemy, "Because their kingdoms are not of this world."

Into these sets Walpole was introduced by his English friends, and his name, as the son of an English minister, backed the introductions. Lady Hervey gave him several, and George Selwyn, a great favorite in Paris, presented him to Madame du Deffand. Her appearance must certainly have been disappointing to him. She was found in a moderate-sized room, with no great attractions, save a few portraits of celebrated beauties, the arms of Madame de Montespan behind the grate, and some other such associations interesting to a dilettante antiquarian like Walpole. In this room, furnished with more comfort than elegance, the "old blind woman" sat in a huge chair, which resembled more than aught else I can remember the seats of the porters of our inns of court or Oxford colleges, very high, very deep, round-backed, low in the seat, and more like a coffin set on end than an easy-chair. Grimm likens it to the tub of Diogenes.

Blind, rather feeble, with her head wrapped in a hood, her old face still delicate and remarkable for its look of cleanliness, she received her new guest. He saw nothing in her, at first, but a merry old woman who said smart things which were repeated wherever he went, and who was much the fashion. As his French was by no means perfect in conversation—even in writing, though generally idiomatic, it is often faulty—and as he confesses that he could not find words enough to join the rapid, noisy gossip of the gay Parisians, it is probable that at first Madame du Deffand cared but little for this new *Anglais*. It was true he bore a celebrated name, was well introduced, and of excellent and easy carriage; and the little he may have said was, we may be sure, of the true Walpolian sort, though in French, displaying the two qualities she could best appreciate—slight satire and complete knowledge of the world. But Walpole was not as yet the fashion.

A clever but unkind squib supplied this one want. Rousseau was at that time a really injured man. The parliament had issued an *arrêt* against him on account of his opinions, and he had been forced to fly to England, where Hume was befriending him. He was therefore in some sense "down;" it was mean in Walpole to kick him. Rousseau's wretched morbid character was as well known to the lord of Strawberry Hill as to every one else. It was known that ridicule was that which he dreaded most in the world, though his conduct throughout was that of a madman. Still, under the circumstances, Walpole might have spared a man who had never thwarted him in any way, and who was at this moment in exile. But Horace could not deny himself the enjoyment of being admired for his wit. He wrote, in capital French, a letter purporting to come from Frederick the Great, offering the Hermit of Montmorency a retreat in his kingdom. This epistle was couched in language which might possibly have been serious, but could easily be detected as satirical. It touched the tenderest points of the philosopher's character, his morbid folly, his perpetual suspicion of real or fancied enemies, his love of appearing in the character of a persecuted man; but all with such delicacy, that it might possibly have been written by the monarch with whose name it was signed, and did indeed mystify the public. Thus with an air of frankness the writer, after expressing his admiration for the philosopher, exclaims: "Show your enemies that you can sometimes be sensible; it will annoy them, and do you no harm. * * * If you persist in racking your brain to discover new misfortunes, choose which you will. I am a king, and can get you as many as you like. * * * And I will leave off persecuting you when you cease to make a glory of being persecuted."

The squib succeeded. It was the amusement first of the salons and then of the newspapers. Widely circulated through France, and causing no little astonishment, it soon crossed the Channel, and appeared in the English journals. Rousseau, infuriated at this new stab, wrote a bitter letter to the editor of the "London Chronicle," to which Walpole, flushed with success, prepared a yet more cutting answer with the signature of "Emile;" but this time his better nature prevailed. He felt, as he wrote to Madame du Deffand, that it was not well to torment a man who had done him no injury, and the fun had gone far enough. At any rate, the *jeu d'esprit* procured him the admiration of all Voltaire's set, and indeed of most of the wits of Paris; and he was soon installed in a seat of honor at most of the supper-tables of that city. At first he wrote of Madame du Deffand in any but a flattering strain; was disgusted with her coarseness, of which he gives quite unrepeatable specimens, and even talks of her company as "dull." But his tone soon changes, and he had not been in Paris four months before he wrote of her in the following strain to his friend Gray:

"She is now very old, and stone blind, but retains all her vivacity, wit, memory, judgment, passions, and agreeableness. She goes to operas, plays, suppers, and Versailles; gives suppers twice a week; has every thing new read to her; makes new songs and epigrams, ay, admirably, and remembers every one that has been made these fourscore years. She corresponds with Voltaire, dictates charming letters to him, contradicts him, and is no bigot to him or any body, and laughs both at the clergy and the philosophers. In a dispute, into which she easily falls, she is very warm, and yet scarce ever in the wrong: her judgment on every subject is as just as possible; on every point of conduct as wrong as possible; for she is all love and hatred, passionate for her friends to enthusiasm, still anxious to be loved—I don't mean by lovers—and a vehement enemy, but openly. As she can have no amusement but conversation, the least solitude and *ennui* are insupportable to her, and put her into the power of several worthless people, who eat her suppers, when they can eat nobody's of higher rank, wink to one another, and laugh at her."

What an unlovable picture, in spite of Walpole's partiality! How unsympathetic this woman, who lived only for society, gave up religion and the hope of heaven for it, and was laughed at by it in her blindness! Walpole's nature had little sympathy in it. He never loved, but he defended eagerly those whom he liked, as he cruelly aspersed those whom he did not. At this time he is full warm in defense of the blind old woman; but in after years he himself was one of those who treated her rudely, and that *because she was in love with him!*

A little later he writes: "Their barbarity and injustice to our good old friend is indescribable. One of the worst is just dead, Madame de Lambert; I am sure you will not regret her. * * * They eat her suppers when they can not go to a more fashionable house, laugh at her, abuse her, nay, try to raise her enemies among her nominal friends."

On a later visit to Paris he writes of her: "Having lived from the most agreeable to the most reasoning age, she has all that is amiable in the last, all that is sensible in this, without the vanity of the former or the pedant impertinence of the latter. * * * Affectionate as Madame de Sévigné, she has none of her prejudices, but a more universal taste; and with the most delicate frame, her spirits hurry her through a life of fatigue that would kill me if I was to continue here. If we return by one in the morning from suppers in the country, she proposes driving to the Boulevard, or to the Foire St. Ovide, because it is too early to go to bed."

It is just to Walpole to say that though he scolded, warned, lectured, and even annoyed this old friend to herself, he never wrote of her to others in any but an affectionate manner. The fact is, that no man was more susceptible to ridicule than that arch-ridiculer, Horace Walpole. And the matter really became ridiculous. He was in Paris some seven months, and perpetually at Madame du Deffand's. If his account of her so-called friends' treatment of her be true, perhaps his kindness may have affected her. Perhaps his wit, as she found it out in spite of his bad French; perhaps, and still more probably, the similarity of their characters and opinions, their common skepticism (though Walpole was more of a skeptic about mankind than about God), their common love of a sneer, and much more that they had in common, may have made Madame du Deffand feel doubly attached to this clever, agreeable man. It was a point of her character—and she is constantly declaring it—that she needed some one to love, and be loved by. It is true she could not love easily. She had passed too selfish, too evil a life to love at all in reality. It was only in her old age that she felt the utter loneliness of her life. She had no religion to console her; no next world to look forward to: she lived for this only, she found it barren, and, true woman that she was, she knew that nothing but love could fertilize it.

The old president was nothing to her by this time. She tyrannized over him too much to love him, and he was really too old for it. Under all these considerations, she tried to fall in love with Horace Walpole. She was bordering upon seventy, he on fifty. Could any thing be more ridiculous? It is true it was only friendship that she offered him, but a friendship of that enthusiastic kind that is quite equivalent to a passion. He had scarcely left Paris when she wrote him her first letter; but in the next we find that Walpole has already been chiding her, and complained of her *indiscrétions* and *emportemens romanesques*. He had, in fact, already suffered from her ridiculous attachment to him. A man must always feel that an attachment in a woman twenty years older than himself partakes of the absurd; but when that woman is seventy years of age, blind and infirm, the absurdity becomes almost painful.

Her letters to Walpole are fitter for a girl of nineteen than a woman of seventy. She talks about being the Héloïse to his Abélard, the Philothée to his St. François de Sales; she submits herself to him as to her master; she tells him freely that she loves him, that she is wretched without him, and so forth, and this strain continues through a correspondence of fifteen years, and no fewer than three hundred and forty-eight letters; so that, deducting Walpole's subsequent visits to Paris, she must have written to him about once a week during that period.

Walpole had not covenanted for this. He had a certain affection, which he occasionally betrays very strongly for his "blind old woman," or, as he calls her sometimes, his "old fairy." Her enthusiasm shocked the son of the daughter of a lord-mayor of London. Walpole, who has often been described as "more than half French," was, in fact, more than wholly English. No one can read his foreign letters without seeing this. He had every English prejudice about the Continent: he gave in, with his usual tact, to Continental manners, and assimilated with them certainly better than Hume, for Walpole was a man of the world, and not a philosopher; but when once at home in his dear Strawberry, he finds French humbug flat and stale, and is almost John Bullish at times in his abuse of it.

He conceived an idea that his letters would be read at the post-office, and the ridicule of a love affair—for so it was on her part—between an old woman of more than seventy and a man of more than fifty exposed to his disadvantage. He therefore continually strove to check her enthusiasm for himself, and was often even rude in his attempts to do so. She was certainly extravagant. She not only wrote in terms of the most vehement affection, but even became jealous of poor Madame de Sévigné, long since in her coffin, but always admired by Walpole as the first of letter-writers. In such a mood she sent him a snuff-box, in which was a portrait of Madame de Sévigné, and within it placed a letter, referred to in that lady's life, and purporting to come from the ghost of Madame de Sévigné herself. This was only one of her pleasantries, in her attempt to make Walpole really as affectionate to her as she was to him.

Less than ten years after the commencement of their friendship, when Madame du Deffand was nearly eighty years old, and reasonable expectations of her death might be entertained, Walpole grew amusingly nervous about his letters, which he thought might possibly be published with others by her executors. He therefore commissioned his great friend, General Conway, who was then in Paris, to obtain them from Madame du Deffand. He writes (1774): "Madame du Deffand has kept a great many of my letters, and as she is very old, I am pained about them. I have written to her to beg she will deliver them up to you, to bring back to me, and I trust she will. If she does, be so good as to take great care of them. If she does not mention them, tell her just before you come away, that I begged you to bring them; and, if she hesitates, convince her how it would hurt me, to have letters written in bad French, and mentioning several people, both French and English, fall into bad hands, and, perhaps, be printed."

It was clearly not the bad French, so much as the ridiculous sentimentality, of which the lord of Strawberry was afraid. She returned the letters, however, very reluctantly, and thus wrote to him on the subject: "You will have material for lighting your fire for a long time, especially if you add my letters to yours; and nothing could be more just. But I trust to your prudence, and will not follow the example of distrust which you set me." But he seems to have left her little peace. "Ha, ha!" she writes to him, "I disturb your gayety, and you fear my letters like actual poison. * * * In the name of Heaven do not scold me * * * bear with my melancholy nature, and the dull passages you find in my letters. I will take care to admit fewer into them. Your severity makes me tremble. Be reassured as to my discretion, and be certain that my acts will always be conformed to your wishes."

Poor old woman! It was certainly a hard fate, that in this latest of her love affairs, and this, too, the first pure one, she should have been "snubbed" and laughed at. Walpole might surely have shown the compassion, which he claimed so eagerly for her at their early acquaintance.

In 1769 he again visited Paris, again in 1771, and, lastly, in 1775. On each occasion the old lady flew to meet him. As a specimen of her want of delicacy, and his too, we may quote his account of her visit on the last occasion. "Madame du Deffand came to me the instant I arrived, and sat by me while I stripped and dressed myself: for as she said, since she can not see, there was no harm in my being stark." She supplied him with ample amusement. Some time after he writes to Conway: "Madame du Deffand has pinned her (Madame de Jonsac) down to meeting me at her house four times before next Tuesday, all parentheses, that are not to interfere with our suppers; and from those suppers I never get to bed before two or three o'clock. In short, I need have the activity of a squirrel, and the strength of a Hercules, to go through my labors, not to count how many *démêlés* I have to *raccommode*, and how many *mémoires* to present against Tonton (Madame du Deffand's favorite dog), who grows the greater favorite the more people he devours. * * * T'other night he flew at Lady Barrymore's face * * * she was terrified; she fell into tears. Madame du Deffand, perceiving she had not beaten Tonton half enough, immediately told us a story of a lady, whose dog having bitten a piece out of a gentleman's leg, the tender dame, in a great fright, cried out, 'Won't it make my dog sick?'"

After her death, Walpole "adopted" this detestable cur, to succeed his late pet, Rosette. He asked for it on the plea that it was "so cross, that nobody else would treat it well." It arrived at Strawberry, was duly installed, and became a great object of attention to his flatterers. "I was going to say, it is incredible how fond I am of it, but I have no occasion to brag of any dogmanity. I dined at Richmond House t'other day, and mentioning whither I was going, the duke said, 'Own the truth: shall you not call at home first, and see Tonton?' He guessed rightly; he is now sitting on my paper as I write—not the duke, but Tonton." He speaks of Rosette as "his poor late favorite." Poor old bachelor! How like are the old bachelor's to the old maid's habits!

To return to Madame du Deffand: her life continued in the same monotonous round of suppers, operas, visits, and gossip. Its main interest was to write to, and receive letters from, her latest lover—Horace Walpole. But the spirit of weariness, the consciousness of the absence of affection, the desire to be loved, preyed upon her daily, and her spirits grew more and more depressed. In such a state of mind she resolved, in 1767, to supply the vacancy caused by Madlle. de l'Espinasse's departure, and engaged as a companion a Madlle. Sanadon.

She was the niece of Père Sanadon, well known for his translation of Horace. She was a much safer person than her predecessor, with none of her talents or liveliness, but much more ready to endure her mistress's ill-humors. Then, too, there was not the same room for jealousy now, for there was no one but Walpole left to be jealous of, and he was in England. The president was still alive and faithful, but he was her slave, and more than eighty. Pont de Veyle was always there, but to him she was indifferent. At seventy years old, too, Madame du Deffand could surely give up being jealous. The fact was, that the fashion of her salon was already giving way to those of younger and less peevish beauties. A certain number of old friends, male and female, remained true to her to the last, and their coterie, though still renowned for wit, had not life enough in it to tempt others to join it. Madame du Deffand did not take much part in politics; she had driven away the philosophers; her main interest was in the gossip of the city, and especially all that related to her own set. Her chief attraction was her wit, which never seemed to flag. Specimens of her bon-mots are scattered through Walpole's letters, and the notices of her life, but a few will be sufficient.

Thus one of her mots was long attributed to Voltaire, namely, that Montesquieu's Esprit *des* Lois was nothing after all but "de l'Esprit* *sur* les lois."

Again, when some very credulous ecclesiastic was relating to her the legend of St. Denis, whose head was cut off at St. Ouen, near Paris, and who thereupon was weak (or strong) enough to walk with it under his arm all the way to the suburb named after him, and explaining the various places at which he stopped to rest, assured her that the first stage had been the most trying; "Ah," cried Madame du Deffand with a look of perfect sincerity, "I can well believe that, for in affairs of that kind, *ce n'est que le premier pas qui coûte*," which has since become a proverb.

Voltaire has preserved a maxim of hers, "Things which can not be known to us are not necessary to us"—a consoling thought for Atheists and Materialists.

On the death of Voltaire, every body that could write verses —and every body did write them in those days—sang his praises in their wretched couplets. "Voltaire suffered the common lot of mortals," said Madame du Deffand "d'être après leur mort la pâture des *vers*."

But far better wit than this, in the more solid form of worldly wisdom, is to be found in her letters; yet it must not be supposed that they are of a very high standard. They are

* *Esprit* meaning both "spirit" and "wit."

clever, amusing, satirical; that is, when they are not mournful, peevish, and ridiculous. But they are the letters of an *ennuyée*, of a woman who, being sick of life, had no religion to reconcile her to it, who, dreading death, had not patience to wait for it. Madame de Sévigné and Madame du Deffand are constantly quoted as the two great letter-writers of France. How infinitely superior is the one to the other! What freshness, what cheerfulness, what nature in the Ste. de Livry, as Walpole called her; what whining misery, what cheerless grumbling in "*ma petite!*" Yet both had their trials. It was a far harder trial to the tender heart of Madame de Sévigné to be separated from the daughter she loved more than all the world, than to Madame du Deffand to lose her eyes, a deprivation which made so little difference in her daily life. The secret is as simple as a child's face. The one had a good conscience and belief in a future world; the other just the reverse. Madame de Sévigné was no bigot, no superstitious Romanist, but she had a fund of belief which sufficed to accept revelation, while it rejected fanaticism. Madame du Deffand was not an avowed atheist, but she was practically a skeptic. She had no power of believing; she lived only for this world, and could not even endure the thought of another. Once or twice she made an attempt to turn *dévote*, according to the fashion of her younger days. But religion in any form was distasteful to her. She could bear to be told of her sins against society, and Walpole's *gronderies* were endured; but she could not bear to be told of her sins against God. "Ask me no questions and preach me no sermons," was the stipulation she made with the confessor, whom she engaged one time to make her a Christian. Blindness, loss of friends, sleepless days and nights, abject misery could not humble her. She believed only in the world, and to her dying day lived in and for it. Let the cheerfulness of the one, and the wretchedness of the other, be a warning to those who would love the world too well. Madame du Deffand, in her old age, though still surrounded by friends, though comfortable in her means, though admired and flattered for her wit, though, even at eighty, sought as a potentate of society, was, to judge from her letters, one of the most miserable women ever born. Let her life be a warning.

There was no striking event in the latter days of Madame du Deffand. Her friendships and their changes were all that made up the sum of her existence. Among the friends of her long old age, the least objectionable and most agreeable was the Duchesse de Choiseul, whom Walpole declared to be his latest and strongest passion. Carmontel, a better dramatist (we hope) than artist, drew a well-known picture of Madame du Deffand receiving a doll from Madame de Choiseul. As we have stated, the latter was always called by the affectionate name of grandmaman, though much younger than Madame du Deffand. In this picture the grandmaman is far from lovely; yet she had the reputation of beauty, and Walpole, who, on receiving the picture, admired the excellence of Madame du Deffand's likeness, indignantly exclaims against that of the duchess. "I should never have guessed it," he writes; "it is a most common face; none of the pretty delicacy of this *esprit personifié*, of this wickedness without malice or affectation; none of that beauty which seems to be an emanation of the soul, which shows itself in the face for fear it should excite awe rather than love. Enfin, enfin, I don't like it."

Still we may judge from this, that Madame de Choiseul had a clever and sparkling rather than beautiful face. She was the wife of the one-time prime minister, afterward disgraced, who, in his will, desired to be buried in the same grave with her, which does not agree with the account of his indifference, given by Walpole in the following agreeable sketch, when he sent Gray a series of portraits of the reigning beauties of Paris.

"The Duchess of Choiseul, the only young one of these heroines, is not very pretty, but has fine eyes, and is a little model in wax-work, which not being allowed to speak for some time as incapable, has a hesitation and modesty, the latter of which the court has not cured, and the former of which is atoned for by the most interesting sound of voice, and forgotten in the most elegant turn and propriety of expression. Oh! it is the gentlest, amiable, civil little creature that ever came out of a fairy egg. So just in its phrases and thoughts, so attentive and good-natured. Every body loves it but its husband, who prefers his own sister, the Duchesse de Grammont, an Amazonian, fierce, haughty dame, who loves and hates arbitrarily, and is detested. Madame de Choiseul, passionately fond of her husband, was the martyr of this union, but at last submitted with a good grace; has gained a good credit with him, and is still believed to idolize him. But I doubt it: she takes too much pains to profess it."

True skeptic—Horace! But Madame de Choiseul is a rare and charming exception to the general rule of Frenchwomen of the day, in the mere fact of having *ever* been in love with her husband.

The loss of the President Hénault took place in November, 1770, when he was eighty-six years old. After being her devoted servant for some thirty or forty years, during which he lived near her alternately as husband, friend, and slave, it is thus that Madame du Deffand writes of his death: "The president died yesterday at seven in the morning * * * Madame de Jonsac (his sister) seemed extremely afflicted; my grief is more moderate; I had so many proofs of his small amount of friendship, that I fancy I have only lost an acquaintance." This is the woman whose good heart Walpole praises!

Her life was henceforward a mixture of selfishness, worldliness, and remorse without repentance. In 1775, when Walpole was in Paris, she was seized with a violent illness. "Madame du Deffand," he writes, "has been so ill, that the day she was seized, I thought she would not live the night * * * She can not lift her head from the pillow without *étourdissements;* and yet her spirits gallop faster than any body's and so do her repartees. She has a great supper to-night for the Duc de Choiseul, and was in such a passion yesterday with her cook about it, and that put Tonton (her dog) into such a rage, that *nos dames de St. Joseph* thought the devil or the philosophers were flying away with their convent. The next day she received a large party, among whom were all the heads of the great French families." At eighty-four, he tells us, she had "all the impetuosity that *was* the character of the French."

At last, in the midst of society, good and bad, the day came when she was to deliver up her soul to her Maker. We would fain not be hard upon a mortal, especially on a woman, and that one dead; but we can not read the last letters of this woman, and the accounts of her last hours, and convince ourselves that she felt the slightest penitence for her life of sin, and it may even be doubted if she died a believer. In 1780, she had reached the great age of eighty-three. She had been given this length of days, that in age, at least, she might repent. She had received repeated warnings since the time she lost her eyesight. She had been made to feel the wretchedness of life within herself; yet while she looked calmly upon death, she viewed it only as a necessary evil, not as the beginning of a great and awful eternity.

On the 22d of August she began to feel her end approaching, and thus wrote to Walpole:—

"I told you in my last that I was not well; it is worse to-day. I feel great weakness and depression; my voice is gone; I can not stand; I can scarcely move; my heart is clogged; I can scarcely think that this state does not announce my end as near. I have no strength to be frightened at it; and since I could not see you again in life, I have nothing to regret. Amuse yourself, my friend, as well as you can, and do not be afflicted by my state; we were almost lost to one another, and could never see one another again; you will regret me, because it is pleasant to feel that one is loved." Her rooms were still crowded with her old friends, to whom she managed to talk, till within eight days of her death. Walpole writes: "So I reckon myself dead to France, where I have kept up no other connection." He does not seem more deeply affected than this. On hearing of her death, he says: "I have heard from Paris of the death of my dear old friend, Madame du Deffand, whom I went thither so often to see. It was not quite unexpected, and was softened by her great age—eighty-four, which forbade distant hopes; and by what I dreaded more than her death, her increasing deafness, which, had it become, like her blindness, total, would have been living after death. Her memory only *began* to impair; her amazing sense and quickness not at all. I have written to her once a week for these last fifteen years, as correspondence and conversation could be her only pleasure."

The Baron de Grimm thus describes her last days: "Her best friends, Madame de Luxembourg, Madame de Choiseul, and Madame de Cambise, scarcely ever quitted her during her last illness: in the excess of their attachment they never ceased playing at *loto* every evening in her chamber till she had breathed her last sigh. *She never would hear either of confession or receiving the sacrament.* All that the minister of the parish, who visited her in virtue of his office, could obtain, after the most earnest exhortations, was, that she should confess herself to her friend the Duc de Choiseul. It can not be doubted, that a confessor so judicially chosen granted her, with the best grace possible, absolution for all her sins, without excepting even an epigram she once made upon himself."

Her faithful servant and secretary, Wiart, wrote to Walpole on her death: "I can not tell you the pain I felt in writing that letter (the last to Horace) at her dictation. I could not finish reading it over to her; my words were choked with sobs. She said to me, '*Then you love me!*' * * * Her death is in the course of nature. She has had no illness, or at least no suffering. When I heard her complaining I asked her if she felt pain any where; she always answered no. The last eight days of her life were a complete lethargy; she had lost all feeling; her death was very easy, although the illness was a long one. * * * She has ordered by her will a most simple burial. Her directions have been executed. She wished to be laid in her parish church, St. Sulpice. The parish would not allow her to be decorated after death with any marks of distinction: these gentlemen were not perfectly satisfied about her. Yet the rector saw her every day, and even began to confess her, but could not proceed, because her head was confused, and she could not receive the sacrament; but M. le Curé behaved excellently, thinking that her end was not so near. I shall keep Tonton (the dog) till the departure of Mr. Thomas Walpole, and take the greatest care of him. He is very good, and bites nobody. He was only naughty when with his mistress. I well remember, sir, that she begged you to take care of it."

That remark of hers, "Then you love me," is touching. This woman had all her life longed to be loved. She had always taken the wrong means to gain this object. Even Walpole, decidedly the most attached of her friends, did not love her enough to put up with her enthusiastic affection. It is a token, too, of that skepticism which made her life so miserable. She never believed in the affection of others. The proof in this case was too strong to doubt. Yet Wiart had been a long time her amanuensis, and must have shown his devotion in his careful attendance on her old age. She would have been happier if she had believed in his affection before. She would have been happier all her life if she had believed any thing.

To Wiart she left about a thousand pounds and an annuity of fifty pounds per annum. Walpole says that she wished to leave to himself her little all, but he protested that if she did so he would never set foot in France again. He consented to receive only a gold box, with a portrait of her dog, and her collection of papers—chiefly letters. Those addressed to Walpole were published in 1810, with a selection of her letters to Voltaire. In the same year appeared a French edition of various letters to D'Alembert, Montesquieu, Hénault, and many other persons of great distinction in their day. Next to Walpole, Voltaire was her chief correspondent. Her letters, and the "Portraits" of her friends, show in the most undeniable manner that she was a woman of high intellectual powers though of poor education. She treats at times of the highest subjects with as much ease as of the gossip and scandal, in which, unfortunately, she seems to have taken greater pleasure. She is an instance of a mind spoiled by the character that accompanied it in the same individual. Able to grasp higher things, she never soars, because she never wished to. Her reflections, though often just and oftener original, are all from a worldly point of view, and leave us, as they left her, sick of a world where all *appears* (namely, in that point of view) so hollow, so rotten, so unworthy of belief. Thank Heaven, the world, bad as it is, is not quite so bad as that; and thank Heaven, too, that women who are as bad and as skeptical as Madame du Deffand—and there may be thousands—have not oftener the opportunity of writing to celebrated men letters which are afterward published. As presenting a view of French society of the day—and most unsatisfactory society it was—her letters have the same value, if not the same interest, as those of Madame de Sévigné.

MRS. ELIZABETH MONTAGU.

Sir Nathaniel Wraxall, in his "Diary," speaks of Mrs. Montagu's "palace, as it would be termed at Rome or Naples, in Portman Square." "The palace" exists: we see it, somewhat secluded from public gaze, yet *not* secluded as in the time of its first owner, when it was encompassed with fields. In spring the earliest budding trees shade its entrance; in autumn the planes and elms near it are the first to shed their leaves. Compared with modern edifices Montagu House is not even stately: it is, at all events, only so because it stands apart; but it has the dignity of tradition. Within those walls, now blackened by London smoke, lived as benevolent a being as ever was intrusted by Providence with a noble fortune. Until lately, the chimney-sweepers, commemorating her consideration for their despised condition, danced every May-day before the door whence she was wont to issue—a grotesque tribute to the kindness that has been exalted into a still higher attribute in the world of spirits. The drawing-rooms in which she assembled the society which was first there called the "Blue Stockings" are still inhabited by her descendants. Montagu House is one of the landmarks of modern society: let us hope that it will not be swept away, but will last, with her memory who built it, to our children's children.

Favored by nature and fortune, Elizabeth Montagu had the advantage of being one of a large family. Her father, Matthew Robinson, a large landed proprietor in Yorkshire, in Cambridgeshire, and in Kent, had by his wife, Elizabeth, the daughter and heiress of Robert Drake, twelve children. How low down in the scale Elizabeth came, her nephew and biographer, who seems anxious to say as little about her as he can, does not inform us. She was, however, descended on her father's side from the Robinsons of Rokeby, who were ennobled in the reign of George II. by the Irish peerage of Rokeby of Armagh.

Elizabeth was born at York on the 2d of October, 1720. Her father, who was a man of considerable acquirements and devoted to society, had made the mistake of marrying at eighteen, and deemed it, therefore, prudent to live chiefly in the country, though pining for the delights of the town. He revenged himself on fortune, nevertheless, and punished his large family for coming into the world by dozens, by giving himself up to occasional fits of the spleen, to which indulgence he naturally considered himself entitled. He was very witty and sarcastic, and soon perceived that his daughter Elizabeth resembled him in those respects: and as she grew up their encounters were ofttimes somewhat sharp.

Mr. Robinson was fond of the arts; and, among the other avocations with which he sought to solace a country life, he undertook to teach his little Elizabeth drawing. But even here her merry spirit broke bounds. "If you design to make any proficiency in that art," she wrote to her friend the Duchess of Portland, "I would advise you not to draw old men's heads. It was the rueful countenance of Socrates or Seneca that first put me out of conceit with it. Had my papa given me the blooming faces of Adonis and Narcissus I might have been a more apt scholar; and when I told him I found those great beards difficult to draw, he gave me St. John's head in a charger; so, to avoid the speculation of dismal faces, which by my art I dismaled ten times more than they were before, I threw away my pencil." Her success did not, indeed, seem to promise well. "I have heard," she adds, "of some who have been famous landscape painters; of others who have been famous battle painters; but I take myself to have been the best hospital painter, for I never drew a figure that was not lame or blind, and they had all something of the horrible in their countenances; and by the arching of their eyebrows and the opening of their mouths they looked so frightened you would have thought they had seen their own faces in the glass."

When she was seven years old a circumstance occurred which gave an impetus to the direction of Elizabeth Robinson's tastes and studies. Her uncle dying, her mother inherited an estate at Coveney, in Cambridgeshire, and of course some months of every year were henceforth passed at that property. Hitherto Mr. Robinson had spent his winters in York, as it was then customary to make the county town a residence for the country families. In the summer he had removed to West Layton, in the same county, and to Edgeley, in Wensleydale. But he now frequently lived at Coveney, near the University of Cambridge, in which he had been a gentleman commoner.

He thus introduced his family into the very heart of all that was witty and talented: more especially as Mrs. Drake, his wife's mother, had for her second husband selected Dr. Conyers Middleton, the author of the "Life of Cicero." Dr. Middleton perceived at once the acuteness of Elizabeth Robinson's understanding and the sensibility which softened her stronger qualities. Elizabeth was the darling of the university; she was surpassingly beautiful as well as intelligent. Like Madame de Staël, before she was eight years old she had listened with interest to the conversations of the learned: all that was said sank deeply into her memory.

Dr. Middleton watched her with delight. He insisted on her repeating to him all she heard; he allowed her age to be no excuse; and she owned, in after life, that she had derived great benefit from the habit of attention thus inculcated. At the same time was engendered a value for learning and for the learned. While her letters were full of all the gayety of a girl, they diverged at times into reflections scarcely to be expected in so young, so flattered, so fashionable a belle. Her studies were Cicero, Plutarch's "Lives," Cornelius Nepos, Pliny. Neither she nor her friend, the Duchess of Portland, appeared to think that there was any thing inconsistent with the character of a fine lady in being well read: in reflecting seriously, and even deeply: in not looking upon this life as one of all pleasure. Her brothers were also devoted to literary pursuits, and became in early life distinguished scholars. So frequent were the arguments in the domestic circles, and so resolute the endeavor to outshine each other, that Mrs. Robinson, gentle and judicious, was often obliged to interpose; hence the bright party around her gave her the name of the "Speaker," and, it may be supposed, bowed to her remonstrances.

Notwithstanding the sensation which the little Elizabeth produced at Cambridge, she found it "the dullest place, affording neither any thing entertaining or ridiculous enough to put into a letter." The love of society dawned in her at a very early period of her life, and this she inherited from her father.

"Though tired of the country, I am not," she wrote when twelve years old, "to my great satisfaction, half so much so as my papa; he is a little vapored; and last night, after two hours' silence, he broke into a great exclamation against the country, and concluded with saying that living in the country was sleeping with one's eyes open. If he sleeps all day, I am sure he dreams very much of London."

Poor Mr. Robinson became, in spite of "saffron in his tea," irretrievably afflicted with the spleen; some provincial gayeties varied, indeed, his existence and that of his gay young daughters; but this was only when they were passing the winter, as sometimes happened, in the less wild regions of Kent instead of Yorkshire. Then for their delight an assembly was set on foot eight miles from Mount Morris. Ten coaches honored the great occasion, and a full moon illumined it: but company was wanting; so the Lady Paramount called in all the parsons, apprentices, tradesmen, apothecaries, and farmers, milliners and haberdashers of small wares to make up the ball. "Here," wrote Elizabeth, in all the impertinence of thirteen, "sails a reverend parson; there skips an apprentice; here jumps a farmer; and then every one has an eye to their trade: the milliner pulls you by the hand till she tears your glove; the mantuamaker treads on your petticoat until she unrips the seams; the shoemaker makes you foot it till you wear out your shoes; the mercer dirties your gown; the apothecary opens the window behind you that you may be sick; and the parson calls out for 'Joan Saunderson.'"

Mr. Robinson, it appeared, enjoyed on this occasion what we should in all our finery now call "a very mixed assembly," with all the spirits of a newly-awakened man; forgot his twenty years of wedlock and his nice children; and "danced as nimbly as any of the quorum." Now and then he was mortified by hearing the ladies cry "Old Mr. Robinson! change sides and turn your daughter." Other ladies, who wished to appear young, exclaim, "Well, there is poor grandpapa, he could no more dance so!" Then an old bachelor of fifty shakes him by the hand and cries, "Why, you dance like one of us young fellows!" Another, by way of compliment, adds, "Who would think you had six fine children taller than yourself?" "I protest if I did not know you I should take you to be young," simpers the most antiquated virgin in the company; "Mr. Robinson wears mighty well: my mother says he looks as well as ever she remembers him. He used to come often to the house when I was a girl." How little is the world changed since then! Mr. Robinson, his saucy daughter observed, had not the "hyp" in this company; "but indeed," she says, "it is a distemper so well bred as never to come but when people are at home and at leisure."

While thus growing up, Elizabeth formed an acquaintance which, like most of those made in early youth, greatly influenced her tastes, if not her destiny. This friend was Lady Margaret Cavendish Harley, the only daughter of Edward, Earl of Oxford and Mortimer by his wife, Lady Henrietta Cavendish, daughter and heiress of John Holles, Duke of Newcastle. Lady Margaret, when first the juvenile friendship was formed with Elizabeth—or, as she wrote to her, "Mrs. Eliza Robinson"—was eighteen years of age, while Elizabeth was scarcely twelve. Lady Margaret was the heiress of a large fortune, and married, long before her friend was old enough to enter into the world, William, the second Duke of Portland, and the leader of the Whig party. After becoming a duchess she proved to be a woman of unbounded munificence, and lived with splendid hospitality, chiefly at Bulstrode, in Buckinghamshire, where persons of high rank, more especially those eminent for talent, resorted. To her this country is deeply indebted for the preservation of the Harleian MSS. in the British Museum, which she gave to the country. To her liberality we also owe the introduction of many valuable objects of art, more especially that of the Barberini or Portland vase, into England.

To this friend Elizabeth Robinson's letters are chiefly addressed. As she grew up she became a *habituée* of that titled and intellectual circle which has perhaps never been surpassed in England. Their friendship lasted many years, and became of the most intimate character. It was the first that Elizabeth ever formed: the esteem she says, "having grown with her" since she first loved the Lady Margaret "and her doll."

From the commencement of this friendship until her marriage, Elizabeth's life seems to have been cloudless. Sometimes we hear of her going eight miles to dance to the music of a blind fiddler, and coming back at two o'clock in the morning "mightily pleased." Sometimes after her and her family dressing for a ball, and "getting into the coach with their ball airs," they were turned back by a brook being swollen, and so much did she take it to heart that she could think of nothing but the ball. "When any one asked me how I did, I cried out 'Tit for tat;' and when they bid me sit down I answered, 'Jack of the Green' "—the names of fashionable dances at that time. Sometimes she writes still merrily of a past illness; she has "swallowed the weight of an apothecary in medicine" and is not the better, except that she is less patient and less credulous. She still confesses to being fond of gadding, and furious with her barrister brother, who goes down to the sessions, and "when he had sold all his law, packed up his salable eloquence, and carried it back to Lincoln's Inn, there to be left till called for," yet he never went to the assize ball. Sometimes she goes to races for "the good of the country," and is always ready to dance to a Whig or a Tory tune; "for she was not like dancing monkeys, who only cut capers for King George." Then we find her banished to Canterbury, on account of the small-pox at home, and staying at a prebend's house, where there were nothing but visits from prebends, "deacons, and the rest of our church militant here on earth." In vain do three out of her seven brothers go to see her: she confesses to be tired of the study of divines. Next she takes her flight to Bath, where she expects that "with the spirits the waters give, and the spirits of the place, she shall be perfect *sal volatile*, and open her mouth and evaporate." Then, not hearing from her friend, whom she always addresses as "your grace," her lively fancy dictates a letter from the shades below; she writes her epistle with the pen with which Mrs. Rowe used to write her letters from the dead to the living, and begs it may be laid where it can not hear the cock crow, or it will vanish, having died a maid. So active, indeed, was the merry Eliza's mind and body that the duchess gave her the name of "la petite Fidget."

At Bath, nevertheless, the "height of her happiness" proved nothing better than a "pair royal at commerce and a peer of threescore," who greatly prefers a queen of spades to her. Still she is amused, and tells, with great gusto, an anecdote of a lady of quality, who was very tall, and who nearly drowned a few women in the cross bath, which she ordered to be filled till it reached her chin, so that those who were below her stature, as well as below her rank, were obliged to "cut or drown."

Her twentieth year came, and found her without any serious thoughts of matrimony, the "more reasonable passion of friendship" filling her heart. Perhaps, from the following passage in one of her letters, it might be that a dower was wanting. "What is a woman," she asks, "without gold or fee simple? —a toy while she is young, a trifle when she is old. Jewels of the first water are good for nothing till they are set; but as for us, we are no brilliants, nobody's money till we have a foil and are encompassed with the precious metal. As for the intrinsic value of a woman, few know it, and nobody cares. Lord Foppington appraised all the female virtues and bought them in under a thousand pounds sterling, and the whole sex have agreed no one better understood the value of womankind." Yet she passed much of her time at Whitehall, the Duke of Portland being in office, and went to every imaginable species of London gayety: sat to Zincke in the dress of Queen Anne Boleyn for her picture, and was evidently one of the belles most in vogue about the middle of the last century. Meantime the number of her correspondents augmented; Mrs. Donnellan, the friend of Swift, and Dr. Freind, afterward Dean of Canterbury, were among those to whom she wrote when in serious mood. In the midst of this hurry of life she was again banished for fear of the fatal small-pox to a Kentish farm-house, with nothing modern about it. Here she sat in an old crimson-velvet chair, that she imagined must have been elder brother to that shown in Westminster Abbey as Edward the Confessor's. Tables there were in the room with more feet than caterpillars; a "toilette that might have been worked by one of Queen Maud's maids of honor; and a looking-glass which

Rosamond or Jane Shore might have dressed their heads in." Then the old clock, which "had struck the blessed minutes of the Reformation, Restoration, Abdication, Revolution, and Accession," seemed, she fancied, from its relation to time to have some to eternity. This banishment, however, had its uses, in weaning from the world to reflection one worthy of being rescued from a mere life of vanity. "Cicero and Plutarch's heroes were her only company." She does not at this period mention those works of religious improvement which afterward formed the consolation of her old age. Yet not long afterward she thus writes: "Few are the hours allowed to freedom, to leisure, to contemplation, to the adoration of our Maker, the examination of ourselves, and the consideration of the things about us." "Few there are that remember their Creator in the days of their youth, and trust to him in their decline. We put off all things but death." It was not until the year 1742, when Elizabeth Robinson was twenty-two years of age, that we find her signing herself E. Montagu. The choice which she made was consistent with that calm good sense which always gave a value to her letters and conversation. Long before she had made up her mind as to what manner of man should be her guide, her companion, and her master. Four years previously she had denied the soft impeachment of being about to marry, and had then described her *beau idéal* to her friend the duchess.

"At present," she wrote, "I will tell you what sort of a man I desire, which is above ten times as good as I deserve. He should have a great deal of sense to instruct me; much wit to divert me; beauty to please me; good-humor to indulge me when I am right, and reprove me gently when I am in the wrong; money enough to afford me more than I can want, and as much as I can wish; and constancy to like me as long as other people do, that is, till my face is wrinkled by age or scarred by the small-pox; and after that I shall expect only civility in the room of love, for, as Mrs. Clive sings—

'All I hope of mortal man
Is to love me while he can.'"

She was, she owned, like Pygmalion, in love with the picture of our own drawing, and had never then seen the original.

The object of her choice proved to be Edward Montagu of Denton Hall, Northumberland, and Sandleford Priory, in Berkshire. He was a man of an ancient and honorable family, and of considerable abilities, which were chiefly employed in the House of Commons in the service of the Whigs. His estates, which he bequeathed to his wife, were considerable, so that one part of her wish was certainly fulfilled. How far the marriage was one, on her part, of attachment, seems questionable. The ceremony of marriage was performed on the 5th of August, 1743, by Dr. Freind, her respected correspondent, to whom she refers, when writing to the Duchess of Portland, to prove that she shed not at the altar "one single tear;" "yet," she adds, "my mind was in no mirthful mood indeed." "I have," she adds, "a great hope of happiness; the world, as you say, speaks well of Mr. Montagu, and I have many obligations to him, which must gain my particular esteem; but such a change of life must furnish one with a thousand anxious thoughts." And with this cool and sensible view she began her married life.

By her friend and preceptor, Conyers Middleton, the union was, however, hailed as between a blooming and intellectual bride with a man "not only of figure and fortune, but of great knowledge and understanding." But it seemed that the very cultivation of that understanding was to Mrs. Montagu a source of sorrow. Mr. Montagu was a great mathematician for that day, but set, to borrow the words of Dr. Beattie, "too much value on mathematical evidence, and piqued himself too much on his knowledge of that science." In other words, he was skeptical; and his wife, when she perceived him in the decline of life, without that light, devoid of which all here is dark indeed, endeavored, through Dr. Beattie, to bring his mind from that fallacious philosophy, in which he fatally confided, to faith and religious hope; but, it appears, without the much-desired effect.

Henceforth a great portion of Mrs. Montagu's life was passed in the country, where her cheerful temper and neighborly habits endeared her to all near the different abodes in which she resided. Atterthorpe, about a day's journey from Doncaster, and beautifully situated on the River Swale, was one of the first places that she visited after a journey of six days from Kent. Here she often went to the almshouse, and the schools founded by her uncle, "where the young were taught industry, the old content;" and found her happiness in her fireside, and that only when it was not "littered with queer creatures." She had not, in the midst of her pining after London and its charms, ceased to take delight in nature, and describes to her friend, Mrs. Donnellan, that wild tract called the Dales with enthusiasm. Yet she owned herself a very swallow, as she could not abide in the country in winter; confessed she had a tendency to dullness; that she loved to be a spectator of the rapid world while her "little machine" was at rest; and that the "lullaby" of country conversation affected her with drowsiness; the news and chat of her own neighborhood affecting her no more than the "Jewish Chronicle" did a modern infidel prime minister. She was, indeed, formed to be the "Queen of the Blues."

Meantime, she was finding out her husband's perfections, his integrity, benevolence, and strong affections. Ill health came, however, to dash her felicity, and Mr. Montagu was obliged to have her at Atterthorpe, and to attend Parliament. "I help him on," she wrote, "with honor's boots, and behold him go without murmuring." He left her sister with her; there was an extraordinary likeness between them, hence Mrs. Montagu always called her sister "Rea." Rea was blessed with a temper of continual sunshine, and made even the dullness of the country endurable to her poor "Fidget."

Mrs. Montagu had now hopes of becoming a mother. This she viewed with her usual good sense, and with the faith that had survived or withstood the contagion of Dr. Huddleston's opinions. She remarked that in our addresses to Heaven, we should only be earnest in thanksgiving. Much as she wished to have children, and that "her affections might be kept living in those she loved," she dared not trust herself to desire objects of so near concern and fondness as children. A son was born; "the young Fidget," as she called him, loved laughing, and dancing, and was worthy of the mother he sprang from. He seemed well and strong, and his mother's letters are, for some time, the short period of his little life, full of hopes, and prayers, and fondness. Her domestic happiness seemed perfect. Early in the September of 1744 her child died of convulsions. The blow was terrible; and no other offspring were ever granted to make it a less fearful blank. "I am well enough," she wrote to the Duchess of Portland, "as to health of body, but God knows the sickness of the soul is far worse. I know it is my duty to be resigned and to submit. I hope time will bring me comfort. I will give it my best endeavors: it is in afflictions like mine that reason ought to exert itself, else one would fall beneath the stroke." She tried to solace herself by reading, and to control her feelings by the example of her afflicted husband. She hoped the same Providence that snatched this dear blessing from her would give her others; but the hope was not fulfilled. Elizabeth Montagu, then twenty-three years of age, had a long life before her. Beauty, talents, fortune, friends, a happy marriage, influence in society, a gay genial temper, were hers. But she was henceforth childless.

She was now in her maturity, of the middle stature, with a slight stoop, so that the fire of her beautiful deep blue eyes was somewhat subdued by an air of modesty; her dark brown hair clustering over her throat and face; her high arched eyebrows; her complexion, notwithstanding the attacks made on it by the envious, singularly brilliant and yet delicate, completed the charms of her person: her manners as dignified as they were polished: with all these advantages she may have been sought by the wisest and best men (who have never any objection to youth and beauty) of her time. The scholar and the politician, the wit, the critic, the orator crowded around her. Her wit was so abundant, so fresh, so involuntary, that she found it difficult to temper it, and to adapt it to society. But her extreme good-nature and good-breeding brought it under control. It was never coarse, never disagreeable. She could curb it at the right point. The gayety of her disposition, her love of society, never drew her into folly. Discreet, correct, the admiration felt for her was that which we feel for purity and elevation of mind.

She was happy in her friends, Mrs. Elizabeth Carter, Young the poet, Gilbert West, Lord Chatham, Stillingfleet, Beattie, Lord Kaimes, Burke, and last, not least, Sir Joshua Reynolds and Garrick, were among those who honored and visited her. She chose her friends for their merits, not for their station; yet she had all society to choose from. She was, nevertheless, accused by Miss Burney and Mrs. Thrale of want of heart, and considered by those two ladies as a character to respect rather than to love: "wanting that *don d'aimer* by which alone love can be made fond or faithful." Nevertheless her affections to her own family are apparent in every line of Mrs. Montagu's letters. It is possible that her circle of friends was too large for her regard for them to be very deep; and years after her marriage we find her writing to Mrs. Elizabeth Carter: "You and I who have never been in love"—a sort of acknowledgment that her marriage was, like almost every other action of her life, the result of reason. So far Miss Burney's opinion of her seems to be confirmed.

Henceforth, Mrs. Montagu appears to belong to society alone. The last century, it has been well remarked, formed an era in all matters of taste: the arts, long dispelled by civil commotions, had been degraded during the reign of Charles II. into the subservient office of portrait painting: they were happily revived, in the very heyday of Mrs. Montagu's life, by the genius of Reynolds. Not only as an artist, but as a man of intellect and refinement, Reynolds infused into the higher classes that love of art which has never since died out among them. The society at his house, easy and inexpensive, though composed almost entirely of the most eminent people of his time, may have suggested to Mrs. Montagu that assemblage of *literati* which soon acquired the name of the "Blue Stockings;" and "to do a bit of blue," as Dr. Burney said, came into vogue.

Reynolds, while at that time painting portraits at twelve guineas a head, used to assemble Dr. Johnson, Richard Cumberland, Edmund Burke, the Thrales, and Mrs. Montagu, not to mention many others who sat around the fire on which sang the tea-kettle which Johnson wished "might never be cold;" Reynolds, "the man who could not," as Johnson well observed, "be spoiled by prosperity," found it essential for his mental powers to mix in intellectual society; and, aided by Johnson, established the "Literary Club." This famous society met at the Turk's Head, in Gerrard Street, Soho, every Monday evening, not to a costly, heavy dinner, but to supper. The standing toast was Mrs. Montagu; who for two successive years invited the club to a dinner at her house, curiosity being her motive, and possibly a desire to mingle with their conversation the charm of her own.

During the early part of her long life Mrs. Montagu had distinguished herself by an "Essay on the Genius and Writings of Shakspeare"—a composition which vindicated our immortal dramatist from the gross attacks of Voltaire. She had also published three "Dialogues of the Dead," which were printed with those of Lord Lyttleton. In the meridian of her days, she delighted to assemble around her, in an easy manner, those whose merits she could so well appreciate. For many years her time was divided between Sandleford Priory, near Newberry, and Hill Street. When in London, she received an assemblage of intellectual persons, at first, unpremeditatedly; and the only difference between these receptions and those of the fashionable world was, that cards were not introduced. The party did not consist, as literary parties are usually thought to do, solely of those who had written something; but was made up of actors, beaux, divines, and pretty or agreeable women. By the side of the learned Elizabeth Carter was found the brilliant Mrs. Boscawen, whose husband, Admiral Boscawen, glancing at Dr. Stillingfleet's gray stockings—that learned divine being an oddity and a sloven—gave these meetings the name of the "Blue Stocking Society," merely meaning that the full dress, then *de rigueur* (as still abroad) in the evening, was to be dispensed with.

"Oh!" cried a foreigner of distinction, catching up the expression, "Les bas bleus!" and the *sobriquet* is still applied to all who assume the literary character.

There was, however, as Hannah More has told us, in her poem on the Blues, no parade of knowledge in this agreeable assembly. Learning was not disfigured by pedantry, nor good taste tinctured by affectation. The general conversation was free from calumny or levity: the presiding genius, graceful and good as she was, seemed to cast her mantle over the whole.

Garrick, who, as Johnson said, "had made his profession respectable, while it made him rich," was a favorite guest of Mrs. Montagu's. "He was the only actor," Johnson remarked, "who had ever been a master both of tragedy and comedy." "And yet," added the great moralist, "I thought him less to be envied on the stage than at the head of a dinner-table;" a sentiment in which Mrs. Montagu concurred.

Destined first for the bar, next a wine-merchant, finally the founder of the modern stage, how pleasant must have been Garrick's anecdote; what a relief after the scholar-like talk of Lord Lyttelton, the responsive pedantry of Mrs. Carter, and the propriety of Mrs. Chapone! One can fancy him telling the anecdote of his sitting to a poor painter, not very skillful, and when a certain progress had been made in the portrait, changing his countenance while the artist's back was turned; and, when the patient man had worked on so as to alter the likeness, and make it what he *then* saw, how he had seized his opportunity, and changed his expression a third time; how the ill-used painter had thrown down his pallet and pencils, exclaiming, that he perceived he was painting the devil, and would touch the canvas no more.

How amusing, also, must it have been to hear Garrick bantering Johnson about the Cock-lane Ghost—a tale which the superstitious Johnson credited, but which the player disbelieved! Horace Walpole, in his prime, when first these meetings were in vogue, but latterly, when Dr. Beattie saw him in 1791, though still "well-bred, and of pleasant discourse, martyred by the gout;" Lord Lyttelton, who was supposed to have felt for Mrs. Montagu a tenderer sentiment than that of friendship; and the great Lord Chatham, were the constant visitors of Mrs. Montagu's house.

In the latter part of the last century, that which was once an intimate circle became so fashionable a resort, that the rooms of Montagu House were thronged, and the intimate, tea-drinking, social character of the assembly merged into one far less agreeable. It must have been then that Mrs. Montagu was sometimes, according to Miss Burney, "brilliant in diamonds, solid in judgment, critical in talk; sometimes flashy, and an immense talker; but still eminently courteous and agreeable."

After Mrs. Montagu took possession of Montagu House, her entertainments were given on a scale of great splendor. Miss

Burney describes a grand breakfast, at which all the company ate enormously, though, as it was remarked, had Mrs. Montagu invited them to dinner at three o'clock, her friends would have exclaimed, "What does it mean? Who can dine at three o'clock?"

The gallery of Montagu House was, on that occasion, thronged by the survivors of those early friends whom Mrs. Montagu had so delighted to collect as her Blue-stocking circle. Seward, the compiler of the "Anecdotes," the Burneys and Boscawens, were there; but Garrick, Johnson, and Reynolds were gone; and the skeptical and intellectual master of the house had disappeared from the scene. In 1755 Mr. Montagu died, as Dr. Beattie affirms, in "extreme old age," so that he must have been many years his wife's senior. His wife's efforts were directed, during his last days, to his eternal welfare, upon which Dr. Beattie held many conferences with him, but, it appears, without any satisfactory result.

Happily, from among her family ties, Mrs. Montagu found still some objects for that affection which only the links of blood can endear. She adopted Matthew, the son of her eldest brother, Matthew Robinson; and bequeathing to him her whole fortune, required him to take the name of Montagu. To this descendant, who became in 1829 fourth Baron Rokeby, we owe the publication of Mrs. Montagu's letters; and on him devolved the office of an editor, which he performed with as little pains and care as possible. The present gallant Lord Rokeby is the great-nephew of Mrs. Montagu. It was of Matthew Montagu that Sir Nathaniel Wraxall related, "that General Montagu Mathew said, in the House of Commons, upon some mistake relative to their identity, 'that there was no more likeness between Montagu Matthew and Matthew Montagu than between a chestnut horse and a horse-chestnut.'" Having been brought up under his aunt's especial care, Mr. Montagu is said to have received an education far more suited to make a man of letters than a statesman. He appears not to have distinguished himself in either of those capacities.

One turns reluctantly from the bright, yet quiet, circle of the original *bas bleus* to the gayer receptions of Mrs. Montagu's later days. In the early part of her reign as a "Queen of Society," her empire was divided with the famous Viscountess Townshend, at whose house a more fashionable, and perhaps a less unexceptionable class of *littérateurs* used to meet without ceremony in the evenings. Lady Townshend, who succeeded Lady Mary Wortley Montagu and Lady Hervey, had figured as a leader of society. Here George Selwyn, Charles Fox, and Sheridan, who was just in the dawn of that career which even

Pitt allowed to be full of eloquence and the powers of fancy, but which he represented to be devoid of reason and truth, shone conspicuously; and in other bright spheres until reckless habits and vices obscured their career. The political and literary clique at Lady Townshend's was now extinct; and Whitehall had ceased to be the centre of wit and fashion since 1788.

Every year, on the other hand, until her death, added to Mrs. Montagu's enlarging circle of votaries. Hers was the very house which is now so greatly wanted in London, where there is no point of union for persons of congenial tastes and pursuits; and no intimate evening society, as in France, in which the pleasures of conversation may be enjoyed with nothing but the *bouillote* on the table, the *brioche* by the fire. Nothing can be worse than the present form of metropolitan society for the intellect, the spirits, the health. "I know half the west end of London," said the late Lord Dudley to the late eminent surgeon, Mr. Copeland, "and yet there is not a house in which I could walk in and ask a cup of tea." Always on the defensive, the English hedge round every thing that is agreeable with exclusiveness, and encumber it with ostentation: and even were Mrs. Montagu, in all her perfection of mind, person, and position, to arise from the dead, to light up the gallery and the drawing-rooms, and call the spirits of the departed from their tombs, we should, I fear, consider her parties as "very mixed." For though she was herself well-born, the associate of duchesses and countesses, rich and gracious, she was un-English enough to call into her presence the lowly born, "under-bred people," if eminent in any way, and harsh enough to banish thence titled sinners of both sexes. We are more liberal now to the sinful, and less indulgent to the unrefined!

Mrs. Montagu, for instance, brought into the unshrinking contact of prime ministers and leaders of *ton* James Beattie, the son of a small retail dealer at Lawrence-Kirk, in the county of Kincardine—his father, a man who kept what is called "the shop" in his native village. She cherished, she assisted him; and, with equal *mauvais ton*, dropped the acquaintance of Thomas, the bad Lord Lyttelton, the pleasantest scapegrace that ever sullied by misdeeds a good name. Thomas, Lord Lyttelton, was a "meteor whose rapid extinction could not be regretted;" but Beattie was like the evening star, whose light we hail as the harbinger of repose. Thomas, Lord Lyttelton, was the spoiled child of fortune. Vain, elegant, and profligate, in the morning, he was, as Mr. Curtis said, "melancholy, squalid, disgusting, and half-repentant; in the evening, the delight, the admiration, and the leader of society; always fearful and superstitious, yet not religious." For a while his youthful and almost handsome face, with the hair turned back over a wide forehead, his bag wig, his exquisite ruffles, and an expression half good-humored, half sarcastic, might be seen in the great assemblies at Montagu House, where he was long tolerated for his father's sake: but he soon became too notorious for any society, and vanished from his own sphere into a lower orbit. His death was predicted to him when in the last stage of decline—at thirty-five years of age—by an apparition in the form of a young lady whom he had seduced. The hour was foretold; and though his friends set the clock on, he expired to the minute that she had predicted. This is the only ghost-story in modern times that has been carefully investigated and minutely recorded; and the short account of it is inscribed on a brass plate in the house near Epsom in which the titled sinner died. The three last years of his existence were passed in penitence, and in an attempt at reform; but the period, as one of his friends wrote, of his emancipation from the fetters of pleasure and indolence also marked his dissolution. Such was the detestation of his character that his funeral took place at night, for fear that the people of Hagley should tear his remains from the coffin in fury.

Thomas, Lord Lyttelton, was a splendid speaker and a wit, a maccaroni (or dandy) of the first class, a man of wonderful fascination; perhaps in the reign of Charles II. he might have been almost respectable; with all his wickedness he must have been a brilliant person in society. Dr. Beattie, on the contrary, educated at the parish-school of Lawrence-Kirk, then himself a schoolmaster, knowing, for many a long year, no better society than that which a peasant's cottage affords; next a professor at Aberdeen, a pedagogue, speaking broad Scotch, must have been one of the most virtuous bores in existence. But he had, though, as we now think, feebly, the seeds of poetic excellence in him: he was pious, hard-working, patient; yet even in his prime he could not have been a very agreeable object. "For have I not," he says to his friend Charles Boyd, "headaches, like Pope? vertigo, like Swift? gray hairs, like Homer? Do I not wear large shoes for fear of corns, like Virgil? and sometimes complain of sore eyes, like Horace?" He seems to have had all the infirmities of these great men without their genius.

When he was thirty-two years of age, he became known to Mrs. Montagu by report. For his own part he regarded her as an honor to her sex and to human nature. Even then he talked of his broken health; but soon afterward a fearful calamity happened to him. His wife, Mary Dun, daughter of the rector of the grammar-school at Aberdeen, had inherited insanity from her mother; and was herself sufficiently wrong-headed to make others wretched, but not to be placed under restraint. Eventually her state, which made poor Beattie inconceivably miserable, broke out into madness.

He had his mother also to support: his means were so limited that he was intoxicated with delight when £52 10*s.* were paid him by the publisher for his famous "Essay on Truth," which it had taken him four years to write, and which he had written three times over; yet the worthy son of the retail dealer is to be envied, in stern comparison with the once idolized heir of the grave and good George, Lord Lyttelton.

In 1771, Beattie went to London, and was introduced by Dr. Gregory, the author of "A Father's Legacy to his Daughters," to Mrs. Montagu. Never, certainly, was an author more plentifully rewarded with fame than was Beattie for his "Essay on Truth;" to say nothing of his poetry. He received a degree at Oxford, and was ordered to Kew Green, where he had an interview with George III. and his queen. "I never stole a book but one," said the kind-hearted monarch, "and that was yours; I stole it from the queen to give it to Lord Hertford to read." Then his majesty, entering into conversation, said he could not believe "that any thinking man could be an Atheist, unless he could bring himself to believe that he made himself"—an idea that seemed so satisfactory that King George repeated it two or three times to the queen. Beattie received also the more substantial benefit of a pension.

Nevertheless, unremitting anxieties marked the career of this good man. It was his fate to lose a beloved son, Mrs. Montagu's godson; to watch over his wife in all the various stages of her malady; and, expiring, to know that she who survived him was hopelessly insane.

He found in music, in which he was a fine performer, a source of infinite consolation. His slouching gait; his large, dark, melancholy eyes; his broad accent, and a kind of simplicity which was always gentle, but yet peculiar, must have marked him out to the derision of the *beau monde* of Portman Square. Short were his periods of peace or rest. "Ever since the commencement of our vacation," he wrote, in 1790, to Sir William Forbes, "I have been passing from one scene of perplexity and sorrow to another." At last all was closed in death. Loved and mourned, he died three years after his kind friend, Mrs. Montagu. The famous Dr. Gregory, writing his epitaph on Mrs. Montagu, said, in 1799: "She has to me on all occasions, ever since 1771, been a faithful and affectionate friend, especially in seasons of distress and difficulty." A simple but heartfelt encomium. To this excellent man was the regard given which was withheld from the dissolute and agreeable peer by the rightly thinking.

Yet the Queen of the Blue Stockings was eminently charitable in her judgments: "I would much rather, even in that very world where charity may be less in fashion than prudence, be accounted a person of inviolable charity than of infallible wisdom. In the hazards of a weak and fallible judgment, I had rather fall into error than into cruel injustice."

Her useful and happy life was now drawing to its close.

She had ever, to use her own words, "enjoyed the present so as not to hurt the future." "Every day," she thought, "ought to be considered as a period apart; some virtue should be exercised; some knowledge improved, and the value of happiness well understood; some pleasure comprehended in it: some duty to ourselves or others must be infringed if any of these things are neglected."

She had never wished for old age; yet length of years is usually allotted to women of letters, and was to her.

Her decline was solaced by her own high thoughts, and cheered by the regard of all who knew her. Though nearly blind for many years, the hours that had never been misspent in cards—the fashionable pastime of that day—were not passed in repining. She had seen the seeds of gambling fostered in early youth. "If I had the education of a child of large fortune, it should not in its earliest infancy play a trick with a court-card. But, alas! it is too late that we taste the wormwood in these things." She had not now to regret that "*whisk*," as she writes it, and quadrille were to her impossible. She had ever esteemed the delights of friendship more highly than those of love; and certainly they failed her not in her old age.

"Many guests," she wrote, "my heart has not admitted; such as there are do it honor, and a long and intimate acquaintance has preceded their admittance: they were invited in it by its best virtues, they passed through the examination of severity, nay, even answered some questions of suspicion that inquired of their constancy and sincerity; but now they are delivered over to the keeping of constant faith and love; for doubt never visits the friend entirely, but only examines such as would come in, lest the way should be too common." What a beautiful definition of friendship!—but it is, alas! of the friendship of the old school. Friends are now made with the speed of railroads, to be dropped at any station in life's journey, to get rid of them when they become a burden.

In her youth she had thus spoken of extreme old age: "If

the near prospect of death is terrible, it is a melancholy thing when every day of added life is a miracle: but such is the happy and merciful order of things that life is eternal, and therefore we can not outlive it. It has for our amusement the midsummer's dream and the winter's tale: the ear, deaf to all other music, is still soothed by its flattering voice."

The Duchess of Portland died nearly fifteen years before Mrs. Montagu. Eight years previous to that event, Mrs. Montagu had visited Bulstrode, "the scene of more tender and sincere joy," when she returned to it, "than any other place." The dignity and piety which distinguished the duchess through life, the excellence of her conduct as a wife, a mother, and a friend, were not excelled by any lady of rank in her day.

Mrs. Montagu, in the decline of life, visited Dr. Gregory, whose daughter long resided with her, at Edinburgh. When at Sandleford Priory, the benevolence of that heart which left a sum for the poor chimney-sweepers to enjoy one holiday in their dark life, showed itself in regard to the haymakers, thirty-six of whom she had at dinner under the shade of a grove in her garden.

When they worked well she loved to see them eat as well as labor, and often sent them a treat to which the haymakers "brought an appetite that gave a better relish than the Madeira wine and Cayenne pepper in which an alderman stews his turtle."

Two years before the close of the last century, Mrs. Montagu continued to receive company at home, although she had ceased to leave her house. "Mrs. Montagu is so broke down," Dr. Burney wrote to his daughter, "as not to go out—almost wholly blind and very feeble." During the ensuing year a report was even prevalent that she was dead: but her decease did not occur till the year 1800, when she expired at Montagu House, aged eighty.

Of this excellent woman Dr. Beattie says: "I have known several ladies in literature, but she excelled them all, and in conversation she had more *wit* than any other person, male or female."

These, he adds, were her slighter accomplishments. "She was a sincere Christian, both in faith and practice, so that by her influence and example she did great good." Yet Mrs. Montagu was not so fortunate as to escape enemies: Dr. Johnson especially disliked one who had often eclipsed him. Nevertheless, Johnson, as Miss Burney asserts, did justice to Mrs. Montagu when others did not praise her improperly. He delighted in seeing her humbled.

"To-morrow, sir," said Mrs. Thrale one day (at Streatham),

MRS. MONTAGU'S ENTERTAINMENT TO THE HAYMAKERS.

"Mrs. Montagu dines with us, and then you will have talk enough." Johnson began to see-saw, and then, turning to Miss Burney, cried, "Down with her, Burney! down with her at once! spare her not! down with her! attack her! you are a rising wit, and she is at the top. So at her, Burney—at her, and down with her."

He had, it seems, put her out of countenance when she had last dined there, out of wanton savageness; but promised now not to contradict her as he did then unless she provoked him again. Yet he acknowledged that she diffused more "knowledge in her conversation than almost any woman he knew—he might almost say, any man;" to which Mrs. Thrale added that she knew no man equal to her, except the doctor, and Burke. Nevertheless, after a time—

"Come, Burney," he resumed, "shall you and I study our parts against Mrs. Montagu comes?"

"I think," said Mrs. Thrale, "you should begin with Miss Gregory, and down with her first."

"No, no!" cried the doctor, "always fly at the eagle—down with Mrs. Montagu herself. I hope she will come full of 'Evelina.'" They could not, however, prevail on Dr. Johnson to stay for this encounter. Early in the day Mrs. Montagu arrived, accompanied by Miss Gregory, a fine-looking young woman. Miss Burney's description of Mrs. Montagu, about the age of sixty, corresponds tolerably with that of others who knew her intimately. She was thin and spare, and looked younger than she really was from that circumstance. Every line of her face showed intelligence; but her eyes had in them an expression of severity and sarcasm which was not attractive. She was very cheerful, with a great flow of words, but apt to become dictatorial and sententious. It is said that this manner was acquired; and indeed one can hardly reconcile, in this stilted, uncompromising woman, the merry, discursive Elizabeth Robinson of former days. Neither was her voice musical, nor her whole style feminine; and while what she said was excellent, it failed, on that account, to charm, though it might often convince.

Then, as she advanced in years, her style of dress by no means suited the decline of her brilliant life. Even when approaching fourscore, she could not relinquish her diamonds and her bows, which formed, of an evening, the perpetual ornament of her emaciated person. Wraxall, who is only equaled in ill-nature by Miss Burney, thought that these glittering appendages of opulence were used to dazzle those whom her literary reputation failed to astound: but they were probably merely the adornments which the habit of using them had rendered almost essential.

Notwithstanding these imperfections, to be invited to Montagu House was the aim of all rising *literati*. Mrs. Montagu was the Madame du Deffand of London; and her fame as the Queen of Society rested not only on her intellect, her "Essay on Shakspeare," her conversational talents, but also on the solid basis of her being the best dinner-giver in London. Sometimes, however, her parties failed; witness the meeting of the Bishop of Chester and Mrs. Thrale, when the bishop waited for Mrs. Thrale to begin speaking, and Mrs. Thrale waited for the bishop, and Mrs. Montagu harangued away, "caring not one fig who spoke, as long as she could herself be listened to." Not to be welcomed to Hill Street, which was an abode of much elegance, or to Mrs. Montagu's new house in Portman Square, would have made the great critic himself miserable. Even at a certain dreaded dinner at Streatham, into which Miss Burney walked with a company step, Johnson could not help asking, in a jocose manner, if he should be invited to see it. And when Mrs. Montagu asked them all to a house-warming, fixing *Easter-day* for their visit, a general emotion of pleasure ran through the party. There was about the close of the eighteenth century so great a change in costume, that the ancient lady in her diamonds and her knots of ribbon must have looked almost like an inhabitant of another period. As Mrs. Montagu came forth in all this finery, she mingled with a fashionable throng who, after the year 1794, were wholly changed in dress and style. Her youth and middle age had been passed with those who in private life wore the costume which is now confined to the levée or drawing-room, but which was then assumed every where and every day. Fox and his clique, affecting a contempt for dress, although formerly coxcombs of the greatest pretensions, first threw a discredit on it; and these new ideas passed from the House of Commons to the clubs, from the clubs to the private assemblies of the capital. Dress was in a sort of atrophy, and Jacobinism gave it its deathblow. Pantaloons, cropped hair, shoe-strings, came into use. Ruffles and buckles went out with powder, and etiquette, in a form, was also vanishing by degrees. Such were the men: while the ladies, casting off their tresses, laying aside their cushions and their curls, their lappets and ribbons, had their locks cut round *à la victime*, as if ready for the stroke of the guillotine.

To carry out the republican phrenzy, the Grecian style was adopted; short waists, sleeves fastened by a button; tight skirts; a drapery suited to the climates of Rome and Greece, but almost death in our foggy atmosphere; and thus distinctions began to be leveled in this country. It was, perhaps, to repel this innovation that the "queen of the blues" was still seen blazing in diamonds—a mark for the ridicule of those who lived in new lights, as the doctrines of revolutionized France were then considered among a certain set or party in the great world.

Another enemy of Mrs. Montagu's was Richard Cumberland, a "Sir Fretful Plagiary," who could endure no one's works but his own. The "Observer," of which he was the editor and chief contributor, was full of personalities; and he attacked Mrs. Montagu, under the name of Vanessa, with much acrimony.

The blue-stocking assemblies, as they were styled, remained in their perfection fifteen years, from 1770 to 1785; but declined after the death of Dr. Johnson, who had formed around him a circle that was then broken up. Horace Walpole was after that period devoured by the gout: Sir Joshua Reynolds could not, from his deafness, contribute to conversation. Mrs. Chapone, who, though a woman of great knowledge, had one of the most repulsive exteriors ever seen, was not calculated, any more than her letters, to enliven. Burke sometimes hovered for a short time in Portman Square, but was absorbed in politics and soon disappeared. Erskine, then a rising barrister, and like many such of his own time and ours, involved in debt, sometimes enchanted the lingerers in what was now comparatively a desert by his vivacity and versatility of talent. Sir William Pepys, Topham Beauclerk, and Bennet Langton were still there, and still welcomed. Hume and Adam Smith, as well as Robertson, lived in Edinburgh, and Gibbon never affected "the blues;" and it is indeed probable that neither he nor Hume nor Smith would have been received by a society so averse to their doctrines and their publications.

To Mrs. Montagu is wholly due the origin of the literary society of the metropolis. It is indeed highly probable that she imbibed her notions of social and intellectual intercourse from the many foreigners expatriated here. The first literary meetings are said to have been held by Hortensia Mancini, niece to Cardinal Mazarin, who assembled in her apartments men of letters, among whom St. Evremond and De Grammont figured.

But no Englishwoman ever succeeded so completely in drawing men from the clubs, and women from the faro-table or quadrille, to the disquisiton of literature and science, so thoroughly as Mrs. Montagu.

She is remembered chiefly for this service done to society; in which, as she had no predecessors, she may be said to have had few successors to be compared to her. As a writer she was respectable; her "Essay on Shakspeare" was praised by

Beattie, who has pronounced it the most elegant piece of criticism in our language or in any other.

Her letters have been also highly eulogized. Ten years after her death they were given to the world, and later the correspondence of her matured years was added to her earlier epistles. These last have, we think, a peculiar charm. Models of pure English as they are, they are easy, sparkling, and sensible. No young person can read them without deriving advantage; without an increased desire for improvement; without finding the sympathies of heart go along with the advancement of the intellect; and it is a satisfaction to know that she who penned those letters, not only thought wisely, but acted well; and living in the world, rose above its follies and meannesses with the aid of faith. To say that she had her weaknesses was but to say that she was mortal: that she had great benevolence, enlarged views, tender feelings for the unhappy, a sincere reverence, above all things, for virtue, is but justice rendered to the merits of Elizabeth Montagu.

MARY, COUNTESS OF PEMBROKE.

CERTAIN families among the English aristocracy have seemed to hold a monopoly of intelligence, honorable ambition, and virtue; several successive generations conferred on the Sidneys and the Herberts especially those distinctive attributes: and these were happily united in the sixteenth century by marriage. Mary Sidney, the sister of that true Christian hero, Sir Philip, in becoming the wife of Henry, Earl of Pembroke, the son of one of the most wealthy and respected of the English peers, and the father of one of the greatest patrons of learning in his time, William, Earl of Pembroke, brought to the splendor of Wilton the gifts and graces of Penshurst.

To the characteristics of Mary, Countess of Pembroke, the term "illustrious" might also be applied. She was distinguished among contemporary wives and mothers for her piety, her abilities, her erudition, and for her social qualities. She stood at the head of society in her age. She influenced the tone of that society; she was its example, its ornament. She befriended genius, and she gathered around her the gifted and the virtuous.

This admirable woman was the daughter of Sir Henry Sidney, of Penshurst Place, in Kent. In that ancient pile, around which ancestral oaks, planted in the reign of Charles the First, and noble elms recall the remembrance of the old Norman line of Sidneys who have successively observed their growth, or delighted in their shade — among these there will come back to the imaginative who ponder on the past, an ancient councilor of Elizabeth's reign, clad in a close ruff, tight doublet, black, yet girded with lace; a steeple-crowned hat, bombasted trunk hose, and nether hose of good linsey, for silk so wise a man would abjure; and, while we view in this phantom of fancy the legislator, the benefactor, the country gentleman, the courtier, we recognize also, in his military bearing, the general and the conqueror. Such, and in so many characters united in one, was Sir Henry Sidney. To him the Countess Mary, of Pembroke, owed her birth. His name is still heard beneath those spreading forest-trees; still are the Sidneys ours; still is Penshurst theirs. The old tenement, more quaint than grand, that witnessed the career of Henry Sidney, the youth of his son, the dawn of his daughter's good and sagacious mind, is still a national boast. Given by Edward the

Sixth to Sir William Sidney, his father's steward of the household and chamberlain, it is picturesque rather than important: a manor-house—neither a castle nor a palace. Penshurst *Place*—or, as the villagers used to call it, retaining the old spelling, "Pencester Place"—could not have been defended: it has a noble hall for hospitality, but no accommodation for a royal progress in those days, or for monster entertainments in ours. It is more interesting than handsome, more traditional than historical. What a repose pervades its park, its pleasaunce! the small village and the old decaying church! How adapted yon glades seem for Sir Henry's walk and talk! How suited the somewhat flat, yet fair expanse of turf for the gravity of old footsteps, or for the revelry of reckless, happy childhood!

Believing in races, with Dr. Arnold, who must have had vast opportunities of studying fully their manifestations at Rugby, one looks far up the roll of names to see whence came the nobility of nature which has made the Sidneys a proverb for honor, for letters, for piety, for courage. We find them descended from Gundred, or Gundreda, the daughter of William the Conqueror. Her tomb was discovered some fifteen years ago in the church at Lewes, in Sussex, after being hidden somehow and somewhere and for some reason, unseen and untold, during all these eventful centuries. The inscription on that tomb is remarkable. Gundred was married to the Earl de Warren, who was governor of Lewes, then a most important trust. Her character is described by all historians as singularly devout, benignant, and high-toned. She was, says the inscription on her tomb, "Mary to her God: Martha to her neighbor." From her, through the marriage of her grand-daughter to the Earl of Warwick, the direct ancestor of the Sidneys, are this fine old race descended.

A more exalted character than that of Sir Henry Sidney is scarcely to be met in history. It is rare in any time to find a consummate legislator, a valiant general, a first-rate privy councilor; a man of the world in every sense, as holy as an anchorite, yet mingling with his love to God human interests and affections which chastened his conduct and elevated his heart. He was the benefactor of the poor Irish; his soul rose nobly above self-aggrandizement, and he scorned to enrich himself as viceroy at the expense of that impoverished country. His wife, the mother of Mary Sidney, was—and it is much to say—worthy of being united to a Sidney. The Lady Mary Dudley whom, wisely, Sir Henry chose for his wife, was the daughter of John, Duke of Northumberland. "As she was of descent," writes the herald Arthur Collins, "of great nobility, so she was by nature of a noble and congenial spirit." Such was the mother of Philip and Mary Sidney.

Never did parents more fondly love their children than this truly noble pair. Their great object was not, however, for present happiness or advancement, but to prepare their treasures for an eternal sphere. In a manuscript letter preserved in the Somers' Collection we find what is endorsed, "A postscript by my Lady Sidney in the skirts of my lord-president's letter to her sayd son Philip:"

"Your noble and carefull father hath taken paynes (with his own hand) to give you in this his letter so wise, so learned, and most requisite precepts for you to follow with a diligent and humble, thankfull minde, as I will not withdrawe your eies from beholding and reverent honoring the same; no, not so long time as to read any letter from me; and, therefore, at this time I will write unto you no other letter than this: whereby I first bless you, with my desire to God to plant you in his grace; and, secondarily, warne you to have alwaies before the eyes of your mind these excellent counsailles of my lord, your deere father, and that you fail not continually once in foure or five daies to reade them over. * * *

"Farewell, my little Philip, and once againe the Lord bless you! Your loving mother, MARIE SIDNEY."

The superficial education given to our grandmothers was the introduction of later times, and must be ascribed to the breaking up of all society during the Rebellion in the first instance; and in the second to the indifference to literature, philosophy, and even to history engendered during the vulgar rule of the three first Georges. Previously, however, to that era, no lady of condition could be deemed properly trained for her station except she were versed in English poetry, in theology, and even in some portion of classical learning. Thus the education of Mary Sidney was conducted with the view to make her an enlightened, agreeable, reflective woman; able to take her place in the colloquies of the divine, as well as to shine in a court gala when she gave her hand to a partner to tread a measure. All politeness was taught her; but true politeness, she was assured, could only be secured by mental cultivation, could only spring from a Christian courtesy. Such was the case in the middle of the sixteenth century, when Lady Mary was born.

But there was another cause of the great pre-eminence of this intellectual woman, even in an age of female excellence. She was blessed with a brother whose name is still uttered to all English boys of condition as an incentive to true glory. In the old gallery of Penshurst hangs a portrait of a fair young man, with a long, narrow face, with a peculiar quickness of eye, and nobleness of brow. That is Sir Philip Sidney. Dates do not exactly show whether he was younger or older than his sister. He was born in 1554, and received the name of Philip, one regrets to say, in compliment to Philip II. of Spain, the husband of Mary Tudor. His education was commenced at Shrewsbury, chosen, perhaps, from its vicinity to Wales, of which Sir Henry Sidney was at one time lord-president. He went to Christ Church, at Oxford, when he was fifteen, studying afterward at Cambridge; even then the academical celebrity of these two great universities being based on different studies, and advantages, special to each, to be met with in them. It is related of the great pride of our nation, Mrs. Somerville, that she acquired her love for mathematics by being present at the instructions given by an eminent professor to her brother, Mr. Gregg. She used to sit by, working, and when the professor went away she wrote down all she had gathered into her comprehensive mind. To that mind the first taste, the propelling force were thus given; and we acknowledge the greatness of her whom Sir James Mackintosh used playfully to call "Queen of the Heavens." In the same way Mary Sidney, it is probable, may have gleaned much of her knowledge, for it is evident that her brother regarded her as his intellectual companion; one who could appreciate his works, who could sympathize in his pursuits. They were, however, frequently separated. Every young man of rank and fortune at that day made the grand tour, but no one could do so without a license from the sovereign. When he was eighteen, Philip Sidney obtained permission from Queen Elizabeth to go to France. Charles IX. then ruled over that country, and Sir Francis Walsingham was embassador. To him Sir Philip had a strong recommendation from Dudley, Earl of Leicester, his maternal uncle, and the favorite of Elizabeth; and, strange to say, Charles IX. took him, on that account, though an Englishman and a Protestant, into his household, and made him one of the gentlemen of his bedchamber.

Mary Sidney, meantime, was pursuing at home the studies which won her the following praise from Osborn, the historian of King James I.: "She was that sister of Sir Philip Sidney to whom he addressed his 'Arcadia,' and of whom he had no other advantage than what he received from the partial benevolence of fortune in making him a man (which yet she did, in some judgments, recompense in beauty); her pen being nothing short of his, as I am ready to attest, having seen some incomparable letters of hers." She won also a tribute from Spenser, who refers to her as

> "The gentle shepherdess that lived that day,
> And most resembling in shape and spirit,
> Her brother dear."

It is difficult to say at what period of her life began that version of the Psalms which obtained the name of the "Sydnean Psalms," and which are said to have been the joint production of Philip and Mary Sidney. But it appears probable that they were the effort of a later period—that of her married life. "The ties of consanguinity," as an historian expresses it, "between this illustrious brother and sister were strengthened by friendship, the effect of congenial sentiments, and similitude of manners."

One of the results of Mary Sidney's muse, however, may have been the result of her comparative seclusion at Penshurst before she became the mistress of Wilton. "A Pastoral Dialogue in praise of Astræa" was given to the world in Davison's "Poetical Rhapsody." Astræa was, of course, Queen Elizabeth. It was a tribute to that extraordinary woman and incomparable queen on the occasion of her visiting either Penshurst or Wilton, *which* is not known; and begins thus:

> *Thenot.* "I sing divine Astræa's praise,
> O Muses, help my wits to raise,
> And heave my verses higher."
> *Piers.* "Thou need'st the truth but plainly tell,
> Which much I doubt thou canst not well,
> Thou art so oft a liar."

Again—

> *Thenot.* "Astræa may be justly said,
> A field in flowery robe arrayed,
> In seasons freshly springing."
> *Piers.* "That spring indures but shortest time
> This never leaves Astræa's clime,
> Thou liest, instead of singing."
>
> *Thenot.* "Then, Piers, of friendship tell me why,
> My meaning true, my words should lie,
> And strive in vaine to raise her?"
> *Piers.* "Words from conceit do onely rise,
> Above conceit her honour flies,
> But silence naught can praise her."

The taste for versifying was increased by the companionship of Spenser, who was only two years younger than Philip Sidney. Connected with the great family of Spenser or Spencer of Althorpe, Edmund Spenser was among the earliest, the most distinguished, the most grateful friends of Philip Sidney. To him the great poet of the Elizabethan era dedicated his "Shepherd's Calendar," under the modest name of *Immerito.* Gabriel Harvey had introduced the two poets to each other. The one, Spenser, poor, ambitious, highly educated, was writhing under the pecuniary difficulties from which he never emerged: the other, Sidney, was in the full tide of fortune; in affluence, aided by powerful friends, with health and hope around him. Yet he forgot not the poor poet, improvident as well as poor: he introduced him to Dudley, Earl of Leicester, by whom Spenser was employed in foreign missions. It is, however, still a matter of doubt to whom the honor of presenting Spenser to the queen is due—whether Raleigh performed that office, or whether to Sir Philip the merit is to be assigned. At all events, Spenser was the associate both of Philip and of his sister, whom he couples together as we have seen. But the pursuits of Mary Sidney were interrupted, though, as it appears, not cut short by her marrying, which took place in 1676.

Previous to that event her brother returned from his travels: they had been both adventurous and improving. When the Massacre of St. Bartholomew was perpetrated, he had taken refuge with Walsingham, the embassador: he had visited Vienna, Hungary, and most of the Italian cities: yet he brought back to his home pure thoughts, high principles, and a blameless practice. His accomplishments were great: nevertheless, there must have been a strong family interest, to procure for him, at the age of twenty-two, the appointment of embassador to the court of Vienna, to which he was accredited. So, after witnessing the nuptials of his sister, he again revisited the Continent. Mary, meantime, was transplanted to the almost princely magnificence of Wilton. Of some, indeed of many of the high-born girls of those days, it was the lot to leave the homes of affection, refinement, and intelligence, to become the wives of dry statesmen, of rough soldiers, or of mere hunting and hawking nobles or squires. But Mary Sidney was, in most respects, far more fortunate than the majority of young women. In all probability, when she was united to Henry, Earl of Pembroke, she acted from her own inclination. It was consistent with the benevolence of her father's character to allow his children, in the most momentous affairs of their existence, the chance of happiness. But in this respect, as in all others, Mary Sidney appears to have been felicitous, when she became the third wife of Henry, the second Earl of Pembroke—in that character the leader of such society as aspired to intellectual eminence, and at the same time maintained a magnificence consistent with their rank.

In this respect the Herberts were unequaled, except, perhaps, by the Arundels. William, Earl of Pembroke, the father of Henry, was one of the most important and magnificent characters of his time. It was then still in remembrance, how he had ridden to his mansion of Baynard Castle with a retinue of three hundred horsemen, a hundred of whom were gentlemen in suits of blue cloth, with chains round their necks, and badges, denoting a sort of bond or servitude, on their sleeves, which bore a dragon worked in gold. Neither did the heralds omit to proclaim what costly largesse there was at this great earl's funeral, when two thousand pounds was spent merely for mourning, every thing else corresponding. It may, therefore, readily be conceived to how grand a pitch every arrangement for the living was raised when such an expenditure was appropriated to the dead.

Henry, Earl of Pembroke, the husband of Mary Sidney, was, when she married him, childless, having been divorced from his first wife, the daughter of Grey, Earl of Suffolk, and having lost his second. The union of Mary Sidney with this nobleman was, however, blessed by the birth of two sons.

She now attracted to Wilton all the illustrious characters of that great period. Of her appearance some portraits give an impression of a plain, long, and somewhat hard face with heavy features; a large, long nose, a small mouth, round which marked lines detracted from the sweetness of the countenance; fine arched eyebrows, and a sleepy, thoughtful eye. Her hair is upraised from a low but broad forehead, and dressed in a thicket of tiny curls, like those of a well-kept poodle: above this intricate mass is a sort of hair trimming, a lock rolled back and forming a frame to the forest beneath. The face is, on the whole, more intellectual than pleasing; the dress very stately, such as one may conceive her to have worn when receiving Queen Elizabeth, or going, with a sickened heart, when a widow, to the wild gayeties patronized by Anne of Denmark. An enormous ruff of delicate lace, vandycked at the edges in a double row, stands out and shows her fair throat and neck, round which two rows of immense pearls are thrown. Over the long tight sleeves of her dress is a velvet mantle edged with minever, that dowager fur which seems to have been designed for queens and courts alone, and which all the dictates of etiquette have appropriated to their use. Two pear-shaped pearls appear beneath the hair, and the long, thin hand holds a Psalter.

In stately form, but in all sweetness and courtesy, did Mary, Countess of Pembroke receive the guests who filled at times the picture-galleries of Wilton. Here Raleigh, with lofty brow, over which a mass of black hair was closely cut square, so as to show that elevated forehead; Raleigh, with his wonderfully searching eyes, his long face, his slight mustache over his faultless mouth, his close-cut pointed beard; Raleigh, with his mind and fancy full, his talk of Ireland, then of Essex, of the queen's last favor, or perchance of Spenser, or of this rare genius—"Will Shakespeare"—was ever a welcome guest, for he had befriended Spenser, and was esteemed by the long-absent, ever-deplored Philip. Here Sir John Harrington, the godson of Queen Elizabeth, talked, one may imagine, against the marriage of bishops, a point with him almost of monomania, but nevertheless acceptable to the queen, his godmother; whom he had almost offended by his having received the order of knighthood from the Earl of Essex on the field of battle. Here, when secrets of state were to be wormed out, crept in he whom King James called his "little beagle," deformed Cecil, Lord Salisbury, the son and successor of the great Burleigh. Cecil was crooked in mind as well as body. One can not imagine him to have been a favorite at Wilton; one can not but portray Lady Pembroke, with her noble sentiments, uncorrupted by fortune's lavish gifts, shrinking from the minister who was envious of Essex and of Raleigh.

But there are associations still more precious with that time, that place, than those with the crooked-minded, crafty, hard-natured Cecil. Among the bondmen who attended on the great Earl William and his son, Earl Henry, was Arthur Massinger, the father of the poet and dramatist, Philip. It is, indeed, probable, though not certain, that the author of the "New Way to pay Old Debts" passed his childhood in the marble halls of Wilton; and that his father was bondman in that house there is no doubt. Shy, poor, somewhat democratic in his views, we must not picture to ourselves the humble poet at the great earl's table; in the lower or servants' hall more probably: but we may venture to conceive him sauntering in that noble park, by that reluctant water in which the airy bridge, the solid mansion, are clearly reflected. We may imagine him there—meditative, apart, abstracted: with a broad, perhaps ungraceful figure, and a noble yet disappointing head: noble, inasmuch as the forehead is magnificent; the eyes soft, kind, thoughtful; the nose well formed; but the mouth small, even to disproportion, shows weakness. We see him full, we may readily suppose, of anxious thoughts, for he was ofttimes obliged to pledge the unworked treasures of his brain—to pawn, to Hinchinbrook the theatrical pawnbroker, the ore before it was wrought out, the play before it was written, to save himself from prison. We may fancy him too proud for confidence, too truthful to disguise, resting beneath the shade of those elms: or meditating, as the pellucid stream flows, on its little resemblance to his own turbid thoughts and adverse destiny.

Within doors, however, Ben Jonson may presume to enter and to abide. How lowly soever his fate, it was one of independence: his father was no bondman. The son, in truth, of a poor but honest parson, Jonson had, it is true, worked with the trowel, and carried probably a hod of mortar on his back. His mother, a woman of rare powers and spirit, married for her second husband a bricklayer: and Ben, as he was called every where, and doubtless at Wilton, had followed for some short period his stepfather's calling. Nevertheless, he had been educated by Camden, the historian, at Westminster; thence had he been to Cambridge, some say to St. John's; but as necessity introduces us to strange company, so does she also, uncompromising fury as she is, bring us into contact with uncongenial employments.

Ben Jonson was, in truth, a far less interesting individual than the indigent, retiring Philip Massinger: yet Ben was a man certain to make a noise in the world; with massive features; a hanging brow shadowing the most searching of all eyes, though with a cast in them; a fine forehead; a complexion seamed and scarred by disease; a great awkward, or, as he called it, ungracious form, which not even the tight-fitting doublet and plain white collar, turned down, of James's time, could reduce to proportion in our view. Then he has a loud, burly voice; wit of the overbearing character; he talks as if he were storming a citadel with his jokes; his assaults are fearful. Yet is he a favorite at Wilton, and he well understands his hostess, on whom he wrote the epitaph, even now so famed for its point.

He visits Wilton, however, as he visits other places, for a special purpose, that of affording amusement to the intellectual great. The masque, an entertainment long out of vogue, was the chief diversion of the rich and noble in the time of Elizabeth and James I. It was almost always acted by persons of the highest class: sometimes by royal personages: almost invariably by the fashionable and noble courtiers of the period. Dancing and music were introduced, and these were also performed by the high-born actors, who learned and rehearsed their parts under the master of the revels. Lawes usually composed the airs to which the exquisite poetry of Ben Jonson was sung; while the scenery, decorations, and dresses were contrived and executed by Inigo Jones. Certain great families copied the example of the court, and ordered masques to be written and *mise en scène* at their own country seats, calling in for their choruses the children of the Chapel Royal, who were regularly trained to take their parts in masques. At Wilton, therefore, at Belvoir Castle, at Whitehall, at Windsor, these charming but costly diversions were carried on sometimes at the cost of more than a thousand pounds. In the time of his health and prosperity, Ben Jonson might be seen in the halls of these stately edifices, encouraging sometimes, but scolding more frequently. His voice might be heard in contest with Inigo, with whom he quarreled, or in approval of Lawes or Lanière. Never was there such a green-room. Princes of the blood—ofttimes, indeed, Queen Anne—peers and peeresses, ministers and generals, all joined in the masque: all commended Jonson, all dreaded his ire, as he cast on them the one eye, which squinted most fearfully in its rage.

But in the midst of all those court gayeties in which the Herbert family continually took a conspicuous part, the Countess of Pembroke's heart was untainted by the world. Among the most esteemed of her contemporaries was Dr. John Donne, that eminent divine and poet, whose life, as written by Izaak Walton, is one of the most beautiful pieces of biography in our language. Donne, although far more happy in his origin and circumstances than many of his brother poets, led a life of vicissitude. He was born, it is true, as Walton tells us, "of good and virtuous parents:" his father being, the same writer adds, masculinely and lineally descended from an ancient family in Wales, his mother from Sir Thomas More. Like Picus Mirandulo, Donne was rather *born* "than *made* by his study." Even in his eleventh year he was thought to be fit for Oxford, when he entered into the small and ancient society called Hart Hall, now merged into Exeter College. Like Jeremy Taylor, Donne had at one time nearly fallen into the errors of Popery, of which persuasion his parents were. He set out in life with a resolution to adopt no other distinction than that of "Christian:" but a careful examination of Father Bellarmin's works brought him to a conviction that the Anglican Church was the purest, and to that he eventually and fervently devoted himself.

His secret and imprudent marriage to a niece of the Lord-chancellor Ellesmere, in whose family he acted as secretary; the anger and vengeance of Sir George More, the young lady's father; his dismissal from his post, with, indeed, this commendation, that the chancellor, in losing him, parted with a "friend and secretary such as was fitter to serve a king than a subject;" his imprisonment for his secret marriage, and not only his but that of the friend who had given the young lady to him, and of the bridegroom's man, another friend also, were adversities which drew Donne from the world, and, in part, influenced him to take orders, leaving the profession of the law, into which he had entered. Strange, indeed, were the times in which an individual could obtain the imprisonment of a young man and his friends on account of a runaway marriage. This misfortune had the effect of stimulating Dr. Donne's exertions, as he thus intimates in one of his poems called "The Will:"

> "I give my reputation to those
> That were my friends, my industry to foes;
> To schoolmen I bequeath my doubtfulness:
> To Nature all that I to rhyme have writ,
> And to my company my wit."

implying that it was his foes who had given him the incentive to work.

When the Countess of Pembroke was established at Wilton, Dr. Donne and his wife were living near Whitehall. He was cherished by the great, valued by the pious. The death of his wife was, however, a life-long trial of this good man: leaving him with seven young children, to whom he gave an assurance that he would never bring them under the subjection of a stepmother: and he kept his word; "Burying with his tears," says old Izaak Walton, "all his earthly joys in his most dear and deserving wife's grave, and betaking himself to a most retired and solitary life." When, after her death, he first went out, it was to preach in St. Clement's Church, where she was buried. His text was taken from the Prophet Jeremiah: "Lo, I am the man that have seen affliction." His congregation, touched, not only by the eloquence that was the delight of Charles I., but by the sorrowful preacher's sobs, were plunged into what Walton calls "a companionable sadness." Donne was said to have preached his own funeral sermon: and he certainly designed his own monument. With regard to the first there was a report that he was dead; after which he appeared, spectral-like, in the pulpit of Lincoln's Inn, of which he was preacher, for the last time, like one risen from the dead. After, Izaak Walton relates, some faint pauses in his zealous prayer, he gave out his text: "To God the Lord belong the issues from death." Many who saw his tears and heard his faint and hollow voice declared that they thought the text prophetically chosen, and that Dr. Donne had "preached his own funeral sermon." While death hovered over him, he was persuaded by his friend, Dr. Fox, to have his monument designed. Walton relates the singular execution of this strange idea in the following words. The monument thus planned is still to be seen in our great national cathedral of St. Paul; it was executed by the famous Nicholas Stone.

"Dr. Donne sent for a carver to make for him in wood the figure of an urn * * * and to bring with it a board of the just height of his body. * * * A choice painter was got to be in readiness to draw his picture, which was taken as followeth. Several charcoal fires being first made in his large study, he brought with him into that place his winding-sheet in his hand, and having put off all his clothes, had this sheet put on him, and so tied with knots at his head and feet, and his hand so placed, as dead bodies are usually fitted to be shrouded and put into their coffin or grave. Upon this urn he thus stood, with his eyes shut, and with so much of the sheet turned aside as might shew his lean, pale, and deathlike face, which was purposely turned toward the east, from whence he expected the second coming of his and our Savior Jesus. In this posture he was drawn at his just height; and when the picture was fully finished, he caused it to be set by his bedside, where it continued and became his hourly object till his death."

Such was one of those able and excellent men whom the reputation which the Countess of Pembroke had acquired for learning and piety drew around her. Her daily life was varied: it was neither continual dissipation nor seclusion. She entered into all the great subjects of the period; she loved poetry; she patronized poets; she could enjoy the wit of Ben Jonson, and not think that her pleasure in masques, or even in plays, could detract from her devotion one shade of warmth, or render her less a companion for the chastened, saintly, yet cheerful and benignant Donne. The human mind, like the body, requires a variety of aliments, and is susceptible of an infinitude of pleasures. As Barrow says, we are meant for this world: we are sent here to live, and "should not be always a-dying."

Blessed with wealth, friends, high estate, and two sons, one of whom, William, was of rare promise, the Countess of Pembroke, one might apprehend, was too greatly endowed with the gifts of fortune for a poor mortal, whose nature can rarely withstand the incessant trials of prosperity any more than those equally perilous of a too unvarying adversity. But she had her trials in life to sustain.

Between her brother Philip and herself the tenderest affection not only subsisted before her marriage but continued to the close of his heroic life.

"Our two souls, therefore, which are one,
Though I must go, endure not yet
A breach, but an expansion,
Like gold to any thinness beat."

Those lines of Dr. Donne's well express the perfect sympathy between the brother and sister; and yet it was the will of God that when they parted, Sir Philip going to the wars, they should never meet again. Philip Sidney was one of the men who proved that high cultivation of mind enhances rather than weakens courage. He had, at an early period, signalized his skill in a tournament before Queen Elizabeth; he next asserted his honor by avenging an insult from Vere, Earl of Oxford, in a tennis-court. It was after this occurrence that he withdrew to Wilton, and there composed the beautiful fragment which he called "Arcadia," and which he dedicated to his sister. It was while he was without any public employment that Sidney married; his choice fell on the beautiful and intellectual daughter of Sir Francis Walsingham. Ben Jonson has written the following lines on this lady:

"TO MISTRESS PHILIP SIDNEY.

"I must believe some miracles still be,
When Sidney's name I hear, or face I see;
For Cupid, who at first took vain delight
In mere out forms until he lost his sight,
Hath changed his soul, and made his object you,
Where, finding so much beauty met with virtue,
He hath not only gained himself his eyes
But in your love, made all his servants wise."

Sidney's felicity now seemed at its acmé. Knighted by Queen Elizabeth—by no means lavish of her distinctions—he was so desirous of fame that he proposed to accompany Sir Francis Drake in one of his expeditions against the Spanish settlements of America. But Elizabeth, hearing of this design, stopped it peremptorily. The thirst for military renown, however, soon impelled the valiant Sir Philip to a new field. He was enthusiastically Protestant. All true English hearts grieved for the oppressions in the Low Countries, and Elizabeth resolved to try her powerful help to succor them. This time the hero was gratified: and he was intrusted with the government of Flushing. He served in this campaign with the young and brave Prince Maurice, the son of Elizabeth of Bohemia, and under the Earl of Leicester, whose incapacity as a general was soon evident to Sidney. One night, in the month of September, he was sent with a detachment, which fell in with a convoy dispatched by the enemy to Zutphen. A fierce action ensued. The gallant Sidney had a horse shot under him: he mounted another, and charged the enemy with all the ardor of a hero. A musket-bullet, at that instant, was aimed at him: he received it in his knee: the bone was broken: the ball penetrated deeply into the thigh. He was conveyed from the field to Leicester's camp. On the way, being very faint and thirsty from loss of blood, he called for water. He was about to drink, when he happened to see a poor soldier in all the agonies of a mortal wound. He immediately gave him the draught, saying those memorable words: "This man's necessity is even greater than mine is." He was carried to Arnheim. Hopes were entertained of his recovery, but on the 17th of October, 1585, mortification having set in, he expired. His death was noble as his life. He had much to resign. To him the world presented many objects of affection—his sister, his wife, his country. But he tranquilly placed himself in the hands of Him who gave him all, and, in a spirit truly worthy to be termed Christian, he prepared himself for the last hour. Thus, at the age of thirty-two, died the good and great Sir Philip Sidney.

The states of Zealand begged to have his body, that they might inter it with honor and reverence; but Queen Elizabeth called the poor remains of her valued warrior home, and he was buried with a public and solemn funeral in St. Paul's. No inscription marked his grave, but the hearts of all his countrymen mourned him: and King James I. composed an elegy on the young and accomplished warrior. His sister undertook a task dear to her heart, but not without its difficulties. Sir Philip had left her his "Arcadia" in scattered fragments. She collected and united these fragments, and carefully revising the whole, published what has thence been often styled "The Countess of Pembroke's Arcadia." The poem is no longer suited to the taste of an age which requires strong excitement, and which disclaims sentiment. In its abstract ideas and calm lofty tone, its exquisite occasional beauty, its noble lessons of morality, the "Arcadia" will recall to the reader, even with all its antiquated diction, some of Tennyson's poetry, which in its lofty sentiments and faith seems to breathe the spirit of Sidney.

After his death, life must have lost much of its charm for his earliest friend and sister. She wrote an elegy on her lamented companion, which is printed in Spenser's "Astrophel." Her interest had, however, a valid source in the education of her two sons, William, who succeeded his father, and became Earl of Pembroke, and Philip, Earl of Pembroke and Montgomery. William inherited his mother's abilities, and emulated the talents and reputation of his uncle: he became the most popular nobleman of his time. Magnificent in his bounty and hospitality, a graceful speaker, full of wit, learning, and courtesy, he had but one failing, and that was perhaps the fault of the age, and to be in some respects excused by a most ill-judged and infelicitous marriage: "for he paid," as Lord Clarendon observes, "too dear for his wife's fortune, by taking her person into the bargain." Married to the Lady Mary Talbot, this nobleman was one of the richest of English peers, and his fortune was much increased by his wife's inheritance; yet he was so lavish that even those vast resources were insufficient for his expenses. In the amours in which he unhappily indulged, he was more attracted by intellectual endowments than by beauty. That he was the slave of his passions was peculiarly inexcusable in one who most highly appreciated virtue, who comprehended all her blessings, all the peace she bestows. To him, the poet's friend as well as patron, Ben Jonson dedicated what he styles the "ripest of his studies," his "Epigrams," and by him Jonson was employed to write that epitaph on the earl's mother which has been deemed a model for similar compositions.

Two anecdotes are related respecting the death of this nobleman. Some years previously to that event, his nativity had been calculated in the presence of a Mr. Allen, of Gloucester Hall. Lord Pembroke died on his fiftieth birth-day, the very day which the astrologer had assigned for his decease; and had he not eaten a very "full and cheerful supper," it might have been supposed that imagination had lent its powerful aid in producing the result, as was, in all probability, the case with the bad Lord Lyttleton. Another curious coincidence is recorded. On the very evening of his death, General Morgan and some other officers were sitting at Maidenhead with some of the earl's dependents. One of the company drank a health to his lordship, who, he thought would be very merry, for he had outlived the day which his tutor Sandford had prognosticated would be that of his death. He was secure now, for it was his birth-day, and he had outlived the prophecy. On the following morning news came of the earl's death.

Still another occurrence startled the superstitious. The body was, of course, to be embalmed: the surgeons prepared to commence operations. On one of these making an incision with his knife, the bystanders were horror-struck; one of the cold hands of the ghastly corpse was instantly lifted up. This anecdote is stated by several writers. It rests also on a tradition which still exists in the family of the Earl of Pembroke, nor is it altogether incredible. Those who have courage to read a most remarkable article on premature interments in the "Encyclopædia Britannica" (the original edition), will find that such events as being buried *too soon* occurred not infrequently in former times, owing to the inadequacy or carelessness of medical men, or to the fear of retaining a corpse in the house after death from infectious distempers. In the dead-house at Munich, where corpses are laid, and where they have a bell attached to the finger to summon the sentinel who parades the garden in case of recovered consciousness, there have been well-authenticated instances of that bell being sounded, to the horror of the unhappy watchman, and to partial though not perfect consciousness being restored. There is a tradition in the Clopton family, living near Stratford-on-Avon, of resuscitation after death. It was when the plague raged, that a young daughter of that old race was interred in the family vault at Stratford. In a short time her brother died also. On opening the vault, the body of the young lady was found out of the coffin, on the pavement of the vault, and the terrible conviction came that she had crawled out in hopes of reaching the door of the vault. And this tale seems to be well authenticated.

It is not, however, required to show that which safer records prove abundantly. The Earl of Pembroke is said to have died of apoplexy. May it not have been catalepsy, which simulates death, and lasts for a considerable time?

Philip, the younger son of Mary, Countess of Pembroke, was the blot upon the scutcheon from which no family had till his time so completely escaped as the loyal, generous, valiant Herberts. He was created Baron Herbert of Solarlands and Earl of Montgomery: he was made chamberlain to King Charles I. and chancellor of Oxford. Yet he meanly changed sides, and was employed to offer to his unfortunate sovereign such terms as would wholly strip him of his prerogative. It was on this occasion that Charles lost his usual self-control. "No, Phil, by —— not for an hour." This Philip actually renounced his rank as a peer to sit in the Parliament over which the monarch no longer presided.

The Countess of Pembroke survived her husband twenty years: "Happy," observes Hartley Coleridge, "as the praises of grateful poets could make her—happy in her fair reputation, and it is to be hoped in the duteous attendance of her elder son—and happy in dying too soon to see her younger offspring

"'——Hold a wing
Quite from the flight of all his ancestors.'"

She had another source of happiness. Her intellect, which had shone in gay assemblies, and had procured for her such a society as even Wilton can never hope to assemble again within its halls, was directed to the service of her Creator. Of her version of the Psalms, Daniel, poet-laureate to Queen Elizabeth, writes—

"Those hymns which thou didst consecrate to Heaven,
Which Israel's singer to his God did frame,

Unto thy voyage eternity hath given,
And make thee dear to him from whence they came."

Upon which Hartley Coleridge remarks "that it is a pity they are not authorized to be sung in churches, for the present versions are a disgrace and a mischief to the Establishment."

The Countess of Pembroke lived, when in London, in Aldersgate Street, where she died in the year 1621—fortunately for herself before the troubles of the Rebellion had even been prognosticated. The locality in which she breathed her last was then both fashionable as a residence, and picturesque. The street was entered by a fine gate, said to have been rebuilt in 1617, when the old one was taken down by Gerard Christmas, the architect of old Northumberland House. James I. had entered London by the old gate—an event which was commemorated by inscriptions on the new gate, on which the heads of several of the regicides were set. The structure suffered in the Fire of London, but was again rebuilt; afterward it was taken down, being first sold for the sum of £91.

This gate, over which John Day, a printer, lived in Elizabeth's time, led to one of the most spacious and uniform streets in the metropolis. The buildings were well placed at convenient distances, or, to use a modern term, detached. Thanet House, the work of Inigo Jones, is now a dispensary. It was once the habitation of Lord Shaftesbury, the "Ashley" of the Cabal. A little higher up the infamous Maitland, Duke of Lauderdale, one of that party, also resided. Great and small tenanted the houses in Aldersgate Street; John Taylor, the water-poet, set out hence to walk penniless to Scotland; and John Milton chose Aldersgate Street for his abode, on account of the pretty garden that his house, situated at the end of an entry, commanded. Here he took a handsome house; here he could find room for his books: quiet, for Aldersgate Street was too grand for petty noises: here he studied in a tranquillity we find it hard to conceive in the present day as having ever blessed the regions of Aldersgate: and here the sister of Sir Philip Sidney expired in a good old age.

Osborn, apologizing, as it were, for having praised this accomplished "Queen of Society" too warmly, says: "Lest I should seem to trespass against truth, which few do unsuborned, as I protest I am, except by her rhetoric, I shall leave the world her epitaph, in which the author doth manifest himself a poet in all things but untruth.

"Underneath this sable hearse
Lies the subject of all verse:
Sidney's sister, Pembroke's mother.
Death! ere thou kill'st such another,
Fair, and good, and learned as she,
Time shall throw a dart at thee."

LA MARQUISE DE MAINTENON.

Born in a prison, bred in poverty, the widow of a cripple, the wife of a king, respectable yet not virtuous, pious yet not religious, the daughter of a needlewoman ruled France in its grandest days. Because she was free from the vices of her age she was hated. Whether there were any other reason for ill-will toward her we shall see. As ruler of France—for she was neither queen nor mistress—her name is historical, her life was political, and she was much more than a "Queen of Society." When she reaches that point we shall make our bow and retire from the august presence. Our business is with her as a "Queen of Society," which she was before her accession. Her life is the most romantic that that of any woman can be, who has never known what it is to love—so it will have its interest.

I am not going to follow a French biographer of this lady and trace her family back to the Romans. It must suffice to say that the D'Aubigné, D'Aubigny, or D'Aubignac family is one of the oldest in France; that it was to be found in Berry, Poitou, and Guienne, and may possibly be represented by some of our English Daubeneys; and that it gave to its country two celebrated people, of whom our Marquise was one and the other rejoiced in the classic prænomen of Agrippa.

This Agrippa, whose full name was Théodore-Agrippa, was a brave Protestant soldier and a man who feared neither king nor kaiser. Born in 1550, he is said to have translated Plato's "Crito" at the age of eight, and might have been a scholar if his Huguenot zeal had not made him a man of war. He had a romantic life, as all the D'Aubignés had; but as we are not writing his memoirs, but his grand-daughter's, it shall suffice to say that he attached himself to the cause of Henry of Navarre, who had made him a gentleman of his bedchamber, governor of Maillezais, and vice-admiral of Guienne and Brittany successively. He spoke his mind out to the king, as if he had been his tutor rather than his servant, and Henri, who brooked this freedom a long time, eventually got disgusted with it. D'Aubigné was the friend and companion in arms of Turenne and others, and himself an intrepid devil-may-care warrior. When the day of the Huguenots had gone by, he took refuge in Geneva, wrote a "Histoire Universelle" in which

Henri III. was abused, and which, therefore, the parliament ordered to be burned, penned his own memoirs and several other pieces, and died in 1630, at the ripe old age of eighty, conscious of having done his best after his own fashion.

His son Constans was a scamp of the first water, and therefore the ladies took care of him. He was always in trouble, and they were always getting him out of it. He rewarded their affections by murdering one—so it was said—and treating another as ill as he could. His, too, was a romantic story, and as it affected the early life of Madame de Maintenon, his daughter, it must be briefly glanced at.

He began his scampish career, as most scamps do, by getting into debt. This was by no means his only or his worst fault. As a young man, he had every vice that the young can have, and he was soon to follow them with crimes. Dear creature! he was just the man to captivate the gallant ladies of the day, and one of them, a rich widow, Madame la Baronne de Chatelaillon, offered him her hand and fortune, both of which he readily accepted.

Good things, too easily gotten, are proverbially despised; and the rich widow soon found that leap-year offers are not productive of much happiness. The scamp abandoned her, and she, to recall him, took the unwise plan of making him jealous. She succeeded a little too well. Her lover, whether real or pretended, and herself were both murdered, and suspicion naturally rested on the husband, though he could not be convicted of the crime. Those were convenient days for criminals, and for a time Constans (or Constant, as the name is also written) was actually received at court, but the relations of the murdered lady succeeded at last in getting him thrown into prison.

Now it is due to truth to say that the story of this first imprisonment, and its romantic consequences, has been disputed and even positively denied. Still it is not refuted, which is quite another matter; and as we can not enter into the arguments, and as, *entre nous*, we love a romantic tale, we will at least give the reader the advantage of it. The governor, then, of the prison of Château-Trompette, at Bordeaux, into which our scamp was said to have been thrown, was a M. de Cardillac, a relative of the Duc d'Epernon, and having for wife a member of the great family of Montalembert. Cardillac had a daughter, young, and of course lovely, who, as the widow had done before, fell in love with Constans, and visited him in his cell. Constans was not the man to neglect an opportunity, ruined the poor girl first, and then induced her to manage his escape. This she did, and it is a consolation to add that Constans married her as soon as they were free. There is no doubt that she loved him ardently, with an affection such as only woman can feel, which forgave every fault, every crime, and which endured in spite of ill-treatment, indifference, and misery. Jeanne de Cardillac was, in fact, a woman of most lovable character. She devoted herself to her husband, and she brought up her children in the best way that poverty and misery permitted. The story goes that the couple fled to America; that after a time the husband abandoned his young wife, returned to France, and was again thrown into the same prison; that she followed him, obtained leave to be imprisoned with him, got him removed to Niort, and there, in a cell, gave birth, in 1635, to a daughter, who was christened Françoise, and who afterward ruled France through France's king.

The misery in which this famous woman began life can scarcely be described. The imprisoned family was reduced almost to starvation, for they had no money by which to extract food from their jailers. The husband, sick and starving, lay on the stone floor, a boy of a few years old was whining for food in a miserable cradle, and the poor mother supplied by turns her husband and her children with the only nourishment she could give them, from her own breast. They were all on the point of starving, when Madame de Villette, a worthy sister of Madame d'Aubigné, heard of their plight, visited them, and insisted on carrying away the young child to be properly nursed in her own house.

But the mother's heart bled at the separation from her child, and, when restored to health, she claimed her again. Madame de Villette was forced to give her up, and thus the famous De Maintenon passed her earliest days in the precincts of a prison. She played and romped with the jailer's little daughter, doubtless unconscious that she was deprived of her liberty; and, as a proof that her poor mother never forgot her own birth, it is related that when the child of the turnkey, who had a pocketful of sous, twitted her companion with having none, the little Françoise drew up proudly as a duchess, and replied, "It is true, I am poor, but I am a lady, and you are not."

Madame d'Aubigné, though a prisoner, never relaxed in her efforts to obtain her husband's release. She applied to all her friends, and petitioned Richelieu, who brusquely told her that the sooner he ridded her of such a husband the better for her. Poor woman! she loved him to madness. However, she succeeded at last, and the family set sail, on his liberation, for America. On the voyage the little Françoise was so ill that she was supposed to be dead. Her brutal father, tired of his wife's sobbing, wanted to throw the body overboard. Madame d'Aubigné asked leave to kiss her infant once more, and placing her hand on the child's heart, declared that it was beating still, and thus saved the future Madame de Maintenon from the waves. When the king's wife in after years related this story to the Bishop de Metz, he replied, like a well-bred ecclesiastic, "Madame, on ne revient pas de si loin pour peu de chose."

In the island of Martinique, whither the family went, there were happier days after all their misery, and Madame d'Aubigné, who had gone through so much, now educated her son and daughter with much care and good sense, until, in 1646–7, the death of her wretched husband left them once more in poverty. The poor widow saw nothing for it but to return to France and claim the aid of her friends; and as she could not pay her debts, she was actually forced to leave her daughter behind as a hostage, hoping to be able to procure the amount when she arrived in her native country. This hope was vain, and the little Françoise might have long remained in pawn if the creditors had not got tired of keeping her. The judge of the place took the child in pity, and sent her off to France. Poor Françoise seemed to have come into the world only to be a plague, and for some time no one could or would keep the future Maintenon. Her great-aunt Montalembert, to whom she was at first dispatched, would have nothing to do with her. Her mother could not afford to maintain her, and it was only the worthy Madame de Villette, who had once rescued the family from starvation, who would have her. This lady was a stanch Calvinist, and soon inspired the young girl with an affection for the religion which her grandfather had fought for. But Madame d'Aubigné soon repented of having "endangered her child's salvation," and took her away again from this kind aunt to place her with another, who was a brute, but a Romanist. This was Madame de Neuillant, who undertook to make her little relative a faithful believer.

At this period Françoise was a sturdy heretic. She refused to accompany her mother to mass; and when Madame d'Aubigné said to her, "Then you do not love me," replied pertly, "I love God more." When to mass she was compelled to go, the little Puritan turned her back on the altar, laughed at the elevation of the host, and behaved in such a manner that her mother boxed her ears. The young heretic turned to her the other cheek. "Strike!" she said, boldly; "it is good to suffer for one's faith."

Madame de Neuillant probably felt that she should deserve the crown of a saint if she managed to convert this young Calvinist, but did not take the right means to do so. After calling in the curé, whom the child answered by appealing to the Bible, after caressing and petting and arguing to no purpose, this charming Romanist determined to treat her young relative as one of the servants. Then the future wife of Louis XIV. might be seen in a morning assisting the coachman to groom the horses, or following a flock of turkeys, with her breakfast in a basket, and on her face a little *loup* to protect her complexion (for Madame de Neuillant was always a Frenchwoman, and remembered that the young heretic was her relation), or combing the hair of the able-bodied peasant who took care of her at home. In after years, when made *dame d'atours* (tire-woman) to the dauphine, she remembered this last circumstance, and declared herself to be a qualified comber of hair. Fortunately, perhaps, for the young girl, who was very pretty, a peasant-boy fell in love with her, and pressed his suit so warmly, that Madame de Neuillant discovering the affair, sent her off to the convent of the Ursulines at Niort. Here were fresh attempts to make a Romanist of her, but all with the same success, till one of the sisters, somewhat cleverer than the rest, took her in hand. It is a curious point in Madame de Maintenon's character that kindness had no effect upon her, but argument always some. She was not old enough or learned enough to resist for long those specious reasonings with which Romanists so well understand how to support the mysteries of their religion, and she gave in so far as to attend mass and even receive the communion. But when the good sisters had got her to this point they felt they had done their duty—they had saved a soul, and were not inclined to look after the body that encased it. So, after keeping her for some time gratuitously, they wrote to her mother that they could do so no longer. In after years she took care to pay these women every penny she had cost them; and when she told the story to her own establishment at St. Cyr, used to add: "My children, let us always do good; it is rarely forgotten by men, but never by God." This was a really Christian view to take of the zealous nuns' conduct.

At this period her mother, Madame d'Aubigné, was supporting herself by needlework at Paris, and it devolved on Madame de Neuillant to take care of the daughter, who was sufficiently pretty to make her proud of having her in her house. Madame d'Aubingé was now engaged in a lawsuit for the recovery of an estate which that rascal, her husband, had alienated in payment of debts. The anxiety was too much for the poor workwoman—for such she was—and in 1649 she succumbed at last, after a life of struggles and misery, leaving to her daughter no heritage but the advice "to fear every thing from men, and hope every thing from God."

A poor orphan, Françoise was now left dependent on the mercies of Madame de Neuillant, and though no longer forced to take care of turkeys or groom the horses, she still felt the odiousness of her position. This lady saw in the promising beauty of her young charge an opening to a good match, and therefore consented to place her with a master of manners.

Good lack! a master of manners! Was there ever such a professor under the sun? Are manners to be taught by a master? There have been hundreds, and are hundreds still. Turveydrop is by no means a peculiar instance. In France, at this time, young ladies were educated by elderly gentlemen with a view solely to their shining in society; they were taught not only what to do, and what to avoid doing, but even the art of wit, for in those days it was an art as easily acquired as that of fencing, dancing, or any other elegant accomplishment. Wit was the first accomplishment of society, and wit must be learned where it was not innate. It was no more to be expected that a young lady should make an apt repartee without being taught, than that she should sit down to a piano and improvise a melody.

The gentleman who undertook this office was a noted wit-trainer. Madame de Lesdiguières, whom he had educated, had said to him, "I want to be witty." "Madame," he had replied, "you shall be so." This ancient Turveydrop was the Chevalier Marquis de Méré, an old gentleman of good family, half philosopher, half courtier, who reduced every principle to what is called decency of feeling and delicacy of manners." He composed dialogues and polite fables for the use of his pupil, and taught her, what, with her strong Calvinistic tendencies, she may have wanted, the art of being charming. He could not, however, resist the untaught graces of his pupil, and even fell in love with her, though, of course, without success. He was proud of having such a pretty disciple, and, wherever he went, heralded her as the *ne plus ultra* of fascination. In this way she obtained a welcome into society, which her poverty and dependent situation would have otherwise rendered doubtful.

Among other houses to which Madame de Neuillant now took her promising *protégée* was that of the poor crippled buffoon, Scarron. This man was an abbé, without having taken orders. At an early age he had been attacked with a disease which doubled his legs up to his chest, and obliged him to write on a desk supported by iron bars close to his face. His figure was often compared to the letter Z. Scarron had brought his maladies upon himself by a most irregular life of self-indulgence, yet he never complained. His disposition was naturally melancholy, yet the very causes which might have fostered it turned its current in the opposite direction; and the more he was afflicted the merrier he became. There are ample instances of such anomalies, but Scarron was perhaps the most extraordinary of them all. His mirth carried him through to the last, as long as he was in company; and on his death-bed, when he saw his friends shedding tears, more or less sincere, he jerked up his head and cried, "You can not weep half as much as I have made you laugh!"

Poor Scarron had the best heart in the world, and not the worst head. True, he was not famous for gratitude: but the fact is, that he saw the ridiculous too strongly in his friends to let them escape his shafts. He was the first to introduce the fashion of burlesque into France, and he burlesqued every thing and every body, including himself. His conversation was utterly unfit for polite ears, and his works are quite unreadable in the present day. But coarseness was only a foible in those times, and if wit supported it, was more admired than condemned. It is not our purpose to give here a sketch of the life of this extraordinary man, who will sit for his portrait in another volume, now in preparation. It must suffice to say that he was the wonder, the buffoon, the recognized fool and wit of Parisian society at that day, and that, with all his faults, he had many good qualities.

Scarron had a benefice in his capacity of abbé, but it was not rich enough to keep him. He therefore petitioned, as every body of any pretension did in those days, for a pension, and when asked what office he, a cripple, could possibly fill, replied, "Le Malade de la Reine." His wit, his works, and his *mots* got him the appointment, though it was quite a new one in any court. His amusing talents brought him all the best society in Paris. Though poor enough to depend on his works for any addition to his fortune, which he spent rapidly and with a reckless hand, he still managed to keep open house in the evenings for all the courtiers and great people who chose to visit him. Scarron's house was, in short, the great centre of all the society of Paris that would not be bored with the stiffness of the court. It was, therefore, just the place at which to introduce a "penniless lass wi' a lang pedigree" and a pretty face for her fortune: and such was Françoise d'Aubigné.

Madame de Neuillant, anxious to make a match for her charge introduced her at Scarron's. The first time she went there her dress was too short (for she was too poor to get a suitable one); and when she found herself among all the *grandes dames* of Paris, dressed within an inch of their lives, she felt so ashamed of her appearance that she burst into tears.

The old cripple was touched, endeavored to reassure her, and felt the first impression of tenderness which perhaps he had ever known. This anxiety about her appearance accompanied Françoise through life. She was not handsome enough to be proud, nor ugly enough to be vain, and she was never satisfied with herself. She was, however, a pretty girl at this period, but her beauty was not of the highest nor even the most pleasing type. The face was too broad above, too tapering toward the chin; the nose, though well formed and graceful, was not beautiful; the eyes, very far apart, had more of sense than depth; there was firmness in the mouth, yet a certain *bonhommie*—if such an expression can be applied to a woman—in the expression. When we add to this a brilliant complexion and soft, fair hair, which clustered round her sensible but unmelting brow, we can easily imagine that her friends thought her charming and her enemies disagreeable.

She left a deep impression on the poor paralytic, who, making the best of his state, laughed at it, at every body, and at every thing, and amused the whole world of healthy Paris with his laughter, unhealthy as he was. She had also a common friend—what more valuable in such affairs?—a Madame de St. Hermant, to whom she wrote frequently, and in confidence, and who occasionally read her letters to the wit. On one occasion Scarron exclaimed on hearing one of them, "Here is a girl as careful to conceal her wit as the rest of her sex are forward to display it: is it at Martinique she has learned to write thus elegantly?" He soon discovered that the poor girl was not happy in her dependent situation, and it was suggested to him that he might rescue her from this position by offering her marriage. He did so, and, perhaps much to his surprise, was accepted. It must, at any rate, have been to every body else's surprise, for Scarron was notoriously the pantaloon of French society. He was accustomed to be looked upon as a miserable creature, who yet had fun enough to amuse those who were more fortunate. And fun he certainly had, and amusement enough for the denizens of Louis's court, who were not particular as to refinement. Indeed, Scarron was famous—or infamous—for his coarseness, the dirtiness of his jokes, the nastiness of his stories. He was a talking Rabelais, and might have discoursed "Tristram Shandy" from beginning to end in easy speeches.

The match naturally excited considerable wonderment. Here was a young and pretty girl joining her fate, of her own will, to an old crippled *debauché* utterly worn out by his wicked ways, and overcome by paralysis.

All this the young Françoise must have known before she

accepted such an offer as that of the buffoon of Paris. Yet she did accept it. There was, no doubt, much in Scarron's character that was lovable, in spite of his vices. Every man who can love is in his way worthy to be loved. It is only those who care for nothing but money who can be detested by women of real feeling, though their tents were bound with gold. Madlle. d'Aubigné had no such idea in uniting herself with poor Scarron. She may not have loved him, probably she did not love him; but she had great pity for his infirmities, and a certain admiration for his wit. In a word, she did what hundreds of girls do daily; accepted the last man she was expected to take, just the very man whom every body thought she would either hate or despise; and the fair young girl married the licensed buffoon in the year 1651.

There was not much fortune on either side to cause any apprehension of disagreement as to settlements. When asked by the notary who prepared the contract what he should put down as the young lady's property, Scarron replied, "Four pounds a year, one pair of modest eyes, a fine figure, one pair of good hands, and plenty of mind." Whether the limb of the law entered these articles we are not told, but we may be sure that it was with unmoved gravity that he proceeded to put the same question relative to the dowry which Scarron was to give his wife. "Immortality," replied the wit. "The names of the wives of kings die with them, but that of *Scarron's* wife will live forever." If he really did make this speech, it is curious to note how exactly his prophecy has been reversed. The lady in question *is* remembered by the name she bore as the king's wife, and she is *not* remembered by that of Scarron, which in after years she attempted to obliterate entirely.

The good buffoon behaved very pleasantly on the occasion. He told her that he saw but one alternative; if she did not marry, she must go into a convent, and he offered to pay the entrance-money for her; if she did marry, it could only be with some one who had an utter contempt for money, and could consent to unite with a penniless girl—a step which is almost a crime in France. In a word, she might choose between a cripple and a convent, and she chose the former. We English, perhaps, can understand and forgive this choice of the fair young girl. Such matches, though contrary to the law of Heaven, do take place repeatedly in this country. I have known a lady—nay, two or three—of youth and attractive appearance, married to men not only much their seniors, but in a state of health which rendered the matrimonial vow a mere mockery. For a time they have been happy, indeed; but in after years a trying restlessness has come over them, and not the greatest affection and the utmost devotion to a patient with the name of a husband were sufficient to make up for a marriage which was no marriage. It may even be asked whether such matches are not in their way as heinous as those which dispense with the ceremony and sacred vows of matrimony altogether.

It may well be a matter of surprise that Madame Scarron, as she now was, retained that virtue for which she has become celebrated, under such circumstances and in such an age. Doubtless, her early Protestant education had a great weight in keeping her in the path of duty. But the wife of Scarron must have had her trials. The society at his house was of the most mixed description; never was there a time, except this and the days of ancient Athens, if even then, when notoriously degraded characters were admitted into so-called "respectable" circles, and met with no scorn. We can understand that the court ladies under Louis XIV. had no stones—not even a pebble or two—to throw at such creatures as Ninon de l'Enclos; but that a virtuous woman, or one who was in her own conduct irreproachable, should have not only admitted her, but formed a firm and lasting friendship with her, seems almost incomprehensible. Yet so it was, and this is the reason that, while according Madame Scarron the meed of respectability, we can not in good conscience call her a strictly virtuous woman. No virtuous woman tolerates the openly profligate in their own sex, whatever they may do for men. There is, indeed, as a rule, too little pardon accorded by women who have overcome the temptation to those who have not overcome it. Men may forgive or pity, since men have been first to blame; but women have no compassion in these matters; they ostracize the victim, and destroy all hope of her return. Ninon could not complain that she was debarred from a chance of becoming respectable. She was bad, not only from circumstances, but from actual inclination. No woman ever served the devil so faithfully or so remorselessly. Neither age nor even decay could terrify her. She managed in some marvelous manner to preserve her beauty, in spite of profligacy; and when she died at eighty was almost as beautiful as when she first erred at eighteen. She was the destruction of all the youth of France; and whatever we may feel of pity for so beautiful a creature, ruined by an early attachment, we can not deny that she was the very representative of hell upon earth in her later days, and well deserved a pension from the Enemy. With this woman the wife of Scarron not only put up, but was intimate. The other members of the set were neither immaculate nor even respectable. Scarron had a reputation for fun, which drew people of all classes and all sentiments to his house. Poor as they were (and of their poverty an idea can be formed from the story that at supper one day the servant whispered to her, "Madame, tell the company another story, for we have no joint to-day)," it was a distinction to be admitted to their rooms, and one, too, not within the reach of princes. Scarron and his wife would not be bored; they would be surrounded by the lively, the clever, and the agreeable, while the great and the wealthy might go elsewhere. Thus their society was made up of various social elements, but of only one set of people—the amusing. The conversation was neither pedantic nor commonplace. Before his marriage, Scarron himself had given to it a disgustingly licentious tone. His young wife soon corrected this, and is said to have improved his mind to an extent which is even traceable in his writings, those published after 1651 being less obscene than the rest. The talk was naturally more or less learned, after the fashion of the day, but it seems to have been free from mere pedantry. Though Madlle. de Scudéry was generally one of the party, they managed to exclude that high-flown classical style which marked out the blue-stockings. Though Ménage, with his wonderful memory and perpetual pedantry, was to be found here, the learning was introduced more as an accessory than for display. There was an ample supply of literary men, song writers like Montreuil and Marigny; poets represented by Charleval; Hénault, the translator of "Lucretius," and many others: for men of the world, there were the elegant De Grammont, the Abbé Têtu, the pet of the ladies; the hideous Pellisson, whom Mademoiselle de Scudéry had made the hero of her twelve-volume novels; the Marquis de la Sablière, and many of the gayest courtiers. Then the Duchesse de Lesdiguières had here an opportunity for displaying that wit which her master, le Chevalier de Méré, had undertaken to impart to her; Madame de Sévigné, always amiable and charming, the Comtesse de la Suze, the Marquise de la Sablière, and, in short, the principal lady-wits of the day, were among the guests at Scarron's.

But though his wife may have purified his mind a little, she does not seem to have thought it at all necessary to purge her society. The least reputable ladies of a very disreputable court were freely admitted, and here a woman so strictly virtuous as Madame de Sévigné was not ashamed to be jostled by one so notoriously licentious as Ninon de l'Enclos. Yet Madame Scarron was not wholly indifferent as to character, and more than one instance is recorded where she endeavored, by advice or assistance, to save that of her friends. She herself was more than once made the object of addresses; and so unusual was virtue among the fashionable women of her day, so completely was she surrounded by the worst in Paris, that the world could not believe she was innocent, and slanders were circulated, which, of course, it has ever since given trouble to refute. Horace Walpole, who lived before she died, speaks of her evidently as if he thought she had at some time been *galante;* and whether her marriage with the king was too strictly kept secret, or from whatever cause, the idea has sufficiently got about that she was not always without reproach. Some of her biographers have taken up the task of her defense; and as the subject is not one we should care to investigate very narrowly, we may be content with adopting the commonly-received opinion, and believe that, whatever other faults she may have had, she was free from that which degraded the women with whom she associated.

It is always a subject of wonder to me how long men and women are permitted to live when really half dead. I have often proposed to myself, as a theme for a Bridgewater Treatise, the possible utility of the life of a toad which for years unnumbered and unnumberable has been known to exist in the centre of a stone. Some design has the Maker in all his works; it is, however, sometimes a puzzle to mankind to discover that secret wisdom. So, too, when I see old men and old women living on long past dotage, when they can do little but groan over their maladies, sit in an ingle-nook, eat voraciously, and talk nonsense, I often ask myself, Why is that poor old sufferer not removed? what end does he serve in this active, progressing world? Is he there as a warning to us, as a picture of death in life, of the degradation possible to the human species? But what can one think when a soul is left in a world with which it has and can have no connection? Such cases are not so very rare. The body dies often by inches, and the mind lives on. At times the body lives vigorously, and the mind seems closed. The "sick of the palsy" are not more rare than are the maniacs; yet often the paralyzed die in body, or seem to die, long before the mind gives up the game.

Poor Scarron! he had been a long time a-dying. Limb after limb had been lost to him as completely as if they had been chopped off by a surgeon. Faculty after faculty left him without resources. He could neither write nor read nor move. He lay a mere lump of human flesh, with just a heart and lungs to keep him alive. Yet with all this, his mind retained the most extraordinary elasticity, as if to contrast with the rigidity of its outer case. He was like the prince in the Arabian Nights whose lower portion was turned into stone. He lived no longer except in wit, and the more his body seemed to congeal, the brighter became his eccentrical mind.

It is said that he had never had any religion, and that it was his wife who recalled him to a sense of his terrible position. He had often made fun of the forms of worship, and still could not withhold his joke. When the curé told him that there was one consolation for his sufferings—that God *visited* him more than most people, he replied, "Well, father, He does me too much honor."

"You should thank Him," replied the priest.

"What for?" said the blasphemer.

But life, as well as death, was all a joke to him. He left a will in wretched verse, but cleverly conceived, bequeathing to Corneille five hundred francs of patience; to Boileau's brother, who had attacked his wife, "la gangrêne et le haut mal," and to the Academy, "the power to change the French language as often as it chose." His bequests to his wife are in the most atrocious taste, replete with insinuations as to his own health. In a word, he was obscene to the last. He confesses that he had never before thought it possible to joke in the presence of death, but he had found it easy enough; yet when he came to speak to his wife, he grew serious and the old melancholy rushed back upon him. Soon after he breathed his last, at the age of fifty-one, and in the year 1660, leaving a wife of five-and-twenty, who had been married to him nine years.

Madame Scarron was, perhaps, still more famous as a widow than as the wife of the great jester. She became the living representative of the importunate widow, and, as in most cases, her importunity succeeded in the long run, though long that run certainly was. She wanted neither assurance nor perseverance. As instances of the former quality several stories are told to show that she did things simply to have it said that she was a strong-minded woman. On one occasion she attended a man who had the small-pox, though she herself had never had it, and confessed that she was influenced to do so by the desire to undertake something which few other women would do. Again, though in good health, she took an emetic one day, in order to show that she did not mind what happened to her.

She now turned her attention to the necessity of living (which Voltaire would not allow), and as Scarron had left her nothing but his name—a very poor legacy—she applied for a continuance of his pension as the queen's patient. She was rudely told by Mazarin that she was in too good health to need it. Her petitions now became too frequent, always beginning with the words "The widow Scarron most humbly supplicates your majesty;" "*Au diable* with *la veuve Scarron*," Louis used to say, "when shall I hear the last of her?" He never heard the last of her, indeed, till on his own death-bed, and more than once he must have blessed the very importunity he was now disgusted with.

Françoise from this time got the regular name of "The widow Scarron:" no one spoke of her in any other terms. The name of Scarron had something ridiculous in it, and the legal form "La veuve Scarron" added not a little to this. How was it, then, that this poor woman managed to become left-handed Queen of France?

Nous allons vous raconter cela. It must be premised that Françoise had a strong attachment to her late husband. Wretched cripple, obscene buffoon that he was, she still plunged beneath, and sounded fathoms of good heart under mere wave and seaweed of talk and vanity. *La veuve Scarron* was not so notoriously importunate, but she had her admirers. She rejected them all and remained poor and single, when men of birth and fortune offered to her. She was, in fact, carrying out her destiny, which had been predicted to her—so goes the tale—by a mason, and of which even Scarron had seemed to have a second sight. Johnson believed in second sight—we may at least quote an old coincidence to illustrate the belief.

It may be doubted if poor Madame Scarron—so poor that, like her mother, she now supported herself by needlework—had any real faith that a king would choose her cut, not for mistress, but for wife. In the present day few women would covet being the wife of such a royal reprobate as Louis XIV., who took the royal road to sin, and incarcerated the husband when he took a fancy to the wife. In those days it was otherwise. Louis, though weakly fond of flattery, selfish, and inconstant, was just such a man as women can not, in spite of their better feelings, help admiring. He was handsome after a Bourbon fashion, elegant, delicate, insinuating, and, in a word, *le grand monarque.*

All this would have had little effect on a woman who was sufficiently without passion to be highly respectable. A mere chance made her the wife of the great French king. The Montespan had a child, whose father was the king. True to the French character, the mistress would not take the trouble to rear it herself. She sought for an *institutrice*, and found one in Madame Scarron, who, though rather ashamed of the office, accepted her proposal. A house in the quiet quarter of the Marais was given her, and the young Duc de Maine was brought up very carefully by her; and the other children soon added to the widow's adopted family.

Louis, at first, took the greatest dislike to her, and even tried to induce the Montespan to get rid of that "strong-minded woman." But he was soon to change. The young duc was sent to Barège for his health. Madame Scarron accompanied him as a matter of course, and the letters which she wrote to the Montespan pleased the king. When she returned, and Louis was beginning to grow weary of his mistress, he was wont to ask the *gouvernante's* advice, and even to take it. This is an old story. How many a widower has married his children's governess! How many a man has broken an engagement to marry the *confidante!* Women do not know their power; and with a vain man, such as Louis was, there is no influence greater than that gained by probing his feelings. In other words, open his heart, if you can. Madame de Maintenon did not, perhaps, view the affair in this light; but she thought she could reform the monarch in her own person, and she did her best toward that object. She has been accused by Voltaire and others of cruelly supplanting the unfortunate Montespan, whom she induced the king to send away; but we respectable English will easily forgive her even such an act of ingratitude; we can think any measure excusable that turns a profligate into a respectable man. Louis was gradually influenced by the powerful mind and strong will of this clever and fascinating woman, and the two were eventually married in the most private manner. Madame de Maintenon—a name she took from an estate which she bought with her own or the king's money, and with which she hoped to obliterate the memory of Scarron—used her influence with her husband in a salutary manner, and the last days of Louis were better than the first. She was two years his senior, and could therefore control him. The king left her a pension of more than three thousand a year. She founded an establishment at St. Cyr, for the education of three hundred young ladies of small means. Perhaps she felt bitterly how her own poverty had been a reproach to her. She was almost worshiped as a saint at that place, and Walpole gives an amusing account of his visit to the establishment, where the young ladies sang Racine's "Athaliah," and performed "proverbs" which their foundress had written for them.

Madame de Maintenon enjoyed the king's favor till his death, and ruled France sternly enough. Of course she made enemies, but she had several friends. Friends and foes, however, both agree in calling her fish-blooded and snow-hearted. She *might* be melted, but, as a rule, she was insoluble. She was at least respectable in a disreputable age, and that is much to say. She died in 1719, at the ripe old age of eighty-four, and perhaps France has not produced many such women, though France boasts of its women even more than of its men.

THE END.

It is a work of real historical value, the result of accurate criticism, written in a liberal spirit, and from first to last deeply interesting.—*Athenæum.*

The style is excellent, clear, vivid, eloquent; and the industry with which original sources have been investigated, and through which new light has been shed over perplexed incidents and characters, entitles Mr. Motley to a high rank in the literature of an age peculiarly rich in history.—*North British Review.*

It abounds in new information, and, as a first work, commands a very cordial recognition, not merely of the promise it gives, but of the extent and importance of the labor actually performed on it.—*London Examiner.*

Mr. Motley's "History" is a work of which any country might be proud.—*Press* (London).

Mr. Motley's History will be a standard book of reference in historical literature.—*London Literary Gazette.*

Mr. Motley has searched the whole range of historical documents necessary to the composition of his work.—*London Leader.*

This is really a great work. It belongs to the class of books in which we range our Grotes, Milmans, Merivales, and Macaulays, as the glories of English literature in the department of history. * * * Mr. Motley's gifts as a historical writer are among the highest and rarest.—*Nonconformist* (London).

Mr. Motley's volumes will well repay perusal. * * * For his learning, his liberal tone, and his generous enthusiasm, we heartily commend him, and bid him good speed for the remainer of his interesting and heroic narrative.—*Saturday Review.*

The story is a noble one, and is worthily treated. * * * Mr. Motley has had the patience to unravel, with unfailing perseverance, the thousand intricate plots of the adversaries of the Prince of Orange; but the details and the literal extracts which he has derived from original documents, and transferred to his pages, give a truthful color and a picturesque effect, which are especially charming.—*London Daily News.*

M. Lothrop Motley dans son magnifique tableau de la formation de notre République.—G. Groen Van Prinsterer.

Our accomplished countryman, Mr. J. Lothrop Motley, who, during the last five years, for the better prosecution of his labors, has established his residence in the neighborhood of the scenes of his narrative. No one acquainted with the fine powers of mind possessed by this scholar, and the earnestness with which he has devoted himself to the task, can doubt that he will do full justice to his important but difficult subject.—W. H. Prescott.

The production of such a work as this astonishes, while it gratifies the pride of the American reader.—*N. Y. Observer.*

The "Rise of the Dutch Republic" at once, and by acclamation, takes its place by the "Decline and Fall of the Roman Empire," as a work which, whether for research, substance, or style, will never be superseded.—*N. Y. Albion.*

A work upon which all who read the English language may congratulate themselves.—*New Yorker Handels Zeitung.*

Mr. Motley's place is now (alluding to this book) with Hallam and Lord Mahon, Alison and Macaulay in the Old Country, and with Washington Irving, Prescott, and Bancroft in this.—*N. Y. Times.*

The authority, in the English tongue, for the history of the period and people to which it refers.—*N. Y. Courier and Enquirer.*

This work at once places the author on the list of American historians which has been so signally illustrated by the names of Irving, Prescott, Bancroft, and Hildreth.—*Boston Times.*

The work is a noble one, and a most desirable acquisition to our historical literature.—*Mobile Advertiser.*

Such a work is an honor to its author, to his country, and to the age in which it was written.—*Ohio Farmer.*

Published by HARPER & BROTHERS,

Franklin Square, New York.

www.ingramcontent.com/pod-product-compliance
Lightning Source LLC
LaVergne TN
LVHW021310110826
845150LV00003B/540

* 9 7 8 1 4 2 5 5 5 9 2 7 4 *